This book is a concise, yet comprehensive, narrative history of Russia from 980 to 1584. Exploring the realm of the Riurikid dynasty from the reign of Vladimir I the Saint, who monopolized political power over the eastern Slav lands, through the reign of Ivan IV the Terrible, who sealed the end of his dynasty's rule, it delves into social and economic issues as well as political history, foreign relations, religion, and culture. Janet Martin's analysis of these issues and emphasis on the dynamic qualities of Russian society form a basis for understanding the mechanisms and results of change in the principalities of Rus'. Her lines of argumentation are clear; her conclusions and interpretations provocative. They combine to make *Medieval Russia, 980–1584* an informative, broadly accessible, up-to-date account of the states and society of early Rus' from the Kievan to the Muscovite eras.

D1489649

Cambridge Medieval Textbooks

MEDIEVAL RUSSIA, 980–1584

Cambridge Medieval Textbooks

This is a series of specially commissioned textbooks for teachers and students, designed to complement the monograph series Cambridge Studies in Medieval Life and Thought by providing introductions to a range of topics in medieval history. This series combines both chronological and thematic approaches, and will deal with British and European topics. All volumes in the series will be published in hard covers and in paperback.

For a list of titles in the series, see end of book.

MEDIEVAL RUSSIA
980–1584

JANET MARTIN

University of Miami

CAMBRIDGE
UNIVERSITY PRESS

PUBLISHED BY THE PRESS SYNDICATE OF THE UNIVERSITY OF CAMBRIDGE
The Pitt Building, Trumpington Street, Cambridge, United Kingdom

CAMBRIDGE UNIVERSITY PRESS
The Edinburgh Building, Cambridge CB2 2RU, UK
40 West 20th Street, New York, NY 10011–4211, USA
477 Williamstown Road, Port Melbourne, VIC 3207, Australia
Ruiz de Alarcón 13, 28014 Madrid, Spain
Dock House, The Waterfront, Cape Town 8001, South Africa

http://www.cambridge.org

© Cambridge University Press 1993

First published 1995
Fourth printing 2003

Printed in the United Kingdom at the University Press, Cambridge

A catalogue record for this book is available from the British Library

Library of Congress Cataloguing in Publication data

Martin, Janet.
Medieval Russia, 980–1584 / Janet Martin.
p.   cm. – (Cambridge medieval textbooks)
Includes bibliographical references and index.
ISBN 0 521 36276 8. – ISBN 0 521 36832 4 (pbk.)
1. Russia – History – To 1533. 2. Russia – History – Ivan IV,
1533–1584. I. Title. II. Series.
DK71.M29 1995
947'.02–dc20 94–42360 CIP

ISBN 0 521 36276 8 hardback
ISBN 0 521 36832 4 paperback

To Daniel

CONTENTS

ILLUSTRATIONS

ACKNOWLEDGMENTS

The history of early Rus' is a rich and fascinating subject. Over centuries it has attracted the attention of literally hundreds upon hundreds of talented and perceptive scribes and scholars who have sifted through evidence, recorded and transcribed it, analyzed and interpreted it. Their efforts have provided for posterity images and understandings of the remarkable society they have studied. For all their work I stand in awe and gratitude. The present volume rests and draws upon a sampling of theirs. I nevertheless take responsibility for the selection from their diverse and, at times, conflicting representations, the balance set among them, the conclusions derived from them, and of course, the omissions that necessarily must occur as well as the errors that should not appear, but inevitably do.

Among the many individuals to whom I owe personal debts of gratitude, I would like to acknowledge particularly Gail D. Lenhoff and Ann M. Kleimola, who generously gave me encouragement, suggestions, and corrections; my former professors Richard Hellie and Edward L. Keenan, who continue to teach me; and a few very special persons who themselves have slipped into history, but whose memory, influence, and inspiration remain very much alive: Alexandre Bennigsen, Arcadius Kahan, and my father, Herman S. Bloch.

This volume would not have been possible without the support of specific institutions as well. I thank the History Department at the University of Miami and especially Jesus Sanchez Reyes; the Reasearch Council of the University of Miami, which awarded me a General Research Fund Grant and a Max Orovitz Research Grant to pursue this project; the Interlibrary Loan Office of Richter Library at the University of Miami; the Summer Research Laboratory on Russia and East Europe as well as the Slavic Library at the University of Illinois; and Cambridge University Press for the opportunity to conduct this project and Publishing Director Richard Fisher for his very kind patience.

NOTE ON NAMES, DATES, AND TRANSLITERATION

The transliteration of personal and place names in the following text has followed a modified version of the Library of Congress system; in a few instances, e.g., Alexander Nevsky, the common English spelling has been used instead. Although epithets, such as Nevsky, are occasionally used, princes are generally identified by name and patronymic, i.e. a form of the name of the prince's father. Thus Alexander Nevsky is also known as Alexander Iaroslavich. For purposes of simplicity proper transliterations have been based on Russian forms of the names.

Most dates are derived from the early Rus' calendar, which had been borrowed from Byzantium. In cases when the conversion is imprecise, dates are given in the form 1271/72 to indicate that an event occurred in either one year or the other.

CHRONOLOGY

<table>
<tr><td>972</td><td>Prince Sviatoslav of Kiev died</td></tr>
<tr><td>972–80</td><td>Prince Iaropolk ruled Kiev</td></tr>
<tr><td>980</td><td>Prince Vladimir Sviatoslavich became grand prince of Kiev</td></tr>
<tr><td>981–82</td><td>Prince Vladimir suppressed Viatichi rebellion</td></tr>
<tr><td>984</td><td>Prince Vladimir conquered the Radimichi</td></tr>
<tr><td>985</td><td>Prince Vladimir conducted campaign against Volga Bulgars</td></tr>
<tr><td>988</td><td>Prince Vladimir converted Kievan Rus' to Christianity</td></tr>
<tr><td>990s–1015</td><td>Rus'–Pecheneg war</td></tr>
<tr><td>996</td><td>Construction of Church of the Tithe completed</td></tr>
<tr><td>1015</td><td>Prince Vladimir died; Prince Sviatopolk murdered Boris, Gleb, and Sviatoslav</td></tr>
<tr><td>1016–19</td><td>Prince Sviatopolk and Prince Iaroslav fought for Kievan throne</td></tr>
<tr><td>1019</td><td>Prince Sviatopolk died</td></tr>
<tr><td>1024</td><td>Prince Mstislav of Tmutorokan' challenged Prince Iaroslav for Kiev; Prince Mstislav established himself as prince of Chernigov</td></tr>
<tr><td>1036</td><td>Prince Mstislav of Chernigov died; Prince Iaroslav became sole grand prince of Kiev; Pechenegs attacked Kiev</td></tr>
<tr><td>1037–46</td><td>Construction and decoration of Church of St. Sophia in Kiev</td></tr>
<tr><td>1042</td><td>Treaty between Kievan Rus' and Poland</td></tr>
<tr><td>1043</td><td>Kievan Rus' campaign against Byzantium</td></tr>
<tr><td>1050</td><td>Construction of Church of St. Sophia in Novgorod completed</td></tr>
</table>

1051	Hilarion became metropolitan of Kiev and all Rus'; Pecherskii Monastery (Cave Monastery) founded
1054	Prince Iaroslav Vladimirovich died; Prince Iziaslav Iaroslavich became grand prince of Kiev
1055	Polovtsy appeared in steppe
1060	Kievan Rus' campaign against Torks
1061	Polovtsy attacked Rus' territories
1067	Prince Vseslav of Polotsk challenged Prince Iziaslav for Kiev
1068	Polovtsy defeated armies of Princes Iziaslav, Sviatoslav, and Vsevolod
1068–69	Prince Vseslav ruled at Kiev
1069	Prince Iziaslav regained Kievan throne
1072	Princes Boris and Gleb Vladimirovich canonized
1073	Princes Sviatoslav Iaroslavich of Chernigov and Vsevolod Iaroslavich of Pereiaslavl' evicted Iziaslav from Kiev; Prince Sviatoslav ruled at Kiev
1076	Prince Sviatoslav died; Prince Iziaslav regained Kievan throne
1078	Prince Oleg Sviatoslavich challenged Iziaslav and Vsevolod for Chernigov; Grand Prince Iziaslav killed; Prince Vsevolod Iaroslavich became grand prince of Kiev
1088	Volga Bulgars attacked Murom
1093	Grand Prince Vsevolod died; Prince Sviatopolk Iziaslavich became grand prince of Kiev
1094	War between Sviatoslavichi and Vladimir Monomakh began
1096	Polovtsy attacked Kiev, burning Pecherskii Monastery
1097	Conference at Liubech
1101	Peace treaty between Kievan Rus' and Polovtsy
1103	Coalition of Kievan Rus' princes defeated Polovtsy
1107	Volga Bulgars attacked Suzdal'
1108	Prince Iurii Dolgorukii of Rostov-Suzdal' founded town of Vladimir
1111	Coalition of Kievan Rus' princes defeated Polovtsy
1113	Grand Prince Sviatopolk Iziaslavich died; Prince Vladimir Monomakh became grand prince of Kiev
1120	Prince Iurii Dolgorukii attacked Volga Bulgar territory
1125	Grand Prince Vladimir Monomakh died; Prince Mstislav Vladimirovich became grand prince of Kiev; Prince Iurii Vladimirovich Dolgorukii became prince of Rostov
1132	Grand Prince Mstislav Vladimirovich died; Prince Iaropolk Vladimirovich became grand prince of Kiev
1132–34	Prince Iurii Dolgorukii attempted to acquire Pereiaslavl'

1136–37	Construction of Cathedral of the Mother of God in Smolensk
1139	Grand Prince Iaropolk Vladimirovich died; Prince Vsevolod Ol'govich of Chernigov became grand prince of Kiev
1146	Grand Prince Vsevolod died; Prince Iziaslav Mstislavich became grand prince of Kiev
1147	First mention in chronicle literature of town of Moscow
1148	Novgorod attacked Iaroslavl'
1152	Volga Bulgars attacked Iaroslavl'
1154	Grand Prince Iziaslav Mstislavich died
1155	Prince Iurii Dolgorukii became grand prince of Kiev
1157	Grand Prince Iurii Dolgorukii died; Prince Andrei Iur'evich Bogoliubskii became prince of Vladimir
1158	Prince Rostislav Mstislavich of Smolensk became grand prince of Kiev; construction of Church of the Dormition in Vladimir began
1164	Prince Andrei Bogoliubskii attacked Volga Bulgars; construction of fortifications around Vladimir completed
1165	Construction of Church of the Intercession on the Nerl' River; construction of Bogoliubovo completed
1167	Grand Prince Rostislav Mstislavich died; Prince Mstislav Iziaslavich of Volynia became grand prince of Kiev
1168	Grand Prince Mstislav Iziaslavich led victorious campaign against Polovtsy
1169	Prince Andrei Bogoliubskii's forces sacked Kiev; Prince Gleb Iur'evich of Pereiaslavl' became grand prince of Kiev
1171	Grand Prince Gleb Iur'evich died; Prince Iaroslav Iziaslavich became grand prince of Kiev; Polovtsy tribes formed coalition under Khan Konchak
1172	Suzdalian forces attacked Volga Bulgars
1175	Prince Andrei Bogoliubskii assassinated
1177	Prince Sviatoslav Vsevolodich of Chernigov overthrew Grand Prince Iaroslav Iziaslavich and became grand prince of Kiev; Prince Vsevolod Iur'evich became prince of Vladimir
1183	Prince Vsevolod Iur'evich attacked Volga Bulgars
1184	Grand Prince Sviatoslav Vsevolodich launched victorious campaign against Polovtsy
1185	Suzdalian forces attacked Volga Bulgars; Prince Igor of Novgorod-Seversk defeated by Polovtsy in campaign that became subject of "Lay of Igor's Campaign"
1191/92	Novgorod concluded commercial treaty with Scandinavians and Germans

1194	Grand Prince Sviatoslav Vsevolodich died; Prince Riurik Rostislavich became grand prince of Kiev
1199	Prince Roman Rostislavich united Volynia and Galicia and challenged Grand Prince Riurik Rostislavich for Kievan throne
1203	Kiev sacked during Roman–Riurik struggle for Kievan throne
1205	Prince Roman Mstislavich died; Suzdalian forces attacked Volga Bulgars
1211	Prince Vsevolod Sviatoslavich Chermnyi evicted Grand Prince Riurik Rostislavich from Kiev and became grand prince of Kiev
1212	Grand Prince Vsevolod Chermnyi removed from Kievan throne and died; Prince Mstislav Romanovich became grand prince of Kiev; Prince Vsevolod of Vladimir died; Prince Konstantin Vsevolodich became prince of Vladimir; Ustiug Velikii founded
1215	Former grand prince Riurik Rostislavich died
1216	Battle of Lipitsa
1218	Prince Konstantin Vsevolodich died; Prince Iurii Vsevolodich became prince of Vladimir; Volga Bulgars attacked Ustiug Velikii
1220	Prince Iurii Vsevolodich of Vladimir attacked Volga Bulgars
1221	Nizhnii Novgorod founded
1223	Battle of Kalka; Grand Prince Mstislav Romanovich died; Prince Vladimir Riurikovich became grand prince of Kiev
1229	Mongol attack on Saksin, Volga Bulgars, Polovtsy
1231	Prince Mikhail Vsevolodich of Chernigov challenged Grand Prince Vladimir Riurikovich for Kievan throne
1232	Mongols attacked Volga Bulgars
1235	Grand Prince Vladimir Riurikovich captured by Polovtsy
1236	Mongol campaign destroyed major cities of Volga Bulgars
1237	Prince Mikhail Vsevolodich became grand prince of Kiev; Livonian Brothers of Sword merged with Teutonic Order; Mongols began invasion of Rus' lands
1238	Mongols conquered Vladimir; Mongols defeated northern Rus' princes at Battle of Sit'; Prince Iurii Vsevolodich of Vladimir killed at Battle of Sit'; Prince Iaroslav Vsevolodich became prince of Vladimir
1239	Mongols conquered Chernigov
1240	Prince Alexander Iaroslavich "Nevsky" defeated Swedes on Neva River; Mongols conquered Kiev

1242	Prince Alexander Nevsky defeated Teutonic Knights at Lake Peipus
1243	Prince Iaroslav Vsevolodich confirmed as prince of Vladimir by Batu
1245	Prince Daniil Romanovich confirmed as prince of Galicia and Volynia by Batu
1246	Prince Mikhail of Chernigov executed by Batu; Prince Iaroslav Vsevolodich of Vladimir died on journey to Mongolia
1247	Prince Sviatoslav Vsevolodich became prince of Vladimir
1248	Prince Andrei Iaroslavich overthrew Prince Sviatoslav of Vladimir
1249	Prince Andrei Iaroslavich confirmed by Mongols as prince of Vladimir
1252	Mongol campaigns against Andrei of Vladimir and Daniil of Volynia; Prince Alexander Iaroslavich Nevsky replaced Andrei as prince of Vladimir
1255	Batu, khan of Golden Horde, died; Sartak became khan of Golden Horde; Prince Andrei Iaroslavich became prince of Suzdal'
1256	Ulagchi succeeded Sartak as khan of Golden Horde
1257	Mongol census taken in Vladimir–Suzdal'
1258	Berke succeeded Sartak as khan of Golden Horde
1259	Mongol census taken in Novgorod enforced by Prince Alexander Nevsky
1262	Golden Horde at war with Ilkhans of Persia; popular uprisings in northeastern Rus'
1263	Prince Alexander Nevsky died; Prince Iaroslav Iaroslavich of Tver' became grand prince of Vladimir
1266/67	Mengu-Timur succeeded Berke as khan of Golden Horde
1269	Novgorod concluded a commercial treaty with German towns
1271/72	Grand Prince Iaroslav Iaroslavich died
1272	Prince Vasily Iaroslavich of Kostroma became grand prince of Vladimir
1277	Grand Prince Vasily Iaroslavich died; Prince Dmitry Aleksandrovich became grand prince of Vladimir
1282/83	Tuda-Mengu succeeded Mengu-Timur as khan of Golden Horde; dispute for grand princely throne between Dmitry Aleksandrovich and his brother Andrei began
1287	Telebuga succeeded Tuda-Mengu as khan of Golden Horde
1291	Tokhta succeeded Telebuga as khan of Golden Horde

1294	Grand Prince Dmitry Aleksandrovich died; Prince Andrei Aleksandrovich became undisputed grand prince of Vladimir
1299	Metropolitan Maksim (Maximus) moved from Kiev to Vladimir; Nogai of the Golden Horde died
1303	Prince Daniil of Moscow died
1304	Grand Prince Andrei Aleksandrovich died; Prince Mikhail Iaroslavich of Tver' became grand prince of Vladimir
1305	Metropolitan Maksim died
1308	Petr succeeded Maksim as metropolitan of Kiev and all Rus'
1313	Uzbek succeeded Tokhta as khan of Golden Horde
1317	Uzbek confirmed Prince Iurii Daniilovich as Grand Prince of Vladimir; battle between Grand Prince Mikhail Iaroslavich and Prince Iurii Daniilovich of Moscow for grand principality of Vladimir
1318	Prince Mikhail of Tver' executed by Uzbek
1322	Uzbek transferred patent for grand principality of Vladimir to Prince Dmitry Mikhailovich of Tver'
1325	Iurii Daniilovich assassinated by Prince Dmitry Mikhailovich of Tver'
1326	Prince Dmitry of Tver' executed by Uzbek; Uzbek confirmed Prince Aleksandr Mikhailovich of Tver' as grand prince of Vladimir; Metropolitan Petr and Prince Ivan Daniilovich of Moscow jointly founded the Church of the Assumption (Dormition) of the Virgin in Moscow kremlin; Metropolitan Petr died
1327	Mongols suppress Tver' uprising; Prince Aleksandr fled
1328	Uzbek confirmed Prince Aleksandr of Suzdal', who shared power with Prince Ivan Daniilovich, as grand prince of Vladimir; Metropolitan Feognost (Theognostus) arrived in northeastern Rus'
1331	Grand Prince Aleksandr died; Prince Ivan Daniilovich Kalita of Moscow became sole grand prince of Vladimir
1340	Lithuania occupied Volynia
1341	Tinibek succeeded Uzbek as khan of Golden Horde; Grand Prince Ivan I Kalita died; Prince Semen Ivanovich became grand prince of Vladimir
1342	Janibek succeeded Tinibek as khan of the Golden Horde
1349	Poland acquired most of Galicia
1353	Grand Prince Semen died of plague; Prince Ivan Ivanovich became grand prince of Vladimir; Metropolitan Feognost died

1354	Metropolitan Aleksei (Alexis) confirmed in office; Moscow became seat of metropolitan; Holy Trinity Monastery founded by Sergei (Sergius) of Radonezh
1357	Berdibek succeeded Janibek as khan of the Golden Horde
1359	Grand Prince Ivan II died; Golden Horde's Great Troubles began; Prince Dmitry Ivanovich claimed his father's throne
1360	Prince Dmitry Konstantinovich of Suzdal' and Nizhnii Novgorod confirmed as grand prince of Vladimir
1362	Prince Dmitry Ivanovich of Moscow received patent for grand principality of Vladimir from khan at Sarai and from Mamai
1367	Hostilities between Grand Prince Dmitry and Prince Mikhail of Tver' began
1370	Mamai issued patent for grand principality of Vladimir to Prince Mikhail of Tver'
1371	Mamai reissued patent for grand principality of Vladimir to Prince Dmitry Ivanovich
1375	Mamai reissued patent for grand principality of Vladimir to Prince Mikhail of Tver'; Prince Dmitry Ivanovich and Prince Mikhail concluded treaty, acknowledging Prince Dmitry as grand prince of Vladimir
1378	Tokhtamysh seized Sarai; Metropolitan Aleksei died
1379	Grand Prince Dmitry Ivanovich rejected Metropolitan Kiprian (Cyprian) in favor of Pimen
1380	Battle of Kulikovo
1381	War between Mamai and Tokhtamysh
1382	Tokhtamysh conducted military expedition against Russian principalities
1389	Grand Prince Dmitry Ivanovich Donskoi died; Vasily Dmitr'evich I became grand prince of Vladimir; Metropolitan Pimen died
1390	Grand Prince Vasily Dmitr'evich married Sofiia, daughter of Vitovt (Vytautas) of Lithuania; Kiprian became undisputed metropolitan
1392	Sergei (Sergius) of Radonezh died
1393	Vitovt became grand duke of Lithuania
1395	Timur invaded lands of Golden Horde
1399	Battle of Vorskla River
1407	Metropolitan Kiprian died
1408	Edigei launched expedition against the Russian principalities; Fotii (Photius) became metropolitan
1411	Edigei driven out of Sarai

1425	Vasily I died; Vasily II Vasil'evich became grand prince of Vladimir
1430	Vitovt of Lithuania died; Andrei Rublev died
1431	Metropolitan Fotii died
1432	Khan Ulu-Muhammed confirmed Vasily II as grand prince of Vladimir
1433	Prince Iurii Dmitr'evich of Galich seized Moscow from his nephew Vasily II, then withdrew
1434	Prince Iurii Dmitr'evich seized Moscow from Vasily II a second time; Prince Iurii Dmitr'evich died
1436	Grand Prince Vasily II defeated his cousin Vasily Iur'evich Kosoi and recovered Moscow
1437	Metropolitan Isadore arrived in Moscow, led delegation to Council of Ferrara-Florence
1441	Cardinal Isadore returned to Moscow, was deposed as metropolitan
1443	Hansa initiated blockade of trade with Novgorod
1445	Grand Prince Vasily II captured by Tatars of Ulu-Muhammed's Horde at Battle of Suzdal', later released
1446	Prince Dmitry Iur'evich Shemiakha captured, blinded, and imprisoned his cousin Vasily II
1447	Grand Prince Vasily II recovered Moscow from Dmitry Shemiakha
1448	Russian bishops named Bishop Iona (of Riazan') metropolitan; Hansa lifted its blockade of trade with Novgorod
1453	Constantinople fell to the Ottoman Turks; Prince Dmitry Shemiakha died in Novgorod
1456	Treaty of Iazhelbitsy
1461	Metropolitan Iona died; Feodosii (Theodosius) became metropolitan
1462	Grand Prince Vasily II died; Prince Ivan Vasil'evich became grand prince Ivan III
1463	Lands of Iaroslavl' principality attached to Muscovy
1464	Metropolitan Feodosii resigned; Filipp became metropolitan
1467	Muscovy launched campaign against Khanate of Kazan'
1469	Muscovy and Kazan' reached peace agreement
1471	Grand Prince Ivan III launched a campaign against Novgorod
1472	Ivan III married Sofiia (Zoe) Palaeologa, his second wife
1473	Metropolitan Filipp died; Gerontii became metropolitan
1475	Ottoman Turks established suzerainty over Crimean Khanate; Aristotle Fioroventi arrived in Moscow

1476	Venetian ambassador Ambrogio Contarini passed through Moscow
1478	Grand Prince Ivan III annexed Novgorod
1479	Monastery of Volokolamsk founded; Cathedral of the Assumption (Dormition) in Moscow kremlin completed
1480	Muscovy and Crimean Khanate formed an alliance; stand on the Ugra
1483–84	Massive confiscations of landed estates in Novgorod
1485	Grand Prince Ivan III annexed Tver'
1487	Muscovy launched campaign against Khanate of Kazan', established Muhammed Amin as khan of Kazan'
1489	Cathedral of Annunciation in Moscow kremlin completed; Metropolitan Gerontii died
1490	Prince Ivan Ivanovich, son of Grand Prince Ivan III, died; Zosima became metropolitan; Church Council found Novgorodian Judaizers guilty of heresy
1492	Ivan III constructed Ivangorod; Muscovite–Lithuanian border war began
1494	Metropolitan Zosima charged with heresy, deposed; Muscovite–Lithuanian treaty; Ivan III closed Hanseatic *dvor* in Novgorod
1495	Grand Prince Aleksandr of Lithuania married Elena, daughter of Ivan III; Semen became metropolitan
1496	First Muscovite ambassador sent to Ottoman Empire
1497	Prince Vasily Ivanovich fell into disgrace; Sudebnik (law code) issued
1498	Coronation of Prince Dmitry Ivanovich as co-ruler and heir of his grandfather, Grand Prince Ivan III
1499	Prince Vasily Ivanovich regained his father's favor
1500	Muscovite–Lithuanian hostilities renewed
1501	Muscovite–Livonian hostilities initiated
1502	Grand Prince Ivan III arrested his grandson, Prince Dmitry Ivanovich; Great Horde destroyed by forces of Crimean Khanate
1503	Muscovite–Lithuanian and Muscovite-Livonian truces concluded; Church council considered issued characterized as "possessor/non-possessor controversy"
1504	Church Council found Judaizers guilty of heresy, condemned their leaders to be burned to death at the stake
1505	Cathedral of the Archangel Michael in the Moscow kremlin was completed; Prince Vasily Ivanovich married Solomoniia

	Saburova; Grand Prince Ivan III died; Prince Vasily Ivanovich became Grand Prince Vasily III
1510	Grand Prince Vasily III annexed Pskov
1511	Metropolitan Semen died; Varlaam became metropolitan
1512	Muscovite–Lithuanian war resumed
1514	Vasily III's forces captured Smolensk
1518	Maksim Grek arrived in Moscow
1520/21	Grand Prince Vasily III annexed Riazan'
1521	Crimean Khanate launched campaign against Muscovy
1522	Muscovite–Lithuanian war concluded; Metropolitan Varlaam deposed; Daniil became metropolitan of the Russian Church
1524	Vasily III sent army against Kazan' khan Sahib-Girey
1525	Maksim Grek found guilty of heresy; marriage of Grand Prince Vasily III and Solomoniia was annulled
1526	Grand Prince Vasily III married Elena Glinskaia
1531	Maksim Grek and Vassian condemned as heretics
1533	Grand Prince Vasily III died; regency for Ivan IV ruled Muscovy
1538	Elena Glinskaia, mother of Ivan IV, died
1539	*Guba* reforms initiated; Metropolitan Daniil deposed; Ioasaf became metropolitan
1542	Metropolitan Ioasaf deposed; Makarii became metropolitan
1547	Ivan IV assumed the throne of Muscovy and the title tsar
1550	Sudebnik (law code) issued
1551	Stoglav Council met
1552	Muscovy conquered Kazan'
1553	Illness of Ivan IV spawned "boyar revolt" over succession; English discovered White Sea route to Muscovy
1556	Muscovy conquered Astrakhan'
1558	Livonian War began
1561	Construction of St. Basil's Cathedral completed
1563	Metropolitan Makarii died; Afanasii (Athanasius) became metropolitan; Prince Iurii Vasil'evich, brother of Ivan IV, died
1565	Ivan IV established the *oprichnina*
1566	*Zemskii sobor* convened; Metropolitan Afanasii retired; Filipp became metropolitan
1568	Metropolitan Filipp deposed; Kirill became metropolitan
1569	Prince Vladimir Andreevich Staritskii forced to commit suicide by his cousin, Tsar Ivan IV; former metropolitan Filipp murdered; Ottoman Turks unsuccessfully attempted to recapture Astrakhan'

1570	*Oprichnina* sacked Novgorod
1571	Crimean Tatars attacked, burned Moscow
1572	*Oprichnina* disbanded
1575	Ivan IV abdicated in favor of Semen Bekbulatovich
1576	Ivan IV resumed his position as tsar
1581	Prince Ivan Ivanovich killed by his father, Ivan IV
1582	Ermak Timofeevich, a Cossack employed by Stroganov family, defeated Khan of Sibir'
1582–3	Livonian War concluded
1584	Ivan IV died

ABBREVIATIONS

CASS   *Canadian-American Slavic Studies*
CMRS   *Cahiers du monde russe et soviétique*
FOG   *Forschungen zur Osteuropäischen Geschichte*
HUS   *Harvard Ukrainian Studies*
IZ   *Istoricheskie zapiski*
JbfGO   *Jahrbücher für Geschichte Osteuropas*
RH   *Russian History*
RR   *Russian Review*
SEER   *Slavonic and East European Review*
SR   *Slavic Review*

I

THE ERA OF VLADIMIR I

In the year 980, an obscure prince landed on the northern shores of a land that became known as Rus' and later, Russia. Almost a decade earlier his father, the ruler of this land, had placed him in charge of the area surrounding one of its towns, the recently founded Novgorod. But after his father died (972) and one of his elder brothers killed the other (977), this prince, Vladimir (Volodimer) Sviatoslavich, fled abroad. After several years of exile he now led a band of Varangians (Norsemen) across the Baltic from Scandinavia. His intention was to depose his half-brother Iaropolk and assume the throne of Kiev.

VLADIMIR'S SEIZURE OF THE KIEVAN THRONE

Upon landing in Rus', Prince Vladimir immediately sought allies to join him against Iaropolk. He turned to the prince of Polotsk (Polatsk), Rogvolod, a fellow Varangian but unrelated to Vladimir and his family, and requested the hand of his daughter Rogneda in marriage. But she haughtily refused him, calling him the "son of a slave" and indicating a preference for Iaropolk. Vladimir responded by leading his Varangian force, along with Slovenes, Chud', and Krivichi from his former domain of Novgorod, against Polotsk. He defeated and killed Rogvolod and his sons, captured Rogneda, and forced her to become his bride. Polotsk was attached to the realm of Vladimir's family, the Riurikid dynasty.

Vladimir then marched toward his brother's capital, the city of Kiev. Growing out of settlements established in the sixth and seventh centuries, Kiev was located far to the south of Novgorod on hills overlooking the

west or right bank of the Dnieper River. By 980 it had become the
political center of a domain, known as Kievan Rus', that extended from
Novgorod on the Volkhov River southward across the divide where the
Volga, the West Dvina, and the Dnieper Rivers all had their origins, and
down the Dnieper just past Kiev. It also included the lower reaches of the
main tributaries of the Dnieper. Arriving at the city, Vladimir entered into
negotiations with his brother. But in the midst of their talks two of
Vladimir's Varangians murdered Iaropolk. Vladimir Sviatoslavich became
the sole prince of Kievan Rus'.

Prince Vladimir's claim to the Kievan throne rested only in part on the
military force he used to secure it. It was also based on heritage. Vladimir
was one of the sons of Sviatoslav, prince of Kiev from 962 to 972. The
Russian Primary Chronicle traces Sviatoslav's lineage back through his
father Igor' and mother Olga to a Norseman named Riurik. The legend
of Riurik claims that in the ninth century a group of quarreling eastern
Slav and Finn tribes that had dwelled in what is now northwestern
Russia invited Riurik and his brothers to come to their lands, rule over
them, and bring peace and order to their peoples.

While the chronicle account incorporates myth and cannot be taken
literally, it does reflect the fact that Scandinavian Vikings, called Rus',[1]
were present in the territories of the eastern Slav and Finn tribes by the
ninth century and that they eventually became rulers or princes over
the native population. Vladimir's ancestors, founders of the dynasty that
was later named after Riurik, led one of those Viking bands; they
ultimately defeated other rival bands and gained ascendancy over enough
of the native tribes to fashion a cohesive principality out of the Slav
territories. Although the Slav tribes shared a common language and there
is some evidence of a federation among them prior to the establishment
of Scandinavian rule, it was their common recognition of the Riurikid
dynasty that bound them into the state that became known as Kievan Rus'.

CONSOLIDATION OF POWER

The lands of Vladimir's realm were populated primarily by eastern Slav
tribes. To the north were the Slovenes of the Novgorod region and the

---

[1] The origin of the term "Rus'" and the populations and territories to which it refers have
been the subjects of lengthy and intense debate. For the sake of simplicity the term will
be used in this chapter to refer to the Scandinavians, including the members of the
Riurikid dynasty, who imposed their rule over the eastern Slavs. In subsequent chapters
the distinction between the Scandinavian Rus' and the Slavs will be dropped and the term
will be applied to the rulers and population of Kievan Rus'. That term will be used
broadly to mean those lands subject to the Riurikid princes.

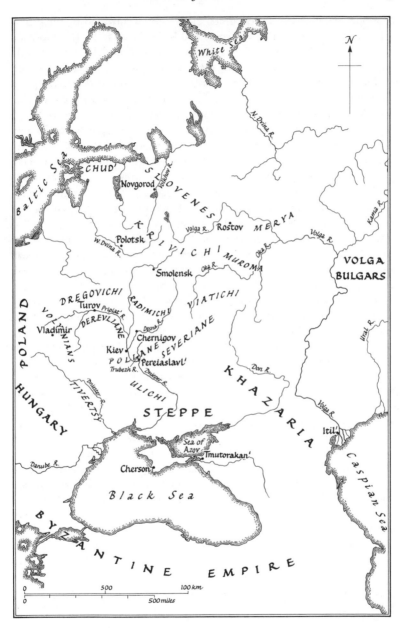

Map 1.1 The tribes of early Rus'

neighboring Krivichi, who occupied the territories surrounding the headwaters of the West Dvina, Dnieper, and Volga Rivers. To the south in
the area around Kiev were the Poliane, a group of Slavicized tribes with
Iranian origins. To their north the Derevliane inhabited the lands west of
the Dnieper extending to its right tributary, the Pripiat' River (Pripet).
On the other side of the Pripiat' were the Dregovichi. West of the
Derevliane dwelled the Volynians; south of them, i.e., southwest of Kiev,
were the Ulichi and Tivertsy tribes. East of the Dnieper along its left
tributary, the Desna River, were Severiane tribes; the Viatichi lived to
their north and east along the upper Oka River. Kievan Rus' was fringed
in the north by the Finnic Chud', and in the northeast by the Muroma
and Merya tribes that occupied the lands on the Oka and Volga Rivers.
To the south its forested lands settled by Slav agriculturalists gave way to
steppelands populated by nomadic herdsmen.

Within Kievan Rus' there were several noteworthy towns by the late
tenth century. Kiev and Novgorod, its southern and northern focal
points, were the most important. In addition, Kievan Rus' contained
Smolensk, a center of the Krivichi, located on the upper Dnieper. West
of Smolensk was the town of Polotsk, which Vladimir had seized from
Rogvolod; it was located on the Polota River which flows into the West
Dvina. South of Polotsk, on the Pripiat' River, was the Dregovich
center of Turov (Turau). On the east side of the Dnieper Chernigov
(Chernihiv), the major center of the Severiane tribes, commanded the
Desna River. Pereiaslavl', situated southeast of Kiev on the Trubezh
River, another tributary of the Dnieper, was the town nearest the steppe
frontier. Rostov, located on Lake Nero in Merya country, had also been
founded by the era of Prince Vladimir.

Kievan Rus' was coalescing amidst other organized states. To the east
was Bulgar, located on the mid-Volga River near its juncture with the
Kama. South of Bulgar and southeast of Kievan Rus' were the remnants
of a once powerful empire, Khazaria. Before the formation of Kievan
Rus' Khazaria had claimed some of the eastern Slav tribes as its tributaries.
And until the reign of Vladimir's father, Sviatoslav, who delivered the
final blow that destroyed it, Khazaria had dominated the region of the
lower Volga and the northern Caucasus and had maintained stability on
the steppe. West of Kiev were Poland and Hungary, which were also
organizing into kingdoms and expanding in the late tenth and early
eleventh centuries. And to the south, beyond the steppe, was the greatest
empire of the age, Byzantium, whose control extended over the northern
coast of the Black Sea and influence into the Balkans.

Once established in Kiev, Vladimir faced the task of consolidating
his personal position and the monopoly on power he had attained for his

family or dynasty over all the lands of Kievan Rus'. After displacing Iaropolk, no relatives were available to challenge him. But he nevertheless had to ensure that all the tribes within his realm would continue to recognize him as their prince and neither withdraw their allegiance nor transfer it to a neighboring power. Their loyalty was symbolized by their payment of tribute or taxes.

Vladimir's most pressing problem in this respect was posed by the Viatichi, who had rebelled when Sviatoslav died in 972. One of Vladimir's first acts (981–82), therefore, was to suppress their rebellion and reestablish Kievan authority over them. In 984, he also expanded Kievan Rus' by subordinating the Radimichi, another Slav tribe that inhabited the lands north of the Severiane and east of the upper Dnieper.

In 985, Vladimir and his uncle Dobrynia also conducted a military campaign against the Volga Bulgars, who dominated the mid-Volga region and exercised some influence over the tribes dwelling to the north and west of their own territories. After the demise of Khazaria, Bulgar was the chief potential rival to Kievan Rus' authority over the peoples, like the Muroma and the Merya, who occupied the lands along the upper Volga and Oka Rivers well to the east of the Kiev and the Dnieper. Vladimir's campaign was militarily successful. Yet significantly, Vladimir, heeding his uncle's advice, did not attempt to reduce the Volga Bulgars to tributary status. Rather, he concluded a treaty with Bulgar that served as the basis for the peaceful relations that lasted between the two states until the late eleventh century. The Rus' victory also removed Bulgar as a potential rival for suzerainty over the tribes on the eastern and northeastern frontiers of Kievan Rus'; in this way it also helped to secure their allegiance to Kiev and the Riurikid dynasty.

CONVERSION TO CHRISTIANITY

In addition to using force to consolidate his ruling position over the tribes of his realm, Vladimir adopted another policy that served twin goals of integrating the diverse tribes into a single society and of introducing an ideology that would legitimize his rule. That policy was the introduction of a uniform common religion for his heterogeneous population. In so doing Vladimir began a process of associating secular political authority with religious institutions and clergy, whose authority and advice were eventually popularly respected. Conversely, pagan priests and tribal leaders, who clung to their local gods, lost their positions, prestige, and power.

Vladimir's first attempt at providing a single faith was undertaken shortly after he assumed the throne in Kiev; it was based on the pagan religions of his subjects. Having witnessed the recent collapse of Khazaria, which had lacked religious unity, and evidently appreciating the political advantages of identifying himself with the broad spectrum of gods worshipped by his diverse subjects, Vladimir sponsored the erection of a pagan temple on a hill at the very heights of the city. The temple was dedicated to six gods; the idols represented several groups within the Kievan population. Perun, the god of thunder and war, was a Norse god favored by members of the prince's *druzhina* (military retinue). Others in the pantheon were the Slav gods of the sky (Stribog) and of light and fertility (Dazhd'bog or Dazhboh); Mokosh', a goddess representing Mother Nature, was worshipped also by Finnish tribes. In addition, Khors, a sun god, and Simargl, another fertility god, both of which had Iranian origins, were included, probably to appeal to the Poliane. For reasons not explained in the chronicles, Vladimir became dissatisfied with this religious arrangement. The alternative he found provided the same unifying advantages and ideological support for his political position. He adopted Christianity.

Christianity had been known in Kievan Rus' for at least a century. Vladimir's grandmother, Olga, had been a Christian, and a Christian church, the Cathedral of St. Elias (Il'ya) had been functioning since at least 944, when Christian retainers of Vladimir's grandfather, Igor', were said to have sworn oaths there. Nevertheless, the selection of Christianity was not a foregone conclusion. Kievan Rus' was familiar not only with Christianity as practiced both in Byzantium and Europe, but with the other monotheistic religions, Judaism and Islam. A chronicle tale relates that Vladimir sent representatives to investigate all the options available to the Rus'. The tale reflects not only the wide range of cultural influences to which Kievan Rus' was exposed, but also the culturally receptive, yet selective character of this emerging state. It explains that Vladimir and his advisers rejected Islam because, among other factors, Muslims were prohibited from drinking alcoholic beverages. They considered Judaism unacceptable because they found it inexplicable that the God of the Jews, if He were truly powerful and favored His people, would have allowed them to be deprived of a country of their own. When comparing the two versions of Christianity, Vladimir's emissaries reported they found no glory in the ceremonies in the "German" or European churches. But when they went to Constantinople and were led by the emperor into "the edifaces where they worship their God," they were overcome with awe: "we knew not whether we were in heaven or on earth," they informed their prince and his court. "For on earth there is no such splendor or such beauty, and we are at a loss how to describe it. We know only that God dwells there among men, and their service is fairer than the ceremonies of other nations."[2]

A continuation of the chronicle tale, however, indicates that the process of adopting Christianity was more mundane and immersed in politics and war. It describes how Vladimir led a campaign against Cherson, a Byzantine commercial outpost on the Crimean peninsula. He laid siege to the town, which surrendered after its water supply had been cut off. Vladimir then held it as ransom while he demanded Emperor Basil's sister Anna in marriage. Despite her declaration that she would prefer to die than wed Vladimir, the emperor agreed to the prince's conditions. Anna reluctantly arrived in Cherson, whereupon Vladimir was baptized, married the Byzantine princess, and returned Cherson to Basil as his bridegroom's gift. Then, accompanied by his wife and Byzantine Christian clergy, he returned to Kiev. Prince Vladimir destroyed the pagan idols that overlooked the city, conducted a mass baptism of the Kievan population in the Dnieper River, and began the process of baptizing the rest of his subjects.

The chronicle tale, an amalgam of legend and fact compiled approximately a century after the events, contains numerous lapses and inconsistencies that have compelled historians, drawing upon supplementary sources, to compose coherent narratives around the events associated with the conversion. Standard descriptions have clung to the chronicle's outline. They add, however, that at the time of these events the Byzantine emperor Basil II (976–1025) had recently suffered a defeat in Bulgaria and was losing control over Anatolia to rebels. Desperate for military support, he sent a delegation to Vladimir with a request for assistance. His need for a Varangian detachment to confront the dangers facing him was so great that the emperor agreed to arrange a marriage between his sister Anna and the Kievan prince. The only conditions were that Vladimir send the troops, convert to Christianity, and forsake his other wives.

As a result of these negotiations, Vladimir did send reinforcements with whose aid Emperor Basil successfully defended Constantinople from the rebels. By spring of 989, the Varangians had finally crushed Basil's opponents. But the emperor seemed to renege on his agreement. Marriage into the ruling house of the Byzantine Empire was a singular honor, rarely granted, and therefore strikingly significant in that it would bestow such high stature on a new addition to the Christian world. The bride herself apparently balked at the idea of marrying a northern

---

[2] *Medieval Russia's Epics, Chronicles, and Tales*, ed. by Serge A. Zenkovsky (New York: E. P. Dutton, 1974), p. 67.

barbarian. It was at this point that Vladimir, impatient at the delays, attacked Cherson.[3]

Some scholars have offered variant scenarios. Andrzej Poppe, for example, proposed that Emperor Basil and his sister Anna, motivated by political and military necessity, honored their commitment to Vladimir in a timely manner. Anna and Vladimir, according to this reconstruction of the events, had already married when the Rus' prince undertook his campaign against Cherson. The objective of the campaign was then not to force the Byzantine emperor to fulfill his pledge, but to assist him, once again, by suppressing rebels in the town who supported his enemies. Poppe justified his revision of the chronicle account by describing it as "a legend 'vested in historical garments'" that had been compiled "over one hundred years after the conversion" not with the intention of accurately recording a chronology of facts, but of "present[ing] . . . a significant religious occurrence" that required no "logical sequence of events" and therefore lacked one.[4]

Although the sources do not provide a consistent set of dates for all the events, the year 988 has been accepted as the traditional date of the formal conversion of Kievan Rus' to Christianity. It marked a triumph for Byzantium and its Church, which acquired potential access to the peoples dwelling as far north as the Gulf of Finland. The achievement was even more dramatic against the background of the recent expansion of the Roman Christian Church into northern, central, and eastern Europe and Islam to the mid-Volga region, where it had been adopted by the Bulgars in 922.

Although written later by Christian monks, the chronicles contain curiously scant information on the history of the Church from 988, the time of the conversion, to 1036, when Vladimir's son Iaroslav gained full authority over the Rus' lands and renewed efforts to spread and fortify the faith in his realm. The lack of information has led to some speculation about the status of the Church during its early years. It is generally accepted, however, that from the time of its inception the Orthodox

---

[3] For examples of this version of the events, see George Vernadsky, *Kievan Russia. A History of Russia*, vol. 2 (New Haven, Conn., and London: Yale University Press, 1948), pp. 62–65, and Dimitri Obolensky, *The Byzantine Commonwealth: Eastern Europe, 500–1453* (Crestwood, N.Y.: St. Vladimir's Seminary Press, 1982), pp. 254–258.

[4] Andrzej Poppe, "The Political Background to the Baptism of Rus': Byzantine–Russian Relations between 986–989," *Dumbarton Oaks Papers*, no. 30 (Washington, D.C.: Dumbarton Oaks Center for Byzantine Studies, 1976), pp. 211–212, 221, 224–228, 241; reprinted in *The Rise of Christian Russia* (London: Variorum Reprints, 1982). The quoted phrases are taken from Poppe's article, "How the Conversion of Rus' Was Understood in the Eleventh Century," *HUS*, vol. 11 (1987), pp. 299–300.

Church in Kievan Rus' had the status of a metropolitanate, whose chief prelate was appointed by the patriarch of Constantinople. It is also widely acknowledged that the seat of the metropolitan was Kiev itself, although other possibilities have been suggested.

The adoption of Christianity had a major impact on Kievan Rus'. It turned the face of Kievan Rus' from the Muslim East, whose wealth had originally drawn the Rus' to the lands of the eastern Slavs, toward Byzantium. The institutions of the Orthodox Church provided, further- more, a vehicle for the influx of a range of cultural influences into Kievan Rus'. They included the Christian religion itself as well as associated cultural traditions.

The most immediately dramatic and obvious impact of the adoption of Christianity was the transformation of Kiev's architectural landscape. Vladimir smashed the pagan idols and hilltop temple he had built just a few years before; in their place arose a church dedicated to St. Basil. Even more spectacular, however, was his construction of an ensemble of buildings set on the central hill of Kiev, outside the old fortifications. Vladimir ordered the grounds of a cemetery that had occupied the place of honor leveled. In a location visible to all inhabitants of the city and with unmistakable symbolism, he built the stone Church of the Holy Virgin, more commonly known as the Church of the Tithe, on the desecrated remains of the pagan dead. The foundations of the church were laid in 989 or 991; it was completed and dedicated in the year 996. The Church of the Tithe has been considered by scholars to have been either the prince's royal cathedral or the first residence of the metropolitan.[5] In either case the grand stone ediface with its elegant interior, including its tile and mosaic floors, its slate and marble detailing, and its vestries, icons, and other religious symbols, was unique among the city's growing number of wooden churches. Vladimir, as an additional confirmation of

---

[5] Among the scholars who have debated this issue, Andrzej Poppe concluded that the Church of the Tithe was a royal chapel. He proposed that the metropolitan's residence was a wooden church, dedicated to St. Sophia (Holy Wisdom). His argument was presented in "The Building of the Church of St. Sophia in Kiev," published in the *Journal of Medieval History*, vol. 7 (1981), and reprinted in his *Rise of Christian Russia*, pp. 18, 24; Ia. N. Shchapov also concluded that the Church of the Tithe was a royal church. His argument is outlined in *State and Church in Early Russia, 10th–13th centuries*, trans. Vic Schneierson (New Rochelle, N.Y., Athens, Moscow: Aristide D. Caratzas, 1993), pp. 25–34. The position that the Church of the Tithe was the original seat of the metropolitan is represented by Petro P. Tolochko in his article "Religious Sites in Kiev during the Reign of Volodimer Sviatoslavich," *HUS*, vol. 11 (1987), p. 322, and in his book, *Drevniaia Rus': Ocherki sotsial'no-politicheskoi istorii* [Ancient Rus': essays on socio- political history] (Kiev: Naukova dumka, 1987), p. 73.

his commitment to Orthodoxy, pledged a tithe or one-tenth of his revenue to support his new church.

Flanking the Church of the Tithe and completing the ensemble were two palatial structures, which served as Vladimir's court buildings. To surround this area that became known as "Vladimir's city," the prince also built new fortifications, consisting of high ramparts and a deep moat that intertwined with the natural ravines cutting into the hillside. These and other construction projects were of such magnitude that within decades of the adoption of Christianity Thietmar, bishop of Merseberg and a contemporary of Vladimir I, recorded a description of Kiev that proclaimed it to be an impressive city, endowed with no fewer than forty churches and eight marketplaces.

The clergy who organized the Church and ministered to the newly converted population were Greeks, sent from Byzantium. The architects and artisans who designed and built the structures, symbolizing the glory of Christian Kievan Rus', were also Byzantine. Thus not only was the city's skyline reshaped, but its population received an infusion of Greeks, who introduced their concepts and designs, applied their teachings and technology, and began to transmit them to native apprentices.

Christian culture also influenced Kievan Rus' literature, which was written in a language that has become known as Old Church Slavonic. Based on the Cyrillic alphabet created by the saints Cyril and Methodius in the ninth century, Church Slavonic drew upon Slavic words and grammar but cast them into Byzantine styles. The language was designed as a vehicle for translating religious texts from Greek into Slavic so Christianity could be disseminated and services could be conducted among the Slav populations of the Balkans. A century later it became the liturgical as well as the formal literary language of Kievan Rus'. Adoption of Christianity thus gave Kievan Rus' access to an array of ecclesiastical literature in a variety of genres, which its society would absorb and use as models for its own compositions. The new Church borrowed earlier translations of some religious literature from the Bulgarians. But the clergymen who came from Cherson and other Byzantine centers also brought with them copies of the Gospels, Psalms of the Old Testament, various Byzantine liturgical texts, sermons and saints' lives, and other ecclesiastical and secular literature, which they translated from Greek into Church Slavonic. Kievan Rus' also gained access to Byzantine chronicles; by the eleventh century clerics in Rus' were imitating them to record the first written histories of the realm of Vladimir and his heirs.

Although Christian culture spread and penetrated Slav society slowly, when it did, it provided a common cultural background to all the tribes within Kievan Rus'. It also furnished the Riurikid dynasty with an ideological foundation for its exclusive rule over Kievan Rus'. The descendants of Vladimir were depicted as God's anointed princes, and Vladimir himself was canonized, although not until the thirteenth century.

DOMESTIC POLITICAL ORGANIZATION

Although Vladimir had formally adopted Christianity for all the lands he ruled and in some circles of society it served to bolster his own legitimacy, among some tribes there was reluctance, even violent resistance to the introduction of Christianity. When Christian clergy arrived in Novgorod and threw the idol of Perun into the Volkhov River, for example, they provoked a popular rebellion. The rebellion was quelled and a stately cathedral, made of oak, surmounted by thirteen domes, and dedicated to St. Sophia, was built under the guidance of the city's first bishop. Nevertheless, the populace remained stubbornly pagan; only gradually through the eleventh century did Novgorodian women, for example, replace the pendants and amulets they wore on their breasts to ward off evil spirits with crucifixes and small icons.

To facilitate the introduction of Christianity around his lands, Vladimir reportedly placed his sons, each with his own *druzhina*, in towns on the frontiers of Kievan Rus'. He thus assigned Novgorod to Vysheslav, Polotsk to Iziaslav, Turov to Sviatopolk, and Rostov to Iaroslav. When Vysheslav, the eldest, died, the chronicle entry indicates that Iaroslav was transferred to Novgorod and their younger brother Boris took his place in Rostov. At that time Gleb was also seated in Murom, Sviatoslav ruled the Derevliane, Vsevolod was the prince in Vladimir (in Volynia), and Mstislav in Tmutorokan'. Another chronicle version adds that bishops, priests, and deacons accompanied each prince. The implication of this notation is that Orthodoxy was formally established in each of the named districts. Some of the towns, such as Novgorod, Polotsk, and Belgorod (an alternate princely seat located just south of Kiev), became the centers of dioceses during Vladimir's reign. Elsewhere the Christian presence was probably little more than a small mission supplemented by the prince, his retainers, and a few converts.

One effect of this policy was to provide the missionaries representing the Church with the protection they would need when they attempted to introduce the new religion, found their churches, and convince local populations and their leaders to reject their traditional gods in favor of the Christian Trinity. But the distribution of princes around the country was probably more successful as a measure to establish direct secular administrative control over the diverse districts of the realm than it was to convert the population within them. Although the two were linked, secular Riurikid authority was more readily accepted than Christianity, which the Slav tribes adopted at a slow pace.

In each of their districts Vladimir's sons not only protected the Christian clerics. They also served as military leaders, as defenders of the frontier, and local administrators. One of their basic functions in the last capacity was to raise revenue. Tribute from the tribes that recognized their suzerainty was their primary source of revenue. When Vladimir's legendary ancestors initially appeared in the Slav and Finn territories, they, like their Viking cousins who ravaged western Europe, had conducted raids on the native populations. They took captives and robbed the populations of their most valuable goods, including furs, wax, and swords, as they made their way down the Volga and Dnieper Rivers to sell their booty at market centers of Bulgar (on the Volga), Itil' (in Khazaria), and Cherson. In return, they received treasures of the great empires of the era, Arab, Persian, and Byzantine: silks and brocades, glassware and jewelry, spices and wine, and silver.

Although the precise stages of the transformation are not clear, some of the Scandinavian raiders, represented by Riurik in the legend, eventually regularized their relations with the Slav tribal society. They became the princes or rulers over the Slavs and substituted an annual collection of regular amounts of tribute for sporadic and destructive raids. In return for those payments and recognition of his suzerainty, a prince protected his subjects from other raiders or competing princes, including other Varangians as well as rulers of neighboring organized states that had previously claimed tribute from the Slavs. Within that framework the tribal societies had generally continued to conduct their internal affairs according to their own customs, laws, and religious ethical codes, guided by their traditional tribal elders or officials.

The method used by the Rus' to collect tribute was described by the Byzantine emperor Constantine Porphyrogenitus in *De Administrando Imperio*, written in the middle of the tenth century. According to his account, the prince with his *druzhina* annually made rounds (*poliudie*) through the subordinated lands and collected tribute.[6] The Primary Chronicle suggests that Vladimir's grandmother Olga may have altered that method. According to the chronicle, her husband Igor' had been killed in 945 by the Derevliane, who were angered when he attempted to collect more than the designated amount of tribute from them. Olga,

---

[6] Constantine Porphyrogenitus, *De Administrando Imperio*, Greek text ed. by Gy. Moravcsik with English translation by R. J. H. Jenkins (Washington, D.C.: Dumbarton Oaks Center for Byzantine Studies, 1967), p. 63.

demonstrating a rare capacity for cunning, exacted a terrible revenge as she resubjugated the tribe. Afterward, she apparently reformed the method of tribute collection. Rather than rely on local chiefs and the system of *poliudie*, she appointed her own officials to gather and deliver it from at least some regions in her domain.

Prince Sviatoslav certainly did appoint his own agents, his sons, to oversee portions of his domain. Shortly before his death in 972, he had designated Iaropolk to rule in Kiev, Oleg among the Derevliane, and Vladimir in Novgorod. That apportionment, however, did not prove to be stable. As noted above, the brothers quarreled after their father's death. Iaropolk went to war first against Oleg, who fled from his brother's advancing forces. As the chronicle graphically describes, he and his forces retreated across a moat to gain the safety of a fortified town called Vruchii; Oleg fell from the bridge and died. It was when Vladimir heard about Oleg's fate that he fled from Novgorod to Scandinavia. Iaropolk appointed his own governor for Novgorod and, as the chronicle notes, ruled the lands of Rus' alone.

When Vladimir took Iaropolk's place, he also ruled alone. But with the assignment of his sons to various parts of his realm, he restored and expanded the administrative arrangement introduced by his grandmother and father. His sons became responsible for maintaining their family's authority over their districts and tribes and for collecting tribute from them. They used a portion of their revenues to support their own *druzhiny* and meet other local expenses, and turned the remainder over to their father in Kiev. But Vladimir's distribution of administrative responsibility was also unstable. His son, Iaroslav, prince in Novgorod, became dissatisfied with the division of revenue. In 1014, he refused to send the required two-thirds of his collections to Kiev; war with his father was imminent and was avoided only by Vladimir's death in 1015.

KIEVAN COMMERCE AND FOREIGN RELATIONS

Collection of tribute was not the only duty Vladimir assigned to his sons. They were also responsible for maintaining order among their subjects, defending the Orthodox missions, and protecting their borders. These functions as well as military engagements for conquest required each prince to have a military force at his disposal. As had their forefathers, Vladimir and his sons each relied on a *druzhina*, which they supported and maintained in permanent service. By dispersing his sons around the country Vladimir also ensured that their military forces would be stationed at some distance from one another where they could defend the frontiers of Kievan Rus' and also be less likely to fight each other. By keeping his sons in positions subordinate to himself, however, he also maintained a capacity to combine his sons' forces with his own if and when it became necessary to assemble a large army. In pressing circumstances any one of the princes could supplement his military force with auxiliary troops, drafted from among the Slav population or hired from abroad.

Although Varangians were originally foot soldiers, the armed forces of the Kievan Rus' princes increasingly became horsemen. Their armor included helmets, cuirasses, and shields; their weapons consisted of swords and spears, maces and battle axes. Bows and arrows were also used, usually by auxiliary troops. Horses, weapons, and equipment as well as general maintenance were costly. A prince's ability to support his retainers and to hire other troops when necessary depended on more than the tribute or taxes he was able to collect from his subjects.

The fur, wax, and honey that the princes collected from the Slav tribes had limited domestic use. They could, however, be converted into valuable items through trade. Commercial opportunities had been one of the most compelling features that had initially attracted the Varangians to the Slavic lands. As Thomas Noonan observed, it was silver that originally drew Norsemen eastward through the Slav lands and motivated them to take the captives and steal the fur pelts and other products that they could exchange at the markets of Bulgar and Itil'.[7] Although they conducted their business in a more orderly manner, Vladimir and his sons essentially followed the same pattern. They sold local products as well as prisoners taken in battle for silver and for commodities that were more useful or valuable to them for military purposes, as status symbols, or after 988, in the conduct of religious services and ceremonies. Vladimir and his sons were thus vitally concerned with commerce and with the protection of the trade routes that ran through their lands.

The vast river system that stretched across Kievan Rus' formed two main trade routes that connected the Baltic Sea in the north with the Black and Caspian Seas in the south. Both were demarcated and dominated by the major towns of Kievan Rus', whose positions along those routes explain the importance the Rus' princes placed on controlling them. Novgorod regulated traffic to and from the Baltic through the Gulf of Finland and a series of rivers leading to the city; in a parallel manner

---

[7] Thomas S. Noonan, "Why the Vikings First Came to Russia," *JbfGO*, vol. 34 (1986), pp. 340, 346; Noonan, "Ninth-Century Dirham Hoards from European Russia: A Preliminary Analysis," *Viking-Age Coinage in the Northern Lands. The Sixth Oxford Symposium on Coinage and Monetary History*, ed. by M. A. S. Blackburn and D. M. Metcalf, BAR International Series 122/1 (Oxford: BAR, 1981), p. 52.

Polotsk guarded access to and from the Baltic along the West Dvina. Smolensk, situated on the upper Dnieper, controlled access from Novgorod or Polotsk to that river and to Kiev, located downstream. Kiev itself commanded the Dnieper and, correspondingly, all traffic that descended that river on its way across the steppe to the Black Sea and to the Byzantine capital and commercial emporium, Constantinople. The river system that encompassed those centers and linked the Baltic and Black Seas via the Dnieper River was known as the route "from the Varangians to the Greeks."

A second route, one of the most important in eastern Europe, followed the Volga River. Long used by the Rus' but well traveled even before their appearance in the region, it connected the forested northlands with the Caspian Sea; by extension it linked the Scandinavian peoples of the Baltic through the Rus' lands with the Muslim empires of the Middle East and Central Asia, located beyond the Caspian. Novgorod controlled transport between the Baltic and the upper Volga, which then flowed through the lands of Rostov toward Bulgar, the main market center on the mid-Volga. From Bulgar the route extended southward to the Caspian; an alternative land route led from Bulgar to the bazaars of Central Asia.

Given their critical importance to commerce, it is not surprising that the Rus' paid serious attention to relations with the Volga states, with Byzantium and the steppe populations, and with Scandinavia. Commercial interests also defined many of the goals of Rus' foreign policy. Vladimir, like his forefathers, sought to subordinate tribes that would deliver goods in tribute, to keep trade routes open and secure, and to attain and preserve trading rights and privileges at foreign markets.

One of the main objects of Rus' concern was the Khazar Empire, which had disintegrated by the beginning of Vladimir's reign. Until the middle of the tenth century, however, it had dominated southeastern Europe. Centered north of the Caspian Sea, the Khazar state had consisted of a largely Muslim and Turkic-speaking population; in contrast, its ruling class, including its ruler or *kagan*, was Jewish. In the ninth and tenth centuries Khazaria controlled territories extending from the north Caucasus to the mid-Volga. But the empire's significance was only partially based on the range of its domain and the tribute collected from its subject peoples. Its location also gave it strategic importance; it preserved stability on the steppe. No traffic of any note, be it river pirates trying to enter the Caspian and raid its shores or mass migrations of nomads seeking fresh pastures west of the Volga River, could cross the Khazar realm or disrupt the region.

Khazaria's geographic position also provided it with commercial advantages. Its capital, Itil', located on one branch of the Volga delta, was the point at which the Volga route leading to the Caspian Sea intersected with a major east–west land route that ran across the steppe. Merchants coming from both the Muslim and Christian worlds followed these routes from north and south, east and west to reach Itil', which became a flourishing commercial center. By the ninth century the Rus' were also coming to its bazaars. Blocked by the Bulgars, who would not allow them to sail down the Volga beyond their own markets, the Rus' reached Itil' by a circuitous route. They traveled down the Dnieper River to the Black Sea, then sailed eastward along its northern coast, where they stopped to trade at Cherson. Resuming their journey, they reached the Sea of Azov and the mouth of the Don River. They then proceeded up the Don to a point where it and the Volga were in closest proximity, crossed over to the Volga, and sailed down the river to Itil'.

The formation and development of Kievan Rus' constituted a direct challenge to Khazaria. The Poliane and the area of Kiev itself had, before the advent of the Rus', formed Khazaria's western frontier. Some of the other Slav tribes that entered Kievan Rus', e.g., the Viatichi whom Sviatoslav conquered in 966, had also been Khazar tributaries. Furthermore, Khazaria controlled all access to the Caspian Sea from the north, and in most instances denied that access to Rus' merchants, adventurers, and pirates alike. Thus despite their commercial accommodation to one another, the Rus' and the Khazars were rivals. In 965, Prince Sviatoslav conducted an attack on Sarkel, a Khazar fortress that stood on the Don River guarding the approaches to the Khazar Empire from the Black Sea, and on Khazar territories in the northern Caucasus. His victory is considered to have delivered a fatal blow to Khazaria, which subsequently collapsed. Its demise, recorded in both the Primary Chronicle and Islamic sources, shocked and destabilized the entire region of the lower Volga, Caspian, and north Caucasus.

Bulgar-on-the-Volga was among the states that, shaken by Khazaria's collapse, competed among themselves even as they tried to establish a new equilibrium. Subordinate to Khazaria until its disintegration, the Volga Bulgars, acting with some local leaders of the north Caucasus, partially restored order along the lower Volga and in the northern Caspian region. They were, however, unable to reestablish the control over the steppe that had been maintained by the Khazars or prevent piracy on the Caspian. But Bulgar did continue to provide Rus' merchants access to their markets. There the Rus' sold their goods for silver coin (until c. 1015) and other Oriental and native products. Bulgar's good relations with the Rus', built upon a mutually favorable pattern of trade, remained consistent from its early encounters with the Varangian pirates through the first centuries of Kievan Rus' existence. Even Vladimir's campaign of 985 resulted in a treaty that outlined mutual trading rights and served as the foundation of stable, peaceful relations until the late eleventh century. Commercial interests also influenced Rus' relations with Byzantium and with the peoples that occupied the steppe separating them. The steppe is the term given to the grassy expanse located directly south of the forested zones settled by the Slav peoples of Kievan Rus'. By the tenth century the area from the Danube to the Don was inhabited by the Pechenegs (known to the Byzantines as Patzinaks and to the Arabs and Persians as Bajanaks), a Turkic-speaking people, who, although exposed to both Islam and Christianity, clung to their pagan gods. They were divided into two wings, each of which was further subdivided. The Pechenegs were nomads. Their basic occupation was animal husbandry, and they easily packed up and moved their felt tents when it became necessary to move their herds of cattle, horses, and sheep from summer to winter grazing areas and back again.

Rus' relations with the Pechenegs were complex. On the one hand, trade relations developed between these two peoples, whose economic activities complemented one another. The Rus' found the horned cattle, horses, sheep, and other livestock raised by the nomads useful for food and clothing, hauling and transport, and for a variety of secondary products such as leather goods. Horses were also important as mounts for warriors. The grain raised by Slav agriculturalists, on the other hand, provided a desirable supplement to the Pecheneg diet of meat and dairy products. The mutual benefit to be derived from trade provided a basis for peaceful relations. From the early tenth century the Primary Chronicle presents an image of relatively tranquil relations between the two peoples; the Pechenegs even joined the Rus' in 944 in a campaign against Byzantium.

Peaceful relations with the Pechenegs were important to the Rus' not just for the opportunity to exchange their goods directly. They were also essential for the princes to conduct their trade with the Byzantines. Initially, the Norsemen had exchanged their booty at the Byzantine colony of Cherson. Rus' offensives against Constantinople in 911 and 944 resulted in treaties that gave Rus' merchants the right to trade in Constantinople as well, and also outlined their commercial rights and privileges. But to reach either Cherson or Constantinople the Rus' had to cross the steppe controlled by the Pechenegs. Emperor Constantine recorded that after the Kievan prince made his rounds to collect tribute from the Slav tribes, he assembled a fleet of river boats, manufactured in Novgorod, Smolensk, Chernigov, and other towns, loaded his goods into them, and conducted this flotilla down the Dnieper River and along the western coast of the Black Sea to sell the products in Constantinople.

Emperor Constantine emphasized that this practice depended upon peaceful relations between the Rus' and the Pechenegs. Well aware of the potential dangers posed by the Pechenegs, who had on occasion attacked Cherson, he observed that these nomads had similarly raided Kievan Rus' and were quite capable of inflicting considerable damage on it. He went on to note:

Nor can the Russians come at this imperial city [Constantinople] . . . either for war or for trade, unless they are at peace with the Pechenegs, because when the Russians come with their ships to the barrages [rapids] of the [Dnieper] river, and cannot pass through them unless they lift their ships off the river and carry them past by porting them on their shoulders, then the men of this nation of the Pechenegs set upon them, and, as they [the Rus'] cannot do two things at once, they are easily routed and cut to pieces.[8]

Shortly after the disintegration of Khazaria in the second half of the century, Rus'–Pecheneg relations became more hostile. Pechenegs raided the frontier of Kievan Rus', seizing crops and captives who were then sold as slaves. They also, as Emperor Constantine had worried, attacked Rus' commercial caravans descending the Dnieper or crossing the steppe on their way to and from Byzantine markets. In 968, Pechenegs attacked the Rus' interior for the first time and laid siege to Kiev. Vladimir's father Sviatoslav, who had not been in Kiev at the time, was later killed during another encounter with the Pechenegs, who "made a cup out of his skull, overlaying it with gold, and . . . drank from it."[9]

The deterioration of Rus'–Pecheneg relations became even more critical after Vladimir adopted Christianity. The consequent establishment of closer ties with Byzantium put a premium on the maintenance of security along the transportation routes that crossed the steppe and gave priority to a policy of neutralizing the Pechenegs, who were becoming more aggressive. In response, Prince Vladimir constructed a series of forts on the tributaries of the Dnieper, near and below Kiev, to guard the southern frontier; they were defended by Slovenes, Krivichi, and Chud' transferred from the north. Almost immediately afterward, just as communication and interaction between Byzantium and Rus' took on heightened importance, war broke out; it was highlighted by a series of Pecheneg attacks on Rus' territory (992, 995, and 997). In one battle (996), which ended in a humiliating defeat, Vladimir personally avoided capture or death only by hiding under a bridge. Afterward, again relying on interregional cooperation, he collected another army in Novgorod and

---

[8] Constantine Porphyrogenitus, *De Administrando Imperio*, pp. 49–53.
[9] *Medieval Russia's Epics, Chronicles, and Tales*, p. 65.

brought it south to continue the war, which persisted through the remainder of his reign. Just before his own death (1015), Vladimir sent his son Boris to lead a campaign against the Pechenegs; on his return Boris was killed by his brother Sviatopolk, who thereby launched a bloody succession struggle, which will be discussed in the next chapter.

The net result of Vladimir's defensive policies, however, was a success. The Pechenegs were driven deeper into the steppe away from Kievan Rus' settlements; the width of the "neutral zone" was doubled from the distance covered in one day's travel to two. Pecheneg auxiliary forces participated in the war of succession fought by Vladimir's sons after his death. But independent Pecheneg attacks on the Rus' lands relaxed.

As a result of his foreign policies, Vladimir secured his borders as well as the trade routes running through his lands. He was thus able to sell the products he and his sons had collected as tribute from the Slav tribes to the Pechenegs and to merchants at Bulgar and Constantinople. At the other end point of the Rus' trading network were the Scandinavian markets on the Baltic coast. The Rus' retained close ties with their Scandinavian compatriots. Vladimir had sought refuge among them when he felt threatened by Iaropolk. He had been able to raise a Varangian force to assist him when he returned to overthrow his brother. Kievan Rus' similarly offered sanctuary to exiled Scandinavians. One example of this reciprocal arrangement is reflected in the legend of the great Viking, Olaf Trygveson. After his father had been murdered, Olaf was trying to escape to the safety of Vladimir's court, where his uncle held high rank; while en route, however, he was captured by pirates. In addition to exchanging exiled princes, the lands of Rus' and Scandinavia also traded a variety of goods. By the time of Vladimir's reign silver coins, silks, glassware, and jewelry from Muslim and Byzantine lands as well as native Slav products were reaching Scandinavian market towns via the lands of Rus'. Some of these items were brought back by Varangian mercenaries, who had been hired by the Rus' princes. But much of it arrived as the result of commercial exchanges that took place, mainly at Novgorod, for a variety of European goods, including woolen cloth, pottery, and weapons.

The achievements of Prince Vladimir, who died in 1015, were notable. He secured the right of his dynasty to rule exclusively in the lands of the eastern Slavs, Kievan Rus'. He overcame competing Varangian dynasties (Polotsk); he held back rival neighboring states; and he gained recognition and legitimacy for his dynasty from the powerful Byzantines and European Christian powers.

With the latter Vladimir maintained generally cordial relations. The main exceptions had occurred early in his reign when he directed campaigns against the Poles for control of Cherven, located southwest of Kiev (981), and against the Lithuanian tribe of Iativigians on the Neman (Niemen) River to the northwest (983). After that, his relations with the central European states of Poland and Hungary as well as his Scandinavian neighbors were peaceful. They demonstrated their respect and acceptance of the Riurikids by intermarrying with Vladimir's children. Sviatopolk married the daughter of King Boleslaw of Poland, while his half-brother Iaroslav wed the daughter of the Swedish king Olaf.

In conjunction with consolidating his personal and his dynasty's position in Kievan Rus', Vladimir also successfully defended his realm from external aggression. He placed his sons with their retinues on the borders, he built forts to defend the southern frontier, and he forced the most aggressive foe of the Rus', the Pechenegs, to retreat. By the end of his reign transit across the steppe was safer and the Pecheneg threat to Kievan Rus' was reduced. Vladimir's administrative and defensive measures also enabled him and his sons to collect the revenue necessary to maintain the armed forces, required for both internal stability and external defense, and to continue commercial exchanges with the great empires of the region.

Vladimir's policies accomplished more than the minimum necessary for his immediate political goals. The distribution of his sons around the country displaced tribal leaders and laid the groundwork for the formation of a political organization based on joint dynastic rule. The adoption of Christianity focused the entire population of his country on a single set of religious principles, which also lent ideological support to his political authority, while the establishment of closer ties to Byzantium and simultaneous maintenance of trade relations with the Muslim East kept Kievan Rus' open to a diverse array of cultural influences and material goods. The transfer of personnel from the north to man the southern forts protecting Kiev reflected an ability to mobilize resources from all over his lands for a single purpose and thereby encouraged a process of social integration. Vladimir's policies thus laid the foundation for the transformation of his domain from a conglomeration of tribes, each of which separately paid tribute to him, into an integrated realm bound by a common religion and cultural ties as well as the political structure provided by a shared dynasty.

2

PRINCES AND POLITICS
(1015–1125)

·

One of Vladimir's major achievements was the confirmation of both domestic and foreign recognition of exclusive Riurikid rule over the eastern Slavs. Following his reign the Riurikid dynasty remained a fundamental and permanent feature of the Kievan Rus' political system. Other aspects of the political system were more fluid. Successive generations of the dynasty, facing ever-changing political circumstances, engaged in a continuous quest for a functional political organization that could maintain the integrity of their realm. Although the dynasty itself remained a constant feature in the political structure of Kievan Rus', the internal divisions of the territory it ruled and their relationship to their princes were in flux. This chapter will examine the dynasty's structure and its evolving patterns of succession; the organization of the territories ruled by the dynasty; and the foreign policies undertaken by its princes.

THE RIURIKID DYNASTY

The political organization observable during Vladimir's reign successfully established and preserved internal and external stability for the Riurikid realm. But that structure, which involved the dispersal of his sons to outlying princely seats around Kievan Rus', provided little to guide his sons in organizing their domain after his death and solving the first problem they confronted – the choice of a successor.

There were competing organizational principles within the dynasty. On the one hand, the dynasty developed a practice of joint rule, shared by all members of a single generation, over all peoples within the realm.

On the other hand there was a tendency toward solitary rule. Both principles were reflected in the legend of Riurik's arrival in the Rus' lands. The legend describes Riurik as initially ruling the tribes around Novgorod, Izborsk, and Beloozero together with his brothers. After his brothers died, however, Riurik ruled the realm alone. The pattern was repeated in 972, when Sviatoslav died and his three sons shared the realm: Iaropolk at Kiev, Oleg among the Derevliane, and Vladimir at Novgorod. Fratricidal warfare resulted in Vladimir becoming the sole prince of all their portions.

Although Vladimir ruled as prince of Kiev alone, his assignment of princely seats throughout his realm to his sons invoked the principle of shared generational authority. When, during their father's reign, Prince Iaroslav replaced his deceased brother in Novgorod and and his younger brother Boris moved into Iaroslav's position in Rostov, a corollary principle of rotation among the princely seats by the princes within a generation was introduced.

Vladimir's death in 1015 sparked a succession struggle. Prince Vladimir, it is important to recall, had had numerous wives and concubines (the chronicles claimed hundreds!) before his conversion to Christianity and marriage to the Byzantine princess Anna. And they had borne at least twelve sons. It is not surprising that disputes among his numerous heirs resulted in a fierce contest for control of Kiev.

The first to take Vladimir's place in Kiev was Sviatopolk, who since 988 had ruled the Dregovich center of Turov, located northwest of Kiev. Almost immediately he turned against potential challengers. His first victim was Boris, who at the time of Vladimir's death was commanding an army that included a large component of his father's *druzhina* in a campaign against the Pechenegs. Indeed, when Sviatopolk assumed the Kievan throne, the city populace did not receive him well because, the chronicler noted, their brothers were serving with Boris. Boris' advisers, the chronicler further recorded, urged him to use the military power at his disposal to seize the throne. But Boris, declaring he could never raise his hand against his brother, refused to act. Sviatopolk, having no such scruples, ordered Boris to be murdered. He then proceeded to assassinate Boris' full brother Gleb and a half-brother, Sviatoslav, who was caught while fleeing to Hungary.

Sviatopolk's bloody rampage aroused Iaroslav, then prince of Novgorod. He gathered an army, marched southward, and in their first encounter (1016) defeated Sviatopolk, who fled to Poland. But Sviatopolk soon returned with his father-in-law, King Boleslaw, and with his Polish troops recovered Kiev and forced Iaroslav back to Novgorod. The two continued their wars with Varangian auxiliaries aiding Iaroslav while

Pechenegs alternated with Poles in support of Sviatopolk until 1019. At that time Sviatopolk, again fleeing westward, became ill and died. Iaroslav assumed the Kievan throne.

Iaroslav was, in turn, challenged by his brother, Mstislav. Mstislav, according to the 988 chronicle entry, had been sent to rule Tmutorokan', a commercial center located on the shore of the Sea of Azov and separated by the steppe from the main centers of Kievan Rus'. In 1024, he advanced from Tmutorokan' toward Kiev. With Iaroslav in Novgorod at the time, the local populace rejected Mstislav, who established himself at Chernigov. This time, when Iaroslav led an army of Varangians south-ward, he was defeated by Mstislav. The two nevertheless resolved their dispute by dividing the lands of Rus' between them. The Dnieper River served as the dividing line. Iaroslav controlled Kiev, the lands west of the river, and those to the north, including Novgorod. Mstislav from his center at Chernigov controlled all the lands east of the Dnieper, including Tmutorokan'.

The fratricidal wars for the Kievan throne were neither random nor simple expressions of sibling rivalry or greed for power. The chronicler attributed them to a failure to honor the Christian tenet of brotherly love, especially on the part of the main villain, Sviatopolk the Damned. Boris and Gleb, in contrast, were depicted as behaving in accordance with that very principle. Their refusal to defend themselves by fighting their brother gave their deaths an aura of martyrdom. In 1072 they were canonized as Kievan Rus' first two native saints.

Despite the chronicle's interpretation, an examination of the interprincely contest reveals that other factors associated with the dynastic and political organization also influenced the events. The combatants all appear to have shared a recognition and respect for at least one principle of succession: the senior member of their generation should inherit Vladimir's throne. It was the definition of seniority they disputed. It could be defined simply in terms of chronological age or, alternatively, seniority could be influenced as well by the status of Vladimir's wives, the various mothers of the competing heirs. Viewed as a contest based on different interpretations of "seniority" within the generation, the succession struggle becomes a key to understanding the evolving system of dynastic control and generational succession within Kievan Rus'.

The Primary Chronicle contains three lists that name Vladimir's sons. One of them also identifies their mothers. It indicates that Iaroslav and Mstislav, as well as Iziaslav, who had died in the year 1001, and Vsevolod were all sons of Rogneda, Vladimir's first, hence principal, wife. Sviatopolk's mother was identified as a Greek woman, the widow of Iaropolk, who had been Vladimir's elder brother and victim. The

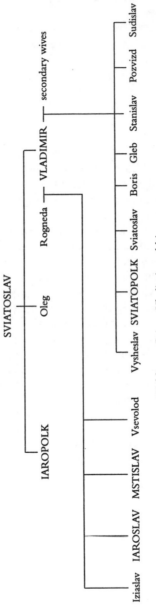

Table 2.1 Prince Vladimir and his sons

chronicler, a Christian monk, stressed Sviatopolk's illegitimacy by pointing out he was actually Iaropolk's, not Vladimir's, son. Boris and Gleb were identified as sons of a Bulgarian woman, while Sviatoslav's mother was a Czech. The chronicle furthermore suggests that the adopted Sviatopolk may have been older than all of Vladimir's sons who had survived to adulthood in 1015.

If so, Sviatopolk inherited the Kievan throne as the eldest member of his generation. The refusal of Boris, who may actually have been Vladimir's choice as successor, to raise his hand against his elder brother may be regarded not only as a sign of his devout Christian beliefs, but as an implicit acknowledgment of Sviatopolk's seniority and right to the throne. An interpretation of seniority defined by age alone would legitimize Sviatopolk's claim.

But Iaroslav and Mstislav, sons of Vladimir's primary wife, Rogneda, did not accept Sviatopolk as the rightful grand prince. A variant interpretation of the principle of seniority, which took into account not merely age but also the status or "legitimacy" of the mother, gave them priority over Sviatopolk. The outcome of their military challenge to Sviatopolk also resolved the political debate and confirmed the righteousness of their interpretation.

The second stage of the succession struggle, the conflict between Iaroslav and Mstislav, also involved the issue of seniority, but the relative status of the rival brothers is even less clear. The various lists recorded in the chronicle provide contradictory information about Mstislav. One (*sub anno* 980) indicates he was older than his brother Iaroslav; if that is accurate, his challenge to Iaroslav was consistent with the principle of succession by seniority within the generation. It would not explain, however, why, after a military victory, he left Kiev to Iaroslav and established his seat at Chernigov. Another entry, which appears later in the chronicle text (*sub anno* 988) but is considered to have been composed earlier and to be more accurate, implies that Mstislav was younger than Iaroslav. If that were the case, then his challenge was without foundation and even the weight of his military victory was insufficient to overturn the legitimacy of Iaroslav's claim to Kiev.

The outcome of the conflict may also have been influenced by the position taken by the Kievan population. Whatever the motivating factors, the brothers reached a compromise, and agreed to share their father's domain. Whatever the reality of the relative ages of the two sons of Rogneda, Mstislav recognized Iaroslav as his "elder brother" or the senior prince with jurisdiction over Kiev. But there is some question as to whether either brother actually sat in the capital. The chronicle indicates that Iaroslav returned to Novgorod, while Mstislav remained at Chernigov.

The very differences in the chronicle entries reflect the centrality of the principle of seniority to legitimacy within the dynasty. Michael Millard examined and dated the three lists that appear in the chronicle. The oldest, composed at the end of the tenth century and inserted *sub anno* 988, is the one that describes Vladimir's distribution of lands among his sons. Sviatopolk is named third, but the two older brothers, Vysheslav and Iziaslav, had both predeceased their father. This is the list that provides the basis for recognizing Sviatopolk as the eldest among Vladimir's surviving heirs. The statement that weakened Sviatopolk's case by naming his mother and alluding to his illegitimacy was the second of the these lists, inserted earlier in the chronicle *sub anno* 980, but composed between 1036 and 1040, i.e., after Iaroslav had achieved full control of Kievan Rus'. The last of the entries, written after 1059 but added to the 988 entry, actually altered the chronological order of the sons, identifying Iaroslav as the eldest surviving son, Sviatopolk as his younger brother, and demoting Mstislav to a position just above Boris and Gleb.[1] By the second half of the eleventh century, when the final list was composed and acceptance of Christianity had made the issue of the status of one's mother both irrelevant and perhaps an embarrassing reminder of the pagan past, the details of birth were reconfigured to make it appear that the succession of 1015–19 had conformed to what in the meantime had become the accepted rule of succession: the grand prince's eldest son was the legitimate heir to the Kievan throne.

Despite the unpromising beginning of his reign, Iaroslav ruled compatibly with Mstislav until the latter's death in 1036; he then ruled alone until 1054. His reign, the highlights of which will be discussed below, proved to be a "Golden Age" for Kievan Rus'.

In an attempt to avoid hostilities like those that had plagued his succession, Iaroslav left a Testament to his sons. No text of the document has survived, but its substance was recorded in the Primary Chronicle. According to the chronicle, Iaroslav, who had imprisoned his only remaining brother in 1036, bestowed Kiev on his eldest son Iziaslav and advised the others to heed Iziaslav as they would their father. He then willed Chernigov to Sviatoslav, Pereiaslavl' to Vsevolod, Smolensk to Viacheslav, and Vladimir in Volynia to Igor'.

Many scholars regard Iaroslav's distribution of territory and political responsibility as the basis of the "rota" or "ladder" system of succession, according to which the Kievan throne passed laterally from one brother to another in order of their ages. They generally add that the princely seats

---

[1] Michael Millard, "Sons of Vladimir, Brothers of Iaroslav," *CMRS*, vol. 12 (1971), pp. 286–295.

assigned by Iaroslav to his sons were arranged in a hierarchy. Thus, the eldest brother ruled from the most important town, Kiev. The next eldest held the second-ranking town, Chernigov; he was followed by the third eldest whose seat was at Pereiaslavl'. If and when a vacancy opened in one of the towns, the next prince in line "rotated" into that position.

Despite Iaroslav's allocations, the Riurikid dynasty endured repeated interprincely conflict. Their experience has convinced other scholars to reject the notion that Iaroslav introduced the rota system. On the contrary, this group of scholars considered the persistently recurring battles as evidence of a complete failure of the Riurikid dynasty to create an orderly pattern of succession that would facilitate the development of a successful political system.

A third view, presented here, suggests that the members of the Riurikid dynasty recognized and adopted common norms of succession. But it does not accept the notion that a fully formed, comprehensive system was introduced at a single stroke by Iaroslav or any other prince. Rather, this interpretation proposes that the succession patterns evolved in conjunction with the growth of the dynasty and the expansion of the state it ruled. The rules of succession, hammered out in battle between members of one generation, were honored by the next. But settlements achieved by previous generations and offered to their descendants as precedents for future successions neither anticipated nor encompassed all the new complications and sources of controversy that their sons and nephews would confront. The issues they faced, generated by the growing size of the dynasty, periodically prompted a need to refine the rules of succession. The princes of younger generations thus also resorted to war. Their conflicts, however, did not reopen the old resolved issues. Instead, they addressed new points of dispute derived from the increasing complexity of an extended ruling family. Each round of combat resulted in the enunciation of a clearer, more precise, and more elaborate definition of the principles guiding the division and transfer of power. Each confrontation may therefore be regarded as a stage in the evolution of the succession system, a process and a system so critical to the political organization that they excited passions of war.

The next phase of intradynastic warfare occurred shortly after Iaroslav's death (1054). Despite his father's precautions, Iziaslav's authority was not unchallenged. His first rival was not any of his brothers, but a cousin, Vseslav of Polotsk. In 988, Prince Vladimir, it will be recalled, had assigned Polotsk to his son Iziaslav (d. 1001). Iziaslav's sons, recognizing that the quarrels of 1015–19 were rightfully confined to their uncles, i.e., the members of the dynasty's eldest generation, did not participate in the succession struggle following Vladimir's death.

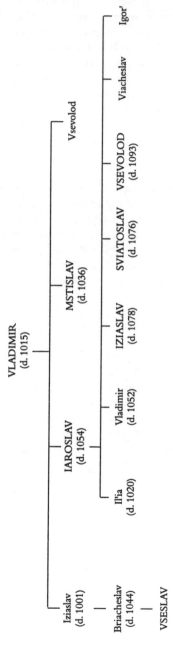

Table 2.2 The descendants of Vladimir: the succession struggles of 1067–1078

But in 1067, Vseslav, the grandson of Iziaslav Vladimirovich, challenged Grand Prince Iziaslav Iaroslavich's right to the throne. As head of the branch of the dynasty descended from Iaroslav's elder brother, Vseslav was claiming seniority over his cousin. His initial attempt ended in failure and his own imprisonment. The following year, however, under pressure from an attack by steppe nomads and a popular uprising in Kiev, Iziaslav fled to Poland. Vseslav was released; he held the throne until Iziaslav returned with a Polish army and recovered Kiev in May 1069.

Vseslav's actions, like those that had spawned conflict a generation earlier, were not necessarily a sign of disorder within the dynasty or the absence of a succession system. Rather, they too were consistent with the principle that called for succession by the senior member of the dynasty. But by the middle of the eleventh century the dynasty had divided into two branches, the descendants of Iziaslav Vladimirovich and those of Iaroslav Vladimirovich. That circumstance defined a new issue and obliged the dynasty to determine which branches should be considered eligible for the succession and, of those, which one should be considered the senior branch. That issue was subject to competing interpretations; its resolution was critical to identifying the senior member of the dynasty, the legitimate heir to the Kievan throne.

Military might once again settled the political debate. Iziaslav's ultimate victory over his cousin Vseslav refined the evolving rules of succession: only those princes whose fathers had actually held the throne of Kiev could succeed to it. The founder of the Polotsk line, Iziaslav Vladimirovich, had predeceased his father and consequently had never been grand prince of Kiev. On that basis his descendants, including his sons and his grandson Vseslav, were eliminated from subsequent succession to the central throne. Polotsk retained an affiliation with Kievan Rus' through its dynastic linkage, but its status was distinct from other territories ruled more directly from the Kievan throne.

The reign of Iziaslav Iaroslavich, however, continued to be troubled. In 1073, he lost the Kievan throne again, this time to his brothers Sviatoslav of Chernigov, who replaced him, and Vsevolod of Pereiaslavl'. When Sviatoslav died three years later, Iziaslav resumed his position in Kiev. Once Iziaslav had reestablished himself in Kiev, he transferred Sviatoslav's former domain, Chernigov, to his brother Vsevolod. He and Vsevolod regarded Chernigov as an integral part of the Kievan realm, control over which was shared by their generation; Vsevolod, the next eldest brother, therefore moved up the ladder or rotated into the position of the deceased Sviatoslav.

But the establishment of Vsevolod on their father's throne was contested by Sviatoslav's sons, who claimed Chernigov as their rightful

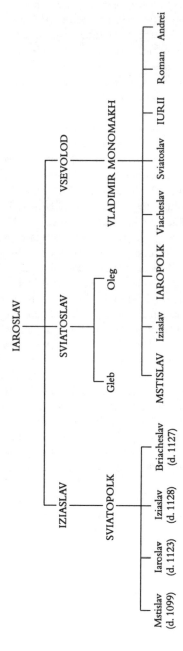

Table 2.3 Succession to the Kievan throne: Prince Iaroslav to the sons of Vladimir Monomakh

legacy. In 1054, when their grandfather, Grand Prince Iaroslav, had distributed the Kievan Rus' lands among his sons, he had assigned Chernigov to their father. They consequently regarded the land as their *otchina* or patrimony to be inherited, similarly to Polotsk, strictly within their branch of the dynasty.

By 1078, Iziaslav and Vsevolod, so recently competitors themselves, joined forces to uphold the principle of generational authority and rotation. They defeated their nephews, forcing Prince Oleg Sviatoslavich to flee to Tmutorokan'. But in the course of the battle Grand Prince Iziaslav was killed. Vsevolod, as the sole surviving member of his generation, succeeded him in a politically orderly, if not entirely peaceful, fashion. Until his death in 1093 he alone ruled the main components of Kievan Rus': Kiev, Chernigov, and Pereiaslavl'.

In 1093, Kievan Rus' passed to the next generation. The princes who claimed eligibility for a place in the rotation for succession to the Kievan throne were by this time divided into three dynastic lines or branches: the sons of Iziaslav, Sviatoslav, and Vsevolod. Sviatopolk Iziaslavich, the eldest son of the senior branch, hence the senior member of his generation, inherited the Kievan throne in accordance with all the guidelines set by his forefathers; he ruled until 1113. But a conflict erupted over which line or branch would follow him. It took the form of a contest for control over Chernigov. And it developed into a feud between the Sviatoslavichi, and their cousins, the descendents of Vsevolod, specifically Vladimir Monomakh and his sons.

During his reign as grand prince Vsevolod had delegated his authority over Chernigov to his son Vladimir Monomakh, who acted as his governor there, although Sviatoslavichi may have continued to control Chernigov's eastern territory, Murom. When Vsevolod died, Monomakh refused to yield Chernigov to Sviatoslav's sons. He not only retained Chernigov, but appointed one of his own sons to rule Murom. Oleg Sviatoslavich aggressively pressed his clan's claim to Chernigov. In 1094, he returned from Tmutorokan' with an armed force and ejected his cousin Vladimir Monomakh from Chernigov.

Monomakh then settled in Pereiaslavl'. His sons, however, still controlled the eastern extensions of the Chernigov principality, including Murom on the Oka River. In 1096, Oleg led an expedition to recover it and killed its prince Iziaslav, a son of Vladimir Monomakh. Oleg then pushed into the Rostov region, which was a possession of the Pereiaslavl' prince. In response, Mstislav, another of Monomakh's sons, led a force from Novgorod against Oleg and chased him out of the Rostov area back to Murom.

As was true of the previous succession struggles, the bloody feud between the Sviatoslavichi and the Monomashichi did not reflect an absence of a political structure recognized by all members of the dynasty. On the contrary, by the end of the eleventh century the principles adopted by several generations of Vladimir's heirs had formed the basis of a well-defined political system in Kievan Rus'. Those principles were: exclusive Riurikid dynastic rule over all the lands of Rus'; shared rule by a single generation of princes over regional centers within Kievan Rus'; lateral succession in order of seniority within a generation; and the limitation of eligibility for succession to the pinnacle of power, the throne at Kiev, to princes whose fathers had themselves been grand princes. These principles afforded mechanisms for the Riurikid dynasty to maintain their exclusive political authority over all the components of Kievan Rus'. They also compensated for the high rates of early death among the warrior-princes to ensure that the dynasty would perpetually be able to provide a militarily strong, experienced adult to fulfill the responsibilities of grand prince of Kiev.

The conflict between the Sviatoslavichi and Monomakh did not seek to upset any of those general principles. Its focus was a refinement of the last one, a more precise definition of the circumstances under which tenure as grand prince would be recognized as a valid basis for future claims to the Kievan throne. The Sviatoslavich claim to Chernigov and by extension to their position in the rotation to the Kievan throne depended on their father's tenure as grand prince. Sviatoslav had reigned as grand prince of Kiev from 1073 to 1076. But he had done so "out of order," only after forcibly evicting his elder brother Iziaslav, who later recovered his throne. The Sviatoslavichi evidently considered their father's tenure as grand prince a legitimate basis for their claim both to Chernigov and to participation in the succession cycle. Their cousins, focusing on Sviatoslav's irregular means of attaining the Kievan throne, rejected that claim. Although warfare was the ultimate means available to these adversaries to resolve their disagreement, their wars were nevertheless conducted within the framework of a set of commonly recognized political principles.

In this instance, however, the contested issue was not resolved by war. Rather, at a conference held in 1097 at Liubech, a town in the Chernigov land, the terms of joint dynastic possession of the realm were altered. At the conference, where all the dynastic branches descending from Iaroslav were represented, the fundamental principle of shared responsiblity for Kievan Rus' was upheld. But within their common realm the princes differentiated distinct principalities by making each one the patrimonial domain of one branch of the dynasty. The conference thus confirmed the existing distribution of lands: Sviatopolk retained Kiev, the "heritage" of his father Iziaslav; Vladimir Monomakh received Pereiaslavl', the domain of his father Vsevolod; Oleg and his brothers were accorded Sviatoslav's possession, Chernigov. Other apportionments of towns and regions to dynastic branches that had been dropped from the central succession were also reaffirmed. Of all the principalities, only Kiev would again become subject to generational rotation across branch lines.

The apparent success of the Liubech conference encouraged the Riurikid princes to reconvene to consider other issues, disputes among themselves as well as matters of war and peace with their neighbors. It also provided the basis for calming intradynastic controversy for the next succession cycles. In exchange for confirmation of patrimonial rights to their principality, the Chernigov princes withdrew from the rotation for the central throne of Kiev. Thus, when Sviatopolk died in 1113, they remained uninvolved despite the transfer of the Kievan throne from Iziaslav's branch of the dynasty, as designated by the conference, to Vsevolod's, specifically to his son Vladimir Monomakh.

In 1113, the citizenry of Kiev invited Vladimir Monomakh to take the throne. By doing so, they were rejecting the decision made at Liubech that placed Kiev under the rule of Iziaslav's descendants; according to that formula Kiev should have passed to Sviatopolk's eldest surviving son, Iaroslav. The Kievans were also bypassing Sviatoslav's sons and thus confirming the ineligibility of his line. The invitation to Vladimir Monomakh was thus a statement in favor of restoring the principle of naming the senior eligible member of the eldest generation of the dynasty to rule as grand prince in the capital city, Kiev.

Prince Vladimir, whose surname derived from his Byzantine mother's family, was at the time prince of Pereiaslavl'. By opposing his Sviatoslavich cousins, he had become a pivotal figure in dynastic politics. He was also a mighty military leader, who had in the preceding decade led, along with Grand Prince Sviatopolk, a series of successful campaigns against the Polovtsy of the steppe and had thereby secured the southern frontier.

Despite his popularity and power, the sixty-year-old Monomakh declined the invitation. Whether he did so out of respect for the terms of the Liubech agreement or a recognition that popular appeal was a relatively weak basis for legitimacy remains unknown. But as the situation in Kiev deteriorated into violent riots, he received a second invitation, this time issued by a broader spectrum of the population. Vladimir then accepted the throne. As noted, his cousins, the Sviatoslavichi, did not oppose him.

Vladimir Monomakh ruled as grand prince from 1113 to 1125. The full dynasty, including the Chernigov princes, accepted his dynastic seniority. The sole exception was Sviatopolk's son, Iaroslav of Volynia. In 1117–18, he expressed opposition to Monomakh, but while he was in Poland and Hungary gathering an army, the grand prince took possession of Volynia. He successively appointed his two youngest sons, first Roman, then Andrei, to rule the region and effectively separated Iaroslav from his base of power.

When Monomakh died in 1125, the Kievan throne passed to the next generation, but remained within his branch of the dynasty. This occurred in accordance with all the rules that had evolved over the preceding century. Only those members of the generation whose fathers had been grand princes of Kiev, i.e., sons of Sviatopolk and Vladimir Monomakh, were eligible to inherit the throne. Sviatopolk's line was effectively eliminated from the succession with the death in 1123 of Iaroslav, then its eldest member, who had earlier lost his seat in Volynia. Monomakh's sons, the princes of Pereiaslavl' and Rostov, thus became the legitimate heirs. Vladimir's eldest son, Mstislav, succeeded to the grand princely throne of Kiev.

Although the most dramatic activities of Riurikid princes were associated with their intradynastic conflicts, discussed above, and their campaigns against foreign foes, discussed below, the princes were also engaged in more mundane functions. Within each prince's realm, he was responsible for collecting tribute and taxes, for providing security and maintaining order, administering justice, and supporting the Church.

In these efforts as well as his military ventures the prince was assisted by his retainers, the members of his *druzhina*. They were, first and foremost, the prince's comrades-in-arms, the core of his army. Whereas other components of his military force, hired mercenaries from abroad or a supplementary citizens' militia, dispersed after a campaign, the prince's retainers generally chose to remain with him. Thus, even when Vladimir Monomakh was forced to abandon Chernigov and withdraw to Pereiaslavl' in 1094, his retinue shared his fate, characterized as three years of hardship and deprivation. Each prince depended upon the members of his *druzhina* not only for military power, but for their political advice and administrative assistance. The prince thus supported his retainers, either by directly absorbing their expenses or by appointing them as his agents to conduct various administrative and judicial duties, for which they would receive fees from the populace. The grand princes of Kiev on occasion even sent members of their retinues rather than members of the dynasty to act as governors in towns within their domain.

Another institution also influenced the politics of Kievan Rus'. This was the *veche* or town assembly. Scholars have debated the constitution of the *veche*. Some have concluded that it truly represented all free male citizens, regardless of wealth or social status. Others have argued that it was fundamentally an instrument of the wealthier class of Kievan society; when members of that class deemed it advantageous, they encouraged merchants and artisans to join in their debate and, thereby, to strengthen their position by force of numbers.

Popular influence on the political process, including the selection of princes, was evident in Kiev in discrete situations during the eleventh and twelfth centuries. The events of 1068–69 provide one example. In that instance, as detailed above, the Kievan citizenry, terrified by the prospect of an onslaught by the Polovtsy, played a pivotal role in placing Vseslav of Polotsk on the Kievan throne, if only briefly. The Kievan populace was similarly involved in pressuring Vladimir Monomakh to accept the grand princely throne in 1113. The *veche* was also influential elsewhere. In Novgorod, where it would in future centuries exercise more power than in any other part of the Riurikid realm, it was rejecting candidates proposed to become the city's princes by the late eleventh century.

THE PRINCIPALITIES OF KIEVAN RUS´

The princes of the Riurikid dynasty, aided by their *druzhiny* and influenced at times by popular pressure exercised through the *veche*, ruled the lands that constituted the state of Kievan Rus'. During the reign of Vladimir I the state consisted of a group of diverse tribes, all of which recognized the suzerainty of the grand prince of Kiev and paid tribute to him, his designated prince, or his agent. At the end of Vladimir's reign Kievan Rus' was politically a single, coherent unit; the posts held by his sons were regional or tribal centers within his realm, not distinct principalities.

As intradynastic relations became more intricate, so the political organization of the Kievan state became more complex. By the reign of Vladimir's namesake, Vladimir Monomakh, the territory that had been internally differentiated by traditional tribal or ethnic divisions had become a federation of distinct principalities. Their princes, all members of the same dynasty, continued to look to Kiev as the center and to its ruler, the grand prince, as the political leader of Kievan Rus'. Yet their relationships to Kiev varied. Some branches of the dynasty, by becoming ineligible for the central throne, presided over principalities that became increasingly independent. Others, deeply involved in the politics of grand princely succession, remained intimately linked with Kiev.

The Polotsk princes reigned over a principality of the first type. By the time Vladimir I died, they had already lost the basis of their claim to the throne of Kiev. After their futile attempt to reenter the order of succession (1067–69), the Polotsk princes withdrew from Kievan succession politics. Their domain, correspondingly, was not considered among the lands directly controlled by the Kievan prince.

By the middle of the eleventh century two other southern Rus' lands were emerging as distinct and politically significant principalities. One, Chernigov, became increasingly independent of Kiev. The other, Pereiaslavl', gained stature through its close affiliation with Kiev. Following the death of Iaroslav (1054) the triad of Kiev, Chernigov, and Pereiaslavl' formed the core of the Riurikid realm. When within six years of Iaroslav's death their brothers Viacheslav and Igor' also died, Iziaslav, Sviatoslav, and Vsevolod, ruling Kiev, Chernigov, and Pereiaslavl' respectively, cooperated so closely that they have been labelled by some scholars as a triumvirate. Their coordinated activity was essential for the successful operation of the state or federation of Kievan Rus'.

The city of Chernigov, located on the Desna River, controlled territories along that river and its tributaries with their population of Severiane; its territories may also have incorporated some Radimichi in the north and Viatichi to the northeast. It had been associated with the Kievan realm even before the reign of Vladimir, but it had not been among the towns recorded in the chronicle *sub anno* 988 as those Vladimir distributed among his sons. Most probably Vladimir had considered it inseparable from Kiev and ruled it personally.

Chernigov became more prominent in 1024, when Prince Mstislav Vladimirovich made it his capital. The center of the eastern half of Kievan Rus', Chernigov was then rich and powerful enough to compete with Kiev. In contrast to the simple state structure of Vladimir's era, the Riurikid realm during the second quarter of the eleventh century was beginning to subdivide. Although Iaroslav reunited the two halves of the dynasty's domain in 1036, Chernigov remained differentiated as a distinct unit, stretching eastward to encompass the lands of Riazan' and Murom, which in his Testament Grand Prince Iaroslav left to his son Sviatoslav.

An indication of the development of Chernigov's internal autonomy may be discerned in a series of incidents concerning Tmutorokan'. After 1054, Sviatoslav's son Gleb ruled Tmutorokan'. When in 1064, however, Gleb's position was threatened by a distant cousin, it was his father, Prince Sviatoslav of Chernigov, who came to his defense. The incident, which was ultimately resolved in Gleb's favor when his opponent was poisoned by a Byzantine official from Cherson, was treated by Grand Prince Iziaslav and the rest of the Riurikid clan as an internal affair of the increasingly independent principality of Chernigov.

During the second half of the eleventh century Chernigov remained closely associated with both Kiev and Pereiaslavl'. But by the middle of the eleventh century it had acquired its own territorial extensions and was engaged in its own political activities. The dynasty's perception of Chernigov as a separate polity was evident during the struggle for control over it following Sviatoslav's death (1076). The result of that conflict, however, left Chernigov under the rule of Grand Prince Vsevolod, who appointed his son Vladimir Monomakh to rule there, while their opponent Oleg Sviatoslavich fled to Tmutorokan'. For the duration of his reign, i.e., until almost of the end of the century, Vsevolod maintained tight bonds between Kiev and the principality of Chernigov.

Chernigov's detachment from Kiev occurred at the end of the century. Oleg Sviatoslavich, who had remained in Tmutorokan' since 1078 with the exception of four years as a captive in Byzantium, took advantage of Vsevolod's death to recover Chernigov for himself and his kin. The consequent wars between the Sviatoslavichi and Monomashichi as well as the Liubech conference led to the withdrawal of the Chernigov princes' claims to the Kievan throne. As a result, the principality of Chernigov acquired a status similar to that of Polotsk. It became the heritage of a specific branch of the Riurikid dynasty. Through its dynastic connection it remained politically affiliated with Kievan Rus'; but with its princes eliminated from the rotation for succession to the central throne of Kiev, it assumed a more independent character.

Pereiaslavl' provides a sharp contrast to the experience of its neighbor, Chernigov. Pereiaslavl', like Chernigov, existed and was associated with Kiev before the reign of Vladimir. But Vladimir evidently built a new city, known by the same name, in 992; it was located on the Trubezh River to the east of the Dnieper River and south of the cities of Kiev and Chernigov. The territories associated with the town of Pereiaslavl' also bordered the steppe and bore the brunt of raids from the steppe nomads. Their critical importance to Kievan Rus' defense dictated a need for cooperation with, if not full attachment to, Kiev. The close relationship between the two centers is reflected by the fact that many of the sites fortified by Vladimir I were located along the Trubezh and Sula Rivers, eastern tributaries of the Dnieper, which ran through Pereiaslavl' territory. When Iaroslav and Mstislav divided their realm, the Pereiaslavl' territories fell into Mstislav's domain. The status of these lands was not clarified until 1054, when in his Testament Grand Prince Iaroslav identified Pereiaslavl' as one of the principalities within Kievan Rus' and assigned it to his son Vsevolod. During the next decades Pereiaslavl', like Chernigov, remained closely affiliated with Kiev.

Although Pereiaslavl's location made it crucial as a guardian of the southern frontier, the principality also gained significance for its north-eastern territorial extensions, the lands known variously as Rostov, Rostov-Suzdal', Suzdalia, and Vladimir-Suzdal'. The original inhabitants of the area, the Finnic Merya tribes, were joined in the ninth and tenth centuries by eastern Slav migrants: Slovenes from the Novgorod region, Krivichi from the Smolensk area, and Viatichi from the Oka River. The chronicle entry *sub anno* 988 reports that Vladimir I assigned this north-eastern district to his son Iaroslav, who continued to oversee it even after he moved on to Novgorod and, ultimately, Kiev. In 1024, while the region was beset with famine, he personally suppressed an uprising provoked by pagan sorcerers. Afterward, he issued a charter defining tribute levies and refining administrative structures for the region.

When Iaroslav died in 1054, Pereiaslavl' with the lands of Rostov was assigned to Prince Vsevolod. Possibly because Vsevolod did not appoint anyone to rule Rostov, little was recorded about its development. It is known that by 1071, the city of Iaroslavl' had been established on the course of the upper Volga River, which ran through Rostov's territory; that year the region experienced another famine and popular uprising. It is also known that Vsevolod's son, Vladimir Monomakh, founded a church in the city of Rostov. But with those exceptions there are few references to the area until the 1090s, when it became, as discussed above, a point of contention between the Sviatoslavichi and the Monomashichi.

The Liubech conference, held in 1097, confirmed Rostov's affiliation with Pereiaslavl', which was assigned to Vsevolod's son, Vladimir Monomakh. Ruling from Pereiaslavl', Monomakh placed his sons in charge of the Rostov region. By 1108, its prince was Iurii Dolgorukii. This youthful prince, just married to the daughter of a Polovtsy khan, established himself at Suzdal'. With his father's support he founded the town of Vladimir on the bank of the Kliaz'ma River (1108), which with another fortified outpost, located downstream on the Kliaz'ma, provided an effective defense against the Bulgars, who had attacked the region the year before; the forts also gave Prince Iurii authority over a major segment of the river systems traversing the Rostov-Suzdal' lands.

While Iurii continued to rule Rostov-Suzdal', his father assumed the grand princely throne in 1113 and placed Iurii's elder brothers, first Sviatoslav (d. 1114), then Iaropolk in Pereiaslavl'. Upon Monomakh's death, his sons had an exclusive claim to the grand princely title, according to established principles of dynastic succession. Mstislav accordingly ruled from 1125 to 1132. His brother Iaropolk, the next eldest among Monomakh's sons, would follow him to the Kievan throne. During Mstislav's reign, however, Iaropolk served as the prince of Pereiaslavl'. When he became heir to the Kievan throne, the principality of Pereiaslavl', which was then also becoming territorially differentiated from Kiev, acquired a special political status. It was not only the principality most closely associated with Kiev, but it began to be regarded as the seat of the heir apparent, the next grand prince of Kiev.

In addition to Chernigov and Pereiaslavl', Novgorod also achieved distinction in the eleventh century. Archeological evidence indicates that the city of Novgorod had been founded in the tenth century just north of Lake Il'men. It dominated the northwestern portion of the Riurikid realm. But its status within that realm was unlike that of the principalities. It never became consistently associated with a single branch of the dynasty.

When Vladimir I appointed his sons to govern the outlying districts of his realm, he assigned Novgorod to his eldest son, Vysheslav. When Vysheslav died, Iaroslav replaced him and was still the prince of Novgorod at the time of Vladimir's death in 1015. It was from his base in Novgorod that Iaroslav launched his drive to win the Kievan throne. The chronicle account indicates that later, when he and his brother Mstislav split the Kievan realm between them, Iaroslav returned to Novgorod, implying that he governed from that city rather than from the capital, Kiev. Other evidence, however, suggests that, like his father, he appointed deputies to rule Novgorod in his place from 1016 through his entire reign.

Vladimir and Iaroslav thus established the practice of designating a governor to rule Novgorod. They generally appointed their sons. But from 1016 to 1030, Iaroslav's deputy in Novgorod was one of his retainers; only after 1030 did he place his sons in Novgorod. This practice was not unique to Novgorod. Grand princes also designated their sons as well as members of their *druzhiny* to administer and protect other portions of the Riurikid realm. But during the period between the reigns of Vladimir I and Vladimir Monomakh other regions became identified with specific branches of the dynasty; Novgorod did not. It continued to be subject to the appointee of the grand prince.

During the eleventh century those governors were usually, but not always, members of the dynasty. Iaroslav and most of his immediate successors appointed their own sons to serve as their delegates in Novgorod. Later in the eleventh century, the grand princes were naming more distant relatives to that post. When the Novgorod throne became vacant in 1088, Grand Prince Vsevolod selected Mstislav, his grandson and the son of Vladimir Monomakh, to fill the vacancy. Although Vsevolod's successor, Sviatopolk, tried to replace Mstislav Vladimirovich with one of his cousins, Novgorod rejected that choice, and the grand prince reappointed Mstislav, who then served in Novgorod until 1117. By that time his father Vladimir Monomakh was grand prince of Kiev; he transferred Mstislav to Belgorod, near Kiev, and replaced him in Novgorod with Vsevolod, his own grandson and Mstislav's son.

Novgorod's special political relationship to Kiev was closely associated with its economic role in the Kievan realm. Novgorod controlled a major portion of the foreign trade conducted by Kievan Rus', particularly the trade with Scandinavian and, increasingly through the eleventh century, German traders from the Baltic Sea community. Also, while the Rostov land was yet relatively undeveloped, Novgorod dominated the Volga trade with the non-Rus' commercial centers of Bulgar-on-the-Volga and those on the Caspian Sea. Details of Novgorod's commercial activities will be discussed in the next chapter.

In order to expand its commerce, Novgorod achieved one of the most singular accomplishments of the Rus' lands in the eleventh century – the conquest of the north. In the seemingly endless expanse stretching to the north-northeast of the city explorers, hunters, and soldiers from Novgorod encountered a variety of Finno-Ugric tribes. Their populations were small and although their resistance to the Rus' was at times fierce, they could not sustain it effectively. By the end of the eleventh century, Novgorod had carved out an empire extending from the city itself northward across Lake Onega to the White Sea and northeastward across the North Dvina and Pechora Rivers to the Ural Mountains.

Although the northern population was sparse, its economic resources were valuable. Novgorod's success in gaining control over them gave it economic advantages unique among the Rus' principalities. But that situation also made other principalities covet Novgorod. By the twelfth century, control over the economically powerful Novgorod became one objective in the continuing wars among the Riurikid princes.

In the meantime Novgorod was also deeply involved in the protection of its trade routes. It thus engaged foreign foes when they threatened to cut off access to the Gulf of Finland and intervened in affairs of the Rostov lands. Iaroslav himself had suppressed disorders in Rostov in 1024. At the end of the century, in 1096, when Oleg Sviatoslavich tried to seize Rostov from the Monomashichi, it was Mstislav Vladimirovich, then prince of Novgorod, who came to Rostov's rescue. His action simultaneously served the interests of his branch of the dynasty and those of Novgorod, whose commercial success depended in part on safe passage along the upper Volga River, which ran through Rostov territory.

By the end of the reign of Vladimir Monomakh, the state of Kievan Rus' was thus more complex than it had been a century earlier. The city of Kiev, which directly controlled a series of towns and fortresses in its immediate vicinity, remained the capital of the realm. Its prince, as the senior member of the dynasty, had an elevated status over his brothers, sons, cousins, and nephews. But various regions were acquiring the character of discrete principalities and were functioning more

Map 2.1 Kievan Rus' in the eleventh century

independently. Over the next century more principalities would similarly separate from Kiev. Among them Volynia and Galicia, Smolensk, and Rostov-Suzdal' would join Chernigov, Pereiaslavl', Novgorod, and Kiev to redefine the political organization of Kievan Rus' from a unitary state into a federation of principalities bound together by dynastic ties and traditions.

FOREIGN AFFAIRS

The foreign policy of Kievan Rus' and its conduct were integrated with the state's internal political structure. The dispersal of Riurikid princes with their *druzhiny* around the realm served the interest of maintaining the dynasty's domestic authority. But because the grand prince of Kiev did not control a tightly centralized monarchy, he held a monopoly neither on the formation of foreign policy nor over military power. Responsibilities for defense, expansion, and the maintenance of the military force as well as the internal administration to fulfill those functions fell to the ruler of each principality. Although the grand prince could usually enlist their cooperation for joint campaigns when necessary, individual princes designed the foreign policies governing relations with those powers closest to them. Thus, the same organizational principle that dispersed the princes of the dynasty and charged them with both administration and defense of their sectors of the realm also imposed on them the practical necessity of conducting relations with the foreign powers in their vicinity. It additionally provided opportunities for individual princes to secure foreign protectors.

Such a division of responsibility enabled the dynasty to sustain its authority over its subjects and defend its lands. But as the dynastic structure and domestic political organization of Kievan Rus' became more complex and dynastic disputes over succession strained the political order, the political and military relations of Kievan Rus' with its neighbors, as well as with more distant foreign powers, correspondingly became more complicated and, at times, inconsistent.

During most of the eleventh century, however, the princes of Kievan Rus', through their multiple sets of foreign relations, formed extensive contacts not only with Byzantium, the center of their Church, and Scandinavia, the source of their dynasty, but with their neighbors to the south and east as well as with a range of European states. The fame and prestige of the dynamic young state became so widespread that Metropolitan Hilarion, possibly with some exaggeration, declared that Kievan Rus' was known in all ends of the earth. In contrast to the disdain, reflected by her reluctance to take her wedding vows, in which the Byzantine princess Anna had allegedly held Vladimir I, members of the Riurikid dynasty were considered in the eleventh century to be prestigious marriage partners; they contracted marital unions with royal houses ranging from France and the Holy Roman Empire to Byzantium itself. The dynasty acquired a cosmopolitan character. Among Iaroslav's sons, for example, Iziaslav was married to the sister of the Polish king, Sviatoslav to the sister of the bishop of Trier, and Vsevolod to a member of the imperial Byzantine family. Vladimir Monomakh, a product of the last union, married an English princess, and is said to have known a variety of foreign languages. His son Mstislav wed the daughter of the king of Sweden. The capital of their realm was correspondingly gaining an impressive international reputation, which was reflected in a statement made by the bishop of Bremen that Kiev was becoming a rival of Constantinople itself.

The main objective of Riurikid foreign policy, however, was not simply to heighten the dynasty's international status. It was essentially to maintain and extend the range of the dynasty's domain, to preserve its monopoly on political authority over the populace that Vladimir I and his predecessors had subordinated. Additionally, the Riurikid princes sought to facilitate commercial and cultural contact with foreign societies; they correspondingly adopted policies either to gain control over or to enforce security along routes of trade and communication connecting their towns with foreign centers. These concerns placed a premium on defense of the realm, which was one of the prevailing objectives of the dynasty as well as a major practical justification for its claim to sovereignty. The following discussion will focus on the political and military aspects of Kievan Rus' foreign relations during the period from the death of Vladimir I through the reign of Vladimir Monomakh. Other forms of interaction, notably commercial and cultural, will be considered in chapter 3.

When Vladimir I distributed the outer portions of his realm among his sons, they each accepted the primary responsibility for defending and expanding their individual domains. Those tasks involved fashioning and implementing policies toward their immediate neighbors. Thus, the princes of Novgorod specialized in conducting relations with the northern neighbors of Kievan Rus'. Their extension of Novgorodian authority over the northlands provides, perhaps, the most spectacular example of their policy toward their Finno-Ugric tribal neighbors. But the Novgorodian princes also expanded westward. Prince Iaroslav defeated local tribes to set the Rus' border west of Lake Chud' (Peipus) in the area that was later known as Livonia and presently as Estonia. To protect that frontier and establish a stronghold from which Novgorod would subsequently subjugate tribes located even further north and west, he founded and fortified the outpost of Iur'ev (Tartu) in 1030. The policies of the Novgorodian princes also included the protection of the trade routes, on which the city's commerce depended, across the north, down the Volga toward Bulgar, and to the Gulf of Finland. For example, Iaroslav's son Prince Vladimir, who ruled Novgorod from 1034 to 1052, went to war against some Finnic tribes to secure the last route, while Prince Gleb Sviatoslavich, who was sent to govern Novgorod c. 1068, died while trying to collect tribute from other northern tribes in 1079.

As the princes of Novgorod engaged in these ventures, they formed close associations with their Scandinavian neighbors, which were epitomized by interdynastic marriages. Prince Iaroslav Vladimirovich married the daughter of the Swedish king, Olaf. He strengthened his bonds with the Scandinavian world by arranging the marriage of his daughter Elizaveta to the king of Norway; when widowed, she married the king of Denmark. Later, Mstislav, the son of Vladimir Monomakh and prince of Novgorod to 1117, also married a Swedish princess. His daughter followed Elizaveta's example, by marrying first a king of Norway, then a king of Denmark. And, as George Vernadsky pointed out, even Vladimir Monomakh's marriage to Gyda, the daughter of Harold II of England, reflected the prince's ties with the king of Denmark more than with England. It had actually been the Danish king who, while acting as host to the exiled Harold after the Battle of Hastings in 1066, had arranged the marriage.[2]

The Scandinavian and Novgorodian princes also exchanged aid. Both Vladimir I and his son Iaroslav had appealed for and obtained Varangian auxiliary troops to secure their positions in Kiev. In a similar manner the lords of Scandinavia looked to the Riurikids, and especially to their kin from Novgorod, for support and refuge. King Olaf of Norway (St. Olaf), defeated and ejected from his throne in 1028, turned to Iaroslav for sanctuary. His half-brother, Harald Hardradi, who would become the husband of Iaroslav's daughter Elizaveta and the king of Norway, also found refuge at Iaroslav's court. He served with the grand prince's retinue for several years before embarking on a series of adventures, including some Byzantine military campaigns, that ultimately led him back to Scandinavia to claim his kingdom.

While Iaroslav, as prince of Novgorod, conducted foreign affairs involving northern tribes and Scandinavia, his brothers focused their attention on other neighbors. Sviatopolk Vladimirovich, who was ruling

Turov, northwest of Kiev, developed ties with Poland. In a manner parallel to Iaroslav, he married the daughter of the Polish king Boleslaw. Their brother Mstislav, who had been accorded Tmutorokan' by Vladimir I, conducted relations with his neighbors on the Black Sea coast. In 1022, for example, he launched a campaign against the Kosogi (Circassians), located to the east of Tmutorokan' on the northeast coast of the Black Sea.

As each prince specialized in the conduct of foreign relations with his closest neighbors, he also secured sources of personal political and military support. The Riurikids took advantage of their foreign connections when they engaged in their succession struggles. As noted, both Vladimir I and Iaroslav had depended upon Varangian military support to depose Iaropolk and Sviatopolk, respectively. Iaroslav again turned to the Scandinavians when he confronted Mstislav. Sviatopolk Vladimirovich, for his part, received aid from his Polish father-in-law in 1015–19. And Mstislav used his foreign contacts in his bid for the Kievan throne. Having subordinated the Kosogi, he added them to the army he led back to central Rus' in his attempt to overthrow Iaroslav. As Grand Prince Iaroslav gained control over the western half and then the entire Kievan realm, he took responsibility for relations with Poland as well as with Byzantium and the steppe nomads. While his son Vladimir ruled in Novgorod (1034–52) and supervised foreign relations in the north, Iaroslav engaged in and resolved clashes with Poland and Byzantium even as he arranged the marriages of his sons and daughters to foreign royalty.

The disturbance with Poland stemmed from the succession struggle in 1015–19, and King Boleslaw's march into Kiev in the futile effort to reestablish his son-in-law Sviatopolk on the throne. The source of the problem was Cherven, a district in Galicia; bordering the western Rus' lands, Bohemia, and Poland, it had been attached to Kievan Rus' by Vladimir I. As the price for his assistance as well as his withdrawal from Kievan Rus', Boleslaw I took possession of Cherven in 1018. Although Princes Iaroslav and Mstislav recovered it in 1031, it was not until 1042 that Iaroslav concluded an agreement with Poland that recognized Cherven as part of Kievan Rus'. The settlement was sealed by a double marriage (1043). Iaroslav gave his sister in marriage to King Casimir (ruled 1038–58), and Casimir's sister, Gertrude, wed Iaroslav's son Iziaslav. As a wedding gift, Casimir repatriated some 800 Rus' prisoners who had been captured by King Boleslaw almost two decades earlier. Iaroslav, in turn, provided Casimir with military support against Mazovia in 1047.

Just as Iaroslav resolved the Cherven issue with Poland, another crisis developed with Byzantium. Much of the Riurikids' contact with the

Byzantine Empire revolved around Church, cultural, and commercial affairs, which will all be discussed in the next chapter. The Rus' and Byzantines also shared an interest in securing the Dnieper route that served as the main conduit for those contacts between Kiev and Constantinople. Their broad range of common concerns provided the basis for generally peaceful relations. Kievans, indeed, regarded Byzantium so favorably that during the crisis of 1069 a group of them threatened to abandon Kiev for Constantinople if their demands were not met. The interests of the two states did not, however, always coincide. And in 1043 they clashed. Grand Prince Iaroslav, having learned of the death of a Rus' visitor to Constantinople, sent a military expedition, led by his son Vladimir, to the city. His force was defeated in the ensuing naval battle; peace was concluded in 1046.

Neither the Russian chronicles nor Byzantine sources, which give a more detailed account of the clash, adequately explain its causes.[3] The underlying reasons for the break in the normally cordial relations between Kievan Rus' and Byzantium have consequently become the subject of scholarly debate. Andrzej Poppe concluded that the episode in 1043, like the Rus' attack on Cherson in 989, was a case of Rus' intervention in Byzantine politics. In this instance, however, Iaroslav sent a military force to support a rebellion against the emperor. But by the time the Rus' fleet approached Constantinople, the challenger had been killed and the campaign had lost its political purpose. Prince Vladimir, holding his position and continuing to threaten the Byzantine capital, negotiated with the emperor, hoping to obtain a ransom payment that would defray the costs of the expedition and substitute for the rewards promised by the deceased pretender to the Byzantine throne. The emperor refused; the Rus' defeat followed.[4]

Most scholars, nevertheless, trace the event to the death of a visiting Rus' merchant in Constantinople. Agreeing that the incident triggered Iaroslav's violent reaction, they disagree about the context in which the events occurred. Some see the murder as an extreme episode arising from a set of restrictive policies on Rus' commerce recently introduced by the Byzantine emperor. M. V. Levchenko, for example, argued that the contemporary Byzantine political situation created unfavorable conditions for the Rus' merchants in Constantinople; the deteriorating commercial

---

[3] For a discussion in English of the substance of the Byzantine accounts of this event, see J. Shepard, "Why Did the Russians Attack Byzantium in 1043?," *Byzantinisch-Neugriechische Jahrbücher*, vol. 22 (1979), pp. 147–182.

[4] A. Poppe, "La dernière expédition russe contre Constantinople," *Byzantinoslavica*, vol. 32 (1971), pp. 1–29, 233–268.

environment provoked the confrontation in 1043.[5] Others regard Iaroslav's actions as part of a long, but otherwise peaceful process, by which the Rus' were attempting to extricate themselves from domineering Byzantine influence. As evidence illustrating the Rus' attitude toward Byzantium its advocates cite not only the 1043 conflict, but also the appointment of the first native Rus', Hilarion, as metropolitan of the Kievan Church (1051). D. Obolensky, rejecting that argument by refuting the evidence used to support it, demonstrated that despite Hilarion's ethnic origins, his appointment was not an act of defiance against Byzantine authorities but was made with the approval of the patriarch.[6] In any case, shortly after the 1043–46 break in relations, the more typical pattern of peaceful multifaceted Rus'–Byzantine interaction resumed. The restoration of good will was symbolized by the wedding of Prince Vsevolod Iaroslavich and a relative of the Byzantine emperor, Constantine IX Monomachus (ruled 1042–55). In 1053, Vladimir Monomakh was born of that union.

Grand Prince Iaroslav thus not only resolved outstanding disputes with Poland and Byzantium, but bound his sons and through them the realm of Kievan Rus' by marital ties to those states. Iziaslav was most closely associated with Poland, Vsevolod with Byzantium. Sviatoslav developed connections with German states by marrying first the sister of the bishop of Trier and subsequently Oda of Saxony. In addition, one of Iaroslav's daughters, Anna, married Henry I of France (1051), while Elizaveta married the Norseman Harald Hardradi.

The most dramatic arena of foreign affairs, however, was not Europe or the Byzantine Empire, but the southern steppe frontier inhabited by nomadic Turkic tribes. At the time of Vladimir I's death (1015), it will be recalled, the steppe was dominated by the Pechenegs. With the exception of their aid to Sviatopolk during the fratricidal conflict of 1015–19, their relations with the Rus' were generally peaceful after Vladimir's death. Nevertheless, in 1032, Prince Iaroslav extended Vladimir's defenses southward to a new line along the Ros' River (a western tributary of the Dnieper), where he settled the Polish captives, seized the year before in his campaign to recover Cherven.

5 M. V. Levchenko, *Ocherki po istorii russko-vizantiiskikh otnoshenii* [Essays on the history of Russian-Byzantine relations] (Moscow: Akademii Nauk SSSR, 1956), pp. 389–396, 400. For further discussion of this view, see also J. Shepard, "Why did the Russians Attack Byzantium in 1043?," pp. 181–183.

6 See, for example, Vernadsky, *Kievan Russia*, pp. 81–82, and Dimitri Obolensky, "Byzantium, Kiev, and Moscow: A Study in Ecclesiastical Relations," Dumbarton Oaks Papers, vol. XI (1957), pp. 61–62; reprinted in *Byzantium and the Slavs: Collected Studies* (London: Variorum Reprints, 1971).

The fortified lines built by Vladimir and Iaroslav provided an effective military defense. And the joint rule of the Riurikid realm by Iaroslav and Mstislav evidently provided the administrative corollary necessary to secure the southern border and pacify Rus' nomadic neighbors. The Pechenegs reappeared in a menacing fashion only one more time; in 1036, they attacked Kiev. Their defeat by Prince Iaroslav before the city's walls was memorialized by the construction of Iaroslav's city, an extension of the fortified zone of Kiev, on the site of the battleground. In its center Iaroslav constructed a complex of buildings, the most striking of which was the St. Sophia Cathedral. And to reach it, he placed in the city's new southern wall the Golden Gate of Kiev, surmounted by the Church of the Annunciation. Iaroslav's victory also marked an end to Pecheneg threats to Kievan Rus'.

During the first half of the eleventh century the organization of the Kievan Rus' state provided the Riurikid princes with a structure that facilitated the successful implementation of their fundamental foreign policies. They were able to defend and expand their realm, which acquired a respected position in the surrounding political community. When Iaroslav died and left Kievan Rus' to his sons, each not only received his own principality, but also a specialized zone of foreign interests, defined by his marital ties and the geographic location of his principality. Thus Iziaslav, who became the grand prince of Kiev, maintained direct ties with Poland, while Vsevolod, who inherited Pereiaslavl', provided the first line of defense against the steppe nomads and also was more closely linked with Byzantium. Division of responsibilities in foreign affairs also provided each prince with a special foreign source of support or protection, a factor that contributed to the maintenance of a balance of power among them.

The foreign ventures of the princes Iziaslav, Sviatoslav, and Vsevolod during most of the third quarter of the century illustrate the functional advantages of these arrangements. Once again, the most active arena was the steppe frontier. In the middle of the eleventh century the Pechenegs were forced to move westward by a group called the Torks. Although they assumed a relatively passive posture toward the Rus', Vsevolod led a campaign against them in 1055, and then in 1060, he was joined by his brother Iziaslav and their cousin Vseslav in another assault.

The Torks were soon displaced, however, by the more aggressive Polovtsy, also known as Cumans or Kipchaks. These Turkish-speaking nomads advanced westward into the steppe north of the Black Sea. Divided into about a dozen tribal groups, they formed a loose federation centered around the Northern Donets River basin. Those Pechenegs and Torks who did not migrate westward either clustered near the Rus' frontier outposts and became irregular border guards or were assimilated by the Polovtsy. Although it had been decades since the Rus' southern frontier had been seriously threatened, the appearance of the Polovtsy renewed all the problems associated with a hostile neighbor in the steppe.

The first mention of the Polovtsy in the Primary Chronicle occurs *sub anno* 1055; at that time Prince Vsevolod of Pereiaslavl' met them and negotiated a peace arrangement. Nevertheless, in 1061, the Polovtsy attacked Rus' territory. Vsevolod led an army against them, but was defeated; the Polovtsy practice of raiding and devastating the Rus' frontier had begun.

Polovtsy raids posed a frightening spectacle for the Rus'. Almost immediately the Polovtsy horsemen were able to penetrate the fortified lines, with whose earthworks and palisades Vladimir I, Iaroslav, and their heirs had so effectively protected their realm. The ability of the Polovtsy during only their second major confrontation with the Rus' in 1068, to reach the Al'ta River (near the city of Pereiaslavl' itself) and there defeat the combined forces of Princes Iziaslav, Sviatoslav, and Vsevolod sent the local population into near, if not total, panic.

The consequences of this attack were profound and extended beyond the immediate devastation inflicted by the booty-hungry raiders who pillaged the countryside. The three princes, having failed to expel the Polovtsy, retreated to the safety of Kiev (Iziaslav and Vsevolod) and Chernigov (Sviatoslav). The rampaging Polovtsy created such havoc that the citizens of Kiev requested arms and horses from the princes so that they could defend themselves. Prince Iziaslav's refusal provoked an uprising in Kiev. It will be recalled that 1068 was also the year that Vseslav of Polotsk had been imprisoned by the triumvirs, Iziaslav, Sviatoslav, and Vsevolod. The frightened and rebellious citizens of Kiev released Vseslav and insisted that he assume both the throne and the task of protecting their lands. Iziaslav fled from Kiev to Poland. There in the land ruled by his wife's nephew, King Boleslaw II (ruled 1058–79), he gathered the support that enabled him to evict Vseslav and recover his position (May 2, 1069).

Meanwhile, Sviatoslav led his retinue against the Polovtsy, who by this time were ravaging the countryside around Chernigov. Despite the reported four-to-one odds against him (12,000 Polovtsy to 3,000 Rus'), Sviatoslav was victorious (November 1). Although the chronicler was not specific, Sviatoslav's victory evidently curbed the Polovtsy campaign that year. After these disturbing encounters, Polovtsy aggression relaxed. With the exception of a conflict in the vicinity of the Ros' River fortifications in 1071, the Polovtsy did not stage any major attacks on the Rus' lands for the next two decades.

These episodes illustrate that each of the ruling princes operated in a clearly delimited sphere of foreign relations and correspondingly had distinct sources of foreign support. Prince Vsevolod of Pereiaslavl' had primary responsibility for dealing with both the Torks and the Polovtsy. When his forces appeared insufficient, the political system allowed for the formation of coalitions to confront a common foe. So Vsevolod gathered his relatives to join in a campaign against the Torks, and he and his brothers pooled their resources to defend their lands against the Polovtsy. Although even their combined forces were incapable of defeating the Polovtsy in 1068–69, the crisis nevertheless demonstrates that the political organization operated smoothly and effectively, facilitating rather than hindering joint cooperative military action. Iziaslav's ability to fall back on his Polish in-laws, who intervened to restore him to power in Kiev while his brothers were preoccupied with the military and social emergency, indicates furthermore the functional value of individual princely ties to specific neighbors.

But throughout the eleventh century the Riurikid princes had repeatedly contested interpretations of the principles guiding their dynastic succession. In the context of their disputes regarding the dynastic order they had also regularly appealed to their individual foreign associates for assistance. By the 1070s and especially in the 1090s, this practice had unusually destabilizing consequences. In these instances the princes extended their domestic competition into the sphere of foreign relations. Intruding into one another's zones of foreign responsibility, they bid against each other for support from foreign neighbors. They thus intensified the bitterness and damaging effects of their domestic disputes, complicated the foreign relations of Kievan Rus', and contributed to a series of political setbacks and failures.

The political crisis following the eviction of Iziaslav from Kiev in 1073 constitutes the first example. After he had lost his throne in 1068, Iziaslav had been able to rely on his Polish relations for help. But in 1073, when his brothers Sviatoslav and Vsevolod expelled him, he was unable to convince King Boleslaw II to come to his rescue again. Sviatoslav was at least partially responsible for Boleslaw's decision. Anxious to prevent Iziaslav from repeating his 1069 restoration of the throne, Sviatoslav intervened in what had been Iziaslav's personal sphere of foreign relations and made direct contact with Boleslaw II. As the new grand prince, he offered him the hand of his daughter as well as military aid against Bohemia (1076). Boleslaw accepted Sviatoslav's proposal and abandoned Iziaslav.

The disappointed Iziaslav turned next to the Holy Roman Emperor Henry IV for assistance. But Sviatoslav once again outmaneuvered him. His offerings of rich gifts dissuaded the emperor from getting involved in the Rus' conflict. Only after Sviatoslav's death in 1076 was Iziaslav able to recover both his position as grand prince and his former relationship with Boleslaw II. Iziaslav's granddaughter, the daughter of Sviatopolk, subsequently married Boleslaw III in 1102.

Sviatoslav's sons similarly refused to recognize the conduct of relations with the steppe nomads as the exclusive prerogative of Prince Vsevolod of Pereiaslavl'. After Sviatoslav died in 1076, possession of Chernigov became, as noted, the focus of dynastic dispute. In 1078, Oleg and Boris Sviatoslavich attempted to recover Chernigov from their uncle Vsevolod. At that time they enlisted aid from the Polovtsy, with whose help they initially defeated Vsevolod. In doing so, the Sviatoslavichi broke the solid front the Rus' princes had erected against the Polovtsy; instead, they invited them to join an invasion of the Rus' lands and become involved in internal Rus' politics. It required the combined armies of Iziaslav and Vsevolod as well as their sons, Iaropolk and Vladimir, to overcome Oleg and his Polovtsy allies. It was at that juncture that Oleg retreated to Tmutorokan'; Vsevolod replaced Prince Iziaslav, who was killed in the battle, on the Kievan throne; and his son Vladimir Monomakh became prince of Chernigov.

Prior to 1073, rival princes had used foreign auxiliary troops in their internecine wars; but they had solicited them from neighbors in their individual sectors of foreign affairs. During the 1070s, Sviatoslav and his sons attempted not only to usurp thrones withheld from them by the then-standard rotation principles; they also infringed on their relatives' exclusive relations with their respective neighbors. By the end of the decade, the rest of the dynasty had curbed the Sviatoslavichi and restored the political order. But the conflicts generated by Sviatoslavich actions demonstrate how precariously the Riurikid political order rested on the delicately balanced distribution of authority, in foreign as well as domestic affairs, among the dynasty's princes.

The challenges to that order in the 1090s would prove even more disruptive. In the 1090s, the Polovtsy resumed their attacks on the southern Rus' frontier. They again penetrated the Rus' defenses and brought terror to the interior of the Kievan lands. The power of their offensive was impressive. Invading repeatedly from 1092 through 1096, they not only laid siege to Iur'ev on the Ros' River (1095), but reached the environs of Kiev itself, where they pillaged and burned the Pecherskii (Crypt or Cave) Monastery (1096). Their strength may have stemmed from the formation of a tighter, if temporary, coalition among the normally autonomous Polovtsy tribal groups.

This series of attacks brought the issue of the effectiveness of the military and political organization developed by the Riurikid princes into sharp focus. The urgency of the situation was further intensified by the fact that Grand Prince Vsevolod died in 1093. Although the dynasty accepted his nephew Sviatopolk Iziaslavich as grand prince without objection, control over Chernigov and the northeastern territories of Murom and Rostov was contested by his cousins. When Oleg Sviatoslavich launched his campaign to recover Chernigov in 1094, he again enlisted the aid of Polovtsy clans that had ties with his branch of the dynasty. His Polovtsy supplementary forces contributed to the general pandemonium. Despite the swift resolution reached between Vladimir Monomakh and Oleg, the latter could not control his Polovtsy allies. Evidently having been attracted to Oleg's cause by promises of rich booty, they persisted in ravaging the Chernigov countryside despite the fact that it had been ceded to their leader. Shortly afterward, while the Polovtsy were destroying the Pecherskii Monastery in 1096, Princes Sviatopolk of Kiev and Vladimir Monomakh of Pereiaslavl' appealed to Chernigov for help, but Oleg Sviatoslavich refused to join his cousins against his former comrades-in-arms.

Meanwhile, the feud between the Sviatoslavichi and the Monomashichi was playing itself out in Murom and Rostov. By this stage of their confrontation, the Monomashichi had formed their own ties with a set of Polovtsy clans, who joined them against Oleg Sviatoslavich. Grand Prince Sviatopolk also entered the bidding for Polovtsy allegiance. When he was unable to stop their attacks militarily, he concluded a short-lived peace agreement, in accordance with which he married the daughter of one of the Polovtsy khans (1094).

The responses to the Polovtsy offensive, coupled with the simultaneous intradynastic wars, left little doubt that their political structure and relationships were preventing the Riurikids from carrying out their basic foreign policy function – defense of their lands. The political organization that distributed principalities and political responsibility, which had evolved through the eleventh century, had provided a means of administering domestic and foreign policies while also supporting multiple *druzhiny*. It also theoretically enabled the members of the entire dynasty to combine their military resources, when necessary, to protect their lands against an external foe. But during the 1090s, no single prince was defining or coordinating policy toward the Polovtsy. On the contrary, dynastic competition and territorial division were not only generating the internal conflicts that hindered joint action against the foreign menace, but were encouraging each of the princes involved in the domestic controversy to pursue independent policies and forge separate alliances that compounded the ferocity of their conflict. The political structure that had been engineered to maintain balance and cohesion, to be a vehicle for cooperative action, was instead contributing to confusion, contradiction, and defeat.

The conference at Liubech the following year was a direct response to the crisis generated by the Polovtsy attacks and the failure of this structural arrangement. Although it had functioned relatively well until the 1090s, the political system, encumbered by intradynastic rivalries, proved to be inadequate to withstand the power of the Polovtsy. The agreement reached at Liubech adjusted intradynastic relationships as well as the political organization of the Riurikid state; it improved the dynasty's ability to cooperate and coordinate military operations.

Favorable results were almost immediately evident. Early in the twelfth century the Rus' princes, continuing to hold conferences for consultation, entered into a series of grand alliances and took the offensive against the Polovtsy. Despite the conclusion of a peace treaty with the Polovtsy in 1101, the Rus' mounted a major expedition against them in 1103. It was led by Princes Sviatopolk of Kiev and Vladimir Monomakh of Pereiaslavl'. Although Oleg Sviatoslavich declined to participate, his brother Davyd joined the coalition, as did several other princes. The expedition made a four-day journey into the steppe before engaging the Polovtsy. The Rus' princes enjoyed a great victory. At the conclusion of the battle twenty Polovtsy khans lay dead. The Rus' also captured valuable booty, including livestock (horses and cattle, sheep and camels) and slaves; and they were able to restore Iur'ev on the Rus' River. Subsequent Polovtsy attacks (1105, 1106) were repulsed; and the Rus' themselves launched several more victorious offensives. The most spectacular was the campaign of 1111. In that venture the combined forces of Princes Sviatopolk, Vladimir Monomakh, and Davyd of Chernigov inflicted two decisive defeats on the Polovtsy as they advanced toward the Don River. Word of their victories, according to the chronicler, spread abroad to the Greeks of Byzantium, through Hungary, Poland, and Bohemia, and as far as distant Rome. By 1116, the Riurikid princes appear to have destroyed the Polovtsy federation of the Northern Donets. Although the Polovtsy would continue to be involved in Rus' domestic quarrels, their offensives ceased and the southern frontier of Kievan Rus' remained stable for the next fifty years.

The extent and nature of the damage resulting from Polovtsy attacks on Rus' lands have led to disagreement among scholars. A traditional view, supported by Soviet scholars, suggests that repeated Polovtsy incursions forced the Slav population to abandon settlements on the frontier and thus lose valuable agricultural lands, which the nomads converted into pastures. Others, however, dispute the idea that the Polovtsy were ever inclined to occupy Rus' agricultural lands, which were only marginally useful as pastures, but had substantial value when they actively produced goods and people, that could be purchased or plundered.

In conjunction with this debate it is also of interest that the targets of some of the raids, including the major offensives of the 1090s, were neither randomly selected settlements nor necessarily those that could have been expected to contain stores of grain and livestock. Rather, they were strategic points on approaches to and/or along the lower Dnieper waterway. The fact that large-scale offensives were mounted in late spring, when the "rivers were swollen," according to the chronicler, suggests that the Polovtsy were more intent on interfering with the commercial flotillas gathering in preparation for their descent down the river than on pillaging agricultural communities, whose stocks would have been more abundant (hence more attractive as plunder) in autumn after the harvest than in spring. The purpose of the raids on the Dnieper route could have been simple pillage. Or they could have been intended to apply pressure so that the Rus' would pay transit fees in exchange for safe passage across the steppe.

However one assesses the intentions of the Polovtsy or the damage they inflicted, it is important to recognize that although they did constitute a serious and frightening menace to Rus' society, they did not always behave as the "godless" perpetrators of destruction depicted by the chroniclers. The pattern of Rus'–Polovtsy relations resembled Rus'–Pecheneg interaction. It was characterized by confrontation and partisan alliances, as well as peaceful and mutually beneficial commercial exchanges. Between bursts of hostilities, and even during them, relations involved intermarriage and trade. During those decades when the Riurikid princes respected the division of authority among themselves, policy toward the Polovtsy was formulated and coordinated by one prince and the frontier remained relatively peaceful and stable.

At the end of the century, however, when the Riurikid political structure was strained, the confrontational character of the relationship between the Rus' and Polovtsy received greater emphasis. Each of the Rus' princes involved in the internal disputes formulated his own policy toward the nomads. The result was that their actions, considered in combination, appeared confused and contradictory. While defending their lands from Polovtsy attacks, they also engaged some Polovtsy tribes as allies against their dynastic rivals. Grand Prince Sviatopolk of Kiev married the daughter of the Polovtsy khan in 1094, yet the year before he had insulted the Polovtsy by arresting their diplomatic envoy. After resuming hostilities that resulted in the death of his father-in-law, Sviatopolk nevertheless honored him by bringing his body back to Rus' for burial at his residence outside Kiev (1096). Vladimir Monomakh, heeding the advice of his *druzhina*, treacherously executed two Polovtsy khans who had come to him seeking peace in 1095; but the very next year his sons were using Polovtsy auxiliaries in their campaign against Oleg Sviatoslavich, and in 1107 Vladimir's son, Iurii Dolgorukii, married the daughter of a Polovtsy khan. Such examples illustrate, as Thomas Noonan has pointed out,[7] that Rus'–Polovtsy relations were complex. Despite the chronicler's depiction of the Polovtsy as the aggressive villains, the Riurikid princes shared responsibility for provoking their wars. The rapid and numerous policy reversals of the Riurikid princes during the crisis of the 1090s are also manifestations of the disruption of their domestic balance of power; when they reached political resolution through the congress of Liubech and subsequent princely conferences, their domestic as well as foreign policies recovered their former coherency and effectiveness.

But the crisis of the 1090s had additional repercussions. It led to the one significant loss of territory sustained by Kievan Rus' in the eleventh century, Tmutorokan'. This principality, geographically separated from the central lands of the Riurikids by the steppe, had been ruled early in the eleventh century by Prince Mstislav Vladimirovich, and even after he returned to central Rus' and established himself at Chernigov, he had continued to control this port city on the straits linking the Black and Azov Seas. During the second half of the century, when the Sviatoslavichi were evicted from Chernigov, Tmutorokan' became their refuge and power base. Yet after 1094, when Oleg Sviatoslavich left Tmutorokan' for Chernigov, Russian chronicles cease to mention it, and by 1118 the Byzantines, who dominated the neighboring Crimean peninsula and the Black Sea, had absorbed it into their empire.

The conflicts also contributed to a deterioration of relations with Bulgar-on-the-Volga. The relations of Kievan Rus' with that polity had been benign since the reign of Vladimir I. But toward the end of the eleventh century they became increasingly hostile. The source of their conflicts lay in Bulgar's dissatisfaction with conditions along the Oka and upper Volga Rivers, the trade routes that linked it to Rus' markets. In 1088, after complaining about thieves along the Oka to the Sviatoslavich princes, who then ruled Murom and were responsible for security on the river, the Bulgars invaded and plundered that region. Their attention and concern were soon thereafter directed toward the Monomashichi, who in conjunction with their own determination to curb the power of the

[7] Thomas S. Noonan, "Polovtsy (Polovtsians)," *Modern Encyclopedia of Russian and Soviet History*, ed. by Joseph L. Wieczynski, vol. 29 (Gulf Breeze, Fla.: Academic International Press, 1982), pp. 16–17.

Sviatoslavichi, took firm charge of the Rostov-Suzdal' area. As they built new towns in the region, they also began to interfere with commercial traffic. By 1107, the Bulgars were attacking Suzdal', and in 1120, Prince Iurii Dolgorukii launched a military campaign against Bulgar territory.

The Riurikid dynasty provided the framework for the political structure and unity of Kievan Rus'. Between the end of the reign of Vladimir I and that of Vladimir Monomakh that structure as well as intradynastic relationships were subjected to stress. Nevertheless, the Riurikids' flexibility, reflected in the changing organizations both of their dynasty and of the territories of their state, enabled them to fulfill their basic functions, maintenance of their own dynastic power and preservation of the integrity and security of their domain. Their interaction with foreign powers, furthermore, reveals not only the ability of the Riurikid princes to expand their domain, but to compete with the states on their borders. Their political structures and military forces were adequate to confront most of those neighbors with relative success. The most serious test of their political institutions, however, was presented by the nomads of the steppe, whose military incursions into the Rus' lands at the end of the eleventh century cast doubt on the functional capacity of the Riurikids to defend their state and society. But in this case too the Riurikids redefined their domestic relationships and gained the strength to overcome their opponents. Fulfillment of its domestic and foreign tasks depended, however, on the dynasty's relationship with the society it governed, on its ability to collect revenues from the society that it was striving to protect. The society of Kievan Rus', its economic activities and resources, and the non-dynastic institutions and concepts that bound its components together will be the subjects of the next chapter.

3

KIEVAN RUS' SOCIETY

·

The Riurikid dynasty and its state organization provided a political frame-work for Kievan Rus' society. Much of the political activity of Kievan Rus', insofar as it revolved around the ruling dynasty and involved the dynasty's internal and foreign affairs, may be understood through an examination of dynastic policies and politics. But the princes of the dynasty constituted only one layer or component of Kievan society. They formed interdependent relationships with other social elements. As Kievan Rus' evolved politically under the Riurikids, the peoples of the state expected their princes to regulate relations with foreign neighbors and defend them from attack, to keep trade routes open and secure, and, as Orthodoxy and princely administration displaced tribal customs, to maintain domestic order and enforce legal norms. The princes, on the other hand, demanded that the population pay tribute and other fees, which they used directly or indirectly to support themselves, their retainers, and the Church.

This chapter will examine the characteristics of Kievan society, its economic activities, and the policies and mechanisms adopted by princes and Church hierarchs to acquire revenue from the main body of the society. Finally, it will consider the effects of the dynamic interaction among the Riurikid dynasty, the Orthodox Church, and general popu-lace, effects that in combination transformed the diverse Slavic tribes that made up Kievan Rus' into an integrated society that could and would retain a significant degree of social and cultural cohesion even when the political ties that united its multiple components loosened.

RURAL SOCIETY

The vast majority of the Kievan Rus' population, who both materially supported the Riurikid princes and depended upon them, were peasant farmers (*smerdy*). Despite variations derived from tribal background, geographic location, and other factors, the peasants of Kievan Rus' shared many characteristics and were regarded as a single undifferentiated social stratum. Among the free members of society, peasant men and women had the lowest social status.

Peasants lived in their own huts with their nuclear families, and farmed their own plots of land using their own tools and livestock. Their households were grouped into rural villages and organized into communes (*vervi* or *miry*), which had their roots in the tribal and clannic ties among the population. By the Kievan era, however, the communes had a territorial identity as much as clannic one. Members of each commune shared common pasture lands, meadows and forests, and fishing and hunting rights. They also, importantly, shared responsibilities for tax payment and other legal obligations.

The lands of Kievan Rus', which these peasants farmed, were located primarily in two climatic zones, the forest belt and the forest-steppe. As their names imply, the vegetation that grew naturally in these regions was forest. The spruce and fir that prevailed in the northern taiga gave way to cedar and birch, then to oak further south. The forest lands were generally well watered. Extensive river systems flowed through them, and they normally received adequate precipitation to sustain agriculture. Their grey and dark grey soils, however, were not particularly rich; fertile black soils were located only west and south of Kiev. Furthermore, the lands of Kievan Rus', most of which were located north of the fiftieth parallel, had short growing seasons.

To accommodate these conditions the Slav peasants most commonly applied a method of farming known as slash-and-burn. To clear a section of forest for cultivation they cut deeply into the bark of the trees and left them to die and dry, then burned them. The resulting ash added to the soil sufficient nutrients to provide a fertile medium for several years. When the nutrients in the soil of one clearing were depleted, the peasants moved their crops to another, which they had prepared in the interim. In some cases, after leaving a clearing fallow for many years, they might clear out the scrub brush and birch trees that had overgrown it and cultivate it once again; this practice is known as a system of long fallow.

The preference for these methods among the variety with which the peasants of Kievan Rus' were familiar was probably based on practical issues. Foremost among them were population density, which influenced a community's available manpower, and the specific physical character of the land. Because fire did most of the heavy work involved in clearing patches for farming, even tiny hamlets populated by just a few households could apply this method and engage in farming. The peasants were similarly selective in their choice of farm implements. The favored instrument was the *sokha*. Pulled across the ground by a draft animal or a farmer, the *sokha*'s forked end, fitted with iron shoes, scratched furrows in the light ash-covered soil of the forest clearings. By fixing the shoes so they were in an almost vertical position in relation to the ground, the farmers were able to maneuver around tree stumps or skip over roots and other impediments that remained in the ground. The Slav farmers also used sickles for reaping, scythes for mowing hay, mattocks, and other implements.

In the forest clearings the farmers generally raised cereal grains: rye in the north, millet in the south, supplemented by wheat, buckwheat, oats, and barley. They also produced other crops, such as peas and lentils, flax and hemp. Peasants maximized their chances for reaping sufficiently large crops by planting twice a year. Archeological evidence suggests that as early as the eleventh and twelfth centuries northern communities were planting both winter and spring crops. Winter rye was typically sown late in the year. The seeds were protected over the winter by an insulating layer of snow and sprouted as the snows melted in the spring. Spring crops were planted after the danger of winter frosts had passed. Once harvested, the grains were stored in pits lined with birch and pine bark or in barns or other buildings.

In addition to grains peasants raised livestock. Horses, cattle, oxen, pigs, sheep, goats, and poultry were the most common animals in Rus' farmyards. During summer they grazed in the forests or in abandoned fallow clearings; in winter they were confined in buildings and fed hay or feed crops. The surrounding forests also supplied the rural population with berries, fruits, nuts, and mushrooms that supplemented their diets. In addition, the peasants regularly fished nearby rivers, lakes, and streams; hunted for game and fur pelts; and kept beehives for the production of wax and honey, which like the fur had both domestic and commercial value.

During the eleventh and twelfth centuries princes and boyars or high-ranking members of their retinues also claimed ownership of rural landed estates. The intrusion of princes and their boyars into the countryside did not necessarily interfere or compete with peasant farming. The main enterprise on these estates appears to have been raising horses, which were so necessary as mounts in combat. They also raised other livestock, mainly cattle and sheep. Grain and other crop production appears to have been a secondary pursuit. The members of the elite, who continued to reside in fortified urban areas, generally turned their estates over to stewards, who oversaw the operations that were conducted by slaves or indentured laborers. Bishoprics and monasteries, which received estates as gifts from princes and boyars, also began to accumulate landed wealth during this era.

Kievan society, including the prince and his retainers, depended upon the rural peasantry for food supplies. Agriculture in the northern climates of Kievan Rus' was precarious and its output was never abundant. At times the system failed. In 1024, for example, a drought in Suzdalia caused a severe famine that prompted the population to purchase grain from the Volga Bulgars. Another famine that affected the Rostov region and the town of Iaroslavl' was recorded in 1071. Near the end of the century (1092) the southern part of Kievan Rus' experienced a famine when a late frost destroyed the young crops that were just beginning to grow after a year-long drought. Droughts, floods, early frosts, and even mild winters that left the land without its blanket of snow and allowed the seed to freeze affected agricultural output adversely throughout the twelfth century as well.

But these events were exceptions and, in most instances, only locally significant. More typically cultivation of the forest zones by means of the slash-and-burn method and the light scratch plow, coupled with the storage of grain reserves, met the society's needs. Contrary to commonly made assertions, these practices did not require large labor forces or abundant livestock, which would have been necessary to haul away tree stumps, pull heavy plows or other equipment, or tend repeatedly planted fields. Rather, the methods selected were well suited to a society whose population was scattered in small communities throughout the vast forested territories that made up Kievan Rus'. Using them the rural sector of the society was able to produce a supply of food that was adequate for its own needs as well as for the growing urban population and also sufficient to pay the fees and tribute, much of which was collected in grain and other food stocks, required by the Riurikid princes.

URBAN SOCIETY

Although the vast majority of the population dwelled in the countryside, Kievan Rus' was known for its towns. M. N. Tikhomirov, one of the foremost Soviet scholars on Rus' cities, identified 89 towns in the eleventh century and another 134 that arose in the twelfth. He estimated that on the eve of the Mongol invasion (1237–40), Kievan Rus' boasted approximately 300 urban centers.[1] Although many of them were not true cities but relatively small fortified posts, some were lively diversified centers of commerce and crafts as well as civil, military, and ecclesiastical administration. Foremost among them was Kiev itself, the "mother of Russian cities."

The largest cities formed around princely strongholds, ecclesiastical seats, and trading posts. Any one or combination of those factors offered opportunities for merchants, master craftsmen, and unskilled workers, who gathered in the vicinity of fortified outposts and produced or exchanged a range of goods and services required by the elite.

Some cities swelled to impressive sizes. Precise numbers for their inhabitants, however, remain elusive. Calculated estimates are frequently based on the land area within a city's limits, the number of domiciles that area contained, and the number of persons per household. Weighing these factors, scholars have offered figures ranging from 36,000 to 50,000 for the population of Kiev at the end of the twelfth century. At either end of the scale Kiev was comparable to Paris and London, whose populations at that time were about 50,000 and 30,000, respectively. Novgorod was also a large city by those standards. Its population grew from 10,000 to 15,000 in the early eleventh century to twice that size by the early thirteenth century. Chernigov, whose land area has been estimated to have exceeded Kiev's as well as Novgorod's by the time of the Mongol invasions, may also have had a larger population.

City populations had a more complex social structure than their rural counterparts. At the apex of the social hierarchy was the prince himself. His military retainers formed a layer beneath him. On a par with them were the hierarchs of the Church. These groups constituted the elite of Kievan Rus' society. But the prince and his retainers, whose residences were in the town, and clergymen made up only a relatively small portion of the urban population. The bulk of the residents were tradesmen, artisans, and unskilled laborers. They too were socially differentiated. Some were foreigners and held a special status. Others were members of the prince's personal household and may have been slaves. Many, however, were free small-scale traders and craftsmen. Their status was slightly higher than the bulk of the population, free unskilled laborers. Slaves and other dependent laborers made up the lowest social stratum.

Social status was reflected in living quarters. In Kiev the prince and metropolitan occupied palatial dwellings atop the central hill; the working population not directly attached to elite households dwelled

[1] M. N. Tikhomirov, *Drevnerusskie goroda* [Ancient Russian towns] (Moscow: Gosudarstvennoe izdatel'stvo politicheskoi literatury, 1956), pp. 36, 39, 43.

primarily in wooden homes in separate sections of the city, located on outlying hilltops or at the base of the bluffs in a district known as the *podol* or *podil*.

In Novgorod dwellings were set in courtyards that lined streets made of logs that had been split in half lengthwise. Their houses were also constructed from logs or timber and built on foundations or decks to protect them from the low, damp ground that was characteristic of the region. Refuse from the inhabitants and their livestock, which were also stalled within the courtyard, typically was simply left in the yard. To provide a relatively dry and clean surface the decaying refuse was covered with twigs; some Novgorodians built log pathways across their yards. Rich and poor lived in these conditions; the sizes of their dwellings, however, varied. The relatively large courtyards and buildings from the eleventh and twelfth centuries probably belonged to members of the social elite whose servants, including craftsmen, lived and worked on their premises.

COMMERCE AND CRAFTS

Most of the urban population in Kievan Rus' was engaged in one of the fundamental elements of the urban economy: intercontinental commerce, domestic trade, and craft production. Of these, the sector of the economy that has, perhaps, attracted the most attention is intercontinental commerce. It had, after all, been the lure of silver and Oriental finery that had brought Varangians to the lands that became Kievan Rus'. The Riurikid princes continued to sponsor and encourage intercontinental trade, which contributed greatly to the wealth and glory of their realm. Commerce with Byzantium, Europe, and the Muslim East was a pivotal component in the economy of Kievan Rus'.

The Kievan economy

Intercontinental commerce Kiev was the main market center for Rus' trade with Byzantium. That trade was already being conducted on a regular basis by the reign of Vladimir, and it expanded after the Rus' adoption of Christianity. During the eleventh and twelfth centuries some elements in the pattern of Rus'–Byzantine trade shifted. Direct princely participation in the trade diminished while princes concentrated more on facilitating commerce by keeping the trade routes open and secure. The trade that in the tenth century had depended upon Rus' flotillas descending the Dnieper and bearing their goods to Constantinople expanded in the following centuries and was supplemented by trade conducted by Greek merchants who visited Kiev as well as other Rus' towns. But while desire for some Byzantine products rose, the demand for others decreased as Rus' merchants adopted Byzantine techniques and manufactured the products domestically.

Despite these variations, the Rus' consistently exported fur pelts, wax, honey, and slaves to Byzantium. Visitors to Constantinople recorded with admiration the presence and quality of Russian goods they found there. And M. N. Tikhomirov concluded that the number of Rus' merchants conducting business in Constantinople by the year 1200 had increased to such proportions that restrictions on them were eased.[2] In exchange for their products the Rus' received a wide variety of goods. Luxury items like silks, satins, brocades, and other rich fabrics, as well as jewelry, glass beads, and bracelets headed the list. Other glass items, such as goblets and other vessels; amphorae filled with wines, olive oil, and naphtha; and combs made of boxwood were also among the Byzantine imports. Spices, fruits, and nuts came to the Rus' lands from Constantinople. The marble used to decorate the Church of the Tithe in Kiev, the Church of the Mother of God in Tmutorokan', and the Cathedral of the Transfiguration in Chernigov was also imported through Byzantium as were glazed tiles and icons.

The flow of goods between Kiev and Constantinople was at times impeded, even interrupted. One source of difficulty was the Polovtsy, who, like the Pechenegs before them, sporadically interfered with the transport of goods across the steppe. Their attacks on the Dnieper during the war against the Rus' at the end of the eleventh century, discussed in the previous chapter, provides one example of their capacity to disrupt commerce. Later, in the 1160s, the Kievan grand prince had found it necessary to take unusual measures to protect the flotillas descending the Dnieper. In contrast, in 1184, even though the Rus' princes were once again at war with the Polovtsy, Rus' merchants were freely crossing the steppe and were well-enough informed to tell the Rus' army where to locate its intended enemy. Although the Polovtsy occasionally threatened Rus' trade, they also exchanged goods with Kievan merchants. The Polovtsy regularly supplied horses and other livestock to the Rus', who in return provided grain as well as clothing, weapons, and other manufactured items.

Of greater consequence to Rus'–Byzantine relations than the Polovtsy were factors affecting the political and economic stability of the Byzantine Empire. In the twelfth century political challenges faced by Byzantium posed commercial dilemmas. The market of Constantinople, it will be recalled, attracted the Rus' as well as other merchants because it was a

2 Tikhomirov, *Drevnerusskie goroda*, pp. 124–126.

collection point for luxury goods from the Orient as well as the products of the Mediterranean and the Byzantine Empire. Yet as early as the eleventh century the trade routes by which this vast array of items was transported to Constantinople began to be disrupted. Turkish invasions in Asia Minor and subsequent wars between the Byzantines and the Turks disturbed the main land route that had brought Oriental goods through Asia Minor to Constantinople. Alternate routes that avoided Asia Minor were opened. One carried Oriental luxury items by sea across the Indian Ocean and the Red Sea to Egypt. By the late twelfth century such diversions of trade were having an impact on Constantinople. Italian merchants, who had become responsible for most of Constantinople's western trade, were moving their business to Alexandria in Egypt and the Crusader states of the Middle East. Donald Queller and Gerald Day, two scholars of the medieval Italian states and Byzantium, have concluded that "by the end of the twelfth century . . . the Byzantine capital was fast losing commercial advantage."[3]

A second route also developed. It passed from Central Asia to the north of the Caspian Sea and proceeded to Sudak on the Crimean peninsula before crossing the Black Sea to reach Constantinople. The flow of goods along this route had repercussions on Kievan trade. With their major trading partner offering fewer goods at more expensive prices Kievan merchants took advantage of the alternate route and met the goods before they reached Constantinople. By the late twelfth century merchant caravans from Kiev were crossing the steppe, in cooperation with the Polovtsy, to the port of Sudak. The activity at Sudak also attracted merchants from the Caucasus and Asia Minor, whose wares (including silver and other metal objects produced in their homelands) were imported by southern Rus' in relatively large quantities during the century preceding the Mongol invasion. Thus, even after Constantinople was sacked by the participants in the Fourth Crusade (1204) and the Central Asian emporium of Urgench was destroyed by the Mongols (1220), Kievan trade activity persisted.

The rerouting of trade resulted also in an expansion of Kievan commercial contacts with central Europe. Kievan merchants not only transferred some of their business from Constantinople to Sudak; they also sold their goods to merchants, including itinerant Jewish traders, who arrived by land from German towns as well as Poland, Bohemia, and Hungary. The intensified use of trade routes between central Europe and Kiev gave economic impetus to the towns of Volynia and Galicia in

---

[3] Donald E. Queller and Gerald W. Day, "Some Arguments in Defense of the Venetians on the Fourth Crusade," *American Historical Review*, vol. 81 (1976), p. 734.

southwestern Rus'. These principalities, as will be discussed in the next chapter, correspondingly gained political prominence in the late twelfth and early thirteenth centuries. Kiev itself thus became a transit center in trade between central Europe and the northern Black Sea ports. By adjusting to Constantinople's commercial difficulties and developing alternate trade routes and new trading partners Kiev was able to maintain its commercial activity throughout the eleventh and twelfth centuries.

Another potential threat to Kiev's economic vitality was the growth of a host of other Rus' cities in developing principalities. Yet Kiev remained economically powerful despite physical attacks on the city by its domestic rivals just as it survived the loss of its chief trading partner, Constantinople. Indeed, indicators such as monumental construction projects, the area the town occupied, and the size of its population provide no evidence that Kiev was declining economically in the decades prior to the Mongol invasion. On the contrary, Kiev remained throughout this period a flourishing cosmopolitan city that not only contained the seats of the grand prince and metropolitan and was a center for intercontinental commerce, but was a thriving center for craft production and an entrepot for domestic trade.

Craft production Craft production in Kiev expanded under the influence of foreign trade and foreign master craftsmen who migrated to Kiev. Evidence of a wide range of occupations has been assembled from archeological artifacts as well as written sources. The Kievan population included blacksmiths and carpenters, potters and leather workers. Jewelers, silver and gold smiths, glass makers, and bone carvers were also represented.

Military activity generated demand for a range of weapons and other products, virtually all of which were crafted domestically. As horsemen replaced infantry on the battlefield, the nature of weapons and armor also changed. Mounted warriors required sabres and swords with which they could unseat an enemy even as they rode at a full gallop. They needed armor and shields for themselves and equipment for their horses. Craftsmen in the workshops of Kievan Rus' towns were kept busy designing and redesigning armaments, making them light enough for the horses to bear but heavy enough to crush an opponent's protective armor, and generally supplying the needs of the military forces of their princes.

Massive building projects that will be discussed below also provided work for a wide variety of laborers: skilled stone cutters who worked in the quarries; artists who carved decorative designs in the buildings' facades, painted frescoes, made and glazed ceramic tiles, and fashioned mosaics; brick makers; carters; and a range of unskilled workers. The craftsmen of Kiev produced items ranging from cathedrals and bridges to clothing and buttons, from weapons to earrings, from armor to glass beads.

The artisans of Kiev were not all native Slavs. After the collapse of the Khazar Empire, skilled workers migrated from its declining cities to Kiev. Particularly after 988, Byzantine craftsmen also came to Kiev to direct the construction and decoration of new cathedrals, including the Church of the Tithe and the Cathedral of St. Sophia in Kiev. These churches, which closely followed Byzantine models, required Greek architects to design them. Artists from Constantinople similarly produced the mosaics that decorated St. Sophia. Byzantine master craftsmen also filled the increasing demand for luxury items generated by the Kievan elite, the Riurikid princes and their retainers as well as the Church hierarchs. Their presence added to the cosmopolitan character of Kiev that had already been created by the mix of Slavs with Varangians and was supplemented by diplomats, merchants, and other visitors from the steppe, the North Caucasus, and Europe.

Domestic trade The flow of Byzantine goods into Kiev and the production of even more items in the city was accompanied by an expansion of domestic trade among the towns of Kievan Rus'. Much of the fur that the Rus' exported to Constantinople, for example, originated in Novgorod's northern empire and reached Kiev through Novgorod. Byzantine goods, including delicacies such as nuts, were sent back to Novgorod. Other Byzantine items, notably amphorae containing olive oil and wine were used not only in Kievan households, but could be found in localities at some distance from the capital. In addition to transporting Byzantine goods beyond Kiev to other Rus' towns, domestic trade provided a means of exchanging items produced within those towns and distributing them throughout the realm of Kievan Rus'. Glass objects produced in Kiev, most prominently glass bracelets, were transported to over two dozen other towns, including Chernigov, Novgorod, and the cities of Rostov-Suzdal'.

Domestic trade was also a vehicle for the transfer of technical skills. Native artisans soon mastered the skills and techniques that foreign craftsmen brought to Kiev. The glassware shipped from Kiev during the eleventh and twelfth centuries, for example, was crafted by Kievan artisans who had borrowed Byzantine techniques, although they had applied them to glass made according to their own formula. Kievan artisans similarly imitated Byzantine methods for glazing pottery and tiles and for producing finely crafted jewelry and other items decorated with inlaid enamel. By the second half of the twelfth century artisans in other towns had learned the processes and were producing their own glassware, beads, window panes, and bracelets in competition with the Kievan artisans. Enameling workshops similarly were established in Novgorod, Vladimir, and other Rus' towns in the twelfth century. Although the art of Byzantine architects and craftsmen dominated the cathedrals constructed in Kiev and Novgorod in the middle of the eleventh century, the wall paintings on Novgorodian churches built during the twelfth century were, according to Dimitri Obolensky, in all probability created by Russian artists who had learned technique and iconographic forms from Byzantine masters.[4] Thus, by the twelfth century artisans in a variety of Rus' towns were adopting methods borrowed from Byzantium but developed in Kiev during the preceding century.

Articles made from a distinctive reddish-colored slate that came exclusively from Ovruch, a region in Volynia northwest of Kiev, have been vivid indicators of widespread domestic trade. One common item made from Ovruch slate was spindle whorls, used in spinning and weaving. They were manufactured at workshops in the area of Ovruch as well as in Kiev. The spindle whorls, however, have been discovered in large numbers not only in Kiev, but in Novgorod, Polotsk, and towns throughout the Rus' lands. The same type of slate was used in Kiev's cathedrals as well as in the Church of the Transfiguration in Chernigov. It had other purposes as well. Molds for making other items were fashioned from it. One such mold, used to make belt mounts, was discovered in Kiev. The mold was marked with an Arabic inscription, suggesting that the artisan who owned it may have moved to Kiev from a Khazar town. The Khazar craftsman working in Kiev with materials originating in Volynia reflects on an individual level the more general image of Kiev as a bustling cosmopolitan economic center, sustained by lively commerce and craft production.

Economic activity in Novgorod and Suzdalia

Novgorod was one of Kiev's main domestic trading partners. It contributed fur and wax that Kiev exported abroad, and it purchased items imported by Kiev as well as goods produced in Kievan workshops. But not all of Novgorod's trade was tied to Kiev. From its inception Novgorod had served as a commercial link between the Baltic Sea and the Volga River. As the main market for exchanging goods coming from both Scandinavia and Bulgar, it was a chief center of Rus' trade with both Europe and the Muslim East.

---

[4] Obolensky, *Byzantine Commonwealth*, p. 456.

In the tenth and eleventh centuries Scandinavian merchants dominated the Baltic trade with Novgorod. Probably in the early and certainly by the middle of the twelfth century they had established their own commercial complex with its Church of St. Olaf on the market side of the city, located across the Volkhov River from St. Sophia. The Scandinavian merchants brought a variety of goods, including woolen cloth, weapons, pottery, and salt to the Novgorodian market. With those items they purchased luxury goods imported by the Rus' from Byzantium and Bulgar: silks and spices, gems and jewelry, and Oriental silver coins or *dirhams*. Novgorodian merchants who traveled to the markets of Sweden and Denmark conducted similar exchanges.

By the twelfth century, however, the character of Novgorod's foreign trade was changing. One difference was its trading partners. During the twelfth century German merchants became more prominent than Scandinavians. By the end of the century they too had established a trading depot, Peterhof, inside Novgorod and presented a serious challenge to their Scandinavian competitors. As Germans joined Scandinavians at Novgorod's market, a second difference in Novgorod's trade patterns became apparent. The goods imported by Novgorod from northern Europe changed. Some items, such as pottery, jewelry, weapons, salt, and alcoholic beverages, remained standard. But a new item appeared: silver.

During the tenth century Novgorod had received *dirhams* from Bulgar and had reexported some of them to Scandinavia. But after the early eleventh century Oriental silver was no longer available. When Bulgar could no longer provide that commodity, Novgorod turned to its new German trading partners to acquire it. During the eleventh century the Novgorodians imported silver coins known as *deniers*; by the twelfth century the coins were replaced by ingots or small silver bars. There is some evidence that fine Flemish cloth may also have been imported by Novgorod as early as the twelfth century.

A new pattern of trade thus developed between the Novgorodians and German merchants. Novgorod imported silver, woolen cloth, and the other items listed above and exported northern fur and wax as well as items obtained from Bulgar and Kiev. The exchange was so beneficial to both parties and so durable that it remained the predominant trade pattern for the next several centuries.

Novgorod also continued to be actively engaged in trade with the Volga Bulgars during the eleventh century. Although it no longer imported silver *dirhams*, Novgorod nevertheless exported furs, isinglass or fish-glue, walrus tusks, and some finished products, such as linen cloth and jewelry, in exchange for Oriental luxury products. By the late eleventh century and through the twelfth century, however, Novgorod and Bulgar encountered an obstacle to their commercial intercourse, the principality of Rostov-Suzdal' and its princes, the Monomashichi.

Novgorod–Bulgar trade depended primarily on a route that followed the upper Volga River. By the second half of the eleventh century Prince Vladimir Monomakh and his heirs were establishing their authority in the Rostov-Suzdal' region, through which the upper Volga River flowed. Over the next century those princes tightened their control over the commercial traffic that crossed their lands. They prevented Novgorodian merchants from passing through their realm to reach Bulgar and likewise obliged Bulgar merchants to sell their goods within Suzdalia. Their successful interception of the traditional Novgorod–Bulgar trade along the Volga River route and concentration of it in their own towns contributed to the development of the towns of Suzdalia into lively commercial emporia, where Catholic, Orthodox, and Jewish merchants from Europe and Byzantium exchanged goods with their Orthodox Rus' and Muslim Bulgar counterparts.

Neither Novgorod nor Bulgar accepted Suzdalia's interference in their trade without protest. On the contrary, the intrusion into their commercial practices became a source of friction that erupted into overt hostilities on several occasions. Bulgar in particular sought alternative means of acquiring the valuable fur pelts it had previously received from Novgorod and sold to merchants from the lower Volga and the Muslim East. But as its own merchants ventured northward, the princes of Vladimir-Suzdal' doggedly pursued them, cut off their supply routes, and absorbed their northern trading posts. By the late twelfth and early thirteenth centuries Bulgar and the princes of Vladimir were engaged in a sharp conflict.

In the meantime Novgorod's fur exports to the east diminished. Novgorodian and Bulgar merchants nevertheless continued to meet in Suzdalian towns and exchanged western for Oriental products. Suzdalian merchants also acquired Oriental goods, which they conveyed to western Rus' towns. Novgorod thus continued to receive Oriental glassware, glazed pottery, pepper, and other items, and Bulgar merchants obtained European and Russian goods, but the exchanges were conducted through Suzdalian markets and intermediaries.

The Bulgars remained a link between the northern Rus' and the market centers of the lower Volga and the Caspian Sea. They conveyed the purchases made in Suzdalia back to Bulgar and either sold them there or transported them down the Volga to another market center, Saksin, where merchants from throughout the Muslim world gathered. In the tenth and eleventh centuries the Volga trade route, which drew Oriental goods to the Caspian Sea and up the Volga River through Bulgar to the lands of Rus', had been dominated by Bulgar and Novgorod. But during the twelfth century Suzdalia physically inserted itself along that route, asserted its control over the passage of goods between those two trading partners, and diverted a significant share of the revenue from the trade between Novgorod and Bulgar to its treasury. Thus, when Kiev's Black Sea and Byzantine trade suffered some disruption and the Volga route acquired added importance, the economic benefits went to Suzdalia.

SOURCES OF REVENUE

Trade, both intercontinental and domestic, craft production, and agriculture were the basic components of the Kievan Rus' economy. The food, goods, and wealth produced by activities in these areas supported the individuals engaged in them and their families with enough surplus to maintain the members of the political and ecclesiastical elites. The princes and Church officials and their retainers contributed other services to society: military, administrative, judicial, and spiritual.

The elites employed a variety of means to obtain the revenue necessary to support themselves. When at war, princely armies pillaged the populations of their opponents and thus obtained some income in the form of booty. The bulk of regular, reliable revenue, however, was gleaned through direct tribute or taxes exacted from the Rus' society; from commercial profits derived from the sale of goods acquired as tribute or produced on privately owned estates; and from a variety of fees imposed on the population for specific administrative services.

Judicial services and fees

Among the administrative services performed by princes and Church hierarchs, judicial functions became one of the chief means of generating revenue. As Riurikid authority supplanted traditional political leadership, the dynasty's laws and courts also replaced local custom. The Primary Chronicle contains an account, probably inserted after the 996 date under which it is presented, that reflects the development of the prince's role in the maintenance of social order and in court procedures. The account relates a discussion between Prince Vladimir and the bishops of Kiev. The bishops were concerned about an increase in the number of homicides (*razboi*) and asked the prince why he was not punishing the criminals. When Vladimir responded that he was afraid of sinning, the bishops assured him that he had been made prince precisely to punish evil and show mercy to the just. Vladimir, heeding them, then began to punish those responsible for the murders. But the bishops returned to him and advised him to replace his form of punishment with a monetary fine, called a bloodwite, which he could then use to arm his retinue.

The Riurikids manifested their concern with the establishment of legal norms and the maintenance of order by issuing a law code, known as Russkaia Pravda. The first version of the law code, known as the Short Pravda, was codified by Grand Prince Iaroslav Vladimirovich. Later in the eleventh century his sons, Iziaslav, Sviatoslav, and Vsevolod, added a second portion to the Short Pravda. As new situations arose in the evolving society, additions were made to the Russkaia Pravda until in the thirteenth century the revised law code, known as the Expanded Pravda, assumed a stable final form.

The added clauses, many of which dealt with commerce, inheritance, slavery, and indentured servants, reflect circumstances and concerns that were becoming sources of conflict in the increasingly complex society and required adjudication and a determination of new standards. The variations in the successive versions of the Russkaia Pravda also reflect a corresponding expansion of princely judicial responsibilities and incomes, which, as the chronicle tale suggests, could be applied to meet their growing administrative and military expenses.

There were two main ways in which the prince and his officers benefitted financially from controlling the judicial system. One method was to collect fines from those found guilty of crimes. A monetary fine or a bloodwite was referred to in the chronicle tale, which also suggested that it had been a traditional form of punishment before the time of Vladimir's reign. Daniel Kaiser, however, has demonstrated that the customary retribution had been a form of revenge undertaken directly by relatives of the victim.[5] Indeed, the Short Pravda recognized vengeance as an acceptable legal response to murder. Monetary compensation was offered as an alternative if there was no appropriate family member to act as the avenger; it was also the norm for other crimes. But when the victim of a crime such as murder, assault, or theft was a member of the prince's household, his steward or stable master, a peasant on one of his estates, or one of his common slaves, the Short Pravda prescribed as punishment a fine levied on the offender and paid to the prince. The code also detailed the division of the fines collected; a small portion went to the sheriff, a tithe went to the Church, and the remainder went to the prince.

Under the terms of the Short Pravda princely revenue from legal suits was relatively minor. The princes issued the law, which confirmed and

[5] Daniel H. Kaiser, "Reconsidering Crime and Punishment in Kievan Rus'," *RH*, vol. 7 (1980), p. 287.

standardized norms for the amount of compensation and clarified procedures for apprehending suspects and determining guilt in the prince's court. But most types of cases covered by the Short Pravda were treated as matters between the offender and the victim. By the time the Expanded Pravda was codified, however, the practice of paying fines to the princes for crimes including murder, assault, and destruction of property had filtered into the statutes and become a standard form of punishment that sometimes supplemented and sometimes replaced compensation to the victims.

The amounts of the fines prescribed in the Russkaia Pravda provide some indication of the social structure in Kievan Rus'. Fines paid to the prince for the murder of his palace or stable steward were twice as high as those required for a page, groom, or cook. A farm steward, craftsman, tutor, or nurse ranked below the latter group; the value of peasants and slaves was even less. The lowest place in the social hierarchy was a female slave. Women in general had a lower status than men. Although murder trials were to be conducted in the same manner regardless of the gender of the victim, the fine assessed for the murder of a woman was half the amount demanded for the murder of a man. Women's property rights also differed from those of men. Women could own their own property, which they received in the form of gifts or dowries; the latter were considered to be their shares of the families' estate. Thus, if the male head of a household died, his sons inherited his estate. But they were legally obligated to arrange marriages for their unmarried sisters and provide their dowries. Among the upper classes, daughters could inherit their fathers' property, but only if there were no surviving sons.

The second method of obtaining income from legal procedures was assessing fees for the performance of judicial services. The Short Pravda, for example, indicated that a bloodwite collector and his assistant regularly traveled around the country to collect fines. While making their rounds, they were entitled to receive provisions from the local populace as well as a cash fee. But even as the law allowed these officers of the prince's court a salary and provisions, it ordered them to complete their tasks in each locality within a week, thereby ensuring that they would not abuse or overburden the local population.

The Russkaia Pravda identified other judicial officials who received fees for their services; they included judges, sheriffs, and scribes. In addition, the code recognized specialized officials, skilled in the technique of administering the "iron ordeal." This was a torture designed to determine the accuracy of testimony, and was found most useful when no verifying witnesses were available. If the application of a hot iron on a person's flesh failed to cause a burn, his statements were accepted as truthful. In most instances, however, swearing an oath was sufficient for testimony to be accepted as truthful. Officers of the court also collected fees for administering the oath.

Ecclesiastical courts

While Prince Vladimir I and his heirs assumed responsibility for introducing a law code, enforcing it, and judging and punishing offenders, their authority in these matters and their right to exercise juridical power was upheld, as suggested by the chronicle tale, by officials of the Orthodox Church. The Riurikids also shared judicial functions with the Church, which not only became responsible for converting the pagan population, but assumed the tasks of introducing Christian norms of behavior and enforcing conformity to them. The princes thus turned over to the bishops responsibilities for rooting out pagan customs and establishing new standards and rites in spheres of human conduct guided by religion and related primarily to family life. These were not trivial tasks.

The primary judicial interests of the Church were to enforce Christian legal and social norms and to adjudicate matters involving its own people, i.e., clergy and individuals who worked for the Church. Although Christianity officially became the official state religion in 988, it was not readily accepted by the general populace, who remained loyal to their pagan gods, influential priests and shamans, and to the customs and rituals that gave meaning to the most basic human activities. The establishment of the Christian church and the distribution of clergy around Kievan Rus' placed pressures on the Slav population not only to abandon their religious beliefs, but to break long-standing traditions, alter the basic patterns of their daily lives, and accept instead Christian norms of behavior.

In extreme cases the reluctance to accept Christianity took the form of open rebellion. The uprising in Novgorod, which occurred when Christianity was introduced, has already been noted. Other uprisings broke out during times of social stress, as during the famines of 1024 and 1071. Such outbursts, although isolated and quickly suppressed, reflect a persistent reluctance to accept Christianity.

The population's unwillingness to internalize Christian precepts and live according to Christian morality was expressed in a variety of other, more passive ways as well. Only gradually did women stop edging their clothing with borders decorated with pagan symbols or give up wearing bracelets, necklaces and headdresses with similar designs worked into them. Marriage ceremonies provide another example. Whereas marriage was an important sacrament for Christians, the chronicler, himself a monk, recorded with dismay and repugnance that several of the Slavic tribes of Kievan Rus', the Radimichi, Viatichi, and Severiane, whom he characterized as living in the forest like beasts, practiced polygamy; he wrote, "they had no marriages, but festivities between villages; and they would gather at the festivities for dancing and for all sorts of devilish songs, and here they took themselves wives, after agreement with them; for they had two or three wives each."[6] Daniel Kaiser noted that according to late eleventh-century canonical texts, church "marriage among ordinary folk had made no headway whatever because the chief competition, the festival dances, continued to dominate marriage arrangements."[7] In the place of Christian ceremonies and norms, customs such as bride abduction and bigamy continued to be practiced in the twelfth century.

Traditional death and burial rites similarly violated Christian norms. The chronicle noted that Slav tribes practiced cremation. After burning the deceased, relatives would place a vessel containing the bones on a roadpost. The Viatichi, according to the chronicler, continued that practice at the time he was writing although others, such as the Krivichi, had abandoned it. Other information suggests that peasants commonly displayed their reverence for dead relatives by keeping their bones in special places of honor in their homes. The Christian Church, however, insisted upon proper burial of dead. Its concern was to perform the holy sacraments and facilitate redemption. But that concern clashed with traditional practices. As a result of this cultural conflict, Christian burials took place, but grave robbery, presumably to recover the bones, was common.

Other remains of disinterred corpses may have been used in potions concocted by pagan magicians. References from twelfth-century Novgorod indicate that Orthodox women whose children had become seriously ill consulted pagan priests, who used special charms to ward off disease. Such evidence suggests that even after local populations had formally accepted Christianity, frightening and stressful circumstances could induce individuals to fall back on their pagan heritage.

To aid the Church in its operations the Riurikid princes formally transferred jurisdiction over family life and related spheres of social

---

[6] Translated by R. E. F. Smith, *The Origins of Farming in Russia* (Paris and The Hague: Mouton, 1959), p. 137.

[7] Daniel H. Kaiser, *The Growth of the Law in Medieval Russia* (Princeton, N.J.: Princeton University Press, 1980), p. 168.

conduct to the Church. Although the acts of transfer were recorded in documents known as Church statutes or charters, it is not known precisely when the Church acquired its judicial authority. The statute of Prince Vladimir I, which also assigned a tithe of the prince's revenue to support his new Church, recognized the establishment of Church courts and gave the Church exclusive legal jurisdiction over its own people. Another charter, known as Iaroslav's statute, gave Church courts jurisdiction over many aspects of family law. But because the earliest surviving copies of both Vladimir's and Iaroslav's statutes were written centuries after the documents were purportedly originally composed and because at least some elements in them do not appear to relate to the tenth and eleventh centuries, caution must be used in describing the Church's role in social and judicial matters in Kievan Rus' on the basis of them exclusively. Other princely charters, attributed to Princes Vsevolod Mstislavich of Novgorod (ruled 1117–36) and Rostislav of Smolensk (ruled 1127–59) similarly assigned matters involving disputes over family affairs and sorcery to the local bishops.

Although the original contents and dates of all these charters remain elusive, although the charters may have been altered over the centuries, and although the surviving copies may not reflect the arrangements originally made between the princes and the bishops, it nevertheless seems probable that the Church courts acquired jurisdiction over specific spheres of social activity during the Kievan era. Furthermore, it is generally acknowledged that during the eleventh and twelfth centuries the number of dioceses within the Rus' metropolitanate increased. During Iaroslav's reign new bishoprics were created in Chernigov and Pereiaslavl'. Rostov also received its own bishop in the eleventh century, and another was appointed to Smolensk in 1136–37. As new bishoprics were established, princes of each region appear to have issued charters that authorized the creation of Church courts and defined their purviews. In the case of Novgorod, where a bishopric and its courts had existed since the late tenth century, the charter attributed to Vsevolod authorized changes in the prince's role and functions. The Church courts generally became responsible for enforcing Christian law, related to marriage, bigamy and polygamy, incest, rape, bride abduction, and other family matters including rights of inheritance. They also became instrumental in suppressing the pagan priesthood, sorcerers, seers, and witches. And in conjunction with the division of judicial responsibilities between secular and ecclesiastical courts, princes also transferred corresponding revenues derived from court fees and fines to the bishops.

The Church with its courts gradually had an impact on Rus' society. As princes and bishops extended their authority to regions well beyond Kiev, not only were monumental cathedrals erected in episcopal and princely capitals, but modest churches in *pogost* or parish centers were scattered throughout the countryside. The extension of ecclesiastical influence placed stronger pressures on the populace to adopt Christian norms of behavior as well as to accept conversion formally. During the twelfth century various indicators, including the popular use of Christian rather than pagan symbols in dress and decorative apparel, signaled that Christian culture was gradually taking hold in Rus' society.

Commercial fees

Princes and Church officials thus shared judicial responsibilities; both political and ecclesiastical treasuries also received revenue for performing those functions. Another realm of social activity that generated income for the ruling elite was commerce. Riurikid princes set and collected customs fees and transit duties. They imposed sales taxes on selected items, as exemplified by a salt tax decreed by Grand Prince Sviatopolk shortly before he died in 1113. They also assumed responsibility for maintaining order in urban marketplaces, which depended in part on eliminating fraud and ensuring that the goods sold were weighed and measured accurately.

Some evidence suggests that Riurikid princes transferred responsibility for safeguarding the weights and measures as well as the fees for using them in commercial transactions to the bishops. Several statutes contain statements that the princes entrusted scales and weights as well as standard measures to the bishops. But because of the problems of dating these charters, it is not known if the princes mentioned actually made such assignments. The statute of Vladimir I contained such a clause, but the earliest extant copy of it dates from the late thirteenth century, and it has not been determined when the particular article concerning weights and measures became a part of the document. The charter of Prince Vsevolod of Novgorod made a similar assignment. It also indicated that in a case of fraud or cheating the bishop shared fines and property confiscated from the offender with the Church of St. Ivan, which was affiliated with the wax merchants' association, and the city of Novgorod.

As the society of Kievan Rus' became more complex and its economy expanded, the functions of both the Riurikid princes and Orthodox Church officials broadened. They provided the guidelines for the orderly conduct of economic and social activities and the power to enforce conformity to prescribed standards. They also benefitted from their expanded roles. They collected transit and customs duties on the transport and sale of goods, and additional fees for weighing and measuring the items at time of sale. They exacted other fees and fines when they were called upon to resolve disputes in court. Such sources of revenue provided not only the means to pay for the prince's military retainers, as recorded in the chronicle tale, but also for the princes' and Church's growing administration and for the officers appointed to perform the tasks derived from the additional responsibilities.

THE GOLDEN AGE AND ITS AFTERMATH

Combined, the tribute, commercial profits, and fees assessed on specific segments of Rus' society provided the Riurikid princes with the revenue necessary to support themselves, their military retainers or armies, and also the Church. In return, the princes provided their subjects with protection and the priests offered spiritual guidance. Together they transformed an agglomeration of settlements surrounding forts, trading posts, and sites for worship into a dynamic state dotted with economically thriving cities adorned with architectural monuments, which heightened the prestige of the members of the secular and ecclesiastical elites who sponsored their construction.

The effects of the mingling of the Riurikid dynasty, the Orthodox Church, and the eastern Slav society were dramatic. By the reign of Prince Iaroslav the Wise Kievan Rus', especially in its urban centers, was experiencing a Golden Age. This era was marked by an unusual degree of political unity and peace. The first version of the Russkaia Pravda and the construction of the Church of St. Sophia with its school and library have been identified as its great achievements. So also have the church statute attributed to Iaroslav and his Testament, in which he left his sons not only portions of his realm, but principles to serve as guides for dynastic tranquility. A spirit of optimism and confidence in the burgeoning new Christian nation also found expression in the literature of this period. The Sermon on Law and Grace, composed c. 1050 by Hilarion, the first native of Kievan Rus' to become metropolitan of the Church, is a prominent example. In it Hilarion celebrated Kievan Rus' and its princes Vladimir I and Iaroslav. Under their inspired guidance Kievan Rus' had become the most recent nation to join the Christian community. Proud of its heritage, it could rejoice in its own achievements and look forward to its future salvation.

Although neither political unity nor peaceful relations would remain stable, other factors identified with the Golden Age would have lasting influence on Kievan Rus'. The emphasis on literacy, education, and piety, so evident in Iaroslav's era, reverberated in the "Instruction" left by Grand Prince Vladimir Monomakh (d. 1125) to his "children or anyone else who happen[ed] to read" it. In this document Monomakh urged his sons to "forget not what useful knowledge you possess, and acquire that with which you are not familiar, even as my father [Vsevolod], though he remained at home in his own country, still understood five languages." But more important even than earthly knowledge, in Monomakh's view, was "the fear of God," which would guide his sons to rule justly and mercifully as good Christians.[8]

The law code introduced by Iaroslav the Wise, was repeatedly adapted to the changing social and economic conditions of the next two centuries and was adopted virtually throughout the realm. The Expanded Russkaia Pravda, as it emerged in the thirteenth century, survived as the legal norm for the Russian principalities through the fourteenth and fifteenth centuries, long after the state of Kievan Rus' had disappeared.

The churches and other monumental structures with which Grand Prince Iaroslav enhanced Kiev similarly became a model and standard for his descendants who sought to elevate the stature of other Rus' towns. Prince Vladimir I, stimulated by the adoption of Christianity, had introduced the practice of princely patronage for constructing churches. With the exception of the Church of the Tithe, most of the cathedrals built in his era were made of wood. But as the Riurikids consolidated their authority and began to accumulate greater wealth, they undertook the construction of more expensive masonry monuments.

Vladimir's sons, like their father, demonstrated both their power and piety by sponsoring the construction of masonry churches. Prince Mstislav, who had built a church in Tmutorokan' in 1022, initiated the construction of the Church of the Transfiguration of Our Savior in Chernigov (c. 1035). Although the church was not yet finished when he died in 1036, Mstislav was buried there. Grand Prince Iaroslav, who assumed full control over Kievan Rus' after Mstislav's death, lavished his attention on Kiev. Perhaps to remind the Rus' community that it was Kiev, not Chernigov, that was their political and ecclesiastical capital, he undertook, as noted in chapter 2, a series of major building projects after the successful repulsion of the Pecheneg attack of 1036. He began the construction of new walls that made the area of the fortified upper city almost ten times larger than it had been. The walls contained several entryways, but the main one was the Golden Gate. The gate itself was an imposing structure built of stone and consisting of two tiers. The lower section included the archway that was the entrance to the city; over the arch was a platform, a defensive parapet. The second tier consisted of

---

[8] *Medieval Russia's Epics, Chronicles, and Tales*, pp. 94, 98.

the Church of the Annunciation (*Blagoveshcheniia*), whose cupola, covered in a gilded copper leaf, probably gave the entire structure its name.

Within the city gates Iaroslav constructed a magnificent architectural ensemble around a central square. Facing it were the palaces of both the prince and the metropolitan. The Churches of St. George and St. Irene also formed parts of the central complex. But the dominating structure of the complex was the Cathedral of St. Sophia, built on the site of the victory over the Pechenegs. The main Cathedral of the Metropolitan of the Orthodox Church in Kievan Rus', St. Sophia was not only large, but richly decorated with mosaics and frescoes, slate and marble. It was built in general according to standard Byzantine architectural models; but it assumed a distinctive style with the striped design on its walls created by the alternation of exposed layers of brick with others covered by mortar, the addition of two apses to the standard three, two tower staircases, and a crown of no less than thirteen cupolas. Progressing from the outer edges to the center, the cupolas rose higher and higher, mounting to a peak that seemingly stretched infinitely upward. This was the church that came to symbolize Orthodoxy in Kievan Rus'. In combination with other edifaces built in this era it inspired the archbishop of Bremen to write in the middle of the eleventh century that Kiev was a jewel in the Orthodox world, rivalling Constantinople itself.

With such a profound transformation of the appearance of the city Iaroslav confirmed the strong bond between his dynasty and Christianity. Although the rural population might have remained indifferent or even hostile to efforts to impose Christianity, in the city of Kiev the influence of the mutually supportive institutions of dynasty and Church provided an economic stimulus and cultural dynamism that could not be ignored. While Iaroslav reaffirmed princely support for his Church by donating a tithe of his revenue and by sponsoring the physical construction of churches and monasteries, the Church reciprocated by venerating holy members of the dynasty, notably Boris and Gleb, and providing ideological support to the dynasty's legitimacy. Its messages were transmitted as much through visual symbols of architecture, icons, and mosaics as through the written and spoken word of chronicles, sermons, saints' lives (vitae), or monks' lives (paterics). Indeed, the vision perceived by the townsmen, visitors approaching the city, and even the invading nomads looking upward from the banks of the Dnieper toward the upper city, must have been awe-inspiring. The walls of the city, curling in and around precipices and ravines directed the observer's eye upward to the Golden Gates, beyond which the glittering cupolas of St. Sophia, towering above the walls, must have almost appeared to touch the

Figure 3.1 The Cathedral of St. Sophia, Novgorod

heavens themselves. The urban population could not avoid those symbols and the recurrent message they conveyed: the Riurikid dynasty, which ruled Kievan Rus', which established and defended social order, had the blessing of all-powerful God, who manifested Himself through the magnificence of His Church.

Novgorod was not slow to follow Kiev's example. In 1045–50, it erected its own stone Church of St. Sophia, which replaced its wooden predecessor that burned down even as the new cathedral was being completed. Set together with the bishop's palace within a citadel, St. Sophia became the cathedral of the Novgorod bishop (archbishop after 1165) and the centerpiece of the Sophia side of the city, i.e., the side on the west bank of the Volkhov River. The Novgorodian churches adopted the basic cruciform floor plan that had been borrowed from Byzantine churches and other features that had become identified with the Kievan architectural style. But the Cathedral of St. Sophia of Novgorod, despite the similarity of many of its elements with its Kievan namesake, was distinguished by its helmet-shaped domes and its more austere appearance. It became the basis for the development of a distinctly Novgorodian variant of the general Rus' architectural style, which evolved with the construction of later churches.

After St. Sophia was completed, masonry construction in Novgorod then lapsed for approximately half a century. During that period, however, Novgorod was emerging as an important political and economic center. Its territories were expanding. The town, filled with Slavs, Finns, and Scandinavians as well as visiting German and Byzantine merchants, acquired, like Kiev, a cosmopolitan character. Its population was also growing. Although its craftsmen acquired some specialized skills and techniques later than their Kievan counterparts, Novgorod too was a center for the manufacture of a variety of goods. Like Kiev, it was thus a thriving commercial center. By the middle of the eleventh century literate members of the Novgorod community had also mastered the art of writing on birchbark and were using that method to exchange brief messages and thereby facilitate the conduct of all types of daily business, personal and commercial.

The wealth and expertise that Novgorod was accumulating provided the means to launch a revival of masonry construction that lasted from the beginning of the twelfth century through the first decades of the thirteenth century and resulted in the appearance of dozens of masonry churches, fortifications, and other buildings in Novgorod proper and its subordinate towns. David Miller's studies reveal that in the century 1138–1237 masonry structures were erected in larger numbers in Novgorod than in any other region of Kievan Rus'; the Novgorodian structures accounted for almost one-quarter (24 per cent) of the total erected in all the Rus' lands.[9]

Novgorod's new churches were not on a scale akin to the central Cathedral of St. Sophia; as many of those built in other regions, they were smaller, simpler in design, and correspondingly less expensive than those of the preceding century. The scale of these structures may reflect a reduction in the surplus wealth that the society could apply to such projects. It may, on the other hand, be an indicator that funds were available in sufficiently large quantities that small-scale churches, normally built with cheaper wooden materials, could be constructed in more expensive masonry. Thus, unusually but consistently with the notion of a broader distribution of the society's wealth, not all of the Novgorodian churches of the twelfth century were sponsored by the prince or the bishop. Novgorod's boyars, including but not exclusively some who held the city's highest offices, as well as members of the merchant class, were also patrons of new churches. Notable among their projects was the Church of Paraskeva-Piatnitsa, built on the market side of the Volkhov River in 1207 by merchants engaged in foreign trade; its architectural style was similar to that of churches constructed in Chernigov and Smolensk near the turn of the century. This source of patronage was, according to Miller, rare; it serves as an indicator of both the unique political arrangements developing in Novgorod in the twelfth century as well as the unusual distribution of wealth among the members of the city's society.

By the twelfth century comparable stone and brick structures were being erected in other towns as well. Prince Rostislav Mstislavich built the Cathedral of Mother of God in Smolensk (1136–37). Two decades later (1158) Prince Andrei Bogoliubskii began the construction of the Church of the Dormition in the town of Vladimir. Prince Andrei's cathedral was a high point in a trend of urban construction in Rostov-Suzdal', which was dependent not only on the region's economic growth, but also on the consolidation of political authority over the region by the Monomashichi, territorial expansion, and a concomitant ' formation of new towns.

The building spree in that region began while Monomakh was still alive. The area of the town of Rostov was enlarged and a church built; Suzdal' received new fortifications and a brick cathedral church; and Vladimir was founded on the Kliaz'ma River in 1108. Iurii Dolgorukii

---

[9] David B. Miller, "Monumental Building and Its Patrons as Indicators of Economic and Political Trends in Rus', 900–1262," *JbfGO*, vol. 38 (1990), p. 335; Miller, "Monumental Building as an Indicator of Economic Trends in Northern Rus' in the Late Kievan and Mongol Periods, 1138–1462," *American Historical Review*, vol. 94 (1989), pp. 366–367.

Figure 3.2 The Cathedral of the Dormition, Vladimir

followed his father's example. He ordered the construction of fortifications on the borders of his realm. In the west those forts defined the boundary between Suzdalia and the Novgorod lands. In the south they demarcated his realm from Chernigov and Smolensk. Moscow, which was first mentioned in chronicle literature under year 1147, was established as one of these frontier posts on the southern border of Suzdalia. Iurii also oversaw the foundation of new towns, such as Iur'ev Pol'skii, Pereiaslavl' Zalesskii, and Dmitrov, in the interior of his lands. Within the towns Iurii was also responsible for major construction projects. It was he who actually sponsored the church construction noted above in Suzdal', which served as his residence and became the central town of the region during his reign.

Prince Andrei Bogoliubskii was Iurii's son and heir in Suzdalia. His activities were continuations of his family's tradition. But Andrei's attention and investment were showered on the town of Vladimir, which his father had assigned to him during in the 1140s. Andrei enlarged his town and between 1158 and 1164 encircled it with fortifications. Four entryways penetrated the walls, but the main one, as in Kiev, was known as the Golden Gate. On the edge of the city on bluffs overlooking the Kliaz'ma River he sponsored the construction of the white stone Cathedral of the Dormition (1158). In addition, he built an entire palace complex at Bogoliubovo in the 1160s not far from Vladimir; and in 1165, in honor of a victory over the Bulgars and in memory of a son who died in the battle, he built the Church of the Intercession on the Nerl' River, located north of Vladimir near Bogoliubovo. Andrei's successors, the first of whom was his brother Prince Vsevolod, continued the building policies. According to David Miller, between 1138 and 1237 thirty-four major construction projects were undertaken in Suzdalia, accounting for over 20 per cent of such projects throughout Rus' lands.[10]

The structures of Vladimir-Suzdal', while employing the same basic floorplan as the churches of Kiev, Novgorod, and other Rus' towns, nevertheless acquired a unique style, distinguished by the commonly used white stone building material, bands of arcading, and the ornate sculpture that decorated the exterior walls. Some of the buildings of the late twelfth and early thirteenth centuries displayed additional departures from familiar models. When Prince Vsevolod in 1185 authorized the restoration of the Church of the Dormition, which had been damaged by a fire, new galleries were added along three walls, four more domes were set atop the structure, and the church assumed a broader, heavier, and

---

[10] Miller, "Monumental Building as an Indicator of Economic Trends in Northern Rus'," pp. 366–367.

Figure 3.3 The Church of the Intercession of the Nerl', near Vladimir

more powerful appearance. Similar effects were achieved in churches erected in the town of Suzdal' in the 1220s. The innovative features may reflect the participation of European designers and craftsmen in these construction projects.

The architectural achievement of Andrei Bogoliubskii and his heirs must have been equally as impressive as that in Kiev. Whether one approached the northeastern capital by river and beheld the Church of the Intercession appearing almost to float above the ground as it sat on a raised mound with its delicate image reflected in the pond beneath, or used a land road and through the surrounding forests caught a glimpse of the golden dome of the Cathedral of the Dormition glittering above the city of Vladimir, a traveler could have no doubt that he was about to enter one of the major centers of the lands of Rus'.

Although smaller and simpler than their eleventh-century predecessors, the edifaces of the twelfth century were appearing in princely seats throughout the Riurikid realm, and their construction in the more recently established principalities, Vladimir-Suzdal', Smolensk, and Galicia-Volynia, was taking place at a faster rate than in the older towns like Kiev and Chernigov. The increase in construction activity in the outlying towns of Kievan Rus' and consequent relative decrease in the portion of structures built in Kiev have been interpreted by some as a sign of decline in the Kievan economy. As discussed above, that conclusion is not entirely warranted.

It has also been suggested that by building some monuments that in size and grandeur were on a scale equal to those in Kiev, the princes of other towns were challenging Kiev's preeminence. The monumental structures built in and around Vladimir by Prince Andrei are particularly cited in this context. Their appearance had the effect of undermining the prestige of Rostov, the center of the local bishopric. But the Church of the Dormition, whose cupolas were four meters higher than those on St. Sophia in Kiev, is also thought to have been built with the conscious intention of rivalling the Kievan cathedral and, by association, its prince and metropolitan. Comparisons have also been made between Prince Andrei's Golden Gate and that of Kiev.

The architectural activity in the lands of Kievan Rus' and particularly in Vladimir-Suzdal' reflects several trends. On the one hand, the upsurge of monumental construction projects stemmed from the growing strength and wealth of peripheral principalities and implicitly challenged Kiev's primacy. Similarly, the development of distinctive regional styles in Novgorod, Suzdalia, and elsewhere were explicit deviations from Kievan norms. On the other hand, underlying such visual statements of independence were themes betraying strong bonds between Kiev and the newer centers. Even as princes of outlying regions competed with one another by erecting magnificent structures, they were adopting fundamentally the same art forms which were identified with Christianity and its social norms. Despite the political or dynastic competition that may have motivated them, all who sponsored the ecclesiastical and secular construction projects used the same architectural models, methods, and technologies of construction, and even communicated in the same symbolic language in which their messages of rivalry and challenge were stated. They thus had all absorbed and were perpetuating a culture that, despite regional stylistic differences, was common to all the lands of Rus'.

In addition to and sometimes in conjunction with monumental building projects, Riurikid princes and other members of the elite strata of Kievan Rus' society contributed to the establishment and growth of monasteries, which were typically built in or very near urban centers. Many of them became centers where literacy, educational activities, and writing, collecting, translating, and copying manuscripts flourished; the establishment and growth of monasteries were thus also significant elements in Kiev's Golden Age and its aftermath.

The Pecherskii Monastery was one of the most prominent and influential of the monasteries in the environs of Kiev. Located three kilometers south of the city, it was founded by a certain Antonii, later St. Antonii, who had traveled to Mount Athos, become a monk, and returned to become a hermit in the solitude of the caves near Kiev. He was, however, soon joined by others and in 1051 a monastery was founded over the caves. In 1089 the Church of the Dormition, an impressive stone structure, was completed at the monastery; it was funded partially by the prince but also by endowments from wealthy members of society who wished to enter the monastery.

The monks of the Pecherskii Monastery collected and translated ecclesiastical manuscripts and built a substantial library. It was also at the Pecherskii Monastery that they compiled the successive versions of the Primary Chronicle, also known as the Tale of Bygone Years. Begun toward the end of the 1030s, the Primary Chronicle was written, edited, and rewritten by a series of at least six chroniclers, including the monks Nikon, who made his contributions c. 1073, and Nestor, whose revisions were made c. 1113. By 1118, the chronicle assumed its final form. It is the oldest surviving written history of Kievan Rus' available to modern historians and has provided the basis of much of what posterity knows of early Rus'. Its form was derived from Byzantine chronicles, but it acquired a distinctive character by incorporating local legends and tales as well as facts and editorials about Rus' affairs. Like Hilarion's Sermon on Law and

Grace, the Primary Chronicle conveyed the pride and self-awareness of a new nation, which by recording its history was proclaiming its place in the Christian community.

By the twelfth century other regional chronicle traditions were also being established, notably in Novgorod and Galicia-Volynia. But the Primary Chronicle, representing the perspective of the central lands of Rus', was incorporated into other chronicles, composed later in widely separated regions of the country. It formed the first part of the Laurentian chronicle, whose later sections, as it was copied in 1377, contained entries that focused on Suzdalian events. The Primary Chronicle also comprised the first section of the early fifteenth-century Hypatian chronicle, which added a Kievan chronicle that extended the coverage to the end of the twelfth century and a Galician-Volynian chronicle for the thirteenth century. Although the later components of the Laurentian and Hypatian chronicles highlight regional developments, emphasize different factors, and provide at times conflicting versions of history, their common use of the Primary Chronicle is another indicator, like religion and architecture, that the diverse regions of Kievan Rus' enjoyed a common culture. In this case the regions accepted a written, standardized statement of their shared history, which testified that no matter how widely the branches or principalities of Kievan Rus' spread apart, they were all growing from common roots.

Prince Vladimir I and his heirs established a political framework for the Kievan Rus' society. The overarching dynasty held together the various regions, populated by related but distinct tribes. Under the influence of its policies, including the introduction of Christianity, the establishment of administrative and legal structures, support for economic and commercial development, and promotion of arts and culture, additional bonds among the components of the realm were forged and tempered.

By the twelfth century, however, dynastic reorganization coupled with shifting trade patterns and a dispersal of craft production had given impetus to the political and economic strengthening of outlying centers. The consequent concentration of wealth and power among the local elites provided the means and desire to glorify their regional centers at the expense of Kievan hegemony. Peripheral Rus' principalities, using a variety of means ranging from territorial expansion to embellishment of their own cities, were exhibiting their individual dynamism and power. These tendencies were underscored by displays of cultural divergence, such as the appearance of regionally distinctive architectural styles and chronicle coverage.

Despite these tendencies toward divergence, interaction between princes and priests on the one hand and peasants and townsmen on the other had an enduring and unifying impact on all members of Kievan Rus' society. It is evident that the reactions to princely policies and their effects on Kievan Rus' society were uneven. The urban population felt the effects of the consolidation of Riurikid rule and the introduction of their policies more directly and immediately than their rural cousins. The latter, remaining remote from much of the princely politics centered in cities, tended to be socially conservative. The rural society, which clung to tribal traditions reinforced by their communal institutions and elders, internalized Christian behavior and secular legal standards at a slower pace than the urban populace. Nevertheless, through the tenth to twelfth centuries distinctions among tribes faded. And in towns especially, customs ranging from preferences for certain styles of clothing accessories to burial practices that had distinguished Slavs from Finns, Scandinavians from emigre Khazars and visiting Byzantines, became more homogenized. Through the eleventh and twelfth centuries the various components of Kievan Rus' society were bound together ever more tightly by a range of economic and cultural ties. A common cultural foundation underlay regional diversity, displayed in the political realm as well as artistic styles. Interaction between the Riurikid princes and their subjects resulted in the formation of a society tightly knit together by economic and cultural threads that would fail to unravel even when its dynastic political framework cracked.

4

KIEVAN RUS': THE
FINAL CENTURY

·

The period between the death of Vladimir I (St. Vladimir) and that of Vladimir Monomakh may be considered politically as one of expansion and consolidation for Kiev and the southern Rus' lands. At the end of Monomakh's reign the Riurikids were the exclusive rulers of a realm that stretched from Galicia and Volynia in the southwest to Rostov and Murom in the northeast, from Pereiaslavl' and Kiev in the south to Novgorod with its own empire reaching the White Sea and the Ural Mountains in the north. With commercial links to Byzantium, the Muslim East, and Europe, Kievan Rus' was a flourishing, powerful state. Its major towns, such as Kiev, Chernigov, and Novgorod, had been transformed into bustling metropoles, inhabited by tens of thousands of people, adorned with stone churches, and protected by strong fortifications; its outposts were becoming centers of dynamic principalities. The dynastic and territorial organization of Kievan Rus' had evolved into what appeared to be relatively stable and effective forms. Kiev, the main political, commercial, and cultural center, continued to be the seat of the senior Riurikid. Members of each branch of the dynasty, as agreed at Liubech in 1097, settled around their own secondary centers, which were transformed into their hereditary principalities.

Within this framework Monomakh and his sons ruled to 1139. But during the next century, preceding the Mongol invasion of 1237–40, political conditions in Kievan Rus' became increasingly complex. The multiplication of dynastic lines, untimely deaths of individual princes, and intradynastic marriages obscured the lines separating dynastic generations and branches and determining the order of succession. The situation was further complicated as more principalities were carved out of Kievan Rus' territory and allocated to specific princes and their offspring, while other existing principalities were subdivided to accommodate their princely families' cadet lines.

By the end of the period in question Kievan Rus' consisted of approximately a dozen principalities. So, Turov and Pinsk, Riazan' and Murom join the more familiar names of Kiev, Chernigov, and Pereiaslavl' that dominated the discussion of political and dynastic events of the tenth and eleventh centuries. But among all the principalities and all the dynastic branches only four were actually contenders for the central seat of Kiev in the period 1125–1240. Neither the emergence of these lines nor their prominence was arbitrary. Rather, their roles derived from the traditions of the succession system coupled with the growing economic and military power of the principalities they individually ruled.

Three of the four lines descended from Vladimir Monomakh. When he died in 1125, his sons, as discussed in chapter 2, were the sole legitimate heirs to the grand princely throne. In 1125, Monomakh's eldest surviving son, Mstislav, ascended the Kievan throne. His reign lasted to 1132. In that year Monomakh's next eldest son, Iaropolk, who had been prince of Pereiaslavl', succeeded Mstislav and remained on the throne to 1139. But as Monomakh's descendants multiplied during the twelfth century, his dynastic line divided. Two of the branches that retained claims to the Kievan throne descended from his first heir, Mstislav. One of them was founded by Mstislav's son Iziaslav and became identified with the principality of Volynia in southwestern Rus'. The other descended from Rostislav Mstislavich and ruled Smolensk. The third line of Monomashichi that played a central role in Kievan politics was that of Mstislav's younger brother, Iurii Dolgorukii. His heirs controlled Suzdalia, including the towns of Rostov, Suzdal', Vladimir, and the border outpost of Moscow. The fourth line that competed for Kiev consisted of the princes of Chernigov, i.e., the heirs of Oleg Sviatoslavich who had withdrawn from the rotation at the end of the eleventh century, but reinserted themselves into it during the twelfth.

Although the Riurikid princes engaged in a series of disputes from 1139 to 1240, the main issue that provoked conflict and shaped the political development of Kievan Rus' in this era remained succession to the Kievan throne. Enlarged populations, lucrative commerce, and compartmentalized foreign concerns and policies enabled the princes to use armies bolstered by supplemental troops and foreign allies in their military engagements. Thus, the continuation of the almost traditional feuding between princes within the dynasty had severe consequences as the rivals brought to their conflicts the greater resources and independence of action that their discrete bases of power, their principalities, afforded them.

The bitter and destructive dynastic warfare that constitutes one of the most striking features of this era has been generally interpreted in two different ways. The first regards the discord as evidence of the decline of Kievan Rus'. Chroniclers as well as the anonymous author of the epic tale, "The Lay of Igor's Campaign," attributed to the late twelfth century, lamented the internecine warfare and discord they witnessed within the Rus' lands. One school of modern scholars has essentially adopted the perspective of its ancient predecessors. Emphasizing the dysfunctional aspects of the conflicts within Kievan Rus', this group has concluded that Kiev itself was in decline during this period and that the Riurikid realm was disintegrating into its component parts.

Some proponents of this view have constructed their argument around a definition of a state or principality that emphasizes the scope and extent of its ruler's power. Accordingly, the integrity of Kievan Rus' is seen to have depended upon the ability of the grand prince of Kiev to perform essential administrative functions, i.e., collect taxes, command the military, and control judicial procedures, within his domain. When other princes fashioned their own hereditary principalities from lands that had previously been directly subject to Kiev, they were effectively reducing the range of the grand prince's authority, causing an erosion of Kiev's resources and contributing to the disintegration of Kievan Rus'. One corollary to that premise is that the center of political gravity moved to the northeast; the principality of Vladimir-Suzdal', especially under its princes Andrei Bogoliubskii (1157–75) and Vsevolod (1177–1212), emerged as the successor to the declining Kiev. Another supplement to this view highlighted demographic trends and commercial patterns; they were seen to have shifted during this era to the detriment of Kiev and contributed thereby to its decline.

A wide range of scholars, including Russian, Soviet, and western historians from the nineteenth and twentieth centuries, supports this point of view partially or wholly. The nineteenth and early twentieth century Russian historians, S. M. Solov'ev and A. E. Presniakov, proposed variants of it. The British scholar John Fennell, although describing Kiev as a coveted princely seat at least among southern Rus' princes as late as the first decades of the thirteenth century, nevertheless considered hereditary acquisition of a principality by one branch of the Riurikid dynasty to have been tantamount to independence from Kiev and implicitly suggested that a division of administrative responsibility

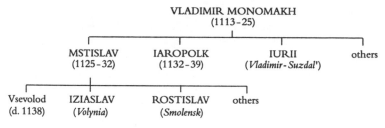

Table 4.1 The division of the house of Monomakh

constitituted a division of the state. Omeljan Pritsak, who characterized "the two destructions of Kiev . . . [in 1169 and 1240 as] coups de grace for the past giant [i.e., Kiev]" and George Vernadsky, who claimed that by 1139 "both the supremacy of Kiev and the unity of Russia were shattered almost beyond recovery," may also be considered as proponents of this view.[1]

Other scholars have offered an alternative interpretation. While acknowledging the increasing strength and political and economic roles of the peripheral principalities, their descriptions of Kievan Rus' conform more to an image of a dynastic realm. Territories governed by any member or branch of the dynasty were components of the realm. An increase in the number of component parts and a distribution of power among them, while diminishing the relative power of Kiev, did not, according to their view, necessarily dilute the strength of the realm as a whole. On the contrary, in the presence of an expansion in both the size of the dynasty and its territories and also in the absence of efficient transportation and communication networks, a division of administrative responsibility, i.e., the formation of individual principalities, was a rational and functional form of organization that, at the time, contributed to stability and order. The examination in chapter 2 of the crises faced by the dynasty in the 1090s provides evidence supporting their view.

Adherents of the second view correspondingly place greater weight on evidence that points to continued prosperity in Kiev itself and to an enduring overarching unity among the Riurikid lands. Some have cited archeological evidence to refute the notion that Kiev's economy and

---

[1] John Fennell, *The Crisis of Medieval Russia, 1200–1304* (London and New York: Longman, 1983), pp. 1, 7; Omeljan Pritsak, "Kievan Rus' and Sixteenth–Seventeenth-Century Ukraine," in *Rethinking Ukrainian History*, ed. by Ivan L. Rudnytsky (Edmonton, Alberta: Canadian Institute of Ukrainian Studies, 1983), p. 5; Vernadsky, *Kievan Russia*, p. 98.

commerce were in a state of decay. They argue that Kiev continued to enjoy economic prosperity in the twelfth and early thirteenth centuries. Others, observing that Orthodox religious institutions and beliefs were being more broadly accepted during this period, suggest that they contributed to a unity among the Rus' lands and society that transcended political division. Similarly, the legal norms, derived from law codes introduced by Prince Iaroslav and his sons in the eleventh century but adopted widely in the early thirteenth, reflect the existence of a common culture binding the Rus' principalities together. These arguments are reflected in the discussion in chapter 3.

Scholars regarding Kievan Rus' from this perspective maintain that its political framework did not essentially change in the twelfth and early thirteenth centuries. It continued to be a dynastic realm, united and even politically defined as an entity by its dynasty. The conflicts among the Riurikid princes, according to this interpretation, represented not a breakdown of the polity, but universal recognition and acknowledgment of a coherent political system, within which there was vigorous competition for seniority, hence for Kiev, which remained their political, economic, and religious capital. The very fact that Kiev remained the focus of their quarrels signifies, according this interpretation, that it continued to be perceived as an object worth winning and the symbol of seniority for the dynasty. In their view, thus, the expansion of Kievan Rus' and the increasing significance of its peripheral principalities redistributed relative power within the realm. But those trends neither destroyed the integrity of Kievan Rus' nor undermined the role of Kiev as its real and symbolic center.

THE PERIPHERAL PRINCIPALITIES

Although the political framework of Kievan Rus' may have been unaltered, the number of principalities within it and the relative power among them was continually changing during the period 1125–1237. In the eleventh century the principalities of Kiev, Chernigov, and Pereiaslavl' formed the core of Kievan Rus' and their princes played the most important political roles in the country. After 1125, several principalities forming on the fringes of the realm assumed greater political importance. They were Volynia, Smolensk, and Suzdalia, all ruled by members of Monomakh's clan. The rulers of these principalities, together with those of Chernigov became the central figures in the political dynamics of Kievan Rus' in the period 1125 to 1237. Novgorod, whose character was changing in the twelfth century, also continued to play a critical role in Kievan politics during this period.

Map 4.1 Kievan Rus' in the twelfth–early thirteenth centuries

Volynia (Volyn'; Volhynia)

Volynia was a principality in southwestern Rus'. Its territories, located along the upper North Bug and the Pripiat' Rivers, bordered Polotsk, Turov, and Kiev on its east, Galicia (Halych) on its southwest, and Poland to the west. Benefitting from the commercial advantages attained during the twelfth century, both Volynia and Galicia experienced marked development, and merged at the end of the century to form a politically powerful principality.

The Galician lands, located south of Volynia along the Dniester River and neighboring Hungary to the west and Kiev and the Polovtsy steppe to the east, were ruled in the late eleventh century by a branch of the Riurikid dynasty that had lost its claim to the position of grand prince of Kiev. This branch descended from Vladimir, a son of Iaroslav the Wise, who had ruled Novgorod but died in 1052, two years before his father. The Liubech congress in 1097 confirmed his heirs' rights to the Galician territories. John Fennell has characterized the establishment of hereditary rights by Vladimir Iaroslavich's descendants to Galicia by the end of the eleventh century as a successful effort to thwart a Kievan attempt to dominate Galicia and the achievement of virtual independence for their domain.[2] Galicia was subdivided among those heirs, however, until the middle of the twelfth century. Only then under the princes of Galich, Vladimir Volodarovich (1141–53) and his son Iaroslav Osmomysl' (1153–87), did Galicia unite and flourish. Despite disputes with his boyars, Iaroslav Osmomysl' became an influential participant in Rus' as well as eastern European political affairs and displayed ambitions toward the neighboring principality of Volynia.

Volynia had been virtually a possession of the Kievan grand prince, until the middle of the twelfth century, and as such had been ruled either directly from Kiev or by an appointee of the grand prince. It was, additionally, influenced by its neighbors, Hungary and Poland, which at times interfered in Volynian politics and Volynian–Galician relations. In the 1140s, the Volynian prince, his father Grand Prince Vsevolod of Kiev (1139–46), and other members of their clan of Ol'govichi successfully resisted the Galician drive to absorb Volynia. Then, while Iziaslav Mstislavich was grand prince (1146–54), Volynia was converted into a patrimony of his descendants. It thus became the patrimony of the senior branch of Monomakh's descendants. As such, rather than becoming further removed from Kiev, it was drawn more deeply into the politics of grand princely succession.

---

[2] Fennell, *Crisis of Medieval Russia,* p. 14.

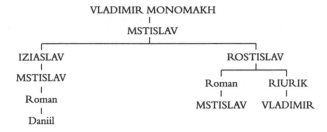

Table 4.2 The descendants of Prince Mstislav Vladimirovich

Despite some internal discord, the princes of Volynia quickly achieved political prominence and influence. In 1158, one of them, Mstislav, son of the late Grand Prince Iziaslav, along with his neighbor Prince Iaroslav Osmomysl' of Galicia, played a decisive role in the succession contest that propelled his uncle Rostislav Mstislavich of Smolensk to the grand princely throne. Mstislav, according to some accounts, acted as co-ruler with the grand prince. In 1167, once again supported by the Galician prince Iaroslav, Mstislav succeeded Rostislav to the Kievan throne. His succession, as will be discussed below, provoked a reaction from other members of the dynasty, determined to remove him.

Volynia reached the pinnacle of its power at the turn of the century. By that time the descendants of Vladimir Iaroslavich had lost their control over Galicia, which was dominated for a period by Hungary. In 1199, Prince Roman Mstislavich of Volynia united Galicia with his own principality. Then, expelling Grand Prince Riurik Rostislavich from Kiev, he assumed effective control over territories ranging from the Dnieper River to the Danube River and Carpathian Mountains and dominated southwestern Rus' until his untimely death during a campaign against Poland in 1205. After Roman's death, his son Daniil had difficulty holding the two principalities together. Galicia, whose boyars assumed a major political role, separated from Volynia and accepted a series of princes from locations ranging from Hungary to Chernigov. Daniil recovered the Galician throne just as the Mongols began their invasion of the Rus' lands.

Smolensk

Even before Volynia became the patrimony of Iziaslav Mstislavich, Smolensk had become the principality of his younger brother, Rostislav (1127–59). Despite its transformation into a distinct hereditary principality, the princes of Smolensk, like those of Volynia, remained legitimate heirs to the Kievan throne. Their principality, inhabited by Krivichi tribes, encompassing the headwaters of the West Dvina, Dnieper, and Volga Rivers, and wedged among Novgorod on the north, Rostov-Suzdal' on the east, Chernigov on the south, and Polotsk on the west, became their base of operation as they participated in central Kievan affairs.

Before Rostislav became its prince Smolensk too had been ruled by appointees of the Kievan grand prince. Grand Prince Iaroslav had left the region to his son Viacheslav, but after his death (1056), Smolensk was not associated with any single branch of the dynasty until 1097. Then, at the Liubech meeting it was attached to the domain of Vladimir Monomakh. Monomakh ruled it through his sons as well as non-Riurikid governors or *posadniki*. Finally, not long after Monomakh died, his grandson Rostislav Mstislavich assumed the Smolensk throne. It then remained the possession of his descendants.

During Rostislav's reign a bishopric was established in Smolensk (1136), and the principality's territory was enlarged; by the early 1220s, it was extending its authority over Polotsk as well. As noted above, Rostislav, supported by his nephew Mstislav Iziaslavich of Volynia, became grand prince of Kiev (1158–67). His sons, Roman and Riurik, similarly involved Smolensk in Kievan conflicts. Riurik Rostislavich in particular was engaged in succession struggles that placed him on the Kievan throne no less than seven times. By the second decade of the thirteenth century, Rostislav's grandsons emerged from the intradynastic conflicts to dominate the lands of western Rus' from Novgorod in the north to Galicia in the southwest. Mstislav Romanovich (1212–23) and his cousin Vladimir Riurikovich (1223–35) continuously held the throne of Kiev until just a few years before the arrival of the Mongols.

Suzdalia

Suzdalia was the name used by the middle of the twelfth century for the Rostov lands located to the northeast of Kiev between the Volga and Oka Rivers. Unlike Volynia and Smolensk, which had been attached to Kiev before becoming distinct principalities, this region, as noted in chapter 2, had been an extension of the principality of Pereiaslavl'. As prince of Pereiaslavl', Vladimir Monomakh had assigned the Rostov lands to several of his sons, who defended them from incursions and challenges from Oleg Sviatoslavich of the Chernigov line in the 1090s; the Monomashichi were confirmed as the region's legitimate and hereditary rulers at the Liubech congress. While some of Monomakh's elder sons proceeded to the Kievan and Pereiaslavl' thrones, one of his younger sons, Iurii Dolgorukii, and his descendants held the princely seat in the Rostov lands.

It was during the reign of Prince Iurii Dolgorukii (prince of Rostov, 1125–57), who favored the city of Suzdal', that the region acquired the name Suzdalia. Iurii's son Andrei Bogoliubskii (ruled 1157–75) shifted his focus to the town of Vladimir with the result that the region is also frequently referred to as Vladimir-Suzdal'. Despite its multiple names, the principality under Andrei and his brother Vsevolod of the Big Nest (ruled 1177–1212) accepted the exclusive rule of the Dolgorukii branch of the Monomashichi.

During the administrations of Iurii Dolgorukii and his sons, the towns of the region multiplied and grew. The outpost of Moscow was only one of the towns constructed by Dolgorukii. The principality itself also expanded. By the end of the first quarter of the thirteenth century it extended to Ustiug, which controlled the intersection of the major river routes across the northlands. Prince Iurii Vsevolodich also extended his lands eastward; in 1221, he founded Nizhnii Novgorod at the juncture of the Oka and Volga Rivers and thereby consolidated his principality's dominance over routes along those rivers as well.

The expansion of Vladimir-Suzdal' to the north and east was undertaken at the expense of the Volga Bulgars. The princes of Suzdalia also extended their influence over some of their Rus' neighbors. Novgorod, which will be discussed below, was one object of their interest. In addition, they exerted pressure on their southern neighbor, the principality of Riazan' (or Murom-Riazan'). The territories of Riazan' encompassed tributaries of the Oka as well as the headwaters of the Don; they thus constituted a linkage between trade routes leading to the Black Sea as well as to Bulgar and the mid-Volga River. From the middle of the eleventh century these territories had been regarded as an appendage of Chernigov, much as Suzdalia had been associated with Pereiaslavl'. After the death of Prince Iaroslav Sviatoslavich in 1129, however, his descendants established themselves as the exclusive dynastic line for both Murom and Riazan', and shed their attachment to Chernigov. Nevertheless, during the second half of the twelfth century, the princes of Murom and Riazan' became dependent upon the princes of Vladimir-Suzdal'.

As a result of their policies, the princes of Vladimir-Suzdal' emerged in the final quarter of the twelfth century as powerful figures in the Rus' lands. Preoccupied with affairs in the northern sectors of those lands, they operated independently of Kiev. With the singular exception of a quarrel over Novgorod that exploded into Andrei Bogoliubskii's interference in Kievan succession, the sack of Kiev in 1169, and the establishment of

Andrei's brother, Prince Gleb Iur'evich of Pereiaslavl' (d. c. 1171), on the Kievan throne, the Suzdalian princes generally refrained from direct involvement in Kievan affairs.

They nevertheless consciously developed their own principality in imitation of and as a rival to Kiev. Andrei Bogoliubskii's effort to transform Vladimir, where he sponsored the construction of half a dozen churches, including the Church of the Dormition (*Uspenskii sobor*), as well as the Golden Gates, into a city whose magnificence was on a par with Kiev's, has already been noted. In a similar manner, chronicle entries describing Andrei's return from southern Rus' to Suzdalia in 1155 emphasize an association between Andrei and his town of Vladimir with the Holy Virgin, a form of imagery normally reserved for Kiev. Thus, Andrei brought the celebrated Byzantine "Mother of God" icon with him from a suburb of Kiev, decorated it with silver, gold, gems, and pearls, and gave it a place of prominence in his church in Vladimir. In subsequent episodes of his reign the Virgin is said to have guided and protected him. Andrei went even further and in 1164 attempted to remove his domain from the Kievan ecclesiastical structure by creating a new metropolitanate for Vladimir. His effort was overruled by the patriarch in Constantinople.

Such policies and rhetoric identified Vladimir, more than any of the other developing centers in the Rus' lands, as the center of the dynasty rivaling Kiev and even as its heir. By the time Grand Prince Sviatoslav Vsevolodich (of the Chernigov line) died in 1194, Andrei's heir Vsevolod was recognized, according to the chronicle accounts, as senior prince of the dynasty. Although he did not claim the Kievan throne for himself, Vsevolod had a decisive voice in determining the succession of Riurik Rostislavich from Smolensk that year.

Even as the Vladimir-Suzdal' principality was growing, acquiring increasing relative power among the Rus' lands, and surpassing its parent principality Pereiaslavl' in political influence, difficulties were arising within it. In contrast to Volynia and Galicia, where local boyars exerted strong political influence, and Novgorod, where the bishops, city officials, and *veche* were dominant, in Suzdalia the princes overshadowed these other social groups and institutions. In an extreme instance in the early 1160s, Andrei Bogoliubskii removed brothers, nephews, some of his father's prominent retainers, and the bishop in an effort to monopolize political authority. Rivalries among servitors based in the various towns of Suzdalia and dissatisfaction with the prince were graphically expressed on June 28, 1175, when twenty of Andrei's own retainers burst into his bedroom at his palace compound of Bogoliubovo and murdered him.

More familiar forms of dispute erupted upon the death of Vsevolod in 1212. Because Andrei's offspring had not survived Vsevolod, the latter's sons were the legitimate heirs to his position as prince of Vladimir. By dynastic convention his eldest surviving son, Konstantin, should have inherited his throne. But Vsevolod, recognizing Konstantin's reluctance to give up his seat at Rostov upon ascending the Vladimir throne, had designated his next son, Iurii, as his successor. As a result, the years following Vsevolod's death were marked by a fractiousness that became intertwined with a dispute over the disposition of Novgorod. It culminated in the Battle of Lipitsa (1216), in which the forces of Konstantin, united with those of the Rostislavichi of Smolensk, defeated his younger brothers, Iurii and Iaroslav, who were favored by the house of Chernigov. Konstantin ruled Vladimir only until 1218; his death in that year enabled Iurii to recover that position, which he held until the arrival of the Mongols.

Novgorod

As discussed above, Volynia, Smolensk, and Suzdalia, as well as most of the regions of Kievan Rus' that had either directly recognized the authority of the Kievan grand prince or accepted an appointed governor from him, had during the twelfth century identified themselves with specific branches of the dynasty. Novgorod also altered its relationship with Kiev, but retained a special political status. As noted in chapter 2, the princes of Kiev had in the tenth and eleventh centuries appointed Novgorod's rulers without regard for the dynastic succession system. Frequently the Kievan princes appointed their eldest sons, but in some cases the appointed ruler was not even a member of the dynasty.

By the late eleventh century, however, this relationship had begun to change. The Russian scholar V. L. Ianin has argued that in 1088, when the twelve-year-old son of Vladimir Monomakh, Prince Mstislav, first assumed the throne of Novgorod, the functions of the *posadnik* of Novgorod, previously interchangeable with those of a prince, were redefined. From that time the Novgorodians themselves, through their *veche*, selected their *posadnik*. By 1120, that office had come to be held exclusively by representatives of the Novgorodian boyars. The functions and authority of the *posadnik* overlapped with those of the prince, who continued to be selected by the Kievan grand prince.[3]

But, while transforming the role of *posadnik* into what was essentially

[3] V. L. Ianin, *Novgorodskie posadniki* [Novgorodian *posadniki*] (Moscow: Moskovskii universitet, 1962), p. 59.

a new office with an old title, Novgorod also began to interject its
voice into the selection of its prince. In 1096 and again in 1102, the
Novgorodians objected to proposed princely replacements and demanded
the return of Mstislav Vladimirovich, who remained at his Novgorodian
post until 1117. Mstislav, reassigned at that time by his father, went on to
become grand prince of Kiev in 1125. He was replaced in Novgorod by
his own son Vsevolod, who served until 1132. In that year Vsevolod's
uncle Iaropolk, the new grand prince of Kiev, transferred him to
Pereiaslavl'. He later returned to Novgorod, but his subjects, annoyed that
he had abandoned them, accused him of having broken his oath to remain
in Novgorod as their prince and only reluctantly reaccepted him as their
prince.

It was during the reign of Vsevolod that the functions of prince and
posadnik became differentiated. The *posadnik*, selected through the *veche*
by fellow Novgorodians, was often juxtaposed to the prince, who was still
officially appointed by the Kievan prince. Princely appointments were,
however, increasingly dependent upon the Novgorodians' approval of a
specific candidate. And in 1136, even the facade of Kievan control over
the selection of Novgorod's princes was removed. In May of that year in
what amounted to a popular uprising the Novgorodians arrested
Vsevolod, imprisoned him in the bishop's palace, and established new
conditions for their princes. The primary principle asserted by the
Novgorodians was their right to select their own prince from among the
Riurikids; no longer would they automatically accept the appointee of
the prince of Kiev. They further restricted the right of their prince and his
retinue to hold landed estates in the Novgorod lands; that privilege was
limited to citizens of Novgorod.

Exercising their newly proclaimed prerogatives, the Novgorodians
expelled Vsevolod on July 15, and four days later invited a member of the
Chernigov branch of the dynasty, Sviatoslav Ol'govich, to be their prince.
In 1137, Vsevolod, encouraged by his supporters in Novgorod, attempted
to recover his former position, but died in the process. By the next spring
Novgorod had expelled Sviatoslav as well and turned to the Suzdalian line
for a prince. The princes of Novgorod not only became subject to the
approval of the Novgorodians; their power was also diminished by an
increase in the *veche*'s influence over other city officials. In 1156, the
Novgorod *veche* for the first time selected the city's bishop, who by 1165
was elevated to the rank of archbishop. By the end of the century it had
also created a new officer, the *tysiatskii* or militia commander, to function
along with the *posadnik* and archbishop as well as the prince to direct the
city's affairs.

From the late eleventh century the *veche* of Novgorod thus gradually asserted a greater and greater voice in the determination of the city's rulers, first by transforming the *posadnik* into an official governing in conjunction with the prince and then in 1136, by firmly establishing its right to name Novgorod's prince as well. One issue that has continued to divide scholars, however, is the character and composition of the *veche*. While some, including V. L. Ianin, have argued that the *veche* was dominated by the boyars of Novgorod, others favor the view that in the eleventh and twelfth centuries this town assembly, which met irregularly at Iaroslav's court on the market side of the city, was a forum for all free townsmen, including merchants and craftsmen as well as the landowning boyars. Nevertheless, internal divisions, especially among the boyar families, coupled with the city's need for a prince to conduct military campaigns and to guide its relations with other Rus' principalities, prevented the *veche* from completely dominating Novgorodian affairs. Rather, the princes selected by the *veche* and often in alliance with one or another of its factions continued to exercise significant authority over the Novgorodian lands.[4]

By transforming its governing institutions Novgorod rejected its politically dependent relationship to Kiev. The loosening of Novgorod's bond with Kiev in some ways paralleled that of other principalities in this era. What distinguished Novgorod's political reorganization was that it did not substitute Kievan authority with that of a particular branch of the dynasty that would perpetually provide it with rulers. Rather, in 1136, Novgorod began a practice of inviting representatives from other, often competing, branches of the dynasty associated with their own principalities to serve as its prince. Thus in 1138, only two years after it had received Sviatoslav Ol'govich from the Chernigov line, Novgorod expelled him and took a prince from the Suzdal' branch of the dynasty. This practice, coupled with the creation of its own set of officials, appeared to serve Novgorod well. In military encounters with other principalities, such as those against Suzdalia in 1148–49 and 1169 (which will be discussed below), it achieved notable victories. The practice also protected Novgorod from domination by any single branch of the dynasty. But at the same time it virtually became an invitation to the main branches of the dynasty to compete for political influence in Novgorod. Indeed, with its extensive trade network and commercial wealth,

---

[4] For a discussion of the debate over the *veche* as well as the corresponding issues of the relative roles and powers of Novgorod's government officials, see Henrik Birnbaum, *Lord Novgorod the Great: Essays in the History and Culture of a Medieval City-State*, UCLA Slavic Studies, vol. 2 (Columbus, Ohio: Slavica, 1981), pp. 45–46, 91ff., and Fennell, *Crisis of Medieval Russia*, pp. 18–19.

Novgorod was perceived as an important asset, control over which provided an advantage that could enhance a prince's position in his struggle for seniority within the Riurikid realm. Ironically, by asserting its "independence," Novgorod made itself vulnerable to pressures and demands of other princes as it became a prized objective in the continuing struggle for power in the lands of Kievan Rus'.

DYNASTIC RELATIONS

The addition of new principalities and the development of older ones made the implementation of the dynastic rules governing succession, hence the relations among the ruling houses in the lands that constituted Kievan Rus', increasingly complex during the period from the death of Vladimir Monomakh (1125) to the Mongol invasion (1237–40). The era was highlighted by sporadic outbreaks of virulent intradynastic conflict, sparked by attempts to revise the traditional dynastic order to accommodate the changing political configurations. The prevailing political relations thus come into sharp focus during a series of crises, which occurred in 1132–34, 1146–59, 1167–77, and the early years of the thirteenth century. The events of those years illustrate that the political organization of Kievan Rus' remained essentially in the form that had evolved during the previous century. The central principalities of Kiev, Chernigov, and Pereiaslavl', as well as the peripheral principalities, were politically joined in a state held together by their common dynasty, the Riurikids. The center of their realm remained Kiev; the senior member of the dynasty continued to reign as grand prince of that city.

The constancy of the political framework did not preclude interprincely disputes within it. The domestic discord that occurred during this period, however, was rooted primarily in contested claims to dynastic seniority, hence to the Kievan throne. The disputes were complicated furthermore by the fact that the real distribution of power among the princes was in the process of shifting; as the peripheral regions became organized politically into principalities and developed economically, they provided their princes with greater resources which they were able to draw upon for their intradynastic rivalries. To offset their opponents' power and increase their own, princes formed alliances among themselves. Such groupings became important in determining the outcome of disputes during this period, while secondary quarrels over dominance in key areas, notably Novgorod, similarly intruded into princely politics.

The chief contenders in the rivalry that developed during this period were members of the dynastic lines mentioned earlier, the descendants of Vladimir Monomakh and the princes of Chernigov (the Ol'govichi). The

Monomashichi, it will be recalled, initially divided into two factions. One consisted of descendants of Monomakh's eldest son, Mstislav. The other, led by Iurii Dolgorukii, included Iurii's sons and other junior members of Monomakh's clan. The wedge that separated Monomakh's offspring was Pereiaslavl'. Possession of that princely seat was valued because it symbolized seniority within Monomakh's branch of the dynasty; the prince of Pereiaslavl' had come to be regarded as heir to the Kievan throne.

When Vladimir Monomakh died in 1125, the political situation, as discussed in chapter 2, appeared far less complicated than it would become later in the century. The range of princes in the rotation for the Kievan throne had narrowed. Iziaslav's grandson, Iaroslav Sviatopolkovich, had died in 1123, thus removing that line from the rotation cycle. Oleg Sviatoslavich and his relatives had accepted the compromise, according to which their rights to Chernigov were confirmed in exchange for their withdrawal of any claims to the Kievan throne. Monomakh's brother had died decades earlier. The succession was confined, therefore, to Monomakh's direct descendants, and his eldest son Mstislav assumed the throne without incident. When Mstislav died in 1132, his brother Iaropolk Vladimirovich, who had ruled at Pereiaslavl' during his brother's reign at Kiev, ascended the Kievan throne. Iaropolk's succession, like his brother's, occurred in complete conformity with the established rules of succession. It also defined the role of Pereiaslavl' as the transition seat for the princely succession to the Kievan throne.

Iaropolk's reign (1132–39) was nevertheless marred by renewed inter-princely conflicts. Although the entire dynasty recognized him as the legitimate heir to Kiev, a dispute arose among the Monomashichi over possession of Pereiaslavl', whose ruler was expected to become Iaropolk's successor. It was as a result of the conflicts generated by this quarrel that George Vernadsky concluded that Iaropolk's reign marked the end of political unity in Kievan Rus'.

The crisis of 1132–1134

The dispute began shortly after Iaropolk assumed the throne in Kiev. One of his first tasks was to install his successor in Pereiaslavl'. But rather than fill the position with one of his younger brothers, the new grand prince recalled his nephew Vsevolod Mstislavich from Novgorod to become prince of Pereiaslavl'. Not only did that action alienate Novgorod, it also provoked Iurii Dolgorukii, prince of Suzdal', to challenge the appointment. As Iaropolk's younger brother, Iurii claimed seniority over their nephew and priority over Vsevolod for possession of the central seat of the family patrimony. Iurii invaded Pereiaslavl' and drove out Vsevolod, then repeated his action when Iaropolk placed another of Mstislav's sons, Iziaslav, on the disputed throne. Despite his military success, Iurii lost his bid to seize personal power in Pereiaslavl'. He nevertheless succeeded in keeping Pereiaslavl' in the hands of his generation; Iaropolk and Iurii agreed to recognize, at least temporarily, their brother Viacheslav as prince of Pereiaslavl'.

In 1134, the conflict was renewed; this time it was a three-way contest, involving both branches of Monomashichi and also the princes of Chernigov. Hostilities revived after Viacheslav decided to leave Pereiaslavl' for his former seat of Turov. Iurii, anxious to secure the center of the Monomakh patrimony, proposed to Iaropolk that he would give up Rostov-Suzdal' in exchange for Pereiaslavl'. But that offer, according to one chronicle version, provoked heated objections from the Chernigov princes. Presumably opposed to any major reallocation of power and principalities, they, supported by their Polovtsy allies, went to war against both Iaropolk and Iurii.

To complicate the situation further, Vsevolod Mstislavich, who had in the meantime returned to Novgorod, attempted to depose Iurii. He led two campaigns from Novgorod down the Volga River against Suzdalia with the intention of establishing his own brother, Iziaslav, in Iurii's place. If successful, he would have consolidated Pereiaslavl' and Suzdalia, i.e., all the territories of the Monomashichi, under the control of the senior branch of that dynastic line, the Mstislavichi. Novgorod would also have benefitted by regaining a measure of control over the upper Volga trade route. But his plan failed. The crisis ended with another compromise: Andrei, the youngest son of Vladimir Monomakh, assumed the throne of Pereiaslavl'. To compensate him for the loss of Pereiaslavl' and then of Suzdalia, Grand Prince Iaropolk gave Volynia to his nephew Iziaslav Mstislavich. It was due to this settlement that Iziaslav's descendants became the hereditary rulers of that principality.

The crisis of 1132–34 shaped dynastic politics for the next several decades. It permanently divided the Monomakh branch of the dynasty. On one side was Iurii Dolgorukii and his successors in Suzdalia, who persistently pursued their claim to the princely seat of Pereiaslavl' and through it Kiev. On the other side were the descendants of Iurii's elder brother, Mstislav, who as the senior branch of the Monomashich clan considered Pereiaslavl' to be their exclusive patrimony.

The crisis also demonstrated the growing importance of principalities outside the central core of Kievan Rus'. Although Pereiaslavl' was considered to be the main seat of the Monomashichi, hence politically more prestigious than the northeastern region of Suzdalia, Iurii drew

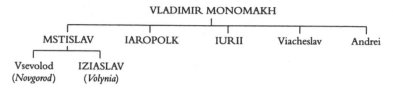

Table 4.3 The princes and dynastic seniority in the crisis of 1132–1134

upon the resources of Suzdalia to stage his bid for control over Pereiaslavl'. Vsevolod Mstislavich used Novgorod, whose commercial interests also provided a motive for antagonism toward Suzdalia, as his base of power to unseat Iurii. Volynia entered the political arena as the seat of Iziaslav Mstislavich. Although Iurii failed to achieve his personal ambition of holding Pereiaslavl', his efforts revealed the heightened significance of the peripheral principalities in shifting the balance of power; they highlight as well the importance attached by the competing princes to controlling the wealthy and powerful land of Novgorod.

The crisis of 1132–34 also drew the Chernigov princes back onto the central stage of Kievan politics. Division within the Monomakh branch offered them an opportunity; the possibility that the quarrels among the Monomashichi would disrupt the balance of power and territory that had made their compromise acceptable provided incentive to take advantage of that opportunity.

The conflict of 1146–1159

When Iaropolk Vladimirovich died in 1139, it was thus Vsevolod Ol'govich of the Chernigov branch of the dynasty who seized the throne of Kiev (ruled 1139–46). Vsevolod had no foundation within the rules of dynastic succession for claiming this position. His father, Oleg Sviatoslavich of Chernigov, had not been grand prince of Kiev, and he therefore should also have been eliminated from the succession. Military might and political circumstances allowed him to circumvent those rules. Although P. P. Tolochko characterizes him as "yesterday's separatist" who became a unifier once on the throne,[5] Vsevolod's dynastic illegitimacy coupled with his attempts to consolidate his position by extending

---

[5] P. P. Tolochko, *Kiev i Kievskaia zemlia v epokhu feodal'noi razdroblennosti XII–XIII vekov* [Kiev and the Kievan land in the epoch of feudal fragmentation of the XII–XIII centuries] (Kiev: Naukova Dumka, 1980), p. 169.

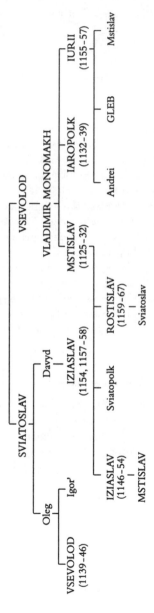

Table 4.4 The princes and dynastic seniority in the succession conflicts of 1146–1159

his authority over both Novgorod and Pereiaslavl' provoked a new round of interprincely conflict.

The Mstislavich line was partially victorious in that struggle. By 1142, they defeated both the Ol'govichi and Dolgorukii and established members of their branch of the dynasty, Iziaslav Mstislavich and his brother Sviatopolk, in Pereiaslavl' and Novgorod respectively. Strengthened through those positions, the Mstislavichi regained control of Kiev after Vsevolod died in 1146. Although Vsevolod's brother (Igor' Ol'govich) was the first to claim the throne, the Kievan *veche* refused to accept him. City notables, returning to only some of the traditions guiding succession, invited Iziaslav Mstislavich, the prince of Pereiaslavl' and the next eldest prince in the Mstislavich line, to be prince of Kiev (ruled 1146–54). Iziaslav installed his own son Mstislav in his place in Pereiaslavl'. Within a few years his relatives were also entrenched in Volynia, Smolensk, and Turov as well as Novgorod, and the Mstislavichi appeared to have prevailed over their rivals and consolidated their dominant position in Kievan Rus'.

Iziaslav's reign was, nevertheless, an uneasy one. Despite the fact that he met some of the criteria for succession, he did not meet them all. He was the senior prince of the Mstislavich line, but not of all the eligible branches of the dynasty. Acceptance of Iziaslav as grand prince would have effectively confined further succession to the Mstislavich branch of the dynasty. Consequently, the Ol'govichi, who wanted to remain in the rotation cycle, and Iurii Dolgorukii, who insisted that his claim to the throne should take precedence over his nephew's, objected vehemently to Iziaslav's succession. Iurii Dolgorukii offered the most energetic challenge to Iziaslav and his Mstislavich relatives, forcing Iziaslav to flee from Kiev on two occasions.

In addition to Kiev itself, their competition involved other issues. One was control over Novgorod's northern possessions and trade routes. Dolgorukii, in conjunction with his effort to undermine the Mstislavichi and also bolster his own power, had tightened his control over the upper Volga River, the main avenue for Novgorodian–Bulgar trade. He also attempted to redirect some northern tribute payments from Novgorod to his own treasury. Grand Prince Iziaslav, incensed at Dolgorukii's disruptions of Novgorod's economic activities, encouraged Novgorod to engage in a series of clashes with Suzdalia. In 1148, supported by the grand prince as well as Smolensk, Novgorod pushed deeply into Suzdalian territory to attack the town of Iaroslavl' on the Volga River; the next year its forces soundly defeated a Suzdalian band that attempted to interfere with its northern tribute collection. Despite Novgorod's victories, Suzdalia's nagging pressure on its economic lifelines continued to be an irritant to its Mstislavich princes, who reigned in Novgorod to 1155.

Another factor in the feud between Dolgorukii and the Mstislavichi was Pereiaslavl'. In 1147, Iurii sent a force, commanded by his son Gleb, with Polovtsy and Chernigov allies to remove Grand Prince Iziaslav's son from that principality. Iziaslav, supported by his brother Rostislav of Smolensk, came to his son's defense. It was partially in response to that offensive that the grand prince, having made peace with the Chernigov princes, encouraged and supported Novgorod's attack on Suzdalia's upper Volga territories in 1148.

Iurii responded to that indecisive campaign with an offer of peace. Its substance illustrates that his primary concern was Pereiaslavl': Iurii offered to recognize his nephew as grand prince if Iziaslav, in return, would transfer Pereiaslavl' to Iurii's son, implicitly making him the heir to the Kievan throne. Iziaslav refused. Iurii went to war once more, and victoriously took possession of Kiev and also placed his son in Pereiaslavl'. Iurii soon withdrew from Kiev, but the battle over Pereiaslavl' persisted. Iurii made a second attempt to evict Iziaslav from Kiev in 1151, but failed completely and lost both Kiev and Pereiaslavl'.

Only after Iziaslav died in 1154 did Iurii Dolgorukii finally secure the long-coveted Kievan throne. Simultaneously, he established his son Gleb in Pereiaslavl'. In 1155, he also arranged the placement of another son, Mstislav, in Novgorod, which throughout Iziaslav's reign had consistently selected Mstislavich princes. For a brief period, until his death in 1157, Iurii and his sons dominated Kievan Rus', holding Kiev, Pereiaslavl', Turov, and Novgorod, as well as their own base, Suzdalia.

Opposition to Iurii was already mounting before his death. One source was the Mstislavich branch of the dynasty. Its leaders were Rostislav of Smolensk and his nephew, the Volynian prince Mstislav, son of the late grand prince. The second source of opposition was the Chernigov line. Its senior member, Iziaslav Davydovich, had briefly seized the Kievan throne after Grand Prince Iziaslav's death (1154), but had been displaced by Iurii. When Iurii died, the Kievan boyars invited Iziaslav Davydovich to return. The Chernigov prince represented Iurii's, i.e., the senior, generation of the dynasty; he also offered a compromise between the fractious branches of Monomashichi. But his father had never served as grand prince of Kiev; hence, according to dynastic tradition, he lacked legitimacy. The new grand prince was neither able to extend his authority to key strongholds nor hold his Kievan position for long. Novgorod accepted a representative of the Smolensk branch of Mstislavichi (Sviatoslav Rostislavich) as its prince in 1157. The Iur'evichi retained Pereiaslavl', which continued to be ruled by Gleb, and Suzdalia, where Iurii's son Andrei Bogoliubskii assumed the throne. In 1158, Rostislav Mstislavich of Smolensk, the senior, fully eligible, and therefore legitimate heir, supported by both the Volynian and Galician princes, easily took the Kievan throne. His reign lasted to 1167.

With the replacement of the Chernigov prince by Rostislav Mstislavich in Kiev, the traditional principles of dynastic succession were restored and the feuds between dynastic branches relaxed. The two branches of Monomashichi jointly dominated the lands of Kievan Rus'. The senior branch, descended from Mstislav Vladimirovich and headed by Grand Prince Rostislav, controlled Kiev, Smolensk, Volynia, and Novgorod. The junior branch, the offspring of Iurii Dolgorukii, held Suzdalia and also Pereiaslavl'; through the latter position they also possessed the key to succession to the Kievan throne. The two branches cooperated. In 1160, for example, when Novgorod turned to Suzdalia for a new prince, Andrei Bogoliubskii and Grand Prince Rostislav Mstislavich quickly reached an agreement to return the displaced Mstislavich prince (Sviatoslav Rostislavich) to his former position. This balance of power, founded on a reaffirmation and universal acceptance of the dynasty's guidelines of legitimacy, provided a basis for political and dynastic stability that lasted through the reign of Rostislav.

The crises of 1167–1177

Discord erupted again, however, when Rostislav died in 1167. Rostislav's brother Vladimir assumed the throne. But he was quickly evicted by Mstislav Iziaslavich, prince of Volynia. Mstislav was Rostislav's nephew; he was the leader of the next generation of Mstislavichi; he had helped Rostislav acquire the Kievan throne and, in the words of P. P. Tolochko, had essentially been the late Rostislav's co-ruler.[6] The close relationship between Rostislav and his nephew is indicative of the fact that until 1167 the entire Mstislavich branch of the dynasty had functioned politically as a single unit even though it had two perceptible branches, the Iziaslavichi who were associated with Volynia and Rostislav's line in Smolensk. But when Mstislav captured the throne in 1167, he opened a breach between these two dynastic lines. His action also effectively disavowed the accord between Rostislav and the Iur'evich princes that had maintained stability by honoring the traditional rules of succession and keeping the Kievan throne in the hands of the dynasty's senior generation; it put the Iziaslavich princes, representing the younger generation, in opposition to their elders. Rostislav's immediate relatives refused to support Mstislav.

---

[6] Tolochko, *Drevniaia Rus'*, p. 134.

Rather, they upheld his bond with the Iur'evichi of Suzdalia and the dynasty's traditional principles of succession.

The premature transfer of the Kievan throne to the next generation not only divided the Mstislavichi, it aroused the opposition of all the dynasty's senior princes. Two opposing camps began to take shape. The first indicator of their formation emanated from Novgorod. Despite the joint efforts of Andrei Bogoliubskii and the Rostislavichi to dissuade it, Novgorod threw its support behind the new grand prince by transferring its allegiance from Sviatoslav Rostislavich, who had first become its prince in 1157, to Grand Prince Mstislav's son Roman (1167–68). The addition of Novgorod to the Iziaslavich camp, which already controlled Kiev and Volynia, triggered the formation of a coalition consisting of the Rostislavichi of Smolensk, the Iur'evichi of Suzdalia and Pereiaslavl', and also the Ol'govichi of Chernigov.

The most prominent member of this group was Andrei Bogoliubskii of Vladimir-Suzdal', who had remained remote from southern, Kievan politics during Grand Prince Rostislav's reign. He reentered that arena in reaction to Mstislav's violation of the rules of collateral succession and to the extension of his influence into the northern part of the Riurikid realm, specifically over Novgorod. The other branches of the dynasty were equally disturbed. The princes of Smolensk and Chernigov joined Andrei to oust Mstislav Iziaslavich from Kiev.

In 1169 Andrei of Suzdal' sent an army against the grand prince. Led by one of his sons, it consisted of the forces of eleven other princes representing three of the main branches of the dynasty (the Iur'evichi of Suzdalia, Rostislavichi of Smolensk, and Ol'govichi of Chernigov) against the fourth, the Iziaslavichi of Volynia. The allies were victorious. Their foe fled, leaving his wife and son to be captured. For three days the victors plundered the city of Kiev, looting its treasures, including, as the chronicler lamented, icons, their valuable metal mountings (*rizas*), and books of the churches and monasteries. They then installed Gleb Iur'evich, the prince of Pereiaslavl' and brother of Andrei Bogoliubskii, on the Kievan throne.

The events of 1169, especially the sack of Kiev, proved shocking to the chroniclers who witnessed and recorded the events. Despite the comments of B. A. Rybakov, who concluded that the description and degree of destruction in Kiev had been exaggerated by the chroniclers,[7] the sack of Kiev has taken on symbolic significance. Many historians

[7] B. A. Rybakov, *Kievskaia Rus' i russkie kniazhestva XII–XIII vv.* [Kievan Rus' and the Russian principalities in the XII–XIII centuries] (Moscow: Nauka, 1982), pp. 493, 550–551.

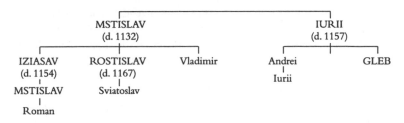

Table 4.5 The princes and dynastic seniority in the crisis of 1167–1169

perceive it as a turning point in the history of Kievan Rus'. It was this event more than any other that gave weight to the argument, discussed at the beginning of this chapter, that Kiev was losing its importance and the entire state of Kievan Rus' was disintegrating.

The defeat and sack of Kiev also signalled, according to this interpretation, the growing power of Vladimir-Suzdal' and its prince Andrei Bogoliubskii, whose authority appeared to be overshadowing that of the grand prince of Kiev. The shift in the center of power was reflected clearly and unambiguously by Andrei's apparent disdain for the official title, grand prince of Kiev. Unlike his father who had devoted himself to attaining that position, Andrei turned command of his armies over to his son. And after the decisive defeat of his rival, he placed Gleb Iur'evich, characterized as a relatively minor prince, on the Kievan throne. Throughout these events Prince Andrei personally stayed in Suzdalia, where he concentrated on developing the city of Vladimir and his palace complex of Bogoliubovo, which he seemingly hoped to elevate above Kiev. In the words of George Vernadsky, "It was characteristic of Andrei that he did not go to Kiev after the seizure of the city by his troops but had the Kievan throne occupied by minor princes whom he treated as his vassals."[8]

A great deal of evidence supports the argument summarized above. But insights into the dynastic structure of Kievan Rus' add credibility to the alternate interpretation of political development in this century. Andrei Bogoliubskii's apparent aloofness from Kievan affairs in the period before 1169 did contrast sharply with his father's intimate involvement in them. But their differences in behavior may be explained by the different political situations each of them faced. Dolgorukii intervened in Kievan succession to defend and restore the dynastic order. In contrast, during the early years of Andrei's reign that order prevailed. Rostislav Mstislavich,

[8] Vernadsky, *Kievan Russia*, p. 221.

who mounted the Kievan throne shortly after Andrei assumed his own in Vladimir-Suzdal', was the senior prince of the dynasty. Andrei as well as the other princes of the realm recognized him as the rightful heir. Andrei, therefore, had no reason to intervene in Kievan politics until 1167, when Rostislav's nephew violated the collateral pattern of succession. His policies toward Kiev were guided by the same views on dynastic legitimacy that his father had held. Thus, although the outcome of the battle of 1169 was determined by the relative power of the principalities making up the two opposing coalitions, Andrei's motives for ousting Mstislav Iziaslavich were rooted, at least in part, in a commitment to restoring the accepted dynastic order, which bound the various components of the realm together, not in a desire to tear that realm apart.

This perspective leads to different conclusions about the status of Kiev and also about the selection of Gleb as grand prince. Andrei's determination to recover the Kievan throne for the elder generation, if not himself personally, suggests that Kiev continued to be the focal point of the realm, its political capital, and the symbol of seniority within the dynasty. The campaign of 1169, authorized by Andrei and undertaken by his son and allies to unseat Mstislav, is not a statement denying or undermining the significance of Kiev, but an acknowledgment of Kiev's continued centrality within the dynastic realm. Similarly, the choice of Gleb was neither arbitrary nor merely the selection of a pliable puppet. As prince of Pereiaslavl', Gleb was the heir apparent, although not the most powerful prince, of the Iur'evich line. He would have, if the traditional norms of succession had been followed, been expected to follow Rostislav's brother to the Kievan throne. Andrei's support for his brother Gleb is thus consistent with the view that he was attempting to restore the traditional patterns of succession within the dynasty and, thereby, domestic stability to the realm.

Andrei's recognition of Kiev's centrality and his commitment to dynastic traditions were not inconsistent with the pursuit of policies designed to benefit his own principality. His actions in 1169 were thus also motivated by his interests in the disposition of Novgorod. Throughout the reign of Grand Prince Rostislav, the northern emporium had been ruled by his son Sviatoslav, who had also enjoyed the support of Andrei. Within the framework of this arrangement Andrei's influence over Novgorod and its northern lands increased. Consequently, when Novgorod evicted Sviatoslav in favor of Mstislav's son Roman in 1167–68, the deposed prince turned to Andrei for assistance. Suzdalian forces responded by closing the roads leading to Novgorod in an effort to force the city to restore Sviatoslav. Failing to convince the Novgorodians, Andrei resorted, also unsuccessfully, to interference with Novgorod's northern tribute collection and finally to a direct attack on the city. In sharp contrast to their success against Kiev, the Suzdalian and allied armies were badly defeated by Novgorod. But Andrei's blockade had greater effect. With their food supplies dwindling, the Novgorodians expelled Roman in 1170 and sued for peace; Andrei responded by selecting first another Rostislavich prince, then his own son Iurii, to hold the Novgorodian throne.

Retention of his influence in Novgorod was equally as important to Andrei as Mstislav's usurpation of the Kievan throne. Indeed, it appears that it was Mstislav's extension of authority over Novgorod that provoked Andrei to take action against him. Thus, even as Andrei was upholding the traditional dynastic system, he was also trying to maintain his role in the northern sphere of the Riurikid realm, whose activities and interests were gradually being differentiated from those of the southern principalities.

As a result of the traumatic events of 1169, the central seats of power in Kievan Rus' were restored to the senior generation of the dynasty. The Iur'evichi benefitted most. Gleb Iur'evich replaced Mstislav Iziaslavich in Kiev. Gleb's son Vladimir (d. 1187) sat in Pereiaslavl'. Andrei Bogoliubskii, the most powerful member of the Iur'evich clan, controlled Vladimir-Suzdal', and by 1171 his son Iurii Andreevich ruled in Novgorod.

Despite the Suzdalian victory, stability remained elusive. Just as Iurii Dolgorukii's reign on the Kievan throne had been shortlived, so his heirs were unable to sustain their dominance. Gleb Iur'evich died under somewhat mysterious circumstances, probably in 1171. With his demise the generational coalitions were resurrected to fight another round in the succession battle. Several members of the senior generation, including Gleb's brothers and Sviatoslav Vsevolodich, the son of Grand Prince Vsevolod (1139–46) of the Chernigov line, were eligible for the throne. Another potential candidate, Grand Prince Rostislav's brother Vladimir, died in 1171. The senior princes closed ranks, bringing together a coalition of Suzdalian, Chernigov, Novgorodian, and some Smolensk forces to place Mikhalko Iur'evich (d. 1176), brother of Andrei Bogoliubskii and the late Gleb, on the Kievan throne.

This impressive assemblage of political and military power was opposed, however, by the leading members of the dynasty's next generation: the Volynian prince Mstislav Iziaslavich, whose eagerness to reach the pinnacle of power had sparked the conflagration of 1167–69, and the junior Rostislavich princes, who abandoned their family's alliance with the Iur'evichi. This group seized Kiev. In response, Andrei launched an offensive with an army made up of the forces of twenty princes. But this

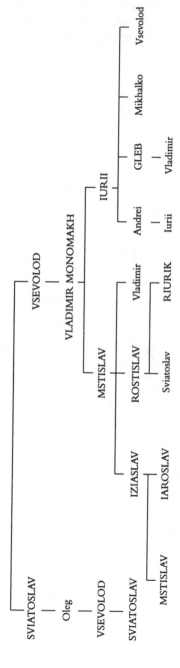

Table 4.6 The princes and dynastic seniority in the succession conflicts of 1171–1177

time the younger generation of Volynian-Smolensk princes were victorious. They placed the Volynian prince Iaroslav, brother of Mstislav Iziaslavich, on the Kievan throne.

The defeat of the Suzdalian alliance contributed to the turmoil within Vladimir-Suzdal' that resulted in Andrei's assassination (1175). His death triggered a struggle within his principality that occupied the attention of its princes and their retainers until 1177, when Vsevolod, Dolgorukii's youngest son, and his Vladimir supporters were victorious. In the course of that struggle Andrei's heirs lost their grip on Novgorod for almost a decade. When Andrei was killed, Novgorod expelled his son Iurii, who had ruled there since 1171, and threw in its lot with one of the losing factions in the fight for control over Vladimir-Suzdal'. Even after Vsevolod won that contest in 1177, he had difficulty gaining Novgorod's confidence; on the contrary, he went to war against the city in 1178. Novgorod juggled princes from Vladimir, Smolensk, and Chernigov until 1187, when it settled more permanently on the house of Vladimir-Suzdal', which with only a brief interlude (1197) provided it with princes to 1209.

The death of Andrei Bogoliubskii also marked the end of an era in dynastic relations within Kievan Rus'. The Iur'evichi, one of the chief contending lines for succession and pillars of support for the traditional order, dropped out of the competition for the grand princely throne. Andrei's brother and successor Vsevolod (ruled 1177 1212), although a member of the older generation and by the end of the century acknowledged accurately as the dynasty's senior prince, focused his attention on his own patrimony, on the neighboring principalities of Riazan' and Murom, and on Novgorod. For most of Vsevolod's reign, his candidates sat on the Novgorodian throne, and Vladimir-Suzdal' dominated the northern and northeastern Rus' lands. But because he never personally ruled as grand prince of Kiev, his own sons and successors were eliminated from the pool of eligible candidates for the Kievan throne and, following his example, devoted themselves to their northern concerns. Thus, the princes of Vladimir-Suzdal' withdrew from southern politics.

Although Vladimir-Suzdal' became enmeshed in its internal power struggle following Andrei's death, the situation in Kiev did not stabilize. The victorious allies, as the chronicler explained, had conferred seniority on Iaroslav Iziaslavich, but neither the Kievan boyars nor the remaining viable candidate for the throne from the senior generation, Sviatoslav Vsevolodich of Chernigov, were prepared to give him their loyalty. For two years control over Kiev vacillated between Iaroslav and Sviatoslav. Finally, Sviatoslav, representing the Chernigov line and the elder generation, reached an accord with Iaroslav's allies, the Rostislavichi of

Smolensk. With this realignment, the Iziaslavichi lost the ability to contend for the throne. Sviatoslav became the unchallenged grand prince. Riurik Rostislavich became, according to some accounts, his co-ruler. Their "duumvirate" introduced a period of stability that lasted until Sviatoslav's death in 1194.

The universal acceptance of Sviatoslav was based in part on the fact that he was a legitimate heir to the throne. He was a member of the senior generation of the dynasty. Although he was a member of the Chernigov branch, which had earlier lost its right of succession, his father, Vsevolod Ol'govich, had served as grand prince (1139–46) and reestablished his descendants' eligibility. Furthermore, by 1177, virtually all the other candidates from Sviatoslav's generation had died. The single exception was the much younger Vsevolod Iur'evich, who acknowledged Sviatoslav's seniority and may also have accepted Riurik as Sviatoslav's intended heir.

As a result of the complex and debilitating struggle of 1167–77, the challenges of the junior generation, led by the Iziaslavichi of Volynia, were overcome and the pattern of collateral succession across the senior generation was again confirmed. The conflict demonstrated that no resolution would be acceptable to a major portion of the dynasty except the establishment of its senior member on the Kievan throne. Political stability thus depended upon adherence to the dynastic principles of succession. But the conflict also demonstrated the growing importance of the peripheral principalities and the roles of their princes in the coalitions that fought for control over Kiev. The shifting position of the Rostislavichi of Smolensk, in particular, had been critical in determining the outcome of the contest that initially had been fought between coalitions formed along generational lines. Stability was achieved only when the two generations reached an accord that recognized the senior prince, Sviatoslav Vsevolodich, as grand prince but also evidently acknowledged Riurik Rostislavich as the senior member of the younger generation and the heir apparent.

The thirteenth century

In 1194, Riurik Rostislavich did inherit the Kievan throne. But his rule was also contested. Interestingly, his chief opponent was not Vsevolod Iur'evich of Vladimir-Suzdal', the single remaining candidate for the throne from the senior generation. Riurik Rostislavich acknowledged Vsevolod's senior status, and, at least according to the Suzdalian chronicle, Vsevolod was responsible for placing Riurik on the Kievan throne. Vsevolod apparently respected the settlement reached in 1177.

Riurik's opposition came instead from Volynia, and then from Chernigov. By the year 1200, he was engaged in a desperate effort to save his throne. Only after another twelve-year battle did the Rostislavichi secure their position in Kiev and reestablish a stable political order that lasted to 1235.

The first challenge to Grand Prince Riurik began in 1199; it came from Prince Roman Mstislavich of Volynia, who had just added Galicia to his domain. Roman was the son of Prince Mstislav Iziaslavich, whose parallel actions in 1167 had precipitated the crisis of 1167–69 and the sack of Kiev. Because his father's brief reign had been illegitimate, Roman's personal claim to the throne was weak. Nevertheless, he drove Riurik out of Kiev. For the next five years, until his own death in 1205, Roman dominated Kiev as well as Volynia and Galicia. But the upsurge of Roman's power, bolstered by the strength of the combined principalities of Volynia and Galicia, provoked resistance from the deposed Riurik and also the Ol'govichi. In 1203 they, together with Polovtsy forces, attacked Kiev, which once again suffered a devastating sack. Riurik, who also had the favor of Vsevolod of Vladimir-Suzdal', recovered his position only to lose it to Roman again. But when Roman was killed on a campaign against Poland, his successors could not hold Galicia, which fell under Chernigov, Hungarian, and then Smolensk authority. Lacking the power provided by the joint principality, the princes of Volynia retreated from the central arena of Kievan politics, at least for the next two decades.

With Vsevolod of Suzdalia engaging only indirectly in Kievan affairs and Volynia temporarily removed from them, only two branches of the dynasty, the Smolensk and the Chernigov princes, continued to compete for dominance. Although they had allied to oppose Roman, they became antagonists almost as soon as he died. The two main figures in the new stage of the competition were Riurik Rostislavich, who had been evicted from the throne by Roman, and Vsevolod Chermnyi, son of the former grand prince, Sviatoslav Vsevolodich (1177–94), of Chernigov.

The objections of the Chernigov prince to the restoration of the Rostislavich prince are hazy. It has been pointed that one of the Chernigov families assumed control over Galicia after Roman died. Perhaps, it was the fact that Vsevolod Chermnyi, who had become prince of Chernigov and head of his clan in 1204, could draw upon this expanded power base that inspired him to make a bid for Kiev. Dynastic considerations may also have provided a motive. In 1204, the last time Roman of Volynia overthrew Riurik, Roman arrested Riurik and forced him to become a monk. When that phase of their struggle ended, it was not Riurik who returned to Kiev, but his son Rostislav Riurikovich. Within a year Roman had died, Riurik had arranged to be released from

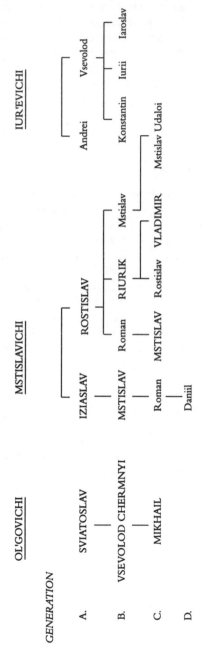

Table 4.7 The princes and dynastic seniority in the succession crisis of the early thirteenth century

his vows, and he resumed his post as grand prince. Vsevolod Chermnyi may have concluded that Riurik had forfeited his rights to the throne. If so, Vsevolod, as a member of Riurik's generation and the son of a former grand prince, was the next in line to inherit the throne, taking precedence over Riurik's son (Riurik's brothers had all died by this time).

Whatever his motives, Vsevolod made his first attempt to seize Kiev in 1206. He made a second attempt the next year. Although he did manage to establish his son in Pereiaslavl' in 1206, on both of those occasions he lost Kiev within a year. He made his third and final try in 1211. Having gained the favor of Vsevolod of Vladimir–Suzdal', he evicted Riurik Rostislavich, who died in Chernigov in 1215, probably in captivity.

The attitude of Vsevolod Iur'evich depended on issues beyond the disposition of the Kievan throne. Pereiaslavl' was one concern. Although Chermnyi had alienated Vsevolod Iur'evich in 1206, when he displaced the Vladimir–Suzdal' prince in Pereiaslavl', he had, in turn, lost that principality to Riurik Rostislavich later that year. Pereiaslavl' was ruled by a member of the Rostislavich clan in 1211. But Vsevolod Iur'evich's reasons for supporting Chermnyi in 1211 may have stemmed more from his interest in Novgorod than the southern principalities. As noted above, Vladimir–Suzdal' princes had been almost consistently chosen to rule in Novgorod since 1187. But in 1209, following some popular disturbances in Novgorod in 1207, Prince Mstislav Mstislavich Udaloi, a nephew of Riurik Rostislavich, seized the Novgorodian throne and added Novgorod's resources to the Rostislavich assets. Almost immediately afterward, Vsevolod gave his support to Rostislavich's opponent, his namesake Vsevolod Chermnyi, who was then able to assume the Kievan throne. Vsevolod of Vladimir–Suzdal' also arranged the marriage of his own son, Iurii, to Vsevolod Chermnyi's daughter in 1211.

Vsevolod Chermnyi's reign lasted less than two years. Other members of the Rostislavich clan removed him in 1212, the same year both he and Vsevolod of Vladimir–Suzdal' died. The death of the two Vsevolods removed all remaining motives for the princes of Vladimir–Suzdal', led by Iurii Vsevolodich and his brother Iaroslav, to interfere further in Kievan affairs. With the defeat and death of Vsevolod Chermnyi, they were left without Iurii's father-in-law, their ally and candidate for the throne. And as noted above, after Vsevolod Iur'evich died, his branch of the dynasty was removed from the succession cycle and could not, therefore, offer any candidates of its own to replace Vsevolod Chermnyi. Those factors encouraged the Vladimir–Suzdal' princes to turn their attention even more exclusively to northern and local concerns.

One of their primary goals was to regain influence over Novgorod. They did not achieve that goal, however, for over a decade. Iaroslav did sit in Novgorod in 1215, but his reign ended quickly and disastrously. Both Iaroslav and Iurii were engaged at the time in their own conflict with their elder brother Konstantin for dominance in Vladimir-Suzdal'. Rather than drawing his new subjects into his camp, Iaroslav alienated them. The Smolensk prince Mstislav Mstislavich Udaloi returned to lead Novgorod in an alliance with Konstantin against Iurii and Iaroslav. Konstantin and Udaloi were victorious at the Battle of Lipitsa in 1216. Prince Mstislav returned to Novgorod, which remained in his family's hands until 1221. Konstantin reigned supreme in Vladimir, but died in 1218, leaving his post to his rival Iurii. It took Novgorod three more years before it turned again to Vladimir for a prince. From 1221, however, members of the house of Vladimir ruled in Novgorod almost exclusively for the next two decades. In contrast to their concerns over Novgorod, Vsevolod's heirs left Kiev to the dominant dynastic branch, the Rostislavichi of Smolensk. Princes from that line held the Kievan throne without a break to 1235.

In 1231 however, Mikhail, son of Vsevolod Chermnyi, renewed his family's bid for supremacy. His attacks forced Grand Prince Vladimir Riurikovich (ruled 1223–35), a Rostislavich, to lean on Volynia, then ruled by Roman's son Daniil, for support. Nevertheless, in 1235, Grand Prince Vladimir was captured by the Polovtsy, who had joined Mikhail in an attack on Kiev. During that campaign Kiev was sacked for the third time. Although Vladimir was released upon payment of a ransom, Mikhail became grand prince of Kiev by 1237, just as the Mongols were launching their offensive on northeastern Rus'. As the invaders began their campaign against the southern principalities in 1239, Mikhail fled to Hungary, leaving the capital the object of contention between the Rostislavichi of Smolensk and Daniil of Volynia and very vulnerable to the forthcoming Mongol onslaught.

The preceding discussion of intradynastic clashes illustrates that the seemingly ceaseless feuding among the Riurikid princes was not an expression of political chaos. The focus of their wars was consistently Kiev. Underlying every episode was an issue derived from the principles of succession that had been fashioned during the course of the eleventh century. The wars of the twelfth century were fundamentally struggles in which one side tried to refine those principles even further, i.e., restrict the range of succession and/or hasten the eligibility of princes of a junior generation, while the other side defended the status quo. The chief contenders were correspondingly the heads of dynastic clans that had legitimate claims to the grand princely throne or were challenging those principles.

The wars of the twelfth century also reflect the growing power, resulting from increased economic and commercial might, of the peripheral principalities. They were the bases upon which their princes were able to mount their drives for power. The coalitions the princes were able to forge, their success in dominating Novgorod, and their ability to attract foreign allies combined to determine the outcome of their battles; but all those factors ultimately depended on the strength of their own principalities. And as their wealth and power developed, some of those principalities, most notably Vladimir-Suzdal', disengaged from central Kievan politics as their princes became preoccupied with discharging their local duties.

Thus, whereas the conflicts reflect a shifting pattern of relative economic power and military might among the lands of Rus', their focus remained Kiev, their objective continued to be elevation to the position of grand prince, and their contenders were limited to dynastic branches that claimed that throne. The withdrawal of Vladimir-Suzdal's princes from the Kievan arena conformed to the principles of succession even as it was consistent with their preoccupation with the development of their own dynamic principality. Furthermore, despite the appearance of virtually continuous confrontation, domestic peace and political stability were attained, sometimes for decades. Those periods occurred when the resolution of the conflicts reaffirmed the traditional dynastic principles of succession, when the revisionists were suppressed.

One way of characterizing the political struggles surrounding Kiev from 1125 to the 1230s is thus as a contest between conservatives and revisionists. The conservatives were committed to preserving the dynastic order and rules of succession in the form that had been developed during the eleventh century and through the reign of Vladimir Monomakh. They, albeit by means of protracted and destructive wars, tended to prevail over the revisionists who attempted to restrict the rights of succession to fewer branches of the dynasty and thereby hasten the eligibility of selected members of the younger generation of the dynasty. It is this recurrent theme in the dynastic conflicts that offers a basis for understanding a range of otherwise problematic issues, e.g., the sharp contrast between the behavior of Iurii Dolgorukii and his son Andrei Bogoliubskii and the relative domestic tranquility during the reigns of Grand Princes Rostislav (1158–67) and Sviatoslav Vsevolodich (1177–94).

It also accounts for the confusion, compounded by the nature of the chronicle accounts, concerning succession in the first decades of the thirteenth century, when dynastic issues become truly hazy. Even then the change was not due to the fact that those issues had lost significance. It had just become harder to define seniority within the dynasty. In the middle of the eleventh century when Grand Prince Iaroslav left his domain to his sons, he had outlined a simple hierarchy among them. Iziaslav, the eldest, ruled first in Kiev, to be followed by Sviatoslav and Vsevolod. By 1125, most of their descendant lines had lost their rights to the throne; only Monomakh's heirs retained a claim to it. The situation became more complicated, however, when the Chernigov line, descendants of Sviatoslav, reestablished their rights to Kiev, but without clarifying their place in the order of succession.

Thus, although the wars of the twelfth century decisively thwarted attempts by the younger generation to usurp the rights of their uncles and senior cousins to the throne of Kiev, relative seniority among the different branches and individual princes within a single generation became difficult to determine. In 1199–1205, there was no question that Riurik Rostislavich's claim to the throne took precedence over that of his challenger Roman of Volynia. In contrast, however, in the conflict of 1206–12, dynastic guidelines offered no means of determining whether Riurik or Vsevolod Chermnyi, both members of the same generation, both sons of former grand princes, had seniority over the other. In the 1206–12 episodes, the issues were even murkier because the actual senior prince of the dynasty, Vsevolod of Vladimir-Suzdal', was alive; although he had evidently renounced his rights to the Kievan throne in 1177, he threw his prestige and his support first behind one candidate and then the other. Similarly in the 1230s, the relative rights of Mikhail, son of Vsevolod Chermnyi, and Vladimir Riurikovich were not obvious. The clashes of the thirteenth century were not, any more than those of the twelfth or the eleventh centuries had been, signs that the political structure of Kievan Rus' had disintegrated. They were indicators that the principles of dynastic order and succession, worked out in the eleventh century and defended during the twelfth, had not anticipated the situations that were emerging in the thirteenth. Before the dynasty had an opportunity to refine its rules to meet new conditions, Kievan Rus' was fractured by the Mongol onslaught.

FOREIGN AFFAIRS

Domestic concerns and politics also played a role in the determination and implementation of foreign policy between 1125 and 1237–40. The range of foreign relations, however, narrowed. The Riurikids continued, for instance, to marry into foreign royal families. But their marriage partners were drawn from the royal houses of their immediate neighbors, for example, Poland, Hungary, and the Polovtsy. They no longer stretched to form ties with ruling families of distant lands, like France and England, as they had in the previous century. The nature of their interaction with some foreign powers also varied. With Byzantium, for example, the Rus' maintained extensive commercial and ecclesiastical ties. But with the exception of the principality of Galicia, which was drawn into the Byzantine–Hungarian conflicts of the middle of the twelfth century, Kievan Rus' did not become involved in Byzantine affairs. It neither conducted its own offensives against Byzantium, nor intervened on its behalf, even when Byzantium was losing its eastern territories to the Seljuk Turks during the twelfth century and then was subjected to the ravages of the Fourth Crusade that created the Latin Empire in 1204.

Rather, the princes of Kievan Rus' devoted their attention and energies in the period 1125–37 to their most immediate neighbors. Their conduct of foreign affairs remained decentralized. Consequently, to the degree that they placed priority on different domestic issues, confronted different neighbors, and also faced different challenges from them, princes in various parts of the realm developed distinct foreign policies and pursued them with varying degrees of success. When several principalities conducted direct relations with the same neighbor however, results were confusing and, at times, had disastrous effects on the Rus' lands.

Novgorod and the northwestern frontier

Novgorod, for example, placed priority on its commerce. Its relations with its neighbors were shaped by that concern. Novgorod's economic need to export northern products dictated a drive to push further to the northeast. During the second half of the twelfth century Novgorod secured the Sukhona River. Then, moving up the Vychegda River, it encountered and subjugated the Perm' and Iugra tribes, whose fur tribute added to Novgorod's foreign exports.

Novgorod's policies toward its Scandinavian and other Baltic neighbors were also shaped by commercial interests. Its goals were consistently to develop its commerce with them while also protecting its trade routes. Its occasional clashes with Sweden arose in response to Swedish interference in Novgorod's passage to the Gulf of Finland (1142) and threats to Ladoga, a crucial point on Novgorod's route both to the Gulf and to its northern possessions (1164). Finnish tribes, at times spurred by the Swedes who were extending their authority over them, similarly nipped at Novgorod's northern and western frontiers. During the first decades of the thirteenth century, however, Novgorod extended its authority over Karelian and Em' tribes in southern Finland and thus improved its own position along the northern coast of the Gulf of Finland.

Changing trade patterns disturbed Novgorod's relations with its foreign neighbors in the late twelfth century. As discussed in chapter 3, German merchants were moving into the eastern Baltic region and becoming more prominent in Novgorod's trade during the second half of the twelfth century. They were followed by missionaries, who were attempting by 1184 to convert the Livonian tribes to Christianity, by bishops who were settled in Riga by 1201, and then, after it was founded in 1202 by the crusading Order of the Brothers of the Sword, which added force to the missionary zeal of the Church. The knights' subordination of local tribes along the West Dvina River weakened the principality of Polotsk, to which they had formerly paid tribute, enabled the German merchants to navigate the river and reach the Rus' towns of Polotsk and Smolensk more safely, and also opened up the lands north of the river to a competition for domination among Germans, Danes, and Rus'.

Novgorod was thus confronted by both commercial and territorial challenges from the Germans. Disputes over territory and trade routes arose. One of the more serious clashes occurred in 1188. On that occasion, after a Karelian attack on the Swedish commercial center of Sigtun, Novgorodian merchants in Swedish ports as well as the German town of Lübeck were arrested. Novgorodian officials similarly refused foreign merchants in their town permission to leave, and prevented their own merchants from embarking on new commercial expeditions. All trade came to a halt. Novgorod's Prince Iaroslav Vladimirovich and city officials then concluded a treaty that defined terms of trade with both Scandinavians and Germans (1191–92).[9]

By the thirteenth century, nevertheless, Novgorod was engaged in clashes with Germans and Danes, as they all vied for control over Livonian territory. Led by Prince Mstislav Udaloi, Novgorod tried in 1212 to subjugate Lett tribes south of Novgorod's outpost of Iur'ev in Livonia. Despite subsequent campaigns conducted by Novgorod under its Suzdalian princes, the Germans conquered Iur'ev in 1224 and the Danes, approaching from the north, gained control of Estonia by 1237. Along that portion of its western frontier, safeguarded by Novgorod, the Rus' borders were being pushed backward. And in 1237, the Livonian Brothers of the Sword merged with the Teutonic Order, which was concluding a crusade against the Prussian tribes; together, the German knights were poised to launch a new drive to the east.

<hr />

[9] These dates are provided by V. L. Ianin in *Novgorodskie akty XII–XV vv.* [Novgorodian acts, XII–XV centuries] (Moscow: Nauka, 1991), p. 81.

Galicia-Volynia and the southwestern frontier

In the northwest by the early thirteenth century the Rus' were losing their authority over tributary populations in Livonia. In the southwest the Riurikids were also in danger of losing territory. Their neighbors in this region were the Poles and Hungarians. Kiev, then Volynia and Galicia, had primary responsibility for maintaining relations with Hungary and Poland. After King Boleslaw III died in 1138, Poland lost its cohesion; although it continued to be involved in Rus' affairs, it yielded its prominent role in Kievan politics, displayed in the previous century, to Hungary. And the Riurikid dynasty almost lost the principality of Galicia to it.

Galicia had become a strong unified principality during an upsurge of commercial activity through its lands and under the administrative guidance of its prince, Iaroslav Osmomysl' (1153–87). It had been Prince Iaroslav who had joined the Volynian prince Mstislav Iziaslavich to place Rostislav on the Kievan throne in 1158–59; he had also supported Mstislav's succession to the throne in 1167. After Iaroslav died, however, his principality fell into political disarray. Hungary took advantage of the situation and seized control of it. The loss of Galicia so disturbed Metropolitan Nikifor that he urged Grand Prince Sviatoslav and his close associate Riurik Rostislavich to recover the principality. They hesitated. But as it turned out, their intervention was unnecessary. Iaroslav's son recovered his throne, and when he died in 1199, leaving no direct heirs, Prince Roman of Volynia attached Galicia to his own patrimony.

When Roman died in 1205, his sons, who were minors, had to flee abroad. Galicia once again became the object of princely competition, involving this time the Riurikids of Chernigov, Smolensk, and Volynia and also the Poles and Hungarians. Galician boyars maneuvered among all of them. After almost two decades of complex squabbling, a Hungarian prince took possession of Galicia. Not until 1235 did Prince Mikhail of Chernigov recover Galicia for the Riurikids; when he became grand prince of Kiev in 1237, he was replaced in Galicia by his rival Prince Daniil Romanovich of Volynia.

Vladimir-Suzdal' and the northeastern frontier

Although their western frontier was vulnerable, the lands of Kievan Rus' were expanding to the northeast. Like the rulers of Novgorod, the princes of Vladimir–Suzdal' also defined their foreign policies, at least in part, around commercial concerns. The territories of Vladimir–Suzdal' spanned a portion of the upper Volga River, which was the main route linking Novgorod with its eastern trading partner, Bulgar-on-the-Volga. The princes of Vladimir sought, as discussed in the previous chapter, to control the commercial traffic along that route, to oblige merchants to conduct their commercial transactions in Suzdalian towns, and to collect customs from those exchanges. Unlike the Novgorodians, whose policies in the twelfth century were geared toward protecting their role in established commercial activities, the Suzdalian princes were attempting to reconfigure those patterns at the expense of both Novgorod and Bulgar-on-the-Volga. Both reacted with hostility. Novgorod's campaigns against Vladimir-Suzdal' in the 1130s and in 1148 were based in part on these considerations. Novgorod's actions found a parallel in an offensive, also directed against Iaroslavl', by Bulgar in 1152.

Despite this venture and two preceding outbreaks of violence (1107, 1120), Rus'–Bulgar relations had generally been benign from 985 to the middle of the twelfth century. But, not long after the 1152 incident, Prince Andrei Bogoliubskii reversed the traditional Rus' posture toward Bulgar and adopted an overtly hostile, aggressive policy toward it. In 1164, he launched the first of a series of campaigns against Bulgar. That offensive, in which the icon of the "Mother of God" is described as having encouraged and protected Andrei and his armies, ended in a splendid victory for the Suzdalian forces. A subsequent campaign, conducted in 1172, however, led to the death of one of Andrei's sons and is considered to have contributed to the disappointment in him that resulted in his assassination not long afterward.

Nevertheless, Andrei's successor Vsevolod continued his brother's policy. In 1183, Suzdalian armies, joined by their neighbors from Murom and Riazan', mounted a campaign that drove deeply into Bulgar territory. For three days the Rus' besieged one of Bulgar's major towns before accepting their opponents' peace offer and retreating. Vsevolod conducted subsequent campaigns in 1185 and 1205. As a result of these efforts, Suzdalian control was extended down the Volga River to its juncture with the Oka.

Suzdal's princes then turned their attention to acquiring political dominance over the Burtas (Mordva) population that dwelled in the region and fortifying their territorial position. In 1221, Prince Iurii Vsevolodich constructed Nizhnii Novgorod at the mouth of the Oka River. The Suzdalian princes also aggressively evicted Bulgar from territories to their north. After Konstantin Vsevolodich, then prince of Rostov, founded the town of Ustiug Velikii at the mouth of the Iug River (1212), Bulgar attacked and briefly gained control of that outpost (1218). Konstantin's brother Iurii, who that year replaced him as prince of

Vladimir, regained possession of it and in 1220 once again invaded Bulgar territory. The net result of all these campaigns was to push back Bulgar's western frontier. Suzdalia, by taking possession of Ustiug and Nizhnii Novgorod, expanded its own territory to the north and the east. In the process it enhanced its own economic base and political authority by incorporating the trade routes upon which Bulgar depended for its northern supplies and its contact with Novgorod.

The steppe frontier

Foreign policy toward the Riurikids' southern neighbors, the Polovtsy, was even more intimately enmeshed in domestic politics and rivalries. The Polovtsy ability to affect trade conducted across the steppe as well as their own trade with the Rus' made commercial interests a significant component in determining the nature of Rus' relations with them. The chronicles, however, depict the Polovtsy as the most dangerous neighbors of the Rus'. They invaded the Rus' lands, caused serious damage, and seized prisoners and booty. Rus' relations with the Polovtsy during the period following Monomakh's death were thus characterized by both the mutually beneficial trade noted in the previous chapter and recurrent hostilities.

There were two types of situations in which the hostile character took precedence. The first consisted of those incidents during which the Polovtsy invaded Rus' territories as allies of a Riurikid prince or clan engaged during a dynastic conflict. Most of the hostile encounters between Rus' and Polovtsy fell into that category. The second type was war between the Rus' on one side and the Polovtsy on the other, uncomplicated by crossover alliances. Instances of this type of clash occurred rarely, mainly in the 1160s–1180s.

Rus' relations with the Polovtsy were affected by several factors. The Polovtsy themselves were divided by the middle of the twelfth century. Scholars have identified between six and twelve distinct Polovtsy groups dwelling in an expanse stretching from the southern Bug River in the west to the lower Volga in the east. From the Rus' perspective a less precise division may have been more significant. The Rus' were concerned mainly with two loose federations of Polovsty tribes. One inhabited the steppe on both sides of the Dnieper River; the other, known as the "wild" Polovtsy, dominated the lands further east. A third steppe population, called the *chernye klobuki* or Black Hoods, was also identifiable by the middle of the century. They were evidently Pechenegs, Torks, and other nomadic peoples who had neither moved westward when the Polovtsy appeared nor been assimilated by them. Hostile particularly toward the "wild" Polovtsy, the *chernye klobuki* not only made peace with the Kievan princes, but occupied lands near the Rus' defense outposts on the Ros' River and served as frontier guards and supplementary troops for Kievan campaigns.

A second factor that complicated steppe relations was that unlike the practice on other Rus' frontiers, where the most proximate principality conducted relations with its foreign neighbors, a variety of Riurikid princes maintained direct relations with at least some of the steppe populations. Kiev had close ties with the *chernye klobuki*. The Chernigov princes and, secondarily, the Suzdalian princes, were allied with the "wild" Polovtsy.

The southern, steppe frontier was correspondingly the most volatile of Kievan Rus' borders. Polovtsy became involved in almost every succession struggle discussed in the previous sections of this chapter. When the Chernigov princes entered the contest between Grand Prince Iaropolk and Iurii Dolgorukii over Pereiaslavl' in 1132–34, they brought Polovtsy forces with them to attack Pereiaslavl' and threaten Kiev itself. During the next round of conflicts, while Iurii Dolgorukii attempted to remove Iziaslav Mstislavich (1146–54) from the Kievan throne, he and his Chernigov allies received military assistance from the "wild" Polovtsy; Iziaslav drew upon the *chernye klobuki* and his Hungarian allies. Not surprisingly, when Iurii did attain the throne in 1155, he encountered difficulties from the *chernye klobuki* as well as the Dnieper Polovtsy until he made peace with them in 1156.

Relations with the steppe populations were also crucial in the succession following Iurii's death in 1157. The first prince to take the throne was a member of the Chernigov clan, Iziaslav Davydovich. He was favored by his family's traditional allies, the "wild" Polovtsy. But that relationship alienated the *chernye klobuki*, usually loyal to the grand prince of Kiev, but who on this occasion gave their support to his opponents, the prince of Galicia and the Volynian prince Mstislav Iziaslavich. They, in turn, helped to transfer the throne from Iziaslav to Rostislav Mstislavich (1158–67). Rostislav's position was secured only after his nephew Mstislav Iziaslavich once again defeated the deposed Iziaslav and his "wild" Polovtsy allies (1161).

Polovtsy involvement in Riurikid partisan politics was also evident later in the period. It was as allies of Riurik Rostislavich, who was attempting to regain his throne, that Polovtsy were involved in the sack of Kiev in 1203; and it was in retaliation that Roman of Volynia and Galicia engaged the Polovtsy in battle in 1204–05. In a similar capacity Polovtsy took part in the princely disputes within Galicia and Volynia in the 1220s and 1230s. They were also involved as allies of Mikhail Vsevolodovich of Chernigov in his defeat of Grand Prince Vladimir Riurikovich and sack of Kiev in 1235.

During the 1160s to the 1180s, however, Rus'–Polovtsy conflicts fall into the second category. The tidy pattern of alliances between "wild" Polovtsy with Chernigov and Suzdalian princes, between Dnieper Polovtsy and *chernye klobuki* with the Kievan grand princes is not consistently apparent. Rather, relations across the frontier appear to have been deteriorating without regard for family ties and traditional alliances. Thus, in 1160 or 1162, Andrei Bogoliubskii, despite the fact that his grandfather had been a Polovtsy khan, sponsored an ill-fated offensive across the Don River into the steppe. By 1167, Rostislav had to send an army to escort the merchants crossing the steppe in order to protect them from Polovtsy raids. The following year, Mstislav Iziaslavich, having claimed the throne, mounted a massive campaign against the Polovtsy. Thirteen princes from all the competing Riurikid clans (the Rostislavichi of Smolensk, Ol'govichi of Chernigov, Iur'evichi of Vladimir-Suzdal', and Iziaslavichi of Volynia) took part. Penetrating deeply into the steppe, they achieved a major victory over the Polovtsy and evidently stabilized conditions along their trade routes.

After the removal of Mstislav and sack of Kiev in 1169, in which the Polovtsy did not take part, the new grand prince Gleb Iur'evich once again relied on the "wild" Polovtsy, while Mstislav, using *chernye klobuki* forces, persisted in challenging him. But about the time of Gleb's death in 1171, according to Peter Golden, the "wild" Polovtsy under Khan Konchak formed a coalition among all groups of Polovtsy. Their combined forces harassed the Rus' frontiers and conducted forays across the border, mainly against Pereiaslavl'.[10] These hostile initiatives, coupled with their intrusion into Rus' politics once again in the early 1180s, provoked Grand Prince Sviatoslav Vsevolodich to gather the Rus' princes and launch another expedition into the steppe. Having been directed to the Polovtsy by merchants returning northward across the steppe, the Rus' armies engaged the Polovtsy in 1184, inflicted a serious defeat on them, and captured several of their khans and other notables. The glory of that victory was only moderately tempered by the defeat the next year of Prince Igor' of Novgorod-Seversk (a subdivision of Chernigov), whose campaign is remembered more for the poetic account of it in "The Lay of Igor's Campaign" than for its military or political significance. The ability of Kievan grand princes Mstislav Iziaslavich and Sviatoslav Vsevolodich to gather such broad coalitions of Rus' princes to fight the Polovtsy has been used to support the argument, discussed earlier, that

[10] Peter Golden, "The *Polovci Dikii*," *HUS*, vol. 3/4 (1979/1980), p. 308.

Kievan Rus' remained a cohesive polity and that its grand prince in the late twelfth century continued to exercise real political influence over other members of the dynasty. The confrontations with the Polovtsy in this period have led some scholars to argue, additionally, that it was actually the perceived threat from the Polovtsy that provided the impetus for the Rus' princes to remain affiliated with one another.

After the mid-1180s, Polovtsy ventures across the frontier were once again coordinated with the interests of their Riurikid allies. By the third decade of the thirteenth century, in the absence of intradynastic warfare, Rus'–Polovtsy relations became more typically cooperative than confrontational. Thus, in 1223, when an army of unknown origin appeared on the steppe, the Polovtsy turned to the Rus' to join forces with them to oppose it. The strangers were Mongols. Having recently conquered Khwarezm in Central Asia, Chingis Khan sent an army to conduct a reconnaissance of the lands to the west. This army had traveled to the south of the Caspian and had just traversed the Caucasus, defeating the Georgians to the south of the mountains and the Ossetians to their north, before entering the Polovtsy steppe. But even the combined Polovtsy and Rus' warriors could not fight them effectively. At the Battle of Kalka, Grand Prince Mstislav Romanovich of Kiev and two other princes were captured and killed; Mstislav Sviatoslavich, the senior prince of Chernigov, and at least five other princes died in battle. The Mongols left the survivors stunned and bewildered, yet unprepared for their return fifteen years later.

Reviews of the domestic political crises and foreign affairs of Kievan Rus' during the era 1125 to 1237 suggest that the society was experiencing two opposing trends simultaneously. The number of its component principalities was increasing. Their economic and military strength was altering the balance of real power among them and reducing the relative significance of Kiev. Under these pressures the political structure of Kievan Rus' was perpetually being tested and adapted to changing political realities. The political flexibility displayed by Kievan Rus' took place, however, within the framework of a consistent and sturdy dynastic structure. Thus, even as the number of principalities multiplied and their princes competed, Kievan Rus' remained the realm of its dynasty.

The political structure of Kievan Rus' thus developed in a manner parallel to other institutions, discussed in the previous chapter. New bishoprics had been created, dispersing the authority previously invested in the metropolitan but nevertheless enhancing the influence of the Orthodox Church around the country. New stone edifaces had been constructed and extensions of chronicles were being written in the burgeoning new towns. Their activities may have diminished the former status of Kiev as the unchallenged cultural center of the realm, but it was Kievan culture the newer centers were emulating, a common culture emanating from Kiev that was becoming more deeply rooted throughout the realm. In the same manner more branches of the dynasty differentiated themselves as they defined and developed their own distinct principalities, at times in unabashed competition with Kiev. But Kiev was also the unquestioned center of their common realm, the seat of the dynasty's senior member. Kiev and the identification of the grand prince were consistently so important that it was precisely disputes over implementation of the dynastic rules and traditions regarding succession to the Kievan throne that caused wars among the princes; and it was the resolution of those issues that provided the foundation for political stability among all the Rus' lands.

Within this political framework, however, each of the princes also took responsibility for conducting foreign relations with his particular neighbors. This practice, although administratively and often militarily practical, revealed through the twelfth and early thirteenth centuries a growing divergence in the economic and political experiences, interests, and goals that formed the bases of the principalities' foreign policies. The result was that although the Riurikid princes found it to be in their common interest to join forces against the Polovtsy, they showed little interest in providing aid to one another on other fronts. While Novgorod was losing control over territory and tributaries to the German knights, Galicia was falling under Hungarian domination. Yet, at virtually the same time Suzdalian princes, preoccupied with the northern fringes of the realm, were evicting the Volga Bulgars from Ustiug. In the conduct of its foreign policy each principality was legitimately pursuing and defending its own interests. But this conduct, more than their domestic conflicts over succession to Kiev, reveals that the princes of the various dynastic branches, especially when they lost eligibility for succession to the Kievan throne, were becoming absorbed in different issues and were striving to attain different objectives. Fissures, dividing the southwest and northeast, were beginning to appear in the structure of Kievan Rus'.

5

THE GOLDEN HORDE

•

During the first decades of the thirteenth century, while the princes of Volynia, Chernigov, and Smolensk were disputing the throne of Kiev and the descendants of Vsevolod were concentrating their attention on their principality of Vladimir-Suzdal', developments were occurring far to the east that would have significant consequences for the Riurikid princes and their peoples. A young Mongol chieftain named Temuchin was subordinating and uniting the Turkic and Mongolian tribes of Mongolia. In 1206 a *quriltai* or an assembly of military and princely dignitaries from those tribes acclaimed Temuchin their great khan and began to organize what would become the Mongol Empire. By the time Chingis Khan, as Temuchin is known to posterity, died in 1227, he had launched an invasion of northern China (which began in 1211 and would continue to 1234) and extended his empire westward to incorporate the domain of the Khwarezm-shah in Central Asia; reconnaissance units of his armies had also explored the Caucasus Mountains and ventured into the steppe north of the Caspian Sea and south of Rus' lands.

When Chingis Khan died, the lands of his empire were distributed among his heirs, the four sons of his first wife. In accordance with Mongol custom Chingis' own *ulus*, the Mongol "heartland," was left to the youngest son Tolui. The third son, Ogedei, became the great khan. The second son, Chagatai, received Central Asia. And the westernmost lands beyond Chagatai's *ulus* and the Aral Sea were assigned to the eldest son, Juchi (Jochi). Because Juchi had died shortly before Chingis Khan, his sons inherited their father's share or *ulus*. The elder son, Orda, received the eastern territories of his father's *ulus*, consisting of western

Siberia, Kazakhstan, and the area around the lower Syr Darya River. An as yet unconquered portion, located further west, was accorded to a second son, Batu.

Batu's *ulus*, to which the lands of Rus' were to be subordinated, has been referred to by many names. All of Juchi's *ulus*, the western sector of the Mongol empire, was designated the White Horde. This term has also been used for Batu's *ulus*. When referring to Batu's and Orda's portions separately, the terms White Horde and Blue Horde have both been used. There is some confusion regarding which term should properly be applied to which half of the *ulus*, but most scholars consider the White Horde to refer to the western half or Batu's *ulus*. His realm, however, has also been referred to by a variety of other names: Desht-i-Kipchak, the Kipchak Khanate, and most commonly although least accurately, the Golden Horde.

After the conquest of northern China was completed, Khan Ogedei and a *quriltai* (1235) decided to conquer those western lands that had been assigned to Juchi, but had never actually been possessed by the Mongols. The ensuing military campaigns, which were led by Batu and the general Subodei, resulted in the Mongol defeat of the Rus' lands.

THE MONGOL INVASION OF THE RUS´ LANDS

The Mongol invasion of the Rus' lands was massive; it was devastating; and it had a lasting impact on the Russian lands. The appearance of the Mongols should not, however, have come as a complete surprise to the Rus'. Although the Mongols had disappeared after their victory over the combined armies of Kiev, Chernigov, Galicia, and the Polovtsy at the Battle of Kalka in 1223, they resurfaced in 1229 to attack Saksin, Bulgar-on-the-Volga, and the Polovtsy, and in 1232 to invade Bulgar again. All their targets were neighbors of the Rus'. Bulgar had, as noted above, maintained close relations with Suzdalia; the two states had also been involved in disputes over control of trade routes as well as dominance over the Mordva. Thus when the Bulgars constructed new fortifications and also eagerly concluded a peace treaty with Suzdalia in the wake of the 1229 attack, their actions if not their discussions certainly alerted Prince Iurii of Vladimir to the Mongol menace. Nevertheless, even after 1236, when the Mongol armies launched an offensive that destroyed the main cities of Bulgar, brought that state as well as its subordinate populations on the mid-Volga into their domain, and stimulated a migration of refugees into the Rus' lands, the Riurikid princes failed to take any extraordinary defensive measures even within Vladimir-Suzdal', much less coordinate a defense for all the Rus' lands.

Map 5.1 The Mongol invasion of the lands of Rus'

VLADIMIR —

Sit' R.

Battle of
Sit' River

Iaroslavl'

•Rostov

S U Z D A L'

Pereiaslavl'   •Suzdal'
Zalesskii   •Vladimir

Moscow

Moscow R.

•Kolomna

Riazan'

R I A Z A N'

CHEREMIS'
(MARI)

Volga R.

VOLGA
BULGARS

M O R D V A

Oka R.

BURTAS'

L A N D S

Don R.

Donets R.

Battle of Kalka River

Kalka R.

Volga R.

Sarai

Saksin

Caspian
Sea

ZOV

N

0   300 km
0   200 miles

The Riurikid princes had, of course, dealt with recurrent aggression from steppe populations before. But nothing in their experience with either the Pechenegs or the Polovtsy had prepared them for their encounter with the Mongols. No attack from the steppe had even approached the scale of the Mongol invasion of 1237–40. Unlike previous incursions from the Pechenegs and Polovtsy, the Mongols carried their devastating campaigns well beyond the southern frontier of the Rus' lands to the northern principalities. And having defeated the Rus' in battle, the Mongols established political suzerainty over the Riurikid princes, drawing them and their lands into the Mongol Empire. As David Morgan put it, "the problem for the Russians was . . . that . . . the Mongols did not go away."[1]

In the winter of 1237, the Mongols launched a campaign against northeastern Rus'. Approaching from the south, they demanded that the prince of Riazan' subject himself and pay tribute to them. He responded by calling upon Iurii of Vladimir for assistance. But while waiting for that aid, Riazan' felt the full impact of the Mongol onslaught. Batu's army besieged the city, bombarded its walls, and within one week in December 1237, captured Riazan'. The "Tale of the Destruction of Riazan' by Batu," recorded in several successive versions long after the events described, reminded its audiences that the Mongols "burned this holy city with all its beauty and wealth . . . And churches of God were destroyed and much blood was spilled on the holy altars. And not one man remained alive in the city. All were dead . . . And there was not even anyone to mourn the dead."[2] So swift in fact was the Mongol victory that the city had fallen before Iurii's reinforcements were able to enter Riazan' territory. The Mongols, however, advancing northward, met the Suzdalian relief force and defeated it near the town of Kolomna, located at the confluence of Moscow and Oka Rivers.

Continuing their sweep northward, the invaders destroyed the fortified outpost of Moscow in January 1238, and reached Vladimir in early February. Prince Iurii, leaving a small force to protect the city, where his wife and two of his sons remained, had departed for the far side of the Volga River, where he was collecting an army. The Mongol forces laid siege to the heavily fortified capital of Suzdalia. Part of the army meanwhile proceeded to the city of Suzdal', which it quickly captured, plundered, and burned. Shortly after it rejoined the main force, the Mongols who had successfully bombarded Vladimir's walls seized that city and sacked it. The combined forces of Iurii and his brothers were too slow

---

[1] David Morgan, *The Mongols* (Oxford: Basil Blackwell, 1986), p. 138.
[2] As translated by Zenkovsky in *Medieval Russia's Epics, Chronicles, and Tales*, p. 202.

even to attempt to save Vladimir. They were defeated in a battle on the Sit' River on March 4, 1238.

After taking Vladimir, the Mongol army fanned out. While one segment was approaching the Sit' River, two others advanced to the north and northwest, reconverged at Tver', and, almost simultaneously with the battle on the Sit', took Torzhok, the gateway from northeastern Rus' to Novgorod. The Mongols did not, however, follow up that victory with an assault on Novgorod. The army was still divided; it was already March, and the expectation that a spring thaw would turn the frozen earth into mud and impede the swift, easy movement of the Mongols' horses before the entire army could regroup may well have convinced them to conclude their offensive. In any case the campaign season of 1237–38 was over.

Later in 1238 the Mongol armies focused their attention on the southern neighbors of the Rus'. They subdued the Polovtsy of the steppe and the Circassians and Ossetians of the north Caucasus. In 1239, they suppressed an uprising among the Mordva, neighbors of the Bulgars. In that year they also directed their forces against the southwestern Rus' principalities. Advancing northward from the steppe, they overwhelmed the Rus' defenses first at Pereiaslavl', which fell in early March 1239, then at Chernigov, which they sacked on October 18, 1239. They directed their final campaign of that year against the Polovtsy in the Crimean peninsula, and in the following spring they focused once again on Derbent in the Caucasian theater.

It was not until the fall of 1240 that the Mongols turned toward Kiev. As noted in the previous chapter, in the years prior to the invasion Kiev had experienced political instability, marked by a rapid succession of princes. The appearance of the Mongols only intensified the crisis stemming from lack of leadership. After the Mongols had taken Chernigov, Prince Mikhail Vsevolodich (of Chernigov's Ol'govich clan) fled to Hungary. Prince Rostislav Mstislavich (of Smolensk) quickly claimed his position in Kiev, but was expelled in turn by Prince Daniil of Volynia. Despite the persistent competition for the title, none of the contenders remained in Kiev. Thus, when the Mongols arrived in November 1240, there was no Riurikid prince personally present to lead the city's defense.

The Mongol armies laid siege to Kiev. Their steady bombardment broke through the city's two sets of fortifications; it took them, according to one chronicle account, written many years after the events, ten weeks to do so. So many residents in their panic sought safety in the Church of the Tithe that its upper floors gave way under their combined weight. Kiev surrendered on December 6, 1240.

After taking Kiev, the Mongols continued westward, forcing the submission of both Galicia and Volynia before pushing beyond the lands of Rus' into Poland and Hungary. The collapse of the Rus' principalities was stunning. It has been attributed to a variety of factors, including, most predominantly, the division among the Riurikid princes. But it has also been argued that even if all the Rus' princes had coordinated their efforts, they would have been unequal to the Mongol military might. Unfamiliar with the siege machines that the Mongols had adopted from their Muslim and Chinese subjects and unprepared for their rapid movement and military tactics, the Rus' princes simply were ill-equipped to defend their lands against this foe.

The Mongols concluded their westward advance only in September 1242, when word reached Batu that the great khan Ogedei had died the previous December. A *quriltai* was to be held to select Ogedei's successor, and Batu had to attend. Political affairs of the empire took precedence over further conquest. Other theories have been proposed to account for the curtailment of the Mongols' westward drive. One suggests that because there were no more good pasturelands beyond Hungary, the nomadic Mongols lost their capability as well as interest in acquiring more territories. Others argue, dubiously, that the Russian defenses had so exhausted the Mongol forces that the latter were too weak to mount a sustained campaign in Europe. Yet another view holds that with their thrust into central Europe the Mongols had already overextended themselves; unable to control all the lands they had already conquered, they ended their campaign.

Whatever their motives, the undefeated Mongols withdrew from central Europe to establish themselves in the steppe north of the Black and Caspian Seas. On the lower Volga Batu built his capital city of Sarai, and from there began to consolidate Mongol authority over the territories of Juchi's *ulus*. Those territories stretched across the steppe from the Danube River in the west to Khwarezm in the east; at their southern end they included the Crimean peninsula and the North Caucasus. North of the steppe were the lands of Rus'. Subordinated by the Golden Horde, they too became adjuncts of the vast Mongol Empire, which at its greatest extent spanned an area from eastern Europe and Persia to China and Korea.

THE ESTABLISHMENT OF THE GOLDEN HORDE

For the Mongols of the Golden Horde, however, the lands of Rus' were on the geographical periphery of their new domain. They and their sedentary populations were also secondary to the Mongols' main concerns, which were to consolidate their position in the steppe, develop and maintain an influential role within the Mongol Empire, and establish relations with foreign powers. The lands of Rus' were significant insofar as they provided means with which they could pursue those aims. After concluding its military campaigns, the Mongol Horde remained predominantly a nomadic society. The Horde's social organization and institutions, founded on tribal and kinship structures, reflected and were permeated with the traditions drawn from their nomadic culture. Similarly, its economic strength derived from pastoral occupations, which were traditional among the ethnic Mongols, who made up the political and social elites of the Horde, as well as among the vast majority of its population, which consisted of other steppe populations, mainly Polovtsy or Kipchaks who were conquered and absorbed into the Horde.

The ruler of the Golden Horde was the khan, known as the tsar in Russian documentary sources. He was subordinate only to the great khan or *kagan* at Karakorum, but by the end of the thirteenth century the practical authority of the *kagan* over the Golden Horde had diminished. The khans of the Horde had to be direct descendants of Juchi and, as such, descendants of Chingis Khan. Thus when Batu died c. 1255, his son Sartak was selected to be his heir. Sartak's younger brother Ulagchi succeeded him in 1256. Subsequent khans of the Golden Horde were: Berke (1258–66), Mengu-Timur (Mongka-Temir; 1266/67–81), Tuda-Mengu (1282/83–87), Telebuga (1287–91), Tokhta (1291–1312), and Uzbek (1313–41).

Tatar society was organized around clans, which were further subdivided into tribes and smaller kinship groupings. The leaders, emirs or beys, of four influential clans served, at least by the first half of the fourteenth century, as the main political advisers to the khan and participated in making policy decisions. Although it is not known precisely when the council of four beys was institutionalized, Charles Halperin has suggested that it replaced the *quriltai* or assembly made up of the Mongol aristocratic elite, i.e., the heads of clans, military commanders, and dynastic dignitaries, whose functions included the selection the khan from among all the eligible candidates.[3] Assigned grazing lands by the khan, the clan leaders wielded power over their own populations by distributing

[3] Charles J. Halperin, *Russia and the Golden Horde* (Bloomington, Ind.: Indiana University Press, 1985), p. 26. For a discussion of the roots of the council of beys in the Mongol Empire, see U. Schamiloglu, "The Qarači Beys of the Later Golden Horde: Notes on the Organization of the Mongol World Empire," *Archivum Eurasiae Medii Aevi*, vol. 4 (1984), pp. 283–297.

pasturages among their kin and subordinates. They were also military commanders, responsible for their clans' contribution of mounted warriors to the khan's military campaigns.

Even as they organized their nomadic society in the steppe, the Mongols incorporated sedentary agricultural populations into their realm; they also built and settled in cities. Batu himself, while living in tents and moving his headquarters seasonally up and down the Volga River, began the construction of Sarai, his capital city, on the lower Volga River. A second city, also known as Sarai, New Sarai, or Sarai-Berke, was later built further up the river. Because of its name, its sponsor has been assumed to have been Khan Berke. Archeological evidence, however, has provided the basis for an alternate conclusion, that Sarai-Berke referred to Batu's Sarai, and that the second capital was built in the 1330s by Khan Uzbek. Even before these cities began to flourish, older towns within their realm, such as Bulgar-on-the-Volga and Khwarezm in Central Asia, showed signs of recovery. Although the khans themselves continued to live according to their nomadic traditions at least part of each year and follow the grazing patterns of their herds, the cities became their administrative and commercial centers. In them there developed cosmopolitan urban populations which included free men and slaves, administrative officials, tradesmen, craftsmen, merchants, and clergy, as well as members of the Tatar elite, who adopted a permanently sedentary, urban manner of living.

One of the chief activities of the cities of the Golden Horde was commerce, which along with animal husbandry became one of the most important elements of the Horde's economy. The entire Mongol Empire was bound together, at least until 1368, by its Great Silk Road, a caravan route that stretched from China to eastern Europe. The Golden Horde controlled the northwestern segment of the route which extended from Urgench in Central Asia through Sarai to Tana (Azov) at the mouth of the Don River, and to Sudak and Caffa on the Crimean coast of the Black Sea. As this commercial pathway became secure, merchant caravans transported silks, spices, gems, ceramics, and other Oriental finery to Sarai. There such goods as well as others obtained along the way were exchanged for slaves, for northern products including luxury fur received from Bulgar and the Russian lands, for locally obtained fish, caviar, salt and hides, and for goods brought from Constantinople, Europe, and Egypt.

Central to this exchange were Italian merchants, who acquired trading privileges from both the Golden Horde khans and the Byzantine emperors. In 1261 Emperor Michael VIII Paleologus granted trading rights in Constantinople and the Black Sea to the Genoese, who were helping him recover Constantinople. Later in the decade, shortly after he became khan in 1266, Mengu-Timur also extended special trading rights to the Genoese, who developed commercial colonies at Sudak and Caffa. The latter became, under the favorable policies of Khan Uzbek, their main market on the northern Black Sea coast. The Genoese, closely followed by their rivals, the Venetians, who centered their trade at Tana, thus provided the key link between the Mongol silk route and Sarai on one end to the Mediterranean world and Constantinople on the other.

In addition to establishing themselves firmly in the steppe, organizing their expanded society and distributing grazing areas among their component clans, building their cities, and developing their commerce, the khans of the Golden Horde maintained close ties with the rest of the Mongol Empire, especially with the *kagans* in Karakorum. Through the thirteenth century the great khans at Karakorum closely observed and supervised the affairs of the Golden Horde and its tributaries, and probably received a significant portion of the tribute collected from them.

The Golden Horde khans were, similarly, intimately involved in Karakorum court affairs. Just as Ogedei's death had precipitated the end of Batu's campaigns and prompted his return to participate in the *quriltai*, so Batu's successors continued to be concerned with issues at the Mongol court. After the great khan Mongke died in 1259, for example, a power struggle, lasting five years, developed in Karakorum between Kubilai and his rival Arik-Buka. Berke, who had become khan of the Golden Horde in 1258 and who supported Arik-Buka, was involved in the intrigues and affected by their outcome.

An imperial decision to expand the empire into the Near East also affected the Golden Horde. The result of that decision was the creation of another branch of the empire, known as the Ilkhan Empire, in the territories of Persia and Iraq. The Golden Horde supported the project, which began with a campaign into Persia in 1253. Golden Horde military forces took part in the capture of Baghdad in 1258.

Prior to the conquest of Persia, however, the Golden Horde khans had exercised influence over the Caucasus and Azerbaijan, even though they were not formally part of Juchi's *ulus*. When those regions, deemed valuable both for their pastures and their caravan routes through mountain passes, then became part of the Ilkhan domain, a rivalry developed between the two neighboring sections of the empire. This relationship mirrored the conflict in Karakorum between Kubilai and his rival Arik-Buka since Hulagu, the Mongol khan in Persia, supported Kubilai whereas Berke was loyal to Arik-Buka.

The rivalry was exacerbated by other factors. Berke, who had personally adopted Islam, was disturbed by the fact that during Hulagu's conquest of Baghdad, the caliph or leader of the Sunni Muslim world had been killed. The establishment of the Ilkhanid branch of the empire, furthermore, created commercial and financial problems for the Golden Horde. The Ilkhans established control over a branch of the silk route that proceeded from Central Asia westward through Persia to the south of the Caspian Sea; it constituted an alternative to the route dominated by the Golden Horde. Transit and customs fees as well as commercial profits derived from trade that had been concentrated in Golden Horde towns were diverted to the Ilkhans. As he consolidated his position, Hulagu also withheld from the Golden Horde its share of tributary income collected from the newly conquered populations. As a result of all these factors, the two branches of the Mongol Empire were at war with one another by 1262.

Its political and commercial rivalry with the Ilkhans was one motivation for the Golden Horde khans, notably Berke and his successor Mengu-Timur, to make diplomatic overtures to the Mamelukes of Egypt and to the newly restored Byzantine emperor, Michael VIII Paleologus. The Golden Horde had entered into close relations with the Mamelukes by the early 1260s. One common interest was their mutual desire to curb the expansion of the Mongols in Persia. In contrast, Emperor Michael VIII was initially favorably inclined toward the Ilkhans and unfriendly toward the Golden Horde. While Emperor Michael interfered with the passage of some embassies between Egypt and Sarai, Berke and his successor Mengu-Timur ordered raids on Byzantine frontiers. But the Italians, concerned about their commerce, pressured the emperor to alter his policy toward the Golden Horde. The more cordial, cooperative relations they developed were symbolized and cemented by marriages. In 1273, Nogai, a powerful Mongol military commander who controlled the western portion of the Golden Horde's territories, married an illegitimate daughter of Emperor Michael. Tokhta would similarly marry an illegitimate daughter of Emperor Andronicus II.

The Golden Horde's diplomatic contacts were extensive. The khans maintained relations with rulers in Europe as well as throughout the Middle East and the rest of the Mongol Empire. Sarai became an intercontinental diplomatic center as envoys and ambassadors representing princes and popes sought audiences with the khans. The Golden Horde also sent its own diplomatic dignitaries, often leading caravans bearing precious gifts of silver and gold, horses and camels, falcons and fur, to foreign capitals.

By the reign of Uzbek (1313–41) the Golden Horde had become a strong, wealthy state, dominating the Kipchak steppe and drawing upon the resources of its northern tributaries. Its growing society, while still clinging to traditional nomadic occupations, adopted Islam under Uzbek's guidance, and absorbed sedentary agrarian cultures and urban activities. Sarai by this time was a cosmopolitan metropolis, enriched by religious ties to the world of Islam, by political and dynastic interests in the remainder of the Mongol Empire, and by diplomatic and commercial intercourse with the Byzantine Empire, Egypt, the Middle East, the Caucasus, Central Asia, the Italian Black Sea colonies, Europe, and the lands of Rus' as well.

RUS' RELATIONS WITH THE GOLDEN HORDE

Invasion and destruction

In the century following the Mongol military onslaught of 1237–40, the Rus' also became a part of this political, diplomatic, and commercial world. But in the immediate wake of the attacks, the lands of Rus' were left defeated, their central cities destroyed, their dynasty depleted. It is difficult to assess the degree of destruction the Mongol invasion inflicted on the Russian principalities. Certainly the physical damage to some cities, such as Riazan', Vladimir, and Kiev, was extreme. Despite the assertion in the fourteenth-century "Tale of the Destruction of Riazan' by Batu" that its prince Ingvar' Ingvarevich "renewed the land of Riazan' and built churches and monasteries," David Miller, who has examined construction records in the post-invasion period, has described Riazan' in the years following the invasion as a "ghost town."[4] The Mongol victory at Vladimir too was accompanied by severe destruction. The Mongol armies broke through the defensive walls, then sacked and burned the city. Among the buildings set afire was the great Cathedral of the Assumption, to which the terrified population, including Iurii's princess and sons, had fled for refuge.

Kiev suffered a similar fate. A Franciscan monk and papal emissary to the great khan in Mongolia, Friar Giovanni de Pian de Carpine (Carpini), left a travel account describing the city five years after its surrender. Although some doubt has been cast on its value as an "eye-witness" statement, Carpine's account asserts that Kiev had been reduced from a great and populous city to "almost nothing," that scarcely two hundred houses remained and the surviving population was held in

---

[4] Miller, "Monumental Building as an Indicator of Economic Trends in Northern Rus'," p. 369.

"abject slavery."[5] The city's population, it will be recalled, numbered between 36,000 and 50,000 people. According to one estimate, they had dwelled in 8,000 homes, and only 2,000 people survived.[6] Although the figures are imprecise, they do offer a sense of the scale of the devastation inflicted on the central cities by the invading Mongol forces.

While there can be no question that these and other towns, e.g., Torzhok in the northwest, Pereiaslavl' and Chernigov in the south, and Galich and Vladimir (in Volynia) in the southwest, which had also been direct targets of the invading armies, were devastated, others fared better. This point was emphasized by both the Soviet historian A. N. Nasonov and the British historian John Fennell, who identified Novgorod, Rostov, Iaroslavl', and Tver' as some of the major centers that escaped undamaged. Fennell, furthermore, while recognizing that damage was inflicted on some cities, expressed doubt that even places like Kiev and Vladimir were harmed as badly as some sources suggest. He argued that the damage was not so great that they were unable to recover relatively rapidly. Other scholars have observed, additionally, that although the Riurikid princes abandoned Kiev as their political capital, the city remained the ecclesiastical center of the lands of Rus'. Metropolitan Kirill (Cyril; 1242–81), although known to have traveled extensively to the various sectors of his see, was also frequently found at Kiev, and his remains were returned there after his death. It was not until 1299, long after the Mongol invasion, that Metropolitan Maksim (Maximus; 1282–1305) vacated Kiev in favor of Vladimir. The Soviet ethnologist, L. N. Gumilev, noting that in the Vladimir principality Batu's armies burned only fourteen wooden towns out of a total of around 300, offered concurring evidence that the scale of destruction may not have been as great as is often proposed.[7]

Although cities were the Mongols' military objectives, the countryside was not immune to their onslaught. Villages and fields surrounding principal towns were also ravaged. The Soviet historian V. V. Kargalov noted that as a result of the initial campaigns as well as fourteen subsequent

5 *The Texts and Versions of John de Plano Carpini and William de Rubruquis*, ed. C. Raymond Beazley (Hakluyt Society, 1903; reprint ed., Nendeln, Liechtenstein: Kraus Reprint Limited, 1967), pp. 87–88, 122. For the doubts about the authenticity of the remarks in Carpine's account, see Donald Ostrowski, "Second-Redaction Additions in Carpini's *Ystoria Mongalorum*," *HUS*, vol. 14 (1990), p. 522.

6 Tolochko, *Kiev i Kievskaia zemlia*, p. 215.

7 A. N. Nasonov, *Mongoly i Rus'* [The Mongols and Rus'] (Moscow and Leningrad: Akademiia Nauk SSSR, 1940; reprint ed., The Hague and Paris: Mouton, 1969), p. 37; Fennell, *Crisis of Medieval Russia*, pp. 87–89; L. N. Gumilev, *Drevniaia Rus' i velikaia step'* [Ancient Rus' and the great steppe] (Moscow: Mysl', 1989), p. 466.

campaigns conducted in northeastern Rus' during the following quarter century, major sections of the countryside suffered depopulation. For the rural areas, just as for towns, the impact of the invasion was not uniform. The effect was most critical in areas around the devastated cities, e.g., Riazan' and Vladimir. Depopulation was less serious elsewhere, e.g., in the regions surrounding Moscow, Tver', and Iaroslavl'. Such areas were even recipients of refugees from the more heavily damaged areas.[8] Thus, David Morgan's general comments about the Mongol conquest of its entire empire may be applied specifically to the lands of Rus' as well: "[T]he Mongol invasions were a truly awful, frequently a final, experience for those who had the misfortune to be in the way of the armies' advance; but . . . the impact was patchy, with some areas escaping fairly lightly or even completely."[9]

The princes of the dynasty, who survived and succeeded those killed defending the Rus' lands, faced multiple problems of consolidating their own positions, reconstructing their lands, and also developing working relationships with their conquerors. In the first years after the invasion, while the Mongols were pursuing military campaigns elsewhere, the remaining Riurikids were virtually left to their own devices to recover and restore order.

Mongol suzerainty

Nevertheless, the invasion of the Rus' lands, although not followed immediately by any formal treaty or Mongol occupation, constituted for practical purposes a conquest. A new, political relationship had to be forged between the Mongol khans and the Riurikid princes. The khans had to find methods of exercising their authority over the defeated lands; and the Rus' princes and their populations had to accept and adjust to the demands of the Horde. The princes of Rus' recognized Batu and his successors as their overlords. The first evidence of this relationship became manifest almost as soon as the Mongols' western campaigns ended. According to chronicle accounts, they began the practice of traveling to the Mongol khan or "going to the Horde" to receive the khan's *iarlyk* or patent, which was an official appointment or confirmation of each prince's right to rule his domain.

[8] V. V. Kargalov, "Posledstviia mongolo-tatarskogo nashestviia XIII v. dlia sel'skikh mestnostei Severo-Vostochnoi Rusi, [The consequences of the thirteenth-century Mongol-Tatar invasion for the countryside of northeastern Rus'], *Voprosy istorii*, no. 3 (1965), pp. 53, 57.

[9] Morgan, *Mongols*, p. 82.

As early as 1243, Prince Iaroslav Vsevolodich, who had replaced his brother Iurii as prince of Vladimir after the latter's death at the Battle on the Sit', made such a trip to the Horde. He was awarded not only the title of grand prince of Vladimir, but also grand prince of Kiev. Three years later Iaroslav returned to Sarai. On that occasion he was sent on to the Mongol capital at Karakorum. He did not survive the journey. Iaroslav's sons, Andrei, who served as prince of Vladimir from 1249 to 1251/52, and Alexander Nevsky, who replaced him in 1252, also traveled to both Sarai and Karakorum. In subsequent years other princes also repeatedly made the trip to the Horde. The Suzdalian princes alone, according to one count, made nineteen visits between 1242 and 1252.

The princes of southwestern Rus' also made trips to the Horde, but with varying results. Prince Daniil of Volynia, who had briefly held the throne of Kiev before the Mongol invasion, had managed with some difficulty to retain Galicia after Batu's forces overwhelmed southwestern Rus'. Several years later, after his westward drive had been concluded, Batu evidently made an effort to consolidate his authority over the western Rus' principalities. In a chronicle entry *sub anno* 1250, but probably referring to events of 1245, Batu demanded that Daniil turn over Galich, which he had recently recovered from Chernigov, to the Tatar officials. Daniil, instead, made a trip to the Horde. The prince submitted to Batu and was confirmed as prince of Volynia and Galicia; he returned to his land, where he reorganized his army along the model of the Mongol forces.

The visit of Prince Mikhail of Chernigov to the Horde was more dramatic and had more tragic results. Mikhail had also been grand prince of Kiev. He assumed that position in 1237, but fled soon afterward (1239 or 1240). He spent the next several years seeking assistance and refuge in Hungary, Poland, and Galicia. After the Tatars sacked Kiev, Mikhail briefly stationed himself outside his former capital, but by 1243, having accepted the Mongols' recognition of Iaroslav Vsevolodich as the senior Riurikid prince, he returned to Chernigov.

Shortly after Daniil "went to the Horde," Mikhail made his journey; he was the last of the major, reigning princes to do so. But when he was ordered to purify himself by walking between two fires and to kowtow before an idol of Chingis Khan, he refused. He is said to have thus aroused Batu's wrath and was executed in September 1246. He was later recognized as a saint in the Russian Orthodox Church. A. N. Nasonov has suggested that the princes of Vladimir influenced Batu against Mikhail and thus reinforced the Mongol khan's decision to recognize their line as the senior branch of the dynasty. George Vernadsky, in contrast, interpreted the execution of Mikhail of Chernigov as a boon to Daniil of Volynia, who was left the most powerful prince in southwestern Rus'.[10]

Another sign of Rus' submission to the Mongols was their payment of tribute to the khans. Initially the Mongols demanded that the Rus' pay a tithe. Upon invading Riazan', according to one chronicle account, the Mongols demanded that the prince turn over a tithe of everything, which meant a tenth of the population, including the princes, of the horses and other livestock, and of other valuables. Carpine made similar observations about Mongol tribute collection in Kiev.

The Rus' whom the Mongols thus removed from their homelands served their new masters in several capacities. Qualified men were drafted into the army, where they were deployed in the most vulnerable forward positions during an offensive. Rus' princes also participated in campaigns of the Golden Horde, although in nobler capacities. Skilled and unskilled laborers were also conscripted. They played significant roles in the construction of cities within the Golden Horde as well as in the production of crafted items for their residents and markets. The removal of skilled labor from the lands of Rus' compounded their economic difficulties, which were occasioned by the invasion but were experienced even in regions that had not been militarily defeated by the Mongols. Other prisoners and conscripts simply served as household slaves or were sold into the thriving slave trade that made up one of the major components of the commerce linking Sarai with the Italian markets at Tana and Sudak, the Caucasian trade centers, and Egypt.

Another factor associated with Mongol suzerainty and tribute collection was the census. As the Mongols consolidated their authority, they took censuses of the Russian population. Such a count may have taken place in the Kievan area in the early 1240s. But there is no record of a similar procedure in Vladimir–Suzdal' until 1257, when the Golden Horde was engaged in the conquest of Persia and Iraq. Using the information they gathered, the Mongols divided the Rus' lands into districts that served as the basis for both drafting military recruits and assessing tribute. There is no scholarly agreement on the timing of this organization; some associate it with the first census, others with changes in Horde administration. Nevertheless, basic units, called *tm'y* (*t'ma* in the singular) in the Russian sources, were created. The term, which is related to the number 10,000, may have referred to a district containing 10,000 households or 10,000 men or, possibly, one that could produce 10,000

[10] Nasonov, *Mongoly i Rus'*, p. 27–28; George Vernadsky, *The Mongols and Russia. A History of Russia*, vol. 3 (New Haven, Conn., and London: Yale University Press, 1953), p. 145.

soldiers. Districts representing subdivisions of the *t'ma* were associated with units of thousands, hundreds, and tens. The census data defined these districts and enabled the Mongols to gather tribute and military conscripts on a more precise basis than the rough estimates used for the original tithe.

The practices of princely travel to the Horde to receive formal approval to rule and payment of tribute marked the subordination of the Rus' lands to the Golden Horde. But the Sarai khans were preoccupied with the affairs of the entire Mongol Empire, rooted in nomadic steppe culture, and disinclined to occupy the alien forested, agricultural, and urban zones of the Rus'. The services of native princes, who enjoyed a legitimacy recognized by their subjects but who also acknowledged the authority of the khan, were essential. But even as Batu affirmed the right of Riurikid princes to continue to rule their principalities, he also superimposed his own appointed officials to oversee administration of the Rus' lands.

The officials had several different titles, but details about the range of their duties as well as their relationships with the Rus' princes are not available. It is known, however, that the officials designated to oversee conscription and tribute collection in the Rus' lands during the thirteenth century were known as *baskaki* (*basqaqi*). The first indication that such personnel were operating in the lands of Rus' pertained to Kiev where, Carpine observed, a *baskak* had been appointed to collect a tithe from the remaining population of that city.

Less is known about when *baskaki* were introduced into northeastern Rus'. If it is understood that in order to conduct their duties, a census had to be taken, then it is plausible to consider 1257, the first year in which a Mongol census in Suzdalia was recorded, also as the date of the introduction of *baskaki* in the region. There is, however, no firm evidence that the census and the appointment of *baskaki* were interdependent.[11] But by 1267, when Khan Mengu-Timur issued a charter exempting the Orthodox Church from the obligations that had been imposed on the rest of Rus' society, *baskaki* were evidently already functioning; they were advised in the *iarlyk* to honor the immunities granted by the khan. *Baskaki* also used military forces at their disposal to carry out their primary duties, to secure roads for safe transport of tribute and commercial goods, and to assist the Rus' princes.

Other officials exercising Mongol authority were present in the Rus' lands during the thirteenth century. They were tax-farmers, usually Muslims from Central Asia, and their duties appear to have overlapped with those of the *baskaki*. Some scholars have suggested that tax-farmers represented the great khans at Karakorum, while others have concluded

---

[11] So Charles J. Halperin pointed out in *Russia and the Golden Horde*, p. 35.

that all tax-collection activities in the lands of Rus' were supervised by the khan of the Golden Horde.[12] If one accepts the concept, discussed by G. A. Fedorov-Davydov, that revenues gathered from any tributaries of the Mongol Empire in the middle of the thirteenth century were shared among the Chingisid rulers,[13] then the debate becomes less significant. As long as the interests of the great khan and the Golden Horde khan coincided and revenues were apportioned according to mutually acceptable patterns, the authority of one reinforced the other. But when the political rivalry between Kubilai and Arik-Buka, paralleled by that between Berke and Hulagu, divided the Chingisids, then the consequences of whom the tax-farmers were serving became more serious. It was under these circumstances that in 1262 several northeastern Rus' towns rebelled against these officials; that episode will be discussed below.

By the fourteenth century the *baskaki* in the northeastern principalities were being replaced by a different Mongol official, known as the *daruga*. Unlike the *baskaki, darugi* were not stationed in the Rus' lands, but remained in Sarai where they functioned chiefly as experts on the lands of Rus' and advised the khan accordingly. Responsibility for collecting and delivering tribute and conscripts was increasingly assumed by the Rus' princes themselves, especially the grand prince of Vladimir. Special ambassadors conveyed directives from the khan to the Rus' princes and, when necessary, enforced them. Khan Tokhta, for example, sent Nevrui as his plenipotentiary to oblige the Rus' princes to settle a dispute over Pereiaslavl' in 1296; another emissary was dispatched to the Rus' lands in 1303.

Rus' resistance to Mongol suzerainty

After Prince Mikhail's execution, the first expressions of resistance to Mongol dominance were made by two other Riurikid princes, Daniil of Volynia and Galicia and Andrei of Vladimir. Prince Daniil appears to have been at the center of their opposition. Although he had been given a relatively favorable reception by Batu when he presented himself at the Horde, Daniil soon afterward began to organize an anti-Tatar coalition. In 1251, by then a widower, he married the niece of the Lithuanian king Mindovg, who had recently adopted Christianity and received his title from the pope. His most prominent domestic ally was Prince Andrei of

---

[12] The first view is represented by Nasonov, *Mongoly i Rus'*, pp. 50–51, 57, the second by Vernadsky, *Mongols and Russia*, p. 160.

[13] G. A. Fedorov-Davydov, *Obshchestvennyi stroi zolotoi ordy* [The social structure of the Golden Horde] (Moscow: Moskovskii universitet, 1973), p. 32.

Vladimir, who with the blessing of Metropolitan Kirill married Daniil's daughter in the same year.

Andrei had traveled with his brother Alexander all the way to Karakorum to receive their princely patents for Vladimir and Kiev, respectively, from the great khan Guyuk. But two years after their return Guyuk died (1251), and the princes were expected to go back to the Horde and receive renewals for their patents from Batu in the name of the new great khan Mongke. Andrei, defiantly, did not make the journey. His decision was received as a challenge to Mongol authority. Khan Batu's son Sartak authorized a punitive campaign against Vladimir. At the same time a twin expedition was sent against Daniil.

Andrei, defeated in battle, fled through Novgorod to Sweden; his brother Alexander replaced him on the Vladimir throne. Only in 1255 did Andrei return to the Rus' lands to become the prince of Suzdal'. Prince Daniil, however, continued to organize alliances against the Tatars; his efforts to arrange marriages for his children with members of ruling families in Hungary, Austria, and Lithuania are consistent with that policy. Daniil also established close ties with the papacy, and in 1253 received a crown and the title of Rex Russae Minoris from Pope Innocent IV. The pope hoped to attract the southwestern Russian principalities to the Roman Church; Daniil hoped that the pope would mount a crusade against the Tatars. When the latter did not materialize, Daniil broke his ties with the pope. Nevertheless, by 1256 Daniil was at war with the Mongols. Four years later he was finally defeated and forced to flee once again to Poland and Hungary. After Daniil's death in 1264, his brother and sons and their heirs ruled his domain under Mongol supervision until the 1320s, when the line died out.

The next display of resistance to Mongol authority occurred in 1259 in Novgorod. Shortly after the Tatars conducted censuses in northeastern Rus' in 1257, they extended the practice to Novgorod. When Tatar officials arrived to gather the customs duties (*tamga*) and a tithe, Novgorodian officials respectfully presented them with gifts for the khan, but refused to cooperate with the tax collection. The Tatars left. But Alexander Nevsky, then the grand prince of Vladimir, who had accompanied the tax collectors to Novgorod, remained after their departure, and punished the Novgorodians for their defiance of the khan's orders.

Nevsky, along with his brothers and Prince Boris of Rostov, were nevertheless ordered to appear before the khan in 1258. Then, in 1259, Novgorod was issued an ultimatum: submit to a census and pay the assessed taxes or face the consequences. Armed forces led by Prince Alexander Nevsky, his brother Andrei, and Boris of Rostov, and accompanied by Tatars then appeared before the city. Illustrating the importance for the Mongols of having both their own officials and loyal, reliable, and effective Riurikid princes on the thrones of the Russian principalities, they waited outside the city while the census officials attempted to count the population. When the Novgorodians again refused to cooperate, the combined Tatar and Russian armies entered the city and forced them to comply with the census takers and pay the corresponding tax.

In 1262, there were also popular uprisings in Rostov, Vladimir, Suzdal', and Iaroslavl'. They were directed against tax farmers licensed by the Mongols. As pointed out above, there is no consensus concerning which khan these officials represented, the great khan Kubilai at Karakorum or Berke, the khan at Sarai. In 1262, the interests of the two clashed. Berke was supporting Kubilai's rival for power at Karakorum and was also preparing for war against Kubilai's ally, Hulagu of the Ilkhans. Under these circumstances either side would have welcomed additional troops and revenue, and either side would have had reason to authorize tax-farmers to make the levies that provoked urban riots among the already heavily burdened populace of northeastern Rus'. Although they may well have been prompted by attempts to collect unusually heavy taxes as a consequence of the political situation within the Mongol Empire, the uprisings, which resulted in the murder of the tax-farmers, are frequently considered indicators of more general and widespread popular discontent with pressures imposed by the new regimen. Despite their display of insubordination and possibly because Alexander Nevsky, shortly after these events, personally presented himself before the khan in what would be his last trip to the Horde (winter 1262–63), no punitive action was taken against the rebellious towns. By the reign of Mengu-Timur, the Golden Horde exercised more autonomy within the empire and regularized the process of tax collection and conscription.

Rus' accommodation to the Golden Horde

One early symbol of Mongol suzerainty was the khan's right to confirm Russian princes on their thrones. A second mark of Mongol authority over the Rus' lands was the collection of tribute and conscripts. The Mongols used their own officials to oversee the accomplishment of these tasks, but gradually during the fourteenth century they transferred that responsibility to the Rus' princes themselves. The interaction between Mongol court officials and Rus' princes involved relatively frequent travel to the Horde. As a result, already in the first decades after the invasion some of the princes were visiting the Horde frequently and/or remaining among the Tatars for prolonged periods. Their attendance at the khan's court enabled them to establish close working relationships with the Mongols.

Alexander Nevsky, who, it has been claimed, developed particularly close ties to Sartak, constitutes a prime example. Virtually every one of the key actions he undertook as grand prince may be associated with a visit to the Horde. It was immediately after such a trip and with the help of Tatar forces, who chased his brother Andrei from the throne, that Alexander achieved power in Vladimir in 1252. He cooperated with the Tatars when they tried to take a census in Novgorod in 1257; then following another trip to the Horde, he used force against the Novgorodians to make them comply with the khan's demands (1259). After the riots in the northeastern Rus' towns, he went once more to the Horde, evidently for consultations. He was returning from that visit when he died (1263). Nevsky's frequent trips to the Horde served his personal political interests; they also reflect his obedience and even loyalty to the khan. Yet especially the last instance suggests that these visits were not simply occasions for the khan to issue orders to a subservient prince, but opportunities for mutual consultation; Nevsky may have by this time wielded some influence with the Mongols, who refrained from taking retribution against the rebellious Rus'.

The princes of the Rostov clan were also frequently at the Horde. By the 1260s and 1270s this branch of the Riurikid dynasty had apparently attained a special position at the khan's court. In the 1260s the chronicles record their visits to the Horde almost exclusively. Some of those princes remained among their Tatar hosts for extended periods and participated in the Golden Horde's military campaigns against Lithuania, the Ilkhans of Persia, and even some other Russian principalities. Some took their wives and children with them to the Horde. Others married within the Horde. The most noteworthy match was that of Fedor Rostislavich. Originally the prince of Mozhaisk, a subdivision of the Smolensk principality, Fedor had married into the Rostov clan and become prince of Iaroslavl'. He retained that position even after his wife died. He nevertheless also lived for a lengthy period at the Horde, participated in Mongol military campaigns in the Caucausus (1278), Bulgaria (1278), and against Pereiaslavl' (1281), and subsequently married the daughter of Khan Mengu-Timur.[14] The Tatars, in turn, assisted Prince Fedor when he met resistance in 1293 while trying to reassume his throne in Iaroslavl'.

[14] Gail Lenhoff has questioned whether a legal marriage actually took place between Prince Fedor and the Mongol tsarevna, whose Christian name was Anna and who bore him two sons; see her *Early Russian Hagiography: The Lives of Prince Fedor the Black* (Berlin: Otto Harvassowitz, 1995), chapter 5.

In addition to establishing their administration over the Rus' lands and forging ties with the Riurikid dynasty, the Mongol court also developed direct relations with the Orthodox Church. During the first four decades after their invasion, the Mongols dealt with Metropolitan Kirill. Appointed as head of the Russian Church in 1242 with the support of Prince Daniil of Volynia and Galicia, Kirill nevertheless ministered to his entire flock. He traveled frequently, visiting the northern principalities of Novgorod and Vladimir as well as Chernigov and Riazan'. Although he actually spent a great deal of time in Kiev and the southwest as well, many scholars interpret his extended stays in the northeastern principalities as evidence that he was deemphasizing the traditional ecclesiastical center in favor of the northeast and correspondingly withdrew his political allegiance from his early sponsor Daniil, whose daughter he had escorted to Vladimir and whose wedding with Prince Andrei Iaroslavich he had conducted. The new focus of his loyalty was Alexander Nevsky, whom he greeted at the Golden Gate of Vladimir when Alexander returned from the Horde in 1252 to assume the throne, at whose funeral he officiated in 1263, and to whose hagiographic biography he was subsequently the chief contributor. Joseph Fuhrmann argued, additionally, that the perceived shift in Kirill's support from Daniil and Andrei, who defied Mongol authority, to Alexander, who complied with it, reflected a parallel change in the Church's posture toward the Golden Horde.[15]

Interaction between the Church and the Horde became more direct and regular after 1261, when during the reign of Khan Berke a bishopric was established at Sarai. The relations that developed were mutually beneficial. The Mongols demonstrated a respect and tolerance for all religious institutions, including, in the Russian case, the Orthodox Church. Although Khans Berke and Tuda-Mengu personally became Muslims and Uzbek oversaw the conversion of the entire Horde to Islam, they never pressured the Russian population to follow their example. On the contrary, the Russian Church enjoyed special privileges. They were specified in a *iarlyk*, which was issued by Khan Mengu-Timur in 1267, and which exempted priests, monks, and laymen associated with the Church from Tatar taxation and military conscription. Those exemptions may also have been extended to the general population dwelling on Church and monastery lands.

In exchange for its privileges the Church regularly prayed for the khan. It also cooperated with the Mongols in more mundane matters. Individual Sarai bishops, appointed by Metropolitan Kirill, served as diplomatic

---

[15] Joseph T. Fuhrmann, "Metropolitan Cyril II (1242–1281) and the Politics of Accommodation," *JbfGO*, vol. 24 (1976), pp. 166, 171.

agents for the khans. Bishop Feognost (Theognostus), representing both his metropolitan and the Golden Horde, traveled on diplomatic missions to Constantinople at least three times during the 1270s, and contributed thereby to adding Byzantium to the Egyptian–Golden Horde alliance against the Ilkhans. The bishop also acted as an emissary to the Russian princes, and thus reinforced the Mongol khan's authority with an implied endorsement by the Church. In 1296, for example, the Sarai bishop Ismail joined the Mongol special ambassador Nevrui who, as noted above, brought instructions to the Russian princes and supervised a conference intended to settle their dispute over the disposition of Pereiaslavl' Zalesskii.

From the 1260s through the remainder of the thirteenth century the political and ecclesiastical elites of the northeastern Rus' lands accommodated themselves, personally and politically, to the Golden Horde khans. In the political framework that developed the Rus' principalities were significant, but not central to the Golden Horde's primary political objectives. The Rus', as a hinterland, could provide men and livestock for the khan's army, and silver and luxury goods for his treasury. Golden Horde policies toward the Rus' were geared to facilitating the smooth and reliable provisioning of those resources, which contributed to their ability to pursue their objectives toward the rest of the empire and their allies.

Within this framework the relationships and relative roles of khans and princes may be characterized by several features. The khans were recognized as suzerains of the Riurikid princes. Within the Rus' lands, however, they exercised their authority primarily through the dynasty. But the khans appointed and confirmed individual princes within the dynasty for each ruling position. Riurikid princes were, accordingly, required to appear personally before the khans to pay obeisance and receive their patents to rule. The khans also named their own officials to supervise tasks carried out on the Horde's behalf and to intervene in Rus' affairs if and when necessary. Initially, *baskaki* representing the Horde were stationed in the Rus' lands. But by the reign of Uzbek, when relations between the Golden Horde and the Rus' principalities had stabilized, *darugi* and special envoys had replaced *baskaki* as the chief agents of the Mongols. The tasks for which they were responsible remained constant. It was their duty to ensure that the Rus' paid tribute and other taxes and sent conscripts for service in the khan's armies. To those ends the Tatars were also involved in conducting censuses, maintaining order, and keeping lines of communication and transportation open and secure.

The presence of Mongol suzerains was burdensome to the Rus' princes and populace alike. But it also afforded some princes opportunities to increase their own stature. And by constituting a higher authority to which they could appeal their cases, the presence of the Golden Horde khan provided a means for competing members of the dynasty to resolve conflicts. As will be discussed in the next chapter, the Daniilovichi of Moscow most successfully took advantage of the opportunities offered by the Horde even as they demonstrated themselves to be the most resourceful and reliable princes in accomplishing the tasks the Mongols set before them.

6

THE RUSSIAN LANDS
WITHIN THE GOLDEN HORDE

The Mongol invasion was a pivotal point in the history of the Russian lands. The Mongol onslaught marked the end of Kievan Rus' as a viable and integrated political entity. The city of Kiev itself, sacked and ravaged, lost its political, commercial, and, ultimately, ecclesiastical centrality. The presence of the Mongols, acting as a mallet driving a wedge into already visible fracture lines, created gaping political and cultural fissures between the southwestern and northeastern principalities. Within a century of the Mongols' arrival, the southwestern lands became attached to Lithuania and Poland, while the northeastern principalities, under Golden Horde dominance, began the process that transformed them into the state of Muscovy.

The precise nature of the Mongol influence over that process has been the subject of wide-ranging debate. At one extreme are the classic views shaped by the Russian historians S. M. Solov'ev and V. O. Kliuchevsky, who saw little or no Mongol imprint on the development of Muscovy. At the opposite extreme is the position that Mongol domination had deep and enduring effects. But the character of those effects, how they were transmitted, and when they manifested themselves are also all topics of debate. These issues, encompassed in an examination of the development of the northeastern Russian lands into the state of Muscovy while under the dominance of the Golden Horde, will be explored in this and the following chapter.

DYNASTIC RECOVERY

One of the most immediate and serious political effects of the Mongol invasion was the decimation of the northeastern Riurikid princes. The reigning prince in Vladimir-Suzdal', Iurii Vsevolodich, three of his sons, and two sons of his late brother Konstantin Vsevolodich, the former prince of Vladimir (1212–18) and prince of Rostov, had all been killed at the battle on the Sit' River in 1238. One of the most urgent tasks for the surviving members of the dynasty was to redistribute themselves throughout their devastated realm.

As they did so, they clung to the patterns of dynastic succession that had been established during the Kievan era. Thus, the grand princely throne was quickly assumed by Iurii's younger brother Iaroslav Vsevolodich, who in turn delegated portions of his domain to his other surviving brothers. Sviatoslav ruled in Suzdal' and had jurisdiction over its associated towns of Nizhnii Novgorod and Gorodets, while Ivan became prince of Starodub. In addition, Iaroslav placed his son Alexander Nevsky in Novgorod.

Even as they reorganized and reaffirmed their dynastic rule, the Riurikids had to defer to their new suzerains, the Mongols. Iaroslav's succession, although in conformity with dynastic tradition, had to be and was confirmed by Khan Batu. When Iaroslav went to Sarai the second time in 1245, however, he was obliged to travel to the Mongol capital of Karakorum. He did not survive the journey. Upon learning of Iaroslav's death (September 30, 1246), his brother Prince Sviatoslav of Suzdal' succeeded him (1247).

One of Sviatoslav's first acts was to divide his domain still further. While leaving the Rostov lands to the descendants of Konstantin Vsevolodich and Starodub to Ivan's direct heirs, he parceled out the territories of Vladimir to his nephews, the sons of Iaroslav, evidently in accordance with their late father's wishes. So, for example, a principality consisting of Galich (located northeast of the city of Vladimir) and Dmitrov (located west of Vladimir) was assigned to Konstantin Iaroslavich; Iaroslav Iaroslavich became the prince of Tver', and Vasily Iaroslavich, although only six years old in 1247, was officially named the prince of Kostroma.

It may have been his dissatisfaction with his allotment. the size and location of which are unknown, that prompted one of Iaroslav's sons, Andrei, to challenge his uncle. Because the chronicles offer differing accounts, the chain of events associated with his action is not precisely clear. Nevertheless, it is evident that the Mongols played a determining role in the ultimate dispensation of the throne.

One version of Andrei's actions indicates that in 1248, he seized the throne of Vladimir from his uncle. Such an act would have both violated dynastic norms and defied Mongol authority. Another version omits that event, but records at about that time Andrei and his elder brother

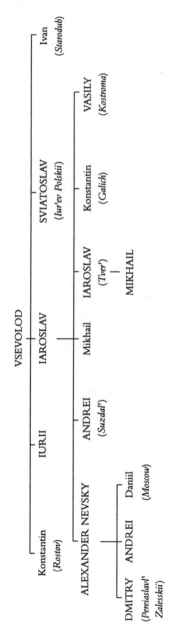

Table 6.1 The princes of Vladimir: the descendants of Prince Vsevolod Iur'evich

Alexander Nevsky made trips to the Horde; from there they were sent on to Karakorum. On their return in 1249, Andrei occupied the Vladimir throne; Alexander had been accorded southern Rus' including, at least nominally, Kiev. Sviatoslav then also presented himself at the Horde. The details and results of his trip are unknown; he died in February 1253 without recovering Vladimir.

After Mongke became the new great khan (1251), however, all the Russian princes were obliged to go to Sarai for a renewal of their patents. Alexander did so. But Andrei refused to make the journey, and immediately after Alexander's visit the Tatars launched simultaneous campaigns against both Andrei in Vladimir and Andrei's father-in-law, Daniil of Galicia. Defeated by the Mongols in their first venture into northeastern Rus' in fifteen years, Andrei fled through Novgorod to Sweden. Alexander, having been thus assisted by the Tatars, assumed the throne of Vladimir.

By the end of Alexander's reign (d. 1263), even more appanage principalities, i.e., principalities that would be inherited within a single branch of the dynasty, had been carved out of Vladimir-Suzdal'. Suzdal' itself, whose status after Sviatoslav became grand prince in 1247 is unclear, was given to Andrei upon his return from exile in 1255. Iur'ev Pol'skii became the domain of the deposed Sviatoslav and his heirs. Alexander's son Dmitry claimed Pereiaslavl' Zalesskii, while Moscow was evidently set aside for his youngest son, the two-year-old Daniil.

Although the territories of Vladimir were divided into appanages ruled by the descendants of Iaroslav Vsevolodich, the principality of Rostov remained the domain of the heirs of Konstantin. The only one of Konstantin's sons to have survived the Mongol invasion died in 1249, thus predeceasing his uncle, Prince Sviatoslav (d. 1253). Konstantin's line had become ineligible for succession by the time the usurper Andrei was displaced. Thus, when the Vladimir throne passed with the Mongols' approval to Alexander Nevsky, he was also the eldest surviving eligible member of his generation, hence the legitimate heir in the view of the dynasty.

Konstantin's grandsons, the same princes who, as discussed in chapter 5, had become so closely attached to the Golden Horde and had spent so much time at Sarai, retained the principality of Rostov. It included the northerly lands of Iaroslavl', Uglich, Ustiug, and Beloozero. Here too a pattern of subdivision was followed. As early as 1238, Beloozero was detached from Rostov; the latter was inherited by Konstantin's grandson, Prince Boris Vasil'kovich; the former became the appanage principality of Prince Gleb Vasil'kovich.

Iaroslavl' also was soon separated from Rostov. The male line of

Konstantin's second son, who had received Iaroslavl', died out in 1249. But rather than revert to the prince of Rostov, Iaroslavl' was transferred through Konstantin's great-granddaughter to her husband, Prince Fedor Rostislavich. The elder of his two sons by his second wife, the daughter of Khan Mengu-Timur, inherited the principality, which through the course of the fourteenth and fifteenth centuries also fragmented into multiple appanages.

The pattern of fragmentation within the northeastern Rus' lands continued and provided the basis for characterizing the era between the fall of Kiev and the rise of a centralized Muscovite state as the appanage period. Subjugated by the Mongol khans and ruling ever smaller principalities, the Riurikid dynasty appeared to be exercising sharply reduced power as the appanage period unfolded. But some of the political tradition of Kievan Rus' survived. The grand prince, located at Vladimir rather than Kiev, represented dynastic unity; the dynasty preserved the cohesion of the realm by continuing to honor its senior member with that position, subject to the khan's approval. Furthermore, just as the multiplication and dispersal of princes had practical value during the Kievan era, so the practice was functional during the critical decades following the Mongol invasion. With the capital city of Vladimir sacked, its population dispersed, and its resources depleted, the princes of the dynasty, distributing themselves among relatively small principalities, were able to carry out their responsibilites for defense, economic recovery, and political and fiscal administration with some effectiveness.

THE WESTERN FRONTIER

Defense of their lands from external foes was foremost among the obligations of the Riurikid princes. Defeat by Batu and severe losses sustained in battles against the Mongols did not prevent the surviving Rus' princes from fulfilling that duty. With their southern and eastern frontiers stabilized by the presence of the powerful Mongol forces, the Rus' faced competitors only on their western borders. They had three main neighbors in the northwest: the Swedes, the German Knights (the Order of the Brothers of the Sword and the Teutonic Knights), and the Lithuanians. At the time the Mongols were invading from the south and east, the Rus' also faced aggression from these neighbors on their northwestern frontier. Alexander Iaroslavich, who acquired the name Nevsky during one of his battles against them, was chiefly responsible for defending this frontier.

Much of the instability in the area may be attributed to the activities of the German Knights. In 1202, the Order of the Brothers of the Sword was founded to conduct a crusade against the pagan Balts and Finns, who dwelled in the Livonian lands lying to the west of the Rus' principalities. Further west, the Teutonic Order similarly launched a crusade in 1230 against Prussian tribes that neighbored Poland. In 1237, shortly after a defeat by Lithuanians, the surviving members of the Brethren merged with the Teutonic Order. Together they placed pressure on the Lithuanian tribes that geographically divided the two sections of the Order; they also targeted the Orthodox Rus'. In response to German pressures Mindovg, who became prince in 1238 and died in 1263, unified, defended, and expanded Lithuanian territories. The Rus', therefore, faced Lithuanian pressures as well as those from the Germans and Swedes.

The most famous battles in defense of the northwestern Rus' lands were the victories of Prince Alexander Iaroslavich against the latter two opponents. The first of these was the Battle of the Neva, fought against the Swedes. Novgorod and Sweden were competitors both for dominance over Finnic tribes north of the Novgorod lands and for control over access to the Gulf of Finland. The Swedish attack on the Neva River in July 1240 was one of a long series of hostile encounters over these issues, not, as is sometimes asserted, a full-scale campaign timed to take advantage of the Russians' adversity and aimed at conquering the entire Novgorodian realm. Nevertheless, Alexander's victory there was celebrated and became the basis for his epithet Nevsky.

Also in 1240, German Knights captured a fortress southwest of Pskov, occupied the city itself, and in the following winter began to establish themselves in lands west of Novgorod, near the Gulf of Finland. In response to appeals from Novgorod, Grand Prince Iaroslav sent Alexander, who with his brother Andrei expelled the knights from Pskov and advanced westward to engage them in a decisive battle. In April 1242, Alexander's army not only defeated the Teutonic Knights at the frozen Lake Peipus (Lake Chud'), but permanently halted the Germans' eastward advance.

The battles are described in the vita or life of Alexander, which emphasizes the heroic nature of Alexander's military ventures and has become a basis for the claim that western aggression, representing the expansionist interests of the Catholic Church, was potentially as threatening to the Russian lands as the Mongol invasion. The implication is that Alexander, unable to expel both, chose to submit to and cooperate with the Mongols while concentrating his military might against his foes in the west. The vita, however, was written in the early 1280s on the basis of information supplied by Metropolitan Kirill who had been both concerned with preserving the integrity of his Church and, as noted in the previous chapter, favorably inclined toward Prince Alexander. Many scholars, therefore, judge its account of these events, and hence the seriousness of the western "threat" to the lands of Rus', to be exaggerated.

These episodes nevertheless illustrate how Grand Prince Iaroslav, while still reeling from the immediate aftermath of the Mongol invasion, continued to regard the protection of the Rus' lands and resources as a fundamental obligation, which he and his heirs honored. Later, even after Alexander Nevsky was awarded Kiev by the great khan at Karakorum, he returned to Novgorod, which he served as prince and continued to defend until with the aid of the Mongols he overthrew and replaced his brother Andrei as grand prince of Vladimir (1252).

The Riurikid princes were less effective in resisting Lithuanian expansion. Although Alexander Nevsky successfully defended Smolensk and Novgorod from Lithuanian attacks in 1239 and 1245 respectively, neither he nor his successors could prevent the Lithuanians from absorbing Polotsk, where Mindovg's nephew became prince, or the western lands of the Turov principality.

Relations between Galicia-Volynia and Lithuania were more complex and variable. Prince Daniil, as discussed in the last chapter, was engaged in building a coalition against the Mongols. In conjunction with that policy he entered into an alliance with Mindovg, who, like Daniil, had been issued a royal crown by the pope. Their union was sealed by ties of marriage (c. 1251, 1254), and Daniil's son Roman ruled for several years in Novgorodok, which had been Mindovg's base. But when relations between Daniil and the Mongols became hostile (1256–60), Mindovg abandoned him and arrested Roman. Daniil, reversing his position, joined the Mongols in a campaign against Lithuania; nevertheless, the Mongols also ordered Daniil to destroy his fortifications. Leaving his brother to carry out the Mongol order, Daniil once again fled to Poland and Hungary.

The southwestern Rus' principalities of Galicia and Volynia continued to be entangled with Lithuania as well as Hungary and Poland after Daniil's death in 1264. But it was not uncommon in the 1270s for the Tatars to assist Daniil's heirs in their campaigns against their western neighbors. When Nogai and Tele-Buga conducted their campaigns in Hungary in 1286 and 1287, troops from Galicia and Volynia joined them. By that time, however, the unity and power of the two principalities were declining. Tatar troops passing through and wintering in Galicia and Volynia during those campaigns destroyed agricultural fields and looted the region. Unable to protect their lands, the Rus' princes lost credibility and authority, and Mongol officials became more directly involved in the southwestern principalities, especially during the height of Nogai's power, than they did in the northeast.

Not long afterward, however, as the Sarai khans consolidated their authority after Nogai's death, their grip on the western principalities relaxed. By the end of the thirteenth century, Daniil's son Lev (d. 1301) and grandson Iurii (d. 1308) were temporarily able to recombine the Volynian and Galician lands. But it was Poland and the rapidly expanding state of Lithuania that ultimately not only replaced the Riurikid princes, but competed effectively and successfully with the Mongols for control over the region. Poland absorbed Galicia by 1349; Lithuania gradually acquired the remainder of the southwestern lands, including Kiev. The divergence of the southwestern from the northeastern Rus' principalities that had become apparent before the Mongol invasion was thus intensified; the two sectors that had previously formed Kievan Rus' split apart.

ECONOMIC RECOVERY

The Riurikid princes were also deeply concerned with and involved in the economic recovery of their lands. Although there is some dispute over the scale of devastation caused by the Mongol invasion, there is little question that the towns and regions that were in the direct path of the Mongol armies suffered extreme social and economic disruption. The demands from their new suzerains to pay tribute and provide military and artisan conscripts both compounded the strains on Rus' society and pressured their rulers to foster and develop their remaining resources.

Recovery was a slow process. John Fennell has argued that the very ability of Prince Alexander Nevsky to mount campaigns to defend the Novgorod lands should be regarded either as an indicator that the damage to the Rus' lands was not as great as is often concluded or that they recovered very rapidly.[1] That activity, however, may well be a reflection of the segmented nature of the defensive system established by the Riurikid princes during the Kievan era and perpetuated after the Mongol invasion as much as a sign of continued military robustness and vigor. In any case, other indicators suggest that economically and socially the Rus' lands, including those undamaged physically, were under severe stress for decades following the invasion.

In his study on the construction of masonry monuments in the northern Russian principalities, David Miller has shown that in the quarter century following the invasion only one small masonry church was built near Vladimir. Even in Novgorod, which had not been initially harmed by the Mongol armies, construction of such buildings was

---

[1] Fennell, *Crisis of Medieval Russia*, p. 89.

suspended for over a quarter of a century, and then only two projects were undertaken between 1263 and 1287. It was not until a full half century had passed that Suzdalia and Novgorod had economically recovered sufficiently to accumulate funds and labor to build churches, fortresses, and other major masonry structures.

In southwestern Rus' the situation was not immediately so grim. Prince Daniil of Galicia and Volynia was able to construct the new fortifications that the Mongols shortly afterward obliged him to dismantle. Daniil also founded new towns and encouraged commerce. He moved his capital city to Kholm, located northeast of Vladimir in Volynia, and developed that town into a vital cultural center. But the prosperity of southwestern Rus' was curbed when the Mongols, after conducting their campaign against Lithuania with the aid of Prince Daniil, returned to Volynia (1259–60); it was at this time that Prince Daniil left for Hungary and Poland, leaving his brother to fulfill the Mongol order to dismantle their recently built fortifications. The consequences of the renewed Mongol incursions of the 1280s further disrupted the economy and compounded the difficulties associated with the political fragmentation that had begun after Daniil's death (1264).

In the northern principalities the princes devoted themselves to economic recovery almost immediately after the Mongol invasion. Prince Iaroslav Vsevolodich, who as noted became prince of Vladimir upon the death of his brother Iurii at the battle on the Sit' River, tried to rebuild Vladimir and encourage its inhabitants to return to that city. Subsequent Mongol raids, however, provoked additional flight, and Vladimir never fully recovered its former glory. But other princes were more successful. Flight from the former capital and other similarly devastated cities resulted in an influx of population in more protected settlements, notably Moscow and Tver', and stimulated their growth.

The commercial center of Novgorod was central to the recovery of the Rus' lands. Its trade with the Scandinavian and German merchants of the Baltic provided a critical means of acquiring profits and wealth, not only for the Novgorodians directly engaged in trade, but for the princes who ruled Novgorod and those who controlled the supplies of goods it exported abroad. During the late thirteenth and into the fourteenth centuries, Novgorod's foreign trade focused increasingly on German merchants who arrived regularly, twice a year, from Riga, Revel', Dorpat, and Lübeck. They conducted their trade activities at Peterhof, the commercial enclave they had established in Novgorod at the end of the twelfth century. By the fourteenth century Peterhof exceeded the importance of the older Scandinavian commercial court in Novgorod, St. Olaf. Novgorod merchants brought batches of fur pelts and blocks of wax to Peterhof. German merchants affiliated with the Hanseatic League and trade representatives of the Teutonic Order purchased those goods with a variety of their own: fine Flemish woolen cloth, beer and wine, salt and herring, metal products and tools. The most important item they brought to Novgorod, however, was silver.

The Golden Horde benefited from and encouraged Novgorod's trade, as did the Rus' princes. Grand Prince Iaroslav Iaroslavich, who succeeded Alexander Nevsky, also removed Alexander's son Dmitry to become prince of Novgorod. Despite some conflict between Iaroslav and the city, the prince became actively involved in Novgorod's trade. His policies were influenced by those of Mengu-Timur, whose reign as khan at Sarai (1266/67–81) overlapped with Iaroslav's reign as grand prince (1263–71/72).

Mengu-Timur encouraged the commercial development of the Golden Horde. He authorized the Genoese to found a trading colony at Caffa on the Black Sea coast and thereby forged the link between the Great Silk Road from China through Sarai to the Black Sea and the Mediterranean. Following Mengu-Timur's example and directives, Iaroslav, even as he was repulsing a German military advance on Novgorodian territory in 1269, joined local Novgorodian officials to negotiate treaties with Gotland, Lübeck, Riga, and other German towns. The treaties, concluded in 1269, established the rules that governed visits of foreign merchants to Novgorod.

Novgorod's ability to conduct its trade depended upon its ability to acquire supplies of fur pelts and wax. The luxury pelts in demand in the thirteenth and first part of the fourteenth century came from the distant northeastern sectors of the Novgorodian lands. They had to be transported along lengthy trade routes that followed the Vychegda, North Dvina, and Sukhona Rivers. Safe passage on these internal trade routes was critical to the success of Novgorod's foreign commerce.

Towns along those routes were economically revitalized as a result of Novgorod's trade; they also gained political importance. Ustiug is a prime example. It was located on the northern outskirts of the Rostov principality near the mouth of the Iug River. That position was commercially strategic. The Iug River flowed into the Sukhona, which joined the Vychegda not far downstream to form the North Dvina River. From Ustiug it was possible to control traffic along all three rivers. Thus, despite its remote location, Ustiug's domination of the rivers connecting Novgorod with its fur hinterlands gave it both economic and political value. While construction of new buildings and the economic health it symbolized still languished in many other regions, Ustiug by 1290 could boast an elaborate new Church of the Assumption. The church's completion was celebrated with the arrival of the bishop of Rostov, a dignitary who brought expensive gifts from the princes of Rostov and consecrated the church.

Other towns gradually became involved in commerce. There was demand for Rus' products not only in northwestern Europe, but also in Sarai. Having become accustomed to northern luxury goods, such as sable and ermine pelts that had been part of early tribute payments, Mongol khans, beys, and other notables continued to encourage Rus' princes to bring offerings of such goods as well as European products in the form of gifts and bribes. Similar items were brought as commercial items to the Sarai market, where they were exchanged for salt and oriental goods. The Russian goods were transported from the far north through Ustiug to Rostov, Tver' and later Moscow for shipment to the Volga. They were then carried down the river to Sarai. From there they were frequently reexported as diplomatic gifts and commercial commodities along the Mongol caravan routes, westward to Egypt or through Italian colonies on the Crimean coast to southern Europe as well as eastward to India and China. Demand for Russian goods emanating from both the khan's court and the commercial marketplace at Sarai served as a stimulant for Russian recovery.

It was on the basis of improving commercial conditions, prompted by both European and Mongol demand for Russian luxury goods, that the more visible signs of recovery became evident by the last quarter of the thirteenth century. Those signs appeared earliest precisely in towns most closely associated with the reviving trade. The construction at Ustiug has been noted. Novgorod was also able in this period to accrue enough wealth to build a costly fort at Kopor'e in 1280 and the Church of St. Nicholas at Lipna, a masonry structure, in the city of Novgorod in 1292. David Miller has demonstrated that the number of masonry structures erected in Novgorod during the next century and a half far exceeded that built in any other northern Russian town.[2] The products of this sustained burst of construction activity expressed the commercial vitality and wealth of the city as well as a unique style in church architecture, distinguished by the buildings' small size, square shape, single domes, trefoil roof lines, limestone slab construction, and singular grace.

Tver', located on the upper Volga, was among the first of the northeastern Rus' towns to demonstrate an economic resurgence. In Tver', Prince Iaroslav Iaroslavich's primary seat, construction work on the Church of the Transfiguration was resumed in the late thirteenth century.

---

[2] Miller, "Monumental Building as an Indicator of Economic Trends in Northern Rus'," pp. 369, 373, 383–385.

In other northeastern towns of Suzdalia monument building was once again underway by the 1320s.

INTRADYNASTIC COMPETITION AND THE GOLDEN HORDE

Following the Mongol invasions the Riurikid princes, with the few noted exceptions, accommodated themselves to the presence of the Golden Horde. But even as they oriented themselves toward Sarai, they also continued to fulfill their traditional functions. They sought to protect their principalities from other invaders and to revitalize the lands devastated by the Mongol onslaught.

The Riurikid princes also continued to engage in their intradynastic rivalries. After 1238, the city of Vladimir itself lost population, wealth, and dominance. But among the northeastern princes the position of grand prince of Vladimir remained a coveted prize. In their quest for that position the Riurikids exploited the presence of the Golden Horde. Individual princes attempted to secure support from powerful Tatars and to use their influence and even military might to achieve recognition as the senior prince within the dynasty and attain the title grand prince of Vladimir.

Initially, the khans of the Golden Horde did not radically alter the political framework of the Rus' lands. The Riurikid dynasty remained in power, and during the second half of the thirteenth century dynastic tradition continued to determine seniority. But the princes' trips to the Horde to receive their patents were not simply symbolic gestures. Succession to the grand princely throne as well as to patrimonial appanage seats depended upon approval by the khans. Until the early fourteenth century, however, the Tatars tended to confirm the candidate generated by Riurikid principles of succession. But then Mongol authority superseded tradition. With the Golden Horde khans supporting them, the princes of Moscow were able to become the grand princes of Vladimir.

Because the Riurikid princes' authority required and was also reinforced by patents from the khans, the latter were in a position to adjudicate the succession disputes that arose among the Riurikid princes. When disagreements arose during the Kievan era, they were commonly resolved by intradynastic warfare. After the Golden Horde had been formed, the Russian princes appealed to a higher authority, the Mongol khan, to settle their disputes. The Mongols functioned in this capacity when they confirmed Prince Andrei, who had overthrown his uncle Sviatoslav, as prince of Vladimir. They did so again when they removed Andrei in favor of Alexander Nevsky. By the time of that decision there was little conflict between dynastic tradition and Mongol authority. After the death of Sviatoslav, the rightful though dispossessed prince, the confirmation of Nevsky, the legitimate heir, by the Mongols amounted to a restoration of the traditional patterns of succession.

The Mongol khan resolved another succession dispute after Alexander Nevsky died. Alexander's brothers Andrei and Iaroslav, the prince of Tver', vied for the post of grand prince of Vladimir. Khan Berke, bypassing the unreliable Andrei, issued the patent to Iaroslav, who reigned until his death during the winter of 1271–72. Iaroslav's reign was then followed, in accordance with the traditional pattern, by that of his younger brother Vasily, prince of Kostroma (1272–77).

Both Iaroslav and Vasily, like their brother Alexander Nevsky, fully accepted the khan as their suzerain. In return, they were able to employ Tatar forces in pursuit of their own military and political objectives. In 1269, according to the Novgorod chronicler, the grand *baskak* of Vladimir, Amragan, accompanied the Rus' princes and regiments in an expedition against Revel' (in Estonia). In 1275, Tatars and Rus' cooperated in an unsuccessful campaign against Lithuania. Similarly, in 1272, Grand Prince Vasily became embroiled with his nephew Dmitry Aleksandrovich in a dispute over Novgorod, whose wealth, highly valued by the Horde, was becoming a critical factor in a grand prince's ability to retain the Horde's favor. Vasily had Tatar troops at his disposal when he pressed his claim to the city's throne. As a result, Dmitry ceded Novgorod to his uncle in 1273, and regained it only when he became grand prince of Vladimir in 1277.

That succession also followed traditional patterns. Upon the death of Vasily, the last member of his generation, the position of grand prince passed to the next generation. According to dynastic guidelines, Dmitry, Alexander Nevsky's eldest surviving son, was the rightful heir, and he indeed inherited the throne.

The Rus' princes were not passive in the succession process. On the contrary, while recognizing Tatar authority over the succession, they actively sought Tatar favor. Following the example of Alexander Nevsky, some, including his brothers and the Rostov princes, were able to enhance their own positions within the Rus' lands by faithfully and exactingly carrying out the Sarai khan's demands. As they established close ties with influential members of the Golden Horde, some Rus' princes also learned to manipulate internal Horde politics to their own advantage. Other Rus' princes, however, did not always simply cooperate with their Mongol suzerain, but exploited Mongol politics to pursue their own political ambitions.

An opportunity to do so presented itself in the last quarter of the century, when during the reigns of khans Tuda-Mengu and his successors

Telebuga and Tokhta, the horde was politically divided. Competing Russian princes took advantage of the situation to gain political and military support from opposing Mongol leaders in return for their pledges of allegiance and tribute. The Russian princes were thus able, as in the pre-Mongol era, to pursue their own rivalries with military might borrowed from their nomadic neighbors of the steppe.

The figure who divided the Golden Horde was Nogai. Leader of the Mangkyt clan and himself a descendant of Juchi, Nogai emerged during the reign of Mengu-Timur (1266/67–81) as a powerful military commander with virtually autonomous control over the western territories of the Golden Horde, i.e., the lands west of the Dnieper reaching to the lower Danube. Nogai's influence was such that he engaged in direct interaction with Byzantium, Egypt, and Hungary and conducted military expeditions as far west as Serbia, Transylvania, and Hungary. When Tuda-Mengu succeeded his brother Mengu-Timur, Nogai's power as clan leader, Horde elder, and military commander was so great that he has been characterized both as a "virtual co-ruler" with the khan and as an independent ruler.[3] Nogai continued to play a powerful role when Tuda-Mengu, having personally converted to Islam (1283), delegated much of his authority and responsibility to his nephew Telebuga.

Horde politics became complicated after Tuda-Mengu actually abdicated in favor of Telebuga (1287). Telebuga had a strong rival in the person of Mengu-Timur's son, Tokhta. But personal political rivalries were exacerbated by consequences of conflicts elsewhere in the Mongol Empire. Telebuga failed in his military campaigns against the Ilkhans to gain control of Azerbaijan (1288, 1290). And, even further away, conflicts between the Chagatai branch of the empire and Kubilai Khan disrupted the empire's trade routes, on which the Golden Horde relied. Under these stressful conditions Tokhta's supporters grew stronger, and Telebuga prepared to arrest their leader. Tokhta fled to Nogai, who gave him sanctuary, cooperated with him in the murder of Telebuga (1291), and then helped him secure the throne at Sarai. Tokhta, however, soon turned against his patron. After one unsuccessful campaign against him (1293 or 1294), Tokhta launched another in 1299. Nogai was killed during that encounter. The tribes that had made up Nogai's Horde reassimilated into Tokhta's; the Golden Horde was reunited.

The political discord within the Horde began shortly after Dmitry Aleksandrovich had succeeded to the grand principality of Vladimir

---

[3] The former characterization was made, for example, by Fennell, *Crisis of Medieval Russia*, p. 145, and Vernadsky, *The Mongols and Russia*, p. 174. The latter was offered by Nasonov, *Mongoly i Rus'*, p. 69.

(1277). As the Horde divided, his political rivals were able to take advantage of the situation. Each side in the ensuing Russian conflict was able to gain Tatar support by appealing to one of the competing camps within the Horde.

From the beginning of his reign Dmitry demonstrated more independence from Sarai than his uncles had. It is not clear that he ever actually received a patent from Mengu-Timur. He did not join his brother Andrei, prince of Kostroma and Gorodets, and the Rostov princes, who went to the Horde in 1277 to participate in the Golden Horde's campaign in the North Caucasus. And in 1281, when Tuda-Mengu became khan and the other Rus' princes presented themselves to him to renew their patents, Dmitry was diverted to Novgorod and failed to appear at Sarai.

Tuda-Mengu promptly transferred the Vladimir throne to the next eligible member of the dynasty, Andrei. The new grand prince, supported by Tatar troops supplemented by those of the Rostov clan and Prince Fedor of Iaroslavl', conducted what has been described as a devastating campaign in northeastern Rus', including the districts of Vladimir, Suzdal', Pereiaslavl' and even some territories belonging to the Rostov princes themselves.

Dmitry fled. But he quickly received support from Nogai, who issued his own patent to Dmitry. Nogai also sent his forces back to Rus' and ousted Andrei from both Vladimir and Novgorod, which had in the meantime also accepted Andrei as its prince. In return Dmitry pledged his allegiance and, evidently, the tribute payments from his domain to Nogai. The episode illustrates how the Rus' princes took advantage of the divisions within the Horde to pursue their own rivalries. Andrei and the Rostov princes, including Prince Fedor of Iaroslavl', remained closely associated with the Sarai khan. Dmitry, evidently supported by Metropolitan Kirill, successfully withstood the challenge from his brother Andrei and Tuda-Mengu by obtaining support from the khan's rival, Nogai.

The situation remained relatively stable with Dmitry on the throne until Tokhta assumed the Sarai throne in 1291. By that time the divisions among the Rus' princes were more pronounced. Princes Mikhail Iaroslavich of Tver' and Daniil of Moscow demonstrated their loyalty to Dmitry by refraining from going to Sarai for a renewal of their patents. Andrei and the Rostov princes, of course, sought Tokhta's confirmation. At about the same time that Tokhta made his first attempt to curb Nogai's power (c. 1293), he also sent an army to the Rus' lands to assist Andrei and Prince Fedor in the removal of Dmitry from Vladimir. The cities of Vladimir, Moscow, and Tver' were all attacked, and the countryside ravaged. Dmitry once again fled, but the conflict over the throne of

Vladimir was resolved only with his death in 1294. Andrei then became the undisputed grand prince of Vladimir.

But in contrast to the Horde, which reunified under Tokhta, the Riurikids of northeastern Rus' remained divided. Although Andrei enjoyed both dynastic legitimacy and Tokhta's support and his position as grand prince was secure, he faced repeated challenges from a coalition made up of Mikhail of Tver', Daniil of Moscow, and Dmitry's son Ivan, who retained the principality of Pereiaslavl' Zalesskii, which his father had also ruled. Possession of the principality of Pereiaslavl' Zalesskii became one of the prime sources of conflict between the two factions.

The point of contention was whether Pereiaslavl' Zalesskii should be regarded as a separate appanage principality, to be inherited within a distinct branch of the dynasty, or as an appendage of the grand principality, to be ruled by the grand prince of Vladimir. Andrei, claiming it for the grand principality, attempted to extend his authority there. It was this event that prompted the 1296 assembly of Rus' princes, attended by Nevrui, the Mongol plenipotentiary sent by Khan Tokhta, and the bishop of Sarai. At the meeting called to consider the issue the factions within the dynasty were clearly discernable. Fedor of Iaroslavl' and Prince Konstantin of Rostov supported Andrei. Princes Mikhail of Tver' and Daniil of Moscow, who were joined by the "men" or boyars of Pereiaslavl' Zalesskii, opposed him. The princes' decision was to leave Pereiaslavl' Zalesskii under the rule of Ivan Dmitr'evich. When Andrei nevertheless tried to seize it later that year and again in 1298, the forces of Tver' and Moscow repeatedly blocked him.

Moscow emerged as the most diligent protector of Pereiaslavl' Zalesskii. At a second princely conference, held in 1300, Daniil was again instrumental in preventing its transfer to Andrei. But the grand prince persisted. When Ivan Dmitr'evich died two years later, he sent his officers to Pereiaslavl' Zalesskii while appealing to Tokhta for a patent. Once more Daniil intervened. His forces quickly ejected Andrei's agents, occupied the city, and physically prevented the grand prince from taking control of it. Finally, in 1303, when Daniil died, Pereiaslavl' Zalesskii gave its throne to his son, Iurii. Andrei again appealed to Tokhta, and again a princely assembly was convened under the watchful eye of Tokhta's emissary. But that body too denied Pereiaslavl' Zalesskii to Andrei. The principality remained in the hands of Iurii Daniilovich, a possession of the Moscow branch of the dynasty. Only several decades later, when Iurii's brother Ivan I Kalita died, was Pereiaslavl' Zalesskii once again considered a component of the grand principality.

The dispute between Alexander Nevsky's two sons, Princes Dmitry and Andrei, reveals another change that was beginning to take place in the

Russian political arena. Before their conflict Mongol hegemony had scarcely interfered with the norms of dynastic succession. But Andrei, who saw an opportunity to take advantage of his elder brother's poor relations with Sarai and hasten his own succession, sought to employ Mongol might to upset those norms. His bid for the grand princely throne was illegitimate in the terms of dynastic tradition and was, accordingly, opposed by a significant portion of the Riurikid princes. And neither of his patrons, Khan Tuda-Mengu or Khan Tokhta, was either powerful or determined enough to overcome that opposition and establish a new basis of legitimacy, derived exclusively from the authority and favor of the khan, at least as long as Dmitry and his allies had the support of Nogai. Andrei was successful only after Dmitry's death in 1294, when he not only had the khan's support, but the dynasty's acceptance.

Andrei and his Mongol mentors failed to remove unambiguously the rightful heir; the khan, certainly under circumstances of dual power within the Horde, was not prepared to overrule dynastic tradition as the basis for the grand prince's legitimacy. But the challenge to traditional dynastic principles, implicit in Andrei's quest for the throne, did not disappear. On the contrary, it manifested itself even more forcefully during the first quarter of the fourteenth century, when a new rivalry for the grand princely throne developed between the princes of Tver' and Moscow. As their conflict reached its conclusion, legitimacy based on the Riurikid custom of generational rotation was discarded in favor of legitimacy based on the might and decree of the Chingisid khan. The Muscovite princes, beneficiaries of this change, were established as the grand princes of Vladimir. Through them the Golden Horde consolidated its authority over the lands of Rus' even more firmly.

THE RIVALRY BETWEEN MOSCOW AND TVER´ (1304–1327)

Andrei died in 1304. At that time a dispute arose between Mikhail of Tver' and Iurii Daniilovich of Moscow and now Pereiaslavl' Zalesskii over the position of grand prince of Vladimir. Tokhta granted the patent to Mikhail, a decision that was once again consistent with Riurikid traditions. Mikhail was Andrei's younger cousin, a member of his generation; both were grandsons of Iaroslav Vsevolodich. Iurii, on the other hand, represented the next generation. Furthermore, his father Daniil, who had died in 1303, had never been grand prince of Vladimir. Iurii was the prince of Pereiaslavl' Zalesskii, namesake of the southern Pereiaslavl' that had been the seat of the designated heir of the grand principality. But according to Riurikid practices and traditions, he had no legitimate claim to the Vladimir throne.

The conflict for the throne that ensued between the Tver' and Moscow lines thus took on a new dimension. It not only reflects Mongol influence in the succession process. Its outcome represents a deviation from the long-standing rules guiding succession and defining eligible princes. According to all the traditional rules, the Moscow line was ineligible. But new factors were becoming more important than the old traditions. The presence of the Mongols gave each prince who sought the dominant position within the Rus' lands opportunities to gain the Horde's support. As *baskaki* were replaced by special envoys, responsibility for maintaining order and, perhaps even more importantly, for collecting and delivering tribute fell increasingly to the Rus' princes. The prince who could best perform those tasks won the favor of the khan. During the course of the Moscow–Tver' rivalry in the early decades of the fourteenth century succession to the grand princely throne came to depend not on the dynasty's customs, but on the khan's approval. His choice was determined in large part by demonstrations of reliable service to him. Eventually the Moscow princes convinced the khans that they could perform those services better than their rivals.

The contest between Tver' and Moscow was played out over several decades and included dramatic episodes of court intrigue, highway robbery, murder, and war. The highlights of the political contest may be summarized in the following manner. When Mikhail of Tver' received the patent for the grand principality of Vladimir from Khan Tokhta, he faced stubborn opposition from his nephew Iurii of Moscow, against whom he waged two military campaigns (1305, 1308) to force compliance. When Tokhta died and Uzbek became khan in 1313, Mikhail returned to the Horde and remained at Uzbek's court for two years. Iurii took advantage of the opportunity to enhance his political power, particularly in Novgorod. When he learned of Iurii's activities, Mikhail convinced Uzbek to send military forces back to Russia with him so that he could reestablish his authority; Iurii was ordered to appear before Uzbek. But while Mikhail was recovering control over Novgorod (1316), Iurii was ingratiating himself with Uzbek. The prince of Moscow married the khan's sister, and returned to Russia with his wife, Uzbek's special envoys, an army, and the patent to rule the grand principality of Vladimir.

In 1317 Iurii, commanding a grand army drawn from all the northeast Rus' principalities and supported by the Tatar contingent led by the Mongol general Kavgadii, advanced against Mikhail. But the Tver' forces won the battle; the Tatar detachment evidently did not fully participate. While Iurii retreated to Novgorod, Mikhail captured both Kavgadii and his rival's wife, the sister of the khan, who died while in his custody.

There are different versions of what happened next. Essentially, Kavgadii, although treated with respect and released by Mikhail, returned to the Horde and accused Mikhail of three crimes: he had fought against the khan's envoy and thus had defied Uzbek's authority; he had withheld tribute; and he was responsible for the death of Uzbek's sister. Iurii too arrived at the Horde with an array of princes and notables from the Suzdalian and Novgorodian lands. Although they may well have gathered to accompany Uzbek on a campaign against the Ilkhans for control over Derbent, Iurii's ability to assemble such a force confirmed his value to the khan and did not help Mikhail's cause. When Mikhail finally arrived at Uzbek's court, he was tried for the named offenses, found guilty, and executed on November 22, 1318. Iurii, both benefitting from and depending on Uzbek's favor, remained grand prince of Vladimir for the next four years.

If Uzbek had expected that by appointing Iurii to be grand prince of Vladimir he would have a reliable agent who could effectively maintain order in the Rus' lands while overseeing the collection and delivery of tribute and troops to the Horde, he was probably disappointed. Iurii evidently encountered lingering resistance to his rule and had some difficulty collecting the tribute due the Horde. While Iurii spent a great deal of his time in Novgorod, Uzbek found it necessary to send four expeditionary forces to the northeastern Russian lands in just the last two years of Iurii's reign (1320–22). Although reported to have been excessively destructive, the Mongol forces were intended to maintain Uzbek's grand prince, keep order, and collect taxes.

Iurii's ineffective performance presented Prince Dmitry of Tver', son of the late Mikhail, with an opportunity to capture the grand princely throne. In 1322, while Iurii was in Novgorod, Dmitry made a journey to the Horde and received the patent for Vladimir from Uzbek. Iurii, taking with him a treasure he had evidently accumulated while in Novgorod, embarked on his own trip to the Horde. But he was waylaid by Dmitry's brother, Aleksandr Mikhailovich, who stole Iurii's treasury. With nothing to offer Uzbek, Iurii fled to Pskov and again took refuge in Novgorod.

In 1325, Iurii finally completed his journey to the Horde. There Prince Dmitry murdered him. The Mongol khan Uzbek, finding this crime uncivilized and intolerable, promptly arrested Dmitry and executed him the following year. He named Dmitry's brother, Aleksandr Mikhailovich, the new grand prince of Vladimir.

The next and final dramatic episode in this saga occurred in 1327. At that time the inhabitants of Tver' staged an uprising against the Mongol Chol-khan, who headed a Tatar force sent by Uzbek to that city. Uzbek's purpose and Chol-khan's mission are unclear. While some scholars argue that Chol-khan had been sent deliberately to provoke a crisis in Tver' because the Mongol court perceived that principality as too powerful, Charles Halperin has suggested quite plausibly that his purpose was to oversee conscription and collection of revenue, which the Horde required in preparation for another campaign against the Ilkhans of Persia over Azerbaijan.[4] Whatever the intention, Chol-khan's methods infuriated the Tverites, who massacred the Tatars.

This time it was the prince of Moscow, Iurii's brother Ivan Daniilovich, who was able to take advantage of Aleksandr's difficulties in fulfilling his obligations to the Horde. Ivan presented himself to Uzbek and returned with a Tatar force. Joined by Prince Aleksandr Vasil'evich of Suzdal', Ivan and the Tatars marched against Tver', sacked the city as well as other towns in the principality, and forced Aleksandr and his brothers to flee. Aleksandr found refuge in Pskov in 1327, but when Metropolitan Feognost (Theognostus) excommunicated the entire populace of the city for allowing him to remain among them, he went to Lithuania (1329). In 1331 however, he returned to Pskov, which he ruled until 1337. He then made a trip to the Horde and was restored to the throne of Tver'. Two years later Aleksandr and his son were recalled to the Horde and executed.

The sack of Tver' and Aleksandr's flight marked an end to this phase of the Tver' princes' participation in the competition for the grand principality of Vladimir. Only once more, in the 1370s, would a Tver' prince attempt, unsuccessfully, to acquire the title. That episode will be discussed in the next chapter.

The grand principality was given to Ivan of Moscow, known as Ivan I Kalita. Although many chronicles indicate he received the patent in 1328, it is more probable that he shared power with Prince Aleksandr of Suzdal', who officially held the title of grand prince of Vladimir, and that Ivan became grand prince only upon Aleksandr's death in 1331. Neither Aleksandr of Suzdal' nor Ivan Daniilovich of Moscow had any claim to the grand princely throne, according to the traditional dynastic rules of succession. By the time the Tver' princes had been eliminated from the competition in 1327, succession to the grand principality depended strictly upon the favor and authority of the Golden Horde. Beginning with Ivan Kalita the position remained in the hands of the Daniilovichi, the princes of Moscow.

---

[4] For an expression of the former view, see J. L. I. Fennell, *The Emergence of Moscow, 1304–1359* (Berkeley and Los Angeles: University of California Press, 1968), pp. 108–109; for the latter, see Halperin, *Russia and the Golden Horde*, p. 54, or *The Tatar Yoke* (Columbus, Ohio: Slavica, 1986), p. 88, by the same author.

THE RISE OF MOSCOW (1327–1359)

Both the principality and the city of Moscow were relatively small in the early fourteenth century. With its wooden fortress or kremlin surrounded by earthen ramparts, artisan quarters, and agricultural settlements, the city of Moscow had a modest rustic character. It hardly appeared as a likely successor to the opulent Kiev or the mighty Vladimir, much less the obvious victor in a competition with Tver', which in 1317 had demonstrated its superiority over the combined strength of the other Russian principalities.

But the Muscovite princes acquired several advantages over their rivals. Scholars have pointed to a variety of factors, ranging from the location of Moscow to the personal characters of its rulers, to account for their success. Some also credit Moscow's improved political fortunes to a manipulative policy adopted by the Golden Horde to bolster Moscow, a relatively weak principality, as a counterweight to Tver', which had been demonstrating its mounting power; the policy, they surmise, aimed at keeping all the Rus' principalities divided and docile. To understand how Moscow became the dominant center in northeastern Rus' during the second quarter of the fourteenth century, however, it is essential to appreciate two basic factors.

The first concerns the domestic situation of the Daniilovichi. Quite simply, the Daniilovichi were illegitimate rulers in terms of dynastic traditions. The second factor concerns the role of the Golden Horde. Because the Daniilovichi lacked dynastic legitimacy, they depended heavily on the Mongol khan as the sole source of their authority. These two factors determined and explain the policies of Ivan I Kalita (1331–41) and his sons and successors, Semen (1341–53) and Ivan II (1353–59). Those policies included submission to the Golden Horde and the assertion of dominance over Novgorod. They also focused on fostering new domestic sources of support, on fashioning new bases of legitimacy.

Dynastic illegitimacy

Each of these policies had its roots in the issue of legitimacy. The remainder of the dynasty did not easily accept the Daniilovichi. Both Iurii and Ivan had become grand prince because Khan Uzbek had selected them, and he had done so when unusual circumstances had limited his alternatives. The trial and execution of the legitimate prince Mikhail of Tver' had paved the way for Iurii to become grand prince. After Iurii's death, however, Uzbek hesitated for years before returning the grand principality to the Daniilovichi. The Horde finally supported Ivan

Daniilovich. But the dynasty's reluctance to accept the Daniilovichi as legitimate heirs would continue to plague them and influence their policies.

Details concerning Ivan's opponents or the manner in which they expressed their dissent are scant. It appears, however, that after 1337, when Aleksandr Mikhailovich was allowed to return to Tver' from Pskov, a coalition that regarded him as the proper member of the dynasty to be grand prince formed around him. The coalition included the princes of Beloozero and Iaroslavl'. As members of the Rostov clan, they had been eliminated from the succession cycle. Their ancestor, Prince Konstantin Vsevolodich, it will be recalled, had died before rotating into the post of grand prince of Vladimir. Despite their close relations with the khans of the Golden Horde, the Rostov princes had accepted a secondary political role within the lands of Rus'. They were, therefore, perhaps among the most offended when the Daniilovichi ignored the very principle that they had honored and which had disqualified them. They were perhaps among the most outraged when, unlike Prince Fedor of Iaroslavl' who had married Khan Mengu-Timur's daughter, Iurii Daniilovich took advantage of his marriage to Uzbek's sister and then manipulated the khan and his court notables with gifts and bribes to gain the grand princely throne.

The Rostov princes also had more concrete grounds for resentment against Ivan Daniilovich. In 1322, that prince had accompanied the khan's envoy, Akhmyl, whose forces had ravaged Iaroslavl' and Rostov territories. Only five years later, when Ivan led the expedition to punish Tver' for its uprising in 1327, his armies again devastated the lands of Rostov. As a result of that incident, according to the fifteenth-century vita of St. Sergei (Sergius) of Radonezh, many inhabitants of the Rostov area lost their property and means of livelihood and were forced to migrate.

Whatever the princes' reasons for supporting Aleksandr, when Khan Uzbek summoned the prince of Tver' to the Horde in 1339, he also ordered his allies, the princes of Beloozero and Iaroslavl', to present themselves. By the end of this visit, Aleksandr had been executed. The fate of the prince of Beloozero was not recorded. The prince of Iaroslavl' persisted in his opposition to the Daniilovichi.

In 1341, he joined forces with the two Princes Konstantin, of Tver' and of Suzdal', to appeal to the khan against the succession of Ivan's son, Semen. The chronicles, referring evasively to a quarrel over the grand principality, do not elaborate on the cause of the dispute. But a review of a dynastic chart suggests their case was founded, once again, in the traditional rules of succession. Konstantin Mikhailovich of Tver' was the son of one grand prince and brother of two others. He was a member of

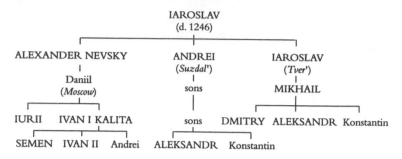

Table 6.2 The Daniilovichi and their dynastic rivals (to 1359)

the same generation as Ivan Kalita. According to the principles of generational rotation, he was not only eligible for the throne, but was the rightful heir. Semen, in contrast, represented the next generation. His right to inherit the throne was furthermore clouded by the fact that although his father had been grand prince, his grandfather Daniil had not. Certainly, his assumption of the throne before Konstantin Mikhailovich violated the traditional dynastic principles of succession.

Semen's other opponent, Prince Konstantin of Suzdal', also had a vague claim to the throne. He was the brother of Prince Aleksandr of Suzdal', who had been selected by Khan Uzbek to be grand prince of Vladimir in 1328, three years before Ivan Kalita acquired that position. Although a member of the same generation as Semen, he could make a case that due to the fact that his brother's reign as grand prince had preceded Ivan Kalita's, he had seniority over Semen. Their arguments did not impress the new khan Janibek, who issued the patent to Semen Ivanovich of Moscow.

The dynasty accepted the khan's ruling, but not Daniilovich legitimacy. In 1353, Grand Prince Semen, his two sons, and his brother Andrei all died of the plague, known as the Black Death. Semen's other brother, Ivan, was the only surviving member of the Daniilovich clan. He received the patent from Sarai, but only over renewed objections from Novgorod and from Prince Konstantin of Suzdal' and Nizhnii Novgorod; the latter principality had merged with Suzdal' in 1341 with approval of Khan Janibek and had grown in strength and wealth over the preceding decade.

Their lack of dynastic legitimacy forced the Daniilovichi to depend exclusively on the khan's favor to hold the position as grand prince. As a result, they served the Horde faithfully. Prince Iurii Daniilovich's not entirely successful efforts to serve Khan Uzbek have been noted. His brother Ivan also maintained a submissive posture. He visited the Horde frequently. Beginning with the trip in 1331–32, when he received the patent for the grand principality, he made four or five trips before his death in 1341. If A. N. Nasonov's estimate that each journey involved at least six months is correct, then he spent a substantial portion of his reign engaged in paying his respects and tribute to the khan and, perhaps, receiving counsel and instructions from Horde officials.[5] Representatives from the Horde were also in evidence at Ivan's court.

Grand Prince Semen continued the practice. Ivan II made trips to the Horde less frequently. In 1357, possibly in reaction to his laxity, the khan sent a "powerful envoy" to him. The embassy caused sufficient stress and suffering in northeastern Rus' that when a new khan Berdibek assumed power at Sarai later that year, Ivan did not delay his journey to pay homage and receive a patent to rule.

Novgorod

More important than any other gesture of obeisance, however, was the delivery of tribute and the offer of valuable gifts to the khan, his relatives, and his beys. For a prince to make these payments consistently it was essential to control Novgorod, the foremost commercial center in the lands of Rus'. Drawing upon resources from its own northern empire as well as from the other lands of Rus', its merchants sold their furs and wax to German merchants for a variety of goods, including fine linen cloth and silver. The latter commodity was most important politically. By the fourteenth century, as the khans transferred responsibility for tribute collection from their own *baskaki* to the Rus' princes, they also demanded that the Russians pay their tribute in silver. Novgorod was the main avenue by which the precious metal entered Russia.

To ensure the flow of silver into Russia, it thus became incumbent upon the grand princes of Vladimir to foster Novgorod's commerce, to protect both its supplies and its interests vis-à-vis its trading partners, and to control the city. Prince Iaroslav Vsevolodich's appointment of his son Alexander Nevsky to Novgorod even as he assumed the grand princely throne in the crisis of 1238, and Nevsky's subsequent devotion to the protection of the city's commercial assets and trade routes testify that Novgorod had long been a principal concern in grand princely policy. Despite his quarrel with Novgorod which expelled him in 1270, Prince Iaroslav Iaroslavich, Nevsky's brother and successor, was also responsible, as noted above, for the conclusion of treaties between Novgorod and the

---

[5] Nasonov, *Mongoly i Rus'*, pp. 109–110.

German merchant groups from Lübeck, Riga, and Gotland. During his reign, Novgorodian merchants were also granted full access to all the northeastern lands of Rus', the lands of Vladimir.

The grand princes of Vladimir regularly regarded themselves as the rightful princes of Novgorod as well. In the few instances in which Novgorod attempted to challenge a grand prince's occupation of its throne, the military might of the latter obliged it to reconsider. From the 1290s, however, it also appears that Novgorod was curtailing the rights of its princes and turning many of their functions, including military, judicial, and commercial responsibilities, over to local officials. By the time Mikhail of Tver' became grand prince in 1304, he openly clashed with Novgorod, which initially rejected Mikhail's governors and only accepted him as its prince in 1307.

Mikhail's problems with Novgorod proved critical; they reduced his ability to collect and deliver tribute for the Horde and to maintain both the khan's confidence and his position as grand prince. Indeed their respective relationships with Novgorod played a major role in the outcome of the contest between the Tver' and Moscow princes for control over the grand princely seat at Vladimir.

It will be recalled that in 1313 Mikhail made a journey to the Horde to curry favor with the new khan Uzbek. Not long before his departure, in 1312, he had taken the extreme measures of withdrawing his governors from Novgorod and blockading the city, presumably to force it to deliver a sum of silver to him. Relations between the city and its prince were tense when Mikhail left to pay homage and present his gifts to the new khan. Mikhail's rival, Prince Iurii of Moscow, was able to take advantage of Novgorod's distress. While Mikhail was absent, he extended his own influence in Novgorod, which offered its throne to him. It was this action that prompted Mikhail to request Uzbek to provide him with the military assistance necessary to restore his position in Russia. By 1316 Mikhail had recovered his post in Novgorod, and Iurii had been ordered to appear at the Horde.

Tver' won that round for control over Novgorod, but the victory was a temporary one. While at the Horde, it will be recalled, Prince Iurii out-maneuvered Mikhail and returned to the Rus' lands with the patent for the grand principality. Charles Halperin has emphasized that Iurii's bid for the throne had hinged on his promise to pay the Horde more in tribute than his rival had been able to deliver.[6]

The Horde continued to regard the ability to deliver tribute as a critical qualification for a prince who sought to obtain or keep the patent

[6] Halperin, *The Tatar Yoke*, p. 81.

for the grand principality of Vladimir. It was precisely the issue of tribute that created difficulties for Iurii after he had been named grand prince. In 1321, one of the Tatar expeditions sent to the Russian lands was aimed against a section of the Tver' principality, specifically to collect overdue taxes. The late Mikhail's son, Prince Dmitry of Tver', was obliged to pay 2,000 silver rubles to Grand Prince Iurii.

But once he had received the payment, Iurii, rather than delivering it to the Horde, took it to Novgorod, where he spent most of his time during the next four years. Iurii's detour to Novgorod was the event that reopened the rivalry between the Tver' and Moscow princes. It gave Dmitry of Tver' his opportunity to journey to the Horde himself. He charged that Iurii had failed to deliver the payment that had been intended for the khan; his accusation was taken seriously enough that Uzbek transferred the grand princely title to him.

Iurii was notified to appear before the khan. Taking with him a delegation of Novgorodians, who presumably could substantiate his reasons for lingering among them, he set off for the Horde. He also took his treasury. Once again, the critical factor in the khan's determination of a prince's value and his qualifications to be grand prince is evident. For Iurii to regain the khan's confidence it was essential to demonstrate his ability to deliver tribute or, as a substitute, to offer gifts, even bribes, of sufficient value to convince the khan and other Tatar notables that he would be able to perform that task. From this perspective the highway robbery conducted by Aleksandr, Dmitry's brother, in which Iurii lost all his valuables, becomes as politically significant as it was melodramatic.

After that episode Iurii returned to Novgorod, where he devoted himself to a series of activities, which to some historians appear inexplic-able in light of the serious nature of his problems with Khan Uzbek.[7] Rather than rush immediately back to the Horde, lay charges against the Tver' princes, and restore his credibility with Uzbek, he dallied in Novgorod. He built a fortress at Orekhov, where the Neva River flows out of Lake Ladoga, and thus secured that waterway against the Swedes. He concluded a treaty between Novgorod and the Swedes, in which their borders were defined. In 1324, he led an expedition to the remote town of Ustiug, which had blocked the passage of Novgorodians traveling to and from the even more distant land of Iugra. That expedition forced Ustiug to restore the customary rights of transit.

Only after these adventures did Iurii set out for the Horde. Although

---

[7] John Fennell, for example, described Iurii as acting "with a single-mindedness strange in one so recently engaged in the unseemly inter-princely struggle for power in Suzdalia . . . " *Emergence of Moscow*, pp. 99–100.

some regard it as a misplaced priority, his attention to Novgorod and its interests, especially interests associated with its commerce, is not difficult to understand. Iurii's single means of regaining Uzbek's confidence and his throne was to convince the khan that he could perform the duty of a grand prince, delivering the tribute. When Prince Aleksandr stole his treasury, he had to accumulate another. Iurii turned to Novgorod, the source of the most abundant wealth in the Russian lands. His services to Novgorod in 1323–24 improved commercial conditions for Novgorod. He secured safe passage along the Neva, the route to the Gulf of Finland and the Baltic, and along the northern route that extended through Ustiug to the Iugra, Novgorod's source of fur supplies. He thus was not engaged in extraneous ventures, but in the central activity of securing Novgorod's profits, the source of a fortune that would enable him to present a compelling case to Uzbek and regain the grand princely title. When he had accumulated a treasury sufficiently impressive to replace the one Aleksandr had stolen and to recover the khan's favor, he resumed his interrupted journey. His plan was thwarted when, upon reaching the Horde, Dmitry murdered him (November 21, 1325).

Novgorod was equally important to Iurii's brother, Ivan Daniilovich. In 1327, immediately after the uprising in Tver' against Chol-khan and his Tatars, Ivan sent his own governors to Novgorod while he personally set off for the Horde. By the time the Tatar army, with which he returned, had ravaged Tver' and turned to Novgorod, that city was prepared to offer a special tribute to the Tatar emissaries as well as rich gifts to the generals. When Khan Uzbek then divided the realm between Aleksandr of Suzdal' and Ivan, the latter received authority over Novgorod.

Throughout his reign, one of Ivan's preoccupations was Novgorod. On several occasions, immediately upon returning from the Horde Ivan applied unusual pressure, including military force, on Novgorod. Using such means, Ivan established his own authority over Novgorod, and also secured additional revenue for the khan, who during the 1330s was once again engaged in war against the Horde's chronic enemies, the Ilkhans of Persia. In 1334–35 particularly, Uzbek, who had established control over the northern Caucasus, mounted a major campaign against Azerbaijan.

The khan's preparations for war may explain Ivan's pressure on Novgorod. In 1332, just after he had received his patent for the grand principality, Ivan demanded that Novgorod pay the *zakamskoe serebro* or silver from beyond the Kama river. In order to force payment he imitated the tactic Mikhail of Tver' had adopted twenty years earlier; he occupied two towns on Novgorod's frontier (Torzhok and Bezhetskii Verkh) and cut Novgorod off from commerce and contact with northeastern Rus'. Although Novgorod's emissaries tried to negotiate, he rejected their offers. It was not until Ivan went and returned once again from the Horde that he normalized relations with Novgorod, which only then formally accepted him as its prince (1334–35).

During this incident Kalita also applied pressure on Novgorod's northern empire, the source of the goods it exported to the German merchants who frequented its markets. He directed his "anger" not just at Novgorod, but also the northern transit town of Ustiug. Both Novgorod and Ustiug were accused of having failed to make tribute payments for the Horde from Vychegda and Pechora, two fur-supplying regions, located to the northeast of Ustiug and subject to Novgorod. In 1337, shortly after his return from another trip to the Horde (1336), Ivan sent armed forces against another of Novgorod's possessions, the North Dvina land, which repulsed his troops.

Again, in 1339, Ivan clashed with Novgorod over tribute. In this instance Novgorod did pay its share of the Tatar tribute when Ivan returned from the horde. But Kalita, in what Novgorod regarded as an unprecedented action, demanded an additional sum. The dispute had not yet been resolved when Ivan died in 1341. His son Semen applied force on the protesting city. He sent an army to collect tribute at the border town of Torzhok. War was avoided, but only when Novgorod conceded, paid the tribute and an additional fine, and reluctantly received Semen's governor. It was not until 1346 that Semen personally visited Novgorod and was formally accepted as its prince. The behavior of both Ivan I Kalita and Semen may account for N. S. Borisov's conclusion that both princes purchased the Mongol khan's support with Novgorodian silver.[8]

Novgorod accepted the authority of Grand Prince Semen, but without enthusiasm. During his reign the city's loyalty to the Daniilovichi eroded further. Prince Iurii Daniilovich had been the last prince of Novgorod to lead its armies. Novgorod did not participate in any of Semen's military ventures. And Semen did not provide adequate defense for Novgorod against Lithuanian incursions. Novgorod was similarly disappointed when in 1348 its officials requested aid from Semen to help them oppose the Swedes, who had attacked Novgorod's northern outposts, seized Orekhov, and threatened Novgorod's control over the Neva River and Lake Ladoga. The grand prince sent his brother Ivan to assist the Novgorodians. Ivan arrived, but refused to go north to recover Orekhov. The Novgorodians evicted the Swedes without grand princely aid.

It was not surprising then that Novgorod raised objections to the succession of Ivan II to the grand principality. The Novgorod chronicle

---

[8] N. S. Borisov, "Moskovskie kniaz'ia i russkie mitropolity XIV veka, [Moscow princes and Russian metropolitans of the fourteenth century] "*Voprosy istorii* no. 8, (1986), p. 35.

indicates that for a year and a half after Ivan II received his patent a state of discord existed between the grand prince and Novgorod; after that Novgorod evidently ignored Ivan II. Its chroniclers made no further mention of him; they did not even record his death.

Power and legitimacy

The Daniilovichi thus depended upon the Golden Horde. The khans favored them with patents for the grand principality, and the Daniilovich princes regularly paid tribute to the horde and made additional irregular payments on demand. Critical to this relationship was control over Novgorod. Despite that city's unwillingness to respond to every "request" from Moscow and Sarai, the Daniilovichi's ability to secure silver from it constituted the key to their success in preserving the favor of the Mongol khan. Even over repeated objections of other Riurikid princes, Uzbek and his successor Janibek placed their confidence in the Moscow clan, whose members consistently obeyed the khan and reliably contributed to his treasury.

But the position of the Daniilovichi was precarious. They, therefore, also attempted to broaden their base of domestic support. On the one hand, the Daniilovichi adopted policies to increase their real power within the northern Rus' lands. Those policies involved expanding their territory and managing the assets they thereby acquired. On the other hand, the princes of Moscow strove to elevate their status and achieve dynastic acceptance. They thus forged ties with other princely houses as well as with the Church to neutralize opposition and to create images of legitimacy.

Territorial expansion The authority of the grand prince of Vladimir rested not just on the patent of the Mongol khan. It also depended upon control over territory within the lands of Rus'. The lands ruled by a prince defined defensive and strategic limits and also provided economic and military resources. Even before they consistently held the grand princely title, the Daniilovichi had attempted to gain control of lands that were associated with the grand principality. Moscow's acquisition of Pereiaslavl' Zalesskii, discussed above, provides one example. Kostroma provides another.

The principality of Kostroma, whose center was located on the Volga River downstream of Iaroslavl', had been ruled by Prince Vasily Iaroslavich. At the time of his death in 1277, it was apparently regarded as part of the grand principality and was assigned by Grand Prince Dmitry Aleksandrovich to his brother and rival Andrei. In 1304, when Iurii

Daniilovich of Moscow initially challenged Mikhail's succession to Vladimir, he sent his own brother Boris to seize Kostroma. But Boris failed, and Mikhail retained Kostroma along with Vladimir. When the Muscovite princes assumed the grand princely title, they gained control of Kostroma as well.

Control over Pereiaslavl' Zalesskii and Kostroma, lands associated with the grand principality, gave both symbolic and practical, if not legal, weight to a claim to the grand princely throne. The implicit argument may have been that the prince who controlled the possessions of the grand principality was the grand prince. If so, Iurii Daniilovich was only partially successful in making this "argument."

The attempts to gain authority over Pereiaslavl' Zalesskii and Kostroma also reveal a tension that existed in the northeastern Rus' lands between subdividing the realm into appanages and consolidating it into larger political units. By fashioning the territories of Vladimir and Rostov into relatively small principalities and assigning them to surviving members of the dynasty after the Mongol invasion, the northeastern Riurikid princes had been able to preserve their authority over their common realm. The practice of subdividing territories continued to serve the interests of those princes who, awaiting succession to the grand principality or excluded from it, could use their principalities as a means of support.

But as the Mongols abandoned the use of *baskaki* and relied increasingly on the Riurikid princes to collect tribute and military conscripts, a premium was placed on aggrandizing territory. Enlarged domains were particularly advantageous to those princes who aspired to the position of grand prince of Vladimir. This was due in part to the fact that the city of Vladimir provided little practical benefit to its prince. Unlike the situation during the era of Kievan Rus', when the central princely seat was a wealthy and influential city, the capital of the grand principality of Vladimir was weak. It had been devastated by the Mongols. Population had migrated from the center to safer locations on the frontiers of the principality, to places in the north, such as Kostroma, and in the west, such as Tver' and Moscow. Prince Iaroslav Vsevolodich's efforts to reinvigorate Vladimir had been largely unsuccessful. The resources of Vladimir proper, the symbolic center, were insufficient to sustain a grand prince, and its associated lands correspondingly acquired increased significance.

The same factors motivated contenders for the position of grand prince, the Daniilovichi prominently among them, to adopt strategies to convert their own domains into populous, wealthy, and strong principalities, whose resources they could use both to win the grand princely position and to supplement those of Vladimir. Thus, in addition to claiming the territories of the grand principality, the Daniilovichi also expanded their own realm of Muscovy. By the early fourteenth century they had added Serpukhov, Kolomna, and Mozhaisk to their domain. Even with these additions, which tripled its size, the principality of Moscow remained relatively small. But the added territories brought strategic advantages to Moscow. With Mozhaisk near its headwaters and Kolomna at its mouth, the entire length of the Moskva or Moscow River was incorporated into Muscovy. Moscow also controlled the stretch of the Oka from Kolomna westward to Serpukhov; the line they formed became the principality's new southern frontier. These additions provided defensive security and also facilitated communication and transportation between Moscow and other towns along both the Oka and Volga Rivers. Continued control over Pereiaslavl' Zalesskii gave the Moscow princes dominance over a route that connected Vladimir on the Kliaz'ma River with the upper Volga and the city of Tver', situated near its headwaters.

Of all the Daniilovichi it was Ivan I Kalita who acquired the greatest reputation for territorial expansion. Scholarly literature portrays Ivan, the "Money-bag," as the purchaser of other principalities, specifically Beloozero and Uglich, which had been parts of the Rostov principality a century earlier, and Galich. The image is derived from the will of Dmitry Donskoi, in which he alluded to his grandfather Ivan's purchases of these lands. A great deal of scholarly debate has been conducted over the meaning of his reference, especially in light of the fact that in their own wills neither Kalita nor his sons mentioned those territories among their possessions. Some scholars argue that Kalita did indeed purchase the principalities, but allowed local princes to retain certain rights over them. Further debate focused on whether Kalita purchased them as additions to the principality of Moscow or to the grand principality of Vladimir. Other scholars reject the notion that he purchased the lands at all, and suggest that Dmitry Donskoi fabricated the story in order to justify his own seizure of them. V. A. Kuchkin has offered an additional interpretation, according to which the "purchase" was actually a payment or bribe made to the Mongol khan for patents to these principalities.[9] With those patents, which would have accorded Ivan Kalita the right to collect and deliver their share of the Tatar tribute, the prince of Moscow would have extended at least his tax-collecting authority over those three principalities. If Kuchkin's view is accurate, then the decision of the prince of Beloozero to support Aleksandr of Tver' in opposition to Ivan I Kalita,

[9] V. A. Kuchkin, "Iz istorii genealogicheskikh i politicheskikh sviazei Moskovskogo kniazheskogo doma v XIV v., [On the history of genealogical and political relations of the Muscovite princely house] "*Istoricheskie zapiski*, vol. 94 (1974), pp. 377–378.

which resulted in his summons to Sarai in 1339, may have been a reaction to Kalita's usurpation of his responsibilities.

Kalita's heirs continued to extend their domain. They acquired Iur'ev Pol'skii to the northeast of Moscow, thereby reinforcing their control over the Kliaz'ma River, and also added the districts of Vereia and Borovsk, located west of Moscow. But by the reign of Ivan II, Muscovy itself was encountering pressure from other principalities. Riazan', located south of the Oka river, engaged Moscow in a border dispute in 1353, while Lithuania's drive eastward was nibbling away at its western frontier. Just as Ivan II was less successful than his predecessors in exercising dominance over Novgorod, so Daniilovich efforts to fortify their political position within northeastern Rus' with territorial acquisitions slackened during his reign.

Assets and management As a result of their territorial expansion during the first half of the fourteenth century, the Muscovite princes accumulated a variety of resources that bolstered their power. In addition to the strategic advantages noted above, Moscow also gained economic resources. Rural and urban populations paid taxes to their prince. The prince also had judicial jurisdiction in territories subordinate to him. Fees associated with court procedures, including fines levied on the guilty, constituted revenue for the princely treasury.

The territories subject to a prince also contributed military resources. Each Rus' prince had his own army, which consisted of a band of military retainers. The richer and more powerful of the retainers maintained their own servicemen, whose military might they contributed to their prince in time of need. Territorial expansion enabled a prince to enlarge his military force. The incident in 1296, noted above, is illustrative. When the "men" or boyars of Pereiaslavl' Zalesskii declared their preference for Prince Ivan Dmitr'evich over his uncle, Grand Prince Andrei Aleksandrovich, they had also in a practical sense pledged their military services to Ivan.

Moscow's princes benefitted in a similar manner. At least some military servicemen from annexed principalities transferred their allegiance to Moscow. Opportunities to gain rewards by capturing booty in battle or by performing administrative or judicial functions for the new and expanding Muscovite court attracted servicemen from other principalities as well. Among the boyars, i.e, top-ranking military and court retainers, who served the Moscow princes in the fourteenth century, one clan is known to have descended from a Kostroma servitor, who had joined Muscovy's ranks early in the century. Another servitor whose descendants became Muscovite boyars hailed from Chernigov. And one mark of

Moscow's victory over Tver' was the departure of many Tver' boyars from the court of Prince Aleksandr Mikhailovich, even as Khan Uzbek restored him to the Tver' throne in 1337, for Moscow and the court of Grand Prince Ivan Daniilovich.

The internal organization of the Muscovite lands during the first half of the fourteenth century contributed to the effective use of the advantages gleaned from territorial expansion. In contrast to their counterparts in the Rostov principality, for example, which subdivided into many small and weak appanages, the princes of Moscow avoided comparable internal division and tried to maintain the cohesiveness of their principality, their base of power. Even when under the terms of Kalita's will Muscovite territories and incomes were distributed among his three sons, they pledged to use their armies jointly under the command of Grand Prince Semen. An agreement drawn up among the brothers in the late 1340s did recognize the territories of each one as appanages, i.e., domains that would be hereditary within their individual lines. Nevertheless, in contrast to Tver', which was experiencing not only subdivision but also interprincely warfare during the 1340s, the Muscovite realm under Prince Semen remained for practical purposes intact; its princes, although not always acting in complete accord, refrained from breaking up the unity of their patrimony. Furthermore, the decimation of the Daniilovich line caused by the Black Plague, which killed Semen, his sons, and his brother Andrei, left Prince Ivan Ivanovich virtually in full control of the Muscovite domain. Only one nephew, Vladimir, who was born shortly after the death of his father, Prince Andrei, held claim to an appanage.

Nevertheless, Muscovite cohesion weakened during the reign of Ivan II (1353–59). Political rivalries among the servitors at court that had remained veiled through the 1340s became more pronounced during that period. As the Daniilovichi attracted servicemen to their military retinues and court, a group of the most influential emerged as leading Moscow boyars by the middle of the century. One of them, Vasilii Protas'evich Vel'iaminov, assumed such stature that he not only held the post of *tysiatskii*, which symbolized high honor among the boyars and at court, but in 1345 his daughter became the wife of the future grand prince, Ivan II.

The marriage caused problems. Although it served to solidify one set of domestic political bonds, it did little to advance interprincely alliances or further elevate Daniilovich stature. On the contrary, it may have contributed to the seeming diminution of Daniilovich prestige during the reign of Ivan II. It also divided Ivan's own boyars. The growing power and prestige of the Vel'iaminov clan evidently caused a reaction among other boyars, including one Aleksei Petrovich Khvost, who managed to replace Vel'iaminov as *tysiatskii*. Khvost's tenure in that office also came to an abrupt end. He was assassinated in 1356, evidently by members of the Vel'iaminov family who vanished to Riazan'. It is unclear whether Ivan II favored his in-laws or Khvost. But within a year he had reconciled any differences he may have had with the former and brought them home to Moscow.

By the time of Ivan II's death, the unity among the Daniilovich princes, which had contributed so significantly to Moscow's strength through the first half of the century, was also endangered. In his will Ivan II not only apportioned Muscovy between his sons, Dmitry and Ivan, but acknowledged the right of his nephew, Vladimir Andreevich, to his father's share of the realm. That share, centered around Serpukhov, then became a true appanage principality with its own capital, court, and military retinue.

Dynastic relations At least until the reign of Ivan II Moscow's growing territorial base strengthened its princes economically. Territorial unity and cooperation among the Daniilovichi also kept their growing military force intact. The Muscovite princes were thus able to convince the Mongols of their worthiness for support, and with consequent Tatar aid they were able to bypass the dynastic norms of legitimacy. In contrast, when Tver', the powerful patrimonial center of the legitimate line of princes, was smashed by the Mongols in 1327, it no longer had the means to remain in the competition and subsequently fragmented into competing appanages.

Although the Daniilovichi successfully expanded their own domain and increased their economic and military power within it, they nevertheless sought support from other princes within the lands of Rus' as well. When the pursuit of their policies required the use of force, as when they suppressed Novgorodian resistance, they depended upon other members of the dynasty to uphold their policies and supplement their military forces. But without the status of dynastic seniority, they could not command obedience from other princes; they had to rely on their ability to rally their cousins, to convince them to join their campaigns.

One method Kalita and his sons employed to gain allegiance and suppport from other princes also provided them with higher status and elevated their prestige within the dynasty. That method was to forge direct marital bonds with other branches of the dynasty. Specifically, Kalita arranged marriages for his daughters with princes of Beloozero, Iaroslavl', and Rostov. In all three cases his sons-in-law acknowledged the seniority of their father-in-law and transferred their political and military support to him and his heirs.

The selection of marriage partners for Kalita's daughters was grounded in intradynastic politics and dissension. His sons-in-law represented a dynastic branch that had challenged Ivan's claim to the grand princely throne. It was to the sons of his opponents from Beloozero and Iaroslavl', who had surfaced in 1339, that Ivan married his daughters. The ties he established with them did not necessarily legitimize the Daniilovich claim to the grand principality; but they did neutralize the most vocal and active challengers to it. Through the marriages Ivan Kalita established his personal, if not dynastic, seniority over princes in Rostov, Iaroslavl' and Beloozero, the three major lines in the Rostov branch of the dynasty.

A similar approach was taken toward the Tver' line. Prince Konstantin Mikhailovich, who ruled Tver' while his brother Aleksandr was in exile in Pskov and Lithuania, was married to Ivan's niece. Ivan's familial relationship to Konstantin paralleled their political relationship; although he would object to Semen's succession, Prince Konstantin regularly accepted Ivan's seniority and authority. Later, in 1347, Grand Prince Semen married Mariia, the daughter of the late Prince Aleksandr Mikhailovich of Tver'. The implied alliance and subordination of Tver' was so important to Semen that he risked alienating Metropolitan Feognost, who refused to sanction this, Semen's third marriage.

The Daniilovichi successfully expanded their territory, enhanced their resources within a cohesive realm, and extended their influence over other Riurikid princes. Nevertheless, during Semen's reign Moscow's dominance over the Rus' principalities was eroding. The grand prince was unable to convince Novgorod, Pskov, Tver', or Riazan' to send troops to join his military campaigns. By the reign of Ivan II (1353–59) Moscow's situation deteriorated further. The inability of Ivan II to continue the expansionist drive of his predecessors, his estrangement from Novgorod, and the problems within his court have already been discussed. His marriage only compounded those difficulties. It is not surprising then that after the death of Ivan II, his young son and heir, Dmitry Ivanovich, guided by his mother's relatives, reverted to the former practice of his ancestors and married into the princely house of Suzdal'-Nizhnii Novgorod, which had not only figured prominently in the opposition to Ivan II's succession but challenged his own as well.

The Church Through the reigns of Ivan Kalita and his sons the Muscovite princely line thus acquired control over key territories, some attached to the grand principality and others to their patrimony. Novgorod also recognized, however reluctantly, the Daniilovichi as its princes. Political authority over these lands added to the economic and military power of the Daniilovichi, who attempted to enhance their prestige and neutralize their opposition through selective marital arrangements. The cultivation of good relations with the Orthodox Church was also important for the Daniilovichi.

Acceptance by, if not active support of, the Church was politically significant. The Church embodied a moral authority, and it symbolized continuity with Kievan Rus'. Ecclesiastical approval of the secular ruler implied a measure of legitimacy, rooted in Rus' culture and traditions, that supplemented and reinforced the authority of the Mongol khans.

At the beginning of the fourteenth century it was not evident that the Church would favor the Moscow princes. On the contrary, it appeared that the Tver' princes had stronger ecclesiastical support than the Daniilovichi. During the reign of Iaroslav Iaroslavich (d. 1271/72) Tver' had become host to its own bishop. In contrast, Moscow was just one component of the Rostov see. Even when Metropolitan Maksim (Maximus) transferred the center of the Russian Orthodox Church from Kiev to Vladimir (1299), it was not evident that Moscow would ultimately reap the advantages afforded by the proximity of the metropolitan. On the contrary, Metropolitan Maksim reportedly tried to dissuade Prince Iurii of Moscow from interfering with the succession of Mikhail of Tver' in 1304.

But after Maksim died in 1305, the situation began to shift. The patriarch in Constantinople did not approve Grand Prince Mikhail's candidate, but selected Petr, the nominee of the prince of Galicia, to be Maksim's successor. The subsequent relationship between Grand Prince Mikhail and the bishop of Tver', on the one hand, and Metropolitan Petr, on the other, was strained. The bishop of Tver' even filed charges against the metropolitan, forcing a Council, attended by an envoy from the patriarch, to be convened at Pereiaslavl' to try Petr. The Council, which met in 1311, found in Petr's favor. By 1316, the bishop had withdrawn to a monastery and Petr had replaced him in Tver' with his own appointee.

Metropolitan Petr also was responsible for appointing Archbishop David in Novgorod in 1309. It will be recalled that while Grand Prince Mikhail was at the Horde in 1313–14, Novgorod called upon Iurii of Moscow to replace Mikhail as its prince. Archbishop David, who held Mikhail's governors captive in his palace, was evidently centrally involved in this action. Metropolitan Petr also named a new bishop to Sarai; that appointment may have similarly had negative political repercussions for Mikhail and the Tver' princes.

Metropolitan Petr's unfavorable disposition toward Tver' ultimately worked to Moscow's benefit. In 1326, he and Prince Ivan of Moscow jointly sponsored the construction of the Church of the Assumption (Dormition) of the Virgin in the Moscow kremlin. Petr, who died a few months after work began on the Church, was buried in a tomb in one of its walls. The resting place of Petr, who was canonized in 1339, became a shrine. Although the seat of the metropolitan was not transferred to Vladimir until 1354, Moscow was gaining prestige as an ecclesiastical center of northeastern Russia.

Church policy was not, however, necessarily determined by internal Rus' politics or motivated by a proclivity toward one princely branch in favor of another. Against the background of the secular political fragmentation of Kievan Rus' into its northeastern and southwestern fractions, the metropolitans of Kiev were struggling to preserve the unity of the Church itself and with it their spiritual authority over the Christian flock in all the lands of Rus'.

That unity was challenged early in the fourteenth century (c. 1303) when the patriarch of Constantinople created a new metropolitan see to include six bishoprics centered around Galicia in southwestern Rus'. Within a few years the see was abolished (1308). But it was during this period that Petr had been selected to succeed Maksim, who died in 1305, as the metropolitan of Kiev and all Rus'. The metropolitanate was reunified, but the candidate of the prince of Galicia served as its head, not the nominee of the prince of Tver'.

Despite the terms of this compromise, a separate see was established for the Lithuanian lands sometime between 1315 and 1319. And, after Petr's death, the new metropolitan, Greek prelate Feognost, had more difficulty. Having traveled through southwestern Rus', he reached the northeast in 1328. When the metropolitan in Lithuania died in 1330, Feognost managed to prevent the appointment of a successor. But by the early 1330s another independent metropolitanate had already been created for southwestern Rus'. It too was quickly abolished, but then in the 1340s Feognost faced the ecclesiastical separation of the southwest once again.

Although he was preoccupied with Church affairs, some of Metropolitan Feognost's actions influenced Rus' politics. It was he, who as noted above, pressured Prince Aleksandr, who had found refuge in Pskov after the Tver' uprising of 1327, to leave that city by threatening its entire population with excommunication. Whether intentionally or not, his action served to reinforce the Daniilovichi's prestige, political success, and appearance of legitimacy. He also, as Petr before him, graced Moscow by favoring it as his residence.

While the metropolitans of the Church indirectly heightened the political stature of Moscow's princes, the Church also contributed to an enhancement of their image. Prince Ivan I Kalita in particular has acquired a reputation in historical accounts as a good and just ruler. That reputation is based in large part on sources that praised his accomplishments and character. Although they were articulated in Church literature surviving from the late fourteenth and early fifteenth centuries and they reflect concerns of that era, the themes in those sources were developed from concepts introduced during or shortly after Ivan's life by secular court scribes.

In a copy of the Gospels transcribed in 1339 expressly for a monastery in the Dvina land, for example, scribes inserted statements lauding Kalita for bringing peace and order, justice and security to his lands. By the end of the century the hierarchs of the Church were incorporating similar images into their own literature. In his version of the vita of Metropolitan Petr, a later metropolitan, Kiprian (Cyprian), described Ivan as a pious prince, "whom the blessed Peter saw resplending in Orthodoxy, merciful to the poor, honouring the holy churches of God and the clergy, loving divine Scriptures, well instructed in the teachings of the books. So the holy hierarch of God [Petr] loved him very much."[10]

The Trinity chronicle, compiled in the early fifteenth century at the court of the metropolitan, even more directly borrowed the characterization of Ivan Kalita that had been promoted at his own court. In its entry announcing the beginning of Ivan's reign as grand prince, the Trinity chronicle not only pushed the date back to 1328, but also editorialized: "[When] grand-prince Ivan Daniilovich obtained the grand principality of all Russia, there came a great peace for forty years; the infidels ceased to fight against the land of the Rus' and kill Christians; the Christians found relief and appeasement away from the great troubles, the many oppressions and from Tatar violence, and there was great peace in all the land."[11] The records incorporated into the Trinity chronicle for the period 1328 to 1389 were, according to John Fennell, originally written in conformity "with the political tendencies of the princes of Moscow" in their own capital.[12]

Ivan Kalita, the prince who "purchased" other principalities, was also hailed as being responsible for beginning the process of "gathering the Russian lands" around Moscow or reunifying Russia. The themes extolling Ivan's personal virtues and public accomplishments elaborated images depicted earlier by the Muscovite court. They were incorporated into Church literature to serve ecclesiastical interests. Nevertheless, they perpetuated the message that even if Ivan Daniilovich had not been the heir to throne according to dynastic traditions, his qualities, achievements,

[10] John Meyendorff, *Byzantium and the Rise of Russia. A Study of Byzantino-Russian Relations in the Fourteenth Century* (Cambridge: Cambridge University Press, 1981), p. 151.
[11] As translated by Meyendorff, *Byzantium and the Rise of Russia*, p. 157.
[12] Fennell, *Emergence of Moscow*, p. 315.

and character constituted proof that he was both qualified and legitimate, according to higher, divine standards.

Just as chronicles and other literary texts portrayed Ivan Kalita in the most favorable terms, so visual architectural symbols enhanced and glorified Moscow, transforming its image from a small wooden rural settlement into a city adorned with impressive stone structures worthy of a political and ecclesiastical capital. In this respect Moscow was directly competing with Tver', which had accumulated sufficient wealth to be the first among the northeastern Rus' towns to build a stone church after the devastating Mongol onslaught. By the 1320s Tver' could boast two such cathedrals, while Moscow had none.

Moscow began its series of construction projects in 1326, with the construction of the Church of the Assumption in the kremlin, jointly sponsored by Prince Ivan and Metropolitan Petr. During the reign of Kalita four more stone churches were built within the kremlin. Later, in the mid-1340s, Byzantine and Russian artists decorated the walls of these churches with frescoes, and five church bells were added to the complex. The construction of these ecclesiastical edifaces were acts of piety. They also represented appeals for divine favor. But on the mundane level they and the special emphasis placed on the Church of the Assumption dedicated to the Holy Virgin gave physical representation to Moscow's bid to be successor to Kiev and Vladimir and its princes' claim to be the legitimate heirs of the grand princely throne.

In the same way as literary themes originated at the grand princely court, church construction was sponsored mainly by members of the Daniilovich line, not members of the Church hierarchy. The multiplication of ecclesiastical buildings in Moscow does not, therefore, demonstrate that the Church hierarchy or the metropolitan had cast their support behind the Daniilovichi. Nevertheless, those princes, by embracing the Church and glorifying Moscow through ecclesiastical imagery, attracted members of the clergy and, ultimately, the metropolitan to their city. On a spiritual plane, the Daniilovichi's contributions to the Church represented gratitude for the good fortune bestowed upon them and appeals for continued protection and grace. But on the material plane, they created the appearance of an alliance between Moscow and Orthodoxy. Their consequent elevation above the remainder of the dynasty, upheld symbolically by association with the Church, complicated matters for other princes who tried to challenge the Daniilovichi and withhold their cooperation even in purely secular, political matters.

Like other Daniilovich policies, the effort to become identified with the Church faltered during the reign of Ivan II. When Metropolitan Feognost died in 1353, he was replaced by Metropolitan Aleksei (Alexis), who was confirmed in his office in 1354. But at that time the Lithuanian see once again received its own metropolitan. This time the activation of the Lithuanian see constituted a serious threat to the unity of the Orthodoxy in the lands of Rus'. Lithuania itself had expanded eastward. It controlled Kiev and was providing an attractive alternative for Novgorod, which was thoroughly disenchanted with the new grand prince Ivan II. The Lithuanian metropolitan courted the Novgorod archbishop as well. During the first years of his tenure Metropolitan Aleksei was thus gravely concerned with the integrity of the Church, and had little time to devote to princely and domestic politics. He strove to regain authority over bishoprics that had fallen under the political domination of Lithuania. He traveled extensively, making several trips to Constantinople and Sarai. He also went to Kiev to establish his authority over southwestern Rus'. But with that action he was directly challenging the reigning Metropolitan there, and Prince Olgerd of Lithuania arrested him in 1358. Aleksei remained a prisoner for two years, and thus returned to the northeastern Rus' only after Ivan II's death.

By the end of Ivan II's reign in 1359, Moscow was the ascendant principality in northeastern Rus'. The Golden Horde had abandoned the traditional Riurikid succession pattern of generational rotation and had placed its confidence in the Moscow princes. The Daniilovichi held power, but their position depended upon the favor of the khan. Retention of that favor required the Daniilovichi to pay tribute and proffer gifts; those demands obliged them in turn to maintain continual domination over Novgorod. Ivan Kalita and his son Semen had tried to broaden their base of support by cultivating good relations with the Church, forging bilateral ties with potentially rival branches of the dynasty, and exploiting all the benefits of territorial expansion.

The Daniilovich position, nevertheless, was not secure. The dynasty did not wholly accept the Moscow princes' legitimacy. At every succession traditionalists challenged the Daniilovich claim to the grand princely throne. Moscow's authority diminished, especially during the reign of Ivan II. At that time the lack of dynastic support became acute. Novgorod, on which Muscovite power pivoted, barely recognized the grand prince. Muscovite territorial expansion seemed to have reached a limit and was even being reversed. Internally, the Moscow boyars, while consolidating their collective political position, were engaged in bitter rivalry, and the principality itself was beginning to divide into appanages. The Church, which had graciously received donations from the Daniilovichi, had also been preoccupied with preserving its own unity and had refrained from unambiguously promoting their interests over those of competing princely branches. While Metropolitan Aleksei worked to reunify his see, Ivan II was deprived even of the level of support the Church had afforded his brother Semen and father Ivan Kalita. Thus, by the time Ivan II died in 1359, the policies that had served the first Daniilovich grand princes well in their process of gaining ascendancy were unravelling. The Daniilovichi of Moscow faced a crisis.

7

THE DANIILOVICH
ASCENSION

•

During the century following the Mongol invasion of the Rus' lands, the Mongol khans and Riurikid princes stabilized their relations. The Riurikid princes acknowledged Golden Horde suzerainty. They paid tribute to the khans, supplemented those payments with gifts to Horde notables, and participated in Mongol military campaigns. The khans issued patents confirming each prince's right to rule. When the occasion demanded, they intervened diplomatically or militarily in interprincely disputes. Despite the devastation caused by their invasion and subsequent military expeditions and despite the loss of capital occasioned by tribute payments, those Mongol demands for tribute coupled with the Rus' involvement through the Horde in the vast Mongol commercial network provided an economic stimulus for the Rus'. The Rus' principalities gradually recovered.

Mongol participation in both the political and economic activity of the Rus' lands slowly altered Rus' political institutions and patterns. Initially the Mongol khans issued patents to princes who, according to dynastic traditions, were also the legitimate heirs to their thrones, including, most significantly, the throne for the grand prince of Vladimir. Ruling princes cooperated with the Mongol officials, the *baskaki,* who oversaw censuses and conscription and tribute collection. As the Mongols shifted responsibility for those functions from their own *baskaki* to the Riurikid princes, they favored those princes who demonstrated the best ability to raise and deliver revenue to the Horde and maintain peace and stability in the Rus' lands. For the Rus' princes who aspired to the grand princely throne, it became increasingly important to dominate the commercial center of

Novgorod, the source of wealth, particularly silver, needed for tribute payments. By the second quarter of the fourteenth century the Golden Horde khans were favoring the Daniilovichi of Moscow over their chief competitors, the princes of Tver'. According to dynastic standards, the Daniilovichi were illegitimate. And other members of the dynasty repeatedly protested the khans' issuance of the grand princely patent to the Moscow princes. Mongol power, however, was sufficient to over-come their objections. An important result of Mongol suzerainty was thus that by the middle of the fourteenth century the dynasty was forced to abandon a significant element of the succession system that had guided it and framed relations among its members for centuries. The principle of collateral succession through generational rotation survived; but the definition of eligibility changed. That issue was no longer determined by a prince's father's service as grand prince. It was decided by the khan.

As the second century of Mongol dominance over the Rus' lands opened, the latter had substantially recovered from the initial economic and political impact of the invasion. The Muscovite branch of the dynasty, buoyed exclusively by Mongol support, had become the grand princes of Vladimir. With the transfer of the grand princely throne to the Muscovite princes, the dependency of the grand prince upon the Horde reached a peak. Without dynastic legitimacy Daniilovich authority rested on the power of the khan, not, as before, on a combination of domestic tradition and Horde confirmation. The Daniilovich princes focused their policies on maintaining Horde support. They were obedient servants of the Horde. They strove to preserve their authority over Novgorod. But they also attempted to broaden their base of power, to create sources of domestic support that might compensate for their lack of dynastic legitimacy. They therefore extended their domain territorially. They forged bilateral bonds with other branches of the dynasty, particularly through marriage ties, and gained recognition of seniority from those branches. Through such means they also gathered a larger, stronger military retinue, which due to the lack of division within the Muscovite principality, remained a united force. Finally, they also bolstered their legitimacy by becoming an ecclesiastical center and creating at least the appearance that their role as grand princes was sanctified by the Church.

By 1359, the princes of Moscow had achieved relative prominence among the northern Russian lands. But their dominance was not assured. During the reign of Ivan II (1353–59), the successes of the Daniilovichi were subsiding, the advantages secured by his predecessors were eroding. Novgorod ignored him, threatening his ability to provide the Horde with its required tribute. Territorial expansion ceased. And his own principality of Moscow as well as his military retinue showed signs of internal division. In addition, two external factors compounded the problems facing Ivan's successors: the political crisis within the Golden Horde and Lithuanian expansion. Those factors created a radically different political context for the next two Muscovite princes, Dmitry Donskoi (1359–89) and Vasily I (1389–1425).

DISCORD WITHIN THE HORDE

Beginning in 1359 the Golden Horde began to experience violent internal political disorder. Its problems were provoked by at least two external circumstances. The first was decimation of the population caused by the Black Death, which had struck down Grand Prince Semen the Proud, his sons and brother, and Metropolitan Feognost in 1353. Bubonic plague, which had spread westward along trade routes from Asia, had attacked the populace of the Golden Horde several years earlier, in 1346–47, as it passed through Sarai, Astrakhan', the Caucasus, and the ports of the Crimea. From those ports it was carried to Europe, where it ravaged the populations of Italy, France, and England as it circled around the continent and returned eastward. On that return sweep the plague reached Pskov and Novgorod (1352), then other lands of western and northeastern Rus' (1353). In 1364 the plague struck Sarai a second time; it then traveled northward to attack the population of Nizhnii Novgorod and, again, virtually all the towns of northeastern Rus' (1365–66). A decade later the Horde and the Rus' lands were visited by the Black Death for the third time.

Bubonic plague, whose symptoms included boils or glandular swellings accompanied by severe pain, high fever, and chills, could kill its victims in as brief a period as one or two days; in other cases the victims suffered longer. In Russian towns, according to chronicle reports, as many as one hundred people died daily during the peak of the epidemic. It has been estimated that the population of the Rus' lands declined by at least 25 per cent as a result of the repeated waves of plague. Such reports are consistent with death tolls recorded for western European towns. In its first sweep through the Crimea the plague is reported to have claimed the lives of three-quarters of the European population; Tana lost half of its Venetian residents. One may assume that the townspeople of the Golden Horde cities perished in comparable numbers. Mongol notables, who had exchanged nomadic for sedentary lifestyles, and Jewish, Italian, Armenian, and Caucasian tradespeople and residents were all among the victims of the epidemic.

The second factor that adversely affected the Golden Horde was its commerce. The Golden Horde controlled the northwestern segment of the Mongols' Great Silk Road. But at virtually the same time that the Horde was suffering the effects of the plague, both ends of the Silk Road were being disrupted. In the west the Genoese and Venetians were engaged in a conflict involving Tana (1350–55). Meanwhile the Ottoman Turks captured Gallipoli, established themselves in the Balkans, and were threatening sea traffic through the straits (1350s). In the east after over a decade of fending off rebellions, the Yuan dynasty, as the Mongol rulers of China were known, was overthrown (1368). The new Ming rulers occupied Beijing and expelled the Mongols to their native lands. The collapse of the Yuan dynasty in China undermined the economic strength of the remainder of the empire, including the Golden Horde. The new Ming rulers reduced commercial contacts with the outside world. The resulting decay of the east–west trade network did not destroy the bazaars of the Golden Horde, but it did weaken its economic underpinnings and contribute to a decline that within half a century would result in its disintegration.

Demographic and economic traumas contributed to political instability, and by the 1360s the Horde was engaged in internally divisive and fatal conflicts. Following the death of Uzbek (1341), who had overseen the peak of the Horde's power, Tinibek (1341–42), Janibek (1342–57), and Janibek's son Berdibek (1357–59) ruled successively as khan. But in 1359, Berdibek's brother overthrew him. That palace coup launched a political upheaval. During the next twenty years the Sarai throne changed hands dozens of times; on occasion two rival khans simultaneously claimed the throne. The range of the Sarai khan's authority also contracted as portions of Horde territory and segments of clans recognized the leadership of local khans. At times as many as seven khans controlled different sections of the Horde's domain, including Bulgar and the Crimea. The power vacuum within the Golden Horde created a force so great that it sucked into its vortex contenders from the eastern half of Juchi's *ulus*.

Non-Chingisid clan leaders and notables played major roles in the general melee. Chief among them was Mamai, whose base of power was the western territories of the Golden Horde. He exercised his influence not only by dominating those lands, but by supporting his own candidates for the Sarai throne and effectively ruling through them when they attained it.

Mamai was challenged, however, by those figures who emerged from the eastern half of the *ulus*. Tokhtamysh, a member of the Chingisid dynasty and a descendant of Juchi, was foremost among them. In 1378, he seized control of Sarai. By 1381, he and Mamai were at war. With his victory over Mamai at a battle on the Kalka River, Tokhtamysh became the unchallenged ruler of both halves of Juchi's *ulus*.

Although Tokhtamysh's ascendancy to power temporarily stabilized the political fluctuations within the Horde, its troubles were not over. Before he had seized Sarai, Tokhtamysh had recognized the suzerainty of Timur (Tamerlane), a non-Chingisid conqueror who was building his own empire centered around Samarkand in Central Asia. Through the 1380s friction between Tokhtamysh and Timur mounted as both sought dominance over Khwarezm and Azerbaijan. In 1391 Timur defeated Tokhtamysh in a major battle east of the Volga River. As a result, Tokhtamysh lost control of the eastern portion of his *ulus*. He continued to rule the western half, the Golden Horde, and from that base he pursued his contest with Timur.

In 1395 Timur defeated Tokhtamysh again at a battle on the Terek River, north of the Caucasus. Timur chased Tokhtamysh toward Bulgar-on-the-Volga, but then, leaving a small force to pacify the area, turned back southward. On his way he passed through southern Riazan', where he rested his troops who pillaged the region. After several weeks, Timur resumed his campaign against his primary targets: Tana (Azak) at the mouth of the Don, Sarai, and Astrakhan' on the lower Volga. He demolished the chief cities of the Golden Horde, then returned to his Central Asian capital, Samarkand. The campaign of 1395–96 not only radically weakened the Golden Horde politically and militarily, but ruined one of the main components of its economy. By wrecking its cities, just as he had destroyed the Central Asian emporium of Urgench in 1387, Timur eliminated the market centers that had formed the Horde's trade route linking Europe and Asia.

After his defeat, Tokhtamysh fled to Lithuania, where he sought refuge and support. The Golden Horde fell under the rule of Edigei, another of Timur's proteges from the eastern half of Juchi's *ulus*. A non-Chingisid himself, Edigei ruled through the khan, Timur-Kutlugh. In 1399, a combined Lithuanian–Tatar army, led by the Lithuanian grand duke Vitovt and Tokhtamysh, met the forces of Timur-Kutlugh and Edigei on the Vorskla River (a tributary of the Dnieper). Once again Tokhtamysh was defeated. This time he fled to western Siberia, where he died a few years later. Timur turned his attention to other conquests and died in February 1405 at Otrar, as he prepared to launch a campaign against China.

Edigei remained the dominant figure in the Golden Horde and, as Tokhtamysh before him, focused on consolidating his authority, reuniting the Horde, and reviving trade. To those ends he seized Khwarezm in 1406. He remained in power until 1411, when his son-in-law drove him from Sarai. Edigei, whose Mangyt clan had been allotted grazing lands in the western steppe (around the lower Bug River), retreated to the steppe, where he exercised local influence until he was killed in 1419.

In the wake of this extended political turmoil, the crumbling of a major pillar supporting its economic structure, and the loss of the strong capable leadership of Edigei, the Golden Horde fragmented. During the next decades competing khans once again acquired power and the loyalty of clans in various portions of the Horde territories. By the 1420s a Crimean khanate was forming independently of Sarai but dependent on Lithuanian protection. It ultimately recognized the rule of Khan Hadji-Girey and his descendants. By 1445, another khanate coalesced around Kazan' on the mid-Volga. It consisted of followers of Ulu-Muhammed (Mahmet), who had ruled briefly at Sarai and had then led his clans and supporters to the Crimea (c. 1427). About ten years later, they appeared in Lithuanian territory in the vicinity of Belev on the upper Oka River; they moved past Moscow in 1439 and ultimately established themselves under Ulu-Muhammed's son on the mid-Volga. The Kazan' khanate absorbed the state of Bulgar.

By the middle of the fifteenth century only a relatively small core, known in Russian sources as the Great Horde, remained of the once formidable Golden Horde. It too disappeared in the early sixteenth century, leaving the Khanate of Astrakhan' on the lower Volga and the Khanate of Sibir' along with the Crimean and Kazan' Khanates as its heirs.

LITHUANIAN EXPANSION

While the Horde was transforming and disintegrating, Lithuania was steadily growing in territory, military power, and political influence. Stimulated by the aggression of the crusading German knights, who as noted in the last chapter were advancing eastward in the thirteenth century, pagan Lithuanian tribes united under Prince Mindovg (d. 1263). Their successful resistance to the knights in 1236 forced the Teutonic Order and the Livonian Brothers of the Sword to unite the following year. Located between Catholic Poland, the crusading Knights, Orthodox Rus', and the Muslim Tatars, Mindovg and his successors adroitly maneuvered among their neighbors, forming and breaking alliances, converting to and renouncing Christianity, and all the while expanding.

Lithuania's territory in the thirteenth century encompassed the lands around the Neman (Niemen) River. Its princes extended their possessions eastward to incorporate principalities that had formerly been associated with Kievan Rus'. Polotsk on the western Dvina River was one of the first to fall under Lithuanian influence; when its Riurikid dynastic line died out in 1307, it became an integral part of Lithuania. In addition, Lithuania encompassed the principalities of modern Belarus: Minsk, Pinsk, and Turov.

During the reigns of its princes Gedymin (Gediminas; 1316–41) and Olgerd (1345–77), it will be recalled, Lithuania expanded into south-western Rus' as well. Among its targets were Galicia and Volynia, which had been dominated immediately after the Mongol invasion by the powerful prince of Volynia and Galicia, Daniil (with whom Mindovg had formed an alliance in the 1250s). Although those regions were weakened after the Mongolian devastation of the area in the 1280s, Daniil's descendants, who continued to rule them, remained invulnerable to their western and northern neighbors due to a continued Tatar presence. Even after that branch of the dynasty died out in the 1320s, Khans Uzbek and Janibek retained authority there, as demonstrated by their ability to use Galician forces and territory in their campaigns against Poland and Hungary.

By Janibek's reign, however, the Golden Horde was diverted by concerns with Persia. It retreated to the Dniester River valley, providing Poland and Lithuania with an opportunity to expand into the south-western Rus' lands. Although they had tended to be allies against the Order, Poland and Lithuania became competitors for dominance in this region. Their struggle, which continued for over a decade, was resolved by Lithuanian occupation of Volynia (1340) and Polish acquisition of most of Galicia (1349).

As the Golden Horde became absorbed in its internal turmoil following Berdibek's death (1359), the Lithuanian prince Olgerd replaced the khan as suzerain over the principalities that had formed the heartland of Kievan Rus', Chernigov, Pereiaslavl', and Kiev itself. The Lithuanian lands reached the shores of the Black Sea.

The Lithuanian–Polish contest revolved not just around political control of territory. They vied for control over commercial markets and routes. As the Horde's grip loosened, Lithuania and Poland each attempted to secure control over land routes connecting the Italian Black Sea colonies with central and northern Europe. King Casimir of Poland (1333–70) explicitly attempted to channel such commercial traffic through the Galician town of Lwow (L'viv or L'vov). Lithuanian princes, by expanding their domain to include territories stretching from the Baltic to the Black Sea, provided alternate routes.

With its incorporation of former Kievan Rus' territories, Lithuania also acquired an increasingly Orthodox population. That population gave its secular allegiance to the Lithuanian grand duke, but continued to look to the metropolitan located in Moscow for spiritual guidance. Lithuanian rulers, as noted in chapter 6, made repeated efforts to establish a separate metropolitanate for their Orthodox subjects. Olgerd, although personally a pagan, appealed to the patriarch of Constantinople to detach Lithuania's lands from the Rus' metropolitanate and create a new see for Kiev and Lithuania. The result was a conflict for ecclesiastical jurisdiction over the Orthodox in Lithuanian territories.

After Metropolitan Feognost died in 1353, the patriarch named Aleksei, the son of a Moscow boyar, to succeed him. But later in 1354, he also created a metropolitanate of Lithuania and consecrated Roman, who was related to Olgerd's wife, herself a princess from Tver', as its primate with ecclesiastical responsibility for Lithuania proper, Kiev, and the western lands of the Chernigov principality. It was in conjunction with the competition between the two prelates that Aleksei formalized the transfer, unofficially made by Metropolitan Maksim at the turn of the century, of the metropolitan seat from Kiev to Vladimir (1354). Aleksei's preoccupation with restoring the unity of his see also accounts for the fact that he provided little assistance to the politically ailing Ivan II and his young successor Dmitry Ivanovich.

Only when Aleksei had returned to Moscow from captivity in Lithuania (1360) and his rival Roman had died (1361), did Aleksei achieve his goal of reunification. But Olgerd of Lithuania as well as the Polish king Casimir complained that Aleksei favored his northeastern Rus' flock to the neglect of those in the southwest. Olgerd argued further that Aleksei abused his ecclesiastical authority by using it to the political advantage of the grand prince of Vladimir and the detriment of other secular princes in his ecclesiastical domain, most particularly himself and the prince of Tver'. In 1371 the patriarch approved the creation of a separate metropolitanate for Galicia, the Orthodox territory within Poland. And in 1375, Kiprian was consecrated as metropolitan of Kiev and Lithuania; it was understood that upon the death of Aleksei (which occurred in 1378), Kiprian would become metropolitan of Kiev and all Rus', once again reuniting the Lithuanian and Russian churches.

Lithuania's intermittent success in its efforts to acquire ecclesiastical recognition contributed to its rulers' legitimacy and the consolidation of their authority in Orthodox territories. Its struggle to gain that recognition also emphasized the competitive nature of Lithuania's relationship with northeastern Rus' and the principality that was emerging as its center, Moscow. That competition was also evident in the relationships of Moscow with Lithuania, the principality of Tver', and the Golden Horde during the reign of Dmitry Ivanovich Donskoi.

THE REIGN OF DMITRY DONSKOI

While the Golden Horde was engaged in its internal conflicts and Lithuania was expanding to its southeast and engaging its neighbors, Poland and the Teutonic Knights, the principality of Moscow was fashioning itself into one of the leading states of eastern Europe. Just as it had been unclear in the beginning of the fourteenth century that the Daniilovichi would transform their domain into the major political and ecclesiastical center among the northern Rus' principalities by the middle of that century, so in 1359 it was scarcely a foregone conclusion that Moscow would become the center of a unified Russian state that would absorb its former Tatar overlords and curb Lithuanian expansion.

On the contrary, during the reign of Ivan II, Daniilovich influence was waning. When Ivan died in 1359, his son and heir Dmitry was only nine years old. The Horde's Great Troubles were just beginning, and the young prince could not rely on the consistent support from Sarai that his father and uncle had received. By the time Metropolitan Aleksei returned to Moscow from his captivity in Lithuania in 1360 and assumed responsibility for advising and protecting Dmitry Ivanovich, the child had already lost his position as grand prince of Vladimir.

When Khan Berdibek was killed in 1359, the Russian princes had gone to Sarai to receive their patents from his successor. Events were transpiring so rapidly that by the time they reached the Horde, yet another khan, Navruz, had assumed the throne. He issued the patent for the grand principality not to Dmitry Ivanovich, but to Dmitry Konstantinovich, the prince of Suzdal' and Nizhnii Novgorod (1360).

Dmitry Konstantinovich was the nephew of Prince Aleksandr of Suzdal', who had held the grand princely title just before Ivan Kalita secured it. Dmitry's father had not been grand prince of Vladimir, but had been among the princes who had opposed the accession of Semen in 1341 and Ivan II in 1353. Although Dmitry Konstantinovich did represent the generation that preceded Dmitry Ivanovich's, he too had no legitimate dynastic claim to the throne, only a tradition of opposition to the Daniilovichi.

Nevertheless, a group of Russian princes, consigned to rule appanages of diminishing size and importance, alienated by Grand Prince Ivan II, and dismayed at the prospect of a minor succeeding him, revived the resistance to Daniilovich domination and formed a coalition around Dmitry Konstantinovich. It included a Rostov prince, Konstantin Vasil'evich, who had married a daughter of Ivan Kalita and had joined in Grand Prince Semen's military campaigns in the 1340s. Prince Ivan Fedorovich of Beloozero, the son of Fedor Romanovich and another of Ivan Kalita's daughters, was also a member, as was Prince Dmitry Borisovich of Dmitrov, an appanage carved out of the former Galich–Dmitrov principality. When Dmitry Konstantinovich was named grand prince, his allies were elevated as well. Konstantin Vasil'evich became prince of all the Rostov lands, Dmitry Borisovich of the full Galich principality.

But the following year their sponsor Navruz was overthrown. Once again the Russian princes obediently went to the Horde to receive their patents. By this time, however, the situation in the Horde was politically more unstable and generally more violent. The Russian princes were subjected to personal abuse and their property was stolen. Thereafter the Russian princes refrained from traveling to the Horde; they sent personal agents to pay homage to the khans and receive the patents on their behalf.

It was under these conditions that Dmitry Ivanovich of Moscow recovered the grand principality of Vladimir and overcame his domestic rivals. He obtained a patent first in 1362 from the Sarai khan. On the basis of that patent the young prince's forces expelled Dmitry Konstantinovich from the city of Vladimir (winter 1362–63). But by this time Mamai, who was supporting his own candidate for khan, had openly attacked their rival at Sarai. Mamai also claimed the Horde's suzerainty over the Rus' lands as well as their tribute for his candidate and, accordingly, issued a second patent for the grand principality to Prince Dmitry Ivanovich. By accepting the second patent, the prince of Moscow alienated his original patron, the Sarai khan, who transferred the grand principality back to Prince Dmitry Konstantinovich. His order was carried from Sarai to Dmitry Konstantinovich by Prince Ivan Fedorovich of Beloozero.

But the prince of Suzdal' and Nizhnii Novgorod was not able to retake Vladimir and other territories belonging to the grand principality. He was physically separated from his Tatar protector by Mamai, who controlled the lands directly south of the Rus' principalities and helped his client, Dmitry Ivanovich, drive Dmitry Konstantinovich back to Suzdal'. By 1364, the two Prince Dmitrys had reached an accord; when yet another Sarai khan offered his patent to Dmitry Konstantinovich that year, he refused it and continued to recognize Dmitry Ivanovich of Moscow as the grand prince of Vladimir.

At about the time the prince of Suzdal'-Nizhnii Novgorod accepted Muscovite leadership, the Muscovite prince also confirmed his authority over the other princes who had been reluctant to recognize his seniority. In 1364, he engineered the eviction of Prince Konstantin Vasil'evich from Rostov to Ustiug; Konstantin's nephew, Andrei Fedorovich, became the prince of Rostov and a faithful ally of Dmitry Ivanovich. The year before the grand prince had also expelled the princes of Starodub and Galich from their lands and attached those principalities to his domain. It may have been in conjunction with this suppression of his political opponents that he assumed control of the other territories (Beloozero and Uglich, in addition to Galich) that he identified in his will as "purchases" made by his grandfather Ivan I Kalita.

In 1363–64, when the Daniilovich prince Dmitry Ivanovich recovered the grand principality of Vladimir, his legitimacy continued to emanate from the Tatars. But in the context of the Horde's Great Troubles, Dmitry's position did not rest with the Sarai khan, as had his predecessors'. Rather his claim to the Vladimir throne depended on the support of a non-Chingisid Tatar lord, Mamai.

Also, like his ancestors, Dmitry Ivanovich lacked a broad base of domestic support at the beginning of his reign. He did, however, benefit from the support and guidance of Metropolitan Aleksei, who, having returned to Moscow in 1360, quickly became one of Dmitry's most influential advisors and coordinated Muscovite princely policy with his own ecclesiastical goal of retaining the unity of his see, which had been achieved after the death of his rival in 1361. As the grand prince overcame the opposition of Prince Dmitry Konstantinovich of Suzdal', he also gained the latter's support. Their new relationship was symbolized by the grand prince's marriage in 1366 to Evdokiia, the daughter of his former rival. Following the example set by his grandfather, Dmitry Ivanovich thus not only neutralized a rival branch of the dynasty, but forged an alliance, symbolized by marriage, with it. The grand prince further consolidated his position by asserting Muscovite dominance over the principalities of Galich and Starodub. And most of the other northeastern Riurikid princes, including the Rostov clan, recognized his seniority. Dmitry Ivanovich, finally, also developed a good working relationship with his cousin, Vladimir Andreevich, who controlled the single appanage of Serpukhov, within the principality of Moscow.

Muscovite relations with Tver' and Lithuania

The major exception to this broad domestic acceptance of Dmitry Ivanovich came from Tver'. During the reigns of Semen and Ivan II that principality had been torn apart by internal strife between rival branches of the Tver' princely family. The princes of the appanage principality of Kashin opposed those of Mikulin. By 1366, Prince Mikhail Aleksandrovich of Mikulin had won the title grand prince of Tver'. He had done so with the aid of his brother-in-law, Grand Duke Olgerd of Lithuania.

In 1367, Dmitry Ivanovich initiated hostilities against Mikhail of Tver'.

The ensuing conflict lasted until 1375. Throughout the contest Mikhail repeatedly turned to Olgerd for assistance. Although they did advance to the very walls of Moscow (1368), Mikhail and Olgerd were unable to penetrate the stone fortifications that Dmitry had constructed the year before. Dmitry, on the other hand, pushed deeply into Tver' territory in 1370, and captured Mikulin, the capital of Mikhail's appanage. Mikhail appealed to Mamai, and received a patent for the grand principality of Vladimir from him (1370). Dmitry refused to yield and quickly recovered the patent.

As the events of 1367–70 suggest, the conflict between Moscow and Tver' engaged not only Lithuania, but also involved the troubled Golden Horde. For the princes who sought the grand princely throne, approval from a Tatar khan remained essential. But rival khans were competing among themselves for control over the sources of revenue and grazing lands that had in the past sustained the Horde's cohesion and power. Each of the khans, therefore, dispensed princely patents to those clients who demonstrated an ability to produce the required tribute and maintain domestic order, especially along trade routes that fed into the Golden Horde's declining commerce. Control over the commercial center of Novgorod as well as over key points along the Russian trade routes was therefore a priority for the competing Russian princes. Each strove to keep the routes safe, to dispense gifts to the Tatar authorities, and to deliver tribute to the appropriate khan.

The discord within the Horde had also contributed to instability along the trade routes. As early as 1360, a band of pirate-adventurers from Novgorod (*ushkuinniki*) were able to take advantage of the weakened authority of Sarai as well as the renewed interprincely rivalry among the Riurikids to seize Zhiukomen (Zhukotin) on the Kama River and threaten Kostroma, a grand princely possession northeast of Moscow and key point on the upper Volga waterway. The khan of Sarai sent envoys to then-Grand Prince Dmitry Konstantinovich, demanding that he maintain order along the trade route. The grand prince convened a princely assembly, captured the *ushkuinniki*, and sent their booty to the khan. The trade routes, however, remained insecure. In 1366, *ushkuinniki* attacked Muslim merchants in Nizhnii Novgorod and approached Bulgar. Dmitry Ivanovich, who had by then become grand prince, held Novgorod responsible and pressured its officials to control the situation. A year later Dmitry's governors were accepted in Novgorod.

The vitality of the trade routes ultimately depended upon Novgorod and the continuation of its trade with the Hanseatic merchants and also the commercial agents of the Teutonic Knights. Beginning in 1367 however, their trade relations began to deteriorate. The Teutonic Order increased military pressure on the Pskov frontier, and Novgorod was drawn into the ensuing conflicts. In 1369, the Hansa imposed duties on its export of silver to Novgorod. These actions may well have disturbed both Novgorod's trade and Grand Prince Dmitry Ivanovich's ability to make the obligatory tribute payments. It may, correspondingly, provide the motive for Mamai's decision in 1370 to transfer the grand princely patent from Dmitry Ivanovich to Tver's prince Mikhail Aleksandrovich.

But Grand Prince Mikhail proved to be less capable of stabilizing the commercial avenues within Rus' and delivering tribute than Dmitry had been. His efforts in 1371 to establish order in Kostroma failed. A year later, Novgorod, allied with Dmitry Ivanovich, evicted Mikhail's governors from another important town on Rus' internal trade routes, Torzhok. By spring of 1373, Mikhail and Novgorod were at war.

In the meantime, Dmitry, who had refused to yield the city of Vladimir to Mikhail, was able to win back Mamai's confidence. While Grand Prince Mikhail sent his son Ivan to represent him at Mamai's camp, Dmitry Ivanovich personally paid homage to the Tatar lord. Dmitry, furthermore, liberally distributed gifts to Mamai, his relatives, and court officials. His presentations convinced Mamai to return the patent to him (1371). Dmitry also paid Mikhail's debt to Mamai, and was allowed to take Ivan Mikhailovich into custody as a hostage (1371). In 1372, Dmitry and Mikhail made peace.

Prelude to Kulikovo

The truce with Tver' constituted a confirmation of Dmitry Ivanovich as grand prince of Vladimir; it also served as an indicator that Moscow was reemerging as the political center of the northern Russian lands. The event that has come to symbolize the might of Moscow and its prince, however, is the Battle of Kulikovo. That battle was fought on September 8, 1380, between Dmitry, who there earned the epithet Donskoi, and his former patron, Mamai. It has commonly been depicted as the courageous stand of an energetic ambitious young prince, who, having united the Russian princes, led them against their common foe, Mamai, in a valiant effort to throw off the oppressive Tatar yoke.

Despite its general acceptance, this interpretation of the Battle of Kulikovo is inherently flawed. One problem, which arises from the previous discussion, derives from the fact that despite their checkered relationship, Dmitry Ivanovich owed his position as grand prince and his legitimacy to Mamai. Rather than regarding Mamai as leader of the oppressive Tatar Horde, Dmitry himself had, shortly before the battle, been courting Mamai's favor. The basis and causes of the conflict between the two may be more clearly understood if the battle is considered in the context of the discord within the Horde and the nature of the obligations of the grand prince of Vladimir to the Horde.

When in 1371, Dmitry visited Mamai and received the patent for the grand principality of Vladimir from him, Dmitry also pledged, according to A. E. Presniakov, to deliver to Mamai the Russian tribute, albeit at a reduced amount.[1] But in 1373, the Hansa cut off its silver export to Novgorod. That ban lasted two years. During that period Dmitry Ivanovich reneged on his obligations; he ceased making any tribute payments to Mamai.

Possibly to compensate for that loss of revenue Mamai focused his own attention on the mid-Volga and its trading centers. He sent his officials to Nizhnii Novgorod, but in 1374 the residents massacred them. *Ushkuinniki* once again rampaged along the Volga, attacking Viatka and Bulgar and then descending the river to Sarai. Faced with Dmitry's refusal to pay tribute, coupled with his own apparent inability to control the chaotic conditions on the Volga commercial avenue, Mamai in 1375 once again issued the grand princely patent to Prince Mikhail of Tver'.

But Mamai could not offer Mikhail substantial military support. His Horde had been decimated the year before by another attack of the plague, and was in no position to send a strong army to enforce his decree. Nor did Mikhail receive aid from Lithuania. His own forces were inadequate to defeat Dmitry's assemblage, which included contingents from virtually all the northeastern Russian principalities as well as Novgorod and Mikhail's long-standing rivals in the Tver' appanage of Kashin. With that army Dmitry successfully defended his throne. Rather than yield his position to Mikhail, he defied Mamai and launched his own offensive, during which he besieged Tver' for four weeks and forced Mikhail to surrender.

The subsequent peace treaty, concluded between Dmitry and Mikhail in 1375, referred to Mikhail by the title of grand prince of Tver', but nevertheless acknowledged Dmitry's seniority by declaring him Mikhail's "elder brother" and the rightful grand prince of Vladimir. Mikhail accordingly renounced all claims to Novgorod. He also recognized the autonomy of Kashin and promised to refrain from conducting independent diplomatic relations with Lithuania and the Golden Horde. Although he would not abide by those last provisions of the treaty, peace was restored.

Once again, Dmitry Ivanovich had regained his grand princely throne.

---

[1] A. E. Presniakov, *The Formation of the Great Russian State*, trans. by A. E. Moorhouse (Chicago: Quadrangle Books, 1970), p. 265.

But he had yet to overcome his difficulties in raising and delivering tribute that had evidently persuaded Mamai to transfer the responsibilites of the grand prince to Mikhail. He too turned his attention to the Volga route and Bulgar, which was then nominally ruled by the khan of Sarai, but still vulnerable to disruptions from *ushkuinniki*. Another band had managed in 1375 to make its way down the entire length of the river, only to be murdered at Astrakhan'. In 1377, Dmitry Ivanovich, joined by Dmitry Konstantinovich of Nizhnii Novgorod and Suzdal', restored a measure of security along the route by attacking Bulgar and forcing it to accept their customs officials.

The following year, however, the grand prince's forces clashed with a Tatar military force subject to Mamai and defeated it on the Vozha River, a tributary of the Oka, in the Riazan' principality. Mamai's force in 1378 may have been responding to the fact that Dmitry, despite his success in reestablishing order and collecting revenue, had not resumed his tribute payments. On the contrary, as the Russian grand prince imposed his authority over the mid-Volga, he was depriving the Tatar chieftain of yet another source of revenue, customs fees from Bulgar. Mamai's deteriorating fiscal position turned into an urgent crisis when Tokhtamysh established himself at Sarai (1378). Mamai had to confront Tokhtamysh, but to do so, he required revenue. And for that he had to force the grand prince of Vladimir, Dmitry Ivanovich, to pay the tribute to him. It was in this context that the Battle of Kulikovo occurred.

The Battle of Kulikovo

In preparation for the confrontation Mamai, between 1378 and 1380, turned to Lithuania. Its grand duke, Jagailo, agreed to provide military support. Mamai also negotiated with Prince Oleg of Riazan'. Finally, he sent messengers to Dmitry Ivanovich with the demand that the grand prince deliver his tribute at, significantly, the higher amount that had been customary during the reigns of Uzbek and Janibek. By the time Dmitry was able, according to some accounts, to collect the tribute and to despatch it to Mamai, the latter's Tatar forces, supplemented by troops hired from the Caucasus and along the Black Sea coast, had begun advancing northward. Dmitry's envoys, seeing little chance of success for their mission, returned without delivering their treasure.

Dmitry then assembled his own army. His successful efforts to consolidate his power enabled him to draw upon the military forces from many of the Russian principalities. The chief exceptions were: Riazan', which, located on the Tatar frontier, had agreed to aid Mamai; Tver', which despite the 1375 treaty, did not on this occasion respect

Dmitry's leadership; Nizhnii Novgorod-Suzdal', whose prince Dmitry Konstantinovich, Donskoi's former rival, was not identified among the participants; and Novgorod Velikii.

The battle took place on a field called Kulikovo Pole (Snipes' Field), near the upper Don River. Mamai had camped there while awaiting the arrival of his Lithuanian allies. The Russian army meanwhile gathered at Kolomna, where it was joined by two of Jagailo's brothers, the princes of Polotsk and Briansk. Grand Prince Dmitry then took the initiative. He led his forces across the Oka and the upper Don, and, before their Lithuanian support arrived, engaged the Tatars.

The battle, as described in the Russian chronicles, was intense. After several hours, Mamai's army appeared to have gained an advantage, and it seemed that the Russian troops, stretched across a seven-mile front, were on the verge of collapse. But at the critical moment, a unit commanded by Dmitry's cousin Prince Vladimir of Serpukhov, which had been held in reserve, was unleashed. This strategy turned the tide of the battle. The exhausted Tatars were no match for the fresh Russian troops. Mamai fled. Dmitry Donskoi was victorious.

Despite its symbolic significance and the historical emphasis placed on the Battle of Kulikovo, the victory had little immediate practical effect on the relationship between the Russian principalities and the Golden Horde. Almost immediately after his defeat, Mamai raised another army and directed it against his main opponent and challenger, Tokhtamysh. At their battle on the Kalka River Mamai again suffered defeat (1381). Mamai's subsequent fate is recorded variously. According to one account, he was captured and executed by Tokhtamysh. Another claims he fled to the Genoese at Caffa, only to be killed there.

Tokhtamysh seized Mamai's treasury and absorbed his family and followers into his own Horde. He also sent envoys to Grand Prince Dmitry Ivanovich, Prince Oleg of Riazan', and the other Russian princes to inform them of his victory and assumption of power as khan of the Golden Horde. The Russian princes respectfully acknowledged the new khan by sending gifts, but declined to attend his court personally to receive their patents. Tokhtamysh quickly asserted his authority. In 1382, he led an expedition against the Russian principalities. Gaining support and cooperation from Oleg of Riazan', he crossed the Oka and approached Moscow. Dmitry Donskoi, hero of Kulikovo, fled to Kostroma. His city was besieged, then sacked by Tokhtamysh's Tatars.

The Russian princes, including those of Tver' and Nizhnii Novgorod, immediately submitted to Tokhtamysh. Dmitry Ivanovich similarly acknowledged the khan's suzerainty and was accorded the grand princely title. But with his title he also reassumed responsibility for collecting and delivering tribute, now set at higher amounts than he had previously paid Mamai. When Dmitry's son Vasily escorted the first payment to Tokhtamysh, the khan held him as a royal hostage at his court.

The causes of the Battle of Kulikovo had thus been rooted in the internal discord within the Horde, particularly Mamai's desperate need to strengthen his position before facing Tokhtamysh. His defeat by Tokhtamysh, however, also ended the division within the Horde and thus removed Dmitry Ivanovich's opportunities for maneuvering among the Tatar competitors. The grand prince of Vladimir and all the Russian principalities were left subordinate to the khan of the Golden Horde, as they had been before the Great Troubles within the Horde had begun.

Nor did the Battle of Kulikovo alter the Muscovite prince's position within the Rus' lands. As discussed above, before Kulikovo Dmitry had overcome his strongest dynastic rivals and asserted dominance over the Rostov and Galich princes and probably those of Beloozero and Uglich as well. As grand prince he commanded obedience from Pereiaslavl', Kostroma, and Iur'ev. The Iaroslavl' princes also appear to have recognized his seniority. He was thus able to gather a large army from the retinues of these numerous principalities in 1380. And when Dmitry died in 1389, no members of the dynasty, except his cousin Vladimir Andreevich and Vladimir's son, raised any objection to the succession of his son Vasily to the grand princely throne. Vasily easily overcame their opposition and ruled from 1389 to 1425.

Nevertheless at the time of the Battle of Kulikovo Dmitry Ivanovich lacked the authority to command the princes or military retinues from Tver', Suzdal'-Nizhnii Novgorod, Riazan', or Novgorod to join his army. And even the prince of Nizhnii Novgorod, who may have cooperated with the campaign, did not submit his retinue to Moscow's command. After returning to Moscow in 1382, Dmitry did send a punitive expedition against Riazan' and temporarily replaced Prince Oleg with his own governors. Even with this expansion of its authority, however, Moscow had not yet achieved supremacy within the Russian lands.

THE POST-KULIKOVO TRANSITION

Although Tokhtamysh rapidly restored Tatar authority, during the next fifty years the relative power of the states of eastern Europe altered dramatically. The Golden Horde fragmented. It was not Moscow, however, that immediately benefitted from its decay. Rather, Lithuania under the capable leadership of its grand duke Vitovt rose to prominence. During the remainder of the reign of Dmitry and that of his son Vasily

(1389–1425), Moscow, although quietly growing in size and economic might, remained relatively weak and under the shadow first of the Golden Horde, then increasingly of Lithuania.

Lithuania

As discussed above, Lithuania had been an expanding power during the fourteenth century. When Olgerd died in 1377, a succession struggle broke out between his sons and his brother, Keistut. By 1381, Keistut had been killed, his son Vitovt (Vytautas) had escaped to the Order, and Jagailo Olgerdovich was ruling Lithuania. Jagailo led his realm into a new relationship with Poland, which earlier in the century had been Lithuania's chief rival. King Casimir, who had competed with Lithuania over Galicia and Volynia, had died in 1370. When his nephew and successor, King Louis of Hungary, also died in 1382, Louis' daughter Jadwiga acceded to the Polish throne. In 1386, she and Jagailo married, joining their two countries in the dynastic union of Krewo.

Jagailo focused his attention on Poland, leaving Lithuania to a viceroy. By 1393, his cousin Vitovt emerged from a renewed power struggle to become grand duke of Lithuania and lead his domain to new heights of power. Under his administration Lithuania extended its influence deeper into the lands of Rus' as well as into the realm of the Golden Horde itself. In addition, in 1410 Vitovt and his cousin, the king of Poland, delivered a debilitating blow to the Teutonic Knights. Although hostilities against the Order continued, the Knights were never able to regain their former power after the Battle of Tannenberg (Grunwald).

But even earlier, before his political victory in Lithuania, Vitovt had begun to extend his authority eastward. Moscow was among the first of the Russian principalities to recognize his seniority. In 1386, Prince Vasily Dmitr'evich escaped from Tokhtamysh's court where he had been held as a hostage. In his flight he reached Lithuania, where he became betrothed to Vitovt's daughter. Vitovt then assisted his return to Moscow. Four years later, Vasily, who had become grand prince in 1389, married his fiancee, Sofiia. In doing so, he implicitly acknowledged his father-in-law, Vitovt, as the senior prince in the region. Thereafter, with the exception of a disagreement over Novgorod in 1406–08, Vasily fully cooperated with Vitovt. Moscow did not intervene even when Vitovt seized Smolensk (1395) and then entered into a decade-long war against Riazan', whose Prince Oleg came to the defense of his own son-in-law, the deposed Smolensk prince. In 1385, the Riazan' prince, after being punished by Dmitry Donskoi for his role at the Battle of Kulikovo and then seeing his domain devastated by Tatar troops as well, had recognized

Dmitry Ivanovich's seniority. Nevertheless, Moscow neglected to protect its client and left Oleg to operate alone in his conflict against Lithuania.

Novgorod was a lingering source of contention between Moscow and Lithuania. And Novgorod's relations with Lithuania were ambivalent. On several occasions during the Lithuanian dynastic quarrels of the 1380s, Novgorod had received Jagailo's displaced relatives and assigned them lands for their sustenance. In 1398 Vitovt, who had been subordinating the junior Lithuanian princes, formed an alliance with the Teutonic Knights to launch a major campaign against Novgorod and Pskov, but the events in the steppe that culminated in the Battle of the Vorskla forced him to abort it.

After he had secured his position in Smolensk, however, Vitovt resumed his efforts to extend his authority over Pskov and Novgorod. His attack on Pskov in 1406 generated a hostile response from his son-in-law, Grand Prince Vasily Dmitr'evich. Nevertheless, although they gathered their armies and sparred for three years, Vitovt and Vasily avoided any serious direct engagements. As their dispute ended, Novgorod again received and set aside lands for a Lithuanian prince, one of Vitovt's cousins, and Vitovt and Vasily concluded a truce (1408).

Nor did their differences over Novgorod upset the basic relationship between Vitovt and Vasily I. In his will Vasily Dmitr'evich included Vitovt in the group of guardians to whom he entrusted the safety and care of his own son and heir, Vasily Vasil'evich, as well as that of his wife and other children. The Lithuanian ruler's authority was so great that when the grand prince died in 1425, no Russian prince dared challenge the succession of Vasily II while the boy's grandfather lived. Only when Vitovt died in 1430 did the young grand prince's uncle and cousins claim the throne and plunge the Russian lands into a civil war that would last a quarter of a century.

Vitovt protected his grandson, but also used his position to strengthen Lithuania. While Moscow passively observed, he concluded a treaty with Tver', in which its prince Boris recognized Vitovt's seniority (1427). Then, after years of pressuring Novgorod, he undertook a final campaign against the city. In 1428, he brought up a cannon so heavy it required forty horses to transport it and placed it before Porkhov, an outpost south-west of Novgorod. When fired, the cannon not only destroyed the fortress tower, but blew itself up along with the German craftsman who had built it. Nevertheless, Novgorod quickly sued for peace, and paid Vitovt a large sum of silver (10,000 rubles). Finally Vitovt, having finally established his governors in Smolensk in 1404, reached an accord with Riazan', whose prince agreed to render his service to Lithuania (1430).

By the time of his death in 1430, Vitovt had incorporated Smolensk, achieved varying forms of supremacy over the grand principality of Vladimir and its possessions as well as Tver' and Riazan', and had intimidated Novgorod. In short, by the end of Vitovt's reign, Lithuania dominated most of the Russian lands. In a similar fashion Vitovt extended Lithuanian political authority into the Tatar realm.

The Golden Horde

Vitovt's ability to expand his sphere of influence was, at least in part, the result of the final decay of the Golden Horde, which was precipitated by Timur's onslaught in 1395–96. After Timur defeated Tokhtamysh, the deposed khan sought refuge with Vitovt. Together the two prepared to confront the new khan of Sarai, Timur-Kutlugh, and his non-Chingisid supporter, Edigei. On August 12, 1399, the two camps met on the banks of a tributary of the Dnieper River. Vitovt adopted a haughty, confident attitude. Unlike Jagailo, who had accepted a junior status in his relations with the Tatars, Vitovt did not. When Edigei and Timur-Kutlugh offered him peace if he would recognize their suzerainty, Vitovt disdainfully refused and made a counter offer, proposing the same terms but in reverse.

Vitovt and Tokhtamysh lost the subsequent Battle of the Vorskla. Tatar forces ravaged Lithuanian possessions, including Kiev, and repossessed the lower Bug River, which since Olgerd's reign had been Lithuania's access to the Black Sea. The defeated Tokhtamysh eventually found sanctuary in western Siberia (Tiumen'), where he died early in the fifteenth century. Despite the outcome of the battle, during the next several decades the Golden Horde deteriorated, while Vitovt's power grew.

Immediately after the Battle of Vorskla, under the guidance of Edigei and the khans he sponsored, the Horde appeared to remain cohesive and powerful. Tatar strength was clearly evident in 1408, when Edigei launched a campaign against the lands of Rus', besieged Moscow, and devastated the Russian lands in his path. But very shortly after that demonstration of his might, Edigei was evicted from the Golden Horde by his son-in-law, Khan Timur-khan (1411). The absence of a strong political and military leader, coupled with its disrupted commerce and economic disarray, resulted in the final disintegration of the Golden Horde.

As the Golden Horde entered another period of political anarchy, Lithuania emerged as the dominant power in the eastern European steppe. Vitovt took advantage of the Horde's weakness to bolster Lithuania's economic potential. By constructing a series of forts between Kiev and the Black Sea, he reasserted Lithuanian control over the steppe and secured the lower Dnieper River. This effort, combined with his territorial expansion into western Russia, gave Vitovt control over the ancient Rus' trade route that connected the Baltic and Black Seas. This asset, acquired just after Timur had inflicted so much damage on the alternate commercial network of the Golden Horde, provided Lithuania with a distinct economic advantage, which he duly exploited.

Lithuania's political influence in the steppe was also heightened. Actively participating in the Horde's power struggle, he supported Tokhtamysh's son after Edigei's flight in 1411. But, by 1419, the Horde's territories were once again divided. The lower Volga was controlled by the Sarai khan, while the lands west of the Volga were dominated by Ulu-Muhammed. Vitovt gave his support to the latter. When he suffered military defeat in 1422, Vitovt offered him sanctuary in Lithuania where he remained until he was able to reestablish his authority in the Crimea (1427).

Ulu-Muhammed did not remain in the Crimea. Ten years later he was again forced out of the area. He led his band northward, where they appeared at Belev on the Lithuanian side of the Oka River in 1437–38, then before Moscow in 1439, and finally settled in the vicinity of Kazan' by 1445. Ulu-Muhammed's son Mahmutek there founded the Khanate of Kazan'.

Ulu-Muhammed was not the only Tatar khan to appeal for and obtain Vitovt's aid. When Ulu-Muhammed established himself in the Crimea in 1427, he forced another Tatar leader, Hadji-Girey, to abandon the area. He too found refuge on Lithuanian soil, where he stayed until 1449, when he returned to the Crimea. He then founded the Crimean Khanate. Hadji-Girey remained a loyal ally of his patrons, the grand dukes of Lithuania.

Moscow

In the immediate post-Kulikovo period the Russian principalities and their Daniilovich grand princes resumed roles subordinate to the Golden Horde. They received their patents from the Golden Horde khan and paid tribute to him. Even as the Horde began to disintegrate, it was not the Russian lands, but Lithuania that initially filled the political vacuum left by the Tatar khans. Western Russian principalities increasingly recognized the hegemony of Vitovt of Lithuania, while the Daniilovichi placed themselves under his protection through the marriage of Vasily Dmitr'evich to Vitovt's daughter. Despite the victory at Kulikovo, the northeastern Russian lands remained subordinate to their more powerful neighbors.

Nevertheless, operating within the evolving political context, facing the fragmentation of the Golden Horde and overshadowed by Lithuania, Dmitry Donskoi and his son Vasily I oversaw the formation of a larger, stronger, and more centralized state of Muscovy. Their motivation, however, stemmed from the issue of dynastic legitimacy. Through the fourteenth century Tatar authority had supplanted the Riurikid dynastic traditions as the basis of the Rus' political structure and legitimacy for its princes. The Daniilovichi had attained their positions by virtue of Tatar favor and support. Internal political disturbances followed by Timur's invasions, however, had shaken the foundations of the Golden Horde. The Daniilovich princes, the chief beneficiaries of the khans' favors, could no longer rely exclusively on their Tatar patrons.

The weakening of the Golden Horde obliged the Daniilovichi, even after they turned to Lithuania for supplementary support, to solidify their domestic political base. Several factors favored Dmitry Donskoi and Vasily I in their pursuit of that objective. In the absence of intra-Daniilovich political disputes, they benefited from the stability at their court and among their boyar elite. They profited from the economic recovery that the Rus' lands were enjoying, but more than any of the others, they added territory and economic resources to their principality. And they basked in the reflected glory of the cultural dynamism of the Orthodox Church, which lent its prestige and influence to Daniilovich hegemony. By the end of the reign of Vasily I in 1425, Moscow did not yet possess the size or strength to rival its neighbors beyond Russian borders, but it had no peer within northeastern Rus'.

The court The size of the Daniilovich branch of the dynasty and the absence of divisive feuds within it gave an advantage to Moscow's princes. Having lost so many relatives to the plague, the Daniilovich princes were able to stem the tendency, frequently practiced by their distant cousins and even tentatively begun in the 1340s during the reign of Semen the Proud, to subdivide their lands into numerous small appanage princi-palities. As a result, Dmitry Donskoi shared the Muscovite realm with only one cousin, Vladimir Andreevich. Vladimir's father, a younger brother of Semen and Ivan II, had also died during the plague in 1353. Vladimir had inherited his father's *otchina*, the appanage principality of Serpukhov. Relations between the cousins, guided by a series of three treaties, were cordial. Vladimir retained rights to rule his own realm and collect revenues from it as well as from one-third of Moscow itself. He was responsible for gathering tribute for the Golden Horde from his domain, but paid it through the grand prince, not directly to the khan. He also acknowledged Dmitry's seniority, supported him in military campaigns, and recognized Dmitry's son, Vasily, as his "elder brother" or the rightful heir to Dmitry's throne.

Dmitry Donskoi was survived not only by Vasily, but also by four other sons. Nevertheless, due to early deaths and the failure of some to have sons of their own, only one more lasting appanage principality, Mozhaisk, was carved out of the Muscovite realm. In the next generation it was subdivided into the principalities of Mozhaisk and Vereia.

The relative unity of the house of Moscow was mirrored by its court, at the peak of which was a small group of boyars. As Moscow's size, power, and prestige grew, its court attracted servitors from all over Rus' as well as from Lithuania. Moscow's military might correspondingly increased. During the reigns of Dmitry and Vasily I the court remained relatively unstructured, allowing some of the new servitors to rise relatively rapidly to prominence; they were drawn into the small elite, consisting of less than two dozen families in middle of Vasily I's reign, whose members were accorded boyar rank.

Although the few appanage princes also maintained their own courts and boyars, they remained in Moscow and no barriers were imposed to inhibit courtiers from transferring service from one prince to another. Regardless of their formal allegiance, all the servitors were expected to join Moscow's military campaigns. Nancy Shields Kollmann has described the boyars' service in this period as virtually interchangeable between the grand prince and his brothers.[2] The harmony among the Daniilovich princes reinforced the stability of the court elite. When a succession did occur, the new prince did not remove his predecessor's closest advisors; on the contrary, the court elite remained constant. As a result, the core of families that achieved elite status at the Muscovite court remained relatively stable and formed strong bonds of mutual dependency and loyalty with the House of Daniil. This core provided the personal advisors upon whom the Daniilovich princes depended for military and administrative assistance. Not the least of these was Metropolitan Aleksei, who came from a boyar family, and who, having returned to Moscow (1360) and reunited the Lithuanian and Russian churches (1361), served as Dmitry Ivanovich's chief counselor.

The boyars' importance became evident at the time of Dmitry Ivanovich's succession. It will be recalled that the nine-year-old Dmitry lost the grand princely throne to Prince Dmitry Konstantinovich of Suzdal' and Nizhnii Novgorod in 1360. The Moscow boyars, however,

2 Nancy Shields Kollmann, *Kinship and Politics: The Making of the Muscovite Political System, 1345–1547* (Stanford, Calif.: Stanford University Press, 1987), p. 44.

remained steadfast in support of their prince. It was largely through their efforts, undertaken despite the political confusion at the Golden Horde, that the Sarai khan issued his patent to Dmitry Ivanovich in 1362. It was their loyalty and refusal to abandon him in favor of his rival that enabled the young prince to mount the military force that expelled Dmitry Konstantinovich from Vladimir and also suppressed the latter's supporters, princes from Rostov and Galich-Dmitrov, as well as the prince of Starodub in 1363–64. They similarly provided the means for him to defeat Prince Mikhail of Tver'.

The character of the Daniilovich court, small enough to function on the basis of personal relationships, flexible enough to absorb selected new arrivals into its highest ranks, and unhampered by division among its princes, became an essential component in the growth and development of Muscovy during the reigns of Dmitry Donskoi and Vasily I. The Daniilovich princes came to depend on their boyars and other servitors, while their court provided an avenue for those servitors to achieve power, wealth, and status.

The economy and territorial expansion Moscow also benefited from a general economic recovery that was evident in the Russian lands by the second half of the fourteenth century. Its vigorous construction programs reflect an economic dynamism, which Moscow was experiencing despite the depletion of its population, including urban workers, resulting from the Black Death; despite the sack of the city by Tokhtamysh in 1382, Edigei's siege in 1408, and the destruction occasioned by their invading Tatar armies; and despite continuing Tatar demands for tribute.

The limestone walls of the kremlin, although they had to be built by peasants drafted from outside the city, were erected by Grand Prince Dmitry Ivanovich in 1367–68, shortly before he began his offensive against Tver'. They constitute but one example of the projects undertaken in and around Moscow. Inside the fortified walls Metropolitan Aleksei founded the Chudov or Miracle Monastery, while to the east and south-east of the city the Andronikov and Simonov monasteries were also constructed in the 1360s and 1370s. A series of other monasteries, built from the 1380s, similarly ringed the northern outskirts of the city. The foundations for the Church of the Assumption within the Simonov monastery were laid in 1378 under the joint sponsorship of the grand prince and the metropolitan. Other fortified monasteries were located in Serpukhov and Kolomna, towns within the Moscow principality on the Oka River. The examples cited were accompanied by many others; according to David Miller, more costly masonry structures were built in

Map 7.1 Northeastern Rus' in the late fourteenth century (1389)

Moscow between 1363 and 1412 than during any other fifty-year period from the time of the Mongol invasion in 1238 to 1462.[3]

The upsurge in construction activity was not confined to Moscow. Monastic expansion, in particular, was evident throughout northern Russia. Unlike the monasteries of earlier eras, most of the new ones were located well outside urban centers in sparsely populated areas. One motive that has been cited for this practice was the influence of hesychasm, a monastic movement that valued mystical experiences, focused on the individual's internal spiritual development, and correspondingly stressed the virtues of self-discipline and a contemplative lifestyle. Isolation from densely populated communities facilitated the monks' ability to purify themselves through prayer and meditation and ultimately achieve their desired goal, a vision of the "Divine Light." The revival and popularity of hesychasm in the Balkans in the first half of the fourteenth century provoked a major controversy in Byzantium. There is, however, little direct evidence that hesychast concepts, specifically, motivated the monastic movement in the lands of northern Rus'. Another reason, not necessarily inconsistent with the first, was the plague. Its disastrous consequences, interpreted to be manifestations of the wrath of God, may well have reinforced the attraction of religious figures to the eremetic life, a spiritual existence far removed from densely populated, sinful, and disease-ridden towns.

St. Sergei of Radonezh (c. 1314–92), originally a hermit who sought sanctuary in the remote forests north of Moscow, was closely associated with the foundation of new monasteries. Committed to a life of asceticism and personal manual labor, he acquired a reputation for holiness and attracted other monks who settled near him. In 1354, they joined together to form the Holy Trinity (St. Sergius) Monastery with Sergei as their abbot. In doing so the hermits exchanged their independence for a cenobitic order, in which they pooled their labor and accepted the monastery's formal organization and communal discipline.

Sergei influenced the development of numerous other monasteries. He founded some personally. In addition, his disciples at the Holy Trinity, having absorbed his teachings, opted to abandon their monastic community in search, once again, of solitary spiritualism. Other monasteries stemmed from the Simonov Monastery. Sergei's nephew, Fedor (Theodore), who grew up at the Holy Trinity Monastery, became abbot of the Simonov Monastery, founded by Metropolitan Aleksei. Subsequently, in 1397, St. Cyril (Kirill) moved from the Simonov Monastery,

---

[3] Miller, "Monumental Building as an Indicator of Economic Trends in Northern Rus'," pp. 372–373.

where he had succeeded Fedor as abbot, to the distant Beloozero, only to attract his own disciples, who became the monks of St. Cyril-Beloozero (Kirillov-Beloozerskii) Monastery. St. Savatii, following the same pattern, abandoned the St. Cyril-Beloozero Monastery in favor of the isolated wilderness of an island in the White Sea, and soon became abbot of his own Solovetskii Monastery (1420s). Similar chains of monasteries were established elsewhere. In less than a century, beginning c. 1350, approximately 150 new monasteries, a significant portion of which were "desert" monasteries modeled after Sergei's Holy Trinity, had formed a network of ecclesiastical communities scattered across the northern countryside.

These monasteries too reflected the economic vitality of the era. When they were first established, the monks themselves constructed churches and other edifices and engaged in a variety of occupations to support themselves. But despite their humble origins, many of the new monasteries ultimately became large wealthy landowning institutions. Their growth was encouraged by local princes, who issued immunity charters, exempting them and settlers on their lands from a variety of taxes. The Holy Trinity Monastery accumulated so many estates, generally by purchase or bequest, that it became one of the largest landholders in the Russian lands. The St. Cyril-Beloozero Monastery took advantage of the effects of the plague. The town of Beloozero was so severely affected by the recurrent epidemic that survivors relocated to a new site. The monastery later, especially after the 1420s, purchased much of the abandoned land in the environs of the original town. The Solovetskii Monastery too developed into a wealthy institution centered around its strong island fortress, but incorporating vast stretches of northern territory. Monastic property, often scattered over numerous districts, consisted not only of agrarian tracts, but urban real estate as well.

Although the monasteries were widespread, the Moscow princes in particular reaped significant benefits from them. Some of the monasteries, strategically located and fortified, contributed specifically to Moscow's defense. Although the Holy Trinity was unable to withstand the attacks from Tokhtamysh and Edigei, it and the monasteries surrounding Moscow doubled as fortresses guarding the approaches to the city. The walled monasteries built by Donskoi in Serpukhov and Kolomna similarly protected his domain at its frontier along the Oka.

Other activities of the Church contributed more substantively to Moscow's political and economic strength. In addition to its monastic expansion, the Orthodox Church was also engaged in missionary activity. One monk associated with the conversion of pagan tribes to Christianity was St. Stefan (Stephen) of Perm' (1340–96). Stefan had taken his vows in

Rostov, where he studied Greek and became a proficient copyist. But he eventually returned to his native town of Ustiug, and there became fascinated with visiting tribal traders from the northeast. In 1379, he set off to explore the lands along the Vychegda and Vym' Rivers. His expedition resulted in the conversion of the local Finno-Ugric population, known as the Zyriane or Komi. Stefan subsequently created an alphabet for them so they could read the Scriptures and other religious texts he translated into their native language. Despite persistent and violent protest from some of the Zyriane and their pagan neighbors, Metropolitan Pimen created a new bishopric of Perm' in 1383, and consecrated Stefan as its first bishop.

The conversion of Zyriane in the area known as Vychegda Perm' and the organization of the region into a new bishopric was not simply an ecclesiastical issue. It had political and economic repercussions for Moscow and, most immediately, for Novgorod. Before the appearance of Stefan, the Zyriane had paid tribute in luxury fur pelts to Novgorod. The archbishop considered their land part of his see and the creation of the Perm' bishopric an infringement upon his authority. In 1385, he sent a Novgorodian army to Perm'. Ustiug took up the defense of Bishop Stefan and defeated Novgorod's forces. Stefan, nevertheless, made a trip to Novgorod the following year and became reconciled with the archbishop. Novgorod ceded Vychegda Perm'. Its tribute subsequently went to Moscow.

The ease with which Moscow secured Vychegda Perm' may have prompted Vasily I to target another of Novgorod's assets, the North Dvina land. This area supplied Novgorod not with luxury fur, but with huge quantities of common grey squirrel pelts, which had become popular during the fourteenth century in northwestern Europe. In 1397, Vasily I sent his governors the North Dvina land and issued a charter to the local inhabitants. Novgorod, however, vigorously defended this possession, and drove out the Muscovite officials. Vasily made two more attempts to seize the area; both were similarly rebuffed by Novgorod.

Nevertheless in the process of attempting to add the North Dvina land to Muscovy, Grand Prince Vasily replaced the prince of Ustiug, a member of the Rostov branch of the dynasty, with his own governor. He thereby gained direct control over the town that controlled the waterways traversing the northlands and immediately built new fortifications around it.

Control over the northern territories of Vychegda Perm' and Ustiug had important implications for Moscow. Expansion to the northeast, although initiated by the Church, enlarged Moscow's economic base and did so at Novgorod's expense. The newly converted Zyriane became subjects of the grand prince, and they transferred their tribute payments, which consisted of rich sable and other thick northern fur pelts, from Novgorod to his treasury. Such resources were particularly valuable to the Muscovite princes in the late fourteenth century.

Novgorod, as discussed above, controlled the inflow of the silver required for the Tatar tribute. Before Moscow's expansion, it had also controlled the sources of fur, one of the main items that served as prized diplomatic gifts as well as exports that were exchanged for silver. But Moscow's relations with Novgorod were deteriorating. In 1380, Novgorod had failed to support Dmitry Ivanovich at Kulikovo. During the following decade it had on several occasions shown favor to Lithuanian princes. In 1386, just after the archbishop's venture to Perm', Novgorod and the Muscovite prince clashed directly. Obliged to deliver increased amounts of tribute to Tokhtamysh, Dmitry Donskoi had been pressuring Novgorod, which objected to making such large contributions. When, in addition, subjects of Novgorod again interfered with traffic along the upper Volga, Dmitry led an expedition against Novgorod. Novgorod lost. It subsequently paid a fine of 8,000 rubles and accepted Dmitry's tax collectors in the city.

But even with its successful use of military force Moscow could not depend on Novgorod's wealth to satisfy Tatar demands. Novgorod was facing its own difficulties in foreign trade. In 1385, a fire in the city had engulfed the German compound and destroyed the bulk of its stores. Hansa merchants demanded compensation. Novgorod, some of whose merchants had been plundered on the Neva River, made counter claims. In 1388, the Hansa, as it had done fifteen years before, forbade the export of precious metals to Novgorod. Then, when the ensuing dispute could not be resolved, trade relations were broken. They were not restored until 1392, when Novgorod concluded a treaty with the Hansa. Under these conditions and even after the restoration of Hansa trade, imports of silver from the Hansa declined, leaving the Teutonic Order as Novgorod's chief source of silver. But the Order's defeat in 1410 by Lithuania and Poland triggered not only its political, but also its economic decline. By 1427, the Order also ceased exporting silver to Novgorod.

Moscow's acquisition of Vychegda Perm' provided supplies of commercial goods that helped compensate for Novgorod's unreliability. Control over Ustiug secured the route that connected that northern reservoir with Moscow. Those northern resources provided Dmitry Donskoi and Vasily Dmitr'evich with the means to offer valuable gifts to regional lords, Tatar and Lithuanian alike; they could export their luxury goods directly to Sarai, Italian merchants of the Crimean colonies, or western markets; they could use their own commercial proceeds to pay their tribute and keep their patents. And they could use any surplus wealth to meet the fiscal needs of their courts and retinues.

Moscow's territorial expansion was not limited to the north. Vasily I also gained control over Nizhnii Novgorod. As the easternmost Russian principality, Suzdal'-Nizhnii Novgorod had responsibility for protecting the frontier and was thus strategically important. It also had commercial importance since the town of Nizhnii Novgorod, located at the juncture of the Oka and Volga Rivers, was the key to the Volga River route that linked the Russian lands to Bulgar and the Golden Horde and through them to the Italian commerical colonies on the Black Sea coast and caravan highways to the east. While Novgorod's exports through the Hansa to northern Europe were subject to interruption, these markets assumed greater significance. *Ushkuinniki,* Tatars, and local princes had all recognized the importance of Nizhnii Novgorod and its role in Volga commerce. For Moscow, which was extending its authority northward and acquiring its own supplies of export items, the cooperation of the Nizhnii Novgorod princes and stability along the Volga route were of paramount importance.

After its prince Dmitry Konstantinovich lost his bid for the grand princely throne, the principality of Suzdal'-Nizhnii Novgorod had remained relatively submissive to Moscow. By 1380, however, the bonds between Moscow and Suzdal'-Nizhnii Novgorod had loosened. And, in 1382, when Tokhtamysh approached Moscow from Bulgar in the east, Dmitry Konstantinovich, still prince of the region, independently opted not to oppose Tatar force and, as a sign of submission, dispatched his sons to Tokhtamysh. His death the following year, however, precipitated a decade-long contest for succession involving his brother and his sons.

In the midst of this chaotic situation Grand Prince Vasily Dmitr'evich obtained the patent for Nizhnii Novgorod, Murom, and Gorodets from Tokhtamysh (1392). Suzdal' remained under the local branch of the dynasty. But for over twenty years the local princes, backed by various Tatars including Edigei, refused to recognize the grand prince's claim to their *otchina.* In 1410, they carried their protest to the city of Vladimir, which they attacked and looted. But soon after Vasily arranged a marriage between his daughter and one of the Suzdal' princes in 1418, he also placed his own governors in Nizhnii Novgorod. He encountered no further resistance from the local dynasty.

By adding Ustiug, Nizhnii Novgorod, and Murom to the Muscovite realm, Vasily I enlarged the territory his father had accumulated. Dmitry's realm had included Galich and much of Beloozero, both of which were located north of the Volga River, as well as Starodub and Uglich. He had

also counted among his possessions the lands of the grand principality of
Vladimir: Vladimir, Pereiaslavl' Zalesskii, Kostroma, and probably Iur'ev.
He left them in his will to his son, Vasily I. At the end of Vasily's reign in
1425, Moscow's lands were not all contiguous. But its southern borders
hugged both the upper and lower ends of the Oka River and it contained
a major segment of the Volga, extending from Kostroma downstream to
Nizhnii Novgorod. Uglich dominated another portion of the Volga,
separating the principalities of Tver' and Iaroslavl'. Through Beloozero
and Ustiug, both located well to the north of the Volga, Moscow had
gained control over the river routes traversing Novgorod's hinterlands.
Moscow had not incorporated all the northeastern Rus' lands by 1425.
The principalities of Tver', Rostov, Iaroslavl', and Riazan' each continued
to recognize princes from its own branch of the dynasty. Nevertheless,
although still smaller than the mighty Lithuania or Novgorod with its
vast northern empire, Muscovy had outstripped the northeastern Rus'
principalities in size and resources by 1425.

The Church The activities of the Orthodox Church in the late fourteenth
and early fifteenth centuries reflected economic conditions in the Rus'
lands and enriched Moscow. Monastic elders also provided a different
type of support for the Daniilovich princes. They, along with the Church
hierarchs of this era, were primarily concerned with issues of Church
leadership and unity. The Orthodox populations of Lithuania and the
Russian lands had been reunified by Metropolitan Aleksei, but divided
again in 1375. When Aleksei died in 1378, control over the Russian see
vacillated between two primates. One was Kiprian, who had been named
metropolitan in Lithuania in 1375 with the intention that he would
eventually succeed Aleksei and reunite the two churches. When he went
to Moscow in 1378 to claim Aleksei's post however, Grand Prince
Dmitry seized him, confiscated his belongings and those of his entourage,
held him in custody overnight, then unceremoniously despatched him
from Moscow.

The second was Pimen, who became Grand Prince Dmitry Ivanovich's
candidate after the death of his first choice Mitiai, and was consecrated as
metropolitan of the Russian lands in 1380. After the Battle of Kulikovo
however, Dmitry Donskoi reversed himself, recognized Kiprian as
metropolitan, and welcomed him in Moscow, where he was in residence
until just before Tokhtamysh reached the city in 1382. Although Pimen
later reassumed responsibilities as head of the Russian Church, the
contest and confusion were not resolved until 1389, when both he and
Dmitry Donskoi died. Kiprian then returned to Moscow in triumph.
His escort included two other Orthodox metropolitans. He was also

accompanied by five bishops, representing both the Lithuanian and the Rus' portions of his see (Chernigov, Smolensk, Riazan', Rostov, and Suzdal') and signifying that he had become chief prelate of both. He continued to function in that capacity until his death in 1407.

If Mitiai and Pimen had been distinguished by their willingness to limit the range of their authority to lands subject to the grand prince's direct rule or influence, Kiprian was identified with the cause of ecclesiastical unity among the entire see. Once he became metropolitan in both Lithuania and the Russian lands, his Church used an array of cultural vehicles to promote that concept. The charismatic monastic leaders, who had acquired perhaps more spiritual influence than the metropolitans in the preceding decades, had supported Kiprian for the post of metropolitan. They too supported a unified Church centered around Moscow. But in the process of fostering ecclesiastical unity, the Church was also, by the middle of the fifteenth century, depicting Moscow's princes with the honor appropriate to the secular rulers of the Orthodox populace. The legitimacy of the Daniilovichi as grand princes of Vladimir was thereby strengthened.

St. Sergei of Radonezh exemplified the monastic elders. His prestige was such that Metropolitan Aleksei, before his own death in 1378, identified Sergei as his choice to succeed him, but Sergei refused to be considered. Sergei died in 1392, but his reputation survived him, and shortly after his death, he began to be venerated. Chronicle entries related to him emphasized his close ties to Grand Prince Dmitry Ivanovich and his family. They recorded that Sergei had officiated at the christening of two of Dmitry's sons, and that he had served as his emissary to Prince Oleg of Riazan' in 1385. He was also in attendance at Dmitry Donskoi's funeral, along with several bishops and other ecclesiastical notables, whereas Metropolitan Pimen, then visiting Constantinople, was noticeably absent.

In addition, Sergei's disciple Epifanii (Epiphanius) the Wise, a monk from Rostov noted for his travels abroad, his scholarship, and a distinctive literary style best reflected in his vita of St. Stefan of Perm' (composed 1396–98), also wrote a vita of Sergei (1417–18). That vita was edited and its style altered by another hagiographer, Pakhomii (Pachomius) the Serb, in the 1430s and 1440s. The vita portrayed Sergei's spiritual qualities and described the miracles attributed to him. Some had political implications. In one miracle the Blessed Virgin appeared to Sergei and assured him that his prayers had been heard and that She would protect his monastery. The Blessed Virgin had been associated with Kiev, and similar miraculous appearances had accompanied each major stage in the transfer of the center of the Church from Kiev to Vladimir. This miracle suggested that the Holy Mother was extending, if not transferring, her special protection to Sergei and, by implication, to those he graced with his blessing.

As the vita was revised, it too incorporated elements that not only highlighted the holiness of Sergei, who was canonized between 1446 and 1448, but by association glorified the grand prince. Thus, in a section that probably had been added to the vita by Pakhomii in the middle of the fifteenth century, Sergei was depicted as blessing Grand Prince Dmitry Ivanovich and his forces on the eve of the Battle of Kulikovo. The imagery implied that the seat of Metropolitan Kiprian was the proper center of Rus' Orthodoxy, the heir of Kiev. The grand prince of Vladimir correspondingly held a special position among the Rus' lands. Dmitry Donskoi was by the middle of the fifteenth century explicitly identified in the vita as one who had both honored Sergei and been honored by him. Sergei had injected Dmitry with the courage to fight Mamai; in gratitude Dmitry sponsored the foundation of a new monastery, the Immaculate Mother of God, for which Sergei selected a location and consecrated its Church of the Assumption of the Blessed Virgin. Once again the image of the Blessed Virgin, identified with the center of the Church, was invoked, in this case in association with Grand Prince Dmitry. Through this and similar images of the blessed St. Sergei respecting and honoring Grand Prince Dmitry the vita not only portrayed the spiritual qualities of the saint and demonstrated the glory of the entire Russian Church, but elevated the prestige of the grand prince and contributed to the new domestic basis for Daniilovich legitimacy that was being constructed during the first half of the fifteenth century.

The literary treatment of Metropolitan Petr, who had been canonized in 1339, had similar effects. His vita, rewritten by Metropolitan Kiprian, emphasized the saint's selection of Moscow as his residence as well as his close association with Ivan I Kalita. The heirs of Kalita and Donskoi, in the absence of both dynastic tradition and Tatar authorization as grounds for legitimacy, benefitted from images of Vladimir as both the ecclesiastical and secular heir of Kiev and characterizations of their forefathers as specially anointed to rule the Orthodox Rus' lands.

Other types of ecclesiastical literature, geared also toward advancing Church unity, served the political goals of the Daniilovichi. At the eparchial courts and monasteries, which were both repositories and purveyors of Christian culture, monks wrote, copied, and preserved literary manuscripts. Among their products were two chronicles distinguished by the broad geographic scope of their subject matter. One of the chronicles was the Laurentian chronicle, copied in 1377 by the monk Lavrentii for the prince of Suzdal', Dmitry Konstantinovich. The Laurentian chronicle, as mentioned in chapter 3, consists of the Primary

Chronicle and a continuation extending to the year 1305. The latter portion had been compiled at the court of Mikhail Iaroslavich, grand prince of Vladimir and prince of Tver'; it combined materials from Novgorod, Riazan', and southern Rus' with others from northeastern Rus'. The broad perspective adopted by the Laurentian chronicle served the interests of a metropolitanate striving to encourage the unity of the Orthodox community.

If the Laurentian chronicle, copied just before the death of Metropolitan Aleksei, evoked an image of a single Orthodox community embodying the diverse lands of Rus', the second chronicle, the Trinity chronicle, placed Moscow in the center of that community. Compiled in 1408 at Metropolitan Kiprian's court in Moscow, it was also based on the 1305 codex. But its entries covering the fourteenth century, while drawn from a variety of local chronicles, had a definite pro-Moscow bias. Its depiction of Ivan I Kalita and its introduction of much of the information suggesting close ties between Dmitry Donskoi and the blessed Sergei of Radonezh typify its tone.

To offset the experience of division within the Church, the premise underlying the Trinity chronicle suggested not only that all the Rus' principalities formed a single community, but that Moscow was historically linked to Kiev, the traditional seat of the Russian metropolitan and origin of the Primary Chronicle, and was replacing it as Orthodoxy's ecclesiastical and cultural center. In the early fifteenth century the Daniilovich princes of Moscow were in no position to assert secular political authority over all the territories within the metropolitan's see. Nevertheless, the literary portrayal of a united metropolitanate implicitly argued for the supremacy of Moscow's secular rulers, the Daniilovichi, as well.

Icon and fresco painting, which reached an artistic peak during the late fourteenth and early fifteenth centuries, beautified Moscow physically and, like the literary texts, symbolically elevated the stature of its religious and secular rulers. Icons and frescoes were used to depict stories from the Scriptures and visually transmit religious messages to the largely illiterate congregations in the many churches that were being built in Moscow, its environs, and its dependent towns. Their artistry also contributed to the spiritual experience of the religious services.

Just as Epifanii's literary style had been affected by the cultural trends he witnessed during his travels, so painting was influenced by trends. Greek artists, like those who decorated the Church of the Assumption in Moscow in the 1340s, had been regularly conveying current styles and techniques to the Russian lands. In 1378, Feofan (Theophanes) the Greek arrived in the northern Russian lands; he decorated churches in

Figure 7.1 The Trinity Icon, by Andrei Rublev

Novgorod and Nizhnii Novgorod before arriving in Moscow, where he painted the iconostasis for the Church of the Annunciation and also worked in the Church of the Archangel Michael.

The greatest exponent of icon and fresco painting of this age was, however, Andrei Rublev (c. 1370–1430). Having spent his early years as a monk at the Holy Trinity Monastery, Rublev was later affiliated with the Andronikov Monastery. By the early fifteenth century he was assisting Feofan the Greek in painting the iconostasis for the Church of the Annunciation. Among his most famous icons were the "Savior" icon for a church in Zvenigorod and the "Old Testament Trinity" icon for the Holy Trinity Monastery. He also painted the frescoes of the Cathedral of the Assumption in Vladimir.

Rublev's style was marked by a combination of graceful, delicate lines and a distinctive use of color that created an ethereal effect for the depiction of heavenly images and a contrasting brighter, more solid appearance for earthly figures. His technique and style were imitated by a "school" of his followers, who continued to embellish the churches of the Muscovite principality with works of distinctive artistry.

But Rublev's work, too, reinforced the message that the center of the Church had shifted from Kiev to Vladimir and Moscow. The Cathedral of the Assumption in Vladimir constitutes an example. It had originally been built by Andrei Bogoliubskii in conscious imitation of Kiev's glory. Thus, when Dmitry Donskoi ordered it rebuilt and his son Vasily I commissioned Rublev to paint the cathedral's frescoes, they were restoring and embellishing a structure that had been identified with the transfer of Kiev's central authority to the northeast. Like the Trinity chronicle, the symbolism of the Cathedral of the Assumption referred to ecclesiastical unity. It suggested that the metropolitan's see, centered in northeastern Rus', was the direct descendant of the Kievan metropolitanate and contained the same lands that had formerly been subject to the Church hierarch based in Kiev. The close association of the grand princes of Vladimir, i.e., the princes of Moscow, with this symbol however, promoted the concept that they were, in a parallel manner, the heirs of the Kievan grand prince. The embellishment of Moscow's churches reinforced that impression.

Through imagery and implication ecclesiastical ceremonies, literature, and art imparted stature, elegance, and grandeur to Moscow, its metropolitan, and its princes. The Church's cultural activities served Metropolitan Kiprian's goal of according permanency to the unity of the Church. They did so in part by characterizing his ecclesiastical seat as heir to Kiev and the center of a single Orthodox community. Although Dmitry Donskoi and Kiprian were never actually reconciled to one another, the metropolitan's efforts to promote ecclesiastical unity had the effect of validating Daniilovich authority, of conferring honor on Donskoi, and of reinforcing his heirs' legitimacy.

The combination of court political developments, territorial and economic expansion, and Church support left the Daniilovichi, whose political position had been precarious in the middle of the fourteenth century, without rival in northeastern Rus' by 1425. Outwardly, the status of Daniilovich princes had not altered. They still acknowledged Tatar suzerainty. When Vasily I assumed his father's throne in 1389, he was confirmed in his position as grand prince by Tokhtamysh's emissary. He also depended heavily upon the protection of his father-in-law, Vitovt of Lithuania.

Within the lands of Rus', however, Dmitry Donskoi and Vasily substantially strengthened their principality and their political position. Grand Prince Dmitry, by defeating Dmitry Konstantinovich of Nizhnii Novgorod-Suzdal' and Mikhail of Tver', had finally curbed the lingering and recurrent dynastic objections to Daniilovich seniority. He reduced the possibility of a resurrection of such resistance by absorbing the lands of Dmitry Konstantinovich's supporters. As a result, when Dmitry Donskoi left to Vasily his throne along with the grand principality of Vladimir, which he treated as his patrimony, virtually no objection was raised by other members of the dynasty, and Vasily was able to extend Muscovy's borders to include Nizhnii Novgorod as well.

Resting on a broad territorial and economic base, supported by the military might derived from a loyal group of courtiers, and benefiting from the ideological expressions emanating from the Church, Dmitry Donskoi and Vasily oversaw not only the construction of new buildings in their expanding realm; they also laid the foundations for a new political structure that had its center at Moscow, contained the lands of northeastern Rus', and recognized the Daniilovich branch of the Riurikid dynasty as its legitimate rulers.

8

THE UNIFICATION AND CENTRALIZATION OF MUSCOVY

Much of the dynamic that drove the domestic politics of the Rus' principalities from the eleventh through the fourteenth century derived from intradynastic relations and concern over succession to the grand princely throne. Before the Mongol invasion the position of grand prince of Kiev had been the focal point of dynastic politics. After the Mongol invasion and the eventual absorption of the southwestern Rus' principalities, including Kiev, into Lithuania and Poland, the role of grand prince of Vladimir assumed a parallel significance for the northeastern Riurikid princes, the descendants of Prince Iaroslav Vsevolodich (d. 1246). Within the northeastern Rus' principalities dynastic tensions continued to shape domestic politics. Defenders of the eroding principles that defined legitimacy and determined the successors to the grand princely seat struggled with the Daniilovichi, whose ascendancy denoted the replacement of those principles by the authority of the khan of the Golden Horde.

By the end of the fourteenth century, the Daniilovich princes, more specifically the descendants of Ivan I Kalita, had monopolized the position of grand prince of Vladimir. By the time Vasily I claimed the throne in 1389, the only murmur of dynastic disagreement came from his father's cousin, Vladimir Andreevich of Serpukhov, who was, as Dmitry Donskoi had been, a grandson of Kalita. Although it is not clear that Prince Vladimir, whose own father Andrei had died in 1353, was challenging Vasily's claim to the throne, the rapid resolution of their dispute effectively confirmed that the field of eligible princes for the grand princely throne had narrowed further to the descendants of Dmitry Donskoi.

When Vasily I died in 1425, the Moscow branch of the dynasty controlled its own principality as well as those that had become possessions of the grand principality. Although Vasily II, the son of Vasily I, ruled as grand prince, he shared control of the family's domain and the revenue from it with his uncles and cousins. Each of them ruled his own appanage principality, inherited from his father or granted by the grand prince and consisting of one or more districts within the common realm. Even authority over and revenues from the city of Moscow itself were divided, albeit unequally, among all the princes in the dynastic line.

By 1425 the grand princes of Vladimir had also annexed territories or exercised strong influence over the princes of territories located beyond the boundaries of Moscow and Vladimir. Some, like Suzdal' and Nizhnii Novgorod, had at the time of the Mongol invasion been part of Iaroslav Vsevolodich's domain and had subsequently been ruled by descendants of his son Andrei. Other territories, the possessions of the Rostov princes that had been transferred to Moscow, for example, had been outside Iaroslav's realm; they had in the early thirteenth century belonged to Iaroslav's brother Konstantin Vsevolodich (d. 1218). In 1425, both Rostov itself as well as Iaroslavl' technically continued to be autonomous principalities, subdivided into their own appanages. Tver' and Riazan' also functioned independently of the prince of Moscow and were even forming close associations with Lithuania, as were Novgorod and Pskov.

Over roughly the next century (1425–1533) dynastic relationships and the political configuration of the northern Rus' principalities changed dramatically. Against the background of the disintegration of the Golden Horde and the receding influence of Lithuania, the princes of Moscow, once again resorting to intradynastic warfare, firmly established a vertical pattern of succession. Proceeding from father to eldest living son, it replaced the centuries-old practice of rotation through the senior generation. In conjunction with the loss of their rights to inherit the grand princely throne, the grand princes' brothers and cousins suffered a diminution of political status, and their appanages were reduced or reabsorbed into the holdings of the grand prince himself. Grand Princes Vasily II (1425–62), Ivan III (1462–1505), and Vasily III (1505–33) were then able not only to consolidate their authority over their ancestral realm, but also to expand it by incorporating the remaining independent principalities of Rostov, Iaroslavl', Novgorod, Tver', Pskov, Riazan', and as a result of war with Lithuania, Smolensk.

THE DMITR´EVICH DYNASTIC WAR AND SUCCESSION

Vasily I died in 1425. In a will written two years earlier, he had designated his son, Vasily Vasil'evich, as heir to both the grand principality and his

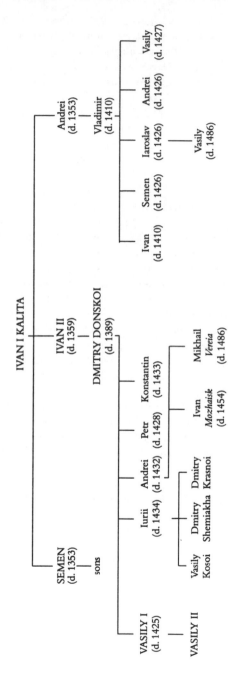

Table 8.1 Prince Ivan I Kalita and his descendants

votchina or personal, patrimonial territories. He thus identified his successor as grand prince just as his father, Dmitry Donskoi, had named him. As guardians for his son, who was ten years old in 1425, Vasily I named two of his brothers, Andrei and Petr; two cousins; and Vitovt of Lithania, the child's grandfather.

Nevertheless, much of the reign of Vasily II was devoted to what has commonly been referred to as a civil war. In fact, it was another dynastic war of succession. By 1425, the dynasty's traditional means of designating its own grand prince had long been supplanted by the selection process of the Golden Horde khan. But while the khans had displayed a preference for the illegitimate Daniilovichi, they had continued to respect the pattern of collateral succession. Some scholars have labeled that principle "anachronistic" in 1425.[1] There is no evidence, however, that it had been abandoned. But since the middle of the fourteenth century those princes who had succeeded to the grand princely throne according to the norms established for generational rotation had, due to peculiarities of family size and early deaths, also established precedents for a vertical system of succession. In practice, the two were temporarily indistinguishable. Dmitry had succeeded his father Ivan II, but at the time none of his uncles were living. Vasily I similarly had succeeded Dmitry, not because collateral succession had unambiguously been replaced, but because he was the senior eligible prince, according to dynastic tradition as well as to the standards of vertical succession. On the other hand, the last case of lateral succession, which had taken place in 1353 when Ivan II succeeded his elder brother Semen, had occurred in the absence of any candidates in the vertical line; all of Semen's sons had died by 1353, the last two having been among the victims of the plague. That succession too conformed to either system.

In 1425, for the first time in generations the deceased grand prince left both lateral and linear heirs; Vasily I was survived by four brothers and by one son. When Vasily I named his son as his heir, he was opting in favor of a new, untested vertical succession system, and his choice was bitterly contested. The opposition came from Iurii Dmitr'evich, the prince of Zvenigorod and Galich and the new grand prince's uncle. As the eldest surviving son of Dmitry Donskoi, he insisted that he was the legitimate heir to the grand princely throne on the basis of the dynasty's traditional principle of lateral succession within the senior generation of its ruling branch.

[1] E.g., Richard Hellie, *Enserfment and Military Change in Muscovy* (Chicago: University of Chicago Press, 1971), p. 78, and Robert O. Crummey, *The Formation of Muscovy, 1304–1613* (London and New York: Longman, 1987), p. 69.

Iurii, who had not been named as a guardian for Vasily Vasil'evich, refused to come to Moscow and swear an oath of allegiance to Vasily II. He also mobilized an army and began to march against him. Metropolitan Fotii (Photius), however, intervened, as did an outbreak of the plague. Iurii, recognizing that Vasily II could also depend on his grandfather Vitovt of Lithuania for protection, negotiated a truce.

The rivalry between Iurii and Vasily II, whose affairs were being conducted by a group of regents led by his mother and the metropolitan, intensified over other issues. In 1427, the last son of Prince Vladimir Andreevich died. Vladimir and his sons, as descendents of Ivan Kalita, had controlled an appanage principality that included Serpukhov and several other districts. In 1427, the entire appanage should have been inherited by Vladimir's single grandson, Vasily Iaroslavich. But the grand prince's regents tampered with his inheritance. They took a portion of it for Vasily II and another portion, Uglich, for his uncle Konstantin, whose loyalty they may have been anxious to secure. The new prince of Serpukhov was left with reduced holdings. In 1428, when one of Vasily's uncles, Petr Dmitr'evich of Dmitrov, died, Vasily's regency absorbed his appanage in toto rather than share it with the deceased's brothers, Vasily's other uncles. Under the protection of Vitovt and the metropolitan the regency was arrogating to the grand prince a status elevated above that of his closest relatives and surmounted upon an expanded territorial base. In the meantime Vitovt of Lithuania was extending his influence over the Rus' principalities of Novgorod, Tver', and Riazan' (1425–30).

In October 1430, Vitovt died. Lithuania quickly became preoccupied with its own succession struggle. Then in July 1431, Metropolitan Fotii also died. The young grand prince of Vladimir was left without his two most influential protectors. Iurii renewed his claim to the throne. But rather than rely on a military solution, Iurii and Vasily placed their dispute before the khan of the Golden Horde. Vasily I may have written a will leaving the grand principality to Vasily II, but when the will was contested, the quarreling parties turned to the khan, the dispenser of the patent for the grand princely throne.

By late summer in 1431 both Vasily and Iurii arrived at the Horde to present their cases and their gifts to Khan Ulu-Muhammed. The khan reached his decision the following June. He issued the grand princely patent to Vasily Vasil'evich, who also assumed responsibility for collecting and delivering the tribute that the khan continued to receive from the grand principality of Vladimir. Iurii was allotted Dmitrov, the principality of his late brother and the other major issue in dispute, as an addition to his own appanage. Vasily was accompanied back to Moscow by the khan's envoy, who formally installed him as grand prince in an official ceremony.

Vasily was supported at this time by most of the members of the house of Kalita. Of his four uncles, Konstantin, who had received Uglich from Vasily in 1427, remained loyal to him. Andrei too favored his nephew. When Andrei died in June 1432, his two sons, Ivan of Mozhaisk and Mikhail of Vereia, almost immediately concluded treaties of friendship with Vasily. Petr had died in 1428 without heirs. Only Iurii opposed him.

The grand prince also improved his relations with Vasily Iaroslavich of Serpukhov, whose lands he had earlier reduced, by marrying his sister. Iurii pointedly did not attend the wedding, which was held in February 1433. And, according to an allegorical tale composed a couple of decades later, when his two elder sons did join the festivities, they were insulted by the groom's mother. Incensed, they returned to Galich ready to do battle.

Iurii was in any case preparing for war. Unwilling to accept the khan's decision and unperturbed by his relatives' solid support for Vasily, he gathered an army, defeated Vasily's forces in an engagement on the Kliaz'ma River in April 1433, and marched into Moscow. Iurii then made peace with Vasily, who had fled from the scene, and granted him Kolomna as an appanage principality.

But Iurii had difficulty holding the power he had seized. Moscow boyars and other servitors, possibly concerned about losing their positions of influence and authority to Iurii's retainers from Galich, drifted to Vasily at Kolomna. Others within Iurii's own entourage were apparently distressed at his lenient behavior toward his rival. Lacking the loyalty of boyars and other courtiers, Iurii within months of his victory ceded Moscow and the grand princely throne and even Dmitrov back to Vasily.

Iurii's withdrawal did not, however, conclude the conflict. His two elder sons, Vasily Kosoi and Dmitry Shemiakha, were not party to their father's agreement. After Iurii returned to Galich, Vasily II launched a campaign against his cousins. Again his army was defeated (September 1433). Iurii, drawn back into the conflict by both his sons' and his nephew's actions, decisively defeated Vasily yet again in March 1434. Abandoning his mother and wife in Moscow, the young prince fled, evidently planning to seek refuge with the khan. Iurii, after besieging Moscow for a week, entered the capital for a second time. He took his nephew's wife and mother captive, and immediately began to consolidate his position. But in the midst of concluding treaties with the circle of princes who had previously supported Vasily, he died (June 5, 1434).

Iurii's death, which followed that of all his younger brothers, placed the Galich princes in an awkward situation. Vasily Kosoi assumed his father's position. But he lacked the foundation in dynastic tradition that had given his father credibility and legitimacy. According to the principle that his father had championed, the throne belonged to the senior member of the next generation. That was Vasily Vasil'evich. Vasily II, on the other hand, could invoke any one of several principles to support his claim: his father's will, the Mongol khan's appointment, and after June 5, 1434, dynastic tradition as well. Kosoi could not hold the throne. His own brothers did not recognize his legitimacy. Despite his persistence, by 1436 he had been defeated, captured, and blinded by his cousin, Vasily II.

The conflict of 1432–36 had been confined to the ruling house; princes of the other principalities had meticulously refrained from getting involved in the quarrel, even declining to grant refuge to exiled participants. After 1434, Vasily II became the legitimate heir according to both the traditional system of succession and a system of primogeniture. But Iurii's death had only postponed, not resolved the issue underlying the conflict, the question of which system took precedence over the other.

The contest between the two branches of Dmitry Donskoi's descendants relaxed for a decade. During that time another of Iurii's sons, Dmitry Krasnoi, died (1440). With Vasily Kosoi removed from political activity until his death in 1447 or 1448, Dmitry Shemiakha became the sole heir to their father's patrimony. During that time also Vasily II had produced a healthy male heir, Ivan (b. 1440). Tensions began to arise between Vasily and Shemiakha. The distribution of Dmitry Krasnoi's appanage territories was one cause of friction. In addition, they disagreed about Shemiakha's contributions to Vasily's military ventures as well as to the Tatar tribute. Nevertheless, the second stage of their dynastic war may be considered to have begun with an event that had little to do with the issues that divided them. But when it did erupt again, its scale broadened to include neighbors of the grand principality of Vladimir, especially the Tatars and Novgorod.

The event that prompted the renewal of the war was the Battle of Suzdal' fought on July 7, 1445, between Vasily II and Tatars belonging to Ulu-Muhammed's Horde. It will be recalled that Khan Ulu-Muhammed, who had invested Vasily II as grand prince, had later been obliged to leave the Crimea and had migrated with his horde to Belev, located on the upper Oka River on the Lithuanian side of the Lithuanian–Rus' frontier. He had been attacked there in 1437 by a Rus' army, led by Dmitry Shemiakha and his brother Dmitry Krasnoi. Although at the time they had acknowledged Vasily II's seniority, it is not unlikely that they launched their attack because they were concerned about the presence of Vasily's patron so near the frontier. Ulu-Muhammed moved eastward. In 1439, a band of his men staged a raid on Moscow; at this time Shemiakha neglected to send military assistance to Vasily and thereby contributed to the deterioration of their relations.

In 1444, Ulu-Muhammed and his followers moved further down the Oka River. They clashed with troops of Vasily II at Murom. When the Tatars continued to harass the area, Vasily II gathered a relatively small force; on his way to confront them, he unexpectedly encountered the Tatars outside Suzdal'. In the ensuing battle (July 7, 1445), the Tatars wounded and captured Grand Prince Vasily II.

The battle represented neither an attempt by the migrating Tatars to gain possession of Rus' lands nor an attempt by the Muscovite ruler to overthrow Tatar domination. Nevertheless, during the next months anxiety overwhelmed Moscow. Fire and fear of further attack prompted Vasily's mother and wife and key boyars to abandon the capital. Ulu-Muhammed, however, retreated to the east. He also sent an emissary to negotiate with Dmitry Shemiakha, who, A. A. Zimin pointed out,[2] was the next senior member of the generation and had assumed the grand princely responsibilities. But even as Dmitry sent the Tatar emissary with his own envoy back to Ulu-Muhammed, the khan yielded to Vasily's entreaties and promises of ransom payments and released him. Vasily's supporters intercepted and arrested Dmitry's envoy, while Vasily returned to Moscow in November 1445. He was accompanied by a detachment of Tatars who were to make sure the ransom as well as tribute, at higher rates than paid previously, were delivered.

Although bypassed by Ulu-Muhammed, Dmitry Shemiakha used the incident to revive his family's claim to the grand princely throne. Having secured the support of Prince Ivan of Mozhaisk and the neutrality of Tver', he waited until the grand prince went on a pilgrimage to the Trinity Monastery, then arrived at Moscow (February 1446), arrested Vasily's mother and wife, and sent a force to capture Vasily. When Vasily was brought back to Moscow, he was accused of showing excessive favoritism toward the Tatars, extravagantly bestowing land, silver, gold, and other valuables on them, and of having blinded Dmitry Shemiakha's brother, Vasily Kosoi. As retribution, Shemiakha blinded Vasily II and confined him with his wife at Uglich.

Reaction among the ruling elite was mixed. Shemiakha was already allied with Prince Ivan of Mozhaisk. But Vasily of Serpukhov adamantly opposed Shemiakha's acts and sought refuge in Lithuania. Some of Vasily II's boyars joined Shemiakha, but others joined the Serpukhov prince across the border. Despite his initial harshness, Shemiakha, pressured by

---

[2] A. A. Zimin, *Vitiaz' na rasput'e: feodal'naia voina v Rossii XV v.* [Hero at the crossroads: the feudal war in Russia, fifteenth century] (Moscow: Mysl', 1991), p. 105.

the senior prelate Iona, released Vasily II and his family to Vologda in September 1446; he demanded only that Vasily renounce his rights to the throne. The ousted grand prince duly swore an oath of allegiance to Shemiakha. But no sooner was he freed than he went on a pilgrimage to Beloozero, where the abbot of the St. Cyril-Beloozero Monastery absolved him of any sin he would commit by breaking that oath. He then began to receive his former boyars and servitors. He also reached an agreement with the prince of Tver', whose daughter was betrothed to Vasily's son Ivan.

More of Vasily's supporters began to assemble. Some returned from Lithuania. In addition, two of Ulu-Muhammed's sons, Kasim and Iakub, joined them. They had fled from the Horde when their elder brother, Mahmutek, murdered their father and founded the Khanate of Kazan'. In the face of this mounting opposition and pursued by Vasily and his Tatar allies, Shemiakha abandoned Moscow for Galich. Almost exactly one year after he had been arrested and blinded, Vasily II returned to his capital in triumph (February 1447).

Vasily was then able to conclude a peace agreement with Ivan of Mozhaisk, but the war with Shemiakha continued. The grand prince inflicted several defeats on his rival, at Kostroma in 1449 and at Galich in 1450. Shemiakha turned to the north. He sought refuge in Novgorod. Then, in 1451–52, he based his operations at Ustiug and tried to extend his authority northeastward over Vychegda Perm'. But Vasily's forces regained Ustiug, and in the winter of 1452–53, Shemiakha made his way again to Novgorod. By the summer of 1453, he was dead, killed by poisoning.

The next year Ivan of Mozhaisk, not trusting that Vasily would honor their treaty, fled to Lithuania. Vasily confiscated Mozhaisk as well as Shemiakha's appanage principality of Galich. In 1456, Prince Vasily of Serpukhov, despite his loyal support for Vasily II during the conflict, was also deprived of his lands, arrested, and exiled.

The war was over. The military victory of Vasily II was also a political triumph for the vertical system of succession. The conclusion of the war brought an end to direct challenges to a new grand prince by relatives who claimed generational seniority. But lateral heirs, the brothers and cousins of the grand prince and of his eldest son, did not become superfluous. A combination of tradition, the absence of a pervasive administrative apparatus, military requirements, and the vagaries of natural calamities that could result in the premature death of a primary heir or a childless grand prince, preserved a place in the political system for them. Thus, while Vasily II and his heirs tried to protect the succession for their own sons, they were bound to honor their brothers and cousins, who provided the dynasty's insurance against disaster and guaranteed that their line would continue to rule.

Even before the conclusion of the war Vasily II acted to ensure the succession of his eldest son. Shortly after his return to the throne in 1447, he named the seven-year-old Ivan as his co-ruler. In 1462, when Vasily II died, Ivan III assumed the throne. By that time his father's brothers had all died; he had no dynastic competitors. Ivan III, however, had four brothers of his own. He too took the precaution of formally declaring his son, also named Ivan, as his heir, before the boy reached his thirteenth birthday. None of the boy's uncles raised an objection. On the contrary, when two of them did engage in a dispute with Ivan III in 1479, their concerns focused on the manner in which Ivan, who already controlled over half of the family domain, was distributing shares of his territorial acquisitions to them and on his treatment of servitors who transferred from his court to theirs, not on his succession to the throne.

Problems arose, however, after the grand prince's eldest son and designated heir, Ivan Ivanovich, died prematurely in 1490. In September 1491, Ivan imprisoned Andrei, the elder of his two surviving brothers. He also arrested Andrei's sons and and boyars, and summoned his other brother, Boris, to Moscow. The reasons cited for the arrest included a series of misdemeanors and transgressions related to earlier disputes as well as the recent refusal by Andrei to participate in a military campaign against the Great Horde. Nonetheless, the possibility remains that Ivan III arrested Andrei in response to the uncertainty about succession generated by the death of Ivan Ivanovich; by removing Andrei, Ivan III effectively safeguarded the succession for his own descendants.

Ivan III thus subdued his brothers. A vertical succession was assured. By 1494, both Andrei and Boris were dead, and the grand prince absorbed virtually all their appanages. The only remaining principality derived from their holdings was Volok, ruled by his nephew Fedor Borisovich. Nevertheless, within a few years a succession crisis occurred at the Muscovite court. The issue was not lateral succession, which was not a viable option, but the choice of a vertical heir.

When Ivan Ivanovich died, he was survived by a son, Dmitry. But Ivan III, who had married for a second time in 1472, had other heirs. His wife, Sofiia (Zoe) Palaeologa, the niece of the last Byzantine emperor, had borne him four more sons by 1490; a fifth was born that year. The eldest of her sons was Vasily. Even though Ivan III's two brothers, who were then still alive, were quickly neutralized and excluded from the pool of princes eligible for succession, the grand prince in 1490 had two potential vertical heirs.

Ivan III was in no hurry to choose between his eldest son, the

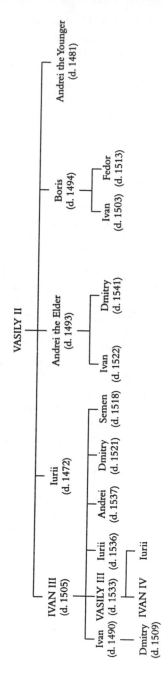

Table 8.2 Prince Vasily II and his descendants

eleven-year-old Vasily, and his six-year-old grandson, Dmitry. But events in 1497 precipitated a decision. In that year a plot to assassinate Dmitry was discovered. Six conspirators, junior courtiers, were arrested and executed; others were imprisoned. Vasily and his mother, the intended beneficiaries and also supporters of the plot, were disgraced; Vasily was temporarily held in confinement. In February 1498, in an elaborate and unprecedented coronation ceremony, conducted at the Cathedral of the Assumption in the kremlin and attended by his full court, Ivan III named his grandson Dmitry his co-ruler.

The coronation itself has attracted scholarly attention. Although some have regarded it as a mark of Ivan III's imperial aspirations and/or a function of foreign policy considerations, George Majeska's explanation of the unusual procedure is probably more accurate. He argued that the elaborate ceremony, highlighted by a blessing from the metropolitan, was rooted in issues of legitimacy and accepted norms of succession. The ceremony was necessary precisely because the selection of Dmitry did not follow those norms. It bypassed a generation. The leap deviated from the simple father-to-son pattern that had become standard for the Daniilovichi in the previous century. It was indeed altogether new in the Riurikid experience. Ivan thus resorted to extravagant fanfare and elicited the blessing of the Church to bolster the legitimacy of his grandson and minimize the possibility of a repetition of the civil wars that had plagued his father's reign.[3]

Despite the pomp of the ceremony, the issue of succession was not settled. By mid-1499, Vasily was restored to his father's good graces. For the next several years court intrigues were quietly playing themselves out. Then, in 1502, for no clearly indicated reason, Dmitry was arrested. The path was cleared for Vasily to inherit his father's throne; in 1505 he duly became Vasily III.

By the beginning of the sixteenth century the tradition of transferring the grand princely throne among eligible members of a single generation had already been replaced by a practice of succession through the vertical line. But the contest between Vasily and his nephew Dmitry, although relatively benign in comparison with the wars half a century earlier, revealed the vagaries of the new system, which had not yet been applied

---

[3] George P. Majeska, "The Moscow Coronation of 1498 Reconsidered," *JbfGO*, vol. 26 (1978), pp. 358–359. For a sample of other views, see John V. A. Fine, Jr., "The Muscovite Dynastic Crisis of 1497–1502," *Canadian Slavonic Papers*, vol. VIII (Toronto: University of Toronto Press, 1966), and Gustave Alef, "Was Grand Prince Dmitrii Ivanovich Ivan III's 'King of the Romans'?," in *Essays in Honor of A. A. Zimin*, ed. by Daniel Clarke Waugh (Columbus, Ohio: Slavica, 1985), pp. 89–101.

to the type of situation those two princes presented. The settlement of their contest equally reflects the successful accumulation of power by the grand prince, the essence of the political system that was being forged. Unlike earlier dynastic contests, this quarrel required neither war nor an appeal to a higher external authority to reach a resolution. The final authority belonged to the grand prince, whose decision in the end was accepted and respected by the dynasty and all Muscovy.

That decision refined the system of vertical succession. It upheld the principle that only the son of a grand prince was eligible for the throne, and further defined the heir as the eldest surviving son of the last ruler. But all vestiges of lateral succession had not yet vanished. The grand prince's younger sons retained important roles. The personal experience of Vasily III demonstrated that the availability of secondary heirs, especially younger brothers of an heir apparent, was vitally important to the dynastic line. The possibility that a grand prince's eldest son would die before assuming the throne, as Ivan Ivanovich had done, was very real. It was equally possible that a grand prince would die before producing an heir, as almost happened with Vasily III who would rule for twenty-five years before producing a son. Younger brothers thus remained critical to the perpetuation of the Muscovite dynasty. But once their elder brother sat on the throne and produced his own sons, their value to the dynasty and the political system evaporated. Thus, when Vasily III died in 1533, his two remaining brothers were quickly arrested, precluding the possibility of an attempt to parlay their potential importance into a real bid for the throne and thereby preserving it for Vasily's elder son, the three-year-old Ivan IV, the future Ivan the Terrible.

TERRITORIAL EXPANSION

After Vasily II's victorious conclusion of the dynastic wars no prince in northern Russia had the strength to withstand the might of Moscow. Vasily II, followed by Ivan III and Vasily III, pursued a deliberate, steady, and aggressive policy of territorial expansion. In the context of evolving ideological concepts, derived from those that will be described in the next section, Moscow's persistent subordination of formerly autonomous principalities came to be regarded as the virtually inevitable unification, or reunification, of the Russian lands. The Muscovite grand prince, correspondingly, was transformed from the senior member of the dynasty into the sovereign of all Rus', who by occasionally using the title "tsar" tentatively arrogated to himself the stature and authority of both the Byzantine emperor or caesar and the Mongol khan, for whom the Russians had previously reserved the term.

Vasily II and his heirs each began his reign sharing the family domain with uncles, brothers, or cousins who controlled appanages within it. But each one also reassembled most of the territories under his personal rule. Thus, by the end of his reign, Vasily II shared his realm only with one loyal cousin, Prince Mikhail Andreevich of Vereia, who died in 1486. Similarly, by the time Ivan III died in 1505, the appanages that had been ruled by Prince Mikhail as well as Ivan's four brothers had almost all reverted to the grand prince; the sole exception was Volok, the appanage of Ivan's nephew Fedor Borisovich (d. 1513).

In addition to maintaining their control over the possessions of Moscow and Vladimir, Vasily II and his heirs expanded their domain. During the reign of Ivan III alone, the size of the territories controlled by the grand prince tripled. Novgorod was the first of the major Rus' lands beyond the possessions of Moscow and Vladimir to become a target of the grand prince. Relations between the grand princes and Novgorod had been troubled for decades. Moscow had been encroaching upon Novgorod's valuable commercial assets. It had asserted authority over Vychegda Perm' and diverted its tribute payments to the Muscovite treasury. Vasily I's repeated attempts to take possession of additional northern territories, notably the Dvina land, had engendered sharp clashes with Novgorod. Novgorod, on the other hand, had developed independent relations with Lithuania, which had repeatedly provided it with princes during the late fourteenth and early fifteenth centuries. When it did accept Russian princes, as was the case from 1412 to 1432, Novgorod found it could not rely on the grand prince for assistance, even when it was directly attacked by Vitovt of Lithuania in 1428. In late 1431, a Lithuanian prince had returned to Novgorod.

Relations were further strained during and immediately after Vasily's dynastic wars. Novgorod had officially remained neutral during the first stage of the war, and refused prolonged sanctuary or assistance to either Vasily II or Iurii and his sons. In 1431, however, it concluded a treaty with the new Lithuanian ruler, Svidrigailo, who was also Iurii's brother-in-law; the Lithuanian prince who came to Novgorod in 1431 was Svidrigailo's nephew. Furthermore, after the death of Metropolitan Fotii (1431), who had refused for over a year to consecrate him, Novgorod's archbishop Evfimii was invested in 1434 in the Smolensk cathedral by a new metropolitan, Gerasim, who had been nominated by Svidrigailo.

In 1435, toward the end of his conflict with Kosoi, Vasily II tried to win Novgorod to his side by promising to negotiate some disputes over territories on Novgorod's eastern frontier. But once his conflict with Kosoi had been resolved, the grand prince reneged on his pledge. In contrast, he wasted no time sending his officials to Novgorod to collect its tribute payment. By the winter of 1440–41, after Novgorod's Lithuanian prince had returned to his homeland, Grand Prince Vasily II mounted a military campaign against Novgorod. Novgorod was able to assuage the grand prince only by paying him an additional sum and pledging to continue paying taxes and rents at former customary rates.

But during the decade of the 1440s Novgorod was ill-prepared to honor its pledge. It became engaged in a war against both the Teutonic Order and the Hanseatic League. In the course of the war the Hansa blockaded Novgorod and abandoned its own trade complex of Peterhof in the city for six years (1443–48). Novgorod's trade and incomes plummeted. Famine and high prices compounded its internal problems. When the second phase of the war began, key points along Novgorod's northern trade routes were placed in jeopardy; with its commercial activities subjected to further disruption, Novgorod supported Dmitry Shemiakha.

It was against the background of all these factors and to punish Novgorod for the position it took during the second phase of the dynastic war that in 1456 that Vasily II gathered a large army and marched against the great city. Novgorod was no more successful against Vasily in 1456 than it had been in 1441. After the Muscovites captured and plundered the Novgorodian town of Staraia Rus', Novgorod sent a heavily armored cavalry force against them. It caught up with the Muscovites after most of the army had retreated with its booty. The outnumbered Muscovites, aiming their arrows at the unprotected Novgorodian mounts, were nonetheless victorious.

Defeated in the battle, Novgorod accepted the Treaty of Iazhelbitsy. Its terms required Novgorod to pay an even larger sum to Vasily II and also take up a special collection for the Tatar tribute. It agreed to pay taxes to the grand prince, to accept the grand prince's judicial officials, to break off relations with Shemiakha's family, to deny any other enemies of the grand prince access to the city, and to issue decrees and conclude treaties with foreign powers only under the seal of the grand prince, that is, with his approval. Novgorod was also obliged to cede northern territories possessed by its own boyars to the grand prince. By 1462, it had lost key sectors of land along the Dvina, the Vaga, and other northern rivers as well as its claims to Vologda.

The Treaty of Iazhelbitsy did not affect the internal structure of the Novgorodian government, which continued to be organized around the *veche* or town assembly. By the fifteenth century each of the five sections or "ends" of the city as well as their subdivisions or "streets" also had its own *veche*. But by that time the significance of the *veche* as a governing body had faded. Its meetings, although still open to all free townsmen, were dominated by several dozen wealthy landowning boyar families. The same boyar families sat on the Council of Lords (*sovet gospod*), which under the leadership of the archbishop of Novgorod functioned as the executive agent of the *veche*. The offices of *tysiatskii* or military commander and *posadnik* or mayor were also filled exclusively by boyars. The latter office had evolved into a collective body, on which virtually every boyar family was represented. The size of its membership swelled from six at the end of the fourteenth century to eighteen by 1416–17 to twenty-four by 1423 and then, during the half century before the final conquest of Novgorod, to thirty-four. The multiple *posadniki* also represented each of the "ends" of the city. A core of six, composed of one boyar for each "end" and a chief mayor, exercised power in the name of the larger group. Through these offices the boyars, rather than the *veche*, dominated Novgorod's political system.

But the boyar oligarchs of Novgorod were not politically homogeneous. In the decades following the conclusion of the Treaty of Iazhelbitsy, two groups became distinguishable. One favored resistance to Muscovy and the formation of closer relations with Lithuania; the other favored accommodation to Muscovy, if only to preserve what remained of Novgorod's autonomy. The first group in particular resisted abiding by the treaty. In 1458, its members requested another Lithuanian prince, but by 1460, when Vasily II visited Novgorod, he had already vanished. During the next decade the Novgorodians challenged the Muscovites in other ways as well. Far to the northeast in territories that had been transferred to the grand prince, Novgorodian bands boldly staged raids and beat, evicted, or killed the stewards and slaves who managed and operated the districts on behalf of their new owners. They chased away any surviving Muscovites and recovered the lands for themselves and Novgorod.

In 1470–71, Novgorod was again actively seeking Lithuanian support. The pro-Lithuanian faction within Novgorod, led by Marfa Boretskaia, who had been married to one *posadnik* and had given birth to another, gained ascendancy. It concluded an agreement with King Casimir, who recognized Novgorod's traditional autonomy, promised to send it a new prince and to protect it. Before the treaty could be implemented however, Ivan III, who had become grand prince in 1462, assembled a large military force, which included contingents from Tver' and some service Tatars, and marched against Novgorod. Once again Novgorod suffered defeat (1471). During the battle Marfa Boretskaia's son as well as several other Novgorodian boyars were taken prisoner; they were later executed. Novgorod was obliged to reconfirm the terms of the Iazhelbitsy

Map 8.1 Muscovy c. 1550

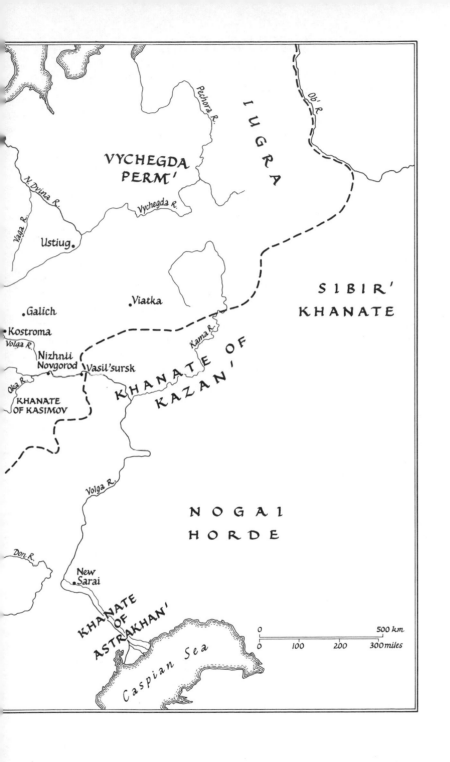

treaty, to pay more reparations to Moscow, to return the lands it had seized, and to break its ties with Lithuania.

In 1478, Ivan III completed the process of subjugating Novgorod. He led another campaign against the city and placed it under siege. Unable to resist militarily, the Novgorodians surrendered after a month. They accepted Ivan's terms. They gave up their rights to select their own prince and recognized the grand prince as their sovereign. They gave up their own *veche* and city officials and accepted the grand prince's administrators. They gave up control over their own lands and finances and subjected them to the authority of the grand prince as well.

As a display of his authority Ivan III removed the *veche* bell, symbol of Novgorod's independence, from the city. He arrested the leaders of the opposition to Muscovite dominance, including Marfa Boretskaia, sent them to Moscow, and seized their vast land holdings. In 1480, he also arrested Novgorod's archbishop, and several years later replaced him with his own unpopular prelate. He appointed his own governors to rule Novgorod, issued new taxes and used Muscovite troops to enforce their collection. But even more devastating to Novgorod's political, social, and economic structure were the land confiscations. As early as 1475–76, Ivan III had confiscated the landed estates of six leading boyars he had arrested for opposing the subordination of Novgorod to Moscow. But by 1489, in a series of similar but much larger actions he had transferred to his government most of Novgorod's privately owned landed estates, held by boyars and by small-scale farmers, his opponents and his supporters. He also confiscated lands belonging to the archbishop and monasteries.

By the time Ivan III had completed his conquest of Novgorod, he had also incorporated the remaining independent portions of Iaroslavl' and Rostov into Muscovy. In 1485 he annexed Tver'. By the time he had completed the confiscations of Novgorodian estates, he had reabsorbed most of the appanages that had been assigned to his brothers. In 1486, when his father's cousin, Prince Mikhail Andreevich of Vereia, died, Ivan inherited his appanage as well. As noted above, at the time of his own death in 1505, Ivan shared the family domain with only one nephew, Fedor Borisovich, who ruled the appanage principality of Volok.

Vasily III completed the process of gathering the northern Russian lands. Although his four brothers also received appanages from their father, Vasily III possessed the overwhelming majority of the vastly enlarged Muscovite realm. He added to it by incorporating Pskov in 1510, the Volok appanage in 1513, and Riazan' in 1520/21. In addition, as a result of wars he and his father conducted against Lithuania, which will be discussed in chapter 10, Vasily III's domain extended deep into territories that had formed the Chernigov and Smolensk principalities of Kievan Rus'.

THE CHURCH AND ITS POLITICAL LEGITIMACY

While Vasily II was fighting the wars against his uncle and cousins, the lands of Rus' were experiencing another series of traumas emanating from the Orthodox Church. The ecclesiastical troubles and their resolution had repercussions for the Muscovite political system and dynasty. They provided a new approach to the creation of an aura of legitimacy for the grand princes who followed Vasily II but could rest their claims to the throne neither on the traditions of the dynasty nor on the authority of the khan.

The problems within the Church began with the death of Metropolitan Fotii in July 1431. Although the patriarch in Constantinople appointed a metropolitan for Lithuania, he did not replace Fotii. Throughout the first stage of the Dmitr'evich war, the Church and the northern Rus' lands under its jurisdiction, although guided unofficially by Bishop Iona of Riazan', lacked a formally designated ecclesiastical chief. After the Lithuanian prelate died in 1435, Vasily II and his advisers nominated Iona as their candidate for metropolitan. In late 1436, Iona set out for Constantinople to be confirmed, but before he arrived, the patriarch and emperor filled the Russian vacancy with their own nominee, Isidore.

Isidore arrived in Moscow in April 1437. His task was not simply to head the Russian Orthodox Church. He was also expected to lead it into a highly controversial union between Orthodoxy and the Catholic Church of Rome. Byzantium had political reasons for favoring union. At the time it was in danger of being annihilated by the Ottoman Turks. Over the previous century the once-powerful empire had lost almost all of its territory, and was confined to the district immediately surrounding the city of Constantinople. Its leaders calculated that their only hope for survival was rescue from Europe. A resolution of Orthodoxy's differences with Rome was regarded as a necessary prerequisite for assistance from the Catholic community. Isidore had been instrumental in preparing for a council devoted to unifying the two Churches. He was sent to Moscow to secure the cooperation of the Russian Orthodox Church and lead its delegation to the council.

Thus in September, less than six months after his arrival, Isidore left Moscow for the Council of Ferrara-Florence. He was accompanied by the bishop of Suzdal' and a complement of clergy that was more impressive for its size than its acquaintance with the issues of Church dogma under debate. At the conclusion of the sessions in July 1439, the Orthodox representatives accepted the Roman Church's views on several of those issues, and the Council of Florence determined that the two Churches were one. Isidore, having become a cardinal and a papal legate, returned to the lands of Rus'. After spending about six months in Kiev and Smolensk, he arrived in Moscow in March 1441.

He was not well received. Vasily II, his courtiers, and the Russian clergy rejected union with Rome. Three days after his arrival, the metropolitan was deposed and imprisoned in the Chudov Monastery within the kremlin walls. He escaped six months later, while awaiting trial. His captors did not pursue him, possibily because they had little enthusiasm for carrying out the mandatory penalty for apostasy, death by burning at the stake or burial alive.

Once again, Moscow and the Rus' lands were functioning without proper ecclesiastical leadership. And within a few years they were once again plunged into civil strife. There was no metropolitan in place when Vasily II was captured by the Tatars, nor when his cousin Dmitry Shemiakha seized Moscow, blinded the grand prince, and confined him at Uglich. By the time Vasily II recovered his throne there was a clearly perceived need to restore order not only at the princely court and in secular society, but in the Church as well. The senior ecclesiastical leadership had not opposed Shemiakha; Iona himself had inclined toward Vasily only after Dmitry reneged on promises he had made regarding the treatment of Vasily's sons. Of equal importance, however, was the awareness that failure to attend to society's spiritual needs and to fill with due piety the Church's highest office had coincided with civil catastrophe and, possibly, occasioned it.

But selection of a new metropolitan posed a dilemma. Normally the appointment of a metropolitan required the approval of Byzantine officials and investiture by them. Yet, the Byzantine patriarch and emperor had espoused union with Rome, which the Russian Church had rejected. Although the Russians stopped short of formally breaking their ties with Constantinople or denouncing its leaders, they were loathe to allow that "heretical" leadership to appoint their metropolitan. The Russian bishops, therefore, in full accordance with the wishes of Vasily II took it upon themselves in December 1448 to name Iona of Riazan' (d. 1461) head of the Russian Orthodox Church.

Vasily II almost immediately reaped political advantage from his support for this measure. The Church lined up behind him to suppress Shemiakha. Iona threatened anyone who assisted Shemiakha with excommunication, and he and other senior clerics traveled with the army to enforce their ban. Only Novgorod, which judged Iona's appointment to be illegal, dared defy him and provide Shemiakha with sanctuary.

Ultimately, the Church provided even greater assistance to the grand prince and his heirs. On May 29, 1453, just a few years after these events, the Ottoman Turks captured Constantinople and finally destroyed the

Byzantine Empire. The Church of Constantinople survived, but under the political authority of an alien Muslim ruler. The Orthodox population of the Rus' lands felt the shock and the loss deeply. Their concern was intensified when in 1458 Lithuania broke its ecclesiastical relations with Moscow and placed its Orthodox population under the jurisdiction of a prelate sent from the Uniate Church in Rome. Yet, from the perspective of Iona and other Orthodox clerics, the fall of Constantinople confirmed the righteousness of the position Vasily II and their Church had taken immediately after the Council of Florence. Constantinople, in their view, had fallen to the Turkish infidels because it had fallen away from the true faith, because it had fallen from Grace.

The issue took on greater dimensions. The unusual manner in which Iona was selected generated opposition. To defend and strengthen his position, Iona identified himself with unquestionably pious and heroic figures. It was probably at his court that a vita of Dmitry Donskoi was composed. In it Dmitry's genealogy was traced back not just to Ivan I Kalita, but to St. Vladimir. Donskoi was repeatedly referred to as "tsar" and ruler of the entire Rus' land. Thus, at a time when the authority of the Church leadership was questionable, its literary spokesmen made a concerted effort to emphasize the link between Moscow and Kiev, the original seat of Rus' Orthodoxy. In a similar manner, shortly after Iona became metropolitan, he began the process of canonizing his predecessor Metropolitan Aleksei.

Although the Daniilovichi themselves may have preferred to ignore their Kievan heritage and therefore not draw attention to their own dynastic illegitimacy, the efforts made to fortify the weak position of Metropolitan Iona indirectly inflated the credentials of his secular counterpart, Grand Prince Vasily II. Other literature, composed in the late 1450s and early 1460s, was more explicit. Chronicle entries and other tracts describing the events of the Council of Florence and subsequent events presented a defense of Vasily II and his unilateral appointment of Iona as metropolitan. That literature developed the theme that in contrast to Constantinople, Moscow had remained true to Orthodoxy. And it emphasized that it was Vasily II personally who had detected Isadore's apostasy, preserved Orthodoxy in Russia, and prevented his people from being deprived of salvation. The grand prince, as Michael Cherniavsky pointed out,[4] was cast in the image of the defender of the faith.

The themes and even the myth of the role of Vasily II were developed in the context of a specific situation. But once enunciated, they infused

[4] Michael Cherniavsky, "The Reception of the Council of Florence in Moscow," *Church History*, vol. 24 (1955), p. 352.

the office of the grand prince with a new function, protection of Orthodoxy. It became a new basis for the grand princes' legitimacy, rooted in the history of the Rus' lands. But it was not the history of the dynasty and its traditions that Vasily II's supporters recalled, nor the history that recorded the grand princes' display of deference to higher external authorities, be they patriarchs, emperors, or khans. Rather, the accounts of these events likened Vasily II to Vladimir I the Saint, who had baptized the Rus'. They thereby set a standard for sovereignty based on emulation of the Blessed Vladimir, on defense of the faith he had brought to his people.

The role they described, however, was one that had been traditionally associated with the Byzantine emperor. It was an intrinsic part of the concept that the Greeks had taught the Russians that the Christian community required both the Church and an empire, a patriarch and an emperor. But Byzantium had collapsed, leaving the lands ruled by Vasily II the largest exclusively Orthodox realm in the world. Set against the background of the fall of Constantinople, the glorification of Vasily II as the righteous defender of the faith carried the implication that Moscow was replacing Constantinople as the center of Orthodoxy and the Muscovite grand prince was assuming the responsibilities and stature within the Orthodox community normally accorded the Byzantine emperor.

The concepts legitimizing the Muscovite grand princes and their heightened authority, formulated by the end of Vasily II's reign, were elaborated during the reign of Ivan III. His occasional use of the title "tsar," his marriage to the Byzantine princess Sofiia Palaeologa, and his employment of Byzantine-style seals and ceremonies, clothed those skeletal theories in grand symbols and imagery. Nevertheless, the Muscovites did not immediately develop the implications of the themes articulated earlier in the century. Only gradually through the next century did those concepts, emanating from the mid-century Church crisis, evolve and mature into a theory that replaced the older and increasingly inadequate and irrelevant principles of legitimacy. The new theory or ideological principles justified the unfolding reality of the accumulation of territory by the grand prince, who governed his expanding realm through an increasingly centralized administration. It provided a basis for understanding, accepting, and celebrating the transfer of power from numerous princes to a single sovereign and the transformation of their dynastic realm into a centralized state with a mandate to expand into an empire.

The theory developed as the Church, once again, confronted a series of troublesome issues, the effects of which compounded and stimulated the enunciation of more fully developed ideological precepts concerning secular power and its relationship to the Church. The last decade of the fifteenth century was a turbulent one, not only for the court which was trying to select an heir, but for the Church. One crisis developed as the year 1492 approached. Byzantine and Russian society had been taught that the world would end after 7,000 years. The year 7,000 in the Orthodox calendar, which began with the creation, corresponded to the year AD 1492.

Anticipation of the apocalypse was mixed with confusion, dread, and doubts about the veracity of Orthodox teachings. In this atmosphere a group of religious dissidents, known in the historical literature as Judaizers, gained momentum and new adherents, especially among the clergy of Novgorod. The origins and tenets of the heresy are known primarily through statements made by their critics and opponents. They claimed that it was rooted in ideas introduced to Novgorod by some Jews who had been in the entourage of the Lithuanian prince invited to the city in 1470–71. It spread to Moscow when Ivan III, having annexed Novgorod in 1478, transferred two Novgorodian priests who had espoused the heretical views to the Cathedral of the Assumption and the Church of the Archangel Michael in Moscow. Ivan's daughter-in-law, the mother of his grandson Dmitry, was one of those influenced by their beliefs.

Among the dissident views with which the Judaizers were charged was their rejection of the Trinity and the year 1492 as the date of earthly destruction. In 1487, the archbishop of Novgorod Gennadii (Gennadius) launched an aggressive campaign to root out the heresy. Using torture among other inquisitorial techniques, he identified the heretics and convinced the grand prince and the new metropolitan, Zosima (1490–94), to convene a church council to suppress their movement. The council of 1490 found nine Novgorodian Judaizers guilty of iconoclasm, anti-Trinitarianism, and Sabbatarianism, i.e., observing the Sabbath on Saturday rather than Sunday. It did not condemn them to death, as advocated by Gennadii and his protege, Iosif (Joseph), the abbot of the Volokolamsk Monastery. Rather, it excommunicated them, banished some, imprisoned others, and sent the rest back to Gennadii who subjected them to public humiliation. The council took no action against Judaizer sympathizers in Moscow. In 1504, although Gennadii had been deposed, another council was held. Dominated by Iosif, it again condemned the Judaizers as heretics and convinced Ivan III to burn their leaders at the stake.

In the meantime the world had not come to an end in 1492. There were a variety of consequences of this non-event. On the one hand there was continued confusion and doubt about the validity of Orthodoxy; on the other there was lingering dread based on the persistent conviction that the apocalypse was yet imminent. On a more practical level the Church had to produce a new paschal calendar to identify when Easter and other holy days would occur; the old calendar had ended in the year 7,000. Metropolitan Zosima approached that task. And in his preface to the new calendar he drew upon the notion, introduced in the middle of the fifteenth century, that Moscow had by default become Constantinople's heir as the center of Orthodoxy and elevated it to a formal premise. He included a statement that Moscow was the new Constantinople and Ivan III was its new emperor.

At Gennadii's court, which became a center for literary activity, where the first complete Slavic translation of the Bible was produced, a variation of the same theme emerged. Gennadii had sent one of his associates, the multilingual Dmitrii Gerasimov, abroad to collect religious texts, which he used in part to develop arguments against the Judaizers. Confronted with the continuation of life on earth, Gennadii also charged Gerasimov to locate and send someone with expertise in astronomy and mathematics to Novgorod to help make the calculations necessary for the formulation of a new calendar. In addition to carrying out these tasks, Gerasimov sent Gennadii a copy of the "Tale of the White Cowl." Although he allowed the archbishop to believe that he had translated it from a text he found at the Vatican archives, Gerasimov himself composed the tale, which told of the transmission of a white cowl, representing Orthodoxy and the "radiant Resurrection," from Rome to Constantinople and finally to Novgorod. The latter transfer occurred after the patriarch of Constantinople, then in possession of the cowl, had a dream. In it he was told:

you must send this holy White Cowl to the Russian land, to the city of Novgorod the Great . . . And when you send it to the Russian land, the Orthodox Faith will be glorified and the cowl will be safe from seizure by the infidel . . . and from the intended profanation by the Latin pope. And the grace, glory, and honor which were taken from Rome, as well as the Grace of the Holy Spirit, will be removed from the imperial city of Constantinople after its capture by the sons of Hagar [in this case, the Turks]. And all holy relics will be given to the Russian land in the predestined moment. And the Russian tsar will be elevated by God above other nations, and under his sway will be many heathen kings. And the power of the patriarch . . . will pass to the Russian land . . . And that land will be called Radiant Russia, which, by the Grace of God, will be glorified with blessings. And its majesty will be strengthened by its Orthodoxy, and it will become more honorable than the two Romes which preceded it.[5]

---

[5] An abbreviated version of the tale in English translation is available in *Medieval Russia's Epics, Chronicles, and Tales*, pp. 325–332; the quoted passage is taken from pp. 328–329.

The "Tale" was elaborating upon the concept that Moscow was the new center of Orthodoxy, hence the heir of Constantinople. It referred to the city of Rome, the original base of the Christian Church, which had succumbed to barbarian invaders in the fifth century AD. At that time, the center of Christianity had relocated to Constantinople, the "second Rome." But Constantinople too had fallen into apostasy and been conquered by the Turks. The center of the Orthodoxy moved to Moscow or, as Zosima had called it, "the new Constantinople."

By the end of the first quarter of the sixteenth century the concept contained in the tale was being repeated, developed, and embellished into what became known as the "Third Rome theory." It was most concisely and powerfully articulated by a monk named Filofei, abbot of the Eleazarov Monastery in Pskov. In a letter, composed c. 1523 and addressed to the *d'iak* or Muscovite state secretary in Pskov, Misiur' Munekhin (d. 1528), Filofei wrote, "Take into account all Christ-loving and God-loving men, how all Christian realms have come to an end and have been reduced to the single realm of our Sovereign, according to the Books of prophecy, that is to the realm of Russia: for two Romes have fallen, the Third stands and there shall be no Fourth."[6]

The notion is contained in two other letters, commonly but not unanimously attributed to Filofei; the dates of their composition are also a subject of debate.[7] The set of letters did not, however, simply praise the grand prince and his realm. Their statements asserting that Moscow was heir to Rome and Constantinople were set in contexts of concern about inappropriate activities conducted by the clergy and appeals to the grand prince to relieve the suffering of the oppressed. They contained a strong note of caution and warning, as expressed in another of the letters, which contained a variation of the passage quoted above: "If thou rulest thine empire rightly, thou wilt be the son of light and a citizen of the heavenly Jerusalem . . . And now, I say unto thee: take care and take heed . . . ; all the empires of Christendom are united . . . in thine, for

---

6 As translated by Nikolay Andreyev in "Filofey and His Epistle to Ivan Vasil'yevich," *SEER*, vol. 38 (1959), p. 28.

7 Nikolay Andreyev, for example, considered the other two to have been written by Filofei to Ivan III and Vasily III, respectively, before the epistle to Misiur' Munekhin. In contrast, A. L. Gol'dberg concluded that they were composed after the Munekhin letter by other unnamed persons, during a period extending from the 1520s to the 1540s. See Andreyev, "Filofey and his Epistle," pp. 10, 13, 26–29 and A. L. Gol'dberg, "Tri 'poslaniia Filofeiia,'" [The three "letters of Filofei"] *Trudy otdela drevnerusskoi literatury*, vol. 29 (1974), pp. 79, 83–85, 92.

two Romes have fallen and the third exists and there will not be a fourth . . . "[8]

The letters attributed to Filofei thus conveyed a dual message. On the one hand, they glorified Moscow, which was placed on a par with imperial Rome and Byzantium and identified as their heir; they thereby accorded Moscow's grand prince with status and power equivalent to their emperors'. But they also issued a warning. The role of the defender of the faith, transferred to the Muscovite grand prince, carried with it solemn responsibilities. Previous guardians had not met the challenges of that role. It was not a foregone conclusion that the Muscovite rulers would perform their duties any more successfully. But should they too fail, the consequences would be more serious because, according to messianic prophecy, this was Christianity's, hence the world's, last chance. There would be no fourth Rome.

The Third Rome theory found further expression during the course of a polemical debate that flared among ecclesiastical scholars and leading monastic figures during the reign of Vasily III. Iosif, who had earlier vilified the Judaizers, and his followers constituted one group of participants. Chief among their opponents was a monk called Vassian. A former boyar, Vassian was born Vasily Ivanovich Patrikeev; in 1499, he had fallen into disgrace, been obliged to give up his career as a diplomat and military commander, and become a monk. He reentered the political arena when Vasily III brought him from virtual exile at the distant St. Cyril-Beloozero Monastery to Moscow (c. 1509). While the Metropolitan Varlaam ruled the Church (1511–22), Vassian exercised significant influence at both the secular and ecclesiastical courts. Among his associates was Maksim Grek (Maxim the Greek), who had been recruited from Mt. Athos by Vasily III to translate Greek religious texts. When he arrived in Moscow in 1518, he was established at the Chudov Monastery where he not only undertook his duties as a translator but composed his own treatises.

The issues of the vitriolic exchanges are often considered a continuation of an earlier debate conducted by Iosif and another monastic leader, Nil Sorskii, over monastic landownership. Coming in the wake of Ivan III's confiscation of Church property in the Novgorod lands, their disagreement, commonly identified as the "possessor/non-possessor controversy," is linked to the adjacent issue of secularization of Church

---

[8] As quoted by Dimitri Stremoukoff, "Moscow the Third Rome: Sources of the Doctrine," reprinted in *The Structure of Russian History: Interpretive Essays*, ed. by Michael Cherniavsky (New York: Random House, 1970), p. 115; originally published in *Speculum*, vol. 28, no. 1 (January 1953).

lands. The "non-possessor" position, attributed to Sorskii, a leader of the trans-Volga eremitic monks and frequently supposed to be Vassian's mentor, renounced monastic wealth and landownership in favor of asceticism, poverty, and spiritualism. Scholars interpret this view, which indirectly favored secularization of the Church's landed estates, as supportive of enhanced grand princely power. In constrast, Iosif, while opposed to the retention of wealth by individual monks, considered institutional wealth a desirable means of supporting the monastery's population and enabling it to carry out its charitable functions, such as caring for the poor.

The issues under debate, according to most accounts, were reviewed by a Church council, held in 1503, which determined that Iosif's views were correct. The council's decision is generally regarded as a compromise between the grand prince, who henceforth respected the sanctity of Church lands, and the Josephites, as Iosif's followers are called, who subsequently emphasized and justified the unlimited nature of the grand prince's authority.

Recent scholarship has challenged the standard version of the controversy. Iakov Lur'e (Jakov Luria), for example, observed that although the existence of "contradictions" between the positions of Iosif and Nil Sorskii has become a "constantly repeated historiographical view," those contradictions have been "insufficiently argued" and have not been proven. Using evidence, including an analysis of handwriting, from early manuscripts, he proposed that rather than being inveterate adversaries, Nil Sorskii and Iosif actually were collaborators, probably before 1504, on a treatise intended to be used against the heretics, whom they both opposed. His findings challenge the commonly held view that the treatise in question, called the "Enlightener" (*Prosvetitel'*), was written by Iosif alone in 1514.[9] Donald Ostrowski, after examining the documentary evidence associated with the controversy, concluded that Iosif, although concerned about moveable Church property, did not discuss landed property and that secularization of Church lands was not an issue at the Church council of 1503.[10]

Nevertheless, by the 1520s and 1530s the "Josephites," on the one hand, and Vassian and Maksim Grek on the other, were exchanging views

[9] Jakov Luria, "Unresolved Issues in the History of the Ideological Movements of the Late Fifteenth Century," in *Medieval Russian Culture*, California Slavic Studies, vol. XII, ed. by Henrik Birnbaum and Michael S. Flier (Berkeley: University of California Press, 1984), pp. 163–179; the quoted remarks are on p. 164.

[10] Donald Ostrowski, "Church Polemics and Monastic Land Acquisition in Sixteenth-Century Muscovy," *SEER*, vol. 64 (1986), pp. 359, 361.

on issues of doctrine, monastic rules, and a variety of other topics, including monastic wealth. In the last years of his life Iosif, who died in 1515, was forbidden to respond to the continuing attacks levied by his opponents. But after 1522, when Metropolitan Varlaam was deposed and replaced by Daniil, who had become a monk at Iosif's Volokolamsk Monastery and later became its abbot, the atmosphere within the Church changed. Vassian lost influence within the Church as well as with Vasily III. In 1525, Maksim Grek was brought to trial, found guilty of heresy, and confined at the Volokolamsk Monastery. He was tried again, along with Vassian, in 1531. Maksim, once again condemned, was transferred to another monastery, where the abbot allowed him to resume his studies and writing. Vassian, who was denounced for his edition of the canonical law and heretical views, was imprisoned at Volokolamsk.

Following these judgments their position, which had been woven into their debates with Iosif and his followers, that the Church, as God's institutional representative on earth, should have broad autonomy and uncontested spiritual authority was overwhelmed by Josephite conceptions. The Josephite views, which easily merged with the Third Rome theory, emphasized grand princely power. That power was to be used to protect the Church and expand the Orthodox domain. But because it emanated from God and was an expression of His authority on earth, it was absolute. The grand prince reigned supreme on earth.

The Third Rome theory and its corollaries were not wholly accepted outside ecclesiastical circles. While imbuing the grand prince, "as the agent of God's will," with virtually unlimited power, those concepts equally imposed on him "responsibilities to obey that will." As Daniel Rowland expressed it, those responsibilities "grew together with his power." Thus, even as the Third Rome theory "magnified the power of the ruler," it "stress[ed] his obligations" as well.[11]

Furthermore, the same literature that described the extensive powers of the grand prince contained passages expressing alternate, even competing, images of his role. In the "Enlightener," which included explicit statements of the ruler's god-like authority, there were also passages cautioning that there were limits to the honor and obedience subjects owed the secular ruler. One portion of the text, which Iakov Lur'e attributed to Nil Sorskii rather than to Iosif, asserted that "If the Tsar who rules men is himself ruled by evil passions and sins . . . , such a Tsar is not God's servant but the Devil's, and he should not be considered a Tsar, but a tormentor . . . " Under such circumstances, there was no obligation to

---

[11] Daniel Rowland, "Did Muscovite Literary Ideology Place Limits on the Power of the Tsar (1540s–1660s)?," *RR*, vol. 49 (1990), pp. 152–153.

obey the ruler.[12] Such qualifications may account for the hesitation of the Muscovite grand princes to embrace the theory that appeared to legitimize their monopolization of power.

The Third Rome theory was not the only set of principles formulated in this period to elevate the grand prince and create justifications for his enhanced powers. Rather, it competed with other notions that evolved simultaneously and similarly tended to legitimize the Muscovite dynastic line. One pointed to Kievan Rus' as the predecessor of Muscovy and to the direct lineage of Muscovite princes from the Kievan princes as the source of their legitimacy. These associations were incorporated into the vita of Dmitry Donskoi. An embroidered version of the theory found its way into the chronicles written at the Muscovite court in the 1470s, just when Ivan III was engaged in subjugating Novgorod. A renewed emphasis on Muscovy as the heir of Kievan Rus' occurred at the turn of the century while Moscow was attempting to wrest political and ecclesiastical control over western Rus' lands, which had formerly been components of Kievan Rus', from Lithuania. In this context it was significant that in a treaty concluded between Muscovy and Lithuania in 1494, the Lithuanians recognized Ivan III's right to use the title "sovereign of all Rus'"; Muscovite-Lithuanian relations will be discussed further in chapter 10. An alternate theory emerged during the reign of Vasily III. It set forth a new fabricated lineage for the Riurikids. The founder of their dynasty was alleged to have been a brother, named Prus, of the Roman emperor Augustus. Like the Third Rome theory, this fable elevated the status of the Muscovite grand princes and imbued them with claims to imperial power.

Although allusions were being made to this false genealogy in the late sixteenth and even in the seventeenth century, it was nevertheless the Third Rome theory that ultimately prevailed over other conceptual frameworks that circulated in Moscow's intellectual circles. During the early years of the reign of Ivan IV, Metropolitan Makarii and his associates elaborated upon its themes in a wide array of media, including literary texts, icons, and ceremonies. In their hands the foreboding and warnings imbedded in "Filofei's letters" receded, allowing the glorification of the Muscovite sovereign and imperial aspirations of his realm to

---

[12] The quoted passage was translated by Marc Szeftel in "Joseph Volotsky's Political Ideas in a New Historical Perspective," *JbfGO*, vol. 13 (1965), p. 20. Lur'e discussed this passage and its authorship in "Unresolved Issues in the History of the Ideological Movements of the Late Fifteenth Century," pp. 166–167. For discussions on the compatibility of seemingly mutually exclusive images of the ruler and his authority, see the full article by Szeftel and Donald Rowland's article cited in the preceding note.

achieve an unencumbered prominence. It would be in the imagery and terminology of this theory, the defense of Orthodoxy and crusades against the infidel Muslims, that events undertaken by the Tsar of all Rus' would be depicted and described, understood and justified.

9

MUSCOVITE
DOMESTIC CONSOLIDATION

•

From the reign of Vasily II through that of Vasily III Muscovy steadily expanded its territory and the Muscovite princes asserted their authority over the annexed principalities. These processes were encouraged and justified by various theoretical principles that not only legitimized the right of the Muscovite line of princes to rule but also justified their enhanced powers. The powers ascribed to the grand princes were portrayed in the familiar ceremonial imagery and literary terminology drawn from Byzantine models and Orthodox religious texts. The theories that described grand princely authority thus reflected Muscovy's Byzantine cultural heritage.

But the political system within which the Muscovite grand princes actually functioned was not Byzantine. It was built upon and shaped by economic resources available to the lands within Muscovy. It was created from and fashioned around social and political groups indigenous to Rus' society. It was constructed to address the problems posed by rapid expansion, to consolidate Muscovite rule in newly acquired lands, to administer and defend them, and to integrate them into a single cohesive state. As Muscovite princes and advisors confronted such issues, they drew upon not only Byzantine concepts but the experience and examples of other neighbors, most prominently the Tatars, to design and organize gradually a political and administrative apparatus to govern the unified centralized state of Muscovy.

THE MUSCOVITE ECONOMY

The rural economy

When the grand princes of Vladimir gathered the other Rus' principalities around Moscow, they also gained access to all their economic resources. They were contained in a land shaped like a huge inverted irregular triangle, with its broad base in the north stretching along the coast of the White Sea from Karelia (eastern Finland) to beyond the Pechora River and its peak formed by the southern tip of the Novgorod-Seversk principality, which included territories that had earlier been part of the Chernigov and Pereiaslavl' principalities. The western side of the triangle was formed by a line extending along the borders of Novgorod, Pskov, Smolensk, Starodub, and Novgorod-Seversk. Its eastern boundary, the third side of the triangle, went south from the northeastern corner of the country, then curved westward to pass through the fortress of Vasil'sursk, constructed in 1523 midway between Nizhnii Novgorod and Kazan'; it then followed the eastern boundaries of Riazan' and finally converged with the western border. Within that expanse the resources were substantial.

The mass of the population engaged in agriculture as its primary means of livelihood. Most of the peasants who cultivated the land lived on "black" or taxable lands that had no private owner, but were subject to the prince and regarded by the peasant community as its own. The remainder dwelled on private lands, owned by a prince, his boyars, Church hierarchs or monasteries, and in some cases even rich merchants. Those peasants were generally obligated to pay a rent known as *obrok* to the landowner, their landlord, for the use of his land. *Obrok* was assessed in cash, in crops, or in other goods produced on the estate (e.g., chickens, eggs, cartloads of wood, sides of bacon or beef). Alternatively, they might be required to pay their rent in the form of labor; but this type of obligation was not common in the late fifteenth and early sixteenth centuries. All peasants, unless they had been specifically released from the obligation, paid taxes to the prince.

The peasant villagers produced a variety of crops. For food they generally raised a crop of winter rye as well as a spring crop of either spring rye, barley, buckwheat, millet, wheat, oats, peas, or some combination of them. In some regions "industrial" crops such as flax, hemp, and hops supplemented edible grains. The peasant farmers also raised livestock, cattle, sheep, hogs, and of course, horses, and raised hay for fodder. They kept bees for wax and honey. They supplemented their crops by hunting for fur pelts and meat, by gathering berries, mushrooms, and wild fruits and nuts from the forest, and by fishing. For some peasants in settlements on rivers and lakes as well as those in coastal villages in the far north fishing became the primary source of livelihood. By the end of the fifteenth century salt production was becoming another important rural economic activity; iron smelting using bog ores and potash, and pitch, tar, and turpentine manufacturing were all important in the sixteenth century as well.

Although agriculture remained a constant feature of the Russian economy, the methods employed by the peasants changed in the fifteenth century. They did so largely in response to increases in population densities, which resulted from a combination of population growth and limited mobility. The Russian population, having sustained the effects of repeated wars and bouts with the plague and other epidemics, was once again growing in the second half of the fifteenth century. By 1500, it had reached its pre-plague levels, and thereafter continued to increase.

But as their numbers grew, a variety of factors tended to inhibit the peasants' mobility: social and family ties; responsibilities to their village and community; agreements with their landlord; debts or other financial obligations; and local legal prohibitions on movement. At the end of the fifteenth century, after Moscow had absorbed most of its neighboring principalities, limits were formally and universally imposed on peasants. The Sudebnik (law code) of 1497 allowed them to move from one location to another only during a two-week period surrounding St. George's Day, which occurred in November after the harvest, and then only if all rents, fees, and other debts had been settled.

The effects of combining an increasing population with restrictions on mobility were the creation of a denser population, i.e., more people dwelled in households, hamlets, and villages, and intensified pressure on the land. Under those conditions traditional methods proved inadequate. The custom had been, as noted, to employ the slash-and-burn method to prepare forested land for agricultural use. That technique had been well suited to a population with limited manpower; peasants simply cut down the trees or slashed and stripped their bark to kill them, then burned the dried wood, and sowed their crops in the resulting forest clearings. Their favored field implement was a scratch plough, a forked instrument sufficient to scratch a furrow into the ashy layer covering the loose forest soil and light enough to move easily around tree stumps or skip over surface roots and other heavy obstacles. Such clearings did not remain fertile for more than a few growing seasons. Farmers regularly prepared new clearings to replace depleted ones, abandoning the older areas to be overgrown with brush and birch trees.

Relatively dense peasant populations, however, had both the means and the incentive to intensify their methods of production. After the middle of the fifteenth century, they increasingly substituted a three-field rotation method of farming for the standard slash-and-burn technique. The new method they adopted had the potential to raise more food from a given land area. Typically, peasants planted one field with a winter crop, one with a spring crop, and left the third fallow. By rotating the fields every year they were able to cultivate the same area repeatedly and thus farm more efficiently. This method required more labor than the traditional slash-and-burn technique because it was necessary to clear fields and then keep them weeded, drained, or irrigated as necessary. It also encouraged peasants to raise livestock, most importantly draft animals, which could be used to remove the heavy stumps and other encumbrances to create open fields and to pull heavier plows. The livestock also produced manure that enriched the repeatedly cultivated soil. As this method of farming became increasingly popular from the latter part of the fifteenth century, it enabled the growing peasant population, whose option to move on to more fertile land was being restricted, to produce sufficient quantities of foodstuffs to sustain themselves, their landlords, a growing urban population, and the government as well.

Forms of land tenure also began to change in the late fifteenth century. It was, as noted above, members of the upper strata of society who owned the hereditary private estates on which many peasants dwelled. They had acquired those estates by the fifteenth century in a variety of ways. Princes had granted some to their relatives, courtiers, and servicemen. Lords of the church, the metropolitan and bishops, also controlled vast tracts of land. Monasteries, which had been multiplying since the second half of the fourteenth century, also gained possession of large estates, some of which were simply appropriated, some granted by local princes, and some presented as gifts by other landowners. But landholdings were useful and lucrative only if kept under production. If peasant villages were not located on their estates, estate owners offered inducements for peasants to move to their lands and work on them. Those inducements might include loans or an exemption from paying taxes and rental obligations for several years. But if a peasant owed rent or was otherwise indebted to his landlord, it was more difficult for him to leave his residence.

Some private landholdings, often consisting of widely scattered parcels, had become in the fifteenth and early sixteenth centuries bases for lucrative economic enterprises. Before Novgorod's demise, its boyars had used their northern lands as the source of goods, primarily squirrel pelts, that they sold through the city's foreign trade market. Monasteries, encouraged by local and grand princes who gave gifts and also, importantly, issued charters granting them immunity or exemptions from a range of princely taxes and administrative fees, became engaged in a range of business activities, including domestic trade.

Toward the end of the fifteenth century, the rate of growth of some monasteries, e.g., the Holy Trinity and St. Cyril-Beloozero Monasteries, slowed considerably. Ivan III and to an even greater degree Vasily III rescinded some of their tax exemptions. But the existing agricultural and non-agricultural enterprises of these monasteries continued to thrive. Moreover, others expanded and new monasteries were founded. The northern Solovetskii Monastery, shortly before the annexation of Novgorod, was the recipient of numerous donations of land from local boyars. Unlike many of the other Novgorodian monasteries, whose lands were confiscated by Ivan III at the end of the century, Solovetskii not only kept its possessions but continued to grow; its control over key islands in the White Sea, stretches of land on its shore and along the rivers emptying into it, gave the monastery control over vast and valuable economic resources, including salt, fish, tallow, and leather. The Volokolamsk Monastery, founded in 1479, provides a second example. Favored first by the appanage prince of Volok and later by Vasily III, it too received gifts of land and the means to purchase additional tracts. Whereas other monasteries lost much of their immunity from taxation, Volokolamsk remained better protected and became an important economic and political as well as spiritual institution.

In the late fifteenth century a new form of land tenure was introduced; it altered conditions for the peasants and ultimately placed even more of them under the authority of private landlords. The new type of estate was known as a *pomest'e* (*pomest'ia* in the plural). The landholder, a *pomeshchik*, had only a conditional title to his estate, which was issued to him by the grand prince. In return for rights to the estate and to the incomes derived from it, the *pomeshchik* owed the grand prince military service.

The *pomest'e* system was introduced on a large scale in the aftermath of the conquest of Novgorod. In the 1470s and 1480s, it will be recalled, Grand Prince Ivan III seized the estates of the Novgorod boyars as well as much of the landed property of the archbishop and the Novgorod monasteries; thus, approximately eighty percent of the private lands of Novgorod passed to the grand prince. Although he kept some of it as court lands, over the next several decades he distributed many of the Novgorodian estates or at least the incomes from them to Muscovite military servicemen. Most were granted to the relatively low-ranking, provincial *deti boiarskie* (literally, boyars' sons), but some estates were distributed to princes from subordinated branches of the dynasty and to boyars from Moscow. At the other end of the social scale, slaves, some of whom had served dispossessed Novgorodian boyars, and others willing to become provincial servicemen also acquired *pomest'ia*. When Pskov, Smolensk, and Riazan' were annexed to Muscovy, similar procedures were followed. The practice of issuing *pomest'ia* to servicemen became standard in the sixteenth century. As the system evolved, servicemen were not content simply to receive income from their allotments. Increasingly through the sixteenth century they settled on their estates, attempted to consolidate their often scattered holdings into contiguous farms, exercised some direction over their operations, and also sought to have them transferred to members of their own family when they died or retired from service.

The confiscations were conducted on a massive scale. Thousands of individuals were uprooted from the annexed territories. Some dispossessed landowners were issued *pomest'ia* in the northeastern principalities. Others were simply imprisoned. The eviction of local landowners dismantled the political and social elites in each of the annexed principalities. With their disappearance the local economies were also disrupted. In Novgorod boyars had carefully organized their estates to supply not only edible food products and livestock, but also the items that were sold to foreign merchants for export. Thus peasants who dwelled on northern estates typically paid their rents to the owners of their lands in fur pelts as well as portions of their crops. When the grand prince confiscated these estates, the peasants were required to pay fixed amounts of grain and/or cash to his treasury. The economic risks of the peasantry, who had to adjust their activities to raise cash, consequently increased, while the supply of goods to the foreign market became less stable. Most of the *pomeshchiki*, who subsequently received estates from the grand prince, changed the rent mix again to reflect their preference for food supplies and other items required for their own sustenance. Through all these changes the total value of the rents collected rose. The increased burden on the peasantry was compounded by a parallel increase in the number of taxes imposed by the Muscovite government.

By the end of the fifteenth century and especially during the 1520s and 1530s, however, inflationary trends were visible. Prices were rising while the value of silver coin was dropping. Such trends benefited those peasants whose rents and obligations were defined in fixed amounts of cash, which were revised only rarely. The same trends may have also motivated the *pomeshchiki*'s desire to collect rent payments in set amounts of goods in kind rather than in cash.

The territorial expansion of Muscovy thus had serious economic and social consequences for the annexed territories. Although there were some exceptions, e.g., Tver', the elites of many of their societies were displaced. The appearance of women, such as Marfa Boretskaia in Novgorod, in prominent political and economic roles virtually ceased. The organization of agriculture on privately held estates was altered and accompanied by a shift in favored crops or products. Increased rents and the multiplication of taxes placed a heavier burden on the peasants. And heightened demand for labor and the need to keep the new *pomest'ia* operative contributed to the decision to restrict peasant mobility.

The urban economy

Nevertheless, the agrarian sector of society produced sufficient quantities of food to support not only the peasants themselves and the landowning groups in Muscovite society, but also growing urban populations. In some towns the number of inhabitants was substantial. Moscow quickly became the country's largest city with a population variously estimated to have been between 50,000 and 100,000 persons in the fifteenth century. One account described it as twice as large as Florence or Prague by about 1520. Sigismund von Herberstein, who visited Muscovy in 1515–16 and again in 1526 as an ambassador from the Holy Roman Empire, noted that according to a recent census, Moscow contained 41,500 households.[1] Novgorod, also considered quite large, had only about 25,000 to 30,000 inhabitants in the middle of the sixteenth century, while towns like Tver' and Nizhnii Novgorod probably each had no more than 10,000 residents.

Herberstein went on to describe Moscow as broad, spacious, and very dirty. "The city itself," he wrote, "is built of wood, and tolerably large, and at a distance appears larger than it really is, for the gardens and spacious court-yards in every house make a great addition to the size of the city, which is again greatly increased by the houses of smiths and other artificers who employ fires. These houses extend in a long row at the end of the city, interspersed with fields and meadows." He also described a section of mills available for public use, and repeated that with the exception of a few stone houses, churches, and monasteries, and of course the masonry walls of the kremlin and its complex of buildings, the city was all wood.[2]

The bulk of the urban dwellers consisted of clergy, merchants, artisans, and slaves. In Moscow, as in other towns before their subordination, the

---

[1] Sigismund von Herberstein, *Notes upon Russia*, Works Issued by the Hakluyt Society, vols. 10 and 12, trans. by R. H. Major (London: Hakluyt, 1851; reprint ed., New York: Burt Franklin, n.d.), vol. 12, p. 5.

[2] von Herberstein, *Notes upon Russia*, vol. 12, pp. 4–5.

prince and his courtiers, i.e., his boyars and retainers of lesser ranks, swelled the number of residents. Some rural landholders also owned property in towns. Before they were dispossessed the Novgorodian boyars, for example, generally lived in the city of Novgorod rather than on any of their vast estates in the surrounding countryside. Rural monasteries frequently maintained agents in towns to oversee their urban business activities. Individuals in these categories could obtain food and other items required for their maintenance directly from the rural estates they owned or represented. But most town residents relied on domestic trade that brought foodstuffs from the villages to town markets and exchanged goods among towns to secure the items they needed.

Ambrogio (Ambrosio) Contarini, a Venetian diplomat who traveled through Muscovy during the reign of Ivan III, described one of the winter markets in Moscow:

The climate is so excessively cold, that the people stay nine months of the year indoors. As it is difficult to travel in the summer time, on account of the thick forests and the great quantity of mud caused by the melting of the ice, they are obliged to get in all their provisions in the spring, for which purpose they use their sani or sledges on which they stow everything, and are easily drawn by one horse. By the end of October the river which passes through the city [Moscow] is frozen over, and the shops and bazaars for the sale of all sorts of things are erected on it, scarcely anything being sold in the town. They do this, as the river, from being surrounded on all sides by the city, and so protected from the wind, is less cold than anywhere else. On this frozen river may be seen, daily, numbers of cows and pigs, great quantities of corn [i.e., grain], wood, hay, and every other necessary, nor does the supply fail during the whole winter. At the end of November, all those who have cows or pigs, kill and bring them, from time to time, to the city market. They are frozen whole, and it is curious to see so many skinned cows standing upright on their feet. The meat that you eat has sometimes been killed three months or more [earlier].[3]

Similar markets operated in other towns. Monasteries, operating under the terms of their immunity charters, participated in the trade of fish and firewood, grain and salt throughout the towns of northern Russia. Vladimir was supplied with grain ground at mills on the Kliaz'ma River. The Novgorod market was the scene for an exchange not only of foodstuffs, honey, wax, and leather goods, but also tallow, flax, and hemp, for which it became renowned by the first decades of the sixteenth century.

---

[3] Josafa Barbaro and Ambrogio Contarini, *Travels to Tana and Persia*, Works Issued by the Hakluyt Society, vol. 49, trans. by William Thomas and S. A. Roy (London: Hakluyt, 1873; reprint ed., Burt Franklin, n.d.), pp. 161–162.

Several industries received special impetus in this period. One of the factors stimulating their expansion was the increasing size of the population. The timber industry was one. Herberstein's comments on Moscow suggest the reason. The expanding city was built almost exclusively of wood. Not only construction of houses and shops for its increasing population, but also the provision and maintenance of bridges, carts, river craft, fences, tools and implements, and fuel created a growing demand for wood. By the time Herberstein made his observations, the forests in the immediate vicinity of Moscow had been depleted, and timber was being transported from other locales, such as Mozhaisk.

The salt-boiling industry provides another example. Salt was an essential item for the Russian society. It was used not only to preserve meats, fish, and other foods, but also to cure hides and to process iron. But locally produced salt had been insufficient to meet the society's needs, and therefore it had regularly been imported to the Russian lands either from the Baltic or from the Black, Azov, and Caspian Sea regions. In the early 1490s, however, Ivan III banned the import of salt. Although the ban was lifted in 1514, a domestic salt industry, operating from points across the Russian northlands from the Novgorod lands through the Dvina land to Sol' Vychegodsk on the Vychegda River in the northeast, gained momentum while the ban was in effect. It continued to be encouraged throughout the reign of Vasily III and successfully competed with foreign imports. Anika Stroganov, the progenitor of the influential Stroganov merchant family, began to build his family's fortune by operating salt-boiling works at Sol' Vychegodsk during this period.

The arms industry provides a third example that displayed marked growth from the late fifteenth century. By the 1470s Russian armies had been using cannon and artillery with gunpowder for almost a century. But it was only at that time that they began to use artillery and firearms in significant quantity and with greater regularity. The army that Ivan III led to Novgorod in 1478, for example, included an artillery unit. The Novgorodians, having experienced the effects of artillery assaults from the Teutonic knights on some of its outlying fortresses, were already familiar with the damage that this weaponry could inflict. They had, as a result, reinforced the walls of those provincial forts as well as the city's own kremlin by 1450. Nevertheless, they were evidently less than confident that their defenses were strong enough to sustain an artillery barrage; Richard Hellie concluded that simply the fact that Ivan III had artillery with him before Novgorod in 1478 frightened its inhabitants into surrendering. Gustave Alef, however, attributed the surrender less to the relatively ineffective cannon than to "hunger and . . . signs of plague."

Both noted that cannon were also used against Tver' in 1485 with similar results.[4]

Possibly because of periodic German and Swedish bans on the export of these items to Muscovy, both the artillery and the gunpowder used in them were being produced domestically by the last quarter of the fifteenth century. The expanded use of these weapons thus stimulated the development of gunpowder production, bronzecasting (the preferred method of making cannon), lead- and then ironcasting for the cannonballs, and the manufacture of auxiliary equipment such as gun carriages to transport the artillery. Their production was assisted by Italian engineers, most notably Aristotle Fioravanti whose architectural expertise was also valued by the Muscovites.

In towns throughout Muscovy artisans were thus engaged in a wide variety of activities. Carpenters, stonemasons, coppersmiths, blacksmiths and armorsmiths, artists, jewelers and silversmiths, potters, weavers, leathermakers, and woodworkers as well as many other types of craftsmen produced items ranging from artillery to frames for precious icons; humble dwellings and workshops to magnificent fortified walls, towers, and cathedrals; simple candlesticks to cathedral chandeliers. Aided by apprentices and unskilled workers, they milled grain and molded candles; they built bridges and dug moats; they cast church bells, fired bricks, and forged cannon. Some of the items were made to order; others were sold at open market in the towns' bustling *posady* or marketplaces, usually set beneath the city walls.

From the middle of the fifteenth century through the reign of Vasily III, Muscovy was thus prospering economically. Despite or, perhaps, because of economic disruption and reorganization in other principalities following their annexations and the imposition of more taxes on their populations, the signs of prosperity were most evident in Moscow itself. In the middle of the fifteenth century Novgorod, based on observations of monumental construction once again, still appeared to be more affluent than Moscow. But its wealth was dispersed among its boyars and merchants, and, especially because the need to rebuild their fortifications absorbed their resources, the number of other expensive construction projects they were able to finance was tapering off.

In contrast, Moscow was undertaking a resurgence in construction activity, which had waned during the dynastic wars. Already in the 1450s new stone structures were being erected in the kremlin. By the last quarter of the fifteenth century Moscow was engaged in a building spree. Within just a few decades the appearance of the centerpiece of the city, its triangular kremlin, was transformed. Upon completion thick new brick walls demarcated by a series of massive towers encased an ensemble of palaces and cathedrals, whose glittering gold cupolas rose above the fortress to shine over the city, the center of Orthodoxy.

The first project was the replacement of the Cathedral of the Assumption (Dormition), which had been built one hundred and fifty years earlier by Ivan I Kalita and Metropolitan Petr and had fallen into decay. Ivan III authorized the construction of a new cathedral to be modeled after the twelfth-century cathedral in Vladimir. Begun in 1472, the structure collapsed in 1474. Ivan III then sent for Italian architects to take over the project. Aristotle Fioravanti, the same figure who contributed to Muscovite artillery production, arrived in Moscow in 1475 to design the cathedral and supervise its construction. The Cathedral of the Assumption was completed in 1479. The cathedral remained true to the traditions of Church architecture in northeastern Rus'. The rectangular structure was surmounted by five cupolas. At its eastern end were five apses, reflecting the internal divisions of the cathedral. The outer face of the southern wall contained a band arcading reminiscent of the facades of Suzdalian churches built in the twelfth and early thirteenth centuries. The result was a grand, elegant cathedral that employed traditional Suzdalian features, but replaced the heavy stolid quality of that school with a simplicity and delicacy characteristic of Novgorodian design blended with the balanced proportions and symmetry that distinguished the Italian Renaissance style. Inside, the cathedral was equally impressive: its iconostasis was painted by Dionysius and his associates, who carried forward the traditions of the school of Andrei Rublev: in 1514–15 frescoes covering its interior walls added to its grandeur. It was in this cathedral that Ivan III held the extravagant coronation ceremony for his grandson in 1498.

After the first attempt to build the Church of the Assumption had begun, a fire in the kremlin destroyed some of the other older churches as well as the residence of the metropolitan. Metropolitan Filipp died at the time of the fire. The disaster created both space and a need for more churches and residences. The Cathedral of the Assumption was consequently joined by the Cathedral of the Annunciation (1484–89), a private chapel for the princely family built by architects from Pskov and distinguished by its ogee arches, and the Church of Our Lady's Vestments (1485–86), which was attached to the metropolitan's residence. In 1505, the Cathedral of Archangel Michael was added to the ensemble on the

Figure 9.1 The Cathedral of the Dormition, Moscow

kremlin's cathedral square. Although its floorplan conformed to standard Orthodox churches, its architect Alevisio Novi of Milan selected red brick for its walls and a contrasting white stone for its decorations, the most outstanding of which were the scalloped or shell-shaped design on the gables. Despite its bright appearance this cathedral housed the tombs of the Daniilovichi.

The construction of these churches required concentrated wealth, expressed the centrality of Muscovite power, and also signified the princes' recognition of their need for divine support and protection. The Cathedral of the Assumption had been initiated in 1472 just after the 1471 defeat of Novgorod. The conscious attempt to reproduce the Vladimir cathedral was an unambiguous signal that Moscow asserted itself as the successor to the former capital. Yet before this symbol of Moscow's triumph could be completed, the kremlin had burned, the metropolitan had died, and the unfinished church had collapsed. Despite their victories, the expansion of their territories, and their aggrandizement of secular attributes of power, the Muscovite grand princes could not ignore such signs, and through the construction of these churches they glorified and paid homage to their God.

Construction was not, however, limited to the kremlin churches. Beside them arose the Palace of Facets, which was built in 1487–91 by the Italian architects Marco Ruffo and Pietro Solario, and used for ceremonial receptions and other court functions; the princes' living quarters were rebuilt between 1491 and 1508; and the Bell Tower of Ivan the Great was begun in 1505. In these, as well as most of the church projects, Italian architects exercised the predominant influence.

Moscow's kremlin walls were also rebuilt and its towers constructed between 1485 and 1495. The thick, strong walls of the enclosure were not only symbols of the power of Muscovy. Punctured by turrets and small apertures through which fixed cannon and soldiers with small arms could shoot at a threatening army, the fortress was also a practical response to the changing style of warfare that had incorporated the use of artillery. The grand prince, accordingly, also rebuilt the fortifications of the city of Novgorod in 1484–90, as well as those of the outlying towns of the Novgorod lands and Pskov.

The grand princes as well as other Muscovite patrons sponsored construction well beyond the kremlin. Bridges, moats, and dams were built around the fortress. Prominent boyars also built palaces for themselves. In the early sixteenth century Vasily III as well as merchants commissioned the construction of churches outside the kremlin in the *posad* or commercial quarter. One of the most innovative efforts of the era was the Church of the Ascension, built by Vasily III in 1532 at the village of Kolomenskoe, outside Moscow. Unlike the standard masonry churches on whose roofs cylindrical drums topped by cupolas were set, the brick Kolomenskoe church was marked by a soaring tent-shaped spire, a form typically reserved for wooden structures. Muscovites also undertook construction projects in newly annexed territories. The reinforcement of Novgorod's fortifications in 1484–90 provides one example. But Vasily III and other Muscovites, most notably merchants who had replaced their evicted counterparts, sponsored churches as well. In the process Muscovy imposed its architectural styles, along with its political authority and economic dominance, on the subordinated city.

POLITICAL CONSOLIDATION

The complex of extravagant new structures in Moscow's kremlin, combined with those elsewhere in the city and around the country, constituted a physical representation of the economic and political power of the Muscovite grand prince. The accumulation of wealth they reflected is even more remarkable when it is considered that their Italian architects demanded large salaries for their services, and, as will be discussed in the next chapter, that Muscovy was at war in the late fifteenth and early sixteenth centuries with Lithuania and Livonia. The projects mounted by the Muscovite grand princes are not only indicative of the country's prosperity, but of their ability to mobilize the society's resources.

As Ivan III and Vasily III completed the process of "gathering the Russian lands" into Muscovy, they acquired an expanded resource base. They concentrated in their own treasury revenues that previously had been dispersed among autonomous princes. They also added new taxes to the customary tribute. Most of them were specifically related to the changing style of warfare, which was based on the use of artillery and firearms. A fee called the *primet*, for example, was being assessed by the early sixteenth century specifically to cover the costs of constructing siege equipment and rebuilding or reinforcing fortifications. Similarly, fees (*gorodchikovaia poshlina*) were assessed to support the officials (*gorodovye prikazchiki*) appointed to construct and maintain fortifications.

In addition to introducing new fees, the grand princes also converted other customary obligations, traditionally paid in labor or in kind, to monetary fees; simultaneously they imposed them on a broader range of the population. Support for the postal service or *iam* falls into that category. The post system had been introduced under the influence of the Mongol khans. During the reign of Ivan III it consisted of a series of relay stations, located along established routes, where official messengers could obtain fresh mounts and sustenance. Around the beginning of the sixteenth century, the service obligation of peasants to supply horses, carts, or sleighs and provisions for couriers as well as to maintain stations and roads in their immediate vicinity was converted into a monetary fee, *iamskie den'gi*. The collection of this fee, which was imposed universally on the tax-paying population, provided the central court treasury with the means to take over the operation of the postal system. Later, the practice of providing labor and fuel for the manufacture of gunpowder, which during the first part of the sixteenth century was required of peasants located near the production centers, was similarly transformed into a gunpowder fee, known as the *iamchuzhnoe delo*, paid in cash and collected from all taxpayers.

The array of taxes collected by the grand prince was used not only to build expensive structures and, as indicated, to improve the country's defenses. More fundamentally, access to increased revenues enabled the grand prince to initiate and develop policies and institutions designed to oversee his expanded realm and to conduct its fiscal, judicial, military, and foreign affairs. The result was the formation of an administrative apparatus capable of carrying out the functions that transformed the diverse collection of principalities accumulated by Ivan III and Vasily III into a unified state centered around the grand prince.

The political institutions that evolved during the reigns of Ivan III and Vasily III were strikingly similar to Tatar government structures. The parallels have led some scholars to the conclusion that as early as the fourteenth century the Muscovites were emulating the administrative apparatus of the Golden Horde.[5] The Horde's political structure was centered around the khan, who depended upon the elders or beys of the Tatar clans for counsel, cooperation, and the conduct of district or provincial administration. He similarly relied upon a vizier to oversee the functions of his court, including his treasury and clerical staff.

By the reign of Ivan III, parallel institutions had become the instruments of administration in Muscovy. But they were used to implement policies in the sedentary society of the amalgamated Rus' principalities. They functioned in the context of Rus' traditions. The concepts that were required to justify and legitimize the expanding power of the grand prince and his government did not, therefore, acknowledge their probable Tatar prototypes, but were drawn from the pervasive Orthodox ideology. Tatar models for organizing and exercising power were encased in Byzantine and Orthodox theory and symbol; they assumed their own Muscovite character and substance.

---

[5] This view is developed in detail by Donald Ostrowski in "The Mongol Origins of Muscovite Political Institutions," *SR*, vol. 49 (1990), pp. 525–542.

The Muscovite court

The Muscovite political system, as it evolved in the late fifteenth and early sixteenth centuries, set the grand prince at its center and vested him with full political power. But despite the centralized character of the political system and the unchallenged concentration of authority in his office and person, the grand prince did not exercise unlimited power. Tradition, practical necessity, and perhaps the wisdom derived from the model of effective Tatar political arrangements placed constraints on the sovereign. In his decisions and functions he depended upon the advice of his relatives, Church hierarchs, and his own servitors. In the implementation of his policies he required the cooperation and loyalty of his courtiers, on the one hand, and a staff of state secretaries, scribes, and clerks, on the other. Both of those groups performed administrative duties at the central and provincial levels.

The grand prince's court was an institution that evolved from the military retinues that every prince in the Riurikid dynasty had customarily maintained. Previously, even when displaced as rulers, northern Rus' princes had owned sufficient landed estates to support themselves; they had also enjoyed the option of offering their military service or administrative expertise to any of the numerous remaining princely courts or even to Lithuania. But as Muscovy expanded, their range of options had narrowed. Entering service of one of the few remaining appanage princes or an ecclesiastic hierarch diminished the status of both the service prince and his family, and transfer to the Lithuanian court ultimately came to be regarded as treasonous. Thus, as members of the elite lost their economic and political freedoms, they became dependent upon the grand prince for their status, position, and wealth.

Although some continued to hold hereditary landed estates, compensation for their service to the grand prince became their main source of income. For those assigned *pomest'ia* , rents and supplies were paid by peasants on their estates. Participation in victorious military ventures supplemented those incomes with booty. In addition, often as a reward for fulfilling military or court assignments, servicemen might be given provincial administrative appointments, for which they also received payment. After Muscovy successfully incorporated most of the other northern Rus' principalities, the chief and preferred source of these personal economic rewards was service to the grand prince. As the issuer of these rewards, however, the grand prince also acquired the power to retract his favor and the benefits he had bestowed.

Prospects of advancement and reward evidently outweighed the associated risks. Displaced princes and their retainers congregated at

Moscow, where they sought positions at the Muscovite court and joined families already in the grand prince's service. The servitors at court were ranked according to their status. The highest ranks were boyar and *okol'nichii*. Below them were additional categories of Moscow courtiers. Other servitors, accorded yet lower ranks, were based outside Moscow in the provinces. Although there was a wide range between the prestige and political influence of boyars and of the *deti boiarskie*, who served from the provinces, all were members of a privileged group in Muscovite society.

Within the court a spirit of rivalry prevailed. Although the Muscovite regime had assumed responsibility for more military and administrative functions in conjunction with its territorial expansion, population growth and the influx of servicemen from annexed territories to the Muscovite court kept the numbers of servitors larger than the numbers of lucrative postings. The ratio of servicemen to desirable posts prompted the competition among the service families.

Gradually, through the reigns of Ivan III and Vasily III, a system known as *mestnichestvo* evolved to assimilate new families into the Muscovite court and to govern the promotion of servitors to higher rank. The system, whose name is derived from the word *mesto* or place, was originally designed as a means of assigning seats at court ceremonies according to status. It was then applied to appointments of high-level servitors to military and civil posts, and later spread to lower ranks as well. *Mestnichestvo* determined the relative "place" or status of each servitor. At the heart of what developed into an intricate system was a simple principle: the closer a servitor's "place" was to that of the grand prince, who stood at the center of the *mestnichestvo* matrix, the higher his status. "Place" or status was calculated by weighing together the service records of an individual and his kin, the status of his family in relation to others, and his seniority within his own clan. An individual's or family's status could be elevated by manipulating any of those factors, for example, by forging marital ties with families of higher rank or by unusual performance in military or administrative assignments. The system thus amalgamated factors of high birth, which served the interests of princely families, and of service, which gave advantages to the untitled Muscovite clans.

Although *mestnichestvo* related fundamentally to status, it also influenced military and civil duty assignments. A record of loyal service was necessary even for members of the most prestigious families to achieve the highest ranks at court. But *mestnichestvo*, as it evolved, incorporated the principle that no serviceman should be required to fill a post deemed inferior to another if the first serviceman's "place" was higher than the second's. By the same token, no serviceman would be assigned as a superior to others who had precedence over him. *Mestnichestvo* did not determine a servitor's specific military or civil posting, but it did require that appointments respect the relative "places" of the servitors.

The atmosphere of competition in which the grand prince's servitors functioned did not dissipate with the development of the *mestnichestvo*. Rather, the system institutionalized disputes and channeled them into the grand prince's administrative machinery. As *mestnichestvo* matured during the second quarter of the sixteenth century, ranking service families sought to elevate their status by serving in high-level positions and marrying into prestigious families. They jealously guarded their own status, tracked their own and others' service appointments, and challenged any assignments they considered dishonorable. Petitions for reassignment were directed to officials of the grand prince; suits were resolved by an expression of his authority.

The system of *mestnichestvo* formalized competition among Muscovite servitors. It muted disputes and defused potentially disruptive feuds among rival clans. It eased the process of transforming autonomous princes and their retainers into servicemen of the grand prince. But it also reinforced the dependency of all the courtiers on the grand prince, who was ultimately responsible for their inclusion in or expulsion from the service elite, for every appointment, promotion, or demotion, and for adjudication of their disputes. Rather than encourage the coalescence of an "aristocracy" that sought to institutionalize its power and prestige at the expense of the grand prince, the competitive nature of the service system functioned to bind even the most highly placed families and individuals in the Muscovite state not to each other, but to the grand prince whose own position was both elevated and strengthened by the dynamics of the court politics surrounding him.

Provincial administration

It was from the ranks of the servitors at the Moscow court that the grand princes appointed provincial administrators. When the Muscovite grand prince annexed a principality, he replaced its prince with his own *namestnik*, variously translated as governor, lieutenant, vice-regent, or viceroy, who was responsible to him and represented his authority. The practice was a continuation of the custom followed in the fourteenth and fifteenth centuries by Muscovite and Tver' princes who had established their governors in Novgorod, for example, and other towns where they asserted their authority. Governors of very important towns were selected from the highest-ranking servicemen, but lower-ranked servicemen from Moscow provided the personnel to fill most of the provincial governorships, just as they occupied other junior administrative posts.

Muscovite governors served for varying periods, sometimes for months, occasionally for decades. Special charters, issued in the name of the grand prince to the local populace, outlined the governors' responsibilities for collecting the prince's tax revenues, preserving public order and safety, and judging legal cases. Immunity charters, on the other hand, removed specific populations, frequently on ecclesiastical lands, from a governor's jurisdiction. Generally, however, the maintenance of roads, bridges, and defensive capabilities were within the purview of the governors. Deputies, constables, and bailiffs assisted them in carrying out these duties. In rural districts *volost'* chiefs (*volosteli*) performed comparable tasks.

Governors and other provincial officials were paid through a system, operative from at least the fourteenth century, known as *kormlenie* or "feeding." According to that system the populace of each locality provided its governor or *volost'* chief with food supplies for himself and his horses. Selected fees, notably those derived from judicial and commercial activities, were assigned to them as supplemental salaries. In the fifteenth century the amounts paid to each official were regulated by the central government, as was the frequency of deliveries. Typically payments were made twice a year, on Christmas and St. Peter's Day (June 29). A third payment, at Easter, became more common in the sixteenth century. Subordinate officials were similarly supported; they received smaller amounts of goods in kind as well as specific fees assessed for transferring certain types of property, serving warrants, issuing official documents, and performing other formal transactions.

With time some of the functions of the governors and *volost'* chiefs were transferred to other specialized officers. The *gorodovye prikazchiki*, for example, were appointed to oversee the reconstruction and maintenance of fortresses and defense. As their duties broadened to supervise local militias as well as to raising revenue and labor for public construction projects, their importance grew at the expense of the governors'. The introduction of other officers with responsibilities for collecting customs and other commercial fees and for legal matters concerning land tenure similarly eroded the powers of the governors. The new officers were not supported by *kormlenie*. Instead, as noted above, special taxes were levied to provide revenue to pay their salaries.

Governors and other officials appointed from the Muscovite court formed the layer of provincial administration that replaced princes from local branches of the dynasty in annexed territories. They were the bearers of Muscovite authority in the provinces. They collected the grand prince's taxes, mustered his military forces, implemented his law and his policies, and thereby bound his diverse lands to Moscow, the center of his extended realm.

The central administration

The duma Although they regularly filled posts in provincial administration, the Muscovite courtiers most commonly performed military duties. They constituted the pool from which officers for the grand prince's regiments were drawn. Servicemen were also called upon to undertake diplomatic duties and travel abroad as special emissaries of the grand prince. A few, selected on the basis of both their prestigious lineage and long, respectable, if not necessarily distinguished, service careers, achieved the highest ranks at court.

Those servitors, the boyars and *okol'nichie*, formed an exclusive elite, commonly although inappropriately called the "boyar duma." Generally numbering only ten to fifteen at any given time, the members of the duma had personal access to the grand prince and regularly advised him on policy decisions and matters of state, including issues regarding war and peace, major financial expenditures, and the selection of marriage partners for members of the royal family.

In addition to counseling the grand prince, boyars participated in court ceremonies. They received foreign envoys with or on behalf of the grand prince; they participated in negotiations; and they were present when treaties were signed. On occasion they were also sent abroad as diplomatic envoys. In addition, boyars exercised direct influence and power in military and civil affairs. They were appointed to be commanders of the grand prince's regiments and governors of particularly important towns. They supervised the functions of administrative units within the court treasury. They served as judges; and they witnessed and co-signed state documents.

The rank of *okol'nichii* carried a somewhat lower status than boyar, but nevertheless connoted high honor. It appears to have been introduced in the late fifteenth century in conjunction with the growing numbers of prestigious families entering Muscovite service. Usually granted to servitors with at least fifteen years' experience, the title was typically accorded to men who were younger than the boyars or had less seniority in their own families; the rank of boyar was bestowed even later in one's career, after an average of twenty years of service.

Some scholars, notably Gustave Alef and Ann Kleimola, discerned in addition a tendency for the career paths of *okol'nichie* and boyars to take different directions. Although acknowledging exceptions, they identified *okol'nichie* with administrative, court, and diplomatic service, but not with the military duties, including regimental commands, that typified careers of servicemen who became boyars.[6] Nancy Shields Kollmann, however, argued that boyars and *okol'nichie* served in essentially the same capacities; the distinction between the two ranks, in her view, was one of status.[7]

Despite the increased size of the grand princely service corps, the number of duma members remained low. Its composition, however, fluctuated. Throughout the fifteenth century virtually all the boyars and *okol'nichie* were selected from untitled, albeit privileged, families. Muscovite expansion, which brought princes of annexed lands into the grand prince's service, also precipitated a challenge to those families that had long and faithfully served Moscow's princes, had achieved the highest ranks, and monopolized the most influential roles at court and in the administration.

During the first three decades of the sixteenth century members of those princely families penetrated the exclusive circle in increasing numbers. The Shuiskii family, descended from the princes of Suzdal'-Nizhnii Novgorod, was among the most eminent in this group. The first member of this family to become a boyar was Prince Vasily Vasil'evich Nemoi Shuiskii, who acquired that rank by 1508/09 after having entered the grand prince's service by 1491/92. The Shuiskii family would figure prominently in political affairs after the death of Vasily III. Similarly, representatives of the dynastic branches of Rostov, Iaroslavl', and Tver', whose ancestors had entered Muscovite service in the 1460s and 1470s, became boyars in the early years of the sixteenth century.

Selected emigre princes, who had voluntarily transferred their service from Lithuania to Muscovy, were also elevated to boyar rank during this period. Among them were members of the Bel'skii family, who would become the Shuiskii clan's chief rivals. Prince Fedor Ivanovich Bel'skii came from Lithuania in 1481 to enter the grand prince's service; he later married Ivan III's niece, and two of his sons became boyars in the 1520s and 1530s. The Glinskii clan, which will be discussed below, constitutes

---

[6] A. M. Kleimola, "Patterns of Duma Recruitment, 1505–1550," *Essays in Honor of A. A. Zimin*, ed. by Daniel Clarke Waugh (Columbus, Ohio: Slavica, 1985), pp. 236–238. See also A. M. Kleimola, "Military Service and Elite Status in Muscovy in the Second Quarter of the Sixteenth Century," *RH*, vol. 7 (1980), pp. 52–53, 55; Gustave Alef, "Reflections on the Boyar Duma in the Reign of Ivan III," *SEER*, vol. 45 (1967), pp. 99, 106–107; and Gustave Alef, "Aristocratic Politics and Royal Policy in Muscovy in the Late Fifteenth and Early Sixteenth Centuries," *FOG*, vol. 27 (1980), p. 87. The last two articles have been reprinted in Alef, *Rulers and Nobles in Fifteenth-Century Muscovy*.

[7] Kollmann, *Kinship and Politics*, pp. 98, 100.

another example of an emigre princely family from Lithuania that gained entrance into Muscovy's elite circle.

When the duma acquired princely members, another distinction between boyars and *okol'nichie* materialized. For untitled servitors experience at the rank of *okol'nichii* became a virtual requirement before advancement to the status of boyar would be approved; but princes tended to skip over the second-level rank and be admitted to the duma as boyars.

Duma politics Although in principle all political power centered in the person of the grand prince, duma members had significant, if informal influence. Tradition, practicality, and the example of the Tatar khans' relationship with their parallel councils of beys,[8] rather than legal or institutional prerogatives guided the informal process of consultation. Acting officially as military commanders, judges, and administrators and unofficially as patrons of courtiers of lower ranks, they were instrumental in implementing the policies adopted by the grand prince through the discharge of their own duties as well as by guiding the conduct of their proteges. Consequently, even in the absence of formal restraints, the exercise of grand princely power was functionally tempered by the influence and advice of his "duma."

But, as was true for the court in general, the boyars and *okol'nichie* functioned in an intensely competitive atmosphere. Their rivalry was driven by the urge, common to all the courtiers, to gain the benefits associated with high status: prestige, political influence, and material wealth. But at the highest levels of court, where the continuing arrival of new servitors, including prestigious princes, was perceived as a challenge and potential threat by the untitled Muscovite families, it was particularly acute.

The task of integrating all the elite families into a single hierarchy of servitors, all loyal and subordinate to the Muscovite grand prince, was not simple. Established duma members attempted to limit access to their status and reserve the honor, wealth, power, and influence associated with it for themselves and their kin. Practicality obliged the grand princes to recognize and respond to the interests of their lieutenants in the duma. As a result, they tended to give priority to relatives and clients of duma members when adding new boyars and *okol'nichie* to that body. Selected families thus acquired "hereditary rights" to the top court ranks.

Nancy Shields Kollmann presented the thesis that once an individual became a boyar, his heirs automatically became eligible for that rank. She

---

[8] Ostrowski, "Mongol Origins of Muscovite Political Institutions," p. 533.

described a pattern of inheritance reminiscent of the lateral succession system that had been traditional among the Riurikids. Within a boyar family the rank was accorded to members of a single generation in order of seniority, then to the sons of those who had achieved boyar rank. Some practices deviated from the old princely model. More than one family member could hold the rank simultaneously. Furthermore, even upon the death of a boyar, the next eligible member of his family might not replace him immediately. Factors such as age, service record, or experience and pressures deriving from the political relationships or balance of power among the remaining boyars might delay a promotion.[9]

Despite this tendency to preserve exclusivity, the composition of the duma was not static. Some eligible servitors did not survive the long apprenticeship, and their descendants lost access to the inner circle. Other boyars lost the grand prince's favor; an individual's disgrace could adversely affect his relatives' status and retard or prevent their promotion to the highest rank. On the other hand, new families gradually gained admission to the duma.

Mestnichestvo offered the mechanism by which both the new princely servitors and the old Muscovite clans could achieve high rank, wealth, and power in the service of the grand prince. It allowed a relatively smooth, but slow and controlled integration of "newcomers" into the Muscovite duma without displacing established Muscovite boyar families. The emphasis on loyal service, which became one of the system's main components, so well preserved the status and opportunities of the Muscovite clans that it was not until the sixteenth century, especially during the final years of Vasily III's reign, that princely candidates, including members of both the Bel'skii and the Shuiskii families, were admitted in any significant numbers to the duma. And it was not until after his reign that princely boyars outnumbered the untitled boyars. *Mestnichestvo* thus provided an orderly method of absorbing the "newcomers" into Muscovite service without sacrificing the honor and experience of the established untitled Muscovite clans.

The grand princes' cognizance and respect for their elite servitors' interests is evident not only in their cautious approach to admitting new families into the duma. They are reflected as well in at least two specific episodes, involving decisions that affected the dynasty, the court, and the Muscovite state. Both episodes suggest that the Muscovite political system, however centralized in principle, had another dimension, represented by the role of duma members in the decision-making process. Among the duma members individual quests for status and power

---

[9] Kollmann, *Kinship and Politics*, p. 119.

intermingled with concerns for state policies and, at times, were indistinguishable. But motivated by personal or public goals, ranking servicemen actively participated in shaping decisions of the grand prince. Both episodes also demonstrate that the grand princes took the interests and concerns of their duma members into account when making those decisions. In one case Ivan III altered his decision to accommodate his duma. In the other Vasily III manipulated duma membership to reduce its influence over his action.

The first episode was the succession crisis of the 1490s, discussed in the previous chapter. The selection of Ivan III's heir was a matter of concern not only to members of the dynasty but to the boyars, whose own status depended upon their close ties to the grand prince. They also had a common interest in preventing any single one of their clans from acquiring a disproportionate share of influence and wealth.

At the time of the crisis one boyar family, headed by Prince Ivan Iur'evich Patrikeev, had achieved preeminence at the court of Ivan III. A descendant of the Lithuanian dynasty, he was also the grand prince's first cousin and his closest advisor. He even opened his home to Ivan III and his family while a masonry palace was being constructed to replace the grand prince's wooden living quarters in the early 1490s. Patrikeev also dominated the duma. By 1494, according to Gustave Alef, seven of the eleven boyars in the duma were his kin. Other members of the duma, as well as servitors whose access to the duma was blocked by the preferential treatment given members of the Patrikeev clan, were disturbed by his growing power. This alone, according to Alef, was sufficient to provoke a reaction from them.[10]

Other scholars relate Patrikeev and his fate to the succession crisis. Although John Fennell argued to the contrary,[11] it appears that after the death of Ivan Ivanovich in 1490, Patrikeev had been instrumental in securing the succession for Dmitry Ivanovich, whose mother was also related to him. Kollmann explained the distress of Patrikeev's opponents not only in terms of his overwhelming influence, but also in terms of the family structures of the two heirs, Dmitry and Vasily. Dmitry had no sisters, and because of his youth it was not expected that any daughters he might produce would reach marriageable age for decades. His succession, by delaying opportunities for other families to marry into the grand prince's family, would have perpetuated the Patrikeev clan's dominance

---

[10] Gustave Alef, "The Origins of Muscovite Autocracy. The Age of Ivan III," *FOG*, vol. 39 (1986), pp. 204–207. See also his "Aristocratic Politics and Royal Policy," p. 81.
[11] In "The Dynastic Crisis 1497–1502," *SEER*, vol. 39 (1960–61), Fennell argued that Patrikeev supported Vasily, not Dmitry. For his conclusions, see pp. 21–22.

at court and in the duma. Vasily, on the other hand, had three sisters who in the late 1490s were already old enough to wed. His candidacy offered other families immediate chances to become the grand prince's in-laws and thereby enhance their status, wealth, and power.

By the beginning of 1499, Patrikeev's rivals were strong enough to prevail upon Ivan III to break up the Patrikeev–Dmitry bloc. Within a year of Dmitry's coronation, the grand prince cast Patrikeev and his son Vasily into disgrace and obliged them to become monks. Patrikeev's second son, also in disgrace, remained in confinement; his son-in-law was executed. Patrikeev's influence and line came to an end. This was no small victory for Patrikeev's enemies. Although Dmitry remained heir to the throne, the Patrikeevs would not benefit from his succession. But by 1502 they achieved an even greater concession from Ivan, who ordered the arrest of his own grandson, Dmitry. In 1505, Vasily Ivanovich, the candidate they had favored, became grand prince.[12]

Although the resolution of the crisis ultimately lay with Ivan III, Dmitry's opponents quietly maneuvered even after his coronation to achieve a reversal of the grand prince's decision. The outcome of the crisis reflects the active role played by duma members and the effective influence they could exert. The incident, furthermore, reveals the ongoing process and difficulties not only of integrating Muscovite retainers and subordinated princes into a single service elite, but of integrating that elite and the Muscovite grand prince into an effective political system.

The second episode occurred during the last decade of Vasily III's reign. It also concerned succession. But the problem that dominated the court's attention in the 1520s was not too many heirs; it was the lack of one. Vasily's wife, Solomoniia Saburova, was barren; as a result, the grand prince had not yet produced a son and heir. In 1523, Vasily raised with his duma the twin issues of obtaining a divorce and remarrying.

The proposal of such actions, which violated the teachings of the Orthodox Church, was perceived in some circles as scandalous. Maksim

---

[12] Kollmann, *Kinship and Politics*, pp. 138–140, and "Consensus Politics: The Dynastic Crisis of the 1490s Reconsidered," *RR*, vol. 45 (1986), pp. 243, 251–253. Some scholars have explained Patrikeev's fall from favor in terms of Muscovy's relations with Lithuania; see K. V. Bazilevich, *Vneshniaia politika russkogo tsentralizovannogo gosudarstva* [The foreign policy of the Russian centralized state] (Moscow: Moskovskii universitet, 1952), pp. 360–376, and Fine, "The Muscovite Dynastic Crisis of 1497–1502," pp. 198–215. Others relate it to a supposed conflict between opponents of centralization and Ivan III. For surveys of the scholarship on these views, see e.g., Alef, "Origins of Muscovite Autocracy," pp. 206–207; Kollmann, "Consensus Politics," pp. 237–241; and Fennell, "Dynastic Crisis," pp. 16–23.

Grek and the monk Vassian, formerly Vasily Patrikeev, who had already lost the confidence of the grand prince, raised their voices in protest against committing such a sacrilege. Maksim Grek's condemnation by the Church council or *sobor* in 1525 was, in part, a response to their criticism of the anticipated divorce, which took place shortly after he was silenced.

The issue also had implications for members of the duma as well as for other aspiring courtiers. A divorce would cause the Saburov family, which had rapidly achieved high status due to its exclusive bond with the grand prince, to suffer an equally abrupt loss of status and influence. The proposed divorce, however, affected the prospects of a broader spectrum of servicemen. In the absence of a vertical heir, the grand prince's younger brother, Prince Iurii of Dmitrov, had become the expected successor. Divorce and remarriage not only threatened Iurii's chance to become grand prince, but the futures of all the servicemen who had gambled that Iurii would succeed Vasily and had sought his favor; that group opposed the divorce. Those who expected to lose influence should Iurii and his supporters take power, on the other hand, encouraged the divorce, which they regarded as Vasily's only means of producing a son and the key to their retention of influential positions. Issues of princely power, dynastic succession, political organization, and personal ambition all overlapped and blended as the debate raged around the grand prince's marriage and proposed divorce.

Despite the controversy and some reservations of his own, Metropolitan Daniil, who had taken office in 1522, approved Vasily's plans. In late 1525 the marriage between Vasily and Solomoniia was annulled. Solomoniia was obliged to enter a convent, and within months the metropolitan officiated at the wedding of Vasily III and Elena Vasil'evna Glinskaia. The new grand princess was from the Glinskii family. Her uncle, Prince Mikhail L'vovich Glinskii, had been an influential political figure in Lithuania during the reign of Aleksandr. In 1508, however, he had staged an unsuccessful uprising against Aleksandr's successor Sigismund. Afterward, he fled to Muscovy and entered Vasily's service.

While the issues had been under consideration, Vasily had allowed the number of boyars in his duma to dwindle by attrition to five. But almost immediately after his remarriage, he began to fill the vacancies that had accumulated. One of his appointees in this period was Prince Dmitrii Fedorovich Bel'skii. Although his father, Prince Fedor Ivanovich Bel'skii, who had fled from Lithuania in 1481, had entered Muscovite service and married the grand prince's niece, Prince Dmitrii was the first member of his family to become a boyar. Gustave Alef has attributed that choice to Vasily's awareness of the powerful coalition within his duma that favored the succession of his brother Iurii. Hoping that his new wife would produce a son, Vasily began to reshape his duma to counterbalance that group. His promotion of Bel'skii to boyar rank was central to that effort.[13] In 1526, he raised two members of the Obolenskii clan, which had first gained admission to the duma in the middle of the fifteenth century, to boyar rank. When Elena's uncle, Prince Mikhail L'vovich Glinskii, married the daughter of one of the new Obolenskii boyars, his position and influence also improved.[14]

In 1530, Elena fulfilled Vasily's expectations and gave birth to a son, the future Ivan IV the Terrible. The next year she bore a second son, Iurii. A vertical line of succession had been created and guaranteed. But the admission of new ambitious boyars into the elite circle also set in place the elements of another power struggle, one that would be conducted among the members of the duma. The struggle would commence when Vasily III died in 1533, and left his two infant sons under the protection of their mother and his new boyars.

The administrative apparatus Functioning side by side with the servicemen both at the central Muscovite court and in the provinces were other administrative officials, state secretaries (*d'iaki*), scribes, and clerks. They conducted much of the business of state and often exercised real authority, but lacked the honorary rank and social status accorded the grand prince's servitors.

Court secretaries and scribes had traditionally been responsible for administering court lands; they had arranged and kept records of gifts presented by the grand prince and had overseen the *kormlenie* system. They functioned within the treasury, which operated as a section of the court; the court was supervised by a servitor, the *dvorskii* or *dvoretskii*, who functioned in a manner akin to the Tatar vizier. Although some later acquired top ranks, the servitors who held the post of *dvoretskii* typically were not duma members.

In conjunction with the expansion of Muscovy's territory and responsibilities, administrative functions, including the need to issue documents and keep records, multiplied. The state secretaries, scribes, and clerks

13 Alef, "Aristocratic Politics and Royal Policy," p. 87.
14 According to Nancy Shields Kollmann, Mikhail L'vovich Glinskii never became a boyar. A. A. Zimin, however, concluded he was elevated to boyar rank in 1533; in their studies Alef and Kleimola, following Zimin, have also counted him as a boyar: Kollmann, *Kinship and Politics*, p. 207; A. A. Zimin, "Sostav boiarskoi dumy v XV–XVI vekakh," [The composition of the boyar duma in the XV–XVI centuries] *Arkheograficheskii ezhegodnik za 1957 god* (Moscow: Akademiia Nauk SSSR, 1958), p. 52; Alef, "Aristocratic Politics and Royal Policy," p. 92; A. M. Kleimola, "Patterns of Duma Recruitment, 1505–1550," p. 254.

responded to the challenges of more complex tax collection and stretched their activities into a variety of arenas beyond fiscal and court matters. By the end of the fifteenth century, the treasury in which they worked was distinguished from the court and during the next three decades began to subdivide into informal, yet identifiable functional units; the treasurer, correspondingly, appears to have assumed increasing importance during those decades.

The new functions of the administrative staff were directly related to the policies adopted by the grand princes. To facilitate the distribution of *pomest'ia*, for example, land surveys and records of land grants were necessary. Beginning in the 1480s, state secretaries and scribes, working together with courtiers, compiled land registers or cadasters (*pistsovye knigi*) for the Novgorod lands. The registers contained descriptions of the estates that had been confiscated, lists of their peasant residents, data on crops and rents, and the history of ownership. Comparable surveys were compiled for Tver', Rostov, Vladimir, and other northeastern Rus' districts. From the 1490s state secretaries were also supervising the distribution of *pomest'ia* and reallocations of *pomest'e* land following the deaths of servicemen. They also made provisions for widows and minor children of deceased servicemen; they processed petitions made by servicemen, typically seeking additional land or permission to exchange their estates with other *pomeshchiki*; and they kept records of all these proceedings, which were entered into revised cadasters that continued to be compiled at irregular intervals. By the reign of Vasily III, a distinct administrative unit that specialized in *pomest'e* affairs had been formed.

Even earlier, in the 1470s, state secretaries and scribes were similarly compiling service rosters, known as *razriady*, in which they collected records pertaining to military duty assignments as well as marriages, participation in court ceremonies, and other activities that became pertinent to determining the relative seniority among members of service families. By the 1530s the compilers of *razriady* formed another distinct operational unit or office, identified as the *Razriad*, within the court administrative apparatus.

During the reign of Ivan III, Muscovy also expanded its diplomatic activities. The exchanges of embassies with neighbors and distant European courts alike generated a growing volume of letters and documents that were sent to foreign rulers and translations of messages received from them, of instructions issued to ambassadors and reports submitted by them, of records of meetings with foreign emissaries and of treaties concluded with them. The administrative staff wrote, copied, translated, and filed these documents. Some of them also traveled abroad on diplomatic missions, at times as the senior or sole emissary; some participated in ceremonies and negotiations conducted at the Muscovite court.

To compile land registers; to register *pomest'e* and military assignments; to keep fiscal and court records; to conduct the correspondence between provincial and central officials as well as between Muscovy and foreign governments; to transcribe charters, decrees, and treaties; and to record, file, and retrieve all these documents a steadily increasing number of state secretaries, clerks, scribes, interpreters, and translators was employed. At the beginning of Ivan III's reign, there were fourteen state secretaries; by the time of his death, there were twenty; midway through Vasily III's reign there were at least two dozen. For every secretary, it has been estimated, there were three or four scribes.

Although they stored documents in separate boxes, distinguished by the type of their subject matter, most of the officials who composed and organized them were not specialists. Rather, they easily transferred their skills, most notably their literacy, from one functional area to another. By Vasily III's reign, however, at least three state secretaries were repeatedly engaged in diplomatic affairs, and may be regarded as "professionals" or experts in that area.[15] During the same period individual secretaries also became more exclusively associated with the functions of the *Razriad*.

The duties of administrative staff officials often overlapped with those of court servicemen and frequently were overseen by members of the duma. The main exception were those associated with the *Razriad*, which maintained lists of military appointments. This unit was headed by the *d'iaki* themselves who, as servants of the grand prince, were his personal agents. Unlike the courtiers, they were initially not dependent upon the system they directed; acting in the name of the grand prince, they stood above it. Lacking any self-interest in the system, they could presumably make balanced and fair judgments affecting even highly placed members of the elite.

The functional units within the court treasury were the embryos of a bureaucratic structure that would mature later in the sixteenth and seventeenth centuries. During the reigns of Ivan III and Vasily III, however, they developed in concert with the needs of the territorially expanding realm of Muscovy. Their staffs provided the mechanisms for implementing the policies of the grand prince, coordinating the activities of his growing number of servitors, and settling disputes among them. In

---

[15] Knud Rasmussen, "The Muscovite Foreign Policy Administration during the Reign of Vasilij III, 1515–1525," *FOG*, vol. 38 (1986), p. 158. See also Robert M. Croskey, *Muscovite Diplomatic Practice in the Reign of Ivan III* (New York and London: Garland, 1987), pp. 86–94.

Moscow and in the provinces state secretaries and other staff officers directly represented the authority of the grand princes. They worked together with the grand prince's servicemen, both assisting them and ensuring that the servicemen, acting as semi-autonomous governors and judges, conformed to the principles and law the grand prince had established. With the servicemen they provided the mechanism for implementing grand princely authority throughout Muscovy.

POLITICAL INTEGRATION

As the court servicemen and staff officers carried out the directives and policies designed in Moscow, they introduced a measure of standardization that served to integrate the diverse principalities subject to the grand prince. Tax collection and the transformation of local labor services into common monetary taxes throughout the realm, discussed above, constitute one example. Monetary reform, which began with the imprint of Muscovite images on coins minted at Novgorod and culminated in 1535 in an attempt to establish a uniform system of coinage for all portions of Muscovy, was another.

Another policy that promoted integration was law enforcement and the conduct of judicial proceedings. In 1497, Ivan III issued a new law code or Sudebnik. Perhaps its provision of longest-lasting significance was the limitation on the right of peasants to leave at will the estate on which they lived and worked. The law code required that peasants confine their departures to a two-week period surrounding St. George's Day (November 26); it also made peasant movement contingent upon the payment of designated fees to their landlords. This article launched a series of restrictions on peasant mobility that eventually resulted in a reduction of their status to serfs, i.e., persons who were bound to the land on which they lived and worked. Other sections of the code focused on land disputes, inheritance laws, and slavery.

The main body of the law code, however, dealt with judicial organization and legal procedures. It identified the officers of the court, their responsibilities, the fees they could charge for their services, and the punishments they could impose; those punishments ranged from fines through confiscation of property and corporal punishment to execution. Provincial governors and *volost'* or district chiefs served as judges in their respective districts. Representatives of the local community were also obliged to witness trials. The judges were assisted by bailiffs who served warrants and arranged bonds to secure court appearances, by scribes who kept records of the court proceedings and composed documents containing the verdicts, by constables and other officers. Litigants were charged fees for each of the services and documents provided by these officials. Some governors and *volost'* chiefs, who held the highest court ranks, had full jurisdictional powers and could resolve virtually any type of case brought before them. Others, who lacked full authority, issued verdicts for petty criminal cases and civil suits. They referred cases involving slaves or serious crimes, along with a record of the preliminary proceedings, to Moscow, to the higher courts conducted by the grand prince, his children, or his boyars and *okol'nichie*.

Like the clause on serfdom, all the other provisions in the Sudebnik, including those that prohibited judges from soliciting or accepting bribes and similarly discouraged officers of the court from using their authority to benefit friends and favorites, applied uniformly to all the lands and people subject to the jurisdiction of the Muscovite grand prince. The law code in essence introduced a standardized judicial system intended for use throughout Muscovy; the only exceptions were the appanage principalities and exempted Church lands. At the center of the judicial system was Moscow, the seat of the highest court, and the grand prince, who was both the issuer of the law and the supreme judge. The Sudebnik of 1497 thus simultaneously limited abuse of authority by provincial officials by establishing guidelines for their conduct and announced the grand prince's legal authority throughout his domain.[16]

Ivan III also began the process of asserting centralized authority over the army. Before his reorganization, the armies available to the grand prince directly reflected the political character of the Russian lands. Each ruling prince, as well as some of the prominent boyars, maintained his own military retinue. This arrangement enabled individual princes to muster forces with relative speed and to defend their sectors of the Russian frontier as well as their internal borders. When a grand prince required a large force, however, he was dependent upon the cooperation of his fellow princes, who neither automatically nor consistently provided their troops. Individual princes, commanding their own retinues, could and did decline to participate in campaigns or unilaterally withdraw from them. The most extreme danger, inherent in such dispersed military authority, had materialized during the dynastic wars fought by Vasily II.

Vasily II addressed the problem by enlarging the military forces directly responsible to him. He welcomed, for example, the arrival of Tatar

[16] The Sudebnik of 1497 is available in an English translation, rendered by H. W. Dewey in *Muscovite Judicial Texts, 1488–1556* (Ann Arbor, Mich.: Michigan Slavic Materials, 1966); it has been republished by Basil Dmytryshyn in *Medieval Russia: A Source Book, 850–1700*, 3rd ed. (Fort Worth, Texas: Holt, Rinehart, and Winston, Inc., 1990), pp. 243–258.

princes, refugees from their own khanates, to his lands. He assigned lands and incomes to them and their followers, and supplemented his own army with theirs. One of the first Tatars to offer his services to Vasily II was Kasim, who had fled from his brother Mahmutek, the khan of Kazan'. He assisted Vasily during his dynastic wars, and was granted a tract of land on the Oka River that became known as the Khanate of Kasimov. The Kasimov khans as well as other Tatar princes who were given similar, but less permanent, land bases placed their retinues at the disposal of the Muscovite grand princes. Ivan III not only continued this practice, but similarly encouraged Lithuanian princes to transfer their allegiance, along with their border lands and the strength of the retainers, to Muscovy during the last decades of the fifteenth century.

This technique gave the grand prince control over a greater portion of the military forces that existed within the Russian lands. Using it, Ivan III was able to gather an impressive force for his campaign against Novgorod in 1471 and again in 1478. But it did not completely resolve the problem. In 1479, Ivan's brothers, Andrei the Elder and Boris, threatened to sever their relations with the grand prince. The prospect of a renewed dynastic war, in which the rebels might obtain Lithuanian support, while the Tatars of the Great Horde were massing across the frontier, convinced Ivan to make concessions to his brothers. They responded by adding their retinues to the defense line opposite the Tatars in 1480. But in 1491 Prince Andrei refused to join a campaign against the Great Horde; four months later he was arrested by Ivan III.

Territorial expansion, the subordination of autonomous princes, the dismantling of their courts, and the absorption of those princes and their boyars into Muscovite court service, gave Ivan III greater control over the military resources within the Russian lands. With those resources Ivan III began to fashion an army, subject to his exclusive authority and based on the same principle of service to the grand prince that permeated central and provincial administrative roles. Members of the service elite generally commanded the grand prince's regiments. Junior officers were drawn from the lower ranks of Moscow servicemen.

The army, however, depended upon the much larger number of provincial servicemen. Most of them were lower-ranking military servicemen who had remained in the provinces when their princes had departed for service in Moscow. Following the subordination of the autonomous princes and the dismantling of their courts, the grand prince gained direct access to those soldiers, but also acquired the responsibility for maintaining them. The conquest of Novgorod and the confiscation of its landowners' private estates in the 1480s provided the means to do so. Having deported the Novgorodian landowners and resettled them in other portions of his realm, he distributed their lands, which had become state property, to approximately 1,500 other servicemen, whom he transferred from Moscow and other northeastern lands.

Ivan III thus inaugurated the *pomest'e* system. The system, it will be recalled, involved the allotment of landed estates, initially the incomes from them, to *deti boiarskie* or provincial soldiers on the condition that they serve in the grand prince's armies. *Pomest'ia* were also granted to princes and courtiers from Moscow. As the pattern of confiscations, deportations, and distributions was repeated in other frontier principalities, central control over the outlying regions was secured while military personnel were positioned near the vulnerable borders of the realm. Military service and the army based on it became increasingly linked to the *pomest'e* system.

The *pomest'e* system, which Jaroslaw Pelenski likened to a form of conditional land tenure developed in the Khanate of Kazan',[17] also became the primary means of acquiring an income for thousands of provincial cavalrymen. A *pomest'e* was virtually the only means available to petty and middle-level servicemen to support themselves and also equip themselves with the arms and horses necessary to retain their roles as cavalrymen, and hence their status in society. Servicemen were consequently eager to accept *pomest'ia* and to respond to the call to join a campaign.

The *pomest'e* system also facilitated an integration of the military servicemen in Muscovite society. Although *pomeshchiki* served in military detachments drawn from distinct regions of Muscovy, the members of each detachment were not all natives of its regional base. Rather they were a combination of local servicemen, other Russians, and possibly servitors who had immigrated from Lithuania and the Tatar khanates, whose primary *pomest'ia* were registered in that province. The officers under whom they served were also appointed from the Muscovite court; they had neither personal ties to the region nor bonds to the warriors they commanded.

The *pomest'e* system did not immediately give the grand prince a full monopoly over military power. Appanage princes continued to maintain their own military retainers. Similarly, holders of large *pomest'ia*, including service princes and boyars, had access to their personal military forces and were, accordingly, expected not only to serve personally, but to maintain and bring to a campaign additional fully equipped cavalrymen in numbers roughly proportionate to the size of their estates. Nevertheless, the

---

[17] Jaroslaw Pelenski, "State and Society in Muscovite Russia and the Mongol–Turkic System in the Sixteenth Century," *FOG*, vol. 27 (1980), pp. 163–164.

pomest'e system enabled the grand prince to support the mass of cavalry-men, to make them dependent upon and loyal to him, and thus to assert his control over the military forces in Muscovy.

The process of converting the Muscovite army from an amalgam of autonomous units into a force subject to the single command of the grand prince took decades. It occurred without abruptly dismantling established retinues of powerful and valuable servitors or straining the financial resources of the state. During the reign of Ivan III appanage princes, Tatar and Lithuanian princes who had entered Muscovite service, and even powerful boyars continued to maintain and command their own retinues. Gradually, however, the grand prince subjected them to his direct authority. Russian princes, having been drawn into the Muscovite court, were given service assignments at great distance from their homelands; the Lithuanian princes who had pledged allegiance to Ivan III similarly lost the autonomy they initially enjoyed, and were absorbed, along with their retainers, into regular court and military service; finally, Vasily III was able to disperse appanage contingents among other units of his army. By Vasily's reign, the crown had accumulated the power and the mechanisms to support, muster, and command an army that was larger and more reliable than the previous collections of princely retinues and militias had been and that was capable of effectively functioning, as will be demonstrated in chapter 10, in both defensive and offensive operations.

Between the reigns of Vasily II and Vasily III the state of Muscovy was formed. Principalities annexed by Moscow were bound together by a dual-faceted administrative apparatus that combined the talents of a social elite, converted into a cadre of dependent servitors, and literate staff officials. Implementing a combination of fiscal, legal, and military policies, this administrative apparatus contributed to the process of integrating those lands into a unified state. Simultaneously, it consolidated grand princely authority, which would be transmitted from each grand prince to his eldest son, throughout the lands that had been absorbed by Moscow.

But the successes achieved by Grand Princes Vasily II, Ivan III, and Vasily III created new problems. The subordination of all members of the social elite, including princely families from annexed territories, to the status of servitors intensified rivalries among them. The competition that had been chronic within the Riurikid dynasty did not disappear. It was merely relocated from one sector of the political arena to another and reshaped from interprincely disputes over succession to competition among the members of the elite for influence over the crown and reflected power over their peers. Under these conditions one of the singular achievements of the Muscovite princes, the confirmation and refinement of vertical succession, became a potential liability for the dynasty and the political stability of their realm. Although he and his predecessors had collaborated in a practice that ensured that their duma was dominated by mature experienced servitors, Vasily III left the position of grand prince itself, the center of the political system and source of all power, not to a capable adult, but to his three-year-old son. The boy and the country were left in the care of the service elite.

10

FOREIGN POLICY
AND FOREIGN TRADE

_____ • _____

During the reign of Ivan III Muscovy conducted diplomatic relations with a wide range of polities. The grand prince exchanged diplomats with heads of state who were as diverse as the Muslim shahs in the Caucasus and the pope at the Vatican; whose realms were as geographically widespread as Denmark in northwestern Europe, Moldavia in south-eastern Europe, and Shirvan in the Caucasus; and whose power was as varied as that of the rulers of city-states of Italy and the Holy Roman and Ottoman emperors. Some of the diplomats representing Muscovy were Italians and Greeks, who were employed by the grand prince for their familiarity with other societies, political systems, and languages. Others were his own court servitors, usually below the duma ranks, and staff personnel. Their activities were overseen by the administrative staff that kept records of their instructions, messages received from abroad, and agreements concluded with foreign rulers.

Muscovy's most intense relations, however, were conducted with its immediate neighbors, Lithuania, Livonia, and Sweden, and also the Tatar khanates that replaced the Golden Horde. The centralized administrative apparatus and the *pomest'e*-based army, which evolved during the reigns of Ivan III and Vasily III, were the instruments the grand princes used to implement their foreign policies. Those policies, which included economic as well as political and military components, were generated by the decline of the Russian principalities' mighty neighbors and the creation of conditions that allowed Muscovite expansion to take place. Although Muscovy maintained bilateral relations with each of them, the policies guiding those relations were shaped by sets of overlapping alliances and rivalries and by the overriding goal to forge and stabilize a new balance of power that would pivot on its own increasingly influential position in the region.

MUSCOVY'S RELATIONS WITH ITS EUROPEAN NEIGHBORS

Relations with Lithuania

For two hundred years before the middle of the fifteenth century the northern Rus' principalities had been contained and dominated by their more powerful neighbors. Surrounded by the Golden Horde to the east and south, Lithuania to the southwest and west, and Livonia and Sweden to the west and northwest, they had little opportunity to expand and few options in defining their foreign policies.

By the middle of the fifteenth century, however, circumstances beyond their borders were radically changing. Most importantly, as discussed in chapter 7, the Golden Horde fragmented. In its place appeared a series of smaller, often competing Tatar khanates. On Muscovy's eastern border appeared the Khanate of Kazan', which was established on the mid-Volga river; to the south the Crimean Khanate coalesced in the steppe and on the Crimean peninsula. The remnants of the Golden Horde, identified as the Great Horde, retained control over the lower Volga and the neighboring steppe. By the early sixteenth century, the Khanate of Astrakhan' replaced the Great Horde in that region. There also the nomadic Nogai Horde occupied lands stretching from the Sea of Azov in the west across the Volga to the Sea of Aral in the east.

Changing regional circumstances coupled with Muscovy's internal development altered its relations with its European neighbors to the west. Among them Lithuania was the largest and most powerful. Although its influence over the northern Rus' principalities had reached its peak during the reign of Vitovt, Lithuania retained vital interests in Russian affairs after his death in 1430.

Lithuania's own borders extended eastward to encompass the lands that had made up the western and central portions of Kievan Rus'. In the north its frontier edged the lands of Pskov and Novgorod; in the northeast it hugged tributaries of the upper Volga and Oka Rivers and reached points that were only 120 miles from Moscow itself. Lithuania was thus master of the strategically and commercially important region that contained the watershed dividing the Volga, Dnieper, and West Dvina River basins. It contained the key passages that connected these river systems and thereby controlled transportation along the routes they defined. Possession of this region gave Lithuania dominance over the western route linking the northern Russian principalities and the south as well as over routes connecting Moscow with central Europe.

Lithuania also maintained direct ties with Novgorod and Tver'. In 1441 or 1442, Lithuania and Novgorod reached an agreement on their common border, on reciprocal rights for their merchants to travel and trade in one another's lands, and on sharing revenue collected in certain border towns, notably Velikie Luki. Lithuania consequently viewed with alarm the conclusion in 1456 of the Treaty of Iazhelbitsy, by which Muscovy asserted its authority over Novgorod and curtailed Novgorodian liberties.

Its concern extended more broadly to Muscovy's westward expansion, which Lithuania regarded as a threat to its own adjacent north-northeastern frontier and its control over the valuable territorial assets those lands contained. The region was subdivided among numerous princes, who ruled relatively small ancestral domains. Politically, they recognized the suzerainty of the Lithuanian grand prince, but they were Orthodox Christians and thus maintained an affiliation with northeastern Rus' and the metropolitan residing in Moscow. But in the late 1450s, after Moscow had rejected the agreement to unify the Orthodox and Catholic Churches reached by the Council of Florence, discussed in chapter 8, the Lithuanian grand prince Casimir supported the appointment of a Uniate metropolitan. Implicitly challenging the legitimacy of Metropolitan Iona in Moscow, he claimed ecclesiastical jurisdiction over Kiev and all Rus' and sought the allegiance of the Orthodox princes of the western Rus' lands.

Lithuania responded to Muscovite expansion in other ways as well. It offered refuge to Riurikid princes and their retainers who, having lost their independence, could not or preferred not to serve the Muscovite grand prince. Thus, at the conclusion of Vasily II's wars of succession, the son of Dmitry Shemiakha, Vasily II's cousin and bitter enemy, was welcomed in Lithuania, as was Prince Ivan of Mozhaisk. Lithuania also tried to stem Muscovite expansion by bolstering the Novgorodian opposition to Muscovite domination. But during the critical years of the 1470s, it provided little meaningful assistance to the pro-Lithuanian camp, and was unable to prevent Ivan III from annexing Novgorod in 1478.

Casimir was, nevertheless, outraged when Muscovy engulfed Novgorod. He not only refused to recognize that latest stage in Muscovy's progressive expansion, but pledged to assist Ahmad of the Great Horde in a joint campaign against Muscovy in 1480, which will be discussed below. Nevertheless, while Ahmad was waiting for Casimir's forces at the Ugra River, the Lithuanians were distracted by Ivan's ally Mengli-Girey, the khan of the Crimean Khanate, who attacked their lands in the south. At virtually the same time a group of Orthodox Lithuanian princes, led by Prince Fedor Ivanovich Bel'skii, revolted against Casimir. As a result, Casimir failed to honor his pledge to Ahmad, and rather than exploding into a decisive battle, the confrontation between the armies of the Great Horde and Muscovy at the Ugra fizzled into mutual retreat.

After 1480, Lithuania remained hostile toward Muscovy. Ivan III's concern over the potential threat posed by his neighbor prompted him to adopt a policy to neutralize Lithuania's allies inside Muscovy; according to Gustave Alef, it was this concern that was responsible for his decisions both to arrest and relocate Novgorodian boyars and to pressure Tver' into submitting to Muscovy.[1] But when Muscovy incorporated Novgorod, it also undertook the defense of the extended western Russian frontier as well as the conduct of relations with its neighbor. Disputes revolving around several issues quickly materialized and tensions between the two countries mounted over the next two decades.

One concerned the respective rights of the two states in districts along the border. According to the treaty concluded between Lithuania and Novgorod in 1441/42, Lithuania had the right to a share of the tax revenues collected from Velikie Luki and other specified towns on the Novgorodian side of the border. But Novgorod's new Muscovite governor, appointed by Ivan III, refused to allow King Casimir's agents across the border to collect the fees due Lithuania.

Another factor contributing to border disputes was the decision of Orthodox princes to transfer their service and allegiance from the Lithuanian to the Muscovite grand prince. Prince Fedor Ivanovich Bel'skii was foremost among them. A descendant of the fourteenth-century Lithuanian grand prince Olgerd, he fled to Moscow in 1481, after his role in the conspiracy against Casimir was discovered. By the late 1480s, Bel'skii was staging raids across the Lithuanian border in cooperation with Ivan III's brothers. Other princes, motivated by Lithuanian political pressures to join the Uniate Church or by a calculated gamble that Muscovy would ultimately incorporate their region, similarly pledged their allegiance to Muscovy. As they joined Ivan's corps of servicemen, they placed their lands, which they continued to hold, under Ivan's protection and participated in raids against their neighbors and relatives who remained loyal to Casimir. In this manner Ivan III was able by the late 1480s to project his border across the Ugra and up the Oka Rivers and, ignoring earlier treaties concluded between Lithuania and Novgorod, to claim the borderlands for Muscovy.

[1] Alef, "Origins of Muscovite Autocracy," p. 124.

Commercial disputes constituted a third source of strained relations. One of the routes that Russian merchants used to travel southward passed through the Lithuanian towns of Briansk, Novgorod-Seversk, and Putivl'. Other routes leading westward toward central Europe went through Toropets or Viaz'ma and Smolensk. But according to diplomatic records from the late 1480s, some merchants had been seized while traveling to Caffa on the Crimean coast and, despite formal requests for their release from Ivan III's envoys, were detained in Lithuania. Others complained that Lithuanian officials were demanding new and higher fees and duties from them and illegally confiscating their goods.

A fourth factor involved the Tatar khanates. Between 1486 and 1491, a conflict between the Crimean Khanate and the Great Horde flared. As will be discussed below, Ivan III and Mengli-Girey of the Crimean Khanate formed an alliance directed against both the Great Horde and Lithuania. By agreeing to join Ivan III, Mengli-Girey had abandoned the traditional patron of his khanate. In response, Lithuania had fashioned a counter-alliance with the Great Horde. Each of the Tatar khans urged his partner to assist him, if only by distracting the other's ally and diverting his military forces from the steppe.

As tensions derived from all these factors mounted, Casimir died (1492). The Lithuanian portion of his realm passed to his son Aleksandr. Aleksandr continued and intensified his father's conflict with Ivan III. He sent an army across the border to seize Mozhaisk. The army was commanded by Prince Semen Ivanovich of Starodub, whose father Prince Ivan of Mozhaisk had fled to Lithuania to escape from Vasily II in 1454. Ivan III, however, counterattacked; his armies seized Viaz'ma as well as other towns on the Lithuanian side of the border. But while he pursued hostilities against Muscovy, Aleksandr also opened negotiations for peace and proposed marriage to Ivan's daughter Elena. In 1494, the border war ended with a treaty and a betrothal.

According to the former, Aleksandr renounced Lithuania's claims to Novgorod, Pskov, and Tver'. He ceded to Muscovy Viaz'ma and the districts along the upper Oka that his armies had captured during the war. Moscow correspondingly recognized Smolensk as a possession of Lithuania. The two then formed an alliance, and the next year celebrated the marriage of Aleksandr and Elena. The union was an acknowledgment of Muscovy's growing regional power. A century earlier the marriage of Vitovt's daughter to Vasily I had reflected the Lithuanian grand prince's seniority; this match, by which Aleksandr became Ivan's son-in-law, symbolized a reversal of that relationship. Within the family Ivan assumed the senior role even as his state challenged and displaced Lithuanian dominance on its western frontier.

Despite the peace settlement and alliance, by 1500 Muscovy, backed by the Crimean Khanate, and Lithuania, joined by the Great Horde, were once again locked in combat. Ivan's stated reason for renewing hostilities against Lithuania was Aleksandr's failure to honor the terms of their 1494 agreement, particularly his pledge to allow Elena to keep her Orthodox faith. According to reports brought to Ivan III, his daughter was being pressured to accept Catholicism.

Muscovy's military objectives, however, were territorial. On the eve of the war more Lithuanian princes and towns declared their preference for Muscovy. The princes included two Semen Ivanoviches, one the prince of Starodub who had so recently led Aleksandr's campaign and the other a brother of Prince Fedor Ivanovich Bel'skii who had hurriedly left Lithuania in 1481. Prince Vasily Ivanovich Shemiachich was another prominent figure in this group. He was the grandson of Dmitry Shemiakha, who had fought against Vasily II in the dynastic wars of the middle of the fifteenth century. At the conclusion of those wars his father, like Ivan of Mozhaisk, had fled to Lithuania, where he had received control over Novgorod-Seversk as well as other lands in the vicinity of Chernigov.

The transfer of these princes, particularly those who were descendants of refugees from Muscovy, may be considered as another reflection of the reversal in the relative roles of Lithuania and Muscovy. Fifty years earlier their ancestors had sought asylum in Lithuania to avoid becoming victims of Muscovite expansion and centralization. In 1500, the new generation linked their futures with the dynamic and increasingly powerful state of Muscovy. Their association with Ivan III also gave Muscovy lands well beyond its former border. During the war that began in 1500, Ivan III's forces, aided by his new service princes, occupied and consolidated Muscovy's control over their lands. While Muscovy was engaged against Lithuania, its ally the Crimean Khanate directed its forces against the Great Horde, which it destroyed in 1502.

In 1503, the combatants declared a truce. Its terms allowed Muscovy to retain the lands it had taken. They included towns near the border, e.g., Toropets, which was an intermediate point on the road linking Moscow to central Europe. They also included Starodub, Briansk, Novgorod-Seversk, and Chernigov, which were located deep within Lithuanian territory. Its acquisitions gave Muscovy control not only over the full length of the Ugra River, which had defined its former border, but also the Desna River, one of the main tributaries of the Dnieper.

The truce remained in effect until 1512, with only a brief interruption in 1507–08, when Prince Mikhail L'vovich Glinskii was staging his abortive revolt, noted in chapter 9, against Sigismund. When hostilities resumed, the focus of the war was the new Muscovite–Lithuanian frontier, its main target, Smolensk. In 1514, Vasily III captured the city. Although the war dragged on until 1522, neither side made any additional major gains.

Muscovy's expansion into Lithuanian territory improved its commercial position. The territories and towns it acquired as a result of the conflicts of 1492–94 and 1500–03 were precisely those that defined the western route between the Russian principalities and the Black Sea. Ivan III took possession of a major portion of that trade route. He then provided the security along it for his merchants, and collected the duties and fees that previously had gone to the Lithuanian treasury. Ivan III's victories had similar effects on Moscow's place in commerce with Europe. One of the major trade routes connecting Moscow and central Europe passed through Toropets and Velikie Luki on the way to Polotsk on the West Dvina and Vil'nius. Another went wesward through Viaz'ma and Smolensk. As a result of their wars with Lithuania, Ivan III and Vasily III incorporated the towns of Toropets, Viaz'ma, and Smolensk, and the roadways they defined.

Muscovy's victories over Lithuania also lent physical substantiation to the theories, discussed in chapter 8, legitimizing the Muscovite princes as the heirs of the grand princes of Kiev. As Muscovy absorbed lands that centuries earlier had been components of Kievan Rus' and approached the former political and ecclesiastical capital itself, it became increasingly difficult to refute the notion that Moscow was Kiev's successor, and that the Muscovite grand prince was the rightful secular ruler of the Orthodox community dwelling in all the lands of Rus'.

Relations with the Baltic countries

In addition to Lithuania Muscovy energetically interacted with two other neighbors on its western frontier, Sweden and Livonia. Muscovy acquired a common border with Sweden when Ivan III annexed Novgorod. In contrast, Livonia was separated from Muscovite territory by the yet independent principality of Pskov. Nevertheless, Muscovy became actively engaged (frequently on behalf of Pskov) with Livonia, whose towns and territories were divided among the Livonian Order, the Hansa, and hierarchs of the Church. Muscovy's foreign policy toward both Baltic lands intertwined commercial, territorial, and defensive objectives, and involved trade, diplomatic negotiations, and war.

Before its subordination to Moscow Novgorod had directly conducted affairs with the various secular and ecclesiastical authorities in Livonia.

After concluding peace in 1448, their relations had remained relatively calm. The most serious exceptions arose from friction between Pskov and the bishopric of Dorpat (Iur'ev). Truces and treaties, concluded in 1460, 1463, and 1474, however, subdued intermittent outbursts of hostilities, defined borders, and regulated the rights and privileges of itinerant merchants as well as fishermen who worked the lakes spanning the border.

After Ivan III absorbed Novgorod, responsibility for security along the northwestern Russian frontier and the conduct of relations with the polities across the border, although regularly referred to the governor of Novgorod, passed to the grand prince. But like Lithuania, the Livonian Order and Sweden were disturbed by the appearance of Muscovy in Novgorod's place in the eastern Baltic and by the destabilization of the regional order Muscovy's expansion represented.

Hostilities soon broke out. In early 1480, the knights of the Livonian Order crossed the border and attacked Pskov. The following year Muscovite forces sent by Ivan III carried the war into Livonian territory and used artillery to attack three fortified towns; their actions convinced the Order to send ambassadors to Novgorod for peace negotiations. The result was a group of treaties outlining terms of peace between Pskov and the Livonian Order, Pskov and Dorpat, and Novgorod and the Order. After lengthy negotiations, new treaties were concluded in 1493.

In 1492, even as his governor in Novgorod was negotiating with the Livonian Order over a renewal of the 1481 treaties, Ivan III constructed a fortress, called Ivangorod, just opposite the Order's town and commercial center of Narva at the mouth of the Narova River on the southern coast of the Gulf of Finland. Then, having secured in the 1493 treaties rights for his merchants to trade at Narva, Ivan III closed the Hanseatic commercial complex or *dvor* in Novgorod (1494) and initiated what became a twenty-year hiatus in Hansa trade at Novgorod.

Both the Hansa and the Livonian Order were gravely disturbed by Muscovy's action, which they interpreted as a prelude to aggression. But it was with Sweden, not with the Livonian authorities, that Muscovy engaged in actual warfare. Russo–Swedish concerns had revolved around their common border, which ran through Finland, and the northeastern coast of the Gulf of Finland, which had commercial and strategic value. In 1495, having concluded an alliance with Denmark, which was already involved in its own dispute with Sweden, Ivan III launched a campaign into Finnish territory controlled by Sweden. His forces attacked, but did not capture, Vyborg, the Swedish outpost guarding the northern shore of the Gulf of Finland. The following year the Swedes seized and destroyed Ivangorod on the opposite shore. By the end of the year, however,

Muscovite forces reoccupied the site and rebuilt the fort. The two belligerents concluded a six-year truce several months later.

Open warfare between Muscovy and Livonia did not break out until the beginning of the sixteenth century. But when the Muscovite–Lithuanian confrontation erupted, Livonia allied itself with Lithuania and joined the war. Although Aleksandr became distracted by the death of his brother, the Polish king, and his own election to the Polish throne, Livonian forces crossed their borders in 1501, and in separate campaigns ravaged districts around Ivangorod and Pskov. Muscovy retaliated and victoriously marched past Dorpat and northward to Narva. In 1503, while Ivan III was conducting negotiations with Lithuanian envoys in Moscow, his officials in Novgorod concluded a six-year truce with the Livonian Order.

At the conclusion of its wars with both Sweden and Livonia, Muscovy's northwestern borders were confirmed. These conflicts had greater impact on commercial patterns than they did on territorial boundaries. Before its annexation by Moscow, Novgorod had regularly hosted Hanseatic merchants as well as commercial agents representing the Livonian Order. Its own merchants, as those from Pskov, reciprocally traveled to Narva, Dorpat, Riga, and Revel' in Livonia. German merchants typically purchased fur and wax from the Russians, who received silver, metal products, woolen cloth, and salt in exchange. The sale of alcoholic beverages, which had been among the traditional items purchased by the Russians, was forbidden by the treaty of 1474. The main avenues for Russian trade with northern Europe had extended from the towns of Livonia to Novgorod. Vyborg, on the Swedish side of the Gulf of Finland, provided an alternate gate to Novgorod for non-Hansa merchants of the Baltic Sea region.

The subordination of Novgorod by Muscovy disrupted those trade patterns. As discussed, Ivan III initiated a series of land confiscations shortly after the annexation. Within fifteen years virtually all the major Novgorodian landowners had been dispossessed. In the process Ivan III also dismantled the mechanism by which large quantities of products had been supplied to the Novgorodian market. Novgorodian boyars had collected rents from peasants on their estates in those commercially valuable goods. Northern estates had supplied squirrel pelts to the boyars, just as Novgorod's northern possessions paid taxes in fur to the city treasury. When Ivan III placed those estates and provinces under his own jurisdiction, he demanded payment of rent and taxes in cash and in grain. When he subsequently redistributed some of the Novgorodian estates to *pomeshchiki*, they collected rents in cash, grain, and other items useful for their personal sustenance. Only the peasants themselves, seeking to convert their goods to the cash required for rents and taxes, continued to sell small quantities of commercial products, which found their way to the market at Novgorod.

In addition, when Ivan III confiscated the Novgorodian boyars' estates and relocated their owners, he similarly removed Novgorod's merchants. Initially, he arrested a few individuals who had supported the opposition to him. But within ten years he had conducted a massive expulsion of merchants from Novgorod. In 1487, fifty merchants were sent to Vladimir. The following year Ivan III forcibly resettled "many" Novgorodian traders in towns throughout northeastern Muscovy. They were replaced by merchants from Moscow and the other northeastern commercial centers. These were the merchants who traded with the Germans visiting the Muscovite town of Novgorod. They were also the merchants who, under the terms of the treaties concluded in 1481 and 1493, traveled to the towns of Livonia and other Hanseatic markets.

The agreements reached with officials of the Livonian Order notwithstanding, the Hansa and the grand prince's officials in Novgorod engaged in a series of commercial disputes. Although the Hansa had refused to join the war against Pskov in 1480, it had issued trade regulations favorable to Livonia. Muscovite officials in Novgorod, on the other hand, imposed new fees and regulations on commercial trans-actions. The ban on importing alcoholic beverages to Novgorod remained in effect. In addition, the import of salt was forbidden.

Their disagreements reached a climax in 1494, when two Russian merchants were sentenced to death by a local court in Revel'. It was in retaliation for this offense that Ivan III closed Peterhof, the Hanseatic complex in Novgorod, arrested the forty-nine merchants who were in residence there, and confiscated their property. Scholars have offered diverse explanations for Ivan's action. Some interpret it as part of a Muscovite scheme to destroy Novgorodian commerce; others consider it pressure on the Hansa to agree to terms that would be more favorable to Russian merchants. Some, regarding it as a component in larger inter-national maneuvers, link it with Ivan's alliance with Denmark against Sweden, which was frequently aided by the Hansa. Others view the incident as a rather ordinary interruption of trade between Novgorod and the Hansa.

During the twenty years that Peterhof was closed merchants from Novgorod continued to trade with the Germans; but they did so by traveling to towns in Livonia. They also exchanged their wares near the mouth of the Neva River, at Vyborg and Narva, and in the Russian towns of Pskov and Ivangorod. By the time Vasily III allowed the Hanseatic *dvor* to reopen in 1514, merchants had rearranged their commercial patterns.

Hansa merchants had lost their virtual monopoly on the role of inter-mediary in trade between Novgorod and northern Europe. Within just a few years of the reconstruction of Ivangorod, following its destruction by the Swedes in 1496, Russian merchants were trading with their Swedish counterparts there. The Dutch and Danes also traded directly with Russians at both Ivangorod and Narva. On the basis of a treaty concluded with Denmark in 1516, Danes joined the Hanseatic merchants in Novgorod; they were followed by the Swedes ten years later. Russian merchants sailed to Copenhagen with their commercial wares in 1517, but, reportedly disappointed with the goods offered in exchange, did not repeat the venture.

Increased use of land routes through Finland and Lithuania also redistributed the trade formerly confined to the Hansa and Novgorod. Russian and European merchants alike traveled eastward through Pskov, annexed by Muscovy in 1510, and Smolensk, conquered in 1514, to Moscow and westward to market centers in Lithuania, Poland, and Germany. Herberstein reported that although Swedes, Livonians, and Germans were regularly directed toward Novgorod to conduct their commercial transactions, Lithuanians and Poles went to Moscow, as did merchants who officially represented the Ottoman and other foreign courts. During the reign of Ivan III, Moscow had firmly established itself in Turco-Tatar commerce. By the reign of Vasily III it also became more directly involved in trade with eastern and central Europe. Moscow was becoming a commercial hub, where trade routes, merchants, and goods associated with the eastern trade with Kazan' and the southern trade with the Black Sea ports met, mingled, and mixed with participants in the western trade with Lithuania and Poland. Joining the two commercial sectors, Moscow was becoming the central marketplace within the Muscovite state as well as in a commercial network spanning an area from central Europe to western Siberia, from the White Sea to the Black.

MUSCOVITE RELATIONS WITH THE TATAR KHANATES

Political relations

Muscovy's expansion to the west was conducted against the background of the disintegration of the Golden Horde and the formation of new, smaller, yet formidable Tatar Khanates. The effects of the dispersal of Tatar might were profound. On the one hand, it enabled the princes of Moscow to pursue their policies of aggrandizing power and territory within the Russian lands without interference from their former suzerain. On the other hand, the disintegration of the Golden Horde produced instability on the steppe and in the new khanates. It thus created both opportunities and dangers for the Russian principalities.

Political disputes within the new khanates resulted in the expulsion of Tatar princes who lost their bids for power. Bands of Tatar warriors, led by displaced princes, roamed the steppe. Although two notable examples, Kasim and Iakub who fled from their brother Khan Mahmutek of Kazan' in 1447, eventually placed themselves at Vasily II's disposal and helped him win his dynastic war, they and others who were later similarly expelled from the Crimean Khanate posed potential hazards on the steppe and threats to the frontiers of established polities on its edge.

In addition to these renegade bands, the Great Horde itself challenged its neighbors. Although it had been left in control of the lands along the lower Volga, the Great Horde lacked the sources of revenue that the Golden Horde had enjoyed. The lower Volga had been one of the Golden Horde's chief assets and commercial traffic along it, one of its main sources of revenue. Despite Timur's destructive attacks on Sarai and Astrakhan' at the end of the fourteenth century and a decline in travel along the east–west routes passing through them, commercial and diplomatic traffic had continued along the lower Volga waterway for several decades. But by the second half of the century conditions had deteriorated there as well, and those who used the route exposed themselves to hardship and personal danger.

The experience of the merchant Afanasii Nikitin is illustrative. Nikitin was unusual for at least two reasons. He left an account of his travels.[2] And his travels took him beyond the markets typically frequented by Rus' merchants, all the way to India. But the beginning of his journey in 1466 or 1468 was relatively normal. He descended the Volga River from his native Tver' to Nizhnii Novgorod, where he planned to meet a Muscovite ambassador and accompany his party down the Volga. When he missed that convoy, Nikitin and nine other Russian merchants as well as some Muslim merchants joined the ambassador from the Caucasian principality of Shirvan, who was returning from his mission to Moscow. Together they sailed down the Volga. Near Astrakhan', however, their group was attacked and plundered. Rather than return home without anything to show for his pains, Nikitin continued his journey to Derbent and Baku. From there he went on, from one market to the next, until he found himself in India.

---

[2] English translations of his account are available in Zenkovsky's anthology *Medieval Russia's Epics, Chronicles, and Tales*, pp. 333–353, and in *India in the Fifteenth Century*, trans. by Count Wielhorsky, Works Issued by the Hakluyt Society, vol. 22 (reprint ed., New York: Burt Franklin, n.d.), pp. 3–32.

Almost a decade later, in 1475–76, Ambrogio Contarini, a Venetian diplomat returning from Persia, encountered comparable difficulties. His property was confiscated at Astrakhan'. In order to retrieve it he had to pay an exorbitant ransom, which he borrowed from the Muscovite ambassador and some Tatar merchants with whom he was traveling. He then accompanied his creditors northward up the Volga River and to Muscovy. He described "the country between [Astrakhan'] and Muscovy . . . [as] a continual desert." The journey was difficult; there were no way stations, no means of obtaining provisions, and even fresh water was not readily available. He did, however, observe some camels and horses; evidently abandoned or lost by a previous and presumably ill-fated caravan, they too were testimony to the dangers of this route.[3]

The deterioration of the lower Volga deprived the Great Horde of transit fees and customs duties. Without access to these revenues, Ahmad Khan resorted to preying upon the caravans laden with goods that crossed the steppe and to exacting booty, ransom, and bribes from the government officials and merchants traveling in them. In addition, the Great Horde raided its sedentary neighbors, including Muscovy. From the late 1440s, i.e., after Ulu-Muhammed left the area and moved his Horde eastward toward the mid-Volga area, the Great Horde repeatedly harassed the Russian frontier along the Oka River. In 1460 the Great Horde staged an attack on Riazan'. In 1465, another major attack was prevented only by the Crimean Tatars, who attacked the Great Horde while it was assembling its forces on the Don River. In 1472, however, Ahmad Khan, urged on by Lithuania, was more successful. His army managed to reach and burn the town of Aleksin, located south of Serpukhov, and to cross the Oka River before its advance was halted by the Russians.

From the middle of the fifteenth century another factor also indirectly affected security for frontier Russian communities. That factor was the conquest of Constantinople by the Ottoman Turks in 1453. Over the next several decades the Turks conquered most of the Black Sea coast. As they did so, they fostered an exchange of goods between the regions north and south of the sea. Istanbul (Constantinople), whose population grew from fewer than 50,000 in the middle of the fifteenth century to 300,000 a century later, benefited from this trade. It was dependent especially upon the provision of grain, meat, and salt from the lands north of the Black Sea. To satisfy the appetites of the Istanbul populace, the Crimean Tatars placed more of their lands under cultivation. But to operate them they required agricultural laborers. They correspondingly

[3] Contarini, "The Travels of the Magnificent M. Ambrosio Contarini," in *Travels to Tana and Persia*, pp. 151–154, 157.

intensified their raids on the borders of their sedentary neighbors to take the necessary captives, who would be employed as slaves in these enterprises. Muscovy, Poland, Lithuania, and Circassia on the northeast coast of the Black Sea were all targets of the Tatar raids.

Thus despite the fragmentation of the Golden Horde, the Tatars remained a potent, if dispersed force in the middle of the fifteenth century. When Vasily II and his uncle Iurii entered into their dispute over succession to the grand princely throne, they had both regarded the khan of the Golden Horde, Ulu-Muhammed, as the appropriate authority to arbitrate and issue the patent for the position of senior prince among the Russians. At that stage, in 1431, Vasily II had been established as grand prince of Vladimir by Ulu-Muhammed.

Even after Ulu-Muhammed had been obliged to leave the steppe, and was leading his Horde in the migration that ended with the foundation of the Khanate of Kazan', his authority was formidable. After Vasily II was captured by his forces in 1445, he was restored to his throne once again by the grace of Ulu-Muhammed, who, as discussed in the preceding chapter, released him in exchange for the pledge of a substantial ransom payment. Two years later Ulu-Muhammed's sons Kasim and Iakub were also instrumental in securing Vasily's throne. These episodes reveal that Tatar authority and military strength continued to have decisive effects on Russian affairs during the middle of the fifteenth century. They also indicate that despite the breakdown of the Golden Horde, Russian princes continued to recognize the seniority of Tatar khans; they both expected and depended upon Tatar involvement in their affairs.

The mid-century, however, marked a turning point in relations between Muscovy and the Tatars. In chapter 8 it was noted that Vasily II enhanced his military strength by enlisting Kasim and his followers into his armed forces. He granted Kasim some territory on the Oka River c. 1452, and assigned him revenues collected from neighboring Riazan'; in the early sixteenth century the grand prince and his brothers contributed to the Kasimov khan's income as well. The territory came to be known as the Khanate of Kasimov. This action was also one of the first indicators of the shift in relative power between Muscovy and its Tatar neighbors; rather than being suzerains of Vasily II, Kasim and all subsequent khans of Kasimov were servitors of the Muscovite grand prince.

Muscovy also took advantage of the fluid political conditions among the Tatars to revive the practice begun almost a century before by Dmitry Donskoi and his son Vasily I when they subjugated the tribes of Vychegda Perm' and to extend its own authority over additional tribes dwelling to its northeast. That practice required a more aggressive posture toward the

Khanate of Kazan'. When the Khanate of Kazan' formed on the mid-Volga, it claimed tribute from tribes on the Kama River and beyond. It also controlled access to the best routes across the Ural Mountains to western Siberia. Between 1458 and 1462, Muscovy initiated several military campaigns into the regions of the Viatka and upper Kama Rivers. Kazan' retaliated by raiding outposts in the vicinity of Ustiug, but was defeated. In 1463, Bishop Iona of Perm' began missionary work among the tribes that dwelled along the upper Kama River in the region identified as Perm' Velikaia, and by 1465 Russian forces were raiding the Iugra tribes of northwestern Siberia and demanding that they too pay tribute to the Muscovite grand prince. Muscovy's policy toward Kazan' was not aimed at defending itself against an intractibly hostile neighbor or, as George Vernadsky described the Khanate of Kazan', a "perennial danger," but at subduing tributaries and gaining access to trade routes controlled by Kazan'.[4]

As the Muscovite–Kazan' contest for dominance over the northeast took shape, Mahmutek, the khan of Kazan', died (1467). He was succeeded by his son Ibrahim. But at least some clan elders in Kazan' preferred Kasim, then khan of Kasimov, over his nephew. Signaling this preference, Mahmutek's widow traveled to Muscovy, where in accordance with Muslim tradition she wed Kasim, her late husband's brother. Ivan III lent military support to Kasim's candidacy, but his efforts to remove Ibrahim and establish Kasim in his place failed. Ivan III and Ibrahim, nevertheless, concluded a peace treaty, which provided a framework for relatively peaceful relations between their two states for the next twenty years. Kasim, having lost his bid for the throne of Kazan', died soon afterward.

Although Vasily II and Ivan III, sensitive to the opportunities afforded by the changing external conditions, undertook these initiatives, they were preoccupied, at least through the third quarter of the century, with achieving and consolidating power within Muscovy and over the remainder of the northern Russian principalities. As those goals were

---

[4] George Vernadsky, *Russia at the Dawn of the Modern Age* (New Haven, Conn., and London: Yale University Press, 1959), p. 18. Similar views have been expressed by other scholars, e.g., Bazilevich, *Vneshniaia politika*, pp. 36, 60, 62, and J. L. I. Fennell, *Ivan the Great of Moscow* (London: Macmillan and New York: St. Martin's Press, 1961), pp. 13, 19. A. A. Zimin, in a variation of the theme on Kazan's hostility, explained Muscovy's policies toward Kazan', especially after 1487, as an effort to prevent the formation of a direct, anti-Muscovite alliance between the Crimean and Kazan' Khanates: *Rossiia na rubezhe XV–XVI stoletii* [Russia at the turn of the XV–XVI centuries] (Moscow: Mysl', 1982), p. 70, and *Rossiia na poroge novogo vremeni* [Russia on the threshold of a new era] (Moscow: Mysl', 1972), p. 68.

achieved, however, and as Muscovy's diplomatic apparatus and military power developed, Ivan III gradually defined and pursued more ambitious foreign policy objectives.

The centerpiece of Ivan III's foreign policy was an alliance with Mengli-Girey, khan of the Crimean Khanate. The Crimean Khanate, which had formed in the 1420s and 1430s, was led in the middle of the century by Hadji-Girey, a descendant of Tokhtamysh, and was protected by Lithuania. Hadji-Girey, recognizing the advantages of keeping the steppe secure for grazing as well as for commercial traffic, was hostile toward the Great Horde, which he perceived to be a disruptive force in the region. It was in this context that he attacked Ahmad's forces on the Don River in 1465.

In 1466, Hadji-Girey died. His sons, Nur-daulet, Aidar (Khaidar), and Mengli-Girey, became entangled in a succession struggle. After the Ottoman Turks captured the Crimean port of Caffa in 1475 however, they helped Mengli-Girey acquire the position of khan in return for his recognition of their suzerainty. By 1478, Mengli-Girey had chased his brothers from his khanate.

During this turbulent period in the Crimean Khanate's domestic politics, Mengli-Girey sought assistance from Ivan III. By 1475, he was requesting that Ivan send Kasim's son, Dan'iar who was then the khan of Kasimov, and another Tatar in Ivan's service to assist in the defense of the Crimean Khanate should it be attacked by Ahmad. Ivan responded that such aid would be forthcoming only if the khan would provide reciprocal help to Muscovy in a confrontation with Lithuania. Before any agreement could be reached, Mengli-Girey was temporarily displaced by Nur-daulet and his ally, Ahmad.

After Mengli-Girey recovered his throne, he resumed his requests for Muscovite aid. In 1480, he sought not only the pledge of Dan'iar's forces, but also cooperation in removing Nur-daulet from Kiev, where the Lithuanian king had granted him refuge and where he remained, poised on his brother's frontier and prepared to continue his challenge. In response to Mengli-Girey's urging, Ivan III thus brought another renegade Tatar prince to Muscovy and into his service. When later that year Ivan sent word that both Nur-daulet and Aidar had arrived in Muscovy, Mengli-Girey agreed to the alliance.

The alliance brought multiple benefits to Muscovy. It redirected Crimean Tatar slave raids from the Russian to the Polish–Lithuanian frontiers. It also gave Muscovy an ally against the Great Horde. Those factors, coupled with the removal of renegade Tatar bands from the steppe and their recruitment into the grand prince's own military service, improved security along Muscovy's southern border.

In response to the Muscovite–Crimean agreement, the Great Horde and Lithuania formed their own alliance. A confrontation between the opposing axes developed almost immediately. In October 1480, Ahmad Khan led his warriors to the Ugra River, a tributary of the Oka. Ivan III sent an army to the opposite bank. The two forces faced each other across the river. Ahmad awaited both his Lithuanian allies and the onset of cold weather, which would freeze the river and enable his forces to cross into Muscovite territory. But the Lithuanians never arrived. They were diverted by Mengli-Girey whose Tatars staged raids on the Polish–Lithuanian border, and by a conspiracy against King Casimir.

Furthermore, according to some accounts, Nur-daulet took advantage of the delay to sail down the Volga with a Russian war party and attacked Ahmad's unprotected base camp. Whether in response to that action or for other reasons, Ahmad soon afterwards abandoned his position. The Russian forces similarly withdrew. No battle took place. The next year Ahmad was killed in an encounter with the Nogai Horde. Despite the military insignificance of the "stand on the Ugra," over the next century Russian bookmen embellished the story of the confrontation; as a consequence the non-battle has commonly, although erroneously, been identified as the event that ended Tatar domination over the Russian lands.

The so-called Battle of the Ugra neither broke the Tatar yoke nor destroyed the close relations Muscovy maintained with its Tatar neighbors. By the time the Russians and the Tatars of the Great Horde faced each other across the Ugra in 1480, the Golden Horde had been decaying for almost a century. Its power over the northern Russian principalities had eroded just as the Horde itself had fragmented. Muscovy and the several Tatar khanates that had formed by 1480 were all heirs of the Golden Horde. The "stand on the Ugra" neither ended Mongol domination over the Russian lands, which had already dissipated, nor did it define the relationships among the polities that replaced the Golden Horde. The confrontation was, rather, one manifestation of the rivalries that had been developing among them as the Golden Horde declined and as they competed to fill the political vacuum it left.

The "stand on the Ugra" was followed by an expansion of the Muscovite–Crimean alliance to include the Kazan' Khanate. Both Ivan III and Mengli-Girey recognized the value of adding Kazan's forces to their own in the effort to suppress the Great Horde and ensure stability on the steppe. But Khan Ibrahim as well as some of the influential clan leaders in Kazan' had close ties with the Great Horde. Ibrahim, however, died c. 1486. Mengli-Girey married his widow. The marriage constituted a major diplomatic victory for the allies. In conjunction with it

Mengli-Girey's new father-in-law also transferred his clan's allegiance from Ahmad to the Crimean khan.

Mengli-Girey then formulated a plan to place his new wife's son, Muhammed Amin, on the Kazan' throne and enlisted the aid of Ivan III to implement it. As he had done twenty years earlier, the Muscovite grand prince in 1486–87 sent armed forces to intervene in a succession struggle in Kazan'. This time his efforts succeeded. The allies, using the military strength of Muscovy, placed Muhammed Amin, the Crimean khan's stepson, on the throne of Kazan'.

Muscovy remained involved in Kazan' affairs. In the late 1490s, it intervened militarily when some factions within Kazan' objected to Muhammed Amin's rule and overthrew him; as a result, Muhammed Amin's brother Abdyl Letif temporarily assumed the Kazan' throne. Vasily III also sent troops to Kazan' in 1506, in response to the detention of a Muscovite ambassador and some merchants there. Normal relations were restored the next year. Muscovy also facilitated communication and cooperation between the two khanates. Diplomatic messages regarding issues ranging from information about mutual enemies to personal notes sent by Mengli-Girey's wife to her sons were conveyed through Moscow.

In none of these activities were the Muscovite princes countering aggression against Russian territory initiated by the Kazan' territories. Nor were they attempting to assert direct Muscovite rule over Kazan'. On the contrary, Ivan III used his military might to uphold the dynastic interests of the Crimean khan in Kazan'. Through their actions he and Vasily III guaranteed that one or the other of their ally's stepsons, Muhammed Amin or Abdyl Letif, was khan of Kazan' until both died in 1517–18. During their reigns Kazan' was a third partner in the alliance, and Muscovy was set firmly in the center of the relations between the two khanates.

Commercial relations

At the height of its power the Golden Horde had drawn its economic strength from commercial traffic along the segments of intercontinental trade routes it controlled. Even when east–west trade along the Great Silk Road deteriorated, the Horde had continued to dominate the exchange of goods between the northern Russian principalities and southern markets, which were linked with both the Mediterranean and the Islamic worlds. As long as the Golden Horde retained its ability to do so, it confined north–south commercial traffic to the Volga River route and concentrated all transactions at Sarai. From the Golden Horde capital goods then flowed eastward to Central Asia, southward to the Caucasus, or westward to Tana and Caffa where they entered the regional Black Sea trade. In these transactions the northern goods exported from the Russian lands were prominently featured.

When the Golden Horde's authority declined, it could no longer channel commerce to its own market center. As it fragmented, control over vital components of its commercial network were redistributed among the polities that replaced it. The Great Horde dominated the lower Volga route. But under its relatively weak authority that route became dangerous and fell into relative disuse. Several alternate routes opened for north–south traffic. One of them passed through Kaluga, Briansk, Novgorod-Seversk, and Putivl', all located within Lithuania, before crossing the steppe; another followed the Don River to Tana; a third cut more directly southward from Muscovy to the Crimean peninsula and the port of Caffa. All of the routes passed through lands controlled by the Crimean khan. It was thus the Crimean Khanate that gained control over access to the Italian commercial colonies of Tana and Caffa, and safe passage to them required the Crimean khan's permission, cooperation, and protection. The Crimean Khanate attempted to secure the steppe routes and the roads to the ports of Caffa and Tana that were attracting the merchants who formerly frequented Sarai.

The Khanate of Kazan' acquired control of another element of the trade network, supplies. Positioned at the juncture of the Volga and Kama Rivers, it commanded the tribute, including luxury furs, from surrounding tribes and dominated the passes across the Ural Mountains leading to western Siberia. Siberian products were among the most valuable goods in demand at the southern markets. Kazan' itself also became a major commercial center, where goods from Siberia as well as from the Caspian region were exchanged for Russian items as well as for European goods channeled through Muscovy.

Like the Tatar heirs to the Golden Horde, Muscovy too sought to capture a role for itself in this commercial network. Its alliance with the Crimean Khanate created a basis for establishing stability on the steppe, which was a necessary prerequisite for Russian participation in the Black Sea trade. Muscovy also tried to acquire control over additional sources of northern products, which it could export across the steppe. The purpose of its conflicts with Kazan' was to gain access to northeastern trade routes and assert dominion over tributaries who would supply northern luxury pelts.

It was Muscovy's alliance with the Crimean Khanate, however, rather than aggressive action against Kazan', that contributed most to the achievement of those goals. By placing Mengli-Girey's stepson on the throne of Kazan', Muscovy drew the khanate into the alliance. Although Kazan' retained a virtual monopoly on the routes leading to western Siberia, a major portion of the goods it received from the east as well as from its southern trading partners were reexported to Moscow. The alliance thus served to carve out a role for Moscow in the regional trade network and to provide Ivan III with revenues derived from commerce that were essential for his expanding and centralizing state. In 1499, Ivan III nevertheless took advantage of the political discord within Kazan' to conduct a campaign against the Iugra tribes of northwestern Siberia and complete their subordination to Muscovy.

Following the steppe routes secured by the Crimean khan, diplomatic and commercial caravans, typically including groups of dozens of merchants, carried goods obtained from the Russian lands, Europe, and Kazan' from the towns of Muscovy to Tana on the Sea of Azov and Caffa on the Crimean coast of the Black Sea. There the Russian merchants met Muslim, Greek, Armenian, Jewish, and Italian merchants and exchanged their furs, hides, leather, and walrus tusks for silks and satins, spices and gems, dyes, incense, and Tatar horses. The grand prince sent similar items as well as hunting birds, silver objects, and fine European woolen cloth as gifts to the khan, his relatives, his advisors, and other notables of the khanate. To ensure the continued cooperation of the Crimean Khanate the merchants from Muscovy paid transit and other fees to Crimean Horde officials. Caravan leaders supplemented those fees with gifts to local Tatar chieftains. The Muscovite alliance with the Crimean Khanate, cemented by generous gifts and military cooperation, thus supported and protected the southern trade.

These southern trade patterns developed during the third quarter of the fifteenth century while the Italians were operating their colonies at Tana and Caffa. They persisted after the Ottoman Turks seized control of the northern coast of the Black Sea in 1475 and the west coast in 1484, displaced the Italians and occupied their port cities, and subordinated the Crimean Khanate. For twenty years after the Ottomans established their authority at Caffa and Azov (Tana), Muscovite merchants traded at those ports. During that period the Crimean khan and his diplomats served as intermediaries in formal discussions between the Ottomans and Muscovites.

In 1492, however, following complaints from his merchants about conditions at the Ottoman market towns, Ivan III cut off trade by forbidding the Russian caravans to go south. The cordial relationship between Muscovy and the Crimean Khanate contributed to a resolution of the commercial crisis and also facilitated the establishment of direct diplomatic relations between Muscovy and the Ottoman Empire. Mengli-Girey, acting as mediator, advised Ivan to write to Sultan Bayazit and encouraged the Ottomans to make concessions in order to resume trade. The sultan appointed his son viceroy of Caffa and authorized Mengli-Girey to resolve the disputes. He also sent an envoy to Moscow. Although the completion of that journey was prevented by Lithuania, Ivan III nevertheless despatched his own emissary to Caffa; he was sent on to the sultan's court.

By 1496, the dispute had been resolved. Commerce at the Ottoman ports resumed, and Muscovite merchants received permission to travel deeper into Ottoman territory to Tokat, Bursa, and Istanbul. For his fruitful mediation the Crimean khan, his relatives, and clan leaders received gifts or *pominki* from Ivan and once again collected transit fees from the traveling merchants. And importantly, the direct Muscovite–Ottoman diplomatic exchanges, initiated during this crisis, continued.

The achievement of stability on the steppe contributed to a rearrangement of the region's commercial patterns and an enhancement of Moscow's role in them. By the end of Ivan III's reign Moscow had become an important commercial center, whose merchants joined their own northern lands with Kazan' and the southern market centers of the Black Sea to form a single commercial network.

THE FOREIGN POLICY OF VASILY III

During the reign of Ivan III Muscovite foreign and commercial policies were successful. They not only carved out a position for the newly unified state of Muscovy and defended it, but established it as a powerful expanding force in the region. The policies also increased the growing state's sources of revenue. Customs, transit, and other transaction fees collected in the annexed market centers were transferred to Muscovite officials or the Muscovite treasury, while the reorganization of commercial patterns attracted customers for expensive luxury goods directly to Moscow.

The success of the policies during the reign of Ivan III, however, created new situations and new problems for his successor, Vasily III. By the time he assumed the throne the Muscovite–Crimean alliance, the knot binding the separate threads of Ivan's foreign policy, was beginning to unravel. The attractiveness of the alliance was diminishing for the Crimean Khanate. Although the Khanate of Astrakhan' quickly replaced the Great Horde as its chief rival in the steppe, the defeat of the Great Horde in 1502 eliminated the main motive for the Crimean Khanate's adherence to the alliance. In addition, Muscovy's victories over Lithuania were the Crimean Khanate's losses; as frontier territories were transferred to Muscovy, they ceased to be acceptable targets for Tatar border raids and sources of booty. Furthermore, unlike his father, who had lavished gifts on Mengli-Girey and other Tatar notables, Vasily III was warned about trying to collect customs fees from the khan's personal commercial agents and gained a reputation among the Crimean Tatars for his stinginess.

Changing conditions similarly altered Muscovy's assessment of the alliance. As it developed direct diplomatic relations with the Ottoman Empire, Muscovy became less dependent upon the Crimean Khanate and its khan's role as an intermediary. Vasily's diminishing reliance upon the khan was most evident in commercial affairs. The sable and ermine pelts sold by Russian merchants quickly became prized at the Ottoman court, where they were used as symbols of high status and office in formal rituals. Their ceremonial use created a growing demand for them, and in 1515 the Ottoman governor at Caffa sent his own agent directly to Moscow to obtain luxury fur pelts as well as hunting birds and other items. This action initiated a shift in Muscovy's trade pattern with the Turks.

Whereas Vasily III was less dependent upon the Crimean khan than his father had been, he nevertheless continued to require the cooperation of the Kazan' Khanate. It was at least partially through Kazan' that Muscovy acquired the goods it sold to the Ottomans as well as to its western customers. The importance of Kazan' for Muscovy's commerce was stressed in 1506, when as noted above, the khan arrested some Russian merchants; his action prompted Vasily to launch a military campaign against him. When the diplomat Sigismund von Herberstein later visited Muscovy, he observed that Kazan' had become so commercially dependent upon Muscovy that Vasily III was able to exercise strong political influence over the khanate. But the dependence was mutual. Herberstein also reported that when Vasily III tried to exercise his influence by cutting off trade with Kazan' in 1523, Muscovy "suffered as much inconvenience as the people of Kazan'; for it produced a scarcity and dearness in many articles," which it had customarily imported from Persia and Armenia through Astrakhan' and Kazan'; among the items the Russians missed were the "finer kinds of fish" that were caught in the vicinity of Kazan'.[5]

Thus, despite its diminishing advantages, Vasily III hesitated to abandon the alliance with Mengli-Girey and risk disrupting his relationship with Kazan' as well. Mengli-Girey basically honored his commitments to Muscovy. But the Crimean khan's son and heir, Muhammed-Girey, was more responsive to Lithuanian ambassadors who visited the Horde and,

[5] von Herberstein, *Notes upon Russia*, vol. 12, pp. 58, 73.

distributing impressive gifts, tried to persuade the khan and his notables to restore the policy of friendship and alliance between the Crimean Khanate and Lithuania. It was under their influence that isolated and officially unauthorized Crimean Tatar raids against the Russian frontier were conducted in 1507, just after Sigismund succeeded his brother Aleksandr as grand prince of Lithuania and king of Poland. One month after Muscovite forces repulsed the Tatar band, Vasily III attacked Lithuania, breaking the truce of 1503. After 1512, when Muscovy and Lithuania renewed their war, which this time lasted until 1522, Muhammed-Girey became increasingly disappointed with Vasily III and doubtful about the wisdom of continuing the alliance with Muscovy.

In addition to the factors noted above, Muhammed-Girey was concerned about Vasily's friendly overtures to his rival, the Khanate of Astrakhan'. Despite repeated requests, Vasily III refrained from assisting Muhammed-Girey in campaigns against the Astrakhan' Tatars. He also welcomed Tatars from Astrakhan' into Muscovy and honored them with positions at his court. One of those Tatars was Sheikh-Aliyar, a nephew of Ahmad of the Great Horde, who had come to Moscow from Astrakhan' in 1502. In 1512, Vasily III named Sheikh-Aliyar the khan of Kasimov.

This act was regarded as an insult by the Crimean khan. Since 1486–87, when Ivan III had assisted in placing Mengli-Girey's stepson on the throne in Kazan', the Khanate of Kasimov had also been held by a member of the Girey family. Muhammed-Girey protested the loss of this position, which he regarded as a possession of his dynasty. He demanded that Vasily transfer Kasimov from his enemy back to one of his relatives. Vasily not only refused, but compounded the insult when, following the deaths of both Muhammed Amin and his brother Abdyl Letif, the throne of Kazan' became vacant. Rather than follow the precedent established by his father and support the candidate of the Crimean Khanate, Vasily III backed Shah Ali (Shigalei), the son of Sheikh-Aliyar, for the post. In 1519, Shah Ali became khan of Kazan'.

By supporting a member of the house of Astrakhan' for the throne in Kazan', Vasily III fashioned a new coalition to dominate the steppe. The alliance included Muscovy, the Khanates of Kazan' and Astrakhan', and, of course, Kasimov. Against the background of this "betrayal," Muhammed-Girey adopted a policy of overt hostility toward Muscovy, and for the next several decades the two former allies engaged in a bitter contest. The main goal of their rivalry was to achieve dominant influence over Kazan'.

The breakdown of the Muscovite–Crimean alliance coincided with the shift in Muscovite–Ottoman trade patterns. In 1519, just as the

Muscovite–Crimean conflict over Kazan' crystallized and passage on the favored commercial route along the Don River was endangered, the Ottoman court began a practice of sending purchasing agents northward to Moscow. They typically used a route that passed through Moldavia, Poland, and Lithuania, and thus avoided the hazards posed by the Crimean khans who objected to the ongoing trade between their suzerain and their enemy. The Ottoman court gradually monopolized the purchase of luxury fur by the empire; the Muscovite treasury received significant quantities of silver and gold from it in the exchange; and the need for Muscovy to rely on the Crimean khan for commercial cooperation evaporated.

The collapse of the Muscovite–Crimean alliance was also accompanied by the renewal of hostilities between Muscovy and Lithuania. While the Muscovite–Lithuanian war dragged on, Muhammed-Girey, supported by the Lithuanians, attempted to reverse the balance of power in the steppe. His plan was to replace Shah Ali in Kazan' with his own brother, force a change of leadership within the Khanate of Astrakhan', and isolate Muscovy by forming his own alliance with those khanates.

Conspiring with anti-Shah Ali factions in Kazan', Muhammed-Girey encouraged them to revolt. Shah Ali escaped to Muscovy, and Kazan' accepted Sahib-Girey, half-brother of both Muhammed-Girey and Muhammed Amin, as its khan. In conjunction with these events Muhammed-Girey, even as he announced his plans to his Ottoman suzerain, launched a campaign against Muscovy in 1521 and thus prevented Vasily III from intervening in Kazan' and restoring Shah Ali. The Crimean offensive, the first major Crimean Tatar attack against Muscovy, pressed deeply into Muscovite territory and reached the city of Moscow, which was placed under siege. Muhammed-Girey retreated only when he received abundant gifts and a promise of tribute from Vasily's brother-in-law, who was himself a Tatar who had converted to Orthodoxy and had been left in command of the city's defenses.

The next year Muhammed-Girey turned his attention to the Khanate of Astrakhan', whose khan fled at his approach. It appeared that Muhammed-Girey had successfully carried out his plan. But almost immediately after his victory, he quarreled with his own supporters over the distribution of power and spoils in Astrakhan' and was killed. Although Saadat-Girey assumed his father's position within the Crimean Khanate, he faced both domestic opposition and hostility from Poland and Lithuania. Under these conditions he could not consolidate his father's gains, and promoted more cordial relations with Muscovy.

Vasily III took advantage of Saadat-Girey's distractions, and consequent inability to protect Sahib-Girey, to reestablish Muscovite influence over

Kazan'. In 1523, after receiving news that his ambassador to Kazan' had been killed, Vasily III ordered his forces to construct a fortress, called Vasil'sursk (Vasil'grad), on the Volga River. He thus established a military base of operations almost 200 km closer to Kazan' than Nizhnii Novgorod, the easternmost major town within Muscovy. In conjunction with these ventures he also, as Sigismund von Herberstein reported, forbade his merchants to trade at Kazan'; he ordered them to conduct their business, instead, at Nizhnii Novgorod. Then, in 1524, Vasily sent an army, led by Shah Ali, to remove Sahib-Girey and recover the throne. Sahib-Girey fled. He was replaced, however, not by Shah Ali, but by another member of the house of Girey, a son of Muhammed-Girey, Safa-Girey.

This outcome represented an uneasy compromise among Muscovy, the Crimean Khanate, and Kazan' itself. The settlement allowed Vasily III, whose own country had suffered from the boycott on trade at the Kazan' market, to restore normal commercial relations. Furthermore, despite another crisis in the 1530s, it provided the basis for stable relations among all the steppe powers for the next quarter century.

Changes in relative power among the eastern European polities had created the opportunity for Muscovy to expand. When it did, it not only further disrupted the status quo in the region, but assumed responsibility for the formulation of foreign policy and the conduct of foreign affairs that had previously been handled by the autonomous principalities it absorbed. Muscovy designed its foreign policies to address the challenges posed by its new neighbors as they, correspondingly, adjusted to the transformation of the complex of loosely affiliated Russian principalities into a unified and potentially dangerous power. Muscovy's foreign policies were aimed at forging a new basis for stability in the region. They resulted in the establishment of Muscovy as a leading and respected, if not yet the dominant, power of eastern Europe.

I I

IVAN IV
THE TERRIBLE

•

During the century preceding the reign of Ivan IV the Muscovite princes had overseen an expansion of their territories, the development of political institutions to administer them, and the formation of a military organization to defend them. They had nurtured economic activities and molded social structures to support and operate their political and military establishments. They had, furthermore, exploited images and ideologies, expressed in a variety of cultural genres for purely ecclesiastical reasons or even to delimit princely authority, to legitimize and justify these developments.

The result was that by the end of Vasily III's reign a centralized political structure had evolved in Muscovy. At its core was the dynasty. But it too had evolved so that the figure of the grand prince, followed by his eldest son and heir, assumed prominence over even his closest relatives. Although the latter princes remained politically significant as secondary heirs, they were steadily pushed to the periphery of the political structure, leaving the grand prince alone at its center. The grand prince was surrounded and assisted by members of other elite families, his highest-ranking servicemen. Administrative officials conducted the business of state, and more remotely, lower ranks of Moscow and provincial servicemen provided the personnel for civil and military posts. With this apparatus the grand princes had gradually tightened their control over key elements, such as the military, tax collection, and the judicial systems, which were essential to the establishment and main-tenance of their authority in all areas of their expanding realm.

Despite the centralized nature of Muscovy's political organization, the grand princes had not accumulated a full monopoly on political, economic, or military power. The brothers and cousins of the grand princes, who filled important roles as guarantors of dynastic rule, retained their appanage principalities, in which they maintained their own military retinues and exercised some judicial and fiscal authority. Other princely and untitled boyar families exercised significant economic and military power on their own extensive patrimonial estates. The chief ecclesiasts held parallel powers in their domains; some monasteries too were exempt from specific state regulations and taxes. The powers of the grand princes within their centralized system were, thus, limited. They were constrained by several factors: the range of activities the central authorities identified as significant for the achievement of their primary goals of establishing, maintaining, and defending both grand princely authority and domestic order in their expanding domain; the traditional control of appanage princes and other members of the secular and ecclesiastical elite over economic and military resources; the grand princes' dependency on the members of that elite to devise and implement both domestic and foreign policies; and the size and capabilities of their administrative apparatus.

Muscovy's institutions, operating within these limits, had been remarkably successful. But they were also fragile. During the next half century they were subjected to severe stress. That period corresponds to the reign of Ivan IV the Terrible (1533–84). Ivan was one of the most colorful figures in the history of both Kievan Rus' and Muscovy. Accounts written by foreign observers as well as domestic literature, including documents attributed to Ivan personally and his contemporaries,[1] have provided more information about Ivan than has been

---

[1] One of the main sources used as a basis for Ivan's personal character is the so-called Ivan–Kurbskii correspondence, which is traditionally regarded as having been initiated by Prince Andrei M. Kurbskii, a once-trusted servitor of the tsar, but who defected to Lithuania in 1564. Edward Keenan argued, however, that the correspondence was a forgery, actually composed in the seventeenth century. His position was bolstered by Inge Auerbach, who presented evidence that Kurbskii was illiterate in Cyrillic and could neither have contributed to the exchange nor composed the history of Ivan's reign attributed to him. Keenan's thesis spawned a voluminous debate, in which most other scholars, including John Fennell, who translated the letters into English, and R. G. Skrynnikov, a noted authority on Ivan the Terrible, disputed Keenan's analysis and concluded the letters and the commentary contained in them were authentic. Edward L. Keenan, *The Kurbskii–Groznyi Apocrypha: The Seventeenth-Century Genesis of the "Correspondence" Attributed to Prince A. M. Kurbskii and Tsar Ivan IV* (Cambridge, Mass.: Harvard University Press, 1971); Inge Auerbach, *Andrej Michajlovič Kurbskij: Leben in Osteuropäischen Adelsgesellschaften des 16. Jahrhunderts* [Andrei Mikhailovich Kurbskii: life in east European noble society in the 16th century] (Munich: Verlag Otto Sagner, 1985);

available for his predecessors. That information yields a portrait of an individual who has been judged by some to have been a ruthless political leader dedicated to the accumulation of absolute power, and by others to have been a madman, a paranoid, possibly suffering from a skeletal disease and mercury poisoning, resulting from medications he took to reduce his pain.[2] But whatever can be said of his personality, neither the political institutions nor the economic and social order they governed were able to withstand the stress generated by Ivan, his formal policies, and his private actions. By the end of Ivan's reign the Muscovite state was experiencing political, social, and economic crises; by the turn of the century those crises resulted in the end of Riurikid dynastic rule, the collapse of central authority, and the onset of civil war, foreign invasion, and economic chaos, collectively known as the Time of Troubles.

THE MINORITY OT IVAN IV

Vasily III, having suffered an illness that had lasted several months, died on December 3, 1533, at the age of fifty-four. He left two sons: Ivan, a child of three, was the elder and the heir; Iurii, born deaf, was a year younger. The fragile nature of the political institutions became apparent almost immediately.

Since the time of his second marriage Vasily had been taking precautions against the possibility of his own premature death. Between 1525 and 1533, in anticipation of the birth of a son, he had, as discussed in chapter 9, appointed a relatively large number of new boyars, including Prince Dmitrii Fedorovich Bel'skii and others from families that had never previously attained duma rank. By more than doubling the number of boyars in the duma, he attempted to forge a balance within it that would protect and support his heir, should a succession occur while the boy was still a minor. During his lingering fatal illness Vasily also wrote a will, in which he named Ivan as his successor and his wife's uncle

---

R. G. Skrynnikov, *Perepiska Groznogo i Kurbskogo: paradoksy Edvarda Kinana* [The Correspondence of Groznyi and Kurbskii: Edward Keenan's paradoxes] (Leningrad: Nauka, 1973; John L. I. Fennell, *The Correspondence between Prince A. M. Kurbskii and Tsar Ivan IV of Russia, 1564–1579* (Cambridge: Cambridge University Press, 1955).

[2] One expression of the first view may be found in S. F. Platonov, *Ivan the Terrible*, ed. and trans. by Joseph L. Wieczynski (Gulf Breeze, Fla.: Academic International Press, 1974). For the latter view, see Richard Hellie, "What Happened? How Did He Get Away With It?: Ivan Groznyi's Paranoia and the Problem of Institutional Restraints," *RH*, vol. 14 (1987), pp. 199–224, and his introduction to the Platonov volume, "In Search of Ivan the Terrible," pp. ix–xxxix. Edward Keenan also discussed Ivan's illnesses in "Ivan IV and the 'King's Evil': Ni maka li to budet?" *RH*, vol. 20 (1993), pp. 5–13.

Prince Mikhail L'vovich Glinskii as his sons' guardian. There is some scholarly dispute concerning the other measures he took. Some conclude that he appointed a special regency council to oversee government affairs during Ivan's minority. Others argue that the full duma was entrusted with those responsibilities.

Despite Vasily's efforts the years of Ivan's minority were troubled. Even his succession did not proceed without incident. Vasily was survived not only by his two sons, but by two brothers. The main threat to Ivan was his uncle, Prince Iurii of Dmitrov. For decades preceding Ivan's birth, it had been assumed that Iurii would inherit Vasily's throne. One week after Vasily's death, Ivan's other surviving uncle, Andrei Staritskii, swore an oath of allegiance to the young grand prince. But Iurii failed to do so. When a member of the prominent Shuiskii family then transferred his service to Prince Iurii, it appeared that he might be amassing forces to challenge his nephew's position. The duma promptly arrested him; he died in prison three years later. Shortly after Iurii's death Ivan's other uncle, Andrei Staritskii, who by that time had produced a son Vladimir, was arrested as well (May 1537). When he too died (December 1537), Ivan's only remaining relatives were his younger brother Iurii and cousin Vladimir; his position appeared to be secure from dynastic contenders.

Nevertheless, for the next decade Muscovy experienced a period of political turbulence. Muscovy's political system pivoted around the grand prince, who, according to political ideology and imagery, controlled all power. But it also depended upon the grand prince's upper-level servitors, his boyars and *okol'nichie*, who were instrumental in the accumulation and the use of the grand prince's power in financial, military, diplomatic, and administrative matters. The status and role of each servitor at court was determined by his relationship to the grand prince. The functional effectiveness of the system was built upon a balanced interdependence between the service elite and the grand prince. When the center of the system softened, the court was also destabilized.

Thus, when Vasily III died and a three-year-old boy became the grand prince of Muscovy, the extreme youth of the heir blurred the lines defining the relationships of members of the elite to the grand prince and among themselves. It weakened the lynchpin that held the other elements of the political structure together and maintained the delicate balance among them. It provided an opportunity for his guardians, including his mother and her uncle, to claim even greater power than they had exercised during the reign of Vasily III and thereby to unleash the rivalries inherent in the relationships among the leading boyar clans. The scene was set for domestic conflict, generated not by competing dynasts seeking the position of grand prince, but by members of the boyar clans who were affected by the disturbance in the equilibrium within the court. Without the presence of a figure, firmly emplaced at the center of the system, to modify their effects, the intensely competitive relationships among the elite families deteriorated into a debilitating struggle for power. Chief among the competitors were the Shuiskiis, descendants of the Suzdal' branch of the Riurikid dynasty; the Bel'skiis, descended from the Lithuanian dynasty; and the Glinskiis, the Lithuanian family of Ivan IV's mother. The contest among these families and their allies was complex, and continued until Ivan IV personally took the throne in January 1547. Their power struggle has been interpreted as a contest between the princely clans and the old Muscovite service families, and alternatively as an attempt by established members of the elite, both titled and untitled, to defend their positions against newly elevated families. But it also reflects the inability of the political system to achieve stability without a functioning grand prince in its central role.

The Shuiskii princes quickly emerged as beneficiaries of the political imbalances that developed at court after Vasily's death. Although its members had been granted the rank of boyar only during Vasily's reign, the family dominated the duma within months of his death. During the following year some of their most influential rivals, including Princes Ivan Fedorovich Bel'skii and Mikhail L'vovich Glinskii, whom Vasily had charged with protecting his heirs, had been arrested. The removal of these figures, however, did not secure exclusive Shuiskii dominance. Rather, Elena Glinskaia herself emerged to lead a regency that ruled Muscovy until her own death in 1538. While she remained at the center of court politics, an equilibrium among the chief clans of the duma was restored. It consisted not only of the Shuiskiis, but included also relatives, the Gorbatyis, and members of the Obolenskii clan, the most influential of whom was Elena's lover, Prince I. F. Ovchina-Telepnev-Obolenskii.

Almost immediately after Elena died, the balance shifted. The Shuiskiis ordered the arrest of Telepnev-Obolenskii and the release of both Ivan Fedorovich Bel'skii and their own clansman who had been confined for aiding Prince Iurii of Dmitrov. Both were recognized as boyars. But the temporary alliance among the powerful boyar clans gave way as the Shuiskiis attempted to add more of their own relatives onto the duma and to elevate their status further by arranging strategic marriages and positioning themselves even closer to the grand prince. As the Shuiskiis renewed their bid for dominance, Prince Ivan Fedorovich Bel'skii was once again arrested and sent, in the fall of 1538, into exile at Beloozero; Metropolitan Daniil was deposed the following February.

The Shuiskiis were no more successful in sustaining their position in 1538–39 than they had been in 1533. By 1540, a reaction to their power and perhaps their abuse of it set in. The new metropolitan Ioasaf arranged for the release and return of Ivan Fedorovich Bel'skii. But neither could Bel'skii organize a stable coalition. A year and a half after his release, in January 1542, the Shuiskiis seized him once more and sent him back to Beloozero, where he died in May 1543. In parallel fashion the Shuiskiis organized the removal of Metropolitan Ioasaf, who was replaced by Makarii (1542). Nevertheless, by the end of 1543, Prince Andrei Mikhailovich Shuiskii had been executed, reportedly thrown to the dogs by the personal order of the young grand prince Ivan IV. The removal of both the Shuiskiis and the Bel'skiis left other duma families, including once again the Glinskiis, in control of political affairs until 1547. By that time at least a dozen prominent figures at court, including members of the ruling family, had been killed and two metropolitans had been forcibly removed from office.

In January 1547 Ivan IV, having reached the formal age of adulthood, personally assumed the throne. His coronation was a spectacular affair, reminiscent of that staged a half century earlier by his grandfather Ivan III for Prince Dmitry Ivanovich. In this ceremony, however, Metropolitan Makarii crowned Ivan IV not only grand prince, but tsar of all Rus'. Shortly thereafter the sixteen-year-old ruler also married Anastasiia Romanovna Iur'eva-Zakhar'ina.

Within months of these events Ivan IV faced a crisis. During the summer of 1547, fire swept through Moscow. Fires were not unusual events in the predominantly wooden towns of Muscovy. But this one, which lasted over ten hours and which followed several others that had occurred just a few months earlier, was catastrophic. In addition to causing massive destruction in many sections of the city, it also engulfed the wooden structures within the walls of the kremlin. Inside stone churches icons and other holy objects were consumed in the conflagration. The event provoked hysteria among the city's population. Concluding that Ivan's grandmother, Anna Glinskaia, was a witch and responsible for the disaster, mobs stormed into the kremlin and captured one of Ivan's uncles, Iurii Glinskii, whom they tortured and murdered. Within days angry crowds followed Ivan to a suburb of Moscow, where he had taken refuge. Demanding retribution against the rest of the Glinskii clan, they retreated only when convinced that the Glinskiis were not in the tsar's company. Although the tsar was evidently in no personal danger, the experience was traumatic; a few months later, when his other uncle, Mikhail Glinskii, attempted to flee to Lithuania, Glinksii dominance over the other boyars came to an end.

The combination of his coronation and marriage and the unceremonious removal of the Glinskii clan enabled Ivan personally to fill the central position in the Muscovite political system. The relationships of elite families to the grand prince on the one hand, and among those families on the other, became more clearly defined. The intensity of the political competition, which had upset the delicate balance in those relationships and erupted in violence during the years of Ivan's minority, relaxed. High-ranking servitors concentrated on their traditional methods of improving their positions in the hierarchy: fashioning political alliances, arranging strategic marriages, and challenging dishonorable appointments. But clan rivalries persisted. And the experience of the minority years had demonstrated that if those rivalries exceeded tolerable limits, the functional effectiveness of the political system, which had guided the growth of Muscovy, enabled it to achieve its strength, and administered its expanding territories at both the central and provincial levels, would be endangered. The reign of Ivan IV the Terrible, which opened with an absence of a stable equilibrium at the center of the Muscovite political system, was marked by continuing efforts to restore and maintain one.

THE POLITICAL SYSTEM

The dynasty and the tsar

The approaches adopted by the young Ivan IV to regain political harmony were shaped by dynastic interests. Those interests were fundamentally to secure recognition of the senior member of the dynasty as the sovereign ruler – tsar and grand prince – and to gain unquestioned acceptance of his heir. From the perspective of the head of the dynasty, political stability, which depended upon the suppression of the untempered rivalries among the members of the service elite and the channeling of their competitive energies toward improved implementation of the grand prince's policies, was essential to the achievement of those goals.

The dynastic interests pursued by Ivan IV had been defined by generations of the Muscovite princes who had directed their efforts toward guaranteeing the legitimacy of their line, and in the process toward narrowing the range of eligible princes within it. The wars of the middle of the fifteenth century had eliminated the practice of lateral succession within a generation. Ivan III's decision to leave the throne to his son Vasily III rather than grandson Dmitry had refined vertical succession to a pattern from father to eldest surviving son. Using a variety of instruments of power and overlaying them with reinforcing ideologies, the process that decreased the number of legitimate princes had also elevated them above their relatives. The exaltation of the grand prince

contributed to his ability to command the respect, obedience, and sub-
servience of his courtiers.

The monopolization of power by a single line within the sprawling
dynasty was reinforced by the elite servicemen who, anticipating each
succession, used their influence and power to reduce the viability of
collateral relatives as heirs and thereby perpetuate their own privileged
positions. This symbiotic relationship between prince and boyars was
manifested early in Ivan's reign by the arrest of Iurii Ivanovich, immediately following the death of his brother, Grand Prince Vasily III.
Nevertheless, while Ivan was a child, neither he nor any of those ruling
in his name had been able to exercise the authority of his office. But when
Ivan personally assumed the throne and adopted the title of tsar of all Rus',
he furthered the cause pursued by his forefathers by elevating himself to
an even higher level, towering above all his servicemen, including the
older and prestigious members of both the Lithuanian and his own
Riurikid dynasties, and by asserting his sovereignty over them.

During Ivan's minority the functional potential of the political system
had been obscured by Ivan's youth and the ambitions of rival boyar clans.
But by 1547, the duma elite was ready to welcome Ivan as tsar and to
celebrate his marriage to Anastasiia Romanovna. Once again, the interests
of the service elite and those of their tsar converged. Ivan's coronation and
marriage reflected, on the one hand, a consensus among the elite families
on the need for political stability and a willingness to create it on the basis
of a new balance of power among themselves. For Ivan, on the other
hand, they provided the means to pursue the dynastic goals set by his
ancestors. A key element in his agenda was ensuring the succession for
his own progeny. Ivan's marriage as soon as he reached his majority
increased his chances of quickly producing an heir. By selecting his wife
from a family that had attained boyar rank earlier, but had not held it
during the recent conflicts, Ivan and his advisors avoided exacerbating
existing rivalries among the boyar families or favoring one of the chief
clans over another.

Ivan furthermore attempted to recreate a duma that would not only
loyally support him, but one that, despite the disastrous experience of his
own minority years, would at any time preserve the throne for his own
future heirs. His marriage identified new candidates for duma rank.
Imitating the pattern begun by his father after 1526 and transformed into
a trend during the years of his minority, Ivan increased the size of the
duma and thereby readjusted the political balance within it. Early in the
sixteenth century the elite circle had consisted of a dozen individuals.
When Vasily III manipulated its membership to build a coalition that
would support his second marriage (from 1526), its size began to increase.

Then, during Ivan's minority each boyar clan tended, when dominant, to attempt to consolidate its advantage by coopting relatives and other loyal supporters onto the duma. As a result the number of individuals holding duma rank rose even more.

After Ivan assumed the throne, he continued the practice. But the magnitude of his appointments was much greater than his father's had been. Between 1547 and 1550 alone, he appointed twenty-three boyars and fifteen *okol'nichie*. Some members of all the major clans continued to hold duma rank. But many of the new appointees were drawn from the untitled Muscovite service families that had lost power to the princely clans in the preceding decades. And Anastasiia's relatives were chief beneficiaries of his policies. In 1547, her uncle Grigorii Iur'evich Zakhar'in and one of her cousins became boyars; her brother Daniil, appointed first an *okol'nichii*, was promoted to boyar within a year. In the next two years they were joined by additional relatives and quickly formed a major bloc within the duma. Ivan's appointments, which benefited the Morozov and Obolenskii clans as well, raised the number of servitors with duma rank, which had previously fluctuated between one and two dozen, to fifty by 1553; for the next decade that number remained in the range of fifty to sixty.

The rapid rise of the Iur'ev–Zakhar'in clan and the consequent adjustments in the balance of power among the other families holding duma rank contributed to ongoing discontent rather than a pacification of rivalries. The young Ivan IV succeeded neither in fashioning an elite circle that regarded him as a feared monarch nor in commanding their unconditional obedience. The divergence of interests between the tsar and his servitors and the resultant vulnerability of the Muscovite political system became evident once again in 1553.

In March of that year Ivan IV, having returned in triumph from the conquest of Kazan' (1552) to greet the birth of his son and heir Dmitry, fell dangerously ill. When his high fever did not break, arrangements were made for his boyars and high officials of the court to swear allegiance to his infant son. Some, however, foresaw a repetition of the political disorder that had characterized Ivan's own minority. Fearing that Anastasiia's relatives, the Zakhar'in clan, which had so rapidly risen to prominence, would dominate a regency, they favored as heir to the throne Ivan's cousin, Prince Vladimir Andreevich of Staritsa, the tsar's closest relative after his passive and infirm brother, and only hestitantly took the required oath to Dmitry.

Ivan's recovery made the issue moot. The boyars' so-called "revolt" of 1553 has been interpreted as an attempt to inhibit the centralizing tendencies of Ivan's predecessors by placing an appanage prince on the throne.[3] But the tsar's own health and the uncertainty that his son would survive suggest that it may also be understood in terms of the potential for renewed instability. The demonstrated inclination toward the tsar's cousin, albeit a secondary and collateral heir, may be regarded as an attempt to maintain a firm center within the centralized apparatus, not to destroy it. The tsar's focus on dynastic interests, i.e., his commitment to a vertical succession within his own line, diverged from his boyars' primary concern, which was to preserve an equilibrium among their own clans and stability for the political system. It was the difference in their priorities that caused their clash over the succession.

Indeed, the reluctance of some boyars to swear allegiance to Dmitry was not unwarranted; the infant died three months later in June 1553. Ivan's second son, who would be named Ivan as well, was not born until March of the following year. Although the tsar, defying Orthodox tradition, ultimately married seven times, he fathered only two sons who would survive him: Fedor, Anastasiia's child, and another Dmitry, the product of his last, uncanonical marriage to Mariia Nagaia.

Ivan's recovery and the death of his son ended the crisis of 1553, but the "disloyalty" of his boyars is often considered to be a factor in Ivan's later policies and behavior. The conclusion of this episode also reconfirmed the vertical pattern of succession within the ruling Muscovite line. Years later, Ivan the Terrible suspected a plot to overthrow him in favor of Vladimir Andreevich; he arrested his cousin and forced him to commit suicide by drinking poison (1569). The "Staritskii affair," as the episode was called, following as it did the death of Ivan's brother Iurii in 1563, eliminated the last potential lateral heir for the Muscovite throne and ensured the succession for the tsar's eldest son.

This development also concluded the Daniilovich dynastic line's long struggle to establish unequivocally the vertical pattern of succession. Ivan's dynastic victory, however, highlights the grand irony of the Daniilovichi's achievement. Their monopolization of the grand princely throne and installation of the pattern of vertical succession had been key factors in the growth and development of the powerful state of Muscovy. But these very factors demonstrated their fatal weakness during the reign of Ivan IV.

In 1581, the heir to the throne Ivan Ivanovich died, the result of a blow to his head administered by his temporarily enraged and deranged father. Consequently, when Ivan IV died on March 19, 1584, the elder of his two surviving sons, the feeble-minded Fedor, succeeded him. During Fedor's reign (1584–98), Ivan's other son, Dmitry, died under mysterious

---

[3] A. A. Zimin, *Reformy Ivana Groznogo* [The reforms of Ivan the Terrible] (Moscow: Sotsial'no-ekonomicheskaia literatura, 1960), p. 414.

circumstances. Fedor himself produced no children. His death constituted the demise of the Muscovite branch of the Riurikid dynasty.

With the deaths of all his sons the full impact of Ivan's elimination of lateral heirs became apparent. Muscovy lacked a tsar. With no heir produced by its dynasty to anchor the other elements of its political system to the center, the court elite, the military, and all the political institutions lost their cohesiveness. The Riurikid dynasty expired, and its state collapsed. Muscovy was plunged into a chaotic period known as the Time of Troubles; torn apart by social uprisings, civil wars, and foreign invasions, it almost ceased to exist.

In retrospect, the cumbersome, clumsy, collateral succession system, which had so often been a source of intradynastic strife during the Kievan Rus' and the early Muscovite eras, had at least been functional. Despite wars, plague, childhood deaths, and the broad range of other factors that conspired to keep life spans short, it had always offered the society a legitimate heir. Its inherent problem had been that too many potential heirs survived to compete for the position of grand prince, not too few. But the system had served the interests of the dynasty as a whole by preserving the realm as their common domain. It had also served the society by guaranteeing an overarching dynastic stability, albeit at the cost of periodic internecine conflict.

In contrast, the system of vertical succession within a single, ever-narrowing dynastic line appeared to be neater, tidier, and more rational. It removed the basis for interprincely wars and, by designating one prince as ruler over all the others, it served the process of centralization and the formation of a state apparatus that replaced autonomous princely administrations. Yet despite all the power that had been accumulated by the tsar and grand prince, who stood as the focal point of the Muscovite political apparatus, the succession pattern that had been created left the state and society in a precarious position. Almost as soon as Ivan IV completed the process of removing the last alternative princely line, his own madness caused the death of his heir and the realm was left to the childless and feeble-minded Fedor. By the end of his reign the succession pattern that had been so painstakingly developed to preserve power for the Moscow princes had also created a political system that had so thoroughly demoted the collateral lines that no prince from any of them had the stature to be recognized by other members of the elite as their sovereign and fill the vacuum at its center. The Muscovite princes, by successfully legitimizing themselves as exclusive rulers of a strong centralized monarchy, laid the basis for the demise of Riurikid authority over the Russian lands and endangered the survival of Muscovy itself.

The victory for the principle of vertical succession within the

Muscovite line achieved by Ivan IV was bolstered by the ideological support offered by the Church, specifically by Metropolitan Makarii. Makarii had become head of the Church in 1542, at the height of the conflicts during Ivan's minority years. In the preceding decade two metropolitans had been deposed for secular partisan reasons. Makarii was thus concerned with reinforcing the status and authority of his own office and the Church itself, even as he guided the young Ivan and supported his assertion of political power.

The metropolitan, who was centrally involved in the decision to have Ivan assume the throne in 1547, officiated at the elaborate coronation ceremony. He used the occasion to instruct Ivan on his duties as ruler. In terms reminiscent of Filofei's warnings decades before, he reminded the tsar of his role as the protector of Orthodoxy on earth and of his responsibilities to honor the Church and its hierarchs. But the political effect was to elevate Ivan's position. Makarii crowned him not only grand prince, but also tsar of all Rus'. His new title symbolized an assumption of powers equivalent and parallel to those held by the former Byzantine caesar and the Tatar khan, both known in Russian sources as tsar.

During the coronation ceremony Ivan IV claimed his throne by invoking his ancestral heritage, which he traced back to the grand princes of Kiev. This legitimizing theme, identifying Muscovy as the heir of Kievan Rus', was repeated in a variety of literary and visual representations, sponsored by Makarii and Ivan. But under Makarii's influence it was interwoven with the sanctity of the dynasty.

At two Church councils, held in 1547 and 1549, the metropolitan oversaw the canonization of thirty-nine Russian saints; he later added eight more. The newly recognized saints included members of the Riurikid dynasty as well as ecclesiastical and monastic figures who had been venerated locally. By their actions, the councils contributed to standardization and unification within the Church. But princely saints then also appeared prominently in the frescoes that were commissioned for a gallery built between the Church of the Annunciation, the chapel of the royal family, and the tsar's palace, both located in the kremlin, as well as in the Cathedral of the Archangel Michael. The images expressed at once both the dynastic legitimacy of the tsar as heir to the princes of Kievan Rus' and his spiritual legitimacy as supreme ruler and protector of Muscovy, the center of Orthodoxy.

The themes were similarly articulated in literary compositions. The Velikie Minei Chetii or Great Menology, whose compilation Makarii directed, was a collection of ecclesiastical literature, including the saints' vitae as well as sermons, polemics against infidels and heretics, and other texts, all organized as daily church readings. In combination they provided arguments for enhanced powers for the Muscovite prince, who as ruler of Moscow, the "Third Rome," was responsible for the protection of Orthodoxy. Chronicles compiled at the metropolitan's court, notably the *Stepennaia Kniga* or "Book of Degrees of the Imperial Genealogy," presented the march of events that led to the placement of Moscow at the center of the Orthodox world and of Ivan, heir to St. Vladimir, as its tsar and grand prince.

Makarii's theocratic concepts of the tsar's role thus emphasized the ruler's sanctity; they highlighted as well his responsibility to use his powers not only to protect, but to extend his Orthodox realm. Makarii's views justified the role of Muscovy as an imperial power. The conquest of Kazan', which will be discussed below, was portrayed as the triumphant outcome of a religious crusade. The Nikon chronicle, a comprehensive compilation that incorporated local redactions, initiated earlier in the sixteenth century and reworked in the late 1550s, focused on the fundamental role of Orthodoxy in the history of the unification and centralization of the Russian lands. Russian encounters with Mongols and Tatars were described in it as episodes in a centuries-long struggle, which culminated in the victory of Orthodoxy over the infidel at Kazan'. Similarly, the icon, known as the "Church Militant," depicted Ivan IV, guided by the Archangel Michael, at the head of a military procession in which Russian princely saints took part and the figure of Vladimir Monomakh was given prominence. The procession, triumphantly leaving one city in flames, approached another. The icon was unusual in representing Ivan, a living person, among the figures. But by doing so, it merged the image of the earthly military victory of the Muscovites over Kazan' with the spiritual triumph of Orthodoxy that paved the way toward heaven even as it reminded the viewer of Ivan's saintly ancestry.

Makarii's ideas and activities did not go unchallenged. Ivan Mikhailovich Viskovatyi, a state secretary or *d'iak* and leading figure in Muscovite foreign affairs, objected to the manner of representation of holy images in some of the icons in the Church of the Annunciation and to some frescoes that had been painted in the "gold room," a throne room, in the tsar's palace. Viskovatyi was brought to trial for his criticisms in 1553; his objections were overruled, but he was released without punishment. Makarii clashed with other influential figures as well. He initiated trials against heretics, and at the Stoglav Council or "Council of One Hundred Chapters," held in 1551, he used his influence to stem a tendency to reduce land ownership by ecclesiastical and monastic institutions; the council considered a variety of other issues, including styles of icon painting and regulations for the behavior of priests and monks, as well.

Despite these controversies, by the time Makarii died in 1563, the concepts he promoted had become fundamental components of Muscovite ideology. Developed from previously formulated principles, encapsulated in the theories of the Third Rome and of the "Josephites," they endowed the Muscovite ruler with a legitimacy that rested on his dynastic lineage; but they also emphasized the saintly aspect of the Riurikids and their holy mission. Ivan IV, as their direct descendant, inherited not only the highest secular position in the land, but an aura of special grace and responsibilities to protect the faith and extend the Orthodox domain. To fulfill his duties as God's servant on earth, he was endowed with absolute political power over his domain. There were tensions between these theoretical formulations and the actual exercise of power, between the theocratic values and secular practicality, between the enhanced authority of the ruler granted by ideology and the informal constraints on it imposed by tradition. But however wide the disparity between the myth of a righteous, all-powerful ruler and the reality of Ivan the Terrible's practices, Makarii provided a conceptual framework in which the Riurikid grand prince was transformed into an unimpeachable tsar and his dynastic realm into an Orthodox empire.

Court and adminstration

The Muscovite court Although significant, the ideological contributions of the Church were not sufficient to reverse the multiple personal and political effects of the traumas experienced during Ivan's minority. Ivan himself, according to some accounts, had been deeply affected. His distress was reported in the first of his letters in the Ivan–Kurbskii correspondence. The letter described how Ivan and his brother were treated with neglect and disrespect after their mother died. The implication is that Ivan nursed grievances against the boyars for the abuse he had endured as a child and that his lingering resentment against them provoked the excessive cruelty with which he later treated them as well as other perceived opponents.

The bitter factionalism, however, had not only disturbed the young tsar. It had distorted the political system and undermined its effectiveness. As leadership at court careered from one boyar clique to another, powerful political figures fell into disgrace and were arrested, exiled, and even executed. The positions of even the highest-ranking courtiers had become insecure. Each of the competing families, when dominant, not only acted to remove its opponents, but attempted to bolster its position by promoting its own members and other loyal supporters to duma rank. One result was an increase in the number of individuals holding the rank of boyar and *okol'nichii*. Another was a reduction in their collective expertise. Unlike their fifteenth-century counterparts who had been elevated to duma rank only after decades of experience in military or civil service, about half of those recruited to the duma during the period of Ivan's minority had careers of less than fifteen years. Shaped by these factors, the duma available to the young Ivan IV in 1547 had diminished value as a reliable advisory body.

Once Ivan IV assumed the throne he almost immediately took measures to restore stability at his court. His coronation and his marriage removed some of the grounds for his boyars' rivalry and clarified their relative positions in the hierarchy. Guided by Metropolitan Makarii and other advisors and employing the services of his boyars and *okol'nichie*, Ivan also attempted to reestablish the credibility and effectiveness of the central Muscovite government throughout his realm. To that end he addressed some of the main domestic problems that had developed during his minority and also mounted some stunning successes in foreign policy. But the balance and functional effectiveness Ivan and his advisors sought proved elusive.

To build consensus and support among the court elite for himself and his future heirs, Ivan IV initially followed the precedent set by his father after 1526 and conferred duma rank on even more of his servitors. While intending to manipulate the political balance within his duma however, he also intensified the trends that had been becoming apparent during his minority. With these appointments he not only further increased the number of his elite counselors, but allowed the standard of experience, which had previously been a qualifying factor for promotion to duma rank, to erode. According to Ann Kleimola's calculations, "the median length of prior service for appointments made from 1547 to 1564 [was] between ten and eleven years . . . Men with twenty or more years of service on their records comprised only about an eighth of the new appointees. At the other end of the scale, a corresponding eighth of those appointees had served three years or less before appointment – a phenomenon unheard of earlier in the century."[4]

The new appointees numerically and politically balanced the older group of boyars and *okol'nichie*; but they did not reliably have the expertise and skills required to counsel the tsar, lead his troops, and supervise administrative and diplomatic functions. Ivan IV increasingly

---

[4] A. M. Kleimola, "Kto kogo: Patterns of Duma Recruitment, 1547–1564," *FOG*, vol. 38 (1986), p. 211; Kleimola summarized her findings from this article in "Reliance on the Tried and True: Ivan IV and Appointments to the Boyar Duma, 1565–1584," *FOG*, vol. 46 (1992), pp. 52, 54–55.

expanded his circle of counselors. Some, such as the Metropolitan Makarii, held positions that traditionally had been included among the grand prince's advisory circle. But others stretched its boundaries. Syl'vestr, a priest at the Church of the Annunciation, became a regular figure at court just after the fire and popular disorders of 1547 left their terrifying impressions on the newly crowned young tsar. Although he engaged in disputes with the metropolitan and appeared to have been sympathetic to those boyars who hesitated to pledge their loyalty to Dmitry Ivanovich in 1553, he did not entirely lose influence until 1560, when he was accused of complicity in the death of Anastasiia and of practicing witchcraft. He was then exiled to the Solovetskii Monastery.

Ivan's pattern of awarding boyar rank reflects an attempt to reestablish a balance among rival clans. Favoritism toward untitled Muscovite families restored a counterweight to the princely clans that had played such a disruptive role during his minority. In a few cases, Ivan also accorded duma rank to members of families that previously had never received such high honor. One example was the Adashev family. Fedor Grigor'evich Adashev, who served as a diplomat, received the rank of *okol'nichii* in 1547; in 1553, he became a boyar. His son Aleksei Adashev, who followed his father into a diplomatic career, became one of the tsar's closest advisors, especially on foreign affairs. Evidently because the status of the Adashev family was relatively low and the traditions governing promotions inhibited his advancement, Aleksei Adashev did not receive high rank while his father remained an *okol'nichii*. He has been identified, however, as a *dumnyi dvorianin*. The new rank recognized his stature as a member of the duma elite, but placed him in the hierarchy below the level of *okol'nichii*. When his father was promoted to boyar rank, Aleksei Adashev became an *okol'nichii*. He never rose beyond that level, however. In 1560, he lost the favor of the tsar, was put on trial with the priest Syl'vestr and imprisoned; he died in 1561. The introduction of the rank of *dumnyi dvorianin*, which became more common after 1565, provided a means of drawing Muscovite servitors from less prestigious families into the court elite.

The creation of another rank, *dumnyi d'iak*, had a parallel effect. The administrative apparatus was expanding in conjunction with the implementation of domestic reforms as well as territorial expansion. The policies adopted by the Muscovite government required improved and more detailed military, *mestnichestvo*, and fiscal records; additional censuses and land surveys; more diplomatic activity; and oversight of new local officials in the provinces as well as in newly acquired lands. As the administrative apparatus assumed these duties, it became divided into an increasing number of specialized branches that by the late 1540s and 1550s were recognized as distinct chancelleries or bureaus, called *izby*; by the end of the century the term *prikaz* replaced *izba*.

Select administrative functionaries who developed high degrees of expertise and directed crucial *izby*, but lacked the qualifying genealogical credentials for the two traditional duma ranks were included in the elite circle by being named *dumnye d'iaki*. Ivan Mikhailovich Viskovatyi, a protégé of the Zakhar'in clan, rose during the 1540s to become the head of the diplomatic branch of the administrative apparatus; in 1549, he received the title *dumnyi d'iak*. Despite his disagreements in 1553 with Makarii, he remained influential until he too lost the favor of the tsar in 1570, and was executed.

Ivan IV thus enlarged the duma not only by appointing more servitors to the rank of *okol'nichii* and boyar, but by creating new lower ranks for servicemen and administrative personnel. Although the *dumnye dvoriane* and *dumnye d'iaki* lacked the status associated with the highest duma ranks, they nevertheless enjoyed the special privileges, received the rewards, and exercised the responsibilities, such as participation in court ceremonies as well as in diplomatic and other civil service activities, that had formerly been the exclusive preserve of boyars and *okol'nichie*. These alterations in the composition of the advisory group, however, diluted the prestige and influence previously associated with duma rank.

The servicemen expressed dismay when the norms that had previously guided appointments and promotions were ignored. In the past both family status and an individual's service record were determinants, along with princely favor, for appointments in service and, for the elite, promotion to duma rank. But during Ivan's minority, when affiliation with more recently elevated clans appeared to outweigh experience, members of established families were obliged to defend their positions. They reacted by initiating *mestnichestvo* cases, in which they challenged the appointments to key posts they considered were in violation of the system of precedence.

The dramatic increase in the number of challenges has led Ann Kleimola, following A. A. Zimin, to regard this period as the time when *mestnichestvo* matured.[5] The elite clans' emphasis on precedence during this period may be understood as an attempt to preserve their status, to formalize their positions, which were endangered by the waiving of

---

[5] Ann Kleimola, "Status, Place, and Politics: The Rise of *Mestnichestvo* during the *Boiarskoe Pravlenie*," *FOG*, vol. 27 (1980), pp. 195–196; A. A. Zimin, "Istochniki po istorii mestnichestva v XV-pervoi treti XVI v.," [Sources on the history of *mestnichestvo* from the XV through the first third of the XVI centuries], *Arkheograficheskii ezhegodnik za 1968 god* (Moscow: 1970), pp. 110, 118.

customary guidelines for appointments in favor of raw nepotism. The resultant institutionalization of *mestnichestvo* may be regarded as a response to the unpredictable fluctuations in the political fortunes of members of the service elite, which had resulted from the power struggle and rapidly shifting political alignments among the duma clans. Although the system did not work with perfect consistency and the places of individuals within the elite circle continued to be affected by political circumstances, the precedence suits did generally protect the status of the older, established service families.

Based on their experience "many members of the elite continued to believe [during the subsequent years of Ivan's reign] that *mestnichestvo* safeguarded their hereditary claims to positions and privilege, limited the arbitrary power of the ruler, and eliminated favoritism."[6] High-ranking servicemen consequently continued to invoke the *mestnichestvo* system when rapid promotions and dubious assignments to military commands and other key posts violated the norms of order. Precedence suits thus replaced more violent means of competition. But they became so numerous that they began to interfere with military effectiveness. Operations against the Crimean and Kazan' Tatars in 1544–45, for example, were compromised as a result of such disputes. In 1549, in conjunction with preparations for a major campaign against Kazan', Ivan issued a decree that clarified seniority among the military commanders, set the appointments to the main command positions outside the precedence system, and ordered that other precedence suits be postponed until after the campaign.

Provincial administration The turbulence of central politics during Ivan's minority had equally unsettling effects on stability and order in the provinces. The policies adopted to reform provincial administration also disturbed Muscovite and provincial servicemen. The political turmoil at court during Ivan's minority and the consequent diminished respect for central authority had spawned both abuse of power by provincial officials and a laxity in law enforcement. In some instances governors (*namestniki*), appointed by their boyar relatives who were temporarily dominating the central apparatus, took advantage of the special protection they enjoyed. As governor of Pskov, for example, Prince Andrei Mikhailovich Shuiskii became notorious for his abuses, which included demanding bribes and free services from the local population as well as levying unusually high fines and fees in judicial proceedings. He was removed from his post in

---

[6] Kleimola, "Status, Place, and Politics," p. 213.

1540 by his family's rivals, the Bel'skiis, while they dominated the duma, and was later executed by order of Ivan. In some localities, the inability or failure of officials to curb criminal activity, notably brigandage, was also causing concern.

The combination of official abuse and popular disorder in the provinces prompted the introduction in 1538–39 of a reform in local government organization, known as the *guba* reform. In response to community petitions, the Moscow government issued special charters, authorizing the local populace to select their own officials or district elders to suppress brigandage and restore order. Despite the community's involvement in the selection process, the reform was not an experiment in local democracy; on the contrary, the provincial servicemen and peasants who served as *guba* elders were responsible to Moscow, where first a special commission and later a branch of the central administrative apparatus, known as the *razboinaia izba* and then the *razboinyi prikaz* or robbery bureau, developed to instruct *guba* elders and oversee their activities. The reform effectively made the entire community responsible to central apparatus for its elder's performance. Although inaugurated while the Shuiskiis were in power and continued under the Bel'skiis, no new *guba* charters were issued from 1543, when the Shuiskiis recovered power, to 1549, after Ivan assumed the throne. While many northern communities operated under existing charters, other sections of the country continued to operate under the older forms of organization and procedures.

In 1550, Ivan's administration also issued a new law code. It repeated many of the clauses contained in the 1497 Sudebnik, including the restrictions on peasant mobility. But it also clarified the relationships between the governors (*namestniki*) and elected officials, and may have been instrumental in extending the *guba* structure to new parts of the realm. In addition, it was stricter than the earlier code in its provisions designed to bring order to the provinces. The 1550 code was particularly adamant on enforcing earlier prohibitions against bribery, falsification of records, and other corrupt practices. Such offenses committed by officers of the provincial law courts were punishable by penalties ranging from heavy fines for judges and state secretaries to public flogging for scribes, bailiffs, and their agents. Removal from office and/or imprisonment were also prescribed. The Sudebnik also reduced opportunities for abuse of power by provincial governors, the *namestniki* and *volosteli*. The governors were relieved of some of their duties; the responsibility for apprehending brigands and bringing them to justice, which was transferred to *guba* elders, is one example. But punishments for violations or excesses, usually fines, were specified for only a few misdeeds.

The *guba* reforms and the law code were followed in the early 1550s by the creation of additional "elected" local officials, known as *zemskie nachal'niki*, who became responsible for tax collection and civil administration, including the settlement of civil judicial cases. In combination, these measures further restricted the range of responsibilities of the provincial governors. Their main functions had been defense, keeping order by subduing felons, and collecting taxes and other fees. The first duty had been transferred to *gorodovye prikazchiki* early in the century. The reforms creating local *guba* and *zemskie* officials removed the remaining functions from them as well. In 1555–56, Ivan's government formally abolished the *kormlenie* system and with it the system of provincial rule by *namestniki* and *volosteli* that it had supported. The old practice did not immediately or entirely disappear. But where it did, new positions, filled by officials drawn from local provincial servicemen, replaced the offices of *namestnik* and *volostel'*, held by centrally appointed members of the Muscovite elite. As they did so, the latter lost access to one of their chief areas of service and sources of reward. Their opportunities for advancement and enrichment were correspondingly limited to military service.

The reforms in provincial administration contributed to another means by which Ivan IV enlarged his circle of elite advisors. Provincial governers, as Richard Hellie has observed, had been principal conveyors of information about the provinces to Moscow. Appointed from the center, they carried information about their regions back with them when their terms expired. When provincial governance by *namestniki* and *volosteli* was abandoned, the central administration also lost its former means of gauging the resources, capabilities, and moods of its provincial subjects. Possibly as a result, the tsar initiated a practice of consulting representatives from a broader range of social groups to consider problems and policies confronting his realm. Some scholars identify the Council of Reconciliation, dated 1549, as the first meeting of this type. Others contend that there is no contemporary evidence confirming the nature of the activities or participants of that particular council. But it was after 1555–56 that the central administration had a more definite need to develop new methods of communication and consultation with its subjects. Thus, in 1566, when Muscovy was engaged in the Livonian War, Ivan IV convened hundreds of representatives from the clergy, elite Muscovite servitors, administrative officials, and Muscovite and provincial merchants to consider the issue of continuing the war. The *zemskii sobor*, the term coined in the nineteenth century to refer to the assemblies of this type that continued to be called at irregular intervals in the late sixteenth and seventeenth centuries, offered an alternative method of information gathering to substitute for the channels of communication that vanished with the centrally appointed provincial governors.[7]

The oprichnina Despite the reform efforts, the balance among the central organs of the political system was not stable. The succession episode of 1553 was one sharp reminder of the differences in interests and priorities that existed between Ivan and at least some of his boyars. The death of Anastasiia in 1560 and Ivan's second marriage in 1561 to a Kabardian princess, who took the Christian name of Mariia, was accompanied by continuing uncertainties regarding succession. Anastasiia's two sons, Ivan and Fedor, were still quite young. And Mariia's son, Vasily, did not survive infancy. The political elite also responded firmly to the appearance of Mariia's brothers at the Muscovite court. Although the Cherkasskii princes, as they were known, converted to Orthodoxy, entered the tsar's service as early as 1558, and formed marital ties with the Iur'ev family, i.e., Anastasiia's clan, they were not accorded duma rank.

In addition to the tensions arising from dynastic concerns and the perpetually competitive atmosphere at court, the flurry of reform activity was not having the desired effects. Each reform, intended to resolve the problems that had become critical during the period of Ivan's minority, also introduced new destabilizing pressures. The policies adopted to correct abuses in provincial government, for example, were partially successful; but they had the added consequences of restricting service opportunities for the elite and contributing to the increased costs and complexity of the central administrative apparatus.

By December of 1564, Ivan IV gave up his attempts to reestablish a balanced equilibrium between tsar and high-ranking courtiers and thus provide firm guidance for the effective functioning of the governmental apparatus. Taking his wife and sons with him, he left Moscow to celebrate the feast of St. Nicholas. Then, early in January, he sent word to the new metropolitan Afanasii (Athanasius) that he was out of patience with the Church hierarchs, his boyars, and his administrative officials. He announced he was abdicating.

The Muscovite political system could not tolerate a vacancy at its center. The ideology that had evolved and legitimized Muscovite princely rule required a divinely selected tsar and grand prince to rule the Orthodox bastion of Muscovy and be God's instrument in secular affairs. The absence of a tsar condemned Muscovite society to betraying the will

---

[7] Richard Hellie, "Zemskii Sobor," in *Modern Encyclopedia of Russian and Soviet History*, ed. by Joseph L. Wieczynski, vol. 45 (Gulf Breeze, Fla.: Academic International Press, 1987), p. 227.

of God. On a more mundane level there was no alternative to the tsar. Ivan's brother Iurii had died in 1563. And although tradition, genealogy, and records of experience gave certain families and individuals exceptional stature, the entire service hierarchy was dependent upon the tsar. All servicemen defined their positions in relation to the tsar and held them at his discretion. Their inherent competition inhibited them from acting collectively as a unified body and prevented them from coalescing around any single one of them and supporting him as a substitute for the sovereign. Without a tsar the other elements of the political system would not be able to function; the realm would lose its cohesion.

A panic-stricken court sent a delegation that pleaded with Ivan to remain on the throne. He did so, but only on condition that they accept his absolute power to deal with his courtiers at will, i.e., to send them into exile, confiscate their property, even execute them without a hearing or any other interference by the Church or his boyars. The delegates accepted the tsar's demands. Ivan returned to Moscow, and a month later announced the formation of the *oprichnina*.

The *oprichnina* was Ivan's private court. He attached to it a corps of guardsmen, known as *oprichniki*, which grew in number from 1,000 to 6,000 men. He also designated regions within Muscovy as *oprichnina* territories and created administrative organs that would oversee those lands and function in a manner parallel to the traditional structures that continued to govern the *zemshchina*, i.e., the rest of Muscovy.

The *oprichniki* were drawn from a variety of sources. The Cherkasskii princes, the tsar's in-laws who had not achieved duma rank, became prominent among them; others were lower-ranking servitors and foreigners. The German Heinrich von Staden, who left an account of his adventures as an *oprichnik*, is among the better known of the latter group.[8] Also among the early leaders of the *oprichnina* was the boyar A. D. Basmanov, a member of one of Moscow's long-established elite families. Indeed, the composition of *oprichnina* corps belies the argument that its main purpose was to destroy the princely and old Muscovite elite families in the interests of enhancing the tsar's exclusive and autocratic powers.[9]

---

[8] For an English edition of his account, see Heinrich von Staden, *The Land and Government of Muscovy*, trans. by Thomas Esper (Stanford, Calif.: Stanford University Press, 1967).

[9] One of the chief spokesmen for this argument was S. F. Platonov. His view is developed in his *Ivan the Terrible*, cited above. R. G. Skrynnikov presented a variant of this view, in which he concluded that the *oprichnina* was initially intended to undermine the power of the princely families by dismantling their landholdings; it later lost its original focus and expanded the range of its victims. See his *Ivan the Terrible*, ed. and trans. by Hugh F. Graham (Gulf Breeze, Fla.: Academic International Press, 1981), especially pp. 87–94. But

The social background of the members of the *oprichnina* court was scarcely distinguishable from that of the members of the *zemshchina* court. The activities of Ivan's new guardsmen were both bizarre and brutal. The *oprichniki* wore dark robes, and attaching brooms and images of dogs' heads to their saddles, they rode around the country, terrorizing the populace as they hunted traitors and opponents. They transformed the tsar's headquarters at Aleksandrova (Aleksandrovskaia Sloboda) into an armed camp and built a stone fortress at Vologda (1567), where they reputedly engaged in debauched behavior. The creation of the *oprichnina* was accompanied by the murders of several courtiers of duma rank, prominent military commanders, and members of princely families. By the time it was disbanded in 1572, Metropolitan Afanasii had been driven from office (1566); his successor Filipp had been deposed (1568) and murdered (1569). The city of Novgorod had been sacked (1570). And Ivan, fearing a reaction against him, had laid plans to escape to England.

The *oprichnina* claimed at least 4,000 lives. Its victims included not only titled and untitled members of the elite, but lower-ranked *pomeshchiki*, administrative officials, commoners, and ultimately members of the *oprichnina* themselves. Three leaders of the 1566 *zemskii sobor* were executed; taking advantage of Ivan's need for the assembly's cooperation in order to pursue the Livonian War, they had used the occasion to protest his excesses, abuses, and deviations from tradition. Other victims were killed for imagined acts of treason. Perhaps the most prominent victim was the tsar's cousin, Prince Vladimir Andreevich of Staritsa who, suspected of being at the center of a plot to overthrow Ivan, was forced to commit suicide in 1569. The sack of Novgorod and execution of hundreds of its residents, probably the single most destructive act committed by the *oprichniki*, was provoked by a similar suspicion that city was harboring and encouraging traitors.

Ivan's experiment in parallel courts and administrations was a dismal failure. His *oprichnina*, despite its attachment of some of the wealthiest lands to its domain and its administrative preoccupation with tax collection, never developed a governmental apparatus comparable to that of the *zemshchina*. Yet its interference in sensitive issues, such as diplomacy, undermined the credibility and effectiveness of the *zemshchina*. Neither was the *oprichnina* able to conduct war. In 1566, as discussed above, Ivan had to assemble representatives from the *zemshchina* to gain support for continuing hostilities against Poland-Lithuania in the Livonian War. And in 1571, as will be discussed below, the *oprichnina* was responsible for

see also Hellie's "In Search of Ivan the Terrible," in which he argued the *oprichnina* had no rational foundation.

allowing the Crimean Tatars to penetrate Muscovite defenses and conduct a devastating attack on Moscow. A *zemshchina* army, however, successfully repulsed the Tatars the next year. Ivan then disbanded his *oprichnina* and reintegrated Muscovite lands, court, and administration. Following the *oprichnina* fiasco there were renewed efforts to bring harmony to the tsar's court. After 1572, Ivan the Terrible raised few servicemen to the rank of boyar or *okol'nichii*, and thus drastically reduced the number of counselors from about sixty in 1565 to eighteen in 1584.[10] Although he also appointed an increasing number of *dumnye dvoriane*, the few he promoted to the highest duma ranks were either members of families that had already achieved that distinction or his own in-laws. They were also distinguished by their long records of service. Ivan thereby restored the standards of genealogy and experience traditionally associated with elevation to duma rank. The effect was to recreate a small elite circle of advisors, whose members were accorded high honor and prestige as well as responsibility.

The restoration of stability at court brought a measure of calm to the Muscovite realm. But the political system continued to be rocked by new traumas. In 1575, Ivan IV once again declared that he was abdicating. On this occasion, however, he transferred his throne to a former Tatar khan of Kasimov, who had been baptized in 1573 as Semen Bekbulatovich. The charade, during which Ivan once again established a separate personal court and maintained his own armed force, lasted one year. Ivan then simply dismissed Bekbulatovich and resumed his position.

Finally, in 1581, as noted above, Ivan murdered his son. The tsar, enraged by the inappropriate attire of his pregnant daughter-in-law, provoked a scene with Ivan Ivanovich. During their fight the tsar struck his son in the head; eleven days later the heir to the throne of Muscovy died. As a result, Fedor succeeded Ivan IV the Terrible rather than his elder brother. But he was unable to produce children. The legitimacy of their half-brother Dmitry, born of Ivan's seventh, uncanonical marriage, was questionable. Dmitry, however, died during Fedor's reign. Ivan IV's cousin Vladimir Andreevich Staritskii had been a victim of the *oprichnina*. The status of other, more distant relatives had been so thoroughly demeaned that they could not be considered potential heirs. The blow Ivan delivered to his son's head not only resulted in the death of Ivan Ivanovich, but in the extinction of the dynasty.

The political system struggled for the rest of the century. But the dynasty's success in elevating the office and person of the tsar so far above other members of the court had reshaped the balanced, interdependent

---

[10] Kleimola, "Reliance on the Tried and True," p. 55.

relationship between the monarch and the political elite that had characterized earlier reigns into a dependency of the court elite on the tsar. Confronted in addition with the consequences of Ivan's *oprichnina* and wars that had adversely affected the economic well-being of Muscovy, the court and country were less prepared to cope with the mounting crisis when the Muscovite line faced oblivion than they had been to meet the less serious situation in 1533, when a toddler had taken the throne.

FOREIGN POLICY

Despite the delicacy of the balance upon which they rested, Muscovy's domestic institutions, especially its the court and administrative apparatus, had served the interests of the dynasty and the state. The strength of those institutions enabled Muscovy to survive the turmoil of Ivan's minority years as well as his radical administrative experiments and cruel methods and to remain an internally cohesive polity. They also were the instruments of the realm's continuing expansion.

Muscovy's most impressive growth during the reign of Ivan the Terrible occurred on its eastern and southeastern frontiers at the expense of the Tatar Khanates of Kazan', Astrakhan', and Sibir'. But its conquests brought new and costly challenges. In addition, Ivan IV engaged Muscovy in a lengthy war against its western neighbors. The Livonian War, which dragged on from 1558 to 1582–83, had devastating effects on the Muscovite realm.

The conquests of Kazan' and Astrakhan'

When Vasily III died, Muscovy was still committed to the terms of the uneasy truce that he had established with the Tatar Khanates of Kazan' and Crimea over a decade earlier. According to that compromise, Safa-Girey, a member of the Crimean dynasty, ruled the Khanate of Kazan' and respected the interests and influence of both the Muscovite grand prince and his fellow dynasts in the Crimean Khanate. Although Safa-Girey's reign was troubled, he had the support of his uncle, Sahib-Girey, khan of the Crimean Khanate, who regarded Kazan' as part of his dynasty's realm. The Muscovite government during the years of Ivan's minority had little appetite to intervene in Kazan' affairs to aid its clients or ability to formulate and implement a new policy toward Kazan'. Muscovy thus also accepted Safa-Girey, who with two interruptions (1532–35 and 1546) held the throne in Kazan' until his death in 1549, and the status quo in Kazan'.

After Ivan IV assumed the throne, however, Muscovy's policy became more active and aggressive. In the autumn of 1547, the newly proclaimed tsar of all Rus' mounted an unsuccessful campaign against Kazan'. Not long afterward, in 1549, the death of Safa-Girey spawned additional political instability in Kazan' and renewed opportunity for Muscovite intervention. Internal support for Safa-Girey's two-year-old son was weak, and the pro-Girey faction appealed to the Crimean khan for a successor. Muscovy took advantage of the situation to launch another military campaign against Kazan' (1549–50). Although it failed to resolve the political crisis, it did prompt another faction from Kazan' to enter into negotiations with Ivan IV. That faction's representatives agreed once again to accept Shah Ali, Muscovy's candidate for the throne of Kazan'.

The agreement that made Shah Ali khan of Kazan' in August 1551 called upon Kazan' to cede territory along with its tribute-paying populations and economic resources to Muscovy. Muscovite troops also accompanied the new khan into Kazan'. Shah Ali, however, quarreled with factions within Kazan' as well as with his Muscovite protectors, and was compelled to abandon his position in March 1552. In his place Ivan IV attempted to seat not another Tatar khan, but a Muscovite governor. The plan aroused opposition from the Kazan' Tatars, their Nogai allies, and the tribes of the newly annexed frontier territories. Most significant, however, was the objection from the Crimean Khanate, which sent a force against Muscovy.

Muscovite forces, however, promptly defeated the Crimean Tatars. They were then able to advance, virtually unhindered, toward Kazan'. Having gathered their forces at Sviiazhsk, a Muscovite fortress constructed in 1550 near the Kazan' border, the Muscovites proceeded into the khanate's territory; on August 23, 1552, they laid siege to the fortified city. The Muscovites' 150,000 troops vastly outnumbered the 30,000 Tatars. They assaulted the city's wooden walls with their 150 pieces of artillery, bombarded its main gate with an eighteen-foot-high siege machine, and blew up its water supply with explosives set in underground tunnels. On October 2, 1552, Kazan' fell.

Muscovite troops sacked the city, and Muscovy annexed the Khanate of Kazan'. But it took another four years before Muscovy overcame the sustained resistance and subdued the Kazan' lands, which nevertheless continued to mount uprisings for decades afterwards. Muscovite efforts to pacify the khanate involved evicting the Muslim population from the city of Kazan' and from the most economically and strategically advantageous locations of the countryside. The Tatars were replaced by Russian colonists, their mosques by Orthodox churches. The city of Kazan' was transformed into a Russian Christian center, and pressures were imposed on the Tatar population to convert to Christianity. As Muscovy

consolidated its control over Kazan', the khan of Sibir', Ediger, agreed to
pay tribute to the Muscovite tsar (1555), and the Great Nogai Horde
similarly recognized his dominance in the region. In 1556, Muscovy also
conquered and annexed the Khanate of Astrakhan', located at the base of
the Volga River.

Muscovy's victories over the Volga khanates reflected the success of
previous achievements, not least of which was the creation of both a
strong and effective army and an administrative apparatus that mobilized
and organized it. By the time of the Volga campaigns the Muscovite army
consisted of a variety of different types of units. In addition to the *pomest'e*-
based cavalry and service Tatars, there were also units specially equipped
and trained in the use of firearms. Such units of arquebusiers (*pishchal'niki*)
had been used in Muscovite campaigns earlier in the sixteenth century,
but had not become a permanent element in the army. Then in 1550,
Ivan's government created six companies of *strel'tsy* or musketeers. These
units differed from the main body of the army. They were standing units
of foot soldiers, and with them the army was able to direct concentrated
firepower at its foes. Their units were commanded by officers, who were
privileged in relation to the rank-and-file musketeers, but were not drawn
from the Muscovite elite and were immune from the debilitating
mestnichestvo quarrels that plagued the cavalry regiments. Also unlike
cavalrymen, the *strel'tsy* were supported primarily with fixed salaries,
derived from a special tax.

The army also contained units of Cossacks. Cossacks were members of
communities that had formed in the steppe, usually along its main waterways but in sectors located beyond the authority of any of the established
states in the neighborhood, i.e., Muscovy, Poland, the Crimean Khanate,
and the Ottoman Empire. Individuals from all those states, seeking
personal freedom, adventure, or relief from burdens such as debt, famine,
onerous taxes, and service obligations, were attracted to Cossack bands
that were generally self-governing under the leadership of elected
atamans. The Cossacks supported themselves by fishing in the rivers, by
brigandage and piracy, and also by selling their military services to the
states surrounding them and becoming border guards, scouts and guides,
and auxiliary cavalrymen for them. By the middle of the sixteenth
century some Cossack bands had entered Muscovite military service on a
permanent basis; as compensation they received land, salaries, supplies,
and tax exemptions from the government. Other "free" Cossacks, mainly
from the Don and Volga regions, while remaining unattached to
Muscovy, made themselves available for temporary duty in exchange for
wages, food and vodka, and other supplies.

Muscovy's Volga conquests also had profound effects. The policy of

Ivan IV had, in imitation of his father's design, initially aimed at establishing stability on the steppe by fashioning an alliance with the Khanates
of Kazan' and Astrakhan'. But it resulted in their subordination. For
Muscovy the annexation of the Tatar khanates meant the addition of vast
territories, the incorporation of major market centers, and the claim to
possession of the entire length of the Volga River. In addition, the
subjugation of the Muslim khanates transformed Muscovy into an empire
and fundamentally altered the balance of power on the steppe.

The incorporation of the Volga khanates also offered Muscovy
opportunities for additional expansion. The conquest of Kazan' initiated a
process that resulted in the annexation of all of Siberia. After Kazan's
subordination, its tributaries recognized Muscovite suzerainty, and the
khan of Sibir' joined them in paying an annual tribute to Moscow.
Although the Muscovite government was cautious about directly
exploiting its new acquisitions, it allowed private entrepreneurial families
to utilize their resources and their access to the routes previously blocked
by Kazan' across the Ural Mountains to Siberia. The Stroganov family, in
particular, having received privileges to do so from the tsar, claimed tracts
of land on the frontier, founded an array of economic enterprises on them,
and established settlements of colonists to work in them and forts manned
by *strel'tsy* and artillerymen to defend them. Their activities, which
steadily encroached upon the lands of tribes subject to the Khanate of
Sibir', provoked border raids and skirmishes. Kuchum, who had become
the Sibir' khan in 1563, discontinued his tribute payments to Muscovy
after 1571. Just over a decade later, in 1582, a Cossack named Ermak
Timofeevich, employed by the Stroganovs, led 540 men armed with
cannon and muskets in an expedition eastward across the Urals,
encountered Kuchum, defeated him in battle, and occupied his capital on
the Irtysh River. Although he was killed in a subsequent encounter with
the Tatars (1585) and the surviving Cossacks of his band, numbering less
than 100, retreated back to Muscovite territory, Ermak had in the
meantime sent word of his victory to Moscow. The tsar despatched troops
to complete the process Ermak had initiated. Although almost all the
members of the first detachments to arrive in 1584 perished from the cold
and lack of supplies, their reinforcements ultimately consolidated and
extended Muscovite control over its newest possession, Siberia.

The annexation of Astrakhan' similarly enabled Muscovy to extend its
influence into the northern Caucasus. After the conquest, the Muscovites
built a fortress ten miles south of the old city of Astrakhan' on an island in
the river. They used their outpost and control over the mouth of the
Volga to penetrate the northern Caucasus. In 1557–58, the Circassians of
Kabarda placed themselves under Muscovite protection, and in 1561,

Ivan, whose first wife Anastasiia had died the year before, married the daughter of their ruler. In 1563, Muscovy constructed a fortress in Kabarda, and in 1567 built another, equipped with cannon, on the Terek River in the Caucasus.

But the conquests and subsequent efforts to consolidate and extend Muscovy's position along the Volga solidified its rivalry with the Crimean Khanate and provoked, for the first time, conflict with the khanate's suzerain, the Ottoman Empire. The motives, interests, and objectives of the Turks and Tatars were not identical. But they shared a desire to expel the tsar of Muscovy from the Volga.

Rather than resolve the competition between Muscovy and the Crimean Khanate for dominance in Kazan', Muscovy's victory in 1552 reignited the animosity of its southern neighbor. Devlet-Girey, who had become khan of the Crimean Tatars in 1551, refused to recognize Muscovite sovereignty over the Muslim khanate, which he too regarded as a possession of the Girey dynasty. The Crimean Khanate's policy of compromise, which had moderated its expressions of hostility toward Muscovy over Kazan', was transformed into rigid unyielding animosity. After failing to prevent the Muscovite campaign that crushed Kazan', the Crimean Tatars appealed to the Turks for aid in liberating their Muslim brethren from infidel, i.e., Orthodox, rule. But Suleiman the Magnificent, who was preoccupied with the expansion of his own empire into the eastern Mediterranean and central Europe, was indifferent to the appeals of the Crimean Tatars. Consequently, after the Livonian War began in 1558, the Crimean Tatars cooperated with the Polish-Lithuanian forces against Muscovy. The persistent pressure from the Crimean Khanate obliged the Muscovites to reinforce and extend their line of defensive fortresses that protected their southern frontier. It also encouraged resistance to Muscovite domination within Kazan'. As a result, the process of consolidating Muscovite rule in Kazan' was lengthier and costlier than anticipated. The need to deploy economic resources and military personnel to Kazan' and the southern defense line furthermore inhibited the success of other foreign policy initiatives.

The repercussions of Muscovy's annexation of the Volga khanates on its relations with the Ottoman Empire became apparent only after 1567, after Selim II succeeded Suleiman (1566) and Muscovy established its stronghold in the Caucasus (1567). The Ottoman Turks' priorities and motives differed from those of the Crimean Tatars. To the latter Muscovy's conquest of the Volga khanates and intrusion into northern Caucasus had appeared as a claim to be the exclusive heir to the Golden Horde khans and had aroused their sharp protest. The Ottoman Turks, however, had not shared the Crimean khan's perspective or attitude toward Muscovy. Rather, they valued their commercial relations with Moscow, and for fifteen years after the fall of Kazan' perceived no direct conflict of interest with it.

The Ottoman Turks changed their policy in response to the consolidation of Muscovy's control in Astrakhan' and its subsequent penetration into the northern Caucasus. Ottoman concern arose from the strategic value of those regions. In addition to its western campaigns, the Ottoman Empire had been engaged in hostilities against its eastern neighbor, the Safavid Empire in Iran (Persia). In the course of its wars it had acquired Baghdad, controlled Azerbaijan, and extended its authority to the western shore of the Caspian Sea. It was particularly the construction of the Muscovite fortress on the Terek, which commanded one of the main passes across the mountains, that attracted Selim's attention. With that action in 1567, Muscovy was encroaching directly on the interests of the Ottoman Turks in the Caucasus, and implicitly threatening their position in that region.

The conduct of the Muscovites at Astrakhan' was also attracting Ottoman attention. The wars between the Ottoman Empire and the Safavid Empire in Iran were disrupting security along the route between Central Asia and the Middle East that had passed through Persian territory south of the Caspian Sea. Central Asian Muslims, traveling westward for commercial purposes, to support Ottoman military forces, or on religious pilgrimages to Mecca opted to use the more northerly route that passed north of the Caspian Sea through Astrakhan' to Azak (Azov, Tana). But reports began to reach the Ottoman officials that the Muscovites were interfering with their passage, and the Ottomans' allies in Central Asia were appealing to them to apply pressure on Muscovy to open the route.

The Ottomans responded in 1569 by undertaking their first aggressive action against Muscovy. Their elaborately designed plan called for an Ottoman force to proceed from Azak up the Don River, build a canal connecting the Don and the Volga Rivers, and then descend the Volga to capture Astrakhan'. Despite the complex planning and provisioning, the Turks were unable to dig their canal. The terrain also impeded them from hauling their ships and cannon from the Don to the Volga. They therefore sent most of their heavy equipment in their ships back to Azak and approached Astrakhan' by land with only light weapons. Without their ships, however, the Turks were unable to reach the island fortress; without their cannon they could not bombard it. Short of provisions and ill-prepared to spend the winter in the vicinity of Astrakhan', the Turks withdrew in late September, just a few weeks after their arrival.

Militarily, the Turkish campaign against Astrakhan' was a failure, and in subsequent negotiations the Turks were silent about a Muscovite retreat from the lower Volga. But they did insist that the Russians open the route through Astrakhan' to Muslim merchants and pilgrims from Central Asia and that they destroy their fort on the Terek River. The Muscovites agreed. The Astrakhan' campaign thus contributed to the achievement of the Ottoman Turks' basic goals.

In contrast, the Crimean Tatars, who were preoccupied with Kazan', remained dissatisfied. Two years after the Turkish expedition, Devlet-Girey mounted a major offensive against Moscow. Setting out in the spring of 1571, his army rode northward and penetrated the Muscovite defenses along the Oka River. On May 24, the Tatars appeared before Moscow. During their attack several fires broke out in the city, which was soon engulfed in a general conflagration. The fire set off explosions of stored gunpowder. It destroyed the church bells ringing warnings to the populace. Ivan IV escaped to Rostov. But thousands of the city's inhabitants, whose numbers had been swollen by refugees who had fled from unprotected neighboring villages to the safety of the city, were trampled, suffocated, or burned to death as terrified crowds poured into the narrow streets, where they were trapped.

In the aftermath of the unexpected devastation of Moscow Devlet-Girey demanded that Ivan IV cede the Khanates of both Kazan' and Astrakhan'. The Ottoman Turks, who had not been party to the Tatar campaign but had received a description of its results from Devlet-Girey, sent a message to Ivan IV in October 1571, in which they similarly demanded that Moscow transfer Kazan' to the Crimean khan and Astrakhan' to the Ottoman sultan. During the negotiations that followed, the Muscovites seriously considered withdrawing from Astrakhan'. But before the negotiations reached a conclusion Devlet-Girey launched another attack on Muscovy. This campaign in 1572, however, ended in victory for the Muscovites. Although the dream of recovering the Volga khanates did not die and the Crimean Tatars would continue to harass Muscovy's southern frontier, neither the Tatars nor the Turks mounted any further offensives specifically directed toward that goal during the reign of Ivan IV the Terrible.

The Livonian War

The Crimean Tatar campaigns against Muscovy in 1571 and 1572 occurred while Muscovy was in the midst of another major engagement, the Livonian War. That war had been initiated by Muscovy in January 1558, and was conducted on its northwestern frontier. It came to an unsuccessful conclusion in 1582–83.

Muscovy's objective in the Livonian War was to acquire the lands west of Pskov. Those territories would have provided Muscovy with control over the Livonian commercial ports and towns that mediated its trade with northern Europe. The acquisition of Livonia, following that of Kazan' and Astrakhan', would also have given Muscovy possession of the entire route connecting the Baltic Sea with the Caspian. Livonia also contained fertile agricultural lands, which were valuable not only for their productive capacity but as supplements to the diminishing pool of land reserves the government used to provide *pomest'ia* to its growing number of military servicemen.[11]

Livonia appeared to be an easy target after the formidable Khanate of Kazan'. The region itself was politically divided among the Livonian Order, bishoprics, and autonomous towns. The Livonian knights, influenced by Lutheranism, were, furthermore, estranged from the Catholic bishops. But almost as soon as the Muscovites demonstrated their intentions by launching twin campaigns in January 1558, and seizing both Dorpat (Tartu) and Narva, other Baltic powers intervened to block Muscovy's expansion and to obtain portions of Livonia for themselves. The war was consequently transformed from a frontier campaign of local dimensions into a regional war, in which Muscovy, Poland–Lithuania, Sweden, and Denmark all participated. The Crimean Tatars, furthermore, disappointed with the Ottoman Turks' reluctance to assist them in liberating Kazan', supported Poland–Lithuania against Muscovy. As a result, when Muscovy launched the Livonian War, it not only provoked hostilities from its European neighbors, but had to face simultaneously the vengeful Crimean Tatars on its southern border.

After its initial victories, Muscovy concluded a six–month truce with its Livonian opponents. During that period Poland became involved by extending its protection over the Order and the bishop of Riga. Denmark, which seized a major island off the Livonian coast, also entered the competition for dominance in the eastern Baltic. And then, when Muscovy launched another offensive in 1560, defeated the Order's army, and established control over central Livonia, the northern towns of Livonia placed themselves under Swedish rule.

As Livonia was carved up among the Baltic powers, Muscovy broadened the range of the war. Forming an alliance with Denmark and concluding a truce with Sweden, it concentrated on Poland–Lithuania and in 1563, captured Polotsk. Although the offensive against Poland–

[11] Ruslan G. Skrynnikov, "The Civil War in Russia at the Beginning of the Seventeenth Century (1603–1607): Its Character and Motive Forces," in *New Perspectives on Muscovite History*, ed. by Lindsey Hughes (London: Macmillan and New York, St. Martin's Press, 1993), p. 72.

Lithuania was halted the next year, Ivan IV rejected the subsequent peace offer extended by Poland-Lithuania. To affirm his position he summoned representatives from various social strata, all drawn from the *zemshchina*, for consultation in 1566. Those attending that *zemskii sobor* expressed a commitment, including pledges of financial support, to a continuation of the war.

Muscovy, however, never again achieved the victories it had won in the early years of the war. In 1569, Poland and Lithuania entered the Union of Lublin. The resultant monarchy, drawing upon the resources of both components of its enlarged realm, was able to repulse Muscovy's subsequent offensives and expand its own possessions in Livonia. In 1579, Stefan Batory, elected king of Poland-Lithuania in 1574 and having completed the process of consolidating his domestic position, began a series of counter-offensives against Muscovy. He recovered Polotsk, and then in 1580 attacked Velikie Luki. The Polish and Lithuanian armies then devastated the southern portion of the Novgorod lands and threatened Pskov. Meanwhile, Swedish forces seized Muscovy's outposts along the coast of the Gulf of Finland, culminating in the capture of Narva in 1581; their advance inland toward Novgorod was halted only at the southern end of Lake Ladoga (1582).

In 1582, Muscovy agreed to a ten-year truce with Poland-Lithuania. Brokered by Antonio Possevino, a papal legate, it obliged Ivan IV to cede his remaining possessions in Livonia to his opponent. The following year Muscovy accepted a truce with Sweden, and gave up all of its coastal territories with the exception of the mouth of the Neva River; Sweden continued to occupy portions of Novgorod's northwestern lands as well.

ECONOMIC AND SOCIAL CONSEQUENCES OF IVAN'S POLICIES

When Vasily III died in 1533, he left his heir a flourishing domain. Despite the turmoil of the period of Ivan's minority, the country's economy continued to thrive through the middle of the century. The Muscovites were able to rebuild after the fire of 1547; they had the means to launch major campaigns against their neighbors; and they continued to construct new costly edifices. They included the architecturally unique Church of the Intercession of the Mother of God, more commonly known as the Church of Vasilii the Blessed or St. Basil's Cathedral, which was constructed between 1555 and 1561 outside the kremlin walls in Moscow in honor of the victory over Kazan', as well as new churches in Kazan' itself. In 1553, when English explorers and merchants discovered a sea route through the Arctic Ocean and the White Sea to northern

Russia, they observed general prosperity throughout the realm. Richard Chancellor, who left one of the earliest accounts of the English impressions of Muscovy, described an economically thriving country, well endowed with a variety of products, which could be found in abundance in numerous market towns.[12]

The main components of the Muscovite economy continued to be agriculture, followed by manufacturing and domestic and foreign trade. Engaged in the various occupations associated with these sectors, the tax-paying rural and urban populace successfully supported the political, military, and ecclesiastical elites of Muscovite society. Ivan's policies, however, had the net effect of increasing political and military costs while simultaneously reducing the ability of Muscovite society to pay them.

Expenditures began to increase as Ivan and his advisors attempted to cope with the consequences of the excesses of his minority years. To restore order and curb the abuses of power in the provinces, the tsar, as outlined above, approved alterations in the structure of provincial administration. But the consequent need to oversee the activities of *guba* and *zemskie* elders prompted the expansion of the central administrative apparatus. Similarly, to restore confidence and harmony among his courtiers, his administration had to adjudicate an increasing number of *mestnichestvo* cases. These and the other rapidly multiplying activities of the government added to the complexity of the administrative apparatus, to the size of its staff, and to its costs.

But even more than administrative expenses, Muscovy's military structure and ventures created needs for additional land, administrative capacity, and revenue. During the sixteenth century Muscovy's cavalrymen were accorded, in addition to their *pomest'ia* and the incomes derived from them, supplemental salaries. A law, issued in 1556, attempted to regularize the amounts of cash servicemen were entitled to receive. The size of their entitlements (*oklady*) depended in part on the size of their *pomest'ia*, but rank and status were also determining factors. The government similarly provided monetary support to other military units, including the *strel'tsy* and standing Cossack detachments that required regular continuous payment. Some of those units were stationed at the forts constructed, also at considerable cost, in the late 1550s and 1560s to improve the southern defense line.

---

[12] There are several published editions of Chancellor's account, including one in *Rude and Barbarous Kingdom*, ed. by Lloyd E. Berry and Robert O. Crummey (Madison, Wis.: University of Wisconsin Press, 1968); see pp. 30–33.

It was the military campaigns themselves, however, that were chiefly responsible for the increasing government expenses. The massive Kazan' campaign of 1552, which entailed 150,000 troops, including units of Cossacks and the newly formed *strel'tsy*, and 150 pieces of artillery, required large expenditures for the men and equipment as well as transportation and provisioning. Subsequent military actions required to pacify the Tatars and consolidate Muscovy's control over the khanate added to the outlay. And even as it struggled to pay for its eastern adventures, Muscovy launched the Livonian War.

Ivan's government adopted a series of measures, beginning in the middle of the century, to raise more revenue. Its main focus was on direct taxes. It continued the practice, which had been pursued during Vasily III's reign, of converting obligations, traditionally paid in labor or in kind, to cash fees. New land surveys, to be conducted virtually throughout the realm, were also authorized. The intention was to obtain an accurate inventory of existing landholdings as well as available arable land and other resources. The data were to be used as a basis for distributing *pomest'ia* as well as for determining taxes.

The surveys employed a new unit of land measurement, called the *bol'shaia sokha*, which took into account both land quality and the social category of the land's owner. By definition a *sokha* of good land was smaller in area than one consisting of poor quality land. A *sokha* of *pomest'e* land was larger in area than one of equivalent quality land possessed by the church, court, or state. The result was that although taxes were nominally assessed at a standard rate based on the *sokha*, peasants on service lands paid less in relation to the real area of land under cultivation than those dwelling elsewhere. These policies, combined with the introduction in 1535 of coins of uniform units and weight throughout the land, served to bring more cash into the treasury.

Horace Dewey concluded that the system of *kormlenie* was abolished in 1555–56 for the same purpose. He argued that although the elimination of *kormlenie* also dismantled the offices of *namestniki* and *volosteli*, which had been dependent upon *kormlenie* payments and whose roles had been gradually circumscribed, its primary purpose was fiscal. It was, he explained, "unquestionably related to the military reforms of the mid-sixteenth century and to the problems of financing the final campaigns against Kazan' and Astrakhan'," which had led to "the bankruptcy of the Moscow treasury." The abolition of *kormlenie* and the virtually simultaneous introduction of the *zemskie* reforms were responses to a fiscal crisis. The former released revenues, previously collected by the provincial governors for their own maintenance, while the latter established a mechanism of provincial administration capable of directing to the treasury "a larger share of income from all areas of the state than had been possible under the *kormlenie* system."[13]

In another initiative the central authorities issued a decree in 1551 that called for the confiscation of all lands that had been transferred from secular landowners to ecclesiastic and monastic institutions by authorization of the duma during the years of Ivan's minority; they also regulated future transfers. The Stoglav council in 1551 correspondingly agreed that future land acquisitions, whether purchased or received as gifts by the Church, would be made only with the consent of the tsar. The return of Church lands to secular ownership was accompanied by a review and reduction of tax exemptions enjoyed by monasteries. Later, in 1572 and 1580, monasteries were forbidden to accept gifts of land. These policies, too, placed more lands and their peasant inhabitants on the state's tax rolls.

All of these factors and the introduction of new fees resulted in both an increased tax burden on the peasantry and tax-paying urban population and an increased income for the state. The amount collected in taxes from the peasantry rose dramatically during the sixteenth century. According to calculations made by Marc Zlotnik, peasants had been paying at a rate of just over 3 rubles per *bol'shaia sokha* at the beginning of Vasily III's reign. By 1533, their total tax bill amounted to just over 9.5 rubles per *bol'shaia sokha*; by 1550, it was closer to 13 rubles, and by 1561, almost 22. Portions of the apparent increase in the tax rate were due to the monetarization of fees and to inflation. But the state's revenues increased correspondingly. G. V. Abramovich, using figures from the Novgorod region, calculated that its share of the state's income rose from 1,725 rubles at the beginning of the century to 3,150 rubles during Ivan's minority, and under the impact of these policies leaped to 13,000 rubles by the mid-1560s.[14]

In addition to its tax policies, Ivan's administration used foreign policy to improve its commercial capacity and its economic situation. Muscovy's conquests of Kazan' and Astrakhan' gave it possession of the markets in those lands and the full length of the Volga River. From its new vantage point on the mid-Volga Muscovy reaped the benefits from Kazan's established trade, which after brief disruptions following the annexation

13 Horace W. Dewey, "The Decline of the Muscovite *Namestnik*," *Oxford Slavonic Papers*, vol. 12 (1965), pp. 37–38, and "The 1550 Sudebnik as an Instrument of Reform," *JbfGO*, vol. 10 (1962), p. 175.

14 Marc Zlotnik, "Muscovite Fiscal Policy," *RH*, vol. 6 (1979), p. 253; G. V. Abramovich, "Gosudarstvennye povinnosti vladel'cheskikh krest'ian severo-zapadnoi Rusi v XVI–pervoi chetverti XVII veka," [State obligations of possessional peasants of north-western Rus' in the XVI and first quarter of the XVII centuries], "*Istoriia SSSR*, no. 3 (1972), p. 81.

of the khanate, continued in its customary manner; it also improved its direct commercial contacts with the Nogai, from whom it purchased horses. Muscovy's income also increased as it collected tribute from the Khanate of Sibir' and small Siberian tribes.

From Astrakhan' Muscovy was able to trade more regularly at Shemiakha, a major market center located on the west coast of the Caspian Sea, which was noted for its silk, and with the Central Asian khanates. It also developed commercial ties, although of dubious quality, with Persia. Richard Cheinie, an English merchant who followed Russian merchants there, advised the directors of his Muscovy Company to send neither "riotous livers, nor drunkards" to conduct their business in Persia; such "vicious living" habits, as one of their number had displayed, he cautioned, might convince the Persians that the English were even "worse than the Russes."[15]

Commercial interests influenced Muscovite policy in Livonia as well. Northern European trade with Muscovy was dominated by the Hansa merchants of Riga and Revel'. Russians had tried to foster direct trade by attracting merchants to Narva, which was not a member of the Hanseatic League and was situated on the Narova River opposite the Russian outpost of Ivangorod. In 1557, Ivan IV encouraged the merchants of Narva to transfer their activities across the river to Ivangorod. Their reluctance contributed to the decision to initiate the military offensive against Livonia the following year. One of the first targets of the Livonian War was Narva. When the Muscovites subsequently failed to capture Riga and Revel', Narva became their chief port in the region.

Its victories during the 1550s thus gave Muscovy control over the route from the Baltic to the Caspian and economic assets that were potentially valuable enough to offset the costs of the wars fought to obtain them, the administrative apparatus required to govern them, and also generally to increase the wealth of the realm.

The English, having discovered their northern route to Muscovy in 1553, were interested in these assets. In 1555, Ivan IV granted the English the privilege of trading throughout his realm without paying the standard customs fees. They valued particularly Muscovy's timber, rope fibers, tallow, and tar, which were all useful for ship construction, as well as its fur and other northern goods. They were also attracted, not unlike the Varangians centuries earlier, by the possibility of opening a route through Muscovy down the Volga to the Caspian Sea and the legendary wealth of Central Asia and Persia. In 1558, Anthony Jenkinson, representing the

---

[15] Richard Cheinie in *The Principal Navigations Voyages Traffiques and Discoveries of the English Nation*, by Richard Hakluyt (London: Macmillan, 1903), vol. 3, p. 43.

Muscovy Company, made his way through Muscovy to Bukhara in Central Asia.

The English found the commercial prospects in Central Asia disappointing. But they did make more trips down the Volga to reach Persia and continued to conduct northern sea voyages, exploring Siberian rivers in search of alternative routes to the Orient. They were also quick to take advantage of Muscovy's capture of Narva, where merchants from throughout the Baltic region congregated. Despite the ongoing war and the German emperor's calls for an embargo on the sale of all militarily useful goods to Muscovy, English, Dutch, and German ships increasingly sailed to Narva, making it one of the busiest and most lucrative ports in the eastern Baltic. The fees generated by its commerce contributed to Muscovy's revenues until the town fell to the Swedes in 1581.

While cultivating eastern trade through its Volga markets and western trade through Narva, Muscovy continued to engage in trade with the Ottoman Empire, which until 1568, just before its expedition against Astrakhan', regularly sent its caravans northward to Muscovy to purchase fur pelts and other northern luxury goods. The assault on Astrakhan' did not interrupt diplomatic communication between the Muscovite and Ottoman courts, and by 1578, normal commercial relations were restored as well. In a single trading venture the Ottomans were known to spend as much as 8,000 rubles' worth of silver and gold. Such a sum, given declining revenues from domestic sources which will be discussed below, constituted a significant amount for the Muscovite treasury and made the Ottoman Turks a highly valued trading partner.

Increased revenues from direct taxation and expanded commercial activity paid for some of the civil and military expenses. But they did not meet all the fiscal needs of the state, especially those generated by the army and its activities. In accordance with the *pomest'e* system, which had been introduced by Ivan IV's grandfather, military servicemen were expected to report for duty fully equipped and prepared for battle. The incomes from their *pomest'ia* were to provide them with the means to obtain their horses, arms, armor, and other equipment.

As the *pomest'e* system developed during the first half of the sixteenth century, it became customary to grant estates to the sons of *pomeshchiki* when the youths enrolled in service at the age of fifteen. Each son's *pomest'e* was typically equal in size to his father's allotment. As the number of servicemen grew, however, it became more difficult for the state to provide *pomest'ia* of sufficient size to all of them. The *pomest'e* system and the effectiveness of the main body of the army, which was dependent upon it, required a reservoir of good agricultural land, populated by peasants. Without such land reserves military servicemen would eventually receive smaller *pomest'ia*; that alternative, however, promised to reduce both the incomes of the servicemen and the effectiveness of the army.

Ivan's government approached the dilemma from several angles. In 1556, it issued the decree on service (*ulozhenie o sluzhbe*), which in addition to designating salary levels for servicemen, specified that for every unit of approximately 400 acres of good land, a landholder was expected to provide one military serviceman with one horse and full armor or with two horses for a distant campaign. The decree applied to *pomeshchiki* as well as secular owners of patrimonial estates (*votchiny*). For providing additional men the landholders received monetary compensation. But failure to supply the required number of men or a cash substitute could mean a fine and/or confiscation of landed property. Using this approach the government attempted to standardize the relationship between landholding and military service requirements.

Ivan IV also relocated some servicemen. In 1550, he ordered over 1,000 provincial servicemen to be granted *pomest'ia* in the immediate vicinity of Moscow. The measure, which A. A. Zimin concluded was never fully implemented, is generally analyzed in political rather than military terms. Zimin regarded the plan as part of a design to favor the provincial servicemen or *dvoriane* at the expense of the boyar clans. Gustave Alef, following Zimin, interpreted it as an attempt to undermine "the influence of the entrenched elite families." John Keep, disagreeing with them, argued that rather than being a "matter of undermining the boyars as a group," the transfer was intended to halt the "grave abuses" that had characterized the period of Ivan's minority by "infusing new blood, mostly from the provinces," into the Muscovite service groups.[16]

New land surveys, proposed in anticipation of Ivan IV's *ulozhenie o sluzhbe*, and his efforts to recover lands that had been transferred to ecclesiastical institutions also served the goal of enlarging the pool of land available for distribution as *pomest'ia*. But the most dramatic means of acquiring lands for the military servicemen was territorial expansion of the realm, a result of war. R. G. Skrynnikov argued that Muscovy's foreign policies were designed for territorial expansion, precisely to satisfy the land requirements of the growing number of military servicemen.[17] Whether or not it was the primary goal of his aggression against Muscovy's neighbors, Ivan IV assigned territories he conquered in

---

[16] Zimin, *Reformy Ivana Groznogo*, pp. 366–371; Gustave Alef, "Bel'skies and Shuiskiis in the XVI Century," *FOG*, vol. 38 (1986), p. 235; John L. H. Keep, *Soldiers of the Tsar: Army and Society in Russia 1462–1874* (Oxford: Clarendon Press, 1985), p. 29.

[17] Skrynnikov, "The Civil War in Russia," p. 72.

Livonia to *pomeshchiki* and, as will be discussed below, issued estates in the Kazan' area, although under somewhat harsher conditions, as well.

But as Ivan's government pursued policies that expanded both Muscovy's territory and its revenue base, the *oprichnina* and the unforeseen duration and ultimate failure of the Livonian War were having counterproductive effects. They contributed to a decline in the agricultural economy of Muscovy and to a related deterioration of the *pomest'e*-based army. They thus resulted in a depletion rather than an enhancement of Muscovy's economic resources. It was consequently from a reduced economic base that the society was called upon to pay the ever-rising costs of Ivan IV the Terrible's policies.

Some aspects of the *oprichnina*, notably the deaths it caused and the political disturbances it created, were discussed above. It also severely affected the economy. When he established his *oprichnina*, Ivan IV designated some regions and towns as its possessions; he later added other districts to them. These districts were scattered throughout the realm. They included sections of the north, notably the Dvina land, portions of the Novgorod lands, and parts of the northeastern core of Muscovy. *Pomeshchiki* and landowners who were not associated with the *oprichnina* were forcibly evicted from their estates in those regions and relocated on *zemshchina* lands. Their estates were redistributed to *oprichniki*. But virtually no restraints were imposed on the new landlords. Some members of the *oprichnina* corps asserted that when granted estates, the *oprichniki* took virtually all that the peasants possessed, forcing them to pay "in one year as much as [they] used to pay in ten . . ."[18] Peasants fled from increased rents and physical abuse; their land was left uncultivated. Thus, although survivors or relatives of the evicted servicemen recovered some of their lands after the *oprichnina* was disbanded, their estates had frequently been ruined by the *oprichniki* who, exercising unprecedented authority over the peasants who worked them, had made excessive demands and provoked their flight.

Disruptions also occurred in the *zemshchina* territory. Records indicate, for example, that a large productive fishing village in the far north was almost completely deserted when in 1568, *oprichniki* whose demand for an extra tax payment was not satisfied physically attacked it. The tsar also confiscated estates in the *zemshchina* sector and removed their owners. One notable example, which was studied by R. G. Skrynnikov, occurred shortly after the *oprichnina* was founded in 1565. In addition to executing prominent members of the elite, Ivan IV ordered hundreds of princely

---

[18] As reported by Jerome Blum, *Lord and Peasant in Russia* (Princeton, N.J.: Princeton University Press, 1961; republished, New York: Atheneum, 1965), p. 156.

servitors, including over 100 princes from the distinguished dynastic branches of Suzdal', Iaroslavl', Rostov, and Starodub, from their ancestral lands and sent them into exile in the recently conquered lands of Kazan'. The estates they received in the Kazan' area were much smaller than those they had lost. And although they were pardoned and some were allowed to return to their native districts a year later, just as Ivan was attempting to muster support from the *zemshchina* for the continuation of the Livonian War, they did not recover all their property. Much of what was returned was economically ruined.[19]

Towns suffered as well. In 1569, the tsar evicted hundreds of families from Novgorod and Pskov. Then early the next year, he ordered the sack of Novgorod. The episode was evidently triggered by an event associated with the Livonian War. In October 1569, two traitors tricked the guards at the fortress of Izborsk, near Pskov, into opening the gates, enabling the Lithuanians to occupy it. Although Ivan recovered Izborsk, his conviction that treason was widespread prompted him to take action against his cousin Vladimir Andreevich and also unleash his *oprichniki* on Novgorod, where some of Prince Vladimir's supporters and retainers dwelled.

But the attack on Novgorod, which R. G. Skrynnikov characterized as the most abominable of all the *oprichnina's* bloody deeds,[20] was conducted on a scale grander than a simple elimination of the retainers of the tsar's cousin. It began with plunder of Tver', which the *oprichniki* passed through as they approached Novgorod. When they reached the outskirts of Novgorod, they were met by Archbishop Pimen, who led a traditional procession to greet the tsar. But Ivan refused the archbishop's blessing, and accused Pimen and all of Novgorod of conspiring to turn the city over to the king of Poland-Lithuania. He arrested the archbishop, and then organized judicial proceedings, during which witnesses were interrogated under torture and the accused, totaling hundreds of Novgorodian servicemen and administrative officials, some of them highly placed and associated with Moscow's elite families, were tried,

[19] Skrynnikov, *Ivan the Terrible*, pp. 93–94, and "Obzor pravleniia Ivana IV," [A review of the government of Ivan IV], *RH*, vol. 14 (1987), pp. 369–371. Skrynnikov's analysis of this episode, which led him to conclude that the *oprichnina* was originally intended to destroy the power of princely clans by subverting their land-based wealth and influence, has been disputed. See, for example, V. B. Kobrin, who argued the incident was neither as massive nor as significant as portrayed by Skrynnikov. V. B. Kobrin, *Vlast' i sobstvennost' v srednevekovoi Rossii (XV–XVI vv.)* [Power and property in medieval Russia (XV–XVI centuries)] (Moscow: Mysl', 1985), pp. 150–154.

[20] Skrynnikov, "Oprichnyi razgrom Novgoroda," [The *oprichnina's* sack of Novgorod] in *Krest'ianstvo i klassovaia bor'ba v feodal'noi Rossii. Sbornik statei pamiati Ivana Ivanovicha Smirnova* [The peasantry and the class struggle in feudal Russia. A collection of articles in memory of Ivan Ivanovich Smirnov] (Leningrad: Nauka, 1967), p. 168.

convicted, and executed. The *oprichniki* also plundered St. Sophia, Novgorod's countryside, especially the estates belonging to the city's monasteries, and the marketplace of the city itself. The six-week-long campaign resulted in the transfer of the wealth of the archbishopric, the Novgorodian monasteries, and the city's artisans and traders to the treasury of the *oprichnina*. But those gains for the *oprichnina* were achieved at the cost not only of the almost 400 lives of the alleged traitors and their families, but of additional hundreds who, driven from their homes in the city and the surrounding villages, subsequently died from cold, hunger, and disease. When the *oprichniki* completed their task in Novgorod, they proceeded to Pskov, where in a somewhat modified fashion they repeated their efforts. In the wake of the Novgorodian rampage, the *oprichnina* turned its punitive forces on its own leaders, most significantly the boyar A. D. Basmanov, who were executed.

Moscow was also affected by the *oprichnina*. Having failed to halt the advance of Devlet-Girey during the Livonian War (1571), the *oprichniki* bore some of the responsibility for allowing the Crimean Tatars to ravage the countryside, take numerous prisoners, and to mount the attack that left Moscow in flames.

The Livonian War exacerbated the social and economic suffering caused by the *oprichnina* in other ways as well. The initial Muscovite victories in Livonia had eased the pressure on Muscovy's land pool by providing Livonian territory for *pomest'e* distribution. But by the end of the war the *pomeshchiki*, who had been given estates in the conquered lands, had to be withdrawn. The final campaigns of the war, furthermore, brought the armies of Stefan Batory across the border into Muscovy. They destroyed vast areas south of Novgorod and near Pskov; the Swedes meanwhile occupied districts north of Novgorod. The war took a terrible toll, militarily and economically, on the Russian lands. In its wake villages were deserted and fields lay untilled. Even when the central authorities granted vacated *pomest'ia* to servicemen, including those transferred from Livonia, there were extremely few peasants available to farm them.

The cumulative effect of these catastrophes was an economic crisis. In contrast to Richard Chancellor's observations thirty-five years earlier, Giles Fletcher, who visited Muscovy in 1588, found a land "with vacant and desolate" villages, abandoned workshops, limited production, and a population prone to "much . . . idleness and drinking."[21] Although some areas that received the fleeing populations demonstrated signs of growth, Fletcher's description accurately described much of Muscovy. It has been

---

[21] *Rude and Barbarous Kingdom*, pp. 125, 170.

estimated that 84 per cent of the arable land in the Moscow district and as much as 90 per cent in the Novgorod lands lay waste.[22] As a result of the consequent low levels of production, food was scarce and prices were high. The labor shortage prompted the government in 1581 to declare a "forbidden year," thus denying peasants their right, guaranteed in the law codes of 1497 and 1550, to relocate their residences during the St. George's period.

The Livonian War had additional negative consequences. The *pomest'e* system, coupled with the development of bureaucratic machinery that made appointments and kept records, had successfully provided a means of maintaining an army that would follow the command of the grand prince and could bring about the territorial expansion that had characterized Muscovite development through the middle of the sixteenth century. But the *pomest'e* system was geared to support military servicemen, who appeared for duty during the annual campaign season, often simply to guard the frontier from possible raids by the Tatars, but who then spent the remainder of their time managing the estates that supplied their horses and the incomes necessary to obtain their weapons, armor, and other equipment.

The lengthy Livonian War conducted by Ivan IV obliged military servicemen to be actively engaged in warfare for prolonged periods. It furthermore provoked the invasions by Tatar, Polish–Lithuanian, and Swedish troops, who overran and ruined their *pomest'ia*, drove their peasants from their villages, took them prisoner, or killed them. Muscovite military servicemen lost their means of support. Consequently, fewer responded when ordered to appear for a campaign. According to figures presented by R. G. Skrynnikov, over 18,000 *pomeshchiki* participated in the campaigns of 1563; their numbers dropped to just under 12,000 in 1572, and 10,500 in 1579.[23] The steady decline in the

---

22 V. I. Koretskii, "Khoziaistvennoe razorenie russkoi derevni vo vtoroi polovine XVI v. i pravitel'stvennaia politika," [Economic destruction of the Russian village in the second half of the sixteenth century and government policy] *Ezhegodnik po agrarnoi istorii vostochnoi Evropy 1965 g.* (Moscow: Moskovskii gosudarstvennyi universitet, 1970), p. 62. Although some scholars consider these figures too high, their revised estimates nevertheless suggest as much as half the arable land was deserted. See, e.g., R. E. F. Smith, *Peasant Farming in Muscovy* (Cambridge: Cambridge University Press, 1977), p. 128.

23 R. G. Skrynnikov, *Rossiia posle oprichniny* [Russia after the *oprichnina*] (Leningrad: Leningradskii universitet, 1975), p. 46; Skrynnikov cited these figures also in his article, "Obzor pravleniia Ivana IV," but identified the last number with 1577 rather than 1579; see p. 369. Other sources suggest different sets of figures. Devlet-Girey, for example, reported to his Ottoman suzerains that in 1571, he faced an army consisting of 30,000 cavalrymen and 6,000 musketeers. But they had to combat, according to Russian sources, 120,000 Tatar warriors. For the size of the Muscovite army, see Chantal Lemercier-

numbers of *pomeshchiki* who were both able and willing to appear for muster left a relatively small force by 1579. Yet it was with that force that Muscovy had to defend itself against offensives launched over the next several years by all three of its opponents, the Polish-Lithuanian, the Swedish, and the Crimean Tatar armies.

Skrynnikov's data support the conclusion that the combination of the *oprichnina* and the Livonian War, which wrought economic havoc on their estates, ruined many *pomeshchiki* and weakened Muscovy's military might. Muscovy, notwithstanding its annexation of Siberia at the end of Ivan IV's reign, was not able to carry out its policy of expansion to the west. The tsar and all his operatives in the political structure had to rely on existing territorial possessions both for revenue and for *pomest'ia*. But the human and economic resources on much of that territory were exhausted.

In order to raise the revenue it required, the state continued to increase taxes. Marc Zlotnik's calculations indicate that the rate of total tax fees per *bol'shaia sokha* jumped from 22 rubles in 1561 to 38.5 in 1584, the year of Ivan's death. Almost all (84 per cent) of the fees in 1584 were devoted to military expenses; the military portion had been 73 per cent in 1561 and 62 per cent in 1533–50. But even though the rate of taxation rose sharply and imposed a heavy burden on the surviving peasants who continued to farm their lands, the area of cultivated land had contracted even more dramatically. The net result was a drastic drop in state revenues. Abramovich's study concluded that the Novgorod regions that had paid 13,000 rubles a year to Moscow in the mid-1560s were able to provide 9,150 rubles in the early 1570s and 6,500 rubles in 1576. By 1583, conditions had so deteriorated that Moscow could collect only 1,110 rubles. Four years after Ivan's death, in 1588, Moscow received a mere 895 rubles from the Novgorod lands, once the wealthiest region in all the Russian lands.[24]

The reign of Ivan IV the Terrible was, in short, a disaster for Muscovy. The long, slow processes overseen by Ivan's Daniilovich ancestors – of firmly entrenching their branch of the dynasty as the sole masters over the Russian lands; of legitimizing their position and fashioning political

Quelquejay, "Les expéditions de Devlet Girây contre Moscou en 1571 et 1572," [The expeditions of Devlet-Giray against Moscow in 1571 and 1572] *CMRS*, vol. 13 (1972), pp. 555, 557; for the Tatar army, Alexandre Bennigsen, "L'expédition turque contre Astrakhan en 1569," [The Turkish expedition against Astrakhan in 1569] *CMRS*, vol. 8 (1967), p. 442.

24 Zlotnik, "Muscovite Fiscal Policy," p. 253; Abramovich, "Gosudarstvennye povinnosti," p. 81.

institutions to administer their power; of defending their domain against their competitive neighbors, expanding it, and transforming it into a prosperous, militarily powerful, centralized state that dominated the region – all came to an abrupt halt. Entrusted to his care, Ivan's dynastic line faced extinction; his subjects were impoverished, his economic resources depleted, his army weakened, and his realm militarily defeated. The political elite, influenced by the ideologies that attributed all power to a divinely selected tsar and hampered by their own dependence on him, were prepared to advise him, command his armies, and administer his policies. But neither those ideologies nor their political character allowed any other individual or institution to replace him. By the time Ivan IV the Terrible died in 1584, Muscovy, from its core, where its centralized political structures depended upon a dying dynasty, to its frontiers, where its villages stood depopulated and its fields lay fallow, was on the brink of ruin. It would not be until it had suffered and survived the additional disasters of the Time of Troubles that it would once again achieve a durable political stability, which would be built around the new Romanov dynasty.

12

CONCLUSIONS AND
CONTROVERSIES

·

Just as the princes of medieval Rus' were frequently engaged in intra-dynastic conflict, so the scholars who have studied them and the society they ruled have often become in embroiled in controversy over interpret-ations of events of the past. The preceding eleven chapters have presented one set of perspectives on the history of the states and society governed by the Riurikid princes from the reign of Prince Vladimir I the Saint (980–1015) through the reign of Ivan IV the Terrible (1533–84). Viewed from those perspectives several themes and arguments were highlighted in the narrative. This chapter will review those themes, but will also offer direction to literature containing both supporting arguments and alternate interpretations of major developments in the history of medieval Rus'.

Five major themes have been developed in the preceding chapters. The first is implied by the definition of their subjects and the time span they cover. The subject matter, the development of the states and society of the lands of Rus', was examined from the reign of Prince Vladimir, who monopolized political power in the eastern Slav lands for his dynasty, and to the death of Ivan IV, who six hundred years later sealed the end of his dynasty's rule. Inherent in these factors is the premise that it is both useful and informative to treat the eras of Kievan Rus', Mongol dominance, and Muscovy together.

Many scholars, including figures such as S. M. Solov'ev and V. O.

This chapter contains references to numerous historians. Full citations of their works are located in the bibliography. In cases of multiple bibliographic entries for a single author, notes are provided with abbreviated titles as guides to the relevant bibliographic listings.

Kliuchevskii, who produced classic studies of Russian history, have treated the developments of Kievan Rus', Vladimir-Suzdal', and Muscovy in a sequence that comprised a single national history. Scholars who have accepted their overview, however, generally point to a dividing line that separated the era of Kievan Rus' from the later stages of development centering around the principalities of northern Rus'.

Most identify the Mongol invasion as the final act that ended the Kievan Rus' era and marked the beginning of the epoch that culminated in the rise of Muscovy. But, as discussed in chapter 4, many also observed a decline in Kievan Rus' prior to that cataclysmic event. Scholars who follow Solov'ev and Kliuchevskii tend to regard Kievan Rus' as having already entered a state of decline and fragmentation by the time of the invasion. Soviet scholarship, represented by B. D. Grekov, V. T. Pashuto, and L. V. Cherepnin, labeled that fragmentation "feudalization." In contrast, B. A. Rybakov, P. P. Tolochko, and Thomas Noonan, among others, have assembled evidence to suggest that Kiev was not in decline, but remained the most important city, politically and economically, in Kievan Rus' until it was destroyed by the Mongols.

Despite such variations, the adherents of this school of thought tend to agree that Kiev had been the center of a coherent polity and that when it did decline, it was replaced first by Vladimir and then by Moscow. The development of the northern Rus' states is regarded as a new stage, even a new historical epoch, differentiated from the Kievan era not only by the geography of the new states, but by their political organization, most significantly by the degree of power held by the grand prince. Thus, while considering them as stages in the history of one nation, this school also emphasizes the discontinuities between Kievan Rus' and its successors. Different conclusions were drawn by Mykhailo Hrushevs'kyi (Mikhail Grushevskii) and his followers. They have argued that the most direct heirs of Kievan Rus' were not Vladimir and Moscow, but its core, i.e., the southwestern principalities, which ultimately formed Ukraine.

Having accepted the "break" between Kievan Rus' and its northern successors, scholars have categorized the Muscovite state in a variety of terms, ranging from a unified patrimonial autocracy, as A. E. Presniakov understood it, to a centralized national monarchy built upon well-developed military and bureaucratic institutions, as Soviet scholars such as L. V. Cherepnin and A. A. Zimin described it.

A few characterizations of the lands of Rus' in the eras following the Mongol invasion, including those of Thomas Noonan and Charles Halperin,[1] have noted the significance of some elements derived from

---

[1] Noonan, "Medieval Russia, the Mongols, and the West"; Halperin, "Kiev and Moscow."

their Kievan Rus' heritage. Expanding upon the implications of their observations, the discussions in the preceding chapters have bypassed the framework of standard periodizations and categorizations, and have instead attempted to explore the political and social institutions whose internal dynamics drove the development of the lands of Rus'. The observations made from this perspective also stress the distinctions between the character and organization of Kievan Rus' and Muscovy. But they highlight as well the fact that two institutions, the dynasty and the Church, transcended the barrier imposed by the Mongol invasion and bound the states and societies that developed in the post-invasion period tightly with Kievan Rus'. They reveal furthermore that it was the responses of those essentially Kievan Rus' institutions, the Riurikid dynasty and the Orthodox Church, to the political environment created in the aftermath of the Mongol invasion that fostered the political ascendancy of Moscow's princes over an expanded territorial realm, enabled them to acquire legitimacy within it, and thus to carve out the state of Muscovy. The development of the dynasty during the era of Kievan Rus' and after the Mongol invasion, the role of the Mongols in its development, and the development and function of the Church thus form three more of the main themes considered in chapters 1 through 11.

The Riurikid dynasty constituted one of the clearest and most direct links between Kievan Rus' and the polities of northern Rus'. Kievan Rus', as elaborated upon in chapters 1 through 4, was a political entity whose components were defined and bound together by their common recognition of Riurikid rule, adoption of Christianity and a religious culture introduced and nurtured by the Riurikids, and a shared popular material culture born of the mixture of the political, military, and legal influences exercised by the Riurikid princes, Christian influences disseminated by the clergy who were supported and defended by the princes and their retinues, and the social and economic traditions of the populace. After the Mongol invasion and the collapse of Kievan Rus', the dynasty continued to give the definition and identity to the lands of Rus' that distinguished them as related and associated principalities. The dynasty continued to be the exclusive provider of legitimate rulers for the Rus' principalities. Subordination to another dynasty or acceptance of a non-Riurikid prince separated the affected principalities from the other lands of Rus', which retained a loose affiliation even when they were not tightly unified around a single center. Additionally, the dynasts of northern Rus' recalled dynastic traditions that were forged during the Kievan Rus' era and followed them in the selection of their rulers in the decades following the Mongol invasion. The enduring influence of those traditions accounts for many of the policies adopted by the Muscovite princes, who defied those traditions, as well as for the responses of other members of the dynasty to them.

Seniority within the dynasty became a central issue that affected relations among individual princes and dynastic branches. Throughout the Kievan Rus' era the dynasty strove to fashion a mechanism to determine seniority and ensure smooth successions. But it was unable to anticipate the complexities that accompanied the enlargement of the dynasty and its territories. As a result, new sources of contention arose even as intradynastic conflicts led to the adoption of guidelines that resolved old ones. Nevertheless, the political development of the lands of northern Rus' and, ultimately, Muscovy proceeded in the context of the dynastic traditions established by the Kievan Rus' princes and of their successful violation by the Muscovite princes.

The transformation of the political structure of the lands of Rus' from a diffuse dynastic realm to a territorially unified and politically centralized monarchy proceeded against the background of the Kievan heritage. The tension between the Muscovite princes, who personified the deviation from Kievan norms, and other members of the dynasty whose efforts to perpetuate Kievan tradition cast them into opposition to Moscow's rulers, contributed to the dynamics that propelled the development of the northern Rus' principalities into the state of Muscovy. The abandonment of Kievan dynastic traditions and political structures generated a need for the Muscovite princes to construct an alternate political order and to adopt new ideologies to legitimize it. The character of the Muscovite state was not a linear continuation of that of Kievan Rus', but it was shaped by the Muscovite princes' rejection and replacement of Kievan patterns of organization and of exercising power. Although Muscovy's political structures contrast sharply with those of Kievan Rus', an understanding of their nature and development is dependent upon a recognition of their relationship to their points of departure, the Kievan institutions and traditions. In this sense, Kievan Rus' and Muscovy were inextricably, if paradoxically, linked.

The issues of the role of the dynasty during the Kievan Rus' era and the continuing influence of its traditions after the Mongol invasion have also received other scholarly interpretations. Many scholars have recognized that the dynasty's pattern of succession was lateral within the senior generation and accepted the notion that a rota or "ladder" system, thought to have been introduced by Iaroslav the Wise, was in operation. This system, discussed in chapter 2, incorporated principles of lateral succession within the dynasty's eldest generation. Described by S. M. Solov'ev and V. O. Kliuchevskii, it was essentially adopted by George Vernadsky, who described it in his *Kievan Russia*. Nancy Shields

Kollmann is among the more recent scholars who generally ascribe to this view. Her treatment of the succession system in Kievan Rus' may be found in "Collateral Succession in Kievan Rus'."

Martin Dimnik offered a variant description of the succession system in his article, "The 'Testament' of Iaroslav 'the Wise'." Although he too observed a pattern of lateral succession for the throne of Kiev, he qualified the findings of others who share that view by refuting the corollary that other towns of Kievan Rus' were ordered in a hierarchy and that heirs to the throne, as they replaced deceased elder brothers, progressed toward the position of grand prince of Kiev by rotating into and ruling those towns in turn, i.e., by moving up the ladder toward Kiev. He argued instead that Grand Prince Iaroslav had divided the territories of his realm and issued them to his sons in the form of permanent hereditary domains. Thus Sviatoslav received Chernigov and Vsevolod acquired Pereiaslavl'. Iziaslav and his direct heirs, Dimnik proposed, gained possession of Turov. Furthermore, Novgorod, which Dimnik maintained had no special status but was treated just like other major principalities by Iaroslav, was assigned to his son Vladimir (d. 1052), whose young son Rostislav inherited his father's position, but never personally took the throne. While sharing access to Kiev, each dynastic branch ruled its own domain and no rotation occurred across dynastic lines.

Among those who recognize that a lateral system of succession was functioning in Kievan Rus' some reached conclusions that are not inconsistent with those expressed in this volume. They have also tended to emphasize, as discussed in chapter 4, the system's failure to function smoothly and its breakdown during the twelfth century. In his article "Kievan Rus' and Sixteenth–Seventeenth Century Ukraine," for example, Omeljan Pritsak noted a continuing inclination among the princes of Kievan Rus' to regard themselves as members of a single ruling family. But he also remarked on their difficulty in effectuating orderly peaceful successions. He attributed their problems to the growth of their family and the consequent multiplication of claimants, each of whom enjoyed the loyalty of their "subclans," to the central Kievan throne. In *The Crisis of Medieval Russia, 1200–1304*, J. L. I. Fennell similarly recognized the tendency among the heirs of Iaroslav the Wise to accept a principle of generational seniority and to be guided by that principle in their successions both to the grand princely throne at Kiev and to the thrones of their own principalities. Yet he, like Pritsak, concluded that as the Riurikid dynasty grew in size, its ability to function waned. Fennell blamed the dynasty's difficulties on the greed of junior princes. The wars they generated coupled with the disintegration of Kievan Rus' that, in his view, resulted from the loss of eligibility for the Kievan throne by one branch of the expanding dynasty after another were counterproductive. Rather than providing the princes a means of ruling their domain, the dynastic succession principles deprived Kievan Rus' of central authority and an effective government. Nevertheless, as Kollmann pointed out, the conflicts among the dynasts reflected an impatience on the part of some princes with the rules of succession, not an absence of such rules. Few who have presented these interpretations of the history of Kievan Rus' and Muscovy, however, have traced the role and significance of the dynastic patterns as surviving beyond the Kievan Rus' era. Whether they characterize dynastic rule and the politics of succession as a binding or dividing force for Kievan Rus', most scholars consider the effects of the fractious Kievan dynastic politics and conflicts to have ceased with the fall of Kiev and with their replacement by the structurally simpler, centralized Muscovite regime.

But other scholars have interpreted interprincely relations within the dynasty, hence the strength and enduring nature of the dynasty's traditions, differently. They have argued that the dynasty lacked organizational cohesiveness or that at a particular time dynastic unity gave way to mayhem and the political unity of Kievan Rus' to fragmentation. Adopting the position of A. E. Presniakov,[2] the most extreme have rejected the entire notion of a lateral or "rota" system of succession. A recent statement of their position was articulated by A. D. Stokes in "The System of Succession to the Thrones of Russia, 1054–1113." He argued that "there was no generally recognized and accepted principle of succession to the senior throne of Kiev" before the reign of Iaroslav, doubted that "such an impractical system [as the rota system] could possibly have been conceived by the 'wise' and undoubtedly ruthless and realistic [I]aroslav," and concluded, therefore, that Iaroslav "instituted no system of succession . . . "

The discussions in chapters 1 through 4 maintained that a system of lateral succession did evolve in Kievan Rus'. It did not guarantee peaceful transfers of power. Not infrequently disputes over interpretations of the "rules" were resolved only by resorting to warfare. In some cases, seemingly legitimate heirs were bypassed. Grand Prince Iaroslav's arrest and confinement of his youngest and only surviving brother Sudislav (d. 1065) helped to secure the succession for his own sons in 1054. Again, the succession from Vladimir Monomakh to his son Mstislav in 1125 took place even though two of Monomakh's nephews, sons of the late Grand Prince Sviatopolk, were still alive. Nancy Shields Kollmann commented

---

[2] Presniakov, *Kniazheskoe pravo drevnei Rusi.*

on these two princes, Iziaslav and Briacheslav, in her article, "Collateral Succession in Kievan Rus'," and P. P. Tolochko included them on the dynastic chart accompanying his book, *Drevniaia Rus'*. But the chronicles contain little information about them other than the dates of their deaths (1128 and 1127, respectively); as a result there is little basis for interpreting the significance of their experience in the evolution of the dynastic succession system. Another exception, noted in chapter 4, is the failure of Vsevolod of Vladimir-Suzdal' to assume the Kievan throne after he had become and was acknowledged as the senior prince of the dynasty. And Mstislav Romanovich, a grandson of Grand Prince Rostislav Mstislavich of the Smolensk branch of the dynasty, ruled as grand prince of Kiev (1212–23) despite the fact that his father had not held that position.

It has been argued above that despite the conflicts and exceptions the Riurikid princes produced a well-defined set of principles that guided succession to the grand princely throne of Kiev. A related argument holds that the traditions guiding the dynasty's succession system were so strong that they exerted a compelling influence on the Riurikid princes long after the Mongols had invaded, Kievan Rus' had collapsed, and the separation of the northern and southwestern Rus' principalities had been completed. With the endorsement of their new overlords the northern princes honored the principles of succession inherited from Kievan Rus' for almost a century after the invasion. Those principles dictated that the sons of Iaroslav Vsevolodich would attain primacy in the second half of the thirteenth century, while others, such as the princes of Rostov, the descendants of Konstantin, would function in more peripheral roles. The only difference was that the center of their realm was Vladimir, not Kiev.

Those traditions also continued to define political relations, including the interprincely conflicts, among the princes of northern Rus'. As during the Kievan era, disputes arose among the princes when attempts were made to violate the established pattern of succession. This factor was central to the clashes, discussed in chapters 5 and 6, between the brothers Andrei and Alexander Nevsky and between Alexander's sons, Dmitry and Andrei, in the thirteenth century and, most significantly, between Mikhail of Tver' and Iurii of Moscow during the first quarter of the fourteenth century.

It was also because the Kievan traditions continued to retain such force that the princes of Moscow, the descendants of Daniil, met sustained domestic opposition when they attempted to acquire and hold the grand princely throne during the fourteenth century. On the basis of the "rules" derived from their Kievan heritage, the Daniilovichi had no legitimate claim to the grand princely seat of Vladimir. As a result, even though they gained the support of the Mongol khans and replaced the princes of Tver' as grand prince of Vladimir from the second quarter of the fourteenth century, representatives of other branches of the dynasty repeatedly protested the appointment of members of the Muscovite line to the grand princely throne of Vladimir.

The Riurikid dynasty survived the devastation wrought by the Mongol invasion. Likewise, the dynastic traditions that defined seniority and determined grand princely succession continued to mold the politics of the northern Rus' principalities long after the collapse of Kievan Rus'. Thus the attainment of the grand princely throne by the Muscovite princes, who lacked traditional dynastic legitimacy, did not occur without serious repercussions. It was in part because of their lack of legitimacy that the Daniilovichi depended so heavily on their Mongol suzerains. It was, furthermore, to consolidate their political power and, especially after the Golden Horde began to weaken, to develop new substitute domestic sources of legitimacy that they adopted the policies that ultimately transformed the dynastic realm of the lands of Rus' into the centralized monarchy of Muscovy.

Those policies resulted in the subordination of previously autonomous principalities to Moscow, in the formation of a central grand princely court and administration, in the conversion of other princes of the dynasty as well as their privileged but untitled advisors and military commanders into servicemen of the grand prince, and in the replacement of the practice of lateral generational succession with a system of vertical succession that ultimately transferred the grand princely throne exclusively from father to eldest son. The new pattern of succession, accompanied by the related reduction in status, power, and independence of other branches and members of the dynasty, was clarified by the dynastic wars of Vasily II and by the succession crisis surrounding the heir of Ivan III. Yet traces of the former lateral system continued to be perceptible during the lengthy childless period of the reign of Vasily III and resurfaced once again during the illness of Ivan IV in 1553, when some of his boyars expressed their reluctance to endorse the succession of his infant son.

Despite the tenacious quality of the patterns rooted in Kievan tradition, the Muscovite princes were successful. Their reordering of dynastic rule, however, led to the breakdown of political order. The removal of potential lateral heirs limited the princes eligible for succession to the sons of Ivan IV. When his son and heir Fedor died in 1598, Riurikid rule over the lands of Rus' came to an end.

Other scholars, implicitly discounting the influence of Kievan tradition, have cited different factors to account for Moscow's ascendancy over the other northern Rus' principalities (Kliuchevskii, Tikhomirov, Semenchenko)[3]. As mentioned in chapter 6, the general factors identified as favoring Moscow have included its geographic location, particularly Moscow's proximity to lucrative rivers that served as trade routes; the unusual personal qualities of the Moscow princes; and their rare ability to avoid the subdivisions of their own domain and the related internal family conflicts that plagued and weakened other northeastern Rus' principalities in the fourteenth century.

Recent scholarship has focused as well on the internal operations and structural arrangement of the Muscovite government. The accumulation of power by the grand prince and the formation of a highly centralized government apparatus have been regarded as the marks of the Muscovite political system. S. B. Veselovskii, A. A. Zimin, S. O. Shmidt, Gustave Alef, Ann M. Kleimola, and Nancy Shields Kollmann have all investigated Moscow's boyars. Advancing beyond early studies, e.g.. Kliuchevskii's *Boiarskaia duma*, they have probed into the identity of the boyars, their family backgrounds, careers, and their roles in the political and governing processes. Alef and Kleimola have offered explanations for the failure of this group, despite its influential position within the political system, to form a counterweight to the grand prince. In "The Crisis of the Muscovite Aristocracy," Alef explored the competitive nature of the relations among the boyar families and proposed that their rivalries prevented them from coalescing into an aristocratic stratum with common interests and power. Kleimola with Horace Dewey emphasized as well the elite's dependency upon the grand prince, who alone held the power both to grant high status and privilege and also, importantly, to punish and withdraw those privileges. The Muscovite rulers' practice, well developed by the sixteenth century, of punishing disloyalty with retributions against a servitor's relatives reinforced other pressures on boyars as well as other servicemen to obey the grand prince rather than attempt to limit his power (Alef, Backus, Dewey, and Kleimola).[4]

In her study, *Kinship and Politics*, Kollmann offered an alternative interpretation. She too observed competition for power and influence among the boyars, but suggested that their goals were achieved as much through forging marital ties and kin relationships as through the performance of military and administrative services. She proposed furthermore that their rivalries generated a common interest in preserving

---

[3] Kliuchevskii, *Sochineniia*; Tikhomirov, "Moskovskie tretniki, tysiatskie i namestniki."

[4] Alef, "Origins of Muscovite Autocracy"; Dewey and Kleimola, "Old Muscovite Amnesties" and "From the Kinship Group to Every Man His Brother's Keeper"; Kleimola, "Changing Face of the Muscovite Aristocracy" and "Up Through Servitude."

stability within the court and balance among their own families. Boyars thus engaged in collective efforts to prevent any single family from gaining too much power. Their preference for stability merged with a similar goal of the grand prince, resulting in a political system in which the sovereign and the political elite tended to function in a cooperative rather than an adversarial manner.

Other potential sources of alternate power, the central administration, and the vehicles of central Muscovite authority have also been subjects of scholarly investigation. Some (e.g., Keep, Nosov, Kashtanov)[5] have delved into methods employed by the Muscovite regime to govern the principalities it annexed, reforms that altered the nature of provincial government, and the relationship of the provinces to the center. Within this group some have considered specifically the role and functions of provincial governors (e.g., Veselovskii, Dewey, Zimin, Zimin and Khoroshkevich, Alef, Davies)[6]. Others have concentrated on the treasury at the court of Moscow, its fiscal policies and activities (Hellie. Zlotnik, Alef),[7] and the development of the bureaucratic offices that grew out of it (Zimin, Kleimola, Brown, Shmidt, Rasmussen, Alef)[8]. Other factors that had the hypothetical potential to limit the power of the grand princes, but functioned to enhance it have attracted the attention of scholars as well. They include the military (Hellie, Alef),[9] the legal system (Kaiser, Dewey, Kleimola, Zimin),[10] and the *zemskie sobory* (Cherepnin, Brown, Hellie).[11] The results of these and other studies, which offer insight into the nature and functional capacity of Muscovite administrative and social institutions, have been incorporated into the discussions of chapters 8, 9, and 11. Those chapters additionally explored the development of those

---

5 Keep, "Bandits and the Law in Muscovy"; Nosov, *Ocherki po istorii mestnogo upravleniia* and "Zemskaia reforma na russkom severe"; Kashtanov, "K probleme mestnogo upravleniia" and "Otrazhenie v zhalovannykh i ukaznykh gramotakh finansovoi sistemy."

6 Dewey, "Decline of the Muscovite *Namestnik*"; Zimin, "Namestnicheskoe upravlenie"; Alef, "Origins of Muscovite Autocracy."

7 Hellie, *Enserfment and Military Change*; Alef, "Origins of Muscovite Autocracy."

8 Zimin, *Reformy Ivana Groznogo* and "D'iacheskii apparat"; Kleimola, "Up Through Servitude"; Brown, "Muscovite Government Bureaus"; Shmidt, *Rossiiskoe gosudarstvo v seredine XVI stoletiia*; Rasmussen, "Muscovite Foreign Policy Administration"; Alef, "Origins of Muscovite Autocracy."

9 Hellie, *Enserfment and Military Change*; Alef, "Muscovite Military Reforms" and "Origins of Muscovite Autocracy."

10 Kaiser, *Growth of the Law*; Dewey, "1497 Sudebnik," "1550 Sudebnik," and *Muscovite Texts, 1488–1556*; Kleimola, "Law and Social Change in Medieval Russia"; Zimin, *Reformy Ivana Groznogo* and *Rossiia na rubezhe XV–XVI stoletii.*

11 Cherepnin, *Zemskie sobory*; Brown, "Zemskii Sobor"; Hellie, "Zemskii Sobor."

institutions in the context of a line of princes seeking the means to consolidate their power in the absence of traditional sources of legitimacy.

Interwoven with the development of the dynasty and the Rus' political systems is an exploration of the role played by the Mongols in the achievement of power by the Muscovite princes. But the degree and nature of Mongol influence on the development of the lands of Rus' after their invasion have posed problems for historians, who have on this issue as well as so many others formed a variety of conclusions. At one extreme, scholars ranging from S. M. Solov'ev and V. O. Kliuchevskii to Nicholas Riasanovsky have found very little evidence of lasting Mongol influence in Russia. To account for the features of Muscovy that so distinguished it from Kievan Rus', some, such as Dimitri Obolensky,[12] have turned to Byzantine models. Michael Cherniavsky's article, "Khan or Basileus," also explored that issue. Others, such as Gustave Alef in "The Origins of the Muscovite Autocracy" explained Muscovy's development in terms of internal factors rather than external influences.

At the other end of the spectrum are those who consider the Mongols to have had a profound impact on the Rus' lands. Within that group some stress aspects of Mongol influence that are judged to be negative. They include the initial devastation, the strain on Russian economic resources, and even the introduction of an "Oriental despotism" into northern Rus' political concepts and norms. Karl A. Wittfogel made the case for the last position in an article entitled "Russia and the East: A Comparison and Constrast."

Others placed greater weight on factors considered to be positive or constructive. The Eurasian school of thought, represented by George Vernadsky, fits into this category. It observed a limited sphere of direct Mongol influence on Rus' society. But it noted as well the dramatic change that took place in the political structure of the Rus' principalities during the period of Mongol domination over them and concluded that Mongol influence contributed in significant ways to the transformation of the northern Rus' principalities into a state unified around Moscow, whose autocratic ruler assumed powers equivalent to those exercised by the Golden Horde khans or tsars. Vernadsky presented his argument in *The Mongols and Russia*.

A. N. Nasonov and J. L. I. Fennell[13] also associated the rise of Muscovy with the Mongols. They attributed the achievement of grand princely status by the Daniilovich line, however, to Mongol manipulation. They explained the khans' decisions to issue the grand princely patents to

---

[12] Obolensky, "Russia's Byzantine Heritage."
[13] Nasonov, *Mongoly i Rus'*; Fennell, *Emergence of Moscow*.

Moscow princes in terms of the Mongols' own overriding concern to maintain a balance of power among the Rus' principalities and prevent any single one of them from becoming too strong. Disturbed in the first decades of the fourteenth century by the growing might of Tver', the khan shifted his support to Moscow with the intention of keeping the Rus' principalities weak and divided, submissive and obedient.

Other scholars have suggested, more specifically, that the Golden Horde and the Tatar khanates that succeeded it provided models for particular political institutions that developed in Muscovy in the fifteenth and sixteenth centuries. In "State and Society in Muscovite Russia and the Mongol–Turkic System in the Sixteenth Century," Jaroslaw Pelenski observed the roots of the Muscovite *zemskii sobor* in the Mongol–Turkic assembly, the *quriltai*; he similarly found a parallel for the *pomest'e* system in a land tenure system employed in Kazan'. Donald Ostrowski argued further that the entire organization of the Muscovite court and administrative apparatus was virtually copied from Tatar models. Charles Halperin tried to explain the dilemma faced by modern historians by demonstrating that the Russian chroniclers themselves placed a veil over the actual nature of Russo–Tatar relations and thereby concealed or distorted some aspects of their interaction.

The position taken in this text falls squarely in the category of those who recognize a significant Mongol influence on the development of the northern Rus' principalities, especially Moscow. The advent of the Mongols created the political conditions in which the Muscovite princes were able to gain preeminence. But some of the effects of the Mongol presence were indirect, even unintentional. In contrast to the conclusions of Nasonov and Fennell, the discussion in chapter 5, reinforced by arguments and evidence presented by Vernadsky, Halperin, Fedorov-Davydov, and Morgan among others,[14] made the point that the primary focus of the Golden Horde was not its Russian subjects, but other components of the larger Mongol Empire. To help support themselves and facilitate their ventures, the Golden Horde khans demanded that the Rus' principalities provide a steady, reliable stream of resources, which were supplied in the form of tribute, gifts, and commercial items.

This set of circumstances created an opportunity for those princes who displayed an outstanding ability to deliver the required goods and personnel to the Horde to gain favor and rewards from the khans. Chief among those rewards was the patent to rule as grand prince of Vladimir. The Moscow princes, who had no claim to the grand princely throne

---

[14] Vernadsky, *Mongols and Russia*; Halperin, *Russia and the Golden Horde* and "Russia in the Mongol Empire"; Fedorov-Davydov, *Obshchestvennyi stroi zolotoi ordy*.

on the basis of domestic dynastic tradition, benefited most from the opportunity created by the establishment of Mongol suzerainty over the lands of Rus'. By demonstrating their reliability and effectiveness they gained the support of the Mongol khans and after 1331, the grand princely throne. They did so despite protests from the legitimately eligible princes from Tver' and later from coalitions of princes who attempted to restore in some form the dynastic traditions.

Their dependency on Mongol support in lieu of dynastic legitimacy obliged the Moscow princes to serve their suzerains obediently. That factor defined many of their actions and policies, including, as discussed in chapters 6 and 7, their determination to collect and deliver tribute to the Mongol khan. The achievement of that objective, in turn, required the Muscovite princes to dominate Novgorod and extend their authority over an ever-increasing number of Rus' principalities. But the policies they pursued, as obedient servants of the Mongols, also began a process of gathering and developing the means, including a larger fiscal base, administrative apparatus, and military force, which ultimately enabled them to dominate the other northern Rus' principalities and overpower their Tatar neighbors.

Viewed from this perspective specific events in the relations between the Rus' and the Tatars are subject to reinterpretation as well. One significant example is the Battle of Kulikovo. The victory of Dmitry Donskoi demonstrated both Muscovy's ability to muster an impressive army drawn from a multitude of principalities and the Tatars' vulnerability. It has thus frequently been regarded as a symbol of Muscovite leadership, which then directed a sustained and concentrated effort to unite the lands of Rus' and mobilize their resources to throw off the Tatar yoke. The Battle of Kulikovo, despite the fact that the Tatars under Tokhtamysh soon afterward defeated the Rus' again, has thus been regarded as a turning point in the history of the Rus' lands and Muscovy. This characterization, which was set forth by S. M. Solov'ev, has been widely disseminated.

The examination of Mongol-Muscovite relations presented in chapter 7 yields a different interpretation: the Battle of Kulikovo was a confrontation between one Tatar commander Mamai, who was preoccupied with a power struggle with other Tatar leaders, and his protégé, Grand Prince Dmitry Ivanovich, over timely delivery of tribute payments, not sovereignty. This conclusion is reinforced by evidence, presented by Charles Halperin, N. S. Borisov, and V. A. Kuchkin among others,[15] that

---

[15] Halperin, "Russian Land and the Russian Tsar" and *Tatar Yoke*; Borisov, "Kulikovskaia bitva"; Kuchkin, "Pobeda na Kulikovskom pole."

dates the texts in which the battle is placed in the context of a nationally unified campaign for independence from Mongol suzerainty no earlier than the fifteenth century.

The view that Muscovite–Mongol relations were characterized by a willingness on the part of the Muscovite princes to cooperate and benefit from their Mongol overlords rather than a determined drive to unite the lands of Rus' in order to overthrow the Tatar yoke also affects perceptions of Muscovite relations with the Tatar khanates in the fifteenth and sixteenth centuries. These relations, which were discussed in chapters 10 and 11, have also been subject to competing interpretations. The most prevalent argues that Moscow's commitment to unifying the Rus' lands and the willingness of other Riurikid princes to subordinate themselves to its leadership were generated by a nationalistic determination to overthrow Tatar hegemony. Having accomplished that goal at the pivotal confrontation on the Ugra River in 1480, Moscow persistently went on to assert a dominating influence over its implacable enemy, the Khanate of Kazan', and ultimately to annex it. The Khanate of Astrakhan' then quickly fell to the Muscovite tsar as well, as did the Khanate of Sibir' a few decades later. Only the Crimean Khanate, protected by the Ottoman Turks, managed to withstand the overpowering might of the Muscovite state. Such views have been expressed by a range of scholars, including K. V. Bazilevich, L. V. Cherepnin, Henry Huttenbach, and Iu. G. Alekseev.[16]

Although many scholars directly or indirectly acknowledge the Muscovite–Crimean Tatar alliance of the late fifteenth and early sixteenth centuries (e.g., Vernadsky, Fennell, Lemercier-Quelquejay, Zimin, Halperin, Alef),[17] the most common characterization of Muscovy's relations with its Tatar neighbors has remained one of hostility. Cordial relations with the Crimean Khanate were sought, it is explained, because Muscovy's main objective in its foreign affairs was the reunification of the western and southwestern Rus' principalities with its own northern possessions. When contemplating war with Lithuania in pursuit of that goal, Muscovite officials negotiated an alliance with the Crimean Khanate, but when relations with Lithuania improved, e.g., after the truce of 1494, Muscovite–Crimean contacts fell off. Similarly, Muscovy's

---

[16] Bazilevich, *Vneshniaia politika russkogo tsentralizovannogo gosudarstva*; Cherepnin, *Obrazovanie russkogo tsentralizovannogo gosudarstva*; Huttenbach, "Muscovy's Conquest of Muslim Kazan and Astrakhan"; Alekseev, *Osvobozhdenie Rusi*.

[17] Vernadsky, *Russia at the Dawn of the Modern Age*; Fennell, *Ivan the Great*; Lemercier-Quelquejay, "Les khanates de Kazan et de Crimée"; Zimin, *Rossiia na rubezhe XV–XVI stoletii*; Halperin, *Russia and the Golden Horde*; Alef, "Origins of Muscovite Autocracy."

posture toward Kazan' has been described as a response to that khanate's repeated acts of aggression against the lands of Rus'. In order to accomplish its goals in the west, Muscovy was compelled to neutralize its eastern enemy. Contributors to and adherents of this view include I. I. Smirnov, K. V. Bazilevich, George Vernadsky, J. L. I. Fennell, and A. A. Zimin.[18]

An alternate interpretation, made by Edward Keenan and supported by Charles Halperin,[19] argued that the Muscovite princes accepted the authority of the Mongol khans well into the fifteenth century. Both Vasily II and his uncle and challenger Iurii Dmitr'evich recognized that authority when they appealed to Khan Ulu-Muhammed to settle their dispute over the Muscovite throne. Keenan as well as Ihor Ševčenko and Alexandre Bennigsen and Chantal Lemercier-Quelquejay[20] are among those who have added that as the Golden Horde decayed, its successor states formed a community of polities. Along with the Tatar khanates Muscovy was one of the members of that community, all of whom remained involved with one another even as they all simultaneously competed for power and attempted to establish a new equilibrium in the region. It was in this context that Vasily II, who regained his throne with the aid of Tatars from Ulu-Muhammed's Horde after 1445, continued to regard Tatar involvement in internal Muscovite affairs as normal and even desirable, and that Ivan III, reversing the pattern, interfered in the domestic affairs of Kazan'. But Ivan's intrusion into Kazan's succession crisis had little to do with conquest; rather he undertook his campaigns in close cooperation with his ally, the khan of the Crimean Khanate.

The growth of Muscovy shifted the balance of power within the post-Golden Horde community in its favor, but Muscovy did not apply its increasing strength to implement a consistent policy aimed at incorporating its Tatar neighbors. Its goal was to reestablish a regional stability, weighted in Muscovy's favor, to replace the equilibrium that had previously been maintained by the Golden Horde but had decayed when the Horde fragmented. In this context Muscovy opposed the Great Horde, most memorably at the Ugra in 1480. But while this confrontation was occurring, Muscovy was also allied with the Crimean Khanate. Muscovite policy was not uniformly hostile toward all its Tatar neighbors;

---

[18] Bazilevich, *Vneshniaia politika russkogo tsentralizovannogo gosudarstva*; Vernadsky, *Russia at the Dawn of the Modern Age*; Fennell, *Ivan the Great*; Zimin, *Rossiia na poroge novogo vremeni* and *Rossiia na rubezhe XV–XVI stoletii*.

[19] Keenan, "Muscovy and Kazan"; Halperin, e.g., *Russia and the Golden Horde*.

[20] Ševčenko, "Muscovy's Conquest of Kazan"; Bennigsen and Lemercier-Quelquejay, "Le Khanat de Crimée."

nor did the Ugra confrontation, as Keenan observed, constitute a significant turning point in Muscovite–Tatar relations. Through the middle of the sixteenth century, the central focus of Muscovy's foreign policy concerns, as described by Charles Halperin,[21] remained the other members of the post-Golden Horde. Only in the middle of the sixteenth century did Muscovy's approaches to implementing its policy, which had included forging alliances and compromising with the khanates, shift to one of conquest and annexation.

The Golden Horde thus had profound effects on the development of the northern Rus' principalities. By extending its suzerainty over those principalities, the Golden Horde drew them into its own political and economic sphere. The princes of northern Rus' became participants in the Horde's political and military affairs. Their involvement in that sphere survived the collapse of the Golden Horde and shaped the direction of Muscovite foreign policy, which placed a priority on relations with its Tatar neighbors until at least the 1550s.

More fundamentally, the establishment of Tatar suzerainty over the Riurikids created conditions in which centuries-old dynastic traditions could be abandoned; the Muscovite branch of the dynasty successfully took advantage of the opportunity to achieve prominence and power. Lacking legitimacy derived from domestic sources, the Muscovite princes relied on the khans, who had appointed them, to maintain them in their positions as the grand princes of Vladimir. But when the Golden Horde itself weakened and fragmented, the Muscovite grand princes' need for domestic sources of support became vitally important. The Church played a critical role in supplying theories that were used to legitimize the preeminence of the Muscovite princes.

Like the dynasty, the Church had developed during the Kievan Rus' era and formed a link between that period and the later stages in the history of northern Rus'. It was also closely related to the dynasty, particularly in its function of providing cohesiveness to the realm and stature to its princes. A variety of issues concerning the Church, beginning with its initial establishment in the lands of Rus' and continuing with its nature as well as its role in Rus' political and social affairs, have been subjects of lengthy discussion and debate among scholars. The circumstances and timing of the conversion of the lands of Rus' to Christianity, which were discussed in Chapter 1, form one area of controversy. Similarly, the status of the new Church has been debated. M. D. Priselkov postulated that the hierarchs of the Kievan Church were under the jurisdiction of the Bulgarian patriarch. Other theories suggested they were subject to Rome.

---

[21] Halperin, *Russia and the Golden Horde.*

And George Vernadsky proposed that the Rus' Church was auto-cephalous until 1037.[22]

The location of the original center of the metropolitan's see has also been a subject of discussion. Vernadsky placed the original center of the Rus' Church at Tmutorokan'. A. D. Stokes argued in his article, "The Status of the Russian Church, 988–1037," that the first metropolis was Pereiaslavl', which had previously been the site of an ancient pagan temple. The selection of Pereiaslavl' as the home of the new Church and the relocation of the town itself to a new site symbolized, in his view, the abandonment of the old gods in favor of Christianity. Later, after Iaroslav became the sole ruler of Kievan Rus' and transferred the metropolitan's seat to Kiev, chroniclers edited out this information, which detracted from the image of Kiev as the secular and ecclesiastical capital of the realm and Iaroslav as its virtuous ruler. Most scholars, however, have accepted the views, enunciated by Dimitri Obolensky, Andrzej Poppe, and Ia. N. Shchapov among others, that Kiev was the original center of the Church in the lands of Rus', and that the Church from the time of its establishment was under the jurisdiction of the patriarch of Constantinople. Ia. N. Shchapov, however, proposed that during the third quarter of the eleventh century there were three Rus' metropolitanates: one centered at Kiev, a second at Chernigov, and the third at Pereiaslavl'.[23]

By providing a uniform religion, introducing cultural standards for architecture, painting, and literature, and by strengthening Kievan ties to Byzantium, the Church generally bolstered the authority and prestige of the Riurikid dynasty. It also added a layer to the identity of Kievan Rus', whose society was distinguished from its neighbors not only by recognition of Riurikid rule but by the eastern Christian religion and culture.

The adoption of Christianity nevertheless had its costs. Prince Vladimir I pledged a tithe of his revenue to the Church. Andrzej Poppe[24] argued that the assignment was designated particularly for the Church of the Tithe (Holy Virgin), which he regarded as Vladimir's royal chapel. His view disputed the more commonly held notion that the tithe was intended to provide financial support for the whole institution of the Orthodox Church in Rus'. This conception is derived from the understanding, expressed for example by Tolochko,[25] that the Church of the

---

[22] Vernadsky, *Kievan Russia*.

[23] Obolensky, "Byzantium, Kiev, and Moscow"; Poppe, "Original Status of the Old-Russian Church" and "Building of the Church of St. Sophia"; Shchapov, *State and Church in Early Russia*.

[24] Poppe, "Building of the Church of St. Sophia."

[25] Tolochko, *Drevniaia Rus'*.

Tithe was the first cathedral of the metropolitan; donations for its main-tenance implicitly constituted contributions for the support of the Church in its entirety. Through the Church statutes, which were issued by the Riurikid princes and have been discussed by Ia. N. Shchapov, Daniel Kaiser, and N. S. Borisov,[26] the princes also transferred jurisdiction and responsibility for matters concerning norms for social and family relation-ships as well as for Church personnel to the ecclesiastical hierarchy. The princes thus shared the power and revenue derived from settling disputes with the Church.

Like the dynasty, the Church survived the Mongol invasion. It gained the right to locate a bishopric at Sarai and enjoyed an array of privileges and tax exemptions under Mongol rule. But unlike the political realm of Kievan Rus', which under the impact of the Mongol invasion split into its northeastern and southwestern components and then subdivided further, the ecclesiastical realm remained intact longer and, as Thomas Noonan pointed out in his article "Medieval Russia, the Mongols, and the West," provided bonds that, despite the absence of political unity, held the Orthodox lands of Rus' together as a cohesive unit. It was not until the end of the thirteenth century that Metropolitan Maksim moved his residence from Kiev to the northeast. And it was only during the fourteenth century, under pressures from their new Polish and Lithuanian secular rulers, that the bishoprics of southwestern Rus' were fashioned into a succession of metropolitanates. At that time an ecclesiastical fissure, parallel to that of the secular, political division of the lands of Rus', began to form in the metropolitanate of Kiev and all Rus'. Other scholars have similarly noted that the Rus' Church was not divided until well after the Mongol invasion; indeed, Robert Crummey,[27] for example, placed the division in 1458, when a permanent metropolitanate was created for the Orthodox population in Lithuania.

But the Rus' ecclesiastical see remained unified only as long as the Golden Horde dominated the lands that had made up Kievan Rus'. During that period all the Rus' principalities, despite their political subdivision, recognized the spiritual authority of the same metropolitan. But when Golden Horde power receded and was replaced in the south-western portions of the Rus' lands by Poland and Lithuania, their new rulers secured the patriarch's cooperation in detaching the Orthodox population in their lands from the Russian see. The first efforts to separate the western bishoprics from the Rus' metropolitanate, described in

---

[26] Shchapov, *Kniazheskie ustavy i tserkov'*; Kaiser, *Growth of the Law*; Borisov, *Russkaia tserkov'*.

[27] Crummey, *Formation of Muscovy*.

chapters 6 and 7, achieved only temporary success. But they were never-theless disturbing enough to the Rus' ecclesiastical leadership to prompt a response. Thus, if the final political division of the southwestern and northern principalities was a direct consequence of the Mongol invasion, the division of the metropolitanate of Kiev and all Rus' a century later may be considered an indirect result of the contraction of Mongol power. And, just as the political development of the northern Rus' principalities was shaped by the dynasty's reactions to the Mongol presence, so ecclesi-astical policies were fashioned in response to the consequences of the Mongol retreat from the southwestern Rus'. The policy adopted by at least some hierarchs and spiritual leaders of the Russian Church was to reunite the Orthodox population of the lands of Rus' into a single see.

The Church's interest in reunifying the Russian lands is commonly perceived in a secular political context and understood as one way in which the Church expressed its undeviating support for the Moscow princes, who during the fourteenth century were not only establishing themselves as grand princes of Vladimir, but were steadily subordinating and unifying the northern Rus' lands. The strength generated by the amalgamation of principalities contributed by 1380 to Grand Prince Dmitry Ivanovich's ability to defy Mongol authority and defeat Mamai at the Battle of Kulikovo.

A. E. Presniakov[28] presented the case for a close identification between metropolitans and Muscovite princes. He traced their relationships from the beginning of the fourteenth century when Petr, favored by Moscow's Prince Iurii, prevailed over Gerontii, the candidate of Grand Prince Mikhail, to become metropolitan and subsequently clashed with the grand prince. Petr's successor Feognost bolstered the position of Moscow's princes by driving Grand Prince Aleksandr Mikhailovich from the Rus' lands after the Tver' uprising of 1327, and thereby clearing the way for Ivan I Kalita to take his place. He, furthermore, depicted Metropolitan Aleksei as an ally, supporter, and close adviser to Grand Prince Dmitry Donskoi. This overview has been generally accepted by a range of scholars, including George Vernadsky, L. A. Dmitriev, Dimitri Obolensky, Omeljan Pritsak, and J. L. I. Fennell.[29]

An alternate version places the forging of tight, mutually supportive relations between the Church and the Muscovite grand princes at a later date. Expressed by N. S. Borisov among others,[30] it stresses the character

---

[28] Presniakov, *Formation of the Great Russian State.*

[29] Vernadsky, *Mongols and Russia*; Obolensky, "Byzantium and Russia"; Pritsak, "Moscow, the Golden Horde, and the Kazan Khanate"; Fennell, *Emergence of Moscow.*

[30] Borisov, *Russkaia tserkov'.*

of the Church as a landowning institution whose possessions were expanding through the fourteenth century. As the metropolitans, bishops, and monasteries became wealthy landowners, whose powers over their estates and the inhabitants who dwelled on them approached those of appanage princes, they entered into an inherent conflict of interest with the Muscovite princes who during the same period were intent upon subordinating autonomous local authorities. The issue became overt late in the fifteenth century, when Ivan III confiscated Church lands in Novgorod. It was resolved and a Church–state alliance formed only in the early sixteenth century, when Ivan III cast his support behind the "possesser" camp in the Church controversy against the "non-possessors." In return, the victors within the Church pledged their loyalty, manifested in part by the formulation of ideologies that enhanced his powers, to the grand prince and his successors.

Other scholars, however, have questioned the validity of various facets of the image of a tight bond between the Church hierarchs and spiritual leaders on the one hand, and the princes of Moscow on the other. Some (e.g., Meyendorff, Dmitriev) have pointed out that the descriptions and characterizations of close, supportive relations between Church leaders and Moscow's princes during the fourteenth century were composed in the fifteenth century. David Miller,[31] examining specifically the signs of support accorded Dmitry Donskoi by Sergei of Radonezh, discussed doubts that have been raised concerning their historicity. He concluded that the accounts of Sergei's "blessing," bestowed on Dmitry and his army on the eve of the Battle of Kulikovo, were among those composed decades later, in the fifteenth century. They should be understood as reflections of the Church's interests at that time.

N. S. Borisov in his 1986 article, furthermore, explained that Metropolitan Petr's conduct was prompted by the hostility he encountered from the grand prince, who came from Tver', not by his personal preference for Moscow's princes. Borisov similarly attributed Feognost's treatment of Grand Prince Aleksandr to the metropolitan's obligation to carry out the will of the khan of the Golden Horde, not to his unambiguous support for Aleksandr's rival, Ivan of Moscow. He also cited other examples of Feognost's official acts, which imply lack of support for the Muscovite princes: his refusal to give his blessing to the third marriage of Grand Prince Semen, which took place in 1347, despite the fact that this match with Aleksandr's daughter Mariia improved the status of the grand prince; his lack of participation in the construction of churches or the compilation of literary texts that glorified Moscow and its princes; and

---

[31] Miller, "Cult of St. Sergius."

his secondary role, in contrast to that of Ivan I Kalita, in the 1339 canon-ization of Petr, who had been so closely associated with Moscow. The image of a long-standing and consistently supportive relationship between the Church and the Muscovite princes is undermined further by the recollection that Bishop Iona, the leading hierarch of the Church in the absence of a metropolitan, was reluctant to support Grand Prince Vasily II in his contest against his uncle. Finally, the argument that the Church's policy culminated in the sixteenth century with an exchange of Church support for virtually autocratic powers for the grand prince in return for property rights for its own institutions has also been cast into doubt by Donald Ostrowski.[32]

The latter set of arguments substantiates the concept, presented in chapter 6, that the interests of the grand prince and the Church did not coincide. The metropolitans of the fourteenth century were preoccupied with maintaining or restoring the unity of their see. The Muscovite grand princes were concerned primarily with holding their positions of power and, to serve that goal, with extending their control over territories in northern Rus', collecting tribute, and satisfying the demands of their Mongol suzerains. Thus, at moments critical to the successful achieve-ment of Daniilovich goals, influential Church leaders were frequently absent or neutral. Some examples were noted above. Another, discussed in chapter 7, revolves around the succession of Dmitry Ivanovich to the grand princely throne. Metropolitan Aleksei, who was being held in Lithuania where he had gone on a mission to rejoin the southwestern bishoprics with his see, was not in Moscow guiding the young prince, who lost his throne almost immediately after ascending it. The lack of uniformity of secular and ecclesiastical interests became apparent again when Dmitry supported Mitiai, then Pimen, to replace Metropolitan Aleksei. But it was Kiprian, who had been named metropolitan in Lithuania (1375) and who was identified with the cause of reunifying the Orthodox community into a single see, who was named Aleksei's successor. Not only did Donskoi oppose him, he humiliated him when he came to Moscow to claim his ecclesiastical throne and ejected him from the city. Donskoi, despite his image as the hero of Kulikovo and unifier of the lands of Rus', did not support the Church's policy of reunifying the metropolitanate of Kiev and all Rus'; under the circum-stances of the late fourteenth century he could not have implemented the concomitant secular policy of uniting the lands of the Orthodox peoples into a single political realm.

Only later did scribes and chroniclers at both ecclesiastical and secular

---

[32] Ostrowski, "Church Polemics and Monastic Land Acquisition."

courts retroactively attempt to depict the grand prince and the Church's most eminent leaders in mutually supportive relationships. The most intensive efforts of the Church to do so came in the middle of the fifteenth century, when, as discussed in chapter 8, its bishops had daringly shed their subordination to Constantinople and assumed the right to name their own metropolitan. The need to justify their actions and legitimize their autocephalous Church generated the development of concepts, enunciated in literature and depicted in icons, that the Church centered at Moscow was the descendant of the Kievan Church, established by St. Vladimir. The Muscovite grand princes, as emphasized by Jaroslaw Pelenski and Charles Halperin,[33] were correspondingly identified with their Kievan ancestors and also cast into the role of defenders of the Church. But as Daniel Rowland pointed out, the dynasts did not always favor the seemingly supportive ideological pronouncements issued by ecclesiasts. In this case, the conclusions of Pelenski and Halperin notwithstanding, the Church's pointed recollection of the Kievan heritage was not necessarily the approach preferred by the Moscow princes, whose own legitimacy could be undermined and weakened by emphasis on their status within the Riurikid lineage. The Church's efforts to fortify its own position nevertheless reflected on the ruling dynasty. Despite the divergence in their motivations and goals, the Church formulated theories that justified the elevation of the tsar and grand prince as well as the accumulation of power exclusively in his hands.

Neither the Church nor the dynasty with their administrative and military appendages could have functioned without the economic support of the Rus' society and the successful use of techniques to channel wealth produced by the mass of society to its elites for their projects and policies. Those techniques, discussed in chapters 3 and 9, included taxation administered and enforced by agents of the princes as well as other devices such as the *pomest'e* system; they were critical tools in the accumulation and exercise of power by the Riurikid princes. The final theme of this volume, however, is the economic activity of the society that underlay the states that developed in the lands of Rus'.

The economic structures and organization of Rus' society have long been recognized as important factors in its political development. They have been the focus of debates as well. In one controversy it has been argued by scholars, led by V. O. Kliuchevskii, that commerce was the most important sector in the Rus' economy. The commercial success of

---

[33] Pelenski, "Origins of the Official Muscovite Claims" and "Emergence of the Muscovite Claims"; Halperin, "Russian Land and the Russian Tsar," "Concept of the *Russkaia zemlia*," and "Kiev and Moscow."

the early Riurikids drove the formation and flourishing of Kievan Rus'; commercial decline was followed by the disintegration of that state; and Moscow's favorable position on commercial trade routes accounted for its political success as well. Opposed to that view are followers of B. D. Grekov, who concluded that agriculture was the primary and most influential component of the Rus' economy.

Other scholars have addressed the broader issue of whether or not the Rus' economy was "backward," particularly in comparison with the economic development of western Europe. Their inquiries have been enveloped in discussions about the appropriateness of categorizing the Rus' economy as "feudal." In that debate B. D. Grekov, L. V. Cherepnin, and V. T. Pashuto, among others, argued that the creation of large landed estates owned by princes and their retainers in the country-side by at least the twelfth century constituted a "feudal" organization of Rus' society and its economy; this organization was equivalent to, not "behind" the forms of organization in western society. George Vernadsky presented a case against classifying Kievan Rus' as a feudal society. I. Ia. Froianov also minimized the extent and importance of elite landownership in the Kievan period and thereby dismissed notions of feudalism as being inapplicable to the Rus' economy. Daniel Kaiser, analyzing economic structures on the basis of Kievan law codes, similarly discounted the notion that members of the political and military elites owned a predominant portion of agricultural land. He observed a dynamic, increasingly complex economy developing in the lands of Rus'.[34]

The discussion in the preceding chapters has been based on the concept that throughout the centuries spanning the Kievan Rus' era through the formation of Muscovy, Rus' society organized and operated its economic activities in response to basic domestic factors, e.g., the climate and physical conditions of the country as well as the size and density of local population groups. Although Russian society was aware of and, at times, borrowed techniques from abroad, its basic units of production, i.e., its farms and workshops, were geared and responsive primarily to the capabilities of the population that performed the basic labor tasks and to the needs and demands of the society's rulers and elites.

Examined from this perspective, the highlighted issues are neither whether Rus' society kept economic pace with others nor the relative importance of the various sectors of the economy. They are instead a determination of the economic activities conducted by the members of

[34] Vernadsky, "Feudalism in Russia" and *Kievan Russia*; Froianov, *Kievskaia Rus'. Ocherki sotsial'no-ekonomicheskoi istorii*; Kaiser, "Economy of Kievan Rus'."

Rus' society; their ability to produce supplies sufficient to satisfy their basic needs and surpluses to support their society's elites engaged in defense and territorial expansion, in administration and the maintenance of domestic order, and in spiritual and cultural activities; and the effectiveness of the means adopted by Rus' society to acquire the commodities its members did not or could not produce or otherwise compensate for the lack of them.

Considered in such terms, the economic functions of Rus' society were successful for centuries. The society operated an agricultural system, described by Jerome Blum, R. E. F. Smith,[35] and James Bater and R. A. French, that evolved in conjunction with a changing availability of both land and labor as well as with urban and territorial expansion and contraction. It was resilient enough to recover from domestic wars, Mongol invasions, and successive attacks of the bubonic plague. With the very real but temporary exceptions of local crop failures and famines, that system reliably produced sufficient supplies of food for the rural peasant farmers as well as for the population engaged in crafts and manufacturing and for the political, administrative, military, spiritual, and cultural elites. Even in the Novgorod lands, which were relatively poor for agriculture and are frequently described as having been dependent upon the northeastern principalities for grain (e.g, Fennell), the agricultural system, studied by I. L. Perel'man, L. V. Danilova, and A. L. Shapiro, et al. among others, generally fed the local population (Raba).[36]

The agricultural system, which sustained Rus' society, was supplemented by sectors that concentrated on crafts and manufacturing and on commerce. Intercontinental trade, i.e., trade with the Byzantine Empire, the Volga River and trans-Caspian markets, and with the Baltic Sea community, afforded Rus' society the means to exchange domestically produced commodities for otherwise unavailable items regarded as economically valuable, politically or militarily useful, and/or socially prestigious. An important example is silver. That precious metal was not among the natural resources of the Rus' lands, yet it played a significant role in the Rus' economy and the political development of the Rus' lands. From the time the Riurikids, whose ancestors had been drawn to the area by the availability of silver at the Volga River markets (Noonan),[37] established their authority over the lands of Rus', they

---

[35] Smith, *Origins of Farming* and *Peasant Farming in Muscovy.*

[36] Fennell, *Emergence of Moscow;* Shapiro, et al., *Agrarnaia istoriia severo-zapada Rossii* and *Agrarnaia istoriia severo-zapada Rossii XVI veka;* Raba, "Novgorod in the Fifteenth Century."

[37] Noonan, "Ninth-Century Dirham Hoards" and "Why the Vikings First Came to Russia."

consistently supported and defended commercial systems designed to import that commodity. Intercontinental trade similarly provided Rus' society with other commodities ranging from the marble and materials for the mosaics and frescoes brought from Byzantium for use in the construction of the Church of St. Sophia (Poppe) to horses purchased centuries later from the Nogai (Bennigsen and Veinstein) and silks and satins obtained from the Ottoman Turks (Syroechkovskii, Fekhner, Martin).[38] Although Paul Bushkovitch suggested that Muscovite interest in trade with the south and east was diminishing by the second half of the sixteenth century in favor of trade with Europe, especially through Muscovy's newly opened northern ports, other scholars (e.g., Bennigsen and Lemercier-Quelquejay, Martin) have observed that the Muscovite court continued to value its commercial interaction with Ottoman and other southern and eastern markets.[39]

In the context of their roles as commercial centers, which were critical to the supply of vital commodities, certain cities, notably Kiev, Novgorod, and Moscow, assumed additional importance. Novgorod has attracted particularly broad attention, both for its unusual political character and for the archeological evidence that has augmented literary sources about the city. Its commercial activities, which have been studied by A. L. Khoroshkevich, N. A. Kazakova, and E. A. Rybina among many others, were critical to the economic success of the Russian lands. Recognizing that factor, some scholars, e.g., M. N. Tikhomirov and B. A. Rybakov, have extended the point to suggest that the merchants and craftsmen of Novgorod played an equally important role in civic affairs of the city. Organizing themselves into merchants' associations and craftsmen's guilds, they exerted a strong influence on political as well as economic affairs. Most scholars, including V. L. Ianin, N. L. Podvigina, N. J. Dejevsky, and Henrik Birnbaum, however, have rejected the notion that such groups were widespread in Novgorod; they regard the one known association of wax merchants, *Ivanovskoe sto*, as unique, not an example of a more general phenomenon.

The conclusions of Tikhomirov and Rybakov, nevertheless, were not inconsistent with an assessment of Novgorod's characteristic features that emphasized popular democratic participation in the city's political institutions, particularly its *veche*. The conceptualization of Novgorod as a

---

[38] Poppe, "Building of the Church of St. Sophia"; Syroechkovskii, *Gosti Surozhane*; Fekhner, *Torgovlia russkogo gosudarstva*; Martin, "Muscovite Travelling Merchants."

[39] Bushkovitch, *Merchants of Moscow*; Bennigsen and Lemercier-Quelquejay, "Les marchands de la Cour ottomane"; Martin, *Treasure of the Land of Darkness*.

democratic republic, which juxtaposed it to the autocratic Muscovite state that eventually engulfed it, was developed in the nineteenth century and favored by scholars such as George Vernadsky[40] in the twentieth. It was refuted, however, by V. L. Ianin.[41] Basing his evaluation on archeological evidence as well as historical literary sources, he described Novgorod as an oligarchy, dominated by its land-owning boyar families whose members controlled the *veche* and also served as the city's governing officials. V. N. Bernadskii, Lawrence Langer, Joel Raba, and Henrik Birnbaum are among those who have shared Ianin's view, at least for fifteenth-century Novgorod. Some of them, however, have stressed the evolutionary process, by which Novgorod's political institutions, which incorporated an element of "democratic" participation, developed into the oligarchic form that prevailed by the fifteenth century.

It was in Novgorod too that unmistakable signs of economic deterioration appeared during the second half of the sixteenth century. Although scholars, including N. F. Ianitskii, A. A. Zimin, S. M. Kashtanov, and A. L. Shapiro et al.,[42] have debated the underlying causes and the initial dates of the economic decline, there is no dispute that by the 1580s Novgorod, as Shapiro and his colleagues demonstrated,[43] and other large sectors of Muscovy were in the midst of an economic crisis that had severe repercussions for the society as well as for the functional capabilities of the entire Muscovite state.

The exploration of the themes, outlined above and undertaken in the preceding chapters, leads to a series of general conclusions concerning medieval Russia. They suggest first of all that the realm of Kievan Rus' received definition and identity both from its dynasty and its Church. The overarching dynasty, despite the conflicts among its members, contributed to the cohesion among the multiplying number of principalities it ruled. Although their interests had begun to diverge earlier, the southwestern and northern principalities of Kievan Rus' separated as a result of the Mongol invasion. Within the northeastern principalities the patterns of intradynastic relations, which had defined seniority, determined succession, and provided legitimacy to the grand prince, remained in force for a century following the Mongol invasion.

[40] Vernadsky, *Kievan Russia.*
[41] Ianin, *Novgorodskie posadniki* and *Ocherki kompleksnogo istochnikovedeniia.*
[42] Zimin, "'Khoziaistvennyi krizis'"; Kashtanov, "K izucheniiu oprichniny"; Shapiro, et al., *Agrarnaia istoriia severo-zapadnoi Rossii XVI veka.*
[43] Shapiro, et al., *Agrarnaia istoriia severo-zapadnoi Rossii XVI veka.*

In the fourteenth century, however, the khans of the Golden Horde, by selecting princes from the Moscow branch of the dynasty to become grand princes of Vladimir, violated the norms of succession derived from the dynasty's Kievan Rus' heritage and terminated the practices based upon them. Lacking traditional dynastic sources of legitimacy, the Muscovite princes held power by virtue of Mongol favor. To satisfy Mongol demands and also develop domestic support they pursued policies that narrowed the definition of eligibility for succession, neutralized their dynastic opponents, extended their authority over additional territory, and tightened their grip on Novgorod and its commercial wealth.

The Muscovite princes were aided in their efforts to hold and consolidate their position not only by their Mongol patrons, but by the Church. Kievan Rus' had been not only a dynastic realm, but an ecclesiastical one. The threats to the unity of the metropolitanate of Kiev and all Rus' in the fourteenth century, followed by the Church's assertion of independence from the patriarch of Constantinople in the fifteenth, prompted the formulation of ideological pronouncements that recalled the glory of the Kievan Rus' era, when Christianity was introduced to the Rus' lands that were united in a single see, and proclaimed Moscow, the new seat of the metropolitan, to be heir to Kiev and Constantinople. Parallel to the ecclesiastical hierarchs, the secular grand princes were cast into roles of heirs of their Kievan forefathers with a mission to defend and reunite the Orthodox community. In conjunction with that role, they were imbued with enhanced and unimpeachable powers.

The development of Muscovy's governmental bodies and the formulation of the ideologies justifying them were the products of different institutions and divergent motives. They nevertheless reinforced one another. Bolstered as well by the economic resources provided by the Rus' society, the grand princes of Muscovy successfully magnified their authority and used it to expand their state and consolidate its role in the region. They imposed on the mass of society the mounting expenses for their activities and for the corresponding administrative and military apparatus designed to conduct those activities. During the second half of the sixteenth century, however, the weight and costs of the long wars and oppressive domestic policies rose beyond the level of the society's and economy's capacity to bear them. Under pressures from a tsar infused by secular and ecclesiastical elites alike with virtually unlimited powers, the society's economic resources were drained and its ability to support the state, its policies, and its elites reduced. By the late sixteenth century the lack of eligible heirs within the ruling dynastic branch combined with the virtually simultaneous depletion of the economy to undermine the stability of the state and weaken its ability to function. Although the Riurikid dynasty would linger through the reign of Fedor Ivanovich (d. 1598), the death of Ivan IV the Terrible in 1584 signaled the end of its six-century reign over the lands of Rus'. The state it had fashioned barely survived its demise.

SELECT BIBLIOGRAPHY

Abramovich, G. V. "Gosudarstvennye povinnosti vladel'cheskikh krest'ian severo-zapadnoi Rusi v XVI–pervoi chetverti XVII veka." *Istoriia SSSR* no. 3 (1972), pp. 65–84.

"Novgorodskoe pomest'e v gody ekonomicheskogo krizisa poslednei treti XVI v." In *Materialy po istorii sel'skogo khoziaistva i krest'ianstva SSSR*, vol. 8, pp. 5–26. Moscow: Nauka, 1974.

Akty, sobrannye v bibliotekakh i arkhivakh Rossiiskoi imperii Arkheograficheskoiu ekpeditseiu imp. Akademii nauk, 4 vols. St. Petersburg: Arkheograficheskaia komissia, 1836–1858.

Alef, Gustave. "Aristocratic Politics and Royal Policy in Muscovy in the Late Fifteenth and Early Sixteenth Centuries." *FOG*, vol. 27 (1980), pp. 77–109. Reprinted in Gustave Alef, *Rulers and Nobles in Fifteenth-Century Muscovy*.

"The Battle of Suzdal' in 1445. An Episode in the Muscovite War of Succession." *FOG*, vol. 25 (1978), pp. 11–20. Reprinted in Gustave Alef, *Rulers and Nobles in Fifteenth-Century Muscovy*.

"Bel'skies and Shuiskiis in the XVI Century." *FOG*, vol. 38 (1986), pp. 221–240.

"The Crisis of the Muscovite Aristocracy: A Factor in the Growth of Monarchical Power." *FOG*, vol. 15 (1970), pp. 15–58.

"Muscovite Military Reforms in the Second-half of the Fifteenth Century," *FOG*, vol. 18 (1973), pp. 73–108. Reprinted in Gustave Alef, *Rulers and Nobles in Fifteenth-Century Muscovy*.

"Muscovy and the Council of Florence." *SR*, vol. 20 (1961), pp. 389–401. Reprinted in Gustave Alef, *Rulers and Nobles in Fifteenth-Century Muscovy*.

"The Origins of Muscovite Autocracy. The Age of Ivan III," *FOG*, vol. 39 (1986), pp. 7–362.

"Reflections on the Boyar Duma in the Reign of Ivan III." *SEER*, vol. 45 (1967), pp. 76–123. Reprinted in Gustave Alef, *Rulers and Nobles in Fifteenth-Century Muscovy*.

Rulers and Nobles in Fifteenth-Century Muscovy. London: Variorum Reprints, 1983.

"Was Grand Prince Dmitrii Ivanovich Ivan III's 'King of the Romans'?" In *Essays in Honor of A. A. Zimin*, pp. 89–101. Ed. by Daniel Clarke Waugh. Columbus, Ohio: Slavica, 1985.

Alekseev, Iu. G. *Gosudar' vseia Rusi*. Novosibirsk: Nauka, 1991.

Osvobozhdenie Rusi ot ordynskogo iga. Leningrad: Nauka, 1989.

Alekseev, Iu. G. and A. I. Kopanev. "Razvitie pomestnoi sistemy v XVI v." In *Dvorianstvo i krepostnoi stroi Rossii XVI–XVIII vv. Sbornik statei, posviashchennyi pamiati Alekseia Andreevicha Novosel'skogo*, pp. 57–69. Moscow: Nauka, 1975.

Allsen, Thomas T. "Mongol Census Taking in Rus'." *HUS*, vol. 5 (1981), pp. 32–53.

Andreyev, Nikolay. "Filofey and His Epistle to Ivan Vasil'yevich." *SEER*, vol. 38 (1959), pp. 1–31.

Attman, Artur. *The Bullion Flow between Europe and the East 1000–1750*. Göteborg: Kungl. Vetenskaps- och Vitterhets-Samhallet, 1981.

The Struggle for Baltic Markets: Powers in Conflict 1558–1618. Göteborg: Kungl. Vetenskaps- och Vitterhets-Samhallet, 1979.

Auerbach, Inge. *Andrej Michajlovič Kurbskij: Leben in Osteuropäischen Adelsgesellschaften des 16. Jahrhunderts*. Munich: Verlag Otto Sagner, 1985.

Backus, Oswald P. "Treason as a Concept and Defections from Moscow to Lithuania in the Sixteenth Century." *FOG*, vol. 15 (1970), pp. 119–144.

Bakhrushin, S. V. *Nauchnye trudy*, 4 vols. Moscow: Akademiia Nauk SSSR, 1952–1959.

Balard, M. "Les Génois en Crimée aux XIIIe–XIVe siècles." *Archeion Pontou*, vol. 35 (1979), pp. 201–217.

Barbaro, Josafa and Ambrogio Contarini. *Travel to Tana and Persia*. Works Issued by the Hakluyt Society, vol. 49. Trans. by William Thomas and S. A. Roy. London: Hakluyt, 1873; reprint edition, Burt Franklin, n.d.

Baron, Samuel H. *Explorations in Muscovite History*. Hampshire, Great Britain and Brookfield, Vermont: Variorum Reprints, 1991.

Muscovite Russia: Collected Essays. London: Variorum Reprints, 1980.

Bater, James H. and R. A. French. *Studies in Russian Historical Geography*, 2 vols. London, New York, Paris: Academic Press, 1983.

Bazilevich, K. V. "Novgorodskie pomeshchiki iz posluzhil'tsev v kontse XV veka." *IZ*, vol. 14 (1945), pp. 62–80.

Vneshniaia politika russkogo tsentralizovannogo gosudarstva. Moscow: Moskovskii universitet, 1952.

Bennigsen, Alexandre. "L'expédition turque contre Astrakhan en 1569." *CMRS*, vol. 8 (1967), pp. 427–446.

Bennigsen, Alexandre and Mihnea Berindei. "Astrakhan et la politique des steppes nord pontiques (1587–1588)." *HUS*, vol. 3/4 (1979–80), pp. 71–91.

Bennigsen, Alexandre and Chantal Lemercier-Quelquejay. "La Grande Horde Nogay et le problème des communications entre l'Empire ottoman et l'Asie Centrale en 1552–1556." *Turcica*, vol. 8 (1976), pp. 203–236.

"Le Khanat de Crimée au début du XVI siècle de la tradition mongole à la suzeraineté Ottomane." *CMRS*, vol. 13 (1972), pp. 321–337.

"Les marchands de la Cour ottomane et le commerce des fourrures moscovites dans la seconde moitié du XVIe siècle." *CMRS*, vol. 11 (1970), pp. 363–390.

Bennigsen, Alexandre and Gilles Veinstein. "La Grande Horde Nogay et le commerce des steppes pontiques." In *Social and Economic History of Turkey*, pp. 49–63. Ed. by O. Okyar and H. Inalcik. Ankara, 1980.

Bennigsen, Alexandre et al. *Le khanat de Crimée dans les Archives du Musée du Palais de Topkapi.* Paris and The Hague: Mouton, 1978.

Berezhkov, M. *O torgovle Rusi s ganzoi do kontsa XV v.* St. Petersburg: V. Bezobrazov, 1879.

Berindei, Mihnea. "Contribution a l'étude du commerce ottoman des foururres moscovites: la route moldavo-polonaise, 1453–1700." *CMRS*, vol. 12 (1971), pp. 393–409.

"L'Empire Ottoman et la 'route Moldave' avant la conquête de Chilia et de Cetatea-Alba (1484)." *Journal of Turkish Studies*, vol. 10 (1986), pp. 47–71.

"Le problème des 'Cosaques' dans la seconde moitié du XVI siècle." *CMRS*, vol. 13 (1972), pp. 338–367.

"Le role des fourrures dans les relations commerciales entre la Russie et l'Empire ottoman avant la conquête de la Sibérie." In *Passé Turco-Tatar Présent Soviétique. Turco-Tatar Past, Soviet Present. Studies presented to Alexandre Bennigsen*, pp. 89–98. Ed. by Ch. Lemercier-Quelquejay, G. Veinstein, and S. E. Wimbush. Paris: Peeters and L'Ecole des Hautes Etudes en Sciences Sociales, 1986.

"Les Vénitiens en Mer Noire. XVI–XVII siècles. Nouveaux documents." *CMRS*, vol. 30 (1989), pp. 207–223.

Berindei, Mihnea and G. M. O'Riordan. "Venise et la Horde d'Or, fin XIII–début XIV s. (a propos d'un document inédit de 1324)." *CMRS*, vol. 29 (1988), pp. 243–256.

Berindei, Mihnea and Gilles Veinstein. "La présence Ottomane au sud de la Crimée et en mer d'Azov dans la première moitié du XVIe siècle." *CMRS*, vol. 20 (1979), pp. 389–465.

Bernadskii, V. N. *Novgorod i Novgorodskaia zemlia v XV veke.* Moscow and Leningrad: Akademiia Nauk SSSR, 1961.

Birnbaum, Henrik. "Did the 1478 Annexation of Novgorod by Muscovy Fundamentally Change the Course of Russian History?" In *New Perspectives on Muscovite History*, pp. 37–50. Ed. by Lindsey Hughes. London: Macmillan and New York: St. Martin's Press, 1993.

Lord Novgorod the Great: Essays in the History and Culture of a Medieval City-State. Columbus, Ohio: Slavica, 1981.

Blum, Jerome. *Lord and Peasant in Russia.* Princeton, N. J.: Princeton University Press, 1961; republished, New York: Atheneum, 1965.

Borisov, N. S. "Kulikovskaia bitva i nekotorye voprosy dukhovnoi zhizni Rusi XIV–XV vv." *Vestnik Moskovskogo universiteta.* Seriia 8, istoriia (1980), pp. 56–66.

"Moskovskie kniaz'ia i russkie mitropolity XIV veka," *Voprosy istorii* no. 8 (1986), pp. 30–43.

Russkaia tserkov' v politicheskoi bor'be XIV–XV vekov. Moscow: Moskovskii universitet, 1986.

Borisov, N. S. and E. N. Mitrofanova. "Iz istorii vzaimootnoshenii moskovskikh kniazei i tserkvi v XIV–XV vv. ('Monastyrskaia reforma')." *Vestnik Moskovskogo universiteta.* Seriia 8, istoriia (1983), pp. 46–57.

Boswell, A. Bruce. "The Kipchak Turks." *Slavonic Review,* vol. 6 (1927–28), pp. 68–85.

Brown, Peter B. "Anthropological Perspective and Early Muscovite Court Politics." *RH,* vol. 16 (1989), pp. 55–66.

"Muscovite Government Bureaus." *RH,* vol. 10 (1983), pp. 269–330.

"The *Zemskii Sobor* in Recent Soviet Historiography." *RH,* vol. 10 (1983), pp. 77–90.

Brumfield, William Craft. *Gold in Azure: One Thousand Years of Russian Architecture.* Boston: David R. Godine, 1983.

A History of Russian Architecture. Cambridge: Cambridge University Press, 1993.

Bushkovitch, Paul. "The Limits of Hesychasm: Some Notes on Monastic Spirituality in Russia 1350–1500." *FOG,* vol. 38 (1986), pp. 97–109.

The Merchants of Moscow, 1580–1650. Cambridge, London, New York: Cambridge University Press, 1980.

Religion and Society in Russia. Sixteenth and Seventeenth Centuries. New York and Oxford: Oxford University Press, 1992.

"*Rus'* in the Ethnic Nomenclature of the *Povest Vremennykh Let.*" *CMRS,* vol. 12 (1971), pp. 296–306.

"Towns and Castles in Kievan Rus': Boyar Residence and Land Ownership in the Eleventh and Twelfth Centuries." *RH,* vol. 7 (1980), pp. 251–264.

Callmer, Johan. "The Archaeology of Kiev to the End of the Earliest Urban Phase." *HUS,* vol. 11 (1987), pp. 323–364.

Cherepnin, L. V. "K voprosu o kharaktere i forme drevnerusskogo gosudarstva X–nachala XIII v." *IZ,* vol. 89 (1972), pp. 353–408.

Obrazovanie russkogo tsentralizovannogo gosudarstva v XIV–XV vekakh. Moscow: Sotsial'no-ekonomicheskaia literatura, 1960.

"Puti i formy politicheskogo razvitiia russkikh zemel' XII–nachala XIII v." In *Pol'sha i Rus',* pp. 23–50. Moscow: Nauka, 1974.

Zemskie sobory russkogo gosudarstva v XVI–XVII vv. Moscow: Nauka, 1978.

Cherniavsky, Michael. "Ivan the Terrible and the Iconography of the Kremlin Cathedral of Archangel Michael." *RH,* vol. 2 (1975), pp. 3–28.

"Khan or Basileus: An Aspect of Russian Mediaeval Political Theory." *Journal of the History of Ideas,* vol. 20 (1959), pp. 459–476. Reprinted in Michael Cherniavsky, ed., *The Structure of Russian History,* pp. 65–79.

"The Reception of the Council of Florence in Moscow," *Church History,* vol. 24 (1955), pp. 347–359.

"Russia." In *National Consciousness, History, and Political Culture in Early Modern Europe*, pp. 118–143. Ed. by Orest Ranum. Baltimore and London: Johns Hopkins University Press, 1975.

Cherniavsky, Michael, ed. *The Structure of Russian History. Interpretive Essays*. New York: Random House, 1970.

Chronicle of Novgorod, 1016–1471, The. Trans. by Robert Michell and Nevill Forbes. Camden 3rd series, vol. 25. London: Royal Historical Society, 1914.

Constantine Porphyrogenitus, *De Administrando Imperio*, Greek text ed. by Gy. Moravcsik with English translation by R. J. H. Jenkins. Washington, D.C.: Dumbarton Oaks Center for Byzantine Studies, 1967.

Croskey, Robert M. *Muscovite Diplomatic Practice in the Reign of Ivan III*. New York and London: Garland, 1987.

Crummey, Robert O. "The Fate of Boyar Clans, 1565–1613." *FOG*, vol. 38 (1986), pp. 241–256.

The Formation of Muscovy, 1304–1613. London and New York: Longman, 1987.

Danilova, L. V. *Ocherki po istorii zemlevladeniia i khoziaistva v Novgorodskoi zemle v XIV–XV vv*. Moscow: Akademiia Nauk, 1955.

Davies, Brian. "The Town Governors in the Reign of Ivan IV." *RH*, vol. 14 (1987), pp. 77–144.

Degtiarev, A. Ia. "Dokhody sluzhilykh zemlevladel'tsev v pervoi polovine XVI v." In *Problemy otechestvennoi i vseobshchei istorii*, pp. 86–90. Leningrad: Leningradskii universitet, 1976.

Dejevsky, Nikolai J. "The Churches of Novgorod: The Overall Pattern." In *Medieval Russian Culture*, pp. 206–223. Ed. by Henrik Birnbaum and Michael S. Flier. Berkeley, Los Angeles, and London: University of California Press, 1984.

"Novgorod: the Origins of a Russian Town." In *European Towns: Their Archaeology and Early History*, pp. 391–403. Ed. by M. W. Barley. London, New York, and San Francisco: Academic Press, 1977.

Dewey, Horace W. "The Decline of the Muscovite *Namestnik*." *Oxford Slavonic Papers*, vol. 12 (1965), pp. 21–39.

"The 1550 Sudebnik as an Instrument of Reform." *JbfGO*, vol. 10 (1962), pp. 161–180.

"The 1497 Sudebnik – Muscovite Russia's First National Law Code." *American Slavic and East European Review*, vol. 15 (1956), pp. 325–338.

"Political Poruka in Muscovite Rus'." *RR*, vol. 46 (1987), pp. 117–134.

Dewey, Horace W., trans. and ed. *Muscovite Judicial Texts, 1488–1556*. Ann Arbor, Mich.: Michigan Slavic Materials, 1966.

Dewey, Horace W. and Ann M. Kleimola. "From the Kinship Group to Every Man His Brother's Keeper: Collective Responsibility in Pre-Petrine Russia." *JbfGO*, vol. 30 (1982), pp. 321–335.

"Old Muscovite Amnesties: Theory and Practice." *RH*, vol. 3 (1976), pp. 49–60.

"Suretyship and Collective Responsibility in Pre-Petrine Russia." *JbfGO*, vol. 18 (1970), pp. 337–354.

Dimnik, Martin. *Mikhail, Prince of Chernigov and Grand Prince of Kiev, 1224–1246*. Toronto: Pontifical Institute of Mediaeval Studies, 1981.

"Oleg Sviatoslavich and his Patronage of the Cult of SS. Boris and Gleb." *Mediaeval Studies*, vol. 50 (1988), pp. 349–370.

"The 'Testament' of Iaroslav 'the Wise': A Re-examination." *Canadian Slavonic Papers*, vol. 29 (1987), pp. 369–386.

Dmitriev, L. A. "Rol' i znachenie mitropolita Kipriana v istorii drevnerusskoi literatury." *Trudy otdela drevnerusskoi literatury*, vol. 19 (1963), pp. 215–254.

Dmytryshyn, Basil, ed. *Medieval Russia: A Source Book, 850–1700*, 3rd ed. Fort Worth, Texas: Holt, Rinehart, and Winston, Inc., 1990.

Dollinger, Philippe. *The German Hansa*. Trans. by D. S. Ault and S. H. Steinberg. Stanford, Calif.: Stanford University Press, 1970.

Drevnerusskie kniazhestva X–XIII vv. Ed. by L. G. Beskrovnyi. Moscow: Nauka, 1975.

Dubov, I. V. *Severo-vostochnaia Rus' v epokhu rannego srednevekov'ia*. Leningrad: Leningradskii universitet, 1982.

Dukhovnye i dogovornye gramoty velikikh i udel'nykh kniazei XIV–XVI vv. Moscow and Leningrad: Akademiia Nauk SSSR, 1950. Reprint ed. Düsseldorf: Brücken Verlag, 1970.

Eaton, Henry L. "Cadasters and Censuses of Muscovy." *SR*, vol. 26 (1967), pp. 54–69.

Egorov, V. L. *Istoricheskaia geografiia Zolotoi Ordy v XIII–XIV vv*. Moscow: Nauka, 1985.

Ekzempliarskii, A. O. *Velikie i udel'nye kniaz'ia severnoi Rusi v Tatarskii period*, 2 vols. St. Petersburg: I. I. Tolstoi, 1889–91. Reprint ed. The Hague: Europe Printing, 1966.

Esper, Thomas. "A Sixteenth-Century Anti-Russian Arms Embargo." *JbfGO*, vol. 15 (1967), pp. 180–196.

Fedorov, G. B. "Unifikatsiia russkoi monetnoi sistemy i ukaz 1535 g." *Izvestiia AN SSSR. Seriia istorii i filosofii*, vol. 7 (1950), pp. 547–548.

Fedorov-Davydov, G. A. *The Culture of the Golden Horde Cities*. BAR International Series, 198. Trans. by H. Bartlett Wells. Oxford: BAR, 1984.

Obshchestvennyi stroi zolotoi ordy. Moscow: Moskovskii universitet, 1973.

Fekhner, M. V. "Izdeliia shelkotkatskikh masterskikh Vizantii v drevnei Rusi." *Sovetskaia arkheologiia*, no. 3 (1977), pp. 130–142.

Torgovlia russkogo gosudarstva so stranami vostoka v XVI veke. Moscow: Gosudarstvennyi istoricheskii muzei, 1956.

Fennell, J. L. I. "Andrej Jaroslavič and the Struggle for Power in 1252: An Investigation of the Sources." *Russia Mediaevalis*, No. 3, 1 (1973), pp. 49–62.

"The Attitude of the Josephians and the Trans-Volga Elders to the Heresy of the Judaisers." *SEER*, No. 3, 29 (1951), pp. 486–509.

The Correspondence between Prince A. M. Kurbskii and Tsar Ivan IV of Russia, 1564–1579. Cambridge: Cambridge University Press, 1955.

The Crisis of Medieval Russia, 1200–1304. London and New York: Longman, 1983.

"The Dynastic Crisis 1497–1502." *SEER*, vol. 39 (1960–61), pp. 1–23.

The Emergence of Moscow, 1304–1359. Berkeley and Los Angeles: University of California Press, 1968.

"The Ideological Role of the Russian Church in the First Half of the Fourteenth Century." In *Gorski Vijenats. A Garland of Essays Offered to Professor Elizabeth Mary Hill*, pp. 105–111. Ed. by R. Auty, L. R. Lewitter, and A. P. Vlasto. Cambridge: The Modern Humanities Research Association, 1970.

Ivan the Great of Moscow. London: Macmillan and New York: St. Martin's Press, 1961.

"The Last Years of Riurik Rostislavich." In *Essays in Honor of A. A. Zimin*, pp. 159–166. Ed. by Daniel Clarke Waugh. Columbus, Ohio: Slavica, 1985.

"Princely Executions in the Horde: 1308–1339." *FOG*, vol. 38 (1986), pp. 241–256.

"The Struggle for Power in North-East Russia, 1246–49." *Oxford Slavonic Papers*, vol. 7, n.s. (1974), pp. 112–121.

"The Tale of Baty's Invasion of North-East Rus' and its Reflexion in the Chronicles of the Thirteenth–Fifteenth Centuries." *Russia Mediaevalis*, vol. 3 (1977), pp. 41–78.

"The Tatar Invasion of 1223: Source Problems." *FOG*, vol. 27 (1980), pp. 18–31.

"The Tver' Uprising of 1327: A Study of the Sources." *JbfGO*, vol. 15 (1967), pp. 161–179.

Fine, John V. A., Jr. *The Late Medieval Balkans. A Critical Survey from the Late Twelfth Century to the Ottoman Conquest.* Ann Arbor, Mich.: The University of Michigan Press, 1987.

"The Muscovite Dynastic Crisis of 1497–1502. *Canadian Slavonic Papers*, vol. VIII, pp. 198–215. Toronto: University of Toronto Press, 1966.

Fisher, Alan. "The Ottoman Crimea in the Sixteenth Century." *HUS*, vol. 5 (1981), pp. 135–170.

Froianov, I. Ia. *Kievskaia Rus'. Ocherki otechestvennoi istoriografii.* Leningrad: Leningradskii universitet, 1990.

Kievskaia Rus'. Ocherki sotsial'no-ekonomicheskoi istorii. Leningrad: Leningradskii universitet, 1974.

Kievskaia Rus'. Ocherki sotsial'no-politicheskoi istorii. Leningrad: Leningradskii universitet, 1980.

"Stanovlenie Novgorodskoi respubliki i sobytiia 1136–1137 gg." *Vestnik Leningradskogo Universiteta.* Series 2, (1986), no. 4, pp. 3–16 and (1987), no. 1, pp. 3–26.

Fuhrmann, Joseph T. "Metropolitan Cyril II (1242–1281) and the Politics of Accommodation." *JbfGO*, vol. 24 (1976), pp. 161–172.

Gol'dberg, A. L. "Tri 'poslaniia Filofeiia.'" *Trudy otdela drevnerusskoi literatury*, vol. 29 (1974), pp. 68–97.

Golden, Peter. "Aspects of the Nomadic Factor in the Economic Development of Kievan Rus'." In *Ukrainian Economic History: Interpretive Essays*, pp. 58–101. Ed. by I. S. Koropeckyj. Cambridge, Mass.: Harvard University Press, 1991.

"Nomads and Their Sedentary Neighbors in Pre-Činggisid Eurasia." *Archivum Eurasiae Medii Aevi*, vol. 7 (1987–91), pp. 41–81.

"The *Polovci Dikii.*" *HUS*, vol. 3/4 (1979/80), pp. 296–309.

Gramoty velikogo Novgoroda i Pskova. Ed. by S. N. Valk. Moscow: Akademiia Nauk, 1949. Reprint ed. Düsseldorf: Brücken Verlag and Vaduz: Europe Printing, 1970.

Grekov, B. D. *Kiev Rus.* Trans. by Y. Sdobnikov. Moscow: Foreign Languages Publishing House, 1959.

Kievskaia Rus'. Moscow and Leningrad: Akademiia Nauk SSSR, 1939.

Gumilev, L. N. *Drevniaia Rus' i velikaia step'.* Moscow: Mysl', 1989.

Hakluyt, Richard. *The Principal Navigations Voyages Traffiques & Discoveries of the English Nation,* 12 vols. Glasgow: J. MacLehose and Sons and New York: Macmillan, 1903–05.

Halperin, Charles J. "The Concept of the Russian Land from the Ninth to the Fourteenth Centuries." *RH*, vol. 2 (1975), pp. 29–38.

"The Concept of the *Ruskaia Zemlia* and Medieval National Consciousness from the Tenth to the Fifteenth Centuries." *Nationalities Papers*, vol. 8 (1980), pp. 75–86.

"Keenan's Heresy Revisited." *JbfGO*, vol. 28 (1980), pp. 481–499.

"Kiev and Moscow: An Aspect of Early Muscovite Thought." *RH*, vol. 7 (1980), pp. 312–321.

"'Know Thy Enemy': Medieval Russian Familiarity with the Mongols of the Golden Horde." *JbfGO*, vol. 30 (1982), pp. 161–175.

"Medieval Myopia and the Mongol Period of Russian History." *RH*, vol. 5 (1978), pp. 188–191.

Russia and the Golden Horde: The Mongol Impact on Medieval Russian History. Bloomington, Ind.: Indiana University Press, 1985.

"Russia and the 'Mongol Yoke': Concepts of Conquest, Liberation, and the Chingissid Idea." *Archivum Eurasiae Medii Aevi*, vol. 2 (1982), pp. 99–107.

"Russia in the Mongol Empire in Comparative Perspective." *Harvard Journal of Asiatic Studies*, vol. 34 (1983), pp. 239–261.

"The Russian Land and the Russian Tsar: The Emergence of Muscovite Ideology, 1380–1408." *FOG*, vol. 23 (1976), pp. 7–103.

The Tatar Yoke. Columbus, Ohio: Slavica, 1986.

"*Tsarev ulus:* Russia in the Golden Horde." *CMRS*, vol. 23 (1982), pp. 257–263.

"Tverian Political Thought in the Fifteenth Century." *CMRS*, vol. 18 (1977), pp. 267–273.

Hellie, Richard. *Enserfment and Military Change in Muscovy.* Chicago: University of Chicago Press, 1971.

Slavery in Russia, 1450–1725. Chicago: University of Chicago Press, 1982.

"What Happened? How Did He Get Away With It?: Ivan Groznyi's Paranoia and the Problem of Institutional Restraints." *RH*, vol. 14 (1987), pp. 199–224.

"Zemskii Sobor." *Modern Encyclopedia of Russian and Soviet History*, vol. 45, pp. 226–234. Ed. by Joseph L. Wieczynski. Gulf Breeze, Fla.: Academic International Press, 1987.

von Herberstein, Sigismund. *Notes upon Russia*. Works Issued by the Hakluyt Society, vols. 10 and 12. Trans. by R. H. Major. London: Hakluyt, 1851; reprint ed., New York: Burt Franklin, n.d.

Hrushevs'kyi, Mykhailo (Mikhail Grushevskii). *Ocherk istorii kievskoi zemli*. Kiev: Tip. Imperatorskii Universiteta Sv. Vladimira V. I. Zavadzkago, 1891. Reprint ed., *Narys istorii Kyivs'koi zemli*. Kiev: Nauk. dumka, 1991.

Hurwitz, Ellen. "Andrei Bogoliubskii: An Image of the Prince." *RH*, vol. 2 (1975), pp. 39–52.

"Kievan Rus' and Medieval Myopia." *RH*, vol. 5 (1978), pp. 176–187.

"Metropolitan Hilarion's Sermon on Law and Grace: Historical Consciousness in Kievan Rus'." *RH*, vol. 7 (1980), pp. 322–333.

Prince Andrej Bogoljubskij: The Man and the Myth. Florence: Licosa Editrice, 1980.

Huttenbach, Henry R. "The Correspondence between Queen Elizabeth I and Tsar Ivan IV: An Examination of its Role in the Documentation of Anglo-Muscovite History." *FOG*, vol. 24 (1978), pp. 101–130.

"Muscovy's Conquest of Muslim Kazan and Astrakhan, 1552–1556. The Conquest of the Volga: Prelude to Empire." In *Russian Colonial Expansion to 1917*, pp. 45–69. Ed. by Michael Rywkin. London and New York: Mansell Publishing Limited, 1988.

"Muscovy's Penetration of Siberia. The Colonization Process 1555–1689. In *Russian Colonial Expansion to 1917*, pp. 70–102. Ed. by Michael Rywkin. London and New York: Mansell Publishing Limited, 1988.

Ianin, V. L. *Novgorodskie akty XII–XV vv*. Moscow: Nauka, 1991.

Novgorodskie posadniki. Moscow: Moskovskii universitet, 1962.

Ocherki kompleksnogo istochnikovedeniia. Srednevekovyi Novgorod. Moscow: Vysshaia shkola, 1977.

"Problemy sotsial'noi organizatsii Novgorodskoi respubliki." In *Rossiia i Italiia*, pp. 69–85. Moscow: Nauka, 1972.

Ianitskii, N. F. *Ekonomicheskii krizis v Novgorodskoi oblasti XVI veka*. Kiev: Imperatorskii universitet Sv. Vladimira, 1915.

Inalcik, Halil. "The Khan and the Tribal Aristocracy: The Crimean Khanate under Sahib Giray I." *HUS*, vols. 3/4 (1979–80), pp. 445–466.

"The Origin of the Ottoman–Russian Rivalry and the Don–Volga Canal (1569)." *Annales de L'Université d'Ankara*. Ankara: University of Ankara, 1947.

"The Question of the Closing of the Black Sea under the Ottomans." *Archeion Pontou*, vol. 35 (1979), pp. 74–110.

India in the Fifteenth Century, Works Issued by the Hakluyt Society, vol. 22. Trans. by Count Wielhorsky. Reprint ed., New York: Burt Franklin, n.d.

Jones, Gwyn. *A History of the Vikings*. London, New York, and Toronto: Oxford University Press, 1968.

Kahan, Arcadius. "Natural Calamities and the Effect upon the Food Supply in Russia (An Introduction to a Catalogue)." *JbfGO*, vol. 16 (1968), pp. 353–377.

Kaiser, Daniel H. "The Economy of Kievan Rus': Evidence from the Pravda Rus'skaia." In *Ukrainian Economic History: Interpretive Essays*, pp. 37–57. Ed. by I. S. Koropeckyj. Cambridge, Mass.: Harvard University Press, 1991.

The Growth of the Law in Medieval Russia. Princeton, N.J.: Princeton University Press, 1980.

"Modernization in Old Russian Law." *RH*, vol. 6 (1979), pp. 230–242.

"Reconsidering Crime and Punishment in Kievan Rus'." *RH*, vol. 7 (1980), pp. 282–293.

"Symbol and Ritual in the Marriages of Ivan IV." *RH*, vol. 14 (1987), pp. 247–262.

Kargalov, V. V. "Posledstviia mongolo-tatarskogo nashestviia XIII v. dlia sel'skikh mestnostei Severo-Vostochnoi Rusi," *Voprosy istorii*, no. 3 (1965), pp. 53–58.

Vneshnepoliticheskie faktory razvitiia feodal'noi Rusi. Feodal'naia Rus' i kochevniki. Moscow: Vysshaia shkola, 1967.

Karger, Mikhail. *Novgorod the Great*. Moscow: Progress Publishers, 1973.

Karpov, S. P. *Ital'ianskie morskie respubliki i Iuzhnoe Prichernomor'e v XIII–XV vv.: Problemy torgovli*. Moscow: Moskovskii universitet, 1990.

Kashtanov, S. M. "K izucheniiu oprichniny Ivana Groznogo." *Istoriia SSSR*, no. 2 (1963), pp. 96–117.

"K probleme mestnogo upravleniia v Rossii pervoi poloviny XVI v." *Istoriia SSSR*, no. 6 (1959), pp. 134–148.

"Otrazhenie v zhalovannykh i ukaznykh gramotakh finansovoi sistemy russkogo gosudarstva pervoi treti XVI v." *IZ*, vol. 70 (1961), pp. 251–275.

"Vnutrenniaia torgovlia i spros krupnykh zemlevladel'tsev na predmety potrebleniia v XIV–XV vekakh." *Istoriia SSSR*, no. 1 (1977), pp. 144–160.

Kazakova, N. A. "Rannye russko-niderlandskie torgovye kontakty." In *Issledovaniia po sotsial'no-politicheskoi istorii Rossii*, pp. 81–88. Leningrad: Nauka, 1971.

Russko-livonskie i russko-ganzeiskie otnosheniia. Leningrad: Nauka, 1975.

Kazhdan, Alexander. "Rus'-Byzantine Princely Marriages in the Eleventh and Twelfth Centuries." *HUS*, vol. 12/13 (1988–89), pp. 414–429.

Keenan, Edward L. "Ivan IV and the 'King's Evil': Ni maka li to budet?" *RH*, vol. 20 (1993), pp. 5–13.

"The Karp/Polikarp Conundrum: Some Light on the History of 'Ivan IV's First Letter.'" In *Essays in Honor of A. A. Zimin*, pp. 205–231. Ed. by Daniel Clarke Waugh. Columbus, Ohio: Slavica, 1985.

The Kurbskii-Groznyi Apocrypha: The Seventeenth-Century Genesis of the "Correspondence" Attributed to Prince A. M. Kurbskii and Tsar Ivan IV. Cambridge, Mass.: Harvard University Press, 1971.

"Muscovy and Kazan: Some Introductory Remarks on the Patterns of Steppe Diplomacy." *SR*, vol. 26 (1967), pp. 548–558.

"Putting Kurbskii in his Place, or: Observations and Suggestions Concerning the Place of the History of the Grand Prince of Muscovy in the History of Muscovite Literary Culture." *FOG*, vol. 24 (1978), pp. 131–161.

Keep, John L. H. "Bandits and the Law in Muscovy." *SEER*, vol. 35 (1956), pp. 202–222.

Soldiers of the Tsar: Army and Society in Russia 1462–1874. Oxford: Clarendon Press, 1985.

Khoroshev, A. S. *Politicheskaia istoriia russkoi kanonizatsii (XI–XVI vv.).* Moscow: Moskovskii universitet, 1986.

Khoroshkevich, A. L. "Iz istorii ganzeiskoi torgovli (Vvoz v Novgorod blagorodnykh metallov v XIV–XV vv.)." In *Srednie veka. Sbornik,* no. 20, pp. 98–120. Moscow: Akademiia Nauk SSSR, 1961.

"Novye Novgorodskie gramoty XIV–XV vv." In *Arkheograficheskii ezhegodnik za 1963 god,* pp. 264–276. Moscow: Nauka, 1964.

Torgovlia Velikogo Novgoroda s pribaltikoi i zapadnoi Evropoi v XIV–XV vekakh. Moscow: Akademiia Nauk SSSR, 1963.

Kirchner, Walther. *Commercial Relations between Russia and Europe 1400–1800. Collected Essays.* Bloomington, Ind.: Indiana University, 1966.

Kirpichnikov, A. N. "Fakty, gipotezy, i zabluzhdeniia v izuchenii russkoi voennoi istorii XIII–XIV vv." In *Drevneishie gosudarstva na territorii SSSR 1984,* pp. 229–243. Moscow: Nauka, 1985.

Kitch, Faith C. *The Literary Style of Epifanij Premudryj Pletenije Sloves.* München: Verlag Otto Sagner, 1976.

Kleimola, Ann M. "The Changing Face of the Muscovite Aristocracy. The Sixteenth Century: Sources of Weakness." *JbfGO*, vol. 25 (1977), pp. 481–493.

"'In Accordance with the Holy Apostles': Muscovite Dowries and Women's Property Rights." *RR*, vol. 51 (1992), pp. 204–229.

"Ivan the Terrible and his 'Go-fers': Aspects of State Security in the 1560s." *RH*, vol. 14 (1987), pp. 283–292.

"Kto kogo: Patterns of Duma Recruitment, 1547–1564." *FOG*, vol. 38 (1986), pp. 205–220.

"Law and Social Change in Medieval Russia: The *Zakon sudnyi lyudem* as a Case Study." *Oxford Slavonic Papers,* vol. 9, n.s. (1976), pp. 17–27.

"Military Service and Elite Status in Muscovy in the Second Quarter of the Sixteenth Century." *RH*, vol. 7 (1980), pp. 47–64.

"Patterns of Duma Recruitment, 1505–1550." In *Essays in Honor of A. A. Zimin,* pp. 232–258. Ed. by Daniel Clarke Waugh. Columbus, Ohio: Slavica, 1985.

"Reliance on the Tried and True: Ivan IV and Appointments to the Boyar Duma, 1565–1584." *FOG*, vol. 46 (1992), pp. 51–63.

"Status, Place, and Politics: The Rise of *Mestnichestvo* during the *Boiarskoe Pravlenie*." *FOG*, vol. 27 (1980), pp. 195–214.

Up Through Servitude: The Changing Condition of the Muscovite Elite in the Sixteenth and Seventeenth Centuries." *RH*, vol. 6 (1979), pp. 210–229.

Kleinenberg, I. E. "Serebro vmesto soli: elementy rannego merkantilizma vo vneshnetorgovoi politike russkogo gosudarstva kontsa XV–nachala XVI veka." *Istoriia SSSR*, no. 2 (1977), pp. 115–124.

Kliuchevskii (Kliuchevsky), V. O. *Boiarskaia duma drevnei Rusi*. St. Petersburg: A. I. Mamontov, 1909. Reprint ed. The Hague: Europe Printing, 1965.

A History of Russia, 5 vols. Trans. by C. J. Hogarth. New York: Russell and Russell, 1960.

Sochineniia v vos'mi tomakh, 8 vols. Moscow: Gosudarstvennoe izdatel'stvo politicheskoi literatury, 1956–59.

Kobrin, V. B. "Iz istorii zemel'noi politiki v gody oprichniny." *Istoricheskii arkhiv*, no. 3 (1958), pp. 152–160.

"Sostav oprichnogo dvora Ivana Groznogo." In *Arkheograficheskii ezhegodnik za 1959 god*, pp. 16–91. Moscow: Akademiia Nauk SSSR, 1960.

"Stanovlenie pomestnoi sistemy." *IZ*, vol. 105 (1980), pp. 150–195.

Vlast' i sobstvennost' v srednevekovoi Rossii (XV–XVI vv.). Moscow: Mysl', 1985.

Kochin, G. E. *Sel'skoe khoziaistvo na Rusi kontsa XIII–nachala XVI v*. Moscow and Leningrad: Nauka, 1965.

Kollmann, Jack E., Jr. "The Stoglav Council and Parish Priests." *RH*, vol. 7 (1980), pp. 65–91.

Kollmann, Nancy Shields. "The Boyar Clan and Court Politics. The Founding of the Muscovite Political System." *CMRS*, vol. 23 (1982), pp. 5–31.

"Collateral Succession in Kievan Rus'." *HUS*, vol. 14 (1990), pp. 377–387.

"Consensus Politics: The Dynastic Crisis of the 1490s Reconsidered." *RR*, vol. 45 (1986), pp. 235–267.

"The Grand Prince in Muscovite Politics: The Problem of Genre in Sources on Ivan's Minority." *RH*, vol. 14 (1987), pp. 293–314.

Kinship and Politics: The Making of the Muscovite Political System, 1345–1547. Stanford, Calif.: Stanford University Press, 1987.

"Was There Honor in Kiev Rus'?" *JbfGO*, vol. 36 (1988), pp. 481–492.

Kolycheva, E. I. *Agrarnyi stroi Rossii XVI veka*. Moscow: Nauka, 1987.

Kopanev, A. I. "O 'kupliakh' Ivana Kality." *IZ*, vol. 20 (1946), pp. 24–37.

Koretskii, V. I. "Khoziaistvennoe razorenie russkoi derevni vo vtoroi polovine XVI v. i pravitel'stvennaia politika." In *Ezhegodnik po agrarnoi istorii vostochnoi Evropy 1965 g.*, pp. 62–70. Moscow: Moskovskii gosudarstvennyi universitet, 1970.

Kostochkin, V. *Drevnerusskie goroda. Old Russian Towns*. Moscow: Iskusstvo, 1974.

Krader, L. "Feudalism and the Tatar Polity of the Middle Ages." *Comparative Studies in Society and History*, vol. 1 (1958), pp. 76–99.

Kuchera, M. P. "Pereiaslavskoe kniazhestvo." In *Drevnerusskie kniazhestva X–XIII vv.*, pp. 118–143.

Kuchkin, V. A. *Formirovanie gosudarstvennoi territorii severo-vostochnoi Rusi v X–XV vv.* Moscow: Nauka, 1984.

"Iz istorii genealogicheskikh i politicheskikh sviazei Moskovskogo kniazheskogo doma v XIV v." *IZ*, vol. 94 (1974), pp. 365–384.

"K biografii Aleksandra Nevskogo." In *Drevneishie gosudarstva na territorii SSSR 1985*, pp. 71–80. Moscow: Nauka, 1986.

"O marshrutakh pokhodov drevnerusskikh kniazei na gosudarstvo volzhskikh Bulgar v XII–pervoi treti XIII v." In *Istoricheskaia geografiia Rossii XII–nachalo XX v*. Moscow: Nauka, 1975.

"Pobeda na Kulikovskom pole." *Voprosy istorii*, no. 8 (1980), pp. 3–21.

"Rol' Moskvy v politicheskom razvitii severo-vostochnoi Rusi kontsa XIII v." In *Novoe o proshlom nashei strani: Pamiati Akad. M. N. Tikhomirova*, pp. 54–64. Moscow: Nauka, 1967.

"Rostovo-Suzdal'skaia zemlia v X–pervoi treti XIII vekov." *Istoriia SSSR* (1969), No. 2, pp. 62–94.

Kulikovskaia bitva v istorii i kul'ture nashei Rodiny. Ed. by N. M. Sidorov. Moscow: Moskovskii universitet, 1983.

Kurat, A. N. "The Turkish Expedition to Astrakhan' in 1569 and the Problem of the Don–Volga Canal." *SEER*, vol. 40 (1961), pp. 7–23.

Kuza, A. V. "Novgorodskaia zemlia." In *Drevnerusskie kniazhestva X–XIII vv.*, pp. 144–201.

Langer, Lawrence N. "The Black Death in Russia: Its Effects upon Urban Labor." *RH*, vol. 2 (1975), pp. 53–67.

"The Medieval Russian Town." In *The City in Russian History*, pp. 11–33. Ed. by Michael Hamm. Lexington, Ky.: University Press of Kentucky, 1976.

"V. L. Ianin and the History of Novgorod." *SR*, vol. 33 (1974), pp. 114–119.

Lazarev, V. N. *Drevnerusskie mozaiki i freski XI–XV vv*. Moscow: Iskusstvo, 1973.

Legacy of St. Vladimir: Byzantium, Russia, America, The. Ed. by J. Breck, J. Meyendorff, and E. Silk. Crestwood, N.Y.: St. Vladimir's Seminary Press, 1990.

Lemercier-Quelquejay, Chantal. "Un condottiere Lithuanien du XVI siècle le Prince Dimitrij Višneveckij et l'origine de la sec zaporogue d'après les Archives ottomanes." *CMRS*, vol. 10 (1969), pp. 258–279.

"Les expéditions de Devlet Girây contre Moscou en 1571 et 1572." *CMRS*, vol. 13 (1972), pp. 555–559.

"Les khanates de Kazan et de Crimée face a la Moscovie en 1521." *CMRS*, vol. 12 (1971), pp. 480–490.

Lenhoff, Gail D. "Canonization and Princely Power in Northeast Rus': The Cult of Leontij Rostovskij." *Die Welt der Slaven*, vol. 37, N.F. 16 (1992), pp. 359–380.

Early Russian Hagiography: The Lives of Prince Fedor the Black. Berlin: Otto Harvassowitz, 1995.

Lenhoff, Gail D. and Janet L. B. Martin. "The Commercial and Cultural Context of Afanasij Nikitin's Journey Beyond Three Seas." *JbfGO*, vol. 37 (1989), pp. 321–344.

Lesnikov, M. P. "Torgovye otnosheniia velikogo Novgoroda s tevtonskim ordenom v kontse XIV i nachale XV veka." *IZ*, vol. 39 (1952), pp. 259–278.

Levchenko, M. V. *Ocherki po istorii russko-vizantiiskikh otnoshenii*. Moscow: Akademii Nauk SSSR, 1956.

Levin, Eve. "Women and Property in Medieval Novgorod: Dependence and Independence." *RH*, vol. 10 (1983), pp. 154–169.

Limonov, Iu. A. "Iz istorii vostochnoi torgovli Vladimiro-suzdal'skogo kniazhestva." In *Mezhdunarodnye sviazi Rossii do XVII veka*, pp. 55–63. Moscow: Akademiia Nauk SSSR, 1961.

Litvarin, G. G. "Osobennosti russko-vizantiiskikh otnoshenii v XII v. (Tezisy)." In *Pol'sha i Rus'*, pp. 208–212. Moscow: Nauka, 1974.

Litvarin, G. G., A. P. Kazhdan and Z. V. Udal'tsova. "Otnosheniia Drevnei Rusi i Vizantii v XI–pervoi polovine XIII v." In *Proceedings of the XIIIth International Congress of Byzantine Studies. Oxford. 5–10 September 1966*, pp. 69–91. Ed. by J. M. Hussey, D. Obolensky, S. Runciman. London, New York, and Toronto: Oxford University Press, 1967.

Longworth, Philip. *The Cossacks.* New York, Chicago, and San Francisco: Holt, Rinehart, and Winston, 1970.

Lur'e, Ia. S. (Jakov Luria). "K istorii prisoedineniia Novgoroda v 1477–1479 gg." In *Issledovaniia po sotsial'no - politicheskoi istorii Rossii*, pp. 89–95. Leningrad: Nauka, 1971.

"Unresolved Issues in the History of the Ideological Movements of the Late Fifteenth Century." In *Medieval Russian Culture*, pp. 163–179.

Majeska, George P. "The Moscow Coronation of 1498 Reconsidered," *JbfGO*, vol. 26 (1978), pp. 353–361.

Maksimov, P. N. "Obshchenatsional'nye i lokal'nye osobennosti russkoi arkhitektury XII–XIV vv." In *Pol'sha i Rus'*, pp. 213–222. Moscow: Nauka, 1974.

Man'kov, A. G. *Tseny i ikh dvizhenie v russkom gosudarstve XVI veka.* Moscow and Leningrad: Akademiia Nauk SSSR, 1951.

Manz, B. F. "The Clans of the Crimean Khanate, 1466–1532." *HUS*, vol. 2 (1978), pp. 282–307.

Martin, Janet. "Economic Development in the Varzuga Fishing Volost' during the Reign of Ivan IV." *RH*, vol. 14 (1987), pp. 315–332.

"The Land of Darkness and the Golden Horde: The Fur Trade under the Mongols XIII–XIVth Centuries." *CMRS*, vol. 19 (1978), pp. 401–421.

"Muscovite Relations with the Khanates of Kazan' and the Crimea (1460s to 1521)." *CASS*, vol. 17 (1983), pp. 435–453.

"Muscovite Travelling Merchants: The Trade with the Muslim East (15th and 16th Centuries)." *Central Asian Survey*, vol. 4 (1985), pp. 21–38.

"Muscovy's Northeastern Expansion: The Context and a Cause." *CMRS*, vol. 24 (1983), pp. 459–470.

"Russian Expansion in the Far North. X to mid-XVI Century. In *Russian Colonial Expansion to 1917*, pp. 23–44. Ed. by Michael Rywkin London and New York: Mansell Publishing Limited, 1988.

"The Tiumen' Khanate's Encounters with Muscovy, 1481–1505." In *Passé Turco-Tatar Présent Soviétique. Turco-Tatar Past, Soviet Present. Studies Presented to Alexandre Bennigsen*, pp. 79–87. Ed. by Ch. Lemercier-Quelquejay, G. Veinstein, and S. E. Wimbush. Paris: Peeters and L'Ecole des Hautes Etudes en Sciences Sociales, 1986.

Treasure of the Land of Darkness: The Fur Trade and its Significance for Medieval Russia. Cambridge, London, New York: Cambridge University Press, 1986.

"Les *Uškujniki* de Novgorod: Marchands ou Pirates?" *CMRS*, vol. 16 (1975), pp. 5–18.

Medieval Russian Culture, California Slavic Studies, vol. XII. Ed. by Henrik

Birnbaum and Michael S. Flier. Berkeley: University of California Press, 1984.

Meyendorff, John. *Byzantium and the Rise of Russia. A Study of Byzantino-Russian Relations in the Fourteenth Century.* Cambridge: Cambridge University Press, 1981.

Mezentsev, Volodymyr I. "The Masonry Churches of Medieval Chernihiv." *HUS*, vol. 11 (1987), pp. 365–383.

"The Territorial and Demographic Development of Medieval Kiev and Other Major Cities of Rus': A Comparative Analysis Based on Recent Archaeological Research." *RR*, vol. 48 (1989), pp. 145–170.

Millard, Michael. "Sons of Vladimir, Brothers of Iaroslav." *CMRS*, vol. 12 (1971), pp. 286–295.

Miller, David B. "The Coronation of Ivan IV of Moscow." *JbfGO*, vol. 15 (1967), pp. 559–574.

"The Cult of St. Sergius and its Political Uses." *SR*, vol. 52 (1993), pp. 680–699.

"The Kievan Principality in the Century before the Mongol Invasion: An Inquiry into Recent Research and Interpretation." *HUS*, vol. 10 (1986), pp. 215–240.

"Monumental Building and Its Patrons as Indicators of Economic and Political Trends in Rus', 900–1262." *JbfGO*, vol. 38 (1990), pp. 321–355.

"Monumental Building as an Indicator of Economic Trends in Northern Rus' in the Late Kievan and Mongol Periods, 1138–1462." *American Historical Review*, vol. 94 (1989), pp. 360–390.

"The Velikie Minei Chetii and the Stepennaia Kniga of Metropolitan Makarii and the Origins of Russian National Consciousness." *FOG*, vol. 26 (1979), pp. 263–382.

"The Viskovatyi Affair of 1553–54: Offical Art, the Emergence of Autocracy and the Disintegration of Medieval Russian Culture." *RH*, vol. 8 (1981), pp. 293–332.

Milner-Gulland, Robin. "Art and Architecture of Old Russia, 988–1700." In *An Introduction to Russian Art and Architecture*, pp. 1–70. Ed. by Robert Auty and Dimitri Obolensky. Cambridge, London, New York: Cambridge University Press, 1980.

Morgan, David. *The Mongols.* Oxford and New York: Basil Blackwell, 1986.

Nasonov, A. N. *Mongoly i Rus'.* Moscow and Leningrad: Akademiia Nauk SSSR, 1940. Reprint ed., Slavistic Printings and Reprintings, no. 223. The Hague and Paris: Mouton, 1969.

"Russkaia zemlia" i obrazovanie territorii drevnerusskogo gosudarstva. Moscow: Akademiia Nauk SSSR, 1951.

Nazarenko, A. V. "Rodovoi siuzerenitet Riurikovichci nad Rus'iu (X–XI vv.)." In *Drevneishie gosudarstva na territorii SSSR 1985*, pp. 149–157. Moscow: Nauka, 1986.

Nazarov, V. D. "Dmitrovskii udel v kontse XIV–seredine XV v." In *Istoricheskaia geografiia Rossii XII–nachalo XX v.*, pp. 46–62. Moscow: Nauka, 1965.

Nikitskii, A. I. *Istoriia ekonomicheskogo byta velikogo Novgoroda.* Reprint ed. The Hague: Mouton, 1967.

Nikonian Chronicle, The, 5 vols. Ed. by Serge A. Zenkovsky and trans. by Serge A. Zenkovsky and Betty Jean Zenkovsky. Princeton, N.J.: Kingston Press and Darwin Press, 1984–89.

Noonan, Thomas S. "Fifty Years of Soviet Scholarship on Kievan History: A Recent Soviet Assessment. Review Article." *RH,* vol. 7 (1980), pp. 334–349.

"The Flourishing of Kiev's International and Domestic Trade, ca. 1100–ca. 1240." In *Ukrainian Economic History: Interpretive Essays,* pp. 102–146. Ed. by I. S. Koropeckyj. Cambridge, Mass.: Harvard University Press, 1991.

"Medieval Russia, the Mongols, and the West: Novgorod's Relations with the Baltic." *Medieval Studies,* vol. 37 (1975), pp. 316–339.

"Monetary Circulation in Early Medieval Rus': A Study of Volga Bulgar Dirham Finds." *RH,* vol. 7 (1980), pp. 294–311.

"The Monetary History of Kiev in the Pre-Mongol Period." *HUS,* vol. 11 (1987), pp. 384–443.

"Ninth-Century Dirham Hoards from European Russia: A Preliminary Analysis." *Viking-Age Coinage in the Northern Lands. The Sixth Oxford Symposium on Coinage and Monetary History,* ed. by M. A. S. Blackburn and D. M. Metcalf. BAR International Series 122/I, pp. 47–117. Oxford: BAR., 1981.

"Pechenegs." *Modern Encyclopedia of Russian and Soviet History,* ed. by Joseph L. Wieczynski, vol. 27, pp. 126–133. Gulf Breeze, Fla.: Academic International Press, 1982.

"Polovtsy (Polovtsians)." *Modern Encyclopedia of Russian and Soviet History,* ed. by Joseph L. Wieczynski, vol. 29, pp. 12–24. Gulf Breeze, Fla.: Academic International Press, 1982.

"Russia's Eastern Trade, 1150–1350: The Archeological Evidence." *Archivum Eurasiae Medii Aevi,* vol. 3 (1983), pp. 201–264.

"Suzdalia's Eastern Trade in the Century before the Mongol Conquest." *CMRS,* vol. 19 (1978), pp. 371–384.

"Why the Vikings First Came to Russia." *JbfGO,* vol. 34 (1986), pp. 321–348.

Nosov, N. E. *Ocherki po istorii mestnogo upravleniia russkogo gosudarstva pervoi poloviny XVI veka.* Moscow and Leningrad: Akademiia Nauk SSSR, 1957.

"Russkii gorod i russkoe kupechestvo v XVI stoletii (K postanovke voprosa)." In *Issledovaniia po sotsial'no-politicheskoi istorii Rossii,* pp. 152–177. Leningrad: Nauka, 1971.

"Russkii gorod v XVI stoletii." In *Rossiia i Italiia,* pp. 41–68. Moscow: Nauka, 1972.

Stanovlenie soslovno-predstavitel'nykh uchrezhdenii v Rossii. Leningrad: Nauka, 1969.

"Zemskaia reforma na russkom severe XVI v. (Ob otmene kormlenii i vvedenii zemskikh uchrezhdenii)." In *Krest'ianstvo i klassovaia bor'ba v feodal'noi Rossii. Sbornik statei pamiati Ivana Ivanovicha Smirnova,* pp. 131–156. Leningrad: Nauka, 1967.

Novgorod Architectural Monuments 11th–17th Centuries. Introduced and compiled by Mikhail Karger. Leningrad: Aurora Art Publishers, 1975.

Novgorodskaia pervaia letopis' starshego i mladshego izvodov. Ed. by N. A. Nasonov.

Moscow and Leningrad: Akademiia Nauk SSSR, 1950. Reprint ed. The Hague: Mouton, 1970.

Novosel'tsev, A. P. and V. T. Pashuto. "Vneshniaia torgovlia drevnei Rusi do serediny XIII v." *Istoriia SSSR*, no. 3 (1967), pp. 81–108.

Obolensky, Dimitri. *The Byzantine Commonwealth: Eastern Europe, 500–1453.* London: Sphere Books, 1974; reprint, Crestwood, N.Y.: St. Vladimir's Seminary Press, 1982.

The Byzantine Inheritance of Eastern Europe. London: Variorum Reprints, 1982.

"Byzantium and Russia in the Late Middle Ages." In *Europe in the Late Middle Ages*, pp. 248–275. Ed. by J. R. Hale, J. R. L. Highfield, and B. Smalley. London: Faber and Faber, 1965. Reprinted in Dimitri Obolensky, *Byzantium and the Slavs: Collected Studies.*

Byzantium and the Slavs: Collected Studies. London: Variorum Reprints, 1971.

"Byzantium, Kiev, and Moscow: A Study in Ecclesiastical Relations." Dumbarton Oaks Papers, vol. XI, pp. 23–78. Cambridge, Mass.: Harvard University Press, 1957. Reprinted in Dimitri Obolensky, *Byzantium and the Slavs: Collected Studies.*

"Russia's Byzantine Heritage." *Oxford Slavonic Papers*, vol. 1 (1950), pp. 37–63. Reprinted in Michael Cherniavsky, ed., *The Structure of Russian History*, pp. 3–28. Revised version in Dimitri Obolensky, *Byzantium and Slavs: Collected Essays.*

Ocherki russkoi kul'tury XVI veka, Part 1. Ed. by A. V. Artsikhovskii. Moscow: Moskovskii universitet, 1977.

Ostrowski, Donald. "The Christianization of Rus' in Soviet Historiography: Attitudes and Interpretations (1920–1960)." *HUS*, vol. 11 (1987), pp. 444–461.

"Church Polemics and Monastic Land Acquisition in Sixteenth-Century Muscovy." *SEER*, vol. 64 (1986), pp. 355–379.

"The Mongol Origins of Muscovite Political Institutions." *SR*, vol. 49 (1990), pp. 525–542.

"Second-Redaction Additions in Carpini's *Ystoria Mongalorum*." *HUS*, vol. 14 (1990), pp. 522–550.

Pamiatniki arkhitektury Vladimira, Suzdalia, Iur'eva-Pol'skogo. Architectural Monuments of Vladimir, Suzdal, Yuriev-Polskoy. In Russian and English. Text written by K. Polunina, trans. by Kate Cook. Photographs by A. Aleksandrov. Leningrad: Aurora Art Publishers, 1974.

Pamiatniki russkogo prava, 8 vols. Moscow: Gosiurizdat, 1952–61.

Pashuto, B. T. *Vneshniaia politika Drevnei Rusi.* Moscow: Nauka, 1968.

Pelenski, Jaroslaw. "The Contest between Lithuania-Rus' and the Golden Horde in the Fourteenth Century for Supremacy over Eastern Europe." *Archivum Eurasiae Medii Aevi*, vol. 2 (1982), pp. 303–320.

"The Emergence of the Muscovite Claims to the Byzantine-Kievan 'Imperial Inheritance'." *HUS*, vol. 7 (1983), pp. 520–531.

"Muscovite Imperial Claims to the Kazan Khanate." *SR*, vol. 26 (1967), pp. 559–576.

"The Origins of the Official Muscovite Claims to the 'Kievan Inheritance'."
HUS, vol. 1 (1977), pp. 29–52.

Russia and Kazan: Conquest and Imperial Ideology (1438–1560s). The Hague and
Paris: Mouton, 1974.

"The Sack of Kiev of 1169: Its Significance for the Succession to Kievan Rus'."
HUS, vol. 11 (1987), pp. 303–316.

"State and Society in Muscovite Russia and the Mongol–Turkic System in the
Sixteenth Century." *FOG*, vol. 27 (1980), pp. 156–167.

Perel'man, I. L. "Novgorodskaia derevnia v XV–XVI vv." *IZ*, vol. 26 (1948),
pp. 128–197.

Platonov, S. F. *Ivan the Terrible*. Ed. and trans. by Joseph L. Wieczynski with
introduction by Richard Hellie. Gulf Breeze, Fla.: Academic International
Press, 1974.

Pletneva, S. A. *Polovtsy*. Moscow: Nauka, 1990.

Podvigina, N. L. *Ocherki sotsial'no-ekonomicheskoi i politicheskoi istorii Novgoroda
Velikogo v XII–XIII vv*. Moscow: Vysshaia shkola, 1976.

Polnoe sobranie russkikh letopisei, 38 vols. to date. St. Petersburg, Moscow, and
Leningrad: Arkheograficheskaia komissiia, Vostochnaia literatura, Nauka,
1846–1989)

Poluboiarinova, M. D. *Russkie liudi v Zolotoi Orde*. Moscow: Nauka, 1978.

Poppe, Andrzej. "The Building of the Church of St. Sophia in Kiev." *Journal of
Medieval History*, vol. 7 (1981), pp. 15–65. Reprinted in Andrzej Poppe, *Rise
of Christian Russia*.

"La dernière expédition russe contre Constantinople." *Byzantinoslavica*, vol. 32
(1971), pp. 1–29, 233–268.

"How the Conversion of Rus' Was Understood in the Eleventh Century,"
HUS, vol. 11 (1987), pp. 287–302.

"The Original Status of the Old-Russian Church." *Acta Poloniae Historica*,
vol. 39 (1979), pp. 7–45. Reprinted in Andrzej Poppe, *Rise of Christian Russia*.

"The Political Background to the Baptism of Rus': Byzantine-
Russian Relations between 986–989." Dumbarton Oaks Papers, no. 30,
pp. 195–244. Washington, D.C.: Dumbarton Oaks Center for Byzantine
Studies, 1976.

The Rise of Christian Russia. London: Variorum Reprints, 1982.

Presniakov, A. E. *The Formation of the Great Russian State*, trans. from Russian by
A. E. Moorhouse. Chicago: Quadrangle Books, 1970.

Kniazheskoe pravo drevnei Rusi. St. Petersburg: Tip. M. A. Aleksandrova, 1909.
Reprint ed. The Hague: Europe Printing, 1966.

Lektsii po russkoi istorii, 2 vols. Moscow: Gosudarstvennoe sotsial'no-
ekonomicheskoe izdatel'stvo, 1938–39. Reprint ed. The Hague: Europe
Printing, 1966.

Priselkov, M. D. *Ocherki po tserkovno-politicheskoi istorii Kievskoi Rusi X–XII vekov*.
St. Petersburg: Tip. M. M. Stasiulevicha, 1913. Reprint ed. The Hague:
Europe Printing, 1966.

Priselkov, M. D., ed. *Troitskaia letopis'; rekonstruktsiia teksta*. Moscow: Akademiia
Nauk SSSR, 1950.

Pritsak, Omeljan. "Kiev and All of Rus': The Fate of a Sacral Idea." *HUS*, vol. 10 (1986), pp. 279–300.

"Kievan Rus' and Sixteenth-Seventeenth–Century Ukraine," in *Rethinking Ukrainian History*, ed. by Ivan L. Rudnytsky, pp. 1–28. Edmonton, Alberta: Canadian Institute of Ukrainian Studies, 1983.

"Moscow, the Golden Horde, and the Kazan Khanate from a Polycultural Point of View." *SR*, vol. 26 (1967), pp. 577–583.

"Non-'Wild' Polovtsians." In *To Honor Roman Jakobson. Essays on the Occasion of His Seventieth Birthday*, pp. 1615–1623. The Hague and Paris: Mouton, 1967.

"The Pečenegs: A Case of Social and Economic Transformation." *Archivum Eurasiae Medii Aevi*, vol. 1 (1975), pp. 211–235.

"Polovcians and Rus'." *Archivum Eurasiae Medii Aevi*, vol. 2 (1982), pp. 321–380.

Pronshtein, A. P. *Velikii Novgorod v XVI veke*. Khar'kov, Ukraine: Khar'kovskii gosudarstvennyi universitet, 1957.

Pskovskie letopisi, 2 vols. Moscow and Leningrad: Akademiia Nauk SSSR, 1941–55. Reprint ed. Düsseldorf: Brücken Verlag and The Hague: Europe Printing, 1967.

Pushkareva, N. L. *Zhenshchiny drevnei Rusi*. Moscow: Mysl', 1989.

Pushkareva, N. L. and E. Levina (Eve Levin). "Zhenshchina v srednevekovom Novgorode XI–XV vv." *Vestnik Moskovskogo Universiteta*. Seriia 8, istoriia (1983), no. 3, pp. 78–89.

Queller, Donald E. and Gerald W. Day, "Some Arguments in Defense of the Venetians on the Fourth Crusade," *American Historical Review*, vol. 81 (1976), pp. 717–737.

Raba, Joel. "The Authority of the Muscovite Ruler at the Dawn of the Modern Era." *JbfGO*, vol. 24 (1976), pp. 321–344.

"Church and Foreign Policy in the Fifteenth-Century Novgorodian State." *CASS*, vol. 13 (1979), pp. 52–58.

"The Fate of the Novgorodian Republic." *SEER*, vol. 45 (1967), pp. 307–323.

"Novgorod in the Fifteenth Century: A Re-examination." *CASS*, vol. 1 (1967), pp. 348–364.

Rapov, O. M. "K voprosu o boiarskom zemlevladenii na Rusi v XII–XIII vv." In *Pol'sha i Rus'*, pp. 190–207. Ed. B. A. Rybakov. Moscow: Nauka, 1974.

"O vremeni i obstoiatel'stvakh kreshcheniia naseleniia Novgoroda Velikogo." *Vestnik Moskovskogo Universiteta*. Seriia 8, istoriia (1988), no. 3, pp. 51–65.

Rappoport, P. A. "O roli Vizantiiskogo vliianiia v razvitii drevnerusskoi arkhitektury." *Vizantiiskii vremennik*, vol. 45 (1984), pp. 185–190.

Rasmussen, Knud. "The Muscovite Foreign Policy Administration during the Reign of Vasilij III, 1515–1525." *FOG*, vol. 38 (1986), pp. 152–167.

"On the Information Level of the Muscovite Posol'skii Prikaz in the Sixteenth Century." *FOG*, vol. 24 (1978), pp. 87–99.

Razvitie russkogo prava v XV–pervoi polovine XVII v. Ed. by V. S. Nersesiants. Moscow: Nauka, 1986.

Riasanovsky, Nicholas. "'Oriental Despotism' and Russia." *SR*, vol. 22 (1963), pp. 644–649.

Rice, Tamara Talbot. *A Concise History of Russian Art*. New York and Washington, D.C.: Frederick A. Praeger, 1963.

Roublev, Michel. "The Periodicity of the Mongol Tribute as Paid by the Russian Princes during the Fourteenth and Fifteenth Centuries. *FOG*, vol. 15 (1970), pp. 7–13.

"Le tribut aux Mongols d'après les Testaments et Accords des Princes Russes." *CMRS*, vol. 7 (1966), pp. 487–530. Translated as "The Mongol Tribute According to the Wills and Agreements of the Russian Princes" and reprinted in Michael Cherniavsky, ed., *The Structure of Russian History*, pp. 29–64.

Rowland, Daniel. "Did Muscovite Literary Ideology Place Limits on the Power of the Tsar (1540s–1660s)?" *RR*, vol. 49 (1990), pp. 125–155.

Rude and Barbarous Kingdom. Ed. by Lloyd E. Berry and Robert O. Crummey. Madison, Wis.: University of Wisconsin Press, 1968.

Russian Primary Chronicle, Laurentian Text, The. Trans. and ed. by Samuel Hazzard Cross and Olgerd P. Sherbowitz-Wetzor. Cambridge, Mass.: Medieval Academy of America, 1953.

Rybakov, B. A. *Drevniaia Rus'. Skazaniia, byliny, letopisi*. Moscow: Akademiia Nauk, 1963.

Kievskaia Rus' i russkie kniazhestva XII–XIII vv. Moscow: Nauka, 1982.

Rybina, E. A. *Arkheologicheskie ocherki istorii Novgorodskoi torgovli*. Moscow: Moskovskii universitet, 1978.

Inozemnye dvory v Novgorode XII–XVII vv. Moscow: Moskovskii universitet, 1986.

Sadikov, P. A. *Ocherki po istorii oprichniny*. Moscow and Leningrad: Akademiia Nauk SSSR, 1950. Reprint ed. The Hague: Mouton, 1969.

Schamiloglu, U. "The Qarači Beys of the Later Golden Horde: Notes on the Organization of the Mongol World Empire." *Archivum Eurasiae Medii Aevi*, vol. 4 (1984), pp. 283–297.

Sedov, V. V. "Smolenskaia zemlia." In *Drevnerusskie kniazhestva X–XIII vv.*, pp. 240–259.

Semenchenko, G. V. "Upravlenie Moskvoi v XIV–XV vv." *IZ*, vol. 105 (1980), pp. 196–228.

Ševčenko, Ihor. "Byzantium and the Eastern Slavs after 1453." *HUS*, vol. 2 (1978), pp. 5–25.

"Byzantium and the Slavs." *HUS*, vol. 8 (1984), pp. 289–303.

"Intellectual Repercussions of the Council of Florence." *Church History*, vol. 24 (1955), pp. 291–323.

"Muscovy's Conquest of Kazan: Two Views Reconciled." *SR*, vol. 26 (1967), pp. 541–547.

"Russo-Byzantine Relations after the Eleventh Century." In *Proceedings of the XIIIth International Congress of Byzantine Studies. Oxford. 5–10 September 1966*, pp. 93–104. Ed. by J. M. Hussey, D. Obolensky, and S. Runciman. Oxford, New York, Toronto: Oxford University Press, 1967.

Shapiro, A. L. "O podsechnom zemledelii na Rusi v XIV–XV vv." In

Ezhegodnik po agrarnoi istorii vostochnoi Evropy 1963 g., pp. 121–131. Vil'nius, Lithuania: MINTS, 1964.

Problemy sotsial'no-ekonomicheskoi istorii Rusi XIV–XV vv. Leningrad: Leningradskii universitet, 1977.

Shapiro, A. L. et al. *Agrarnaia istoriia severo-zapada Rossii.* Leningrad: Nauka, 1971.

Agrarnaia istoriia severo-zapada Rossii XVI veka. Leningrad: Nauka, 1974.

Shchapov, Ia. N. (Yaroslav Nikolaevich). "Formirovanie i razvitie tserkovnoi organizatsii na Rusi v kontse X–XII v." In *Drevneishie gosudarstva na territorii SSSR 1985*, pp. 58–63. Moscow: Nauka, 1986.

"K istorii sootnosheniia svetskoi i tserkovnoi iurisdiktsii na Rusi v XII–XIV vv." In *Pol'sha i Rus'*, pp. 172–189. Moscow: Nauka, 1974.

Kniazheskie ustavy i tserkov' v Drevnei Rusi XI–XIV vv. Moscow: Nauka, 1972.

"Pamiatniki tserkovnogo prava IX–XII vv." *IZ*, vol. 107 (1982), pp. 304–332.

State and Church in Early Russia 10th–13th Centuries. Trans. by Vic Schneierson. New Rochelle, N.Y., Athens, Moscow: Aristide D. Caratzas, 1993.

"Tserkov' v sisteme gosudarstvennoi vlasti drevnei Rusi." In *Drevnerusskoe gosudarstvo i ego mezhdunarodnoe znachenie*, pp. 279–352. Moscow: Nauka, 1965.

Shchapov, Ia. N., ed. *Drevnerusskie kniazheskie ustavy XI–XV vv.* Moscow: Nauka, 1976.

Shchapova, Iu. L. "Drevnerusskie stekliannye izdeliia kak istochnik dlia istorii russko-vizantiiskikh otnoshenii v XI–XII vv." *Vizantiiskii vremennik*, vol. 19 (1961), pp. 60–75.

Shepard, J. "The Russian Steppe-Frontier and the Black Sea Zone." *Archeion Pontou*, vol. 35 (1979), pp. 218–237.

"Some Problems of Russo-Byzantine Relations c. 860–c. 1050." *SEER*, vol. 52 (1974), pp. 10–33.

"Why Did the Russians Attack Byzantium in 1043?" *Byzantinisch-Neugriechische Jahrbücher*, vol. 22 (1979), pp. 147–212.

Shmidt, S. O. "O vremeni sostavleniia 'vypisi' o vtorom brake Vasiliia III." In *Novoe o proshlom nashei strany*, pp. 110–122. Moscow: Nauka, 1967.

Rossiiskoe gosudarstvo v seredine XVI stoletiia. Moscow: Nauka, 1984.

Skrynnikov, R. G. "The Civil War in Russia at the Beginning of the Seventeenth Century (1603–1607): Its Character and Motive Forces." In *New Perspectives on Muscovite History*, pp. 61–79. Ed. by Lindsey Hughes. London: Macmillan and New York, St. Martin's Press, 1993.

"Ermak's Siberian Expedition." Trans. by Hugh F. Graham. *RH*, vol. 13 (1986), pp. 1–40.

Ivan the Terrible. Ed. and trans. by Hugh F. Graham. Gulf Breeze, Fla.: Academic International Press, 1981.

"Obzor pravleniia Ivana IV." *RH*, vol. 14 (1987), pp. 361–376.

"Oprichnaia zemel'naia reforma Groznogo 1565 g." *IZ*, vol. 70 (1961), pp. 223–250.

"Oprichnyi razgrom Novgoroda." In *Krest'ianstvo i klassovaia bor'ba v feodal'noi Rossii. Sbornik statei pamiati Ivana Ivanovicha Smirnova*, pp. 157–171. Leningrad: Nauka, 1967.

Oprichnyi terror. Leningrad: Leningradskii universitet, 1969.

Perepiska Groznogo i Kurbskogo: paradoksy Edvarda Kinana. Leningrad: Nauka, 1973.

Rossiia posle oprichniny. Leningrad: Leningradskii universitet, 1975.

Tsarstvo terrora. St. Petersburg: Nauka, 1992.

Smirnov, I. I. "Vostochnaia politika Vasiliia III." *IZ*, vol. 27 (1948), pp. 18–66.

Smith, Dianne L. "Muscovite Logistics, 1462–1598." *SEER*, vol. 71 (1993), pp. 35–65.

Smith, R. E. F. *The Origins of Farming in Russia.* The Hague and Paris: Mouton, 1959.

Peasant Farming in Muscovy. Cambridge: Cambridge University Press, 1977.

Solov'ev (Soloviev), S. M. *History of Russia*, 16 vols. to date. Ed. by G. Edward Orchard. Gulf Breeze, Fla.: Academic International Press, 1976– .

Istoriia Rossii s drevneishikh vremen, 29 vols. in 15 books. Moscow: Izdatel'stvo sotsial'no-ekonomicheskoi literatury, 1959–66.

von Staden, Heinrich. *The Land and Government of Muscovy.* Trans. by Thomas Esper. Stanford, Calif.: Stanford University Press, 1967.

Stokes, A. D. "The Status of the Russian Church, 988–1037." *SEER*, vol. 37 (1958–59), pp. 430–442.

"The System of Succession to the Thrones of Russia, 1054–1113." In *Gorski Vijenats. A Garland of Essays Offered to Professor Elizabeth Mary Hill*, pp. 268–275. Ed. by R. Auty, L. R. Lewitter, and A. P. Vlasto. Cambridge: Modern Humanities Research Association, 1970.

Stremoukoff, Dimitri. "Moscow the Third Rome: Sources of the Doctrine." *Speculum*, vol. 28, no. 1 (January 1953), pp. 84–101. Reprinted in Michael Cherniavsky, ed., *The Structure of Russian History: Interpretive Essays*, pp. 108–125.

Syroechkovskii, V. E. *Gosti-Surozhane.* Moscow and Leningrad: Gosudarstvennoe sotsial'no-ekonomicheskoe izdatel'stvo, 1935.

"Mukhammed-Gerai i ego vassaly." *Uchenye zapiski Moskovskogo ordena Lenina gosudarstvennogo universiteta im. M. V. Lomonosova*, vol. 61 (1940), pp. 3–71.

"Puti i usloviia snoshenii Moskvy s Krymom na rubezhe XVI veka." *Izvestiia AN SSSR.* Seriia 7, otdelenie obshchestvennykh nauk (1932), pp. 193–237.

Szeftel, Marc. "Joseph Volotsky's Political Ideas in a New Historical Perspective," *JbfGO*, vol. 13 (1965), p. 19–29.

Texts and Versions of John de Plano Carpini and William de Rubruquis, The, Ed. C. Raymond Beazley. London: Hakluyt Society, 1903; reprint ed., Nendeln, Liechtenstein: Kraus Reprint Limited, 1967.

Thiriet, Freddy. "Les Vénetiens en mer noire organisation et trafics (XIIIe–XIVe siècles). *Archeion Pontou*, vol. 35 (1978), pp. 38–53.

Thompson, M. W. *Novgorod the Great.* New York and Washington: Frederick A. Praeger, 1967.

Tikhomirov, M. N. *Drevnerusskie goroda.* 2nd ed. Moscow: Gosudarstvennoe izdatel'stvo politicheskoi literatury, 1956. Trans. by Y. Sdobnikov: *The*

Towns of Ancient Russia. Moscow: Foreign Languages Publishing House, 1959.

"K voprosu o vypisi o vtorom brake tsaria Vasiliia III." In *Istoricheskie sviazi Rossii so slavianskimi stranami i Vizantiei*, pp. 78–82. Moscow: Nauka, 1969.

"Moskovskie tretniki, tysiatskie, i namestniki." *Izvestiia Akademii Nauk SSSR*, Seriia istorii i filosofii, vol. 3 (1946), pp. 309–320.

"Rossiia i Vizantiia v XIV–XV stoletiiakh." In *Istoricheskie sviazi Rossii so slavianskimi stranami i Vizantiei*, pp. 27–47. Moscow: Nauka, 1969.

Rossiia v XVI stoletii. Moscow: Akademiia Nauk SSSR, 1962.

Tolochko, Petro P. *Drevniaia Rus'. Ocherki sotsial'no-politicheskoi istorii.* Kiev: Naukova Dumka, 1987.

"Kiev i iuzhnaia Rus' v period feodal'noi razdroblennosti." In *Pol'sha i Rus'*, pp. 223–233. Moscow: Nauka, 1974.

Kiev i Kievskaia zemlia v epokhu feodal'noi razdroblennosti XII–XIII vekov. Kiev: Naukova Dumka, 1980.

"Kievskaia zemlia." In *Drevnerusskie kniazhestva X–XIII vv.*, pp. 5–56.

"Religious Sites in Kiev during the Reign of Volodimer Sviatoslavich," *HUS*, vol. 11 (1987), pp. 317–322.

Udal'tsova, Z. V., et al. "Drevniaia Rus' – zona vstrechi tsivilizatsii." *Voprosy istorii*, no. 7 (1980), pp. 41–60.

Vasiliev, Alexander. "Economic Relations between Byzantium and Old Russia." *Journal of Economic and Business History*, vol. 4 (1932), pp. 314–334.

Veinstein, Gilles. "Prélude au Problème Cosaque à travers les registres de dommages ottomans des années 1545–1555." *CMRS*, vol. 30 (1989), pp. 329–362.

Vernadsky, George. "Feudalism in Russia." *Speculum*, vol. 14 (1939), pp. 300–323.

"Ivan Groznyi i Simeon Bekbulatovich." In *To Honor Roman Jakobson. Essays on the Occasion of his Seventieth Birthday*, pp. 2133–2151. The Hague and Paris: Mouton, 1967.

Kievan Russia. A History of Russia, vol. 2. New Haven, Conn., and London: Yale University Press, 1948.

The Mongols and Russia. A History of Russia, vol. 3. New Haven, Conn., and London: Yale University Press, 1953.

Russia at the Dawn of the Modern Age. A History of Russia, vol. 4. New Haven, Conn., and London: Yale University Press, 1959.

The Tsardom of Moscow 1547–1682, 2 vols. *A History of Russia*, vols. 5 and 6. New Haven, Conn., and London: Yale University Press, 1969.

Vernadsky, George, trans. *Medieval Russian Laws.* New York: Columbia University Press, 1947; paperback ed. New York: W. W. Norton, 1969.

Veselovskii, S. B. *Feodal'noe zemlevladenie v severo-vostochnoi Rusi*, vol. 1. Moscow and Leningrad: Akademiia Nauk SSSR, 1947.

Issledovanniia po istorii oprichniny. Moscow: Akademiia Nauk SSSR, 1963.

Vodoff, Wladimir. "A propos des 'achats' (kupli) d'Ivan Ier de Moscou." *Journal des Savants* (1974), pp. 95–127.

"Un 'partie theocratique' dans la Russie du XII siècle?" *Cahier de civilization medievale*, vol. 17 (1974), pp. 193–215.

"La place du grand-prince de Tver' dans les structures politiques russes de la fin du XIVe et du XVe siècle." *FOG*, vol. 27 (1980), pp. 33–63.

"Quand a pu être le Panégyrique du grand-prince Dmitrii Ivanovich, tsar' russe?" *CASS*, vol. 13 (1979), pp. 82–101.

Vodov, V. A. "Zarozhdenie kantseliarii moskovskikh velikikh kniazei." *IZ*, vol. 103 (1979), pp. 325–350.

Voyce, Arthur. *The Art and Architecture of Medieval Russia.* Norman, Okla.: University of Oklahoma Press, 1967.

Westergaard, Waldemar. "Denmark, Russia, and the Swedish Revolution, 1480–1503." *SEER*, vol. 16 (1937–38), pp. 129–140.

Wieczynski, Joseph L. "Archbishop Gennadius and the West: The Impact of Catholic Ideas upon the Church of Novgorod." *CASS*, vol. 6 (1972), pp. 374–389.

Wittfogel, Karl A. "Russia and the East: A Comparison and Contrast." *SR*, vol. 22 (1963), pp. 627–643.

Zdan, Michael. "The Dependence of Halych–Volyn' on the Golden Horde." *SEER*, vol. 35 (1957), pp. 505–522.

Zenkovsky, Serge A., ed. *Medieval Russia's Epics, Chronicles, and Tales.* New York: E. P. Dutton, 1974.

Zimin, A. A. "D'iacheskii apparat v Rossii vtoroi poloviny XV–pervoi treti XVI v." *IZ*, vol. 87 (1971), pp. 219–286.

"Istochniki po istorii mestnichestva v XV–pervoi treti XVI v." *Arkheograficheskii ezhegodnik za 1968 god*, pp. 109–118. Moscow: Nauka, 1970.

"'Khoziaistvennyi krizis' 60–70-kh godov XVI v. i russkoe krest'ianstvo." In *Materialy po istorii sel'skogo khoziaistva i krest'ianstva SSSR*, vol. 5, pp. 11–20. Moscow: Akademiia Nauk SSSR, 1962.

"Kniazheskaia znat' i formirovanie sostava boiarskoi dumy vo vtoroi treti XVI v." *IZ*, vol. 103 (1979), pp. 195–241.

Krupnaia feodal'naia votchina i sotsial'no-politicheskaia bor'ba v Rossii (konets XV–XVI v.). Moscow: Nauka, 1977.

"Namestnicheskoe upravlenie v russkom gosudarstve vtoroi poloviny XV–pervoi treti XVI v." *IZ*, vol. 94 (1974), pp. 271–301.

Oprichnina Ivana Groznogo. Moscow: Mysl', 1964.

Reformy Ivana Groznogo. Moscow: Sotsial'no-ekonomicheskaia literatura, 1960.

Rossiia na poroge novogo vremeni. Moscow: Mysl', 1972.

Rossiia na rubezhe XV–XVI stoletii. Moscow: Mysl', 1982.

"Sobytiia 1499 g. i bor'ba politicheskikh gruppirovok pri dvore Ivana III." In *Novoe o proshlom nashei strany*, pp. 91–103. Moscow: Nauka, 1967.

"Sostav boiarskoi dumy v XV–XVI vekakh." *Arkheograficheskii ezhegodnik za 1957 god*, pp. 41–87. Moscow: Akademiia Nauk SSSR, 1958.

Vitiaz' na rasput'e: feodal'naia voina v Rossii XV v. Moscow: Mysl, 1991.

Zimin, A. A. and A. L. Khoroshkevich. *Rossiia vremeni Ivana Groznogo.* Moscow: Nauka, 1982.

Zlotnik, Marc. "Muscovite Fiscal Policy." *RH*, vol. 6 (1979), pp. 243–258.

INDEX

(Italicized page numbers refer to tables or figures)

Riurik Rostislavich (grand prince of Kiev), 97, *97*, 98, 100, *116*, 118–21, 124, 127, 130
Riurikid dynasty (Riurikid princes), 2, 33, 34, 36, 37, 39, 42–3, 44, 45, 48, 52, 55, 56, 57, 58, 60, 62, 66, 70, 71, 76, 77, 78, 89, 91, 96, 98, 100, 101, 102, 103, 124, 127, 129, 130, 131, 132, 133, 134, 135, 138, 139, 140, 146, 147, 156, 158, 162, 164, 165, 192, 197, 209, 235, 258, 265, 331, 367, 394, 395
  and Church, 10–11, 12, 73, 74, 76, 81, 87, 258, 338, 340, 374, 388, 389, 393
  end of rule, 329, 337, 379, 399
  intradynastic warfare, 22–3, 27, 29, 31, 37, 45, 50, 51, 52, 53, 91–2, 97, 98, 104–24, 133, 169, 171–7, 209–11, 212, 217, 239–44, 300, 378
  loss of territorial possessions, 55, 127, 158, 165, 205
  and Mongol suzerainty, 147, 148, 150, 153, 154, 155, 156, 159, 162, 169–70, 174–5, 180, 186, 187, 199–200, 220, 236, 239, 379, 385, 387
  succession systems, principles of, 22, 23, 25–7, 29, 31, 32, 33, 34, 37, 50, 101, 104–5, 111, 113–14, 118, 122–4, 159, 162, 169–70, 173, 174–5, 179–80, 199–200, 220, 236–7, 239, 247–8, 289, 293, 300–1, 333–4, 336–7, 375–9, 387, 397–8
  see also Daniilovichi
Rogneda, 1, 23, 25
Rogvolod, 1, 4
Roman (metropolitan of Lithuania), 206
Roman Mstislavich (prince of Volynia and Galicia), 97, *113*, *120*, 122
  and conflicts over Kievan throne, 97, 119, 124, 130
  death, 97, 119, 127
  as prince of Novgorod, 112, 114–15
  and unification of Galicia and Volynia, 97, 119, 127
Roman Rostislavich (prince of Smolensk), 97, 98
Romanov dynasty, 371
Ros' River, 47, 49, 51, 53

Rostislav Mstislavich (prince of Smolensk and grand prince of Kiev), 91, *93*, 97, 97–8, *108*, 111, 112, *113*, 114, 115, *116*, *120*, 123, 378
  acquisition of Kievan throne, 97, 98, 111, 113–14, 127, 130
  death, 111
  and Iurii Dolgorukii, 110
  and Mstislav Iziaslavich, 97, 110, 111, 127, 130
  and Orthodox Church, 75, 82, 98
  and Polovtsy, 130, 131
Rostislav Riurikovich, 119, *120*
Rostislav Vladimirovich, 376
Rostislavichi (descendants of Rostislav Mstislavich), 101, 112, 115, 117–18, 119, 121, 122, 131
Rostov, 4, 11, 22, 38, 60, 90, 91, 99, 101, 154, 167, 172, 229, 357
  commerce, 15, 40, 168
  contests over, 31, 52
  division into appanage principalities, 161–2, 187, 188, 190
  and Mongols, 146, 153, 154, 170, 172, 179
  and Novgorod, 31, 40
  and Orthodox Church, 75, 82, 86, 193, 225–6, 230
  and Pereiaslavl', 31, 34, 37–8
  subordination to Moscow, 191–2, 208, 209, 215, 222, 237, 254
  see also Rostov-Suzdal'; Suzdalia; Vladimir-Suzdal'
Rostov, princes of, 34, 38, 91, 99, 154, 159, 161, 170, 172, 179, 209, 215, 222, 226, 237, 378
  marriages with Daniilovichi, 191–2, 207
  opposition to Daniilovichi, 179, 207–8
  and *oprichnina*, 367
  see also individual princes by name
Rostov-Suzdal', 37, 38, 42, 56, 66, 69, 82, 98, 99, 106
  see also Suzdalia; Vladimir-Suzdal'
Rowland, Daniel, 264, 393
Rublev, Andrei, 233–4, 277
Ruffo, Marco, 279
Russkaia Pravda, 71–3, 77, 78

Cambridge Medieval Textbooks

Already published

Germany in the High Middle Ages *c.* 1050–1200
HORST FUHRMANN

The Hundred Years War
England and France at War *c.* 1300–*c.* 1450
CHRISTOPHER ALLMAND

Standards of Living in the Later Middle Ages:
Social Change in England, *c.* 1200–1520
CHRISTOPHER DYER

Magic in the Middle Ages
RICHARD KIECKHEFER

The Papacy 1073–1198: Continuity and Innovation
I. S. ROBINSON

Medieval Wales
DAVID WALKER

England in the Reign of Edward III
SCOTT L. WAUGH

The Norman Kingdom of Sicily
DONALD MATTHEW

Political Thought in Europe 1250–1450
ANTONY BLACK

The Church in Western Europe from the Tenth
to the Early Twelfth Century
GERD TELLENBACH
Translated by Timothy Reuter

The Medieval Spains
BERNARD F. REILLY

England in the Thirteenth Century
ALAN HARDING

Monastic and Religious Orders in Britain 1000–1300
JANET BURTON

Religion and Devotion in Europe *c.* 1215–*c.* 1515
R. N. SWANSON

Medieval Russia, 980–1584
JANET MARTIN

The Wars of the Roses: Politics and the Constitution in England,
c. 1437–1509
CHRISTINE CARPENTER

The Waldensian Dissent: Persecution and Survival, *c.* 1170–*c.* 1570
GABRIEL AUDISIO
Translated by Claire Davison

The Crusades, *c.* 1071–*c.* 1291
JEAN RICHARD
Translated by Jean Birrell

Other titles are in preparation